RHETT

Sen. Robert Barnwell Rhett, ca. 1852
(South Carolina Historical Society, Charleston)

RHETT

THE TURBULENT LIFE AND TIMES OF A FIRE-EATER

William C. Davis

UNIVERSITY OF SOUTH CAROLINA PRESS

UNIVERSITY OF SOUTH CAROLINA *BICENTENNIAL*

Published in Columbia, South Carolina, by the
University of South Carolina Press

Manufactured in the United States of America

05 04 03 02 01   5 4 3 2 1

Library of Congress Cataloging-in-Publication Data
Davis, William C., 1946–
    Rhett : the turbulent life and times of a fire-eater / William C. Davis.
    p. cm.
    Includes bibliographical references and index.
    ISBN 1-57003-439-7 (Hardcover : alk. paper)
    1. Rhett, Robert Barnwell, 1800–1876. 2. Legislators—South Carolina—Biography.
3. South Carolina—Politics and government—1775–1865. 4. Secession—South
Carolina. 5. Legislators—United States—Biography. 6. United States. Congress.
Senate—Biography. 7. Statesmen—Confederate States of America—Biography.
8. Confederate States of America—Politics and government. I. Title.
F273 .R48 D38 2001
973.7'13'092—dc21   2001005098

In oligarchies, where men vie with each other in
the service of the commonwealth, fierce enmities are apt
to arise between man and man,
each wishing to be leader, and to carry his own measures;
whence violent quarrels come, which lead to open strife,
often ending in bloodshed.

> Darius in "Thalia," from *The History of Herodotus,*
> ca. 446 B.C.

NAPOLEON: "Do you see yonder star?"
CARDINAL FESCH: "No Sire."
NAPOLEON: "But I see it."

Pride and envy together include all wickedness

> Otanes in "Thalia," from *The History of Herodotus,*
> ca. 446 B.C.

Contents

Illustrations

Acknowledgments

DEBTS ARE THE WRITING HISTORIAN'S constant companions, and happily so, for without the assistance of professional colleagues and personal friends alike, few books would be written, especially books like this one with material from a wide and disparate range of sources. All of the archives—state, local, and university—that were consulted have provided helpful and accommodating assistance. Special mention is due to the major archives used for this book, starting with David O. Percy, C. Patton Hash, and Kathryn M. Meehan at the delightful South Carolina Historical Society in Charleston, worth a visit just for the experience, let alone the fine materials in its collections. Mary Giles and Sarah Foss of the Charleston Museum were also especially helpful with the little-known Aiken Rhett Collection in their archives, so vital for reconstructing Robert Barnwell Rhett's postwar memoir. Allen Stokes and the staff at the South Caroliniana Library of the University of South Carolina in Columbia did yeoman service during long research days of constant questions and requests generated by their own excellent holdings.

Also very helpful were John Coski at the Museum of the Confederacy in Richmond, Virginia; J. Tracy Power of the South Carolina Department of Archives and History in Columbia; Olga Tsapina of the Henry E. Huntington Library and Art Gallery, San Marino, California; and Nelson Lankford at the Virginia Historical Society in Richmond. Of course, hardly any book that involves research in the Civil War period can escape a debt to Michael Musick of the National Archives in Washington, D.C., an old and dear friend, and a national treasure for historians.

Many other friends helped in their way. Gary W. Gallagher, T. Michael Parrish, Robert K. Krick, and Emory Thomas all gave assistance in tracking down the odd elusive article or book, and Robert N. Smith, graduate student at the University of Georgia, was especially helpful with material from the Thomas R. R. Cobb Letters. Shinaan Krakowsky of Encino, California, graciously gave me the use of three outstanding Rhett letters written during the exciting days of making the Confederacy in February 1861, perhaps the most informative of all Rhett's letters from that period. Richard M. McMurry did a bit of scouting and provided some very useful material for judging the accuracy of some of Rhett's sources in his memoir, and Karen Anderson was a delightful guide to Beaufort and the scenes of Rhett's youth. It is here appropriate to interject that original spelling has been retained without the intruding "*sic*" where words are misspelled, unless meaning could be obscured.

A special word needs to be said about Michael Reynolds of Columbia, South Carolina. Working on a master's thesis on Rhett's Civil War career, he has offered invaluable aid and insight as we have traded sources during the course of our respective projects, showing that fine spirit of generosity that has always characterized the best scholars. He has also read and critiqued this work, and I am obligated to him for his comments, as I am to my old friend Eric H. Walther of the University of Houston, distinguished student of the Fire-eaters, whose biography of Rhett's soul mate William L. Yancey was being written even as this work on Rhett was completed, and whose evaluation of this book has been of inestimable benefit.

Several members of the Rhett family have been most helpful, especially Dr. William P. Rhett Jr. of Charleston, and Harry Moore Rhett III of Nashville and his sister Leslie Crosby of Huntsville, Alabama, who opened to me the home of Robert Barnwell Rhett Jr. and gave me access to his surviving papers. Thanks are also due to Alexander Moore of the University of South Carolina Press for numerous favors during the writing of the book and to another friend of many years, director Catherine Fry, for being patient.

I would be remiss if I failed to acknowledge Jennifer Davis, whose own patience with a writer's schedule and habits was remarkable and who bore up wonderfully during the period that I seemed to be taking on some of the less felicitous aspects of Rhett's personality while spending so much time with him.

The Signing

The cheering erupted as more than three thousand Carolinians exploded in enthusiasm. It had begun.

"Edward Noble."

Ladies in the balcony fluttered white handkerchiefs and added their voices as one after another the men solemnly stood and stepped forward.

"James L. Orr."

On the stage the governor, the clerk, and other officers of the legislature sat watching as one after another the delegates' names were called by John Sloan, clerk of the state house of representatives.

"James Chesnut."

Out in the streets and down on the Battery militia loaded cannon, preparing to fire a sustained salute, while men stationed themselves in every church tower in the city ready to ring their bells.

"Langdon Cheves."

The men were being called alphabetically by election district, and after almost ninety minutes the cheering still had not stopped.

"Andrew Gordon Magrath."

Suddenly the roar grew louder. The clerk had finally reached the names of men from St. Michael's and St. Philip's, the Charleston delegates, and this was a Charleston crowd.

"William Porcher Miles."

They had been at it for almost ninety minutes, and then at last the crowd heard the name they had been waiting for.

"Robert Barnwell Rhett."

At once the greatest shout yet went up as a sixty-year-old man, slim and erect at six feet, arose and began to walk down the aisle. Blue eyes behind gold-rimmed spectacles acknowledged the accolades of the multitude and saw the shimmering array of white silk handkerchiefs as he nodded a well-formed, balding head at those he knew. Before him on the stage he saw Governor Francis Pickens; his old friend David Jamison, president of the convention; the clerk;

and behind them the scenes of Southern industry and culture painted by the nephew of another toiler for freedom, the Italian liberator Garibaldi. They were all together now, at last.

Red-faced as usual, with a small white plaster covering an annoying pimple beside his nose, he reached the simple two-drawered table on which the ordinance of secession lay for signature. Suddenly he fell to his knees, lifted his hands upward toward the heavens, and bowed his head in prayer. It was high drama, and high theater as well, and the crowd exploded in cheers as he said his silent thanks. Everyone else arose, men took their hats in their hands, and the handkerchiefs went to eyes tearing over at the emotion of the moment. Then he stood, took the pen, and wrote his name midway down the fourth column of signatures, immediately to the right of his old friend Maxcy Gregg's. That done, he returned to his seat, no doubt mildly chagrined that the next to be called was his old enemy Christopher G. Memminger, whose name would go right below his own. Memminger would bear watching, not only for who he was, but for the danger that he and his kind posed to the great movement.[1]

Another half an hour and it was done. Jamison stood to say, "I proclaim the State of South Carolina an Independent Commonwealth," and as they poured out of Institute Hall the cannon and bells commenced in a symphony that lasted long into the night. A few blocks away at the office of the *Charleston Mercury*, Rhett's editor son printed an extra, a broadside proclaiming that "THE UNION IS DISSOLVED!"

It had taken Robert Barnwell Rhett more than thirty years to come to this day, turbulent years of controversy and ceaseless turmoil, many of them filled with defeat and rejection, but he had persevered as he always persevered. Now he had received his reward. His whole career had led him to this point. At last the people of South Carolina had caught up to him and were ready for his lead. If the rest of the slave states did the same, a glorious future awaited them all, free and independent. No wonder it was the greatest moment of his life. In this hour of his triumph he could scarcely imagine that he would need more than prayers in the days ahead, nor that an angry future awaited with vengeance to repay him for the past.

RHETT

ONE

Madam Modesty
1666–1819

HE NEVER TIRED OF BOASTING of his distinguished English ancestors. They were one of the two earliest sources of pride for a man in whose character pride was not just a feature but also a defining element. Sixty years after his birth, even in the midst of the greatest crisis of his generation, Robert Barnwell Rhett could not resist impressing upon an English visitor the fact that he came from the finest British stock. The other source, of course, was that those Englishmen had shown the good sense to come to South Carolina, and moreover that he numbered among them the very first settler of the colony. He would only have been prouder, perhaps, if his patrilineal forebears had come under a more distinguished surname, but that was something he could remedy himself.[1]

The enterprising English felt interest in settling and exploiting future South Carolina at least from 1629, though a few Frenchmen got there half a century before, erecting and then abandoning what they called Charles Fort. The first settlers came from Virginia in 1633 under a royal charter granted to Sir Robert Heath. Thereafter for thirty years adventurers concentrated their efforts on Barbados, which also came under their charter. Then in 1663 a venture, under a new charter to the newly formed Lords Proprietors of Carolina, explored the coastline but chose future North Carolina to begin a settlement called Charles Town on the Cape Fear River. Two years later, however, Charles II gave the Lords Proprietors a second charter. That, and the pressure to expand their sugar cane planting from Barbados to the mainland, impelled the adventurers to look more closely at the region south of Charles Town. They sent a vessel south from the Cape Fear in 1666, exploring the coastline as far south as Port Royal, and before they returned they left behind a single man, Henry Woodward, to learn the local aboriginal tongues. He was the first settler of the future South Carolina.[2]

More ancestors followed close behind. After several missteps, storms at sea, ships wrecked, and ships blown off course, two sloops, one of them the *Carolina,* finally dropped anchor in the Ashley River in May 1670. When the men went ashore they began their new settlement called Charles Town, among them Henry Woodward, who was destined to achieve prominence as a physician, student of the native languages, explorer, and entrepreneur. Another passenger on the *Carolina,* or else on the somewhat later *William and Ralph,* which was loaded with settlers given grants from the Lords Proprietors, was a young man from Exeter named Smith.

Thomas Smith of South Devon was a man of more than average property and standing in the middle of the seventeenth century, though as a Protestant dissenter from the Church of England he was a tacit—if not active—sympathizer with the parliamentarians under Oliver Cromwell in the late civil war. His son Thomas was born in 1648, the year before triumphant Roundheads condemned King Charles I to the headsman's ax. As a result, the younger Thomas Smith grew to a teenager under the Commonwealth but far enough away in the west country not to be much affected by its troubled incumbency, for the royalist pockets of continuing resistance and the occasional mutinies and uprisings that followed 1648 were mostly in the north, the Channel Islands, and Ireland.

The Smiths' role in the civil war certainly was not active enough to bring them harm when Charles II resumed the throne in 1661. Their social standing by 1670 was at least such that the junior Thomas could woo and wed the young widow Barbara Atkins. It was a productive match and perhaps one of convenience for them both. She brought to the nuptials a grant from the Lords Proprietors of a "barony" of twelve thousand acres in the new Carolina colony, no doubt left to her by her late spouse, but she could hardly claim and exploit it without a husband. Smith had the wit and the will to rise in the world and at least enough substance of his own to attract the confidence of the Proprietors. Her grant promised to make him a man of increased wealth and importance, and his youth and strength could make of that grant something she could not for herself. If there was love in the bargain, so much the better. By the time they boarded their ship for the voyage they already had an infant son named Thomas.[3]

The Smiths prospered in the new colony, the family itself increasing almost on their arrival with the birth of another son. As for their land grant, it all but guaranteed success if they could bring it under cultivation. The crown had made the Lords Proprietors virtually a power unto themselves where Carolina was concerned. They could make laws, appoint governors and lower officials, grant land, and more entirely at their own will, subject to no oversight from Parliament and answerable only to the king. They were an aristocracy in their own right. None of them would move to the new colony, but those who served them well by making Carolina profitable for growing and trading could expect to win their favor.

Thomas Smith won that approval. In 1680 the Proprietors secured his wife's twelve-thousand–acre grant in title to Smith, and eleven years later they granted directly to him four more such baronies on Goose Creek in St. James Parish at an annual rent of one penny an acre, building his holdings to sixty thousand acres. Meanwhile Smith had already acquired Oyster Point, where the Ashley and Cooper Rivers converged in a great harbor, which he bought for six shillings in 1688 and which was now the site of the growing community of Charles Town. At the same time, on May 13, 1691, concluding that Smith was a man of "singular merit" gifted with "wisdom, prudence, integrity and loyalty," they gave him the hereditary title of landgrave, or count, with full authority over a small portion of the colony, subject to the laws of the Lords Proprietors and their appointed governor. The year before, the planters had named him interim governor to succeed the deceased Sir Peter Colleton, but the Proprietors' own appointee arrived before Smith could take office. Two years later, in 1693, they appointed him governor of the colony in his own right.[4]

One event in particular from Landgrave Smith's life would be remembered and passed down through the generations, perhaps embellished and confused by fallible memory along the way, yet its influence on the future South Carolina and on Smith's descendants was such that the grain of the story cannot have been much altered in its basic features. In its earliest form the family story told of a brigantine from Madagascar that stopped in Charleston in 1694 while he was governor, perhaps bringing slaves but almost certainly intending to take on barreled beef and pork. The Carolinians planted nothing more than subsistence crops. They were livestock breeders, some of them running considerable herds that foraged freely on the virgin land. One of the reasons the Proprietors had settled the mainland, in fact, had been the need for large grazing areas unavailable on Barbados and Bermuda to raise meat for the islands as well as for shipment to England. That same year Governor Smith started the practice of keeping a register of livestock brands and marks in order to establish ownership in disputes and prevent theft.[5]

Before the ship left for England, its captain named Thurber met with Smith and gave him a bag of seed rice from Madagascar. The governor divided the seed among a number of his friends, and they all experimented with planting and harvesting it in the rich upland that they cleared, leaving it to natural rainfall to nurture the grain. They discovered that it grew well in Carolina, providing some variety in their diet and enough seed to expand the planting. Eventually Carolinians found that the yield was even greater if they planted it in the marshy tidal lowlands along the coastal plain. Thus Landgrave Thomas Smith introduced to Carolina the staple crop that would make it famous and form the basis for its greatest fortunes.[6]

First told more than a century after the fact, the story, like many after the passage of several generations, certainly muddled the facts and unconsciously amalgamated Smith's involvement—if any—with other dimly recalled tales. Rice had been known and planted on a household scale in the colony since the early 1670s but was of so little importance other than as a subsistence crop that it attracted no attention to its commercial value. Captain Thurber probably made landing at Charles Town around 1685 and may have left some Madagascan seed rice behind, but nothing connects Smith with the event. By 1690, well before the landgrave's elevation to governor, some were seeing commercial possibilities in the grain as an export, and ten years later it had become the major staple crop of the colony, bringing with it a new demand for cheap field labor that the livestock raising had never required. That meant slaves, and by 1705, even as the white population remained static or even declined, the numbers of newly imported blacks from Africa grew dramatically.

Whether or not Landgrave Thomas Smith had anything to do with it or not, his posterity would fervently believe that he had, and generation after generation they told all who listened of how their ancestor inaugurated Carolina's path to wealth and power.[7] If he did contribute to the introduction of rice, Smith did not live to see the crop's success. He was already in poor health when he assumed the one-year term as governor and soon resigned, but he continued to hold office while awaiting his successor. Before he could be relieved of office, he died on November 16, 1694.[8]

Just hours after Smith's burial another man destined to be a revered ancestor arrived in the colony. When William of Orange arrived in England in 1688 to take the throne of the deposed James II, Sir Gwalter de Raedt of The Hague came with him, and the new king soon made him a baron and later governor of the Bahamas. Raedt had brought with him his son William, born September 4, 1666, and in time both of them anglicized the family name to Rhett.[9] William felt an affinity for affairs nautical and military, it seems, and must have seen some time at sea, for around 1693 he and Nicholas Trott, then governor of the Bahamas, and his kinsman John Trott, a London merchant, fitted out the 1,250-ton frigate *Providence* with Rhett in command for a trading voyage to Gambia on the western African coast. The voyage was a success, Rhett exchanging a cargo of iron bars—the standard currency for trade with the natives—for gold, elephant ivory, and most of all slaves. That done, he sailed across the Atlantic to land at Charles Town on November 19, 1694 while the town still mourned the late Governor Smith. Just what he did with his cargo is uncertain, though five years later his partners, the Trotts, still had not received their share of the goods and commenced court proceedings against him in London, seeking to seize his property and personal slaves in compensation. Somehow Rhett settled with the Trotts in the end, but for some time thereafter his name carried about it vague rumors of piracy.[10]

Rhett prospered in spite of rumor. He had married the daughter of one of the Lords Proprietors, which undoubtedly gained him some dowry of land, and brought her and their child William with him, choosing to live in Charles Town rather than on the plantation. The boy William died, unfortunately, but the Rhetts would have six more children in the colony, including his daughter Catherine, born in 1705. Meanwhile his standing in the colony rose. He was appointed captain of the province, later colonel of the militia, and by 1717 was surveyor and controller of customs. His duties included enforcement of a 10-percent importation duty passed by the Carolina assembly on all goods introduced from England as a means of raising colonial revenue. Rhett objected strenuously to the tariff, warning that it would "discourage the Fair Trade" and encourage smugglers, though at the same time it would foster any inclination the colonists might have to manufacture their own goods, especially woolens. In time the solicitor general in London would overturn the tax, closing the first, but by no means last, affair connecting the name Rhett with a tariff.[11]

Rhett also added the title of vice admiral of the colony's tiny navy to his honors and sailed more than once out of Charles Town to patrol the coast for smugglers and pirates. In the autumn of 1718 he took two sloops and 130 men after the notorious freebooter Stede Bonnet after the pirate captured a slave ship off Charles Town harbor, and they caught up with him off Cape Fear on September 27. In the five-hour fight that followed, Rhett bested Bonnet's eight-gun sloop and brought the pirate back to Charles Town to hang.[12] The feat made Rhett a local hero and earned him lasting fame for generations, but just a year later some of those who cheered him were shooting at him.

Relations between the colonists and the Lords Proprietors deteriorated throughout the early 1700s, Rhett and his onetime partner Nicholas Trott standing in defense of the Proprietors. In 1717 they had sent Robert Johnson as a new governor charged to rule firmly and keep the local assembly in its place, but he and Rhett disagreed, and Rhett behind his back tried to weaken him with the Proprietors and no doubt encouraged local disaffection as well. Though Rhett had favored repeal of the tariff on imports when it came, it did not sit well with the colonists who would now be taxed on their own property instead. The Proprietors also moved to cut the flow of paper money being used in lieu of scarce specie, causing a currency crisis, and then in a final ill-advised blow they closed off all further land sales. The result was a hard check not only on immigration but, more importantly, on the expansion of existing colonists' holdings.[13]

Finding themselves threatened with inadequate currency, looming taxes on their property, and curbs on their future expansion in land and wealth, the colonists rebelled. In November 1719 they deposed Johnson and his governing council and installed their own governor, the current Speaker of the assembly, James Moore. Moore and his own council virtually usurped the power of the Proprietors in hopes that the king would assume authority, and meanwhile they openly resisted all vestiges of control by their former rulers. Rhett's customs boats were fired upon, and an outcry arose against him despite his recent popularity. Smugglers lay at the root of some of the outcry, for with the customs operation disrupted they could operate more blatantly. In December someone, either a smuggler or another dissident, shot Rhett through the body when he was seizing pirated goods being smuggled ashore.[14]

Rhett recovered from the wound, and the crown took up the reins of control in 1721. Rhett regained his popularity rather quickly, but he may never have recovered his health entirely. On January 11, 1723, aged fifty-six, he suffered a stroke or apoplectic seizure that left him speechless. He died the next day and was buried in Charles Town's St. Philip's churchyard on January 14. Most of the town came out for his funeral, all wearing their best gloves and scarves in his honor, while the ships in the harbor ran their flags to half-mast and fired salutes. His passing was noted as far away as Boston in the Massachusetts Bay Colony, where the press praised him as "a Gentleman who greatly promoted both that Place and its Trade."[15] Like many of the ruling elite in the days of the Lords Proprietors, when Rhett died he had his own family arms, a Latin cross, against which appeared an arm, bent and brandishing a broken spear. What he could not leave behind was his name to carry those arms. All of his surviving children were women, and with his passing the Rhett name disappeared from South Carolina and America. Yet there would be generations of Rhetts to come for whom that broken lance would provide inspiration and admonishment.

Ironically, Rhett's daughter Catherine married Roger Moore, sometimes called "King Roger," who was the son of the rebel governor James Moore of 1719 and grandson of an earlier governor, James Moore, and whose maternal grandfather had been Sir John Yeamans, governor of Barbados and founder of Charles Town. Thus their daughter Sarah, born in 1728, brought a distinguished Carolina lineage to her marriage around 1750.[16] Her husband was to be Thomas Smith of Cape Fear, great-grandson of the old landgrave. At his death the first Thomas Smith's property and title had gone to his eldest son, Thomas, then aged about thirty-five and already nicknamed "the little Englishman" thanks to his infancy when he arrived in the colony. He had married Anna Van Myddagh and built the first brick house in the colony at his plantation on Back River and another in the growing city at Charles Town. He held his title as landgrave until 1729 when, after years of friction between the colonists and the Lords Proprietors, the crown assumed full control of the colony, and its feudal titles and powers dissolved as Carolina was absorbed into England's rule of all its American colonies. Still "the little Englishman" remained a man of influence until his death in 1738, leaving behind him wealth and property and some twenty children, the beginning of a family tradition of remarkable fecundity.[17]

One of those twenty offspring was a daughter named Sabina, who coincidentally wed a man named Thomas Smith. Her husband, in fact, was the latest of three straight generations of Thomas Smiths originating in Boston and possibly some distant relation.[18] Compounding the confusion, or reflecting an utter disdain of variety, when Sabina and her husband had their first son in 1719 they named him, too, Thomas Smith. Unlike his mother Smith's ancestors, and perhaps reflecting the New England side of his ancestry, this Thomas Smith made his way as a merchant in Charles Town—now called Charleston—accumulating considerable wealth from importing and investment by the time of his marriage to Sarah Moore. Not surprisingly, this Thomas was called "the Banker" by the family, and if his profession showed his Yankee lineage, his twelve children reflected the unceasing fertility of the Carolina Smiths. Certainly he had a banker's temperament. "Full of candor towards all men, he behaved as if he thought no evil of them," recalled his son James, "yet prudently guarded against their possible treachery." He enjoyed a reputation for veracity and discretion, and he lived simply, even frugally, observing the most regular of habits. "He used this world happily without abusing it," said James, and eschewed the temptation to pride. The Banker appeared grave at home and abroad, yet enjoyed good cheer in others and was known to show courtesy and kindness to all regardless of their social station. "His religion was love & rejoicing," recalled his son. Often Smith took his children individually with him to a room at their plantation on Goose Creek, off the Cooper River, and there prayed privately with them, especially the youngest son, James, who became his favorite.[19]

James had been born November 2, 1761 and was just old enough to start being politically aware when echoes of the old revolt against the Lords Proprietors were heard in 1775 as the several colonies rebelled against Great Britain. Thomas Smith had just set up his son Roger as a banker with four hundred thousand dollars in capital when protest erupted into armed revolution. The Smiths never forgot the scene in Charleston the next year when South Carolina framed its new independent constitution and then cheered for the first time a governor and council whom they had elected by their own franchise as freemen.

One of the sons, probably Roger, went briefly to Massachusetts where he spoke with the patriot leader John Adams and described the scene in Charleston that day and the tears in the eyes of those who realized that they had elected a government of their own. He told Adams that "their People will never give up this Government."[20]

Much of the family fortune disappeared in the turbulent years to follow, and Roger left banking to raise and command the Silk Stocking Company of light infantry, composed of the sons of leading gentlemen from Charleston. By 1779 his brother James was old enough to join the company and serve with it when the British laid siege to nearby Savannah, Georgia, in October. Soon afterward the Smiths and their company joined the defenders as Charleston endured its own siege, and when it fell in May 1780, young James found himself aboard a British prison ship. Only his father's influence prevented his being shipped away. Pleading the boy's youth, Thomas Smith persuaded Gen. Henry Clinton to release James on parole until he could be properly exchanged for a British prisoner of war. But Thomas had no intention of letting his favorite son return to war after exchange. Immediately after the parole he sent James abroad for education.

James Smith was still in London when the Revolution ended in 1783 and England acknowledged the independence of the new United States. James persuaded his father to allow him to remain there to complete his education, and Thomas agreed on the understanding that the boy would support himself out of his inheritance. He studied law, applying himself so tenaciously that he later believed he ruined his eyesight, for he had to hire someone to read aloud to him some of the literature he studied. One such reader possessed such an amazing memory that James could send him to church and the man would return and recite verbatim the sermon. James Smith eventually progressed so far that he was admitted to practice in the courts of equity at the Middle Temple in London. He stayed seven years abroad without seeing his beloved father and family, but it softened the loneliness somewhat to discover that he had other kin in the city. His brother's acquaintance with John Adams was not entirely accidental. Adams's wife was born Abigail Smith, the great-granddaughter of that same Thomas Smith of Boston whose grandson Thomas married Sabina Smith. Thus James Smith and Abigail Adams were third cousins once removed, and now her husband was in London as the new minister from the United States to the court of George III. Somehow she learned that James was in the city, and though surely they had never met, she invited him to their home and thereafter entertained him almost every Sunday at dinner, where he probably met his younger teenaged cousin John Quincy Adams. John Adams even secured the young man an introduction to the king. Though he returned to South Carolina in 1787, James Smith never forgot the hospitality of the Adamses, especially of Abigail, whom he believed to be an admirable woman.

Quickly other concerns occupied his more immediate attention. He joined the Charleston bar but never practiced much, for in 1789 his father, Thomas, died and James inherited fifty thousand dollars that he used to buy a plantation on the Combahee River in Colleton District and a summer home in the small community of Beaufort in St. Helena Parish. There were more changes in store too, for on December 22, 1791 he married Marianna Gough.[21] She was the only child of Capt. Richard Gough and Elizabeth Barnwell, parents who never lived well together. Two months after her birth in 1773 Marianna's mother left Gough and moved to Beaufort where she raised her daughter on her own. Elizabeth's strength and independence showed a streak that had run in the Barnwells since her grandfather John Barnwell first left Ireland to settle in Carolina. He early established himself as one of the first settlers near Beaufort and began acquiring thousands of acres of plantation land. In 1711–12, after a series of clashes and raids by local natives, he was chosen to command a retaliatory raid against the Tuscarora at Cape Fear, his victories earning him the sobriquet "Tuscarora Jack."

By the time of Marianna Gough's marriage to James Smith, her grandfather was a part of South Carolina legend. Moreover, when Marianna's father, Nathaniel Barnwell, married the great-granddaughter of that very first English settler, Henry Woodward, the assemblage of ancestors for worship was complete. The first Carolinian, half a dozen governors, two landgraves, an admiral and pirate-catcher—and perhaps a bit of a pirate himself—and Tuscarora Jack all combined to ensure that the next generation of Smiths would have title to an ancestral pride second to none in the state. Moreover, the myriad aunts, uncles, and cousins in the unfailingly fertile family allied them with the Middletons, Heywards, Stuarts, and virtually every other prominent family in Carolina.[22]

James Smith's distinguished bloodline could not save him from himself, however. He simply did not have his father's gift for prosperity. "He was totally unsuited for planting or for any money-making occupation," one of his future sons would say of him. The rice plantations that he bought did not thrive, partially, no doubt, from his own neglect, for he was an inattentive planter. He loved books and gardening passionately but ignored most else, and his first-born would later describe him as "a mere child in the practical means of life." Everybody managed to hoodwink and cheat this gentle but utterly guileless man, even his own slaves. Only in one realm did he equal his ancestors' productivity, and that was in the nursery. James and Marianna's first child—Thomas, of course—appeared in 1794, and over the next twenty years they would have fourteen more, ten of whom lived to adulthood. After Thomas came James in 1797, then Benjamin in 1798 and Marianna in 1799. As the close of the year 1800 approached, Marianna was pregnant yet again, and on December 21 she gave birth to a fourth boy at their Beaufort home. In honor of her uncle Robert Barnwell, they named him Robert Barnwell Smith, but from an early age they would call him Barnwell.[23]

During the next several years as his family increased by two more girls, Claudia in 1802 and Emma the next year, James Rhett's fortunes continued their decline. Cotton had become the second staple crop of the state, but neither at that fiber nor rice could he make a profit from his land. His interests naturally led him to the secluded pursuits of the scholar, and instead of managing his land he spent his time studying early South Carolina and compiling family history. Moreover, he had no head for handling money and was easily duped out of his dwindling fortune thanks to a nature more trusting than the Banker's. By the time he and his wife acted as sponsors for the baptism of Barnwell and several of the other children at their home on April 30, 1805, it was beginning to look doubtful that they would keep that home indefinitely.[24]

Thus it came as something of a godsend when James's older and much more successful brother Benjamin Smith, now governor of North Carolina, contacted him in 1807 and suggested that he sell out and come to Cape Fear to invest with him in a rice plantation. With Marianna pregnant yet again and no prospects in South Carolina, James wisely agreed, but when the parents moved, they took only the daughters with them. The four boys, Thomas, James, Benjamin, and Barnwell, were to stay behind to be educated in Beaufort, where they could live with their grandmother Elizabeth Barnwell Gough.[25]

For the next five years young Barnwell Smith would know his grandmother's three-story house on Carteret Street as home. Though not so grand as many another planter's town house, still it was large and elegant. It sat just two streets back from a wide bay in the Port Royal River and enjoyed the cool evening breezes that came in off the river much of the year. Beaufort itself was a small town, its inhabitants almost entirely planters whose families had held plantations in the vicinity for nearly a century going back to Tuscarora Jack. In that day it concentrated probably more wealth and educational attainments for its population than any other community in the state, and so inbred were its families that the same surnames predominated, most of them in some way descended from or connected to the Barnwells. Some claimed that given a little time they could name up to a thousand persons in the town and parish to whom they were related.

Beaufort society was different too. Though the nearby river instilled in most townspeople a love of sporting on the water, they were in other matters remarkably restrained. Society, said one, was "checked and tamed by the very rigid notions prevalent there as to the frivolity and sinfulness of many amusements highly attractive to the young and gay." Though almost all of them, including the Smiths, were Episcopalians whose faith hardly frowned on a little overt indulgence in fun and sport, Beaufort society somehow dampened that behavior in young and old alike.[26] The citizens preferred to keep it that way, looking to the vice in Charleston and other larger centers of population as an object lesson on the perils of amusement unchecked. Young William Grayson recalled Beaufort as having the property of "standing still," its people self-satisfied, pious, moral, "and not a little addicted to mental cultivation." In short, Beaufort may not have been the most enjoyable place to be a child just then, but certainly Barnwell and his brothers found themselves not wanting for attention or affection from their grandmother and all those other relatives, particularly their great-uncle Robert Gibbes Barnwell, whose son Robert Woodward Barnwell was just eight months younger than Barnwell Smith and soon became his closest companion.

Among Beaufort's other distinctions, thanks to that addiction for learning, it harbored almost no illiteracy among its white inhabitants. There were tutors for the wealthy, literate parents to provide rudimentary learning at home and the Beaufort Library Society's public library, founded in 1802 and already grown to several hundred volumes. One of the Barnwells always remembered the twin allurements of the river and the Library Society's books, calling Beaufort "this old town of note, where each man had a library and every man a boat." For the younger boys there was also a primary school opened in 1804 by Milton and Virgil Maxcy, which young Barnwell Smith probably started attending before his parents left for North Carolina and where he would have continued until his early teen years.[27]

In 1812, with war breaking out once again with England, James Smith sent to Beaufort for his sons to come join him at the rice plantation he owned with his brother Benjamin on the Cape Fear River. The three older boys went, but their uncle Robert Barnwell asked that young Barnwell be allowed to remain, to live with him, be a companion to his own son Robert, and finish his education. Robert Gibbes Barnwell was the same age as James Smith, had served in the legislature, was elected to the Continental Congress, and later served in the United States Congress. He staunchly defended the Constitution in the ratification debates in South Carolina and as a Federalist argued that it was necessary to relinquish some local powers in the greater common good of a strong government that could protect the rights of all. Thereafter he served in the state senate as a progressive proponent of free public education and abolition of the African slave trade. Such an uncle was bound to be an influence on his nephew, as indeed he was throughout Beaufort. "He maintained a sort of intellectual dictatorship in our society," recalled William Grayson, "which no one was disposed to dispute." Barnwell presided over the Conversation Club, at whose meetings local men presented papers and debated current topics, and around his home there was always the ferment of discussion and lively thought. He gave young Smith the example of one who, while he listened politely to opposing views, remained inflexible in adhering to his own opinions. Though others might disagree with his positions, no one doubted that he held them sincerely.[28]

Away from his father, with whom he seemed to have little in common other than a studious nature and a diffidence toward business, young Barnwell Smith must naturally have looked up to and in some degree emulated his uncle, certainly the most distinguished family member of his immediate acquaintance. Even if he did not accept Barnwell's Federalist leanings, young Smith certainly learned from the elder statesman's manner in debate and noted the force and tenacity with which he held to his opinions. Indeed, the shyness and want of self-confidence already evident in the boy may well have been encouraged by an uncle who, in serious conversation at least, could seem overbearing and intimidating.

The elder Barnwell was also a passionate supporter of Beaufort College, which had opened in a new frame building in January 1804 on a site overlooking the river just a few blocks away from Elizabeth Gough's house. Its founders had hoped to create there a source of liberal education for all classes of the white community, one to rival South Carolina College in distant Columbia, the state capital. Though Beaufort College never realized those aspirations, still it quickly became one of the finest preparatory schools in the region. Barnwell sent his sons Robert Woodward and William Gibbes there, and young Smith may have been enrolled already when he went to live with his uncle. Among the other boys there were Richard deTreville, born in Beaufort just a few months after Smith; young William F. Colcock, son of Judge Charles Colcock; Edward Peronneau; and Richard Fuller.[29]

Barnwell Smith was soon a favorite, especially with the Reverend John Hedly, professor of languages and a strict disciplinarian who yet developed an affection for the quiet youngster. In fact, Smith benefited from a remarkably fine faculty for such a small school. Dr. Thomas Fuller, one of the founders of the college and its current president, was a leading apologist for slavery on religious grounds, and young Smith, a distant cousin, always felt he owed a great deal to his kinsman's attention and influence while there.[30] The Maxcy brothers also taught there, and the Reverend Martin Luther Hurlbut from Maine would be there until 1814, when the Reverend William Brantly and William Grayson also began to teach.[31] From January 1811 onward James L. Petigru was part of the staff, acting also as temporary president. With his round saucer-shaped face and what one called his "Irish mother wit," Petigru especially won the affection of Barnwell Smith.[32] Though himself a stern disciplinarian, he spun tops and shot marbles with the boys when not at their lessons, and Smith formed an attachment to him that lasted half a century.

Petigru's adherence to principle, even when unpopular, always impressed Smith. He had hoped to be elected permanent president of the college, but something—perhaps his adherence to the Federalist Party—cost him the election, and Hurlbut took the post instead until succeeded by Brandy.[33] Looking back on Petigru, who left a few months after the election, Smith recalled that "with the great multitude of men, in public affairs, *place* is *success.*" Men hid their unpopular opinions for the sake of expedience and subordinated their principles to popularity in order to achieve position. Petigru had refused to do that, though it may have cost him the presidency of the college, and it was a lesson Smith never forgot. "It is only the strong man—strong in conscious rectitude, strong in convictions of truth, strong in the never-failing and eternal vindications of time—who can put aside the temptations of present power, and patiently submit to official inferiority," he would say of Petigru. "Superficial observers may not understand," he said, "the greatness of such a man."[34] It was a kind of greatness he would emulate if he could.

The rote method of teaching could be hard on a boy, especially when, in the classroom at least, the instructors could seem so stern. Brantly sometimes browbeat the boys when they were slow at their lessons, calling then "dunces," and no doubt Smith came in for his share.[35] It is no wonder such men encouraged Smith's natural diffidence and shyness, and before long his schoolmates teased him with the nickname "Madam Modesty."[36] Still, if he was retiring, Smith thus had all the more time to apply to his learning. Beaufort College possessed an excellent library, and the students enjoyed the use of the holdings of the Beaufort Library Society as well, and Smith demonstrated early a capacity for study and memorization.[37]

During the April through October terms he was exposed to many of the standards of classical literature, the works of Homer, Herodotus, and Virgil. Latin came handily enough for him to be comfortable with it for the rest of his life, and Greek to a lesser extent. He also read Edward Gibbon's *Decline and Fall of the Roman Empire,* with all the lessons it implies on the hazards of civil laxity and corruption, several histories of the world, and no doubt some of the literature of the new nation, including biographies of George Washington and the history of the Revolution. There was philosophy, of course, both the ancients and the modern, such as the Scot David Hume—whose ideas took little hold on Smith—

and mathematics and classical mythology. He also read a little poetry, though in later life the only verses he still had memorized—albeit imperfectly—were a few stanzas from Lord Byron's new *Childe Harold's Pilgrimage*. They were words that spoke of isolation: "This is to be alone; this—this is solitude" is what he remembered Byron saying in the third canto. Perhaps he also recalled a later verse that declared: "I have not loved the world, nor the world me. I stood among them, but not of them." These were feelings of which he already knew much. There was also rhetoric and oratory, and Smith's first lessons in elocution. Under his uncle Edmund's advice he took a few lessons from a local teacher but quickly found them not worth attending. The boy preferred instead the classical rules of declamation, stressing the importance of saying the right thing to the right audience at the right time. Even a feeble speaker could succeed, they argued, if the time were right. It could give the common man untutored in oratory, even a shy and modest person like young Smith, the power to sway an audience and best even the most experienced orator.[38]

All progressed well until the fall of 1814. On October 24, Robert Gibbes Barnwell died suddenly. With the disruption in the family that followed, it was no longer feasible for Barnwell Smith to stay with them. He may have returned to his grandmother's for a few months, but she was elderly, and meanwhile there came a renewed summons from James Smith in North Carolina. Though scarcely past his fourteenth birthday, Smith had to leave Beaufort College. While the sons of the prosperous planters who had named him Madam Modesty went on to South Carolina College and northern schools such as Yale and Harvard and the College of New Jersey, James Smith could spend nothing more on formal education for his son Barnwell. Thereafter he would largely have to educate himself.[39]

James Smith did not prosper in North Carolina any more than he had at Beaufort. He finally settled on a small plantation called Exeter near Smithfield. James spent the winters on the Kendall plantation operated with his brother Benjamin, and he spent summers at Exeter. The family at least grew, with Edmund born in 1808, Albert two years later, another who died in infancy in 1814, and Elizabeth shortly after young Barnwell rejoined the family.[40] But if he could not run a plantation, at least James Smith could continue Barnwell's education. For the next few years father privately tutored son. At the same time young Barnwell got to renew associations with his siblings, special favorites being the sickly Claudia, his confidante, and little Albert, for whom he formed an early admiration.[41]

It was not long before more disruption upset the family's life. Exeter finally failed, and at almost the same time Elizabeth Gough died on October 10, 1817, probably during a yellow fever epidemic in Beaufort that so ravaged the community's population that Beaufort College had to close for want of students and the building was razed to the ground for fear of infection. Marianna Smith was Elizabeth's only heir, and thus she inherited the house on Carteret Street. That and the failure of the plantation in North Carolina brought the Smiths back to Beaufort, where they could live comfortably, if not in wealth, from the inheritance and what little remained of James's own fortune.[42] For the next two years Barnwell Smith continued his learning at home. If Beaufort College's doors were closed, at least the many private libraries in the town were open to him, and his reading and study proceeded. He could spend spring afternoons at the house on Carteret enjoying the delicacy of his mother's strawberries with sweet cream and sugar, lessons with his father, and the company of his boyhood friends who were not sent away to college, as his cousin Robert Barnwell had been to Harvard. There, too, he absorbed a lifelong admiration for James Smith, who, though a failure professionally, certainly succeeded as a model for character. A model of domestic purity, his children were often awakened by the sound of James Smith singing a hymn before starting the day. "He was the most truthful man I ever knew," Smith's eldest son recalled. Often he paused in conversation to rethink his words and then correct himself to make certain his meaning was absolutely precise. Patient, forgiving, ceaselessly kind, and indulgent, he never lost his temper with his children, and even when he was agitated, the strongest oath ever heard from him was to call the object of his displeasure a "Son of a Gun." He gave them an example, if nothing more.[43]

Increasingly Barnwell mused on what he should do when learning inevitably must give way to earning. One certainty was that he must look to himself for a living. There was no remaining Smith fortune and no family land on which to set himself up as a planter. His father's remaining fortune had all but disappeared just as James Smith's older sons were about of an age to start life. He would leave no inheritance other than perhaps a few remaining slaves, for no man of James Smith's family and station would be without slaves, no matter how low his fortunes might sink. All his family and ancestors had been slaveowners, accustomed from birth to the assumptions of natural superiority of white over black, and necessarily his son Barnwell was inculcated with those notions from earliest cognizance. It was natural to his blood that he would own slaves too, regardless of his future profession, even though his inclinations, like his father's, ran toward more intellectual pursuits than farming. That being the case, there were inevitably only three choices of profession before him: the law, medicine, or the church. He had already seen enough of the physician's life with his sickly sister Claudia, the infant deaths of several of his siblings, and the occasional fever epidemics to know that it held no appeal. As for religion, though Episcopalian like most of his family, he was not entirely comfortable with the laxity of a denomination that was going through some crisis itself at the moment, and for several years yet he remained uneasy and unsettled in his faith. That left the law, his father's avowed profession, for what little good it had done him. At least it was the calling of a gentleman, which he yearned to be, and a life with books. It also promised a code of conduct and a body of laws that, while hardly perfect in their precision, still offered his literal temperament that certainty of right and wrong and of his place on the firmament that the rife quackery of medicine and the unending doctrinal debates of the church did not. When just past his nineteenth birthday he borrowed his first law books from a cousin, attorney Thomas Grimké of Charleston, who thereafter guided Barnwell's study, both instructing and examining him by correspondence.[44]

There was another part of Barnwell Smith's education that had been continuing virtually since his birth, and that was his political acculturation as a "Low-country" South Carolinian. Beaufort had started as a staunchly Federalist area in the early days of the republic and remained so after much of the rest of the South abandoned the party for Thomas Jefferson's new Republicans and even after the virtual death of the Federalist Party itself in 1816. Just a few weeks before Barnwell Smith's birth, Jefferson defeated incumbent John Adams for the presidency, but Beaufort's electoral district sent to Congress Federalist Thomas Lowndes, an ardent nationalist like Petigru, Charles Pinckney, and the rising young John C. Calhoun.[45]

By the time Barnwell took up his law studies in 1819, however, the nationalist hold on Beaufort was crumbling, and over the same issues that politically divided the nation: money and power. There were only two sources of income for the federal government: sale of public lands, and customs and excise. With the former, few had any quarrel, but it was on the tariff that men and parties—and eventually sections—began to divide. The issue of contention was a simple one in theory. There were two kinds of tariff, a lower rate on imports designed solely as a means of raising revenue for the operation of the government, and a higher rate as a punitive or "protective" tariff to give domestic goods an advantage in the marketplace over otherwise cheaper foreign exports. No one objected in principle to a revenue tariff, for all parties agreed that the government must be funded somehow. But opinions divided sharply on protection, for it benefited domestic producers by forcing domestic consumers to pay higher prices.

The outcry commenced with the very first tariff passed by the new Congress in 1789, for though it was basically a revenue measure, still it allowed additional duties to be imposed to protect some chiefly Northern manufactures and a few agricultural products. Being mainly agricultural producers and manufacture consumers, the Southern states felt the tariff falling harder on them than on the North, and just the next year, in 1790, South Carolina senator Pierce Butler spoke in Congress warning that the doctrine of protective tariffs, if pursued, might one day destroy the Union.[46] Federalist support of the tariff had helped defeat Adams, though Beaufort continued to support the old party, helping reelect Lowndes in 1802. But then the cracks started to show. Lowndes was defeated in 1804 and again when he ran four years later, as the district three times elected the more moderate Robert Marion. Then in 1810, with Beaufort and Colleton Districts for the first time forming their own congressional district, they chose William Lowndes for the first of five consecutive terms. He was still an ardent national-ist like his brother Thomas and had been a Federalist, but he was shifting to the Jeffersonians on some issues. In 1816, in the face of opposition from his con-stituents, Lowndes supported a new tariff that protected both industry and agri-culture, especially cotton, a measure also backed by Calhoun. Still the South saw itself as the loser and moreover felt threatened by the alliance of the New Eng-land and middle Atlantic states that pushed the tariff through. Even though the measure was supposed to encourage cotton in states such as South Carolina, the sudden availability of cheaper fiber from new states such as Louisiana and Mis-sissippi undercut the seacoast planters.

All the while there raged the struggle for power. From the first the Federalists, led by Secretary of the Treasury Alexander Hamilton, urged a strong central government with considerable control over the finances of the nation, including a national bank, and the sort of liberal construction of the Constitution that would allow Washington to be an active agent in pursuing commercial prosper-ity, of which protectionism was a part. Against that Jefferson and his followers argued for limitations on federal power, a more literal view of the Constitution, and hands off the monetary system. Inevitably the two parties gradually became increasingly sectional, with the moneyed interests concentrated in the North and those resisting its grasp for influence dominant in the South. Then came the second war with Britain, opposed by the Federalists and much of the North, and enthusiastically supported by the Republicans and most of the South. Not the least of their reasons for prosecuting the war was the promise of adding new ter-ritory to the west. The South could claim three of the four presidents to hold office as of 1812, but the only means of being certain to defeat protectionism and contain the growth of central power in Washington was to maintain parity in Congress. The North already outstripped it in the population-based House of Representatives, but in the Senate, where each state had two elected representa-tives, they could block objectionable legislation so long as Southern states equaled or outnumbered Northern states. That meant new territory was needed for Southern planters to settle into new states, and remaining British territory in America offered the solution. Directly or indirectly, the outcome of the war pushed them toward the ultimate acquisition of Florida, Alabama, and Mississippi, and a precarious—and temporary—balance of power.

Barnwell Smith could hardly be unaware of the national scene during these formative years in Beaufort. In contrast with most of the community, James Smith was a Jeffersonian Republican, suspicious of too much power in the central government and jealous of local prerogatives. He planted the first seeds of his son's later attitudes toward the course of the nation, past and present. From the earliest moment that he could form political opinions, the younger Smith believed, they were molded by Jeffersonian Republican ideas. "I was . . . raised & nurtured a Republican, in the faith & principles of my Father," he recalled in after years. Harkening back to his father's war, Barnwell erroneously believed—or at least maintained—that whereas Southern soldiers served in the Continental forces north of the Potomac, not a single regiment from New England helped out in the Carolinas.[47] It may have been true, but he saw it in a sectional light, the North refusing to give as good as it got by helping the South, conveniently ignoring the fact that when Washington and his army were in Virginia in 1781, the majority of his soldiers were Northerners.

As with the Revolution, so with much of what happened since. Smith came to believe that James Madison was not the so-called "father of the Constitution" and that instead it was South Carolina's Charles Pinckney, who had presented his own plan to the constitutional convention in 1789. Then after Washington took office as president, Barnwell believed that Hamilton was the real power behind the throne, imposing "false construction and usurpation" by the government and a Federalist "latitudinarian-construction policy" on the nation. Hamilton's policy of federal assumption of state debts after the Revolution was clearly unconstitutional to him, and the creation of the Bank of the United States was worse, while the funding system of maintaining federal deposits on the one hand and an unpaid national debt on the other struck him as ridiculous and simply another means for the financial manipulators of the Northeast to profit. It was the maintenance of that debt, he believed—or was told—that led to the imposition of high tariffs in the first place and started a system of increasing protection that was only one more tool by which Yankee moneyed interests sought to concentrate power in their hands through the government. If there had been no national debt, there would have been no need for duties, and the nation would enjoy the benefits of free trade and a free market with the world. His ancestor William Rhett's old plea for "the Fair Trade" echoed within him.

Barnwell laid it to what he called the corrupt bargain between Secretary of State Jefferson and Secretary of the Treasury Hamilton in 1791. Hamilton wanted the debts assumed, and Jefferson wanted the national capital moved to the Potomac

River. Each was able to give the other what he wanted, but to Smith, Jefferson had sold out the South and the Constitution, an attitude that helped account for Beaufort's continuing opposition to the Republicans.[48] "From the commencement of the Government of the United States, the money power of the north, controlled the North, and hovered over the Government like a vulture seeking its prey," he would say.[49] After that, one usurpation easily led to another, as Smith saw the matter. Soon the Federalists followed up with legislation against new immigrants, who, arriving without capital of their own, had nothing in common with the money interests and leaned toward the Jeffersonians, and at the same time struck at opposition to their party in the press by passing the Alien and Sedition Acts of 1798.[50]

Then came the War of 1812. It commenced shortly before the death of Robert Gibbes Barnwell, whose opposition could not have been unknown to the nephew then living with him, but the Smiths supported it along with most of the rest of their political brethren in the Southern states. Beaufort, especially, felt vulnerable to British naval attack, and though none came, the sound off the Port Royal River was blockaded for a few weeks in 1813. Barnwell came under the belief—probably passed to him by his uncle and later his father—that the Southern states pushed for the war from altruistic motives, to avenge the wrongs inflicted on Yankee ships and seamen. Nothing was said of the South's own preeminent self-interest in gaining more territory. Instead, Barnwell Smith believed that the Yankees were making so much profit from the embargo on foreign goods following the outbreak of war that they had no desire to fight it to a conclusion. And when in 1814 three New England states met at Hartford to propose constitutional amendments that would limit future federal power to make war and impose other restrictions to preserve state rights, Smith believed they were intent on seceding and disrupting the Union in order to protect their financial interest.[51]

Immediately after the war came the 1816 tariff, which, though it actually launched protectionism, Smith regarded as "anti-protective," since it provided for reduced duties over succeeding years as New England industry recovered from the war and became more competitive with foreign manufactures. Despite support for the tariff from Calhoun and Congressman Lowndes, local planters sent a complaint to Congress, another sign of the shift away from their old Federalist ideals, and the Smiths would have been fully behind the protest. Indeed, as 1820 approached there was a younger generation coming of age in Beaufort and Colleton, men such as Barnwell Smith who were born too late to pass through the experiences that made ardent nationalists of Petigru and Calhoun. Growing up in the shadow of events since 1800 and encouraged by a few older Jeffersonians such as James Smith, they regarded the North and the Washington government with increasing suspicion and resentment, and more and more saw South Carolina threatened from without.[52]

And there was another threat. At Beaufort College, Barnwell Smith absorbed from Petigru a detestation of the "pernicious dogmas" of what Smith called "the whole batch of French atheists and philosophers, who, by denying the weakness of our fallen nature, would set man against his fellow man, in vain efforts for abstract justice and equality, and vainer efforts for human perfectibility."[53] He rejected almost the whole of the Age of Reason out of hand. "Reason is a faculty of the mind—not a principle," he would conclude. Noble as that faculty was, however, it was the most easily perverted. Men could twist reason to support the most flagrant sophistries, and the French in 1792 made it the basis of their postrevolutionary government as he saw it. Passion was natural and thus reasonable, and therefore not to be suppressed. If reason could dictate moral rectitude, then anything could be justified, no matter how unjust or perverse.[54] Clearly Smith was no believer in the Enlightenment, and his views were only reinforced by the time he studied law under Grimké and could see the shifting population of South Carolina. The white population of the Lowcountry was sparse thanks to all the land given over to large plantations. Meanwhile inland, in the Upcountry, the numbers of poor whites grew much more rapidly, threatening a shift in the electoral balance in the legislature and in the congressional delegation that made the old planter aristocracy fearful for their hold on state politics. From an early age Smith fully accepted the prevailing myth that the South had been settled by the descendants of the noble, high-toned English Cavalier aristocrats, while the narrow, bigoted Puritan stock populated the North. It was a fiction contradicted by his own solidly middle-class ancestors, as well as by his Smith cousins in Massachusetts, but nevertheless a prevalent idea that only reinforced the belief that certain people were destined by birth and blood to rule, and others to be ruled.[55]

South Carolina had been an oligarchy from its founding, a few influential families connected by intermarriage virtually dominating politics at all levels, and they intended for that to continue. Arguments for universal white male suffrage threatened to ruin the oligarchy, and the peril in the state was only a microcosm of the threat in the nation as a whole.[56] Even Smith's readings in the classics that he so much favored reinforced his distrust of the direction American democracy was headed. He had studied Herodotus, and from more than twenty-three centuries in the past the words of Megabyzus came to him from "Thalia" in the *History*. "There is nothing so void of understanding, nothing so full of wantonness, as the unwieldy rabble," he said. It was folly for well-born men to yield their affairs to the will of a mob that could rush in any direction on a whim, like a swollen river. The will of such a majority could spell disaster. "Let us choose out from the citizens a certain number of the worthiest, and put the government into their hands," Megabyzus went on. "For thus both we ourselves shall be among the governors, and power being entrusted to the best men, it is likely that the best counsels will prevail in the state."

With all that Barnwell Smith had heard from his father, what he had read, what he had learned from his teachers, and what he had seen for himself in his adolescent years, the ancient Greek's words seemed a credo for South Carolina's survival in the increasingly complex and threatening world of American politics. More than that, it sounded like a call for those "worthiest" and "best men," men with the determined and principled example of Petigru and Robert Gibbes Barnwell, in the face of opposition and unpopularity, to step forward and take their rightful place and power and "be among the governors." It was what his ancestors would have expected.

TWO

All Passion, Excitement and Fire

1819–1828

A GREAT DEAL HAPPENED IN BEAUFORT the same year that Barnwell Smith commenced reading law. The planters felt a tremendous credit crunch from a financial collapse that year. Moreover, the argument over admitting Missouri to statehood renewed the controversy over parity for the slave states in Washington. Thus perhaps it was a blessing that Beaufort's attention could be diverted, however briefly, by the arrival of a distinguished visitor. President James Monroe took an extensive trip down the eastern seaboard that spring, and on May 6 he arrived at the Port Royal ferry, six miles from Beaufort.

The townspeople turned out in numbers to meet him at the ferry and ride along with him back to their community. If he was at all able, Barnwell Smith would have been among them, and his father as well, for Monroe was a Jeffersonian in the main, though rather less strict in his construction of the Constitution than many in the South would have liked. Even more of a reason for the Smiths to attend, however, was the president's traveling companion, the secretary of war. By now John C. Calhoun was the blazing young star of South Carolina politics; he was just thirty-seven, previously a congressman and intimate ally of Monroe in prosecuting the war with Britain, and an ardent nationalist. Though he also supported the unpopular national bank and was something of a protectionist, still the new generation of Carolinian Republicans looked on him as their ideal. Surely this visit to Beaufort marked young Smith's first sight of Calhoun, and in the round of introductions that followed during the reception festivities, he would have been presented to both the president and the secretary of war. Monroe would have had no reason to remember the introduction in later years. Calhoun would.[1]

Having seen great men in the flesh for the first time, Smith could scarcely help a bit of daydreaming and admiration, envy even, of the acclaim they received. "Madam Modesty" may have been starting to emerge from that shell of diffidence that shadowed his earlier youth, but the example of such men, especially Calhoun, could only inspire him to try all the more, for life in the public eye had an undeniable allure if a man could be comfortable before the people and confident of himself. His law studies provided a natural push in that direction, for an attorney was a public man. Smith kept at Grimké's books for two years, then in the fall of 1821 went to Charleston to finish reading at Grimké's office directly under his guidance and also with his old mentor Petigru. Grimké influenced Smith almost as much as Petigru before him, even though both varied dramatically from him in their ideas of government and society. Like James Smith, Thomas Grimké was more at home with ancient and modern literature than with the law, and when he did practice it was often pro bono work for the poor. Smith found him affectionate as a relation and patient, though firm as a tutor, a man courteous to all and reluctant to offend any. Years later he would look back fondly on his time with Grimké as he "drank from the full fountain of his legal acquirements," and drank well enough that the following spring he went before the local examiners and passed their scrutiny.[2] Just a few months past his twenty-first birthday Barnwell Smith was admitted to the bar.[3]

With a profession before him and a family in Beaufort that increasingly strained James Smith's resources, the new attorney naturally went out on his own. He borrowed fifteen hundred dollars and went to Coosawhatchie on the river of the same name, the small but important crossroads district seat several miles inland from Beaufort, and there he commenced his practice, modestly at first. His first case involved a suit over the malicious killing of a horse. Smith argued it before Judge Daniel E. Huger, one of the state's leading nationalists, and won, and within a year this case plus others to come allowed him to repay the loan.[4]

It was a crowded bar, however, and with the country still just emerging from the depression of 1819, he found little business to suit him. In 1823 he moved to Walterborough, seat of adjacent Colleton District. The move promised not only more clients, but also the chance to form a partnership with his cousin Robert Woodward Barnwell, recently graduated from Harvard.[5] Apparently the partnership prospered. Smith was admitted to practice in the courts of equity, and on March 15, 1824 the court of appeals admitted him to practice, along with his sister Claudia's new husband John A. Stuart. A painter, poet, orator, and devotee of the works of Shakespeare, Stuart was just nine months older than Smith, and though he would set up his own practice in Charleston, he was restless at the law. Animated by the same political leanings as his brother-in-law, his literary inclinations may already have turned his eye toward journalism instead.[6]

For the next two years Smith and Barnwell gradually built their practice, and Barnwell Smith showed some aptitude at the calling. He performed capable research in the statutes and judicial opinions of South Carolina and nearby

Georgia, gained some authority especially in cases involving inheritance, and demonstrated some considerable forensic skill in marshaling arguments for his pleadings. His chief handicap, and one that he would never overcome, was an abominable handwriting that made reading his briefs next to impossible for anyone but himself.[7] Smith was in his middle twenties now, scarcely under six feet tall in his stockings, and trim at 180 pounds. He revealed a fair, rather florid complexion topped by brown hair that was already thinning atop his small but well-formed head. Blue-gray eyes sat above a prominent nose and a rather small mouth whose agreeable smile revealed perfect teeth. He smiled freely too and was quick to laugh, showing that however retiring he may have been as a child, he was no stranger to fun. Smith relished a good jest, so long as it was not vulgar, and he liked to impart jokes, reportedly telling them well. Nor was he at all puritanical, despite his discomfort with the laxity of the Church of England. Certainly he held distinct opinions on vice and morality, looking with contempt on the sinfulness that he believed epidemic in the North. While he eschewed coffee, which he was convinced was bad for the health, he condemned ardent spirits and referred to himself as a "cold-water" man, though he perhaps took an occasional glass of claret at meals and certainly did not object to candy flavored with brandy.[8]

Smith believed that a person's character was fully formed by the age of ten. "All the great elements of character are stamped into the mind before childhood, or boyhood, has ended," he maintained. "Here begins the moral inequality of men, by which one is raised to honor, and another to dishonor." Those early elements rarely changed thereafter, he felt. "We then act upon them, as they are grown within us, and carry them out in the moral warfare of life, for good or evil, to others and ourselves."[9]

Certainly by the summer of 1826, at twenty-five, Barnwell Smith believed that his own character had formed fully enough for him to engage at a different level in that warfare and to seek some position of honor beyond his profession in which he could do good for others, or at the least prevent evil being done to them. And he had seen enough of what he took for evil coming out of Washington, the North, and even from the state capital in Columbia to believe firmly that South Carolinians needed protection. In 1820, as he still pored over his law books, Congress settled the Missouri controversy with a compromise that in his view was no compromise at all but rather a betrayal of Southern rights by limiting the formation of new slave states to the territories below the 36° 30' parallel. To his mind, and those of most Carolinians, the federal territories belonged to all the peoples of the Union, and therefore Congress had no right to exclude Southern slaveholders implicitly from taking their slave property with them north of that line. It was a matter of rights, certainly, but also one of power. With the free and slave states at equal numbers for the moment, anything that threatened Southern expansion and the formation of more slave states by men of Jeffersonian persuasion only increased the danger of a Northern majority in the Senate and thereby utter Yankee domination of Congress and national affairs. That could mean more tariffs, more protectionism, and eventually even a threat to slavery itself.

In 1824, as he and Barnwell opened their new practice, the next tariff arrived, and he regarded it as a repudiation—indeed, a violation—of the spirit of the 1816 law. Now that the terms of expiration on protected manufactured goods were to expire, the money interests that he saw controlling Northern politicians forced through a new law that not only kept the protective rates in force but raised them and extended the tariff to even more products. Beaufort sent another protest to Congress, and Smith complained that "it was nothing but robbery." Just as bad was what he saw as the workings of a rising political party tied to commercialism. The remnants of the old Federalists and some nationalistic Jeffersonian Republicans coalesced around Smith's kinsman and the new president, John Quincy Adams, and Henry Clay of Kentucky, seeking to expand federal authority. To Smith's view, they were motivated increasingly not by principle and conviction but by ambition. Political influence was driven by money, the money was in the North, and therefore these men played to the Yankee galleries. "The Party thus became, but little more than a mere association to obtain office and power," Smith grumbled. Moreover, not only was Southern security threatened by the precarious balance in Congress, but now he could no longer count on the old solidarity of the Republicans to protect local interests, as party loyalties seemed to start breaking down beneath the weight of ambition.[10]

All of these controversies played themselves out in smaller compass on the South Carolina stage, especially given the automatic division of interests between the wealthy Lowcountry planters, and the more populous but less affluent Upcountry people. The same battle for control between ancient aristocrats and the unwashed mob that Megabyzus so feared faced the state now, further confirming Smith's conviction that absolute democracy pointed a dagger at the heart of what he liked to call "Free Government." As a proud descendant of those blue bloods who founded the state, as a firm believer in the natural right to supremacy of the oligarchy as the protector of every man's rights, as a defender of the class to which his family had belonged and into which he hoped to propel their fortunes once more, and as a young man who had a taste of ambition for public prominence as perhaps an antidote to that old modesty he was now shedding, he had a call to answer. Smith's success at the bar encouraged him to believe that he could win votes as well as judgments. Moreover, his family associations and Beaufort College friends gave him the ear of the most influential families, while among his contemporaries the fact that, like many of them, he was completely the product of a provincial upbringing and education, untainted by European philosophy or Northern universities, made him one of them.[11]

That summer he decided to seek one of Colleton District's seats in the state assembly representing Walterborough's parish, St. Bartholomew's. He could have gone back to Beaufort to run for office, but undoubtedly he discussed the prospect with his partner Barnwell, who decided to try for another Colleton seat for himself. His cousin could have reminded Smith of what Petigru had said to one or both of them around 1819, when perhaps they first discussed glimmers of political expectations. Petigru warned that they would never get ahead in politics if they remained in Beaufort. Their hometown was too tied to the old aristocracy, and their families, ill at ease with the spreading social democracy in state affairs, would not encourage their entry into such an increasingly plebeian arena.[12] Moreover, even though there was an increasing shift away from the old Federalist leanings in the face of the turmoil of the 1820s, Beaufort had not yet caught up to young Smith's Jeffersonian leanings.

He announced himself as a candidate that summer as a Republican and in the polls emerged at the head of the list of candidates, Barnwell right behind him.[13] Thus the boyhood friends who commenced the law together would now enter the state house together as well. They took their seats at the opening of the Twenty-seventh General Assembly on November 27, 1826, and Smith was at once impressed with some of the other legislators as men of ability and note. There was Waddy Thompson, a freshman, from the western part of the state. There were Hugh Legaré of Charleston, fervent antiprotectionist; Isaac E. Holmes; the budding legal scholar John B. O'Neall; and Benjamin F. Dunkin.[14] Most of them he was meeting for the first time, and the newer members were largely his own age.

Of course the business of the state house was chiefly parochial. The Speaker appointed Smith to the committees on claims and the judiciary, and when not sitting with them he came well prepared to represent the wants and needs of Colleton. Smith presented his first petition from his constituents just the day after taking his oath, a request to construct a road in the district, and thereafter he was frequently on the floor introducing reports of the parish school commissioners, petitions for articles of incorporation of a fraternal lodge, and most of all the claims for compensation that would be referred to his own committee. There were ceremonial duties as well, even an adjournment on December 4 for all of the legislators to participate in the commencement ceremonies for

South Carolina College. In keeping with the state's tight rein on democracy, the governor, the attorney general, and United States senators were all elected not by the people but by the legislature, and Smith helped make John Taylor governor and his old mentor Petigru attorney general, and helped send William Smith to the Senate in Washington.[15]

On December 2, Rhett introduced the first bill of his own, designed to alter the sitting times of the courts of common pleas and general sessions in the circuit that included Colleton. It was referred to his own Judiciary Committee and made its way to the state senate before the end of the session. Indeed, it was in committee that the legislator's real work was done. In the Judiciary Committee he had to ponder requests for the purchase of law libraries, oversight of some grand jury decisions from the several districts, alteration of the procedures for electing tax collectors, suggestions for amendment of the state constitution, and even a proposal to ban billiard tables within a certain radius of the capital.[16]

Far more significant of the times, and of affairs beyond state borders in the South at large, were the issues he faced on both his committees relating to slavery. Of course Smith had grown up in a society inseparable from its system of labor. The Smiths for generations had been slaveowners, and though his father's failed plantations would have obviated possession of any substantial number of field hands and their families, still even a somewhat frayed middle-class family such as the current generation of Smiths would have had domestic servants. More than half the population of Beaufort District was made up of slaves; the system was the loom weaving the fabric of Southern economy and life. Though he had said nothing publicly as yet, there can be no doubt whatever that Barnwell Smith not only condoned slavery but regarded it as a positive political, social, economic, and moral blessing to both races, one more reason for his rejection of the sophistries of the Enlightenment.

Throughout this first session Smith faced in committee the mounting social and political problems posed by slavery, both from the slaves themselves and from outside antislavery agitation. He saw cases of slaves convicted and executed for assault, burglary, and rape, and when an owner submitted a petition for compensation, Smith's Claims Committee had to decide how much to pay, usually $120, and in the case of rape they made the owner split for reimbursement with the victim. When a slave was injured or killed while helping a master chase a runaway slave, the committee had to determine if the owner was entitled to compensation for his damaged or lost property. Occasionally a local court tried to dodge jurisdiction in trying slaves and free blacks, bumping these cases to the state instead. Sometimes he even had to consider bills that regulated the behavior of slaves on their masters' plantations, as with a measure to prohibit blacks

from planting their own cotton in their little gardens, thus potentially competing with whites.

Most troubling of all to Smith and the others, however, were the petitions
from men who wanted to free their slaves. In June 1822 a free mulatto named
Denmark Vesey allegedly assembled a band of 130 blacks who began hoarding
weapons with the apparent intent of attacking and capturing Charleston. They
were discovered and hanged or deported before they could act, but the wave of
fear and near hysteria over the plot drove South Carolina and much of the South
into a course of draconian repression of its blacks, free and slave. Not surprisingly in such a climate, Smith's committee denied every emancipation petition
that came before them. "Notwithstanding the conclusion to which a course of
reasoning upon abstract rights might lead the necessary policy," the committee
report read, "the general welfare and absolute safety of the citizens of this state
forbid the emancipation of slaves." Smith firmly believed that the Vesey plot had
been instigated by Northerners scheming against "the property and the lives of
the people of the South."[17] Not only did they not want their own slaves made
free, but the committee also denied entry into South Carolina to slaves from other
states who had been convicted of crimes but reprieved on condition of leaving.
Uneasy with the potential consequences of slaves acquiring too much learning,
they reported favorably a bill prohibiting the public instruction of blacks. The
clear imperative driving the legislature's policy was that blacks were untrustworthy and sank easily into degradation and crime, and for the benefit of everyone
needed to be kept in ignorance and under firm control. It was an opinion that
Smith certainly already held before he went to Columbia but that beyond question his initial legislative experience confirmed.[18]

Inevitably echoes of broader national issues confronted Smith and his colleagues. In reaction to the coalition of old Federalists and monetarist Republicans that had elected John Quincy Adams to the presidency in 1824, a new
Jeffersonian party was growing up around Andrew Jackson of Tennessee, calling
themselves Democratic Republicans, soon to be shortened simply to Democrats.
William Smith was one of those new Democrats when the legislature elected
him to the Senate. Unhappy with the presidential outcome in 1824, when the
election went to the House of Representatives with Jackson having a plurality of
electoral votes until Henry Clay shifted his electors to Adams, the legislature in
committee of the whole recommended an amendment to the Constitution to
reform the electoral process that had denied the South what would have been
its fourth consecutive Jeffersonian president.

On that increasingly vexing question of the tariff, Charleston sent to Columbia a memorial protesting that despite all the commerce that passed through its

wharves, the duty revenue it produced as the second largest port in the South all seemed to be going to the North and the West thanks to the 1824 tariff and what its greatest advocate Clay called the "American System." The protective duties imposed by the "System" financed internal improvements designed to improve transportation and thus foster industry, thus to free America from dependence on foreign markets. Customs revenue from Charleston and other ports of importation was being spent on building roads and canals and improving navigable rivers and harbors, most of which seemed to be in the Mississippi Valley and in the North, where all of the raw materials and industry for manufacturing were located. The South and South Carolina, blessed with numerous navigable rivers all leading to the seacoast, scarcely needed improvements to get their agricultural products to market, while their politicians in Washington mainly opposed internal improvements in principle and therefore made no effort to secure what might have seemed a fair share of such seeming "pork barrel" appropriations for their region. Calhoun was somewhat friendly to internal improvements, but he now sat as Adams's vice president, an office virtually powerless. When the legislature received Charleston's protest, all Smith and his colleagues could do was acknowledge the injustice and send a recommendation to their congressional delegation in Washington to try to address it in Congress. At least Smith could help prevent the corruption happening on a national scale from infecting state affairs. When a bill appeared for an appropriation to encourage agriculture in South Carolina, he joined the majority in defeating it. Even in his home state public moneys should not be spent to favor any particular commercial enterprise or industry. That was the essence of a free market.[19]

By the close of that brief first session in mid-December, Smith had established himself as a firm adherent to a strict construction of the Constitution, an unwavering opponent to any interference or special encouragement from government with business and industry, and a strong advocate of the protection of slavery and slaveholder interests. Smith also showed that "Madam Modesty" was all but dead. He rose to speak frequently, more so than most of the other freshman legislators. Young Benjamin F. Perry, then studying law in Columbia, met Smith for the first time during this session and observed that he "always spoke with great fervor and animation." Indeed, by the end of that session Perry found that Smith "was then regarded as a very brilliant and promising young man."[20]

Certainly he showed no fear or favor. During the previous legislature it was learned that while he was governor a few years earlier John L. Wilson drew several thousand dollars from the state contingency fund and had not yet paid it back. He was notified of the amount due, $4,816, but took no steps to return it, and since he was a noted duelist, no one in Columbia seemed inclined to take

Wilson to task over the money. On November 29, Wilson finally submitted a note on the matter, requesting a statement of the amount due, and it was referred to a special committee of five including Smith. Six days later the committee reported back to the body that the amount was still outstanding and offered a resolution apparently written by Smith calling on the comptroller general to report to them the following day on whether or not the money had been repaid. A copy of their resolution was also handed to Wilson, then in Columbia, and the implicit suggestion was obvious that if he did not make restitution immediately, he might face legal proceedings. Smith may even have called on the floor for such action, just to make it perfectly clear. Years later Smith claimed that he was prepared for the possibility that Wilson, who happened to be co-author with John Ash of a dueling manual called *The Code of Honor,* might well make the matter personal and that Ash, then sitting in the legislature, admired Smith's audacity. Wilson apparently did grumble and make some veiled threats, but by the next morning his friends raised the money for the comptroller, who reported it paid in full to the house, ending the matter. Wilson and Smith later shook hands when they met.[21]

Smith impressed others as well and had one in particular on his mind by the close of the session. Until then no one had been as close to him in his life as his immediate family, and his closest friend was cousin Robert Barnwell, with whom he spent most of his time in Columbia.[22] But within two months of the close of the session he had a new intimate. He must have been courting Elizabeth Washington Burnet for some time before he went to Columbia. She was much younger than Smith, just turning seventeen at the close of the session, yet was noted for her beauty and intelligence. The Burnets were not of the aristocracy, but her mother had been a DeSaussure from one of the most distinguished Huguenot families. Perry, like many others, found her to be "a most amiable, mild and gentle lady," and for the rest of Smith's life she would be and remain his first and deepest love. They married on February 21, 1827 and set up housekeeping in Walterborough while Smith returned to his practice and prepared for the next winter's second session.[23] Certainly he expected to maintain the Smith tradition of fertility, for when he left for Columbia that November, Elizabeth was already six months pregnant with their first child.

By then Smith had already passed another milestone "first" in his career. On May 11, 1827 a group of citizens met in Walterborough in answer to a general call. They elected William C. Pinckney chairman, their purpose being to send a memorial to Congress to protest the protective tariffs in general and an 1826 Woolen Bill in particular that had come up in the last session in Washington. Smith attended and moved that a committee be appointed to draft the memorial, and Pinckney appointed him and eight others to frame the document, with Smith as chairman. Quite clearly this had all been planned ahead of time, for the committee retired only a few minutes before returning to report a lengthy draft that must have been written sometime before, most likely by Smith.

They protested the inordinate benefits to "the monopolist" and his "grasping cupidity" afforded by protectionism. While they stopped short of accusing Congress of framing sectional legislation, still they affirmed that "from the moderation of our Northern Brethren, who for the last ten years have been beating at your doors for monopolies—we have renounced all hope." They rehearsed the history of increasing tariff legislation, until the Woolen Bill asked for a staggering 92 percent duty on imported goods. This was nothing but "tyranny and injustice," argued the memorial. "It is immaterial whether that money is received by one man called a King or by thousands termed Manufacturers." The South was already producing two-thirds of American domestic exports. They argued that production encourages consumption, foreign imports could only be purchased by domestic production, and therefore the South must of necessity consume more imports than the North. Thus that region bore an unnatural proportion of the burden of duty, since "the revenue of the United States is chiefly raised from the Southern States." The Constitution was a "charter between sovereignties" and did not allow protectionism to favor one section over another. Americans were only a single nation with respect to other nations, but so far as relations among the several states, they were really "separate and independent." Governments could not create capital but could only shift it from one place to another, but by the protective policy Washington was trying to aid industry that needed no aid.

"Free commerce is the true interest of every nation," they affirmed. Government's only real utility was in preserving social order and protecting people in their rights of person and property within the nation and against foreign threats. Any efforts to go beyond that to direct domestic industry "is not less futile, than criminal." Smith and his committee admitted that they did not expect their memorial to influence Congress but nevertheless had a duty to make this protest. If the protection doctrine were allowed to go unabated, it must lead inevitably to prohibition of some categories of trade entirely, a crippling of the American merchant fleet, an end to export income that funded the government, and a last resort to "the desperate alternative of direct taxation." If the government went that far, it would not be long before "its glory will have departed from you." Then Southerners must face the question of "how far the patience of the people of the South exceeds their indignation; and at what precise point, resistance may begin, and submission end."

Never before had Colleton sent a memorial to Congress, and in doing so now the committee members affirmed that they did not seek to intimidate by its strong language. But they warned that "error, here, may be ruin." Their region was already ridden with debt, and they pleaded, "do not add oppression to embarrassment, and alienate our affections from the home our fathers together raised." That said, they raised again the threat of something stronger than words. "Do not believe us regenerate from our sires," it said, "and that we will either bear or dare less, when the time for suffering or resistance comes." The message of threat was unmistakable. If pushed to the wall they would resist, though they did not say how. The mention of suffering might suggest a self-imposed embargo on their imports, thus strapping the national government for money even at the cost of their own comfort, just as their ancestors had done in response to British duties on tea and other luxuries before the Revolution. The mention of resistance could well suggest something even more radical.

The meeting adopted the memorial unanimously, condemning not only the tariff but also the policy of federally funded internal improvements financed by high import duties, and copies of the memorial were circulated throughout the state and to Washington. Smith and nine others were appointed to a "Committee of Vigilance and Correspondence" to see to the task, a resonant echo of the committees of correspondence that in the 1770s began to arouse and maintain resistance among the colonies.[24] While Smith had said little before this time in the public forum to establish the dimensions and tenor of his feelings on the tariff controversy, his subsequent declarations make it evident that he played a heavy authorship role in formulating this memorial. All the hallmarks of his future approach were there—protestations of loyalty to the union, denial of any intent to threaten, and yet repeated hints and threats of "resistance" with, moreover, the harkening back to their revolutionary forefathers as an example to emulate in rising up to defend themselves against wrongs. It was no call to arms but certainly suggested that such a call would be their rightful alternative if the North ignored their demands of justice. Most important of all, however, while other communities in the slave states were also protesting the Woolen Bill, Smith's Colleton memorial was the first really strident protest to hint at something more. Smith was all but inaugurating an escalation in the sectional debate that suggested that remonstration might be only a step on the road to outright resistance. Equally significant, he was going considerably beyond the idolized Calhoun in his rhetoric, actually speaking in opposition to the orthodoxy that Calhoun was trying to establish as he cemented his hold on South Carolina. Calhoun and the Union could expect trouble from Barnwell Smith.

No immediate furor developed from the Colleton memorial. Indeed, many outside the district seem not to have taken much notice of it, though the public discussion on the tariff continued warmly. But when Smith reached Columbia in November for the new session of the assembly, his agenda was already laid out for him on other lines and had probably been in planning in the Judiciary Committee the year before. The old judicial system lay badly in need of reform. For a start, the fact that the courts of equity and law were separate tribunals for last-resort adjudication frequently led to conflict between their decisions. Much worse than this, however, was the notorious intemperance of some incumbents on the bench, especially William D. James. Secure in their lifetime tenure, some appeared in court while drunk, and others did not bother to appear at all or issued irrational and capricious judgments. Smith's mentor Grimké was an outspoken proponent of legal reform, and this very year he had called for the legislature to codify state statutes rather than leaving management of the laws in the haphazard hands of judges. Current laws, he argued, no doubt influencing his cousin and pupil, were the grave rather than the cradle of principles.[25] Certainly Smith intended to redress one weakness in the system, and as soon as the legislature assembled on November 19, quite possibly by prior arrangement, the Judiciary Committee met to plan a remedy to the complaints against drunken judges.

On the third day of the session Smith stood up on behalf of the committee and introduced a resolution that "the Honbl William Dobbin James is guilty of the high crime and misdemeanor of habitual intemperance in the discharge of his office as a Judge of the Courts of Common Law in the State of South Carolina." A copy of the resolution was sent to James, and the Speaker appointed a committee of five, including Robert Barnwell and Waddy Thompson, with the power of subpoena, to look into the matter and report. At the head of the committee he placed Barnwell Smith.[26] Meanwhile, Smith had hardly had time to commence the investigation when James Gregg, chairman of the Judiciary Committee, proposed several resolutions to eliminate life tenure on the bench in favor of ten-year elective terms, an approach that enjoyed some favor, especially with the influential Speaker, John B. O'Neall. It did not meet the approval of Barnwell Smith, however.[27] From the opening of the discussion in committee he opposed a popularly elected judiciary. Judges must be "free from popular favor or rage," he argued.[28] What he did not have to say was that it would also upset a careful balance put in place by the old oligarchy to preserve its control on the state. Through a combination of gerrymandering, making property holding a condition for service in the legislature, and retaining in that body the power to elect the governor, state cabinet officers, and senators, the old elite still had a firm grip on South Carolina. The legislature also chose the president of South Carolina College and even ferry operators, and made the appointments of all judges. The retention of power in this body preserved the status quo and, in Smith's mind, protected the state—and its ruling elite—from the threat of mobocracy, the irrational, fickle, and ultimately destructive will of the majority.[29]

Smith preferred another alternative that had lain before them all along but which no one seemed either to remember or to be willing to pursue. On November 22, as the house was considering an alteration in the state constitution respecting the appointment of judges, he rose and introduced a resolution of his own. He proposed that "every civil officer may be impeached for any misdemeanor in office, or for any act committed or omitted during, or with a view to his office, which shall degrade his office, or impede the administration of Justice."[30] In the lengthy debate that ensued, Smith made his case well. "You complain of the state of the judiciary. Will the House inform me who occasioned its abuse?" he asked. The legislature had tried imposing more qualifications on judicial candidates some years before with the express view of purging the judiciary of the inept and inefficient, and still men like James had been chosen. "You place party-leaders-weary-pleaders, and mere rhetorical declaimers on the bench, and then clamor at their inefficiency, and when the justice of the state is disregarded or broken in their hands you shrink from the responsibility of impeachment," he chided them. If appointment by the legislature could not ensure competent and conscientious men on the bench, how would popular election by an easily swayed and deceived populace do any better? "Let us not attribute to the system our own follies," he implored. Impeachment could remedy individual evils without jeopardizing the foundation of the system itself. The power was theirs; they had only to use it.[31]

For the next few days the debate continued intermittently, and then on November 28, Smith offered a resolution that his special committee formally investigate James's conduct, take testimony recorded by solicitors, and report their opinions to the house. While Smith's committee began seeing witnesses and gathering information, the house again debated the proposed amendment providing for popular election and Smith's own resolution providing for impeachment instead. On November 29 in the vote on a ten-year term limit resolution, Smith stood against it with the minority but at the same time sided with a majority that rejected another alternative providing for removal of a judge by a simple two-thirds vote of both houses of the legislature. Finally the house passed a substitute amendment to Smith's that achieved his intent of broadening the powers of impeachment, thus accepting and sending on to the senate his principle, if not his actual resolution. Eventually an amendment to the state

constitution was drafted and passed, the first and last piece of constitutional legislation Smith would initiate.[32]

Meanwhile Smith and his own committee completed their investigation, and
on December 11 he reported their finding that James ought to be impeached.
For the next two days the committee of the whole heard debate on the report,
with Dunkin leading the opposition to impeachment, and a resolution was
finally passed to impeach the judge by a vote of ninety-nine to twelve. The
Speaker ordered Smith and his committee to draft the articles of impeachment,
which Smith presented on December 17 in a damning indictment enumerating
instances of James appearing drunk on the streets, losing official papers, ignoring
his duties, bungling sentencing, appearing in open court while intoxicated, and
even refusing to hear evidence in cases and making his decisions solely on the
bases of indictments. That same day, on instructions from the house, Smith presented the articles to the senate, which would conduct the trial after the holiday
recess, with Smith heading the trial managers from the house in prosecution.[33]

The judicial reform debate and the James investigation had so dominated the
first month of the session that Smith had had little time for other matters. He
missed a number of votes and was absent entirely on several days, but when
there he continued positions first espoused the previous session, including supporting a bill that prohibited the education of persons of color, free or slave, and
another that banned the introduction of all free blacks into the state. Yet there
was a charitable side to him that ..either he nor his contemporaries would have
seen as out of keeping with his opposition to rights for blacks, and he gladly
voted for an appropriation of twelve thousand dollars to aid transient poor whites
in the state. He supported an appropriation to continue an internal improvement, the completion of the Rocky Mount Canal, also not inconsistent in his
view. The canal was already started, and thus if not completed, what was already
spent would be wasted. Moreover, it was South Carolina's money alone that
would pay for it. Though in principle he normally opposed even that kind of
subsidized encouragement to commerce, at least it was South Carolina tax money
being spent inside the state rather than siphoned to Pennsylvania or Kentucky.[34]

After the holiday recess the legislature assembled on January 3, 1828, and the
most immediate business was the senate trial of James. Smith, Barnwell, Butler,
James Irby, and David L. Wardlaw presented the evidence for impeachment,
and William Preston, a rising Columbia attorney, acted for James's defense. James
entered a plea of not guilty, and Smith believed that Preston conducted an able
and eloquent defense that occasionally moved some senators to tears. Gen. David
Williams, onetime congressman, officer in the War of 1812, and former governor, put his head on his desk and wept openly, for James was well liked in spite

of his intemperance. No one, including Smith, could take pleasure in the humiliation of an old friend. In the end, however, their duty gave them no choice, and they voted to impeach. That shifted the attention back on the house to convict or acquit. On January 28, Smith, Butler, Irby, and Wardlaw each spoke in succession and at some length. The next evening Preston presented his defense for two hours, the senate sitting in the gallery to hear arguments that displayed sound research and eloquent advocacy on both sides. On January 30 the house voted seventy-four to twenty-six to convict on three of five counts in yet another moving scene. That same morning James went before the senate to appeal for leniency, and despite his immediate removal from office, he was allowed to draw his salary until the end of the year. The recommendation required the concurrence of the house, which agreed, with even Smith voting in favor of the charitable terms of dismissal. That done, the house offered its thanks to the impeachment managers, and Smith responded on their behalf.[35]

It is surprising that such an event as the impeachment of one inebriate judge would attract so much attention, but all of the principal presses in the state covered the trial, and many of the legislators and others who witnessed it ever after regarded the affair as a landmark in reform.[36] Certainly it established the precedent for removal of life appointees without resorting to the—for South Carolina—extreme measures of term limits or popular election, thus preserving the all-important old order. Barnwell Smith stood at the center of much of that attention, and the James trial and constitutional amendment made him a reputation that immediately elevated him considerably beyond the other first-term assemblymen. Certainly he was young enough, and human enough, to feel a bit of hubris at his newfound celebrity. Judge James, if he did nothing else, put the last nail in the coffin of "Madam Modesty."

The adjournment of the session barely gave Smith time enough to hurry home for something even more exhilarating. Staying with her family in Charleston in the last weeks of her pregnancy, Elizabeth gave birth to a son on February 5, 1828, and the proud father probably got there in time for the birth. With commendable restraint, they broke the tradition of the past several generations and did not name him Thomas. Smith was a man of growing importance in his own right now, and he could start a new tradition of his own. They named the boy Robert Barnwell Smith Jr., later to call him "Barny" within the family, and for the rest of their lives this son would have the closest relationship of all his siblings to his father and become in turn the one most like him.[37]

The excitement of fatherhood, and even the consciousness of spreading reputation with all that promised, could never entirely obscure more ominous events over the northern horizon. Despite all the execration that his fellow Republicans had heaped on President John Quincy Adams and his own opposition to his distant cousin's policies and associations, Smith still gave Adams credit for the economy and integrity of his administration. He never countenanced one charge of corruption or venality against the president.[38] Nevertheless, Smith, like other Carolinians, saw affairs tending steadily in an ever more dangerous direction. Reflecting national events, the Republicans in South Carolina were splitting along lines of nationalism versus state sovereignty on the tariff question and for and against protectionism and internal improvements, all of it confused by personal and political loyalties.

The year before Barnwell Smith won his seat, the legislature enacted resolutions championed by William Smith anathematizing internal improvements and protective tariffs, denying Congress the power to enact either. In 1826 the fight to elect a senator put that same Smith in office, but only after a battle that revealed serious cracks in the old party alignments in the state, for William Smith's ardent strict constructionism positioned him directly against the nationalistic and moderately protectionist Vice President Calhoun, South Carolina's popular and powerful favorite son who had his eye on the presidential election in 1828. Meanwhile there were voices in South Carolina speaking out more and more stridently against the central authority in Washington, and when the issue of the tariff arose again in Congress in 1827, it all went to the boil. That year Smith's brother-in-law John Stuart gave up the law and started publishing the *Gazette* in Beaufort, his editorials taking a hard stance against any further extension of protectionism. In July, Dr. Thomas Cooper, president of South Carolina College, a strong supporter of state sovereignty, publicly speculated that the state might one day have to put the value of the Union to South Carolina on the balance against the cost to the state of remaining in it. Robert J. Turnbull, writing as "Brutus," published a series of essays in the *Charleston Mercury* that year that he reissued in book form as *The Crisis: or, Essays on the Usurpations of the Federal Government*. The title said it all, and in the essays Turnbull called for an assertive policy upholding the compact theory of government by which a state, as a member of the compact, yielded some of its sovereignty to the Union on sufferance of good behavior, with the reserved right to withdraw and reclaim that sovereignty at will.[39]

Barnwell Smith took in all of this. He knew Cooper in Columbia. He read Turnbull's essays and book. He saw and heard from his family how Beaufort by now had completed its shift from the old nationalist days and was firmly in the state sovereignty camp.[40] Even Calhoun was reevaluating his nationalist stance as a result of what was happening within the South Carolina electorate, and Smith had never from the outset felt Calhoun's degree of attachment to the central government. Regarding the 1824 tariff as robbery, he could only view anything other than reduction as merely a continuation of the crime against South Carolina and her sister states. As with all evils, if not confronted and halted in its progress early, it would only get worse.

The legislature, with Smith in support, sent its resolution to Congress in December and echoed Smith's Colleton memorial in declaring that Washington had no authority to pass tariff laws that favored domestic industry, though in more temperate language. The majority in Congress were unwilling to be swayed, however, and in May 1828, just before the end of the current session of Congress, a new tariff passed that raised duties on almost everything. Even New England was unhappy with some of the new duties, but for the South it quickly became the "Tariff of Abominations." South Carolina's congressional delegation toyed with walking out, and George McDuffie spoke of urging the state to leave the Union. In the end they did neither, for fear of the damage that creating a confrontation at that moment might do to the presidential hopes of fellow Southerner and slaveholder Andrew Jackson and his running mate Calhoun that fall. It was better to keep the lid on protest until after the election when South Carolina could hope for reform.

They reckoned without assemblyman Smith. Heavily occupied with the James trial and other legislative business, and then with his growing family, he said nothing publicly as the congressional debates on the tariff progressed in early 1828. Certainly he discussed the issues in private with Barnwell and others, but so long as Congress remained in session and so long as the legislature had instructed the delegation in Washington in its course of opposition, there was nothing a state legislator could do in the matter, and he may well have felt it improper in any case. But when Congress adjourned on May 26, with the tariff an accomplished fact and the defeated South Carolina delegation on its way home, he felt free to act. He printed a handbill and circulated it throughout Colleton, urging the people not to submit to the tariff and calling another meeting of the citizens for June 12, 1828, at the new courthouse in Walterborough.[41]

It was evident from the outset that Smith had in mind an audience far more substantial than the few hundred who met on the appointed day. After a few formalities he took the floor and, instead of making a speech, read two addresses he had prepared. Wisely, he read them not as expressions of his own sentiments—the opinions of one man—but as declarations to be promulgated on their behalf to the people of South Carolina at large, and to Gov. John Taylor.

"What shall we do?" he asked in their name. Their congressmen had warned the government that the tariff violated their sovereign rights and would present them the grim alternative of "submitting in shame, or resistance in sorrow." In spite of that, their memorials lay buried on the table, ignored, and the abominable measure had passed and proved tenfold worse even than they had feared, with no consideration of the constitutionality of the measure. "What course is left to us to pursue?" he asked. "We have done by words all that words can do. To talk more must be a dastard's refuge."

He saw but one course: "If we have the common pride of men, or the determination of freemen, we must resist." They must stand committed rather than standing still. "We must either retrograde in dishonor and in shame, and receive the contempt & scorn of our brethren, superadded to our wrongs, and their system of oppression, strengthened by our toleration; or, we must, 'by opposing, end them.'" But unlike Hamlet, he did not contemplate suicide. He proposed that they array themselves "in open resistance to the Laws of the Union," even at the cost of their blood, and laid before them his own credo and, he hoped, theirs. South Carolina entered the Union as a sovereign state and retained to herself every power not specifically and expressly granted to the central government. Therefore, the Constitution itself possessed only limited and expressed powers and had none other than those specifically enumerated, and protective tariffs and internal improvements were not among them, the fostering of domestic manufactures by duties and imposts being expressly retained by the individual states.

Moreover, they could not seek remedy in the Supreme Court. "With a timid fraud well becoming the tyranny it covers," the new tariff purported to be a revenue measure and thus could only be judged in that context. The oppressions that propelled their fathers into revolution against Great Britain "are weak and trivial when compared with those upon which we now stand." Perhaps it was inevitable, he mused, for throughout history government, even constitutional government, invariably tended toward oppression and consolidation. It was a basic view of human nature and government that he would never amend. They had unwisely hoped for better, but history was against them, and Congress was steadily taking more and more power to itself. Without saying its name, he hinted at something more than the tariff threat, a danger to slavery itself. "All the property we possess, we hold by their boon, and a majority in Congress, may, at any moment, deprive us of it and transfer it northward, or offer it up on the bloody altar of a bigot's philanthropy."

The people were deluded if they thought there was any security for them in this government unless it was jerked back to the basic principles of the Constitution. Reminding them of how they had suffered in the Revolution to establish their freedom, he then revealed for the first time an instinct to indulge in hyperbole and disregard inconvenient facts when he asserted that in 1775 the South had no real complaints with Britain and only went to war to help New

England. He went on to claim that in 1812 another war "was waged, and maintained by us in the defense of Northern Interests." Despite this selfless support of the North, Congress, dominated by Yankees, had imposed tariffs that he maintained resulted in South Carolina paying more revenue per citizen into the general government than any other state. Yet the state's politicians, "in the fulness of their love and confidence," had yielded this to Washington. "We have done these things from love to our Brethren," he said.

Therefore, now when they stood up to demand their rights in the face of ingratitude and oppression, they did it "not, then, from a desire of disunion, or to destroy the Constitution, but it is that we may preserve the Union, and bring back the Constitution to its original uncorrupted principles." Usurpation was marching rapidly, and if they did not halt its progress now, "the day of open opposition to the pretended powers of the Constitution cannot be far off; and it is that it may not go down in blood that we now call upon you to resist." By all that was holy, by all their fathers had fought for, "we must resist," and do so "as becomes a Free, Sovereign and Independent People." And they must do so now.

Smith called on South Carolina to convene a special convention, or else call on the legislature, to determine its specific course. Without saying what he felt that course ought to be, he made it clear that he favored taking resistance to the last extremity if necessary, calling on them to "follow up your principles wherever they may lead, to their very last consequence," even to the loss of life rather than honor. "Impotent resistance will add vengeance to your ruin," he warned. There was almost a sneer as he closed with an admonition: "Live in smiling peace with your insatiable Oppressors, and die with the noble consolation, that your submissive patience will survive triumphant your beggary and despair."

The address to Governor Taylor asked him to convene a special session of the legislature to determine what should be done, and there followed resolutions at the meeting, after which those present unanimously approved Smith's address and ordered it printed for circulation throughout the state, with Smith on the committee appointed to see to the printing.[42] Even while these formalities proceeded, though, the crowd at Walterborough stirred. Smith had written the address entirely on his own and felt proud of it.[43] Indeed, he pitched it not just to the planter aristocracy that still dominated the Lowcountry, but to the much broader constituency that spreading democracy had produced among the middle and even lower classes. He told them that they all shared the same patrimony and were all the offspring of the Revolution, and he appealed to their universal manly instincts. Though his sympathies and family associations were all with the oligarchy, he presented himself as one of the yeomen and urged action not to defend the interests of the planters—the ones chiefly threatened—but to protect the rights of them all as freemen, even invoking veiled allusions to their enslavement and the inflammatory suggestion of invasion. He was not seeking to lead the people, he implied rather disingenuously, but wanted them to lead that he might follow. It was his first real statement on a stage larger than his own little district, and though the address was exaggerated and inflated, emotional in places, and long on invective and short on substance, still he had been true to those ancient precepts of Greek oratory learned in boyhood. Weak though the address was in logic and rhetoric, it spoke to the right topic at the right time and before the right audience. He might distrust the will of the people, but he would use it to achieve his ends if he could.[44]

He produced an instant sensation. While everyone else tried to stay quiet and keep the tariff issue contained before the coming election, Smith was the first to step forward and call for open resistance, though those who were paying attention would have remembered that his 1827 Colleton memorial clearly paved the way for this. "He was all passion, excitement and fire," his friend Perry observed.[45] In an instant he had leapt ahead of Cooper and Turnbull and other theorists of confrontation by advocating it in actuality and calling on the governor to put the process in motion. The *Charleston Mercury* published the address and lauded Smith for being "forceable eloquent and impressive, and embodying at once the political creed, the popular feeling and probably the determined policy of the state." Moreover, it praised him for his "fearless and independent" language.[46] The address was reprinted as far away as Baltimore as an "extraordinary" expression of political opinion, with again a notice of Smith's language of resistance, though this time called "strange."[47] Stuart and his partner in the *Beaufort Gazette*, William Grayson, immediately adopted Smith's position.[48] When less radical men attacked the speech in the state's press, there was no shortage of defenders whose letters to the editors, especially in the *Mercury*, revealed that Smith had struck a responsive chord among the radical conservatives.[49]

He said nothing new at Walterborough, but it was the way he said it, and the fact that he issued a call to action, that attracted so much attention. Moreover, by bringing the matter out in the open as a challenge, Smith virtually forced men in South Carolina to make a choice between resistance and submission. Among those disposed to resist the tariff, the discussion arose at once of how best to achieve their end, and Smith saw that the discussion was a warm one. A week after the Walterborough speech McDuffie suggested that South Carolina even the score by imposing a special tariff of its own on northern manufactured goods brought into the state, and others advocated anew a walkout by their congressional delegation, promising that such a move would be hailed by bonfires all across the state. Stuart wrote and published a "Disunion Drama" in his *Gazette*, and Beaufort suddenly found itself the state's hotbed of radical resistance sentiment, proud that a native son had been the first to call for confrontation.[50]

Capitalizing on the moment, and at the same time responding to criticism of his address from other quarters, Smith sought to lay out a course of action, no doubt to take the high ground before a special session of the legislature could convene. Either the assembly or a specially elected convention should prepare an ultimatum to Congress demanding that it back away from this tariff and future such usurpations, or else South Carolina would secede from the Union and resume its sovereignty in toto. Should Congress attempt to persevere even after that, then the governor should put the state in a posture for defense, open its ports to the commerce of the world with duties collected by the state alone, and instruct all state officials to support the governor, with an indemnity against any presumed violation of federal law that would then no longer be recognized. It was not a call to arms necessarily. Smith suggested no overtly hostile acts. However, all other states feeling a similar indignation at federal excesses would naturally join with South Carolina in resistance. Such a united stand of resistance would force the North to honor the Constitution.[51]

It was a radical and dangerous course at every level. First Smith asked South Carolina to act alone, taking the first step of resistance. If none of the other Southern states chose to join her, she would be on her own to face the ire and might of the Union. Even if other states did join with her in principle, they might stop short of the secession he proposed, and she would still be alone. And should several others secede after she led the way, the whole scheme would collapse in disaster if the North failed to do what Smith expected and refused to back down but instead chose to assert federal law and authority by force. South Carolina and any others in her camp would then face the choice of a humiliating submission, or civil war. It was not his design to break up the Union, but rather to use the threat of its dissolution to bring Congress to its senses. The trouble with ultimata, of course, is that they only work when the other party is willing enough, or weak enough, to be coerced. Barnwell Smith was counting a great deal on bluff to get the North's attention.

Calhoun paid attention. Beside the fact that he was too much a nationalist at this time to countenance the divisive noises Smith had been making for a year, he also knew that anything that split South Carolinians into factions, let alone causing this kind of furor, endangered his and Jackson's election prospects. He could not ignore the meetings sprouting all across the Lowcountry, especially the July 4 celebrations that mixed patriotic orations, political invective, and fireworks into an intoxicating cocktail. Smith's outline of action proved even more provocative, and Calhoun quickly sent out the word to his friends in the state to quell the uprising. Governor Taylor decided not to act on the call for a special session of the legislature, and the editors of the *Mercury* and other Calhoun organs were quietly told to back away from the Walterborough address.

Yet Calhoun could not make Smith's challenge go away by quelling discussion. Just as Smith's address forced everyone else to take sides, it meant that Calhoun most of all, if he wished to retain his leadership, must state a position. Moreover, the legislature had asked him to prepare for it a statement of grievances against the new tariff for its consideration. Yet whichever way he turned, for resistance or for submission, he stood to weaken his base of power in the state and compromise chances for the fall election. Side with Smith and he risked losing the North; oppose resistance and he would lose much of the South. He had to find a third way, one that took constitutional ground, that afforded South Carolina an opportunity to stand up for its rights, yet short of the outright and immediate confrontation advocated by Barnwell Smith.

He found it that summer and may indeed have been formulating such a policy even before the Walterborough meeting, for Smith was not the only radical threatening the peace of that summer, only the loudest. He may also have had some help in composing his solution, though likely not from Smith, for there is nothing to suggest that the two were yet acquainted other than that probable introduction in Beaufort nearly ten years earlier. Calhoun's closest associates were Gen. James Hamilton, the congressman, Calhoun's cousin Francis Pickens, the planter James Henry Hammond, and Congressman Robert Y. Hayne. These and others formed an inner circle of confidants and managers who saw to Calhoun's interests in the state and in Washington, and most were more radical than their leader when it came to resistance. Hamilton and Pickens would accept secession as a necessary last resort, while Hammond and Hayne were closer to Smith's point of view. What Calhoun produced from his own contemplation and their contributions was a new theory that would soon be known as *The Exposition and Protest.*

He did not wait until the convening of the legislature late that fall to reveal his plan. It got its first outing, and very little notice, at a public meeting in Abbeville that summer. But then Smith organized a public dinner at Walterborough, this one to honor Hamilton, who would be the chief champion of Calhoun's new plan in the state. On October 21, Hamilton, accompanied by Hayne, arrived for the celebration, and in speeches by both of them the people heard what Calhoun proposed. It was nullification.

The idea itself was not that new, having been proposed by Madison and Jefferson in the Virginia and Kentucky Resolutions of 1798 and 1799. Taking the view that the Union was a compact among sovereign states and that the

Constitution was the creation of the states for their common government, those resolutions argued that the states themselves were the proper judges of when that document was being violated by the central authority. Thus, having created the government, the states were not in law bound to obey its dictates when it exceeded its constitutional authority. There had been occasional attempts to put this into practice before, but what Calhoun had done, and what Hamilton revealed in Walterborough, was the first concrete plan of procedure. Nullification of the Tariff of 1828—or any other violation of the Constitution—could be achieved by a specially convened state convention asserting its veto. That would only suspend the operation of a law within a state's borders, not throughout the Union, for it was up to each state to determine the matter for itself. Such a state of things could not endure indefinitely, of course, but upon a declaration of nullification by any state, a convention of all the states should be called to act in their sovereign capacity and rule on the law in question. If three-fourths or more upheld the nullified law, then—and only then—the state or states aggrieved would make the choice of acquiescence or secession.

Smith thought Hamilton's speech at Walterborough the best of the congressman's long career, and Hayne, too, ably expostulated the new doctrine. When it came time for Smith to make an address of his own at the dinner, however, he declined to get entirely in line. The controversy at hand was not just about the tariff, he said. There were more issues at stake, and the whole framework of the South was endangered. He did not have to spell it out for everyone to know that he meant slavery. He saw the tariff as only the first battle in a larger war, which was why he felt they had to take the strongest possible stand at the earliest moment to stop the policy of federal aggression now. A defeat today on the tariff only ensured that tomorrow the next assault would be on slavery itself. "Unyielding resistance," he told them, was "absolutely necessary to avert oppressing danger to our home institutions." He would support nullification, he said—given Calhoun's power he could do nothing else but fall in step on that—but he told them freely that he did not believe that nullification by itself would bring them "a peaceful remedy."[52]

Just what alternative to "a peaceful remedy" he expected to result he did not say, but soon enough the battle would be joined and they would all see where it led. Barnwell Smith had taken the cork from a dangerous bottle indeed. Let others attempt to force the evil jinn back inside, since it would still be there waiting to escape again. Better to confront the spirit now, even if in the battle to come they risked breaking the bottle itself. Already he held a personal motto to govern himself now and forever in such matters: "perseverance will ensure success."[53]

THREE

I Am a Disunionist!

1828–1832

BARNWELL SMITH HANDILY WON REELECTION for another term that fall, only to discover that by the time the legislature convened on November 24, 1828 Calhoun's *Exposition* was already calming tempers as he had intended, presenting the orderly procedure that Smith's fevered call had not. Indeed, while Smith realized—and always would—that for an iron to burn it must be used at its hottest, Calhoun's nullification plan had built into it so much time for state and then national conventions that almost inevitably tempers would cool, compromises arise, and the crisis end short of disunion, which he personally abhorred. Nullification, and Calhoun's control of much of the press and leading men, took the heat from Smith's iron, if not from the legislator himself.

In recognition of Smith's growing influence, the Speaker gave him new committee appointments, including the important ways and means. For the first week of the session he went about the routine business of school reports, ferry charters, and tax collection, though everyone knew that the major issue would be Calhoun's *Exposition* when it came. Meanwhile, on December 2, Smith joined Hugh Legaré, Waddy Thompson, and others in submitting individual nullification resolutions to be communicated to all of the states through their representatives in Congress. Smith's declared all protective duties unconstitutional and violations of South Carolina's sovereignty, yet protesting that the peace and harmony of the Union were so valuable that the state should regard "the necessity of any measures that may jeopardize its existence" as a great calamity. He never said secession, but that was what he meant. He wanted a copy of his resolution sent to the delegation in Washington to put before Congress, and should that body not reject protectionism, then the legislature ought to be convened at once. He did not say for what purpose, but again his implication was clear enough. It was his earlier ultimatum, softened only a little.[1] That same month William Preston introduced a motion embodying essentially what Smith had proposed at Walterborough, calling for the assembling of a convention a year hence on December 1, 1829 "to enquire and decide whether the several acts of the General Government imposing imposts and duties are of such oppressive and unconstitutional character as to require that Convention, representing the Sovereignty of the State, then to interfere for the purpose of annulling the said acts or any of them" by declaring them unconstitutional and void for South Carolina.

A week later the debate began, with Smith in the middle from the outset, and he came ready. Opponents of calling a convention argued that granting it power to give Congress an ultimatum or declare secession would mean an abrogation of legislative power and virtually an alteration of the state constitution without proper procedure. Smith rose and argued to the contrary that historic practice in the state had limited conventions only to the consideration of matters assigned by the legislature, and thus the assembly retained to itself the power of amendment exclusively. Good lawyer that he was, he placed copies of the proceedings of previous state conventions on the Speaker's table to support his point, then proceeded to spend rather too much time making that same point repeatedly, as had become his wont.

To charges that the convention might stray from its assignment and change the basis of representation in the assembly, altering the balance of power built into the state constitution for the protection of the Lowcountry and Upcountry alike, he replied with ridicule:

> What, Sir, when the whole State shall have been driven together by the ruthless and desolating tempest of oppression—when we are to hold council together, whether our vital liberties can be maintained or not—whether we can exist as a free people and an independent State, or shall give up all freedom, independence, nay, national existence itself to the all-powerful, overwhelming energy of usurpation—at such a night-time of national difficulty and calamity, when all our united wisdom, united strength and united patriotism, will be necessary to work out our joint salvation—that one section of the State shall seize upon the opportunity our common distress and ruin affords, to tear from another section a little power, which can be wanted for no purpose, unless to carry on the very system of sectional tyranny which they are all assembled to oppose, and to sink down the whole State into one miserable contentious mass of factious slaves—

The very idea was ridiculous, he said, and "too base and idle for elaborate refutation," having just indulged himself in spending more attention and invective on it than he said it was worth.

Having spent too much time on peripherals, Smith finally addressed the heart of the convention debate. All around him he heard other members call for patience and tolerance, and rebukes for his rashness. "When patience under tyranny is the dogma to be taught," he responded, "it were well to call up the example of crushed and trampled slaves, who have been only fit for the heel of a despot, by their abject submission to his will, and base apostasy to the liberties of their race." Everyone invoked their ancestors before the Revolution and their forbearance. He remembered their stand against despotism, their maintenance of their rights. "These men threatened not to threaten again—raved not in words in weak apology for action, but they simply spoke, and the energy of their actions as simply corresponded with their words." They did not wait for oppression to grind them down. They acted. But "when I turn to the language I have heard upon this floor," he said, "I do indeed feel weighed down with the consciousness, that their posterity have fallen."

That said, he gave them a history lesson on the revolutionary era to remind them of what he assumed they had forgotten, admonishing them to "talk not then of the example of these pure and noble votaries of freedom, when you bid us bow the neck to the oppressor's wrong." Rather than pervert their ancestors' memory, they should imitate their courage and principle. "Strike," he railed, "and casting all—property, liberty and life, on the hazard of one mighty, uncompromising and decisive struggle, call upon the example of your Fathers in exulting imitation. Then sound their glory, and it shall not curdle your blood in humiliation and shame." He reminded them of that "glorious, unalienable right, which every people possesses of throwing off their government, whenever they deem it useless or oppressive to them." They had that right, and rather than submit, they should use it. If they did not use it now, surely they would have to tomorrow.

"We may fail now in this momentous struggle," he said to those who stood by him that day. The majority might call them blind and rash and foolish, preferring its own "superior wisdom in forbearance, and superior patience in toleration," he said with contempt in his sarcasm if not in his manner. Nevertheless, in the end, "we'll not fail." Glorying in liberty, their cause was "the cause of a people, not yet so ignorant, as not to distinguish between their friends and foes, nor yet so wasted by tyranny, as to be incapable of one great—one glorious, and if it must be, one dying effort for their blood-bought heritage of freedom.— Despair we will leave to the weak,—ours will be the energy of those who know that they contend for all that to freemen is worth living for, is worth dying for." For his own part, he would fight to the last breath, and if South Carolina were to go down in ruin and shame without a struggle, into the dark abyss of slavery, "a land of slaves shall never be mine." Rather than "lay the bones of a slave beside those of a free ancestry," he would leave for another land.[2]

It was quite a performance, neither a good nor an effective speech, but it revealed that the characteristics of every paper and public address he would make for the rest of his life were already fixed in his mind. The didactic posture and the tendency to overkill with example were all there, and so were the hyperbole and lack of proportion, the intolerance of opposing viewpoints and the hint of contempt for those who disagreed. There, too, was the willingness to misrepresent opponents' arguments in order to ridicule and refute them, to ignore or distort contrary facts, and most of all there was the reductio ad absurdum. The issue before South Carolina was the tax on imported pianos and shovels, but Smith was talking of oppression, subjugation, and slavery. Throughout it all there ran the sinister rhetoric not just of resistance but of warfare against an evil host in the North bent on conquest and even the destruction of slavery and their way of life, and the call to the sacrifice of property and martyrdom of a people, to death before dishonor.

Just how long Smith had been couching his views in such extreme terms is uncertain. Though his Walterborough address a few months before certainly struck many as inflammatory, it was temperate compared to this eruption. He may well have acquired the habit of extended preparation by research, and overindulgence in lecturing an audience, in debating studies at Beaufort College, and of course a few years practicing law certainly sharpened any natural inclination he may have had to overstate his own case and misrepresent the opposition. But there was more here than he should have acquired in lessons and example, and that certainly he did not imitate from mentors James Petigru or Thomas Grimké or even Robert Gibbes Barnwell. There was something excessive in his speech. The contempt and derision went beyond customary boundaries of political decorum. The self-righteousness and posture of infallible rectitude were even more pretentious than most public men could straight-facedly assume. The appeal to fear and passion and prejudice, and most of all the easy resort to the language of confrontation and violence as logical and even welcome eventualities had to come from something within.

A tender and adoring husband, a kind and indulgent father to his growing family, a man of deep though unsettled religion, with a charitable nature to fellowmen and not a hint of outward violence in his nature, still Smith began to reveal in this speech an alter ego of hidden resentments and bitterness, violent passion, an instinct for the jugular out of all proportion to the matter at hand, and a tendency to become so carried away by the groundswell of emotion and argument that clearly he was not the master of his passions, but rather they of him. Perhaps these traits were always there, suppressed beneath the shyness of "Madam Modesty," and maybe some were even the products of a reaction to

that early diffidence and lack of self-confidence, the sense of isolation and alone-
ness that he never put behind him. No doubt their origins lay in the unfath-
omable mystery of human nature itself, shaped by experiences good and bad,
tempered in the sometimes unbearable flames of adolescence, and revealed at
last when the growing confidence of maturity allowed them to escape. For the
rest of his life he would fight a battle between his self-restraint and this inner
nature, and he would admit to himself more than once that he actually feared
this demon within him.

Even as he addressed the house Smith knew, of course, that the convention
motion would fail, as it did by a vote of eighty to forty-one, Smith voting with
the minority. The defeat revealed just how much tempers had calmed. When a
member offered a substitute calling for another remonstrance to Congress instead,
Smith voted against it as pointless, but it carried, and on another motion to make
the remonstrance stronger in language he voted against that too. By now it
should have been clear that the sentiment of the house stood two-to-one against
him. Memories of Robert Gibbes Barnwell and James L. Petigru and their uncompromising stands on principle in the face of overwhelming opposition might
well have come to him at that point, as for the first time he found himself in the
sort of position in which he had once seen and admired them. It would not be
the last time. Indeed, in years to come one of his chief sources of pride would
be the number of times he stood outnumbered, even alone, refusing to bend to
popular will.[3]

Though rebuffed, Smith was hardly rejected, and when the motion for a
stronger remonstrance passed, the Speaker appointed him to a committee with
Legaré, Preston, Hayne, and others to draft the memorial. The result was the
Protest that Smith believed to have been written by Legaré but undoubtedly had
much influence from Calhoun.[4] Smith surely had some impact on the changes
from Calhoun's original draft and later learned that the elder statesman was not
entirely happy with the changes.[5] On December 19 they presented it to the
house, which ordered five thousand copies to be printed and sent throughout
the Union. The next evening they took up the matter once again, having now
to merge their report with one produced by a senate committee. The differences
were such that a conference committee of the two houses was required to agree
on a final version. Citing two previous ignored protests to Congress, the protest
referred to the 1828 tariff as a "further aggression" and stated that the legislature
only refrained from imposing its sovereignty in the form of calling a nullification convention out of hope for the "magnanimity and justice of the good
people of the Union," a phrase which Smith himself would never have written,
thinking the idea absurd. If thereafter South Carolina should have to pursue

stronger measures, the protest declared that such would emanate from expediency and not from a want of allegiance. The protest concluded by calling for its circulation to the governors of other states to be laid before their legislatures. Though South Carolina might not choose to take action at that time, it behooved her to make certain that sister states in disgruntlement knew what she was about and to seek their sympathy and support.[6]

Smith entertained little faith, and less hope, in the *Protest,* regarding it as but little more than submission with a whimper, but the moderates who backed Calhoun were in control of the legislature, and it was the best that could be gotten. In fact, it was the only really important business of the session, other than the threatened impeachment of his friend Waddy Thompson as state chancellor and, perhaps significantly in the crisis, Smith's advocacy of a four-thousand-dollar appropriation to augment the guard on the state arsenal.[7] While the *Protest* went to Washington, the real activity was back in his district that spring and summer. As Calhoun's forces worked to continue the calm and lay their strategies for implementation of the nullification plan in a deliberate and temperate atmosphere, Beaufort and Colleton remained hothouses thanks to Smith. John Stuart kept his readers inflamed in the editorials of the *Gazette,* and a radical new organization called the South Carolina Association met in Charleston on July 23 and toasted Smith and Colleton as "the nurse of lofty sentiment; the fannuiel hall where the cradle of Southern Sovereignty is constantly rocked," not neglecting more toasts of resistance to the tyranny of Congress and its tariff.[8]

Smith worked to keep the flame burning. In August he furnished the *Mercury* a text of his speech in the legislature and at the same time issued a written address to his constituents explaining his course in defending "your falling liberties, and violated rights." He challenged them to say he was not representing their views, for if not, then they should reject him at the next election if they thought there was no threat of oppression before them, or—loading the question—if they were "willing passively to be crushed." But if they agreed with him that they were "oppressed, wrongfully, grievously, unconstitutionally oppressed—oppressed beyond the toleration of any *free* people, since the sun rose upon man in the enjoyment of his rights," then they should rely upon no one man, not even him, but rather should rely upon themselves "for self protection." They must speak by their votes to command their representatives. It was time to forget about electing men to go on with the normal petty local affairs of state government. They should base their votes upon the one great issue before them; otherwise they risked becoming "victims of a consolidated Empire & sectional tyranny." He denied any ill feeling toward those who differed with him—"conscientiously differed from me," he qualified the denial—

and wished to accuse no one. The question before them all now was would their representatives act, and "act RIGHT," and ability counted now for less than commitment to their interest. But he made it clear that any legislator who did not stand to protect their rights and property was hostile to them. "Talent and integrity give power," he warned, "and if you are to intrust your interests to your foes, the greater knaves and fools you select as your Representatives, the wiser will be your conduct because they will be the less efficient instruments for your destruction."[9]

South Carolina stayed rather quiet for the balance of 1829, and even Smith backed off after August, once again focusing his attention on an impending addition to the family when, on October 18, Elizabeth gave birth to Alfred Moore. The second session of the legislature, convening November 1, presented mostly the customary business. Smith introduced a bill amending the punishment accorded to whites who murdered slaves, reflecting his firm belief that though inferior to whites in every way, blacks were still entitled to the right to life and that ownership of slaves carried with it the high obligation to provide considerate and humane treatment. Nevertheless, he also supported a measure prohibiting whites from engaging in any commerce with slaves, remaining consistent in his conviction that nothing should allow a black, free or slave, to deal with a white on any basis of equality, even commercial.[10] Having championed the use of impeachment to rid the state of incompetents, he backed the indictment of another drunken judge that term. Though the offender resigned before trial, impeachment was now firmly fixed as the proper remedy.[11]

Of course the pressing issue, though in the background for the moment, could not be ignored entirely, and Smith missed no opportunity to keep the wound open. Late in November he presented a resolution calling on the state's delegation in Congress to oppose all appropriations for internal improvements, and he then addressed the house at some length and with some animation, especially censuring the new South Carolina Rail Road & Canal Company for applying to Congress for funds. For any state corporation or private citizen to accept such funds would compromise Carolinians' whole stand against internal improvements. Though the resolution was repeatedly tabled, he kept calling it up, and finally on December 2 it went to final debate, with Preston supporting him while Hayne and Legaré opposed it as unnecessary. Several other members spoke, many of them ardently in favor of the railroad's application in spite of one observer's assertion that accepting any federal money would make them all hypocrites. Not surprisingly, the debate turned heated, one member complaining that Smith, "a member from an obscure parish[,] should presume to dictate the course" of their congressmen, but in the end the resolution passed ninety to

twenty and included a clause stipulating that any internal improvement appropriation for South Carolina should be especially discountenanced. Smith was
hardly opposed to the railroad itself, however, and later in the session, when a
bill arose to lend the company money to get going, he kept it alive, and at the
end of the session he voted in favor of a one-hundred-thousand-dollar loan.[12]

The situation in Washington hovered over them throughout. The governor
sent in a message at the opening of the session that condemned unwarranted
federal assumption of power. Smith sat on the committee that took the message
under consideration and on December 16 voted with the majority in approving
the governor's conduct and that of their delegates in Congress, and calling on
him to correspond with them on relations with the central government on the
tariff. Smith's committee expressed confidence in President Jackson but regretted that he did not stand with them in opposition to the 1828 tariff, and then
in a passage probably drafted by Smith he declared that no modification of that
tariff would satisfy "the spirit in which South Carolina has resisted it." They
would be patient and wait for justice to the state after their protest but warned
that if Congress should "satisfy all minds that the Government which in the language of His Excellency 'is the best in theory' may be so perverted as to be made
the worst in practice: and that our Constitution Confederacy is overthrown by
a combination of interested majorities, against which there is no conservative
power," then they would have to resort to that power "which resides in the States
as sovereigns."[13] Smith and those of like mind intended to keep the pressure on
Washington and the issue ever present in the minds of South Carolinians.

At the end of the session Smith returned to Walterborough, smarting somewhat
under the criticism for opposing the railroad appropriation. When a Charleston
meeting ignored the house resolution and issued a memorial to Congress
appealing for an appropriation, Smith responded at once by calling another
meeting of his constituents, this time aided by his friend and fellow local attorney Franklin H. Elmore, and issuing another address. No one doubted, he least
of all, that the railroad would be an economic blessing to the state, but if it were
built with federal money they would be compromised in a Faustian bargain that
bartered their freedom, their liberty, and their constitutional principles for a
few miles of track. Once more, as he would again and again, he stressed resistance, not only to the siren temptation of government money raised from unlawful tariffs, but to the government itself. Again his voice carried beyond the state's
borders, and in Baltimore an editor condemned Smith's views as "disreputable,"
worse even than the supposedly secessionist sentiments of the Hartford Convention. Words such as "traitor" and "disunionist" were not used yet, but they
were coming.[14]

Indeed, sentiment in the state was warming again, catching up to Smith as South Carolinians found that the new president had no inclination to reduce or rescind the 1828 tariff, and even Calhoun, once enthusiastic about "Old Hickory," grew rapidly disillusioned—all of which made his nullification proposal assume renewed life now that there was no hope of the *Protest* being effective. Calhoun's cousin Francis W. Pickens believed that the people were ahead of their elected officials on the issue, the politicians being "a class of lawyers particularly, who have mediocrity of intellect & make some pretensions to reputation, who are afraid of their own shadows, & for fear of losing what they imagine to be their prosperity by being branded with disunion, are too timid even to assert their rights." Smith would have been in complete agreement, though he did not share Pickens's belief that they still should keep disunion talk quiet in favor of a continued pressure on the bold state rights and sovereignty stance.[15]

Certainly the people were not ahead of Smith. Rather, especially in Colleton and Beaufort, he seemed precisely in step with the Lowcountry. At a July 4 celebration in Walterborough, after the usual parade and speeches, his cousin Barnwell made a speech expressing his like mind, and then William C. Pinckney offered a toast to "R. Barnwell Smith—The Constitution and State Rights! 'War, Pestilence and Famine' may crush, but never *disjoin* them." The hint was unmistakable that while the Constitution and the rights of the states could not be disjoined, the Union itself could. Smith responded with a long address on their rights and closed with a heated call for the legislature to summon a convention when it convened that fall. "*The State of South Carolina*," he shouted. "Her citizens look to her for protection—honor, interest, liberty, demand that she affords it."[16]

He would go farther yet, farther than Pickens. He continued in the same vein at "State Rights Meetings" elsewhere as he pursued his successful bid for reelection, and then in a meeting at Columbia on September 29, its location virtually a challenge to the legislature to act, he took his most extreme ground yet. Along with the usual history lesson, he showed that Jefferson and Madison had both countenanced the idea of nullification in response to the unlawful actions of the Federalists and acknowledged that the doctrine had been stigmatized endlessly since. "This doctrine should be hated and feared by all Government dependants, and speculators in the grand lottery of the American System," he said. But what should they expect from those in an oppressive majority that chose to construct and interpret the Constitution to profit themselves? "Gentlemen, it has been so long since the public liberty has been endangered, that our citizens have fallen asleep upon their rights." The lines that once clearly defined the old parties in the Union had become blurred and lost. Some men now actually called themselves Republicans and state rights advocates, and at the same time denounced nullification. "To me, it sounds more like solemn merriment than reason."

Deny the states their right to impose their sovereignty, and talk of states' rights and republicanism was inane. "The States have no rights—there are no limitations upon the powers of the General Government,—and ye are the vassals and slaves of a consolidated empire." It was imperative that Jefferson's and Madison's principles be enforced—"peacibly . . . constitutionally enforced" he added—by South Carolina's interposition. "She must now settle the question of submission, or resistance forever." The time for words and protests was over. "If we halt, we halt from fear. Our foot is on the base of the battlement, and we must advance or leave the field." Were they ready to submit, he asked? If so, they must forfeit every totem of their proud history of liberty.

These were times for men to speak frankly and without possibility of misunderstanding. To dissemble now was cowardice, if not perfidy. "I will speak my opinions without regarding misconstructions, or consequences," he declared. He had been born in this Union and he hoped to die in it and would, moreover, gladly die *for* it if necessary. But it must be a Union of equal rights, one that protected all sections alike and that recognized the sovereignty of the states.

> If the Union is to be perverted from the high and just ends for which it was created, and to absorb the rights of the States—if instead of a Union to protect us from abroad, it becomes a Union for the regulation and government of our internal affairs—if instead of guaranteeing to us the safe possession of our property, it becomes an instrument in the hands of a plundering majority, to wrest it from our possession—offering to us no resource for redress, but the mercy or avarice of this interested majority . . . ; I say with Mr. Jefferson, give me disunion rather than a consolidated government. Aye—disunion, rather, into a thousand fragments. . . . Because under such a Government I would be a slave—a fearful slave, ruled despotically by those who do not represent me . . . with every base and destructive passion of man bearing upon my shieldless destiny—love of domination—avarice—long rankling jealousy —and, worst of all, the fell spirit of bigotry, which would exult over my dwelling in flames, and my children given to slaughter.

Smith could not stop the invective, captured once more in that seizure of passionate rhetoric in him that could assume a being of its own. "Will some blattant sycophant in office, or base pander to power cry out 'a disunionist!— a traitor!'" he cried. "I will tell the slave, 'take the words, if they will serve you.'" Washington, Samuel Adams, Patrick Henry, Jefferson, and more "were all disunionists and traitors" in their time, and they broke the British Empire and redrew the map of the world with the sword. "Shall we tremble at epithets, or shake when a tongue rails?" And what was a disunionist anyhow? Was it one who stood up for constitutional rights against a self-aggrandizing centrality, or was it one who meekly acquiesced to usurpation and tyranny? Did anyone there really believe that the Union as it was could be preserved under an unlimited government in which one section, its interests differing from the other, sought to dominate the whole? "It is impossible—utterly impossible, unless all the people of these States are slaves," he cried.

"The Union must be dissolved under its present course of administration. It requires no conspiracy to destroy—no exertion on our part to drag it to its dissolution. It goes down with the inevitable weight of its own gravitation, into that dark abyss of anarchy and ruin, where all tyrannies have fallen." The only way to save it was Jefferson's way, Calhoun's way, by nullification, and they must do it now "while yet some warmth of affection lingers in our bosoms—now, whilst we have the respect of our brethren, and contempt from our vacillation and pusilanimity, may not tempt a resort to force and blood." How could he be any more explicit than that? He knew the answer. "If to think, to speak, to feel such sentiments as these, constitute me a disunionist and a traitor, according to the English language as now understood in Carolina," he declared in closing, "then gentlemen, I am a Disunionist!—I am a Traitor!"[17]

The speech was electrifying, still overblown, with all of the flaws in argument and hyperbole that he had revealed earlier, but powerful nevertheless in its sheer extremity. At one and the same time he had moderated his own previous stand to the point now of embracing nullification, and yet he had become even more radical in his rhetoric. Seeing that Calhoun's policy was more broadly acceptable than his own, he realized the importance of pushing it all the more stridently to force an early resolution. Half a loaf might be better than none, but if not eaten right away it would stale the faster. Smith's speech put an immediate fright into the antinullification forces in the state, especially since Calhoun's supporters would control at least a majority in both houses of the legislature in the coming session, though possibly short of the necessary two-thirds vote to force a convention.[18] Soon a rumor arose in Columbia that if the legislature did not call a convention to nullify, then the state rights majority would pass a law requiring a popular referendum instead.[19]

It was in an atmosphere of suspicion and portent that the assembly convened on November 22, and Smith's growing prominence became immediately apparent as the battle for control of the house began at the first gavel. Calhoun's forces scored their initial victory with the election of Henry L. Pinckney to the Speakership, and one of his first acts was to give Smith, though only commencing his third term, the chairmanship of the powerful Ways and Means Committee. Though Smith began a qualified support of Calhoun in 1828, after his own resolution for a convention failed in the face of the nullification solution, this was the first tangible sign of a budding alliance between Smith and the vice president.[20]

Each faction accused the other of irregularities in the recent elections, and with control of the house and the issue of a convention in the balance, challenges to seating some members were inevitable. Smith started it on the second day of the session when he introduced a resolution to unseat antinullifier Rene Godard and call a special election to fill the vacancy. At once his old friend Judge Daniel Huger arose and offered a similar challenge to several state rights members. Huger suggested referring the Godard case to the Committee on Elections, and though Smith fought him, Huger's motion won. Almost immediately that committee reported against Godard, declaring his seat vacant by a vote of forty-one to three, and in the house at large the committee recommendation carried with only one dissenting vote, showing just how powerful the nullifiers were now. Huger argued for reconsideration, pleading that there was no candidate with a better claim to the seat, but again Smith replied, and Huger failed.[21]

The next day Smith moved discussion of a resolution by Preston calling for creation of a standing Federal Relations Committee, and Smith rose to second the motion spiritedly. It was a logical first step, for such a committee could produce a report declaring an impasse on the tariff issue and calling on the legislature for a convention summons. Again Huger rose in opposition, denouncing what he called "a plan or scheme" by the nullifiers. He agreed that the tariff was unconstitutional and oppressive and that South Carolina ought to resist it, but only through the existing laws. Smith jumped to his feet to compliment Huger on agreeing with him that the state should not be prostrated before Washington, and when the vote came Preston's resolution carried handsomely, Smith being appointed to the committee as expected. Then they received the governor's annual message containing his assertion that the legislature had the right to determine what constituted treason against the rights of the state, meaning the tariff and nullification. Huger proposed referring that part of the message to the Judiciary Committee, to keep it out of the hands of Smith's new committee, while warning of the dangerous attitude that it reflected in the state at large. Smith stood once more and contemptuously dismissed Huger's fears. This house, he said, was not the place "to introduce the cry of the Alarmists and Bloody Bones" that had so frightened the state in the recent hotly contested elections. It was Huger and the antinullifiers, he said, and not the Calhoun men, who were the fear mongers. When Huger defended himself, Smith replied in what a reporter called "a storm of fervid eloquence" and successfully moved that the text in question be referred instead to his committee. The "plan or scheme" that Huger feared was working.[22]

Smith was on the floor several times a day now, clearly one of the leaders among the nullifiers and just as clearly contributing to the rising tempers in the house, with Huger his chief opponent. The judge had resigned his seat on the bench that year to win a place in the house where he could fight the rising tide of nullification, and Smith had written expressions of support for Huger's candidacy for the *Mercury*.[23] Just over fifty, the old Federalist had been Petigru's law partner and shared his devotion to the Union.[24] Though he and Smith had been friends, and Smith won his first case before the judge, their exchanges now grew increasingly heated.

When Smith and Andrew P. Butler wrote their committee's resolutions, they chose careful language, a phrase or two borrowed from the benchmark Virginia and Kentucky Resolutions, starting with an expression of firm determination to uphold the Constitution "against any aggression, either foreign or domestic." Second, they declared that the legislature had a duty to protect the Union from infractions of constitutional principles "which constitute the only basis of that Union because a faithful observance of them can alone secure its existence." Then came the third resolution, stating that all federal power resulted from the compact between the states "limited by the plain sense and intention" of the Constitution, "and in case of a deliberate and palpable and dangerous exercise of other powers not granted by the said compact, the States who are parties thereto have the right and are in duty bound to interpose for arresting the progress of the evil." Nowhere did they use the word *nullification*. The resolutions simply proposed that the convention do what was needed to protect South Carolina's rights and preserve the Constitution. Of course Smith *meant* nullification, but by not stating it explicitly he and Butler hoped to win enough support among those wavering between the two camps to carry the vote.[25]

When Smith's Federal Relations Committee delivered the report, he and Preston largely managed the ensuing debate. They pressed for immediate consideration, but opponents won at least a stay of a few days to prepare their response, and predictably, Huger was their chief spokesman. By December 13 the debate was under way, and at once Huger and opponents pointed out what they saw as an attempt at subterfuge by omitting mention of nullification, for no one doubted that such was the resolutions' intent.[26] Tempers rapidly began to fray, and Smith for one showed that the passion that seemingly carried him away in his Columbia speech was quite genuine. On December 16 he lost control. Huger went after the resolutions for being deceptive, part of the scheme he had warned of, and introduced an amendment to the third resolution stating explicitly that no state had the lawful power to nullify. That brought the whole matter out into the open, and Huger, warming himself after weeks of constant adversarial debate, taunted the nullifiers for trying to hide behind wordplay. Freely he declared that the purpose of his amendment was precisely to bring out the truth "that the Convention party *did* mean to nullify, and were afraid to avow it—that now that they had come up to the mark, they were for flinching and concealing their intention and deceiving the people."[27]

That was too much for Barnwell Smith. Now and hereafter he would show little inclination to accept criticism, most especially when he was caught in error, and his response would be quick and heated. Moreover, he later said that he feared that Huger's pointed attack threatened to demoralize or even break down the nullification supporters in the house if not abruptly checked.[28] Thus he arose and in a posture of scorn and indignation offered a transparent rationalization to explain the absence of the offensive word. Nullification meant different things to different people, he said, ignoring entirely the fact that it meant one thing and one thing only to him and Butler, the authors of the resolutions. Their only object for the proposed convention, he said, was for it to declare the tariff and internal improvements unconstitutional. He was not lying, certainly, for he and the nullifiers did indeed want the convention to make such a declaration. He just evaded admitting what they wanted and expected the convention to do after that. In so doing, Smith revealed yet one more constituent of his increasingly complex public character, a willingness to bend or even violate the truth when convenient or necessary. That said, he pointed his finger at Huger and snarled in contempt that as to the charge of fear which the judge had applied to him and his associates, he answered for all that he "scorned and despised the imputation."[29]

While a sensation at the outburst passed through the members, Huger rose to reply, coolly and calmly pointing out that Smith still evaded the issue just as had the resolutions. As for the final outburst, that had crossed the boundary between public debate and personal attack, and he would not intrude a matter of personalities onto the floor of the legislature. The implication was inescapable that he would respond to Smith's provocation in another manner.[30] Almost immediately Huger wrote out a challenge to a duel and gave it to his cousin and state senator Alfred Huger to deliver to Smith. Still hot from the debate, Smith accepted and specified the next morning at dawn as the time for the meeting, naming former Governor Hamilton as his second and leaving further arrangements in his hands.

No one, most of all the nullifiers, wanted to see the two friends come to violence, especially because the inevitable excitement and attention would all work further against the hope of a convention. Even opponents of nullification such as Petigru were amazed that Smith had "pushed against the Judge offensively, considering the attraction of party is so strong in keeping them united that agree."[31] In principle both were united on the evils and unconstitutionality of the tariff. It was in the interest of all such opponents not to quarrel among themselves, but Smith's now-passionate temper had shown that it easily propelled him beyond the wise restraints of policy. He could lash out at friend as well as foe.

Friends went to work that evening to prevent a tragedy. Smith was in bed asleep at midnight when Hamilton knocked at the door of his lodging. His second and Huger's had met and adjusted the matter, calling on each to make an explanation to the other and public withdrawal in the house of any intention of personal insult.[32] The next day a reporter listened to what he called "a very handsome explanation between Barnwell Smith and Judge Huger." Smith admitted that he had been harsh and intemperate, but since Huger had since stated that he meant nothing personal in his own remarks, he now happily recalled his own animadversions. Moreover, he renewed his expressions of esteem for Huger as a gentleman, and Huger responded in kind, stating that he had always regarded Smith with esteem, though noting impishly that his friend's "high character had undergone, for a moment yesterday, a slight eclipse in his estimation."[33]

The episode acted as a valve to release much of the pressure accumulating in the house over the resolutions. Smith and Huger remained friends, and henceforward the tone of the debate was considerably more polite.[34] In fact, immediately after the mutual apologies the house went into committee of the whole where Smith moved to cut off further debate and got a vote approving the resolutions and referring them to the general house, which proceeded to pass all three of them without incident. When Huger again introduced an additional resolution, in place of his earlier amendment, stating that South Carolina did not recognize the right of a state to nullify a law of Congress, it went through some amendment, and finally was narrowly defeated. Four more resolutions covered a statement of the compact theory of government and the right of a state to be a judge of infractions of the Constitution, the assertion that expansion of federal power threatened the sovereignty of the states, a declaration that the tariff was unconstitutional and dictatorial and the state had a right to "interpose in its sovereign capacity," and finally the opinion that redress from Congress was hopeless, thus requiring a call for a state convention. Smith, having co-authored that last portion about abandoning hope, now moved to remove it, no doubt as a minor concession to the more moderate in the chamber. All of the resolutions passed, but the crucial final one only bettered a tie by two votes, falling far short of the two-thirds needed to call the convention.[35]

It was a galling failure, making the few achievements of the session pale. But the effort advanced Smith's cause nevertheless. First it had brought him into even more prominence personally, establishing him firmly among the highest echelon of ardent state rights proponents. The fact that his duel never materialized did not alter the fact that no man in South Carolina ever suffered in reputation from *almost* coming to the dueling field. Best of all, from his point of view, the more moderate approach of the Calhoun men who sought to stop short of aggressive assertion of nullification had failed. Seeing that, over the next several months some of Calhoun's most influential backers saw no choice but to shift to the right, bringing them more in harmony with Smith's harder line. In losing a battle Barnwell Smith had gone a long way toward winning his war for South Carolina's political posture.

Backed by his brother-in-law John A. Stuart and the *Beaufort Gazette,* Smith kept up the pressure by helping to organize the State Rights and Free Trade Party, a new splinter from the old Republicans as the various antitariff and anti-internal improvements conservatives in the South still felt their way toward a firmer definition of the new Democratic Party. Smith served on the Arrangements Committee for its massive July 4 celebration in Charleston, with Gov. James Hamilton in the chair and Hayne delivering the principal address fresh from an epic debate with Daniel Webster in Congress. Significant of the uncertainty and fluid political climate, elsewhere in the city that day a rival Union and State Rights Party was holding its own celebration, and both groups vied for the citizens' loyalty. The Union meeting had invited President Jackson to attend, and in declining he had nevertheless approved their conduct and made a Union appeal to the state, which outraged Smith, who saw Jackson's comments as an interference in the internal affairs of South Carolina. Governor Hamilton offered a toast to the Union, saying that it must be preserved but that "violence and corruption" could dissolve it, and Smith followed him with an effusive toast to Langdon Cheves, a former congressman and Speaker of the house, and one of the state's most distinguished elder statesmen, a moderate whom both rival meetings that day sought to woo. Significant of his increased stature in the state rights movement, Smith was the only member of the Arrangements Committee allowed to offer a toast along with the chairman, all the rest having to wait until the end of the meeting.[36]

A week later the State Rights and Free Trade Party held an organizational meeting in Charleston and asked Stuart to start publishing the *States Rights and Free Trade Evening Post* there. There would be more public meetings of the party throughout the summer and fall, and even a Free Trade convention in Philadelphia in October, but Smith stayed in his home district managing affairs there.[37]

All hope of Jackson coming to their aid seemed finally dashed when the president plainly told Hayne earlier that year that he regarded nullification as unconstitutional and those attempting it as disunionists. Instead, Jackson sent his endorsement to the Huger faction in the state, making it appear implicit that if the state did try to nullify, not only would Jackson not acquiesce, but he might use force to put down what he considered treason. To Smith, of course, such a posture was only a challenge to renewed assertion of the state's rights. He called another meeting at Walterborough in early August that adopted defiant resolutions that loyalty to the Union was never more than a temporal adherence and revocable at any time, whereas a South Carolinian carried from birth an indissoluble allegiance to the state. Daring Jackson to rise to their challenge, Smith sent the resolutions to the White House, where Jackson simply ignored them.[38]

Smith felt his position gradually gaining strength as the second session of the legislature approached. In July, Calhoun released another exposition of his nullification doctrine that showed him moving closer to the radical position. Then on August 21 an uprising in Virginia led by a slave named Nat Turner electrified the South. More violent than Denmark Vesey's abortive rebellion, it was no less unsuccessful, but the outrage and panic in response spread quickly to South Carolina where it worked to the nullifiers' advantage as people imagined conspiracies for a nationwide slave revolt planned by the same Yankees who imposed the abominable tariffs on the South. Calhoun was in Columbia when the legislators gathered and, now that the ground was growing more common beneath them, probably met with both the radicals and the moderates, including Smith, a father yet again after the September 28 birth of his third son, Andrew Burnet. To the extent that they had gotten to know one another by now, Smith and Calhoun found themselves of congenial tastes and character, though Calhoun would always be a bit guarded at Smith's radicalism. But beyond question the younger man was winning the vice president's esteem as a man of reckoning in the state and perhaps one day on a grander scale.[39]

Shrewdly the Free Trade and Southern Rights Associations in the state—their name seemed always in flux—scheduled a statewide convention in Camden to coincide with the session. As a delegate to the convention from St. Bartholomew's, Smith was absent from the house for two days, no doubt helping prepare the address that his Distribution Committee sent throughout the state reiterating the by-now-familiar complaints against Congress and affirming the necessity for resistance.[40] The regular business session afforded little interest other than Smith's report from ways and means on the condition of the state bank and his move to have the trustees of South Carolina College investigate its president Thomas Cooper for his unorthodox and, Smith thought, atheistic views. Even though Cooper was a fellow radical, Smith's convictions of religious propriety took precedence in this case, but Cooper would be retained.[41]

On December 14, however, they took up consideration of a recent letter from Jackson in which he averred that the tariff was too high and ought to come down in a new tariff act anticipated for 1832, while at the same time making it clear that he regarded any action by any state to interfere with the law of Congress as unlawful and treasonous. Smith's Federal Relations Committee returned a report on Jackson's letter that commended him for saying the tariff should be reduced, but when a resolution was introduced complimenting the administration, Smith voted with a large minority that tried to strike the praise from the report. He declined to engage in debate since he knew he would lose, and in that case he wanted to "avoid all angry feeling and excitement," suggesting that he briefly learned a lesson from the Huger affair. He went on, however, to condemn Jackson's interfering letter to the Union and State Rights Party meeting the previous summer and for his several instances of veiled threats. "Is this legislature," he asked, "to legislate under the suspended sword of the Commander-in-chief?" Once more he raised the old specter of slavery if they did not resist.[42]

For the time being the initiative rested with Jackson, and until they saw the proposed new tariff, the nullifiers could do nothing more by way of another try for a convention. As for Smith, he had personal concerns after the adjournment. By early 1832 he had spent three terms in the legislature and had already developed what would be a lifelong habit of paying too little attention to his own business while engrossed in politics. "For the last six years I have neglected my profession, from the belief that its practice tended to injure my popularity, and would jeopardize my continuing in the service of the State," he told a friend in February. How practicing law would impair his popularity he did not explain, though with the state in another financial depression he would certainly have angered financially strapped clients by efforts to collect fees for his services, or more likely in representing their suits for collection of debts due them. His brother Edmund, recently graduated from Yale—Smith expressed no jealousy that his father was now finding money to educate his younger sons at fine universities—was now reading law under him, which was an extra expense, and even when Smith did take a case, he seemed to lack the necessary predatory instinct that came so easily to him in politics. Pressing a suit, he would eschew court orders when he could, saying, "I intend however trying gentle means first."[43] He feared that he "must now however abandon public life," even though he was at the height of his influence, unless he could establish a comfortable security for his family. Yet if he did retire to his practice, he believed it unlikely that he would make enough even to educate his children.

He had heard that Hugh S. Legaré, currently attorney general of the state, was being offered a diplomatic post in Belgium, and he began to circulate the word that he would happily accept the vacated post, which would pay enough for him to move his family to Charleston where his brother Edmund, as a partner, could run the practice when he had to be away. Piously he begged his friends for no special favors, saying that the cabinet post—chosen by the legislature—should go to the most deserving man. Meanwhile he asked his friends to sound the sentiment for him in the state, especially in the Upcountry where his friends were few and members of the antinullification party most numerous. He determined that if not appointed, he would still seek reelection one more time in the fall, but that would be his last. "I must endeavor to strain on through the present crisis," he said with resignation.[44]

Legaré's replacement would not be chosen until the end of the year in the next legislature, and even with the prospect of self-imposed retirement before him, Smith continued the tariff fight while the battle to shape the tariff itself raged all that season in Congress. He could even see the division in his own family. His oldest brother, Thomas, stood far from Barnwell Smith's ardent state rights position, while the next eldest, James, was an out-and-out opponent of nullification and a Unionist. Benjamin, next oldest to Barnwell, was closer to his own stance, while younger Edmund was absorbing his legislator brother's views wholeheartedly. That summer, even while Barnwell Smith addressed audiences in Colleton to promote a convention and nullification, James spoke before a Union meeting in opposition.[45]

Barnwell Smith's own high point in the summer campaign came predictably at the annual July 4 event in Walterborough. His associate Elmore was the principal speaker, but Smith stood out clearly as the man of the moment. He was toasted as "the ardent and uncompromising advocate of State Rights, and from whom the first voice of resistance to unconstitutional taxation was heard." Of course Smith was prepared for such a moment and responded at great length. All of his now-customary arguments were there. It was their right and their duty to resist unlawful taxation. Indeed, the defense of the principle itself was "worth more than the existence of nations and empires." The demons of power and greed were sweeping like Tartar hordes down upon them from the North, justifying their acts as the will of the majority. Against that South Carolina had tried "seven years of imbecile petition and remonstrance," to what avail? What else remained but resistance? As to how they should resist, he replied, "any way, every way, provided it is downright effectual resistance." The only check to oppressive power was an equal power, and if nullification offered that course, they must take it. Beyond that, however, once resolved to resist, what did it matter what form that act took, so long as it was constitutional? All South Carolinians should cooperate with the nullifiers, since they all sought the same end, and weaker means had failed. If the worst happened, nullification failed, and they found themselves facing military coercion, truly they would be in revolt. "Revolution!" He said the word repeatedly, then asked what had they ever gained but by revolution. "It is the dearest and the holiest word, to the brave and free." He felt no chills of fear at the sound of the word. Far worse was the alternative of slavery, the ironic enslavement of South Carolinians who themselves "own our *peculiar property.*" He said nothing direct in reference to their own slavery but repeated "our *peculiar property*" a second time to emphasize the hinted threat that if the North defeated them on the tariff, the next attack would be on slavery itself.

Rather than that, rather than lose their property and see their families and posterity shamed, he cried, "give us Revolution rather—aye, the battle-field rather; and sword in hand, and freemen by our side." They demanded nothing of the North but their rights, but if "the fire and the sword of war are to be brought to our dwellings, why, then, Sir, I say, let them come!" Over and over again he repeated, "let them come!" He asked if they thought his words too bold and free, or if he did not echo their own feelings. They had proclaimed "resist" in 1828, even though they were a lone voice and attacked from all sides. But now their prescience had been vindicated. "What was once the solitary voice of Colleton District, is now the stern demand of Carolina." He urged them all to keep before them ever the inspiration of "the Men of 76—They dared all things but to be Slaves."[46]

The reaction was predictably enthusiastic. One militiaman responded to Smith's final toast by giving one of his own: "The spirit of '76—I have heard of it, and seen its blessed fruits; but now my eyes see it embodied in the gentleman who last addressed us." Another spoke with pride that it was there four years before that Smith "aroused and animated us, sending forth the very first voice in Carolina, which proclaimed resistance to unjust and oppressive taxation." Just as predictably, opponents in the state attacked him anew for his intemperance. The object of Smith and the nullifiers, they said, "is civil war." They were mistaken in that. For all his overblown rhetoric of war and battle and blood and disunion—he had used the word *revolution* fourteen times—he still wanted the political solution that nullification might offer.[47] Disunion and the bloodshed that he took for granted would be the inevitable result were not the end he had in mind; they were only the last resort if nullification failed and Washington sought to use force to impose its laws. His foes could not see the difference, but it is evident that his manner had become so inflammatory and intemperate that even those on his side of the issue were not certain where hyperbole left off and intention began, and for the next several weeks others in the nullification ranks strove to backtrack from his extremism. His cousin Barnwell declared that nullification was in no way a hostile or aggressive act, and Calhoun and others quickly reiterated that it was a peaceful and constitutional means of redress whose outcome would depend not upon South Carolina rising to face the government, but on a convention of all the states.[48]

Smith backed down not a syllable, and his Walterborough speech helped to crystallize the remaining summer campaign in the state. Smith and the radicals wanted a state convention to nullify unilaterally and take the consequences. If the convention would not, or if the legislature could not get the two-thirds majority needed to call a convention, then they wanted the legislature to vote to nullify.[49] The Unionists made it clear that they would support a state convention only so that it could call for a convention of all Southern states, so that there might be united action through cooperation. Independent action was too fraught with peril and, they thought, too weak.[50] Meanwhile in Charleston an ardent opponent of the nullifiers named Christopher G. Memminger issued an anonymous satire whose authorship soon became generally known. He called it the *Book of Nullification,* a biblical parody that ridiculed Smith as "Robert the Nullifier" and "Robert the Disunionist." Smith would never forgive him.[51] Then on July 14, 1832 Congress passed the new tariff, and the battle was joined.

FOUR

Perseverance Will Ensure Success

1832–1834

CERTAINLY THE NEW TARIFF DID not surprise Barnwell Smith. Rather, it only confirmed his now-settled distrust of the character and motives of the majority controlling Congress, most of them Northerners. The 1828 tariff had imposed so much duty that a considerable surplus accumulated in the Treasury, and Smith felt that the government had no business now collecting unnecessary taxes.[1] Even the protectionists could not ignore a growing balance that argued against continuing the rates and the increasing political unrest that threatened to disrupt the Union. Clay and others backed and passed a new measure that took many of the most controversial imports off the tariff list and made them duty free, while reducing the levels of tax on the balance of goods to or slightly below the 1824 level. Had this been done four years earlier, it might have been seen as a compromise, or even a gain. But years of growing opposition across the political spectrum in the state, and exacerbated by Smith and the radicals, had created a climate in which almost any tariff revision or reform would not be enough, especially since Smith and a few others were starting to raise the stakes by equating government tariff policy as only the tip of a wedge whose broad end would be an attack on what he called "our *peculiar institution.*"

Indeed, that atmosphere contained more flammable gases than just political vapor. A palpable sense of fear had grown steadily, started by the Vesey plot and dramatically spread by the Nat Turner rebellion. Hearing slavery increasingly attacked by abolitionists in the North and abroad and seeing slaveowners murdered in their beds in Virginia, South Carolinians and other Southerners shifted more and more toward a siege mentality, a sense of being constantly under threat to which Smith's militant rhetoric played eloquently. At the coming session of the legislature Smith would chair a committee to consider yet another bill making it unlawful to educate slaves. It is hardly coincidental that in such a climate of apprehension a religious revival should have taken hold, starting in 1831. Especially potent was Daniel Baker, an evangelist who held meetings in Beaufort and Walterborough before audiences that easily accepted the laxity of their old Episcopal faith as one of the reasons for their current predicament. They needed now a religion that preached firmness, passionate rectitude, and unflinching adherence to principle, a faith that instead of weakening their social and political fabric, would act in its defense. Baker's evangelism answered the need. Though a Presbyterian, he crossed denominations to convince people of their sin and need for salvation. It was not difficult for them, especially the planter aristocracy, to hear his sermons in a political and social as well as a metaphysical voice for their times.[2]

Smith had been uncertain, somehow uncomfortable in his Episcopalian faith for several years, probably because it simply did not fit his conservative character or his often passionate temperament. "I had lovely children, and personal distinction, and affluence seemed beckoning me on, in the path of life," he later recalled. "Yet my spirit was not satisfied." His parents gave him a pious upbringing, and for all his other differences with his friend Petigru, the teacher certainly had reinforced his conservative view of religion and the need for ceremony and form. But by and large the rest of the Smiths were not that devout, and he observed that "it is a strange history, but it is true, whenever piety was in our family we prospered, but as soon as a disregard of God prevailed, we have sunk."[3] Perhaps he attributed his own financial straits to this rather than to his palpable neglect of his practice, for more and more recently Smith turned to the Bible "to see if in that I could find any light, any relief." He read daily in the New Testament and began trying to proselytize his brothers. Often he discussed religion with his political associates as well and took much to heart Hugh Legaré's assertion that the sermon on the mount was a greater proof of deliverance than all of Christ's miracles.[4] The idea that Jesus' greatest accomplishment had been made in a revolutionary speech cannot have been lost on Barnwell Smith. "Religion is a personal matter," he believed, "the most personal of all matters, since no other human being can stand between us and the Deity." Man and God were alone together, he felt, and he fully upheld the separation of church and state.[5]

His cousin the Reverend William Barnwell, brother of Robert Barnwell, heard of Baker's successes elsewhere and invited him to come preach in Beaufort in 1831. It was the evangelist's most successful appearance to date, and 140 of his auditors joined the churches in town, helping to shift all denominations in a more fundamentalist direction. The next year, in the heat of the campaign over the convention and nullification, he converted 500 more, many of them men who now walked armed in public due to the heightened passions of party strife. William J. Grayson became a convert, as did Henry Pinckney, founder and editor of the *Mercury;* several of the Elliotts; and more. Baker preached not on the fine points of dogma but the simple religion of sin as the source of evil, and repentance and redemption as the road to salvation. He made sinners feel they were fools if they did not pray and repent.[6]

That was precisely the kind of faith that Barnwell Smith needed, and that summer he and his cousin Robert Barnwell stepped forward and confessed to Baker their sins and gave testimony that they personally accepted Christ and sought forgiveness. Smith would thereafter remain a member of the Protestant Episcopal Church. "Strong religious faith characterized and sustained him amid the trials of a stormy life, [and] the temptations of strong passions," a nephew later remembered.[7] In fact, for Smith this newfound faith was a literal godsend, not just for him but for South Carolina. "I fear some signal chastisement may yet be in store for us, from our long hardened rebellion towards God," he confessed.[8] That chastisement could only be the trials facing the state and the Union, threatening, as he reminded everyone, not just constitutional government but civil war. His conversion surprised some, but not Petigru, who knew Smith so well. He told Hugh Legaré that he had some hope that the revival of faith would moderate political and social passions in those inflammatory days, but he was not at all sure it was for the best when it came to his former pupil. "Fanaticism of all kinds spreads," he lamented. "Barnwell Smith and Robert Barnwell are full of the Holy Ghost." Yet he found Smith's conversion "like Mahomets faith. They combine war and devotion—and in fact it seems to me that fanaticism of every kind is on the increase."[9]

Petigru saw confirmation of that in the fall election for the new legislature. Smith won handily, of course. Across South Carolina the state rights candidates took twenty-three thousand votes, to seventeen thousand for the Unionists. When they gathered in Columbia in November the nullifiers would have control of both houses by majorities more than large enough to get the two-thirds necessary to call a convention.[10] Seeing this result, Governor Hamilton did not wait but called them into special session on October 22. Smith was involved in the management of things from the start, especially sitting on the Privileges and Elections Committee. After two days the house passed a bill to call a convention by a vote of ninety-six to twenty-five, Smith heartily with the majority, and sent it to the senate. Even though this initial vote in the house showed 80 percent in favor, Smith feared that erosion might still threaten the call and as a safeguard introduced a bill to eliminate the requirement for a two-thirds majority. He need not have bothered. The same majority held on the second reading of the bill the next day, and on October 26 it passed both houses, with Smith moving the immediate printing and distribution of the act.[11]

In hastily arranged voting St. Bartholomew's elected Smith a delegate to the convention, but when it met on November 19 sickness kept him from attending.

Having so long fought for this moment, it must have been a serious illness to keep him away, but his unhappiness was more than relieved five days later when the convention reported an ordinance nullifying the tariffs of both 1832 and 1828. "The knell of *submission* is rung," exulted the *Mercury*.[12] Smith reached Columbia on November 26, but the convention allowed him to affix his signature to the historic document that, after all, owed much to him for its existence. It declared that collection of import duties in the state would be unlawful after February 1, 1833 and that any attempt to do so forcibly would absolve South Carolinians from any future obligation to the other peoples of the United States, and they would then secede and organize their own government. The sense of necessity was made all the more palpable by Jackson's easy reelection that month to a second term as president, and the fact that he had already ordered the federal forts in and around Charleston harbor to be reinforced, leaving little doubt that he would be prepared to use military power to enforce the tariff and put down nullification.[13]

While the majority gathering in Columbia had cause for rejoicing, Smith came with special impetus. Whether or not his membership on the Elections Committee during the special session helped his cause, it cannot have hurt, and on November 29 that committee reported Smith's own election as attorney general to replace the departing Legaré. But there were other things to take care of before assuming his new office. Almost at once the house began consideration of the convention's nullification ordinance. Smith joined the majority in rejecting a motion from the opposition that would have raised constitutional complications for nullification by requiring the governor to take a special oath to uphold the actions of the convention, beyond his customary oath of office. Then on December 10 they passed a bill carrying the ordinance into effect, ninety-one to twenty-four. The next day governor-elect Robert Y. Hayne took his oath, his election another manifestation of the sentiment for nullification.

Two days later Smith supported a resolution from the Federal Relations Committee approving Hayne's call on Congress to summon the other states for a constitutional convention that would precisely define the existing Constitution by strict construction, or else amend it. The resolution also proclaimed that the tariff and internal improvements were making of the Union something different from what South Carolina and other states had joined in ratifying the Constitution. "As she never has been a voluntary member of such a Confederacy," they said, "she reserves to herself the right of determining whether she ever will be." That, of course, meant secession without actually saying the word. On December 15, Calhoun having resigned the vice presidency as his differences with Jackson became more profound, the senate across the lobby elected him to fill the seat in the United States Senate vacated by the resignation of Hayne when he assumed the governorship.

Of course it all had the appearance of a well-planned scheme to cement control of the state in the crisis. With Calhoun in the Senate in Washington, Hayne in the governor's mansion, and Smith as attorney general, the nullifiers' hold would be unshakable. That the crisis lay before them, few could doubt. Minutes after Calhoun's election was announced in the house, they broke the tradition of a generation by not adjourning to attend the graduation ceremonies of the college. Instead they considered a resolution of condemnation of Jackson for his denunciation of South Carolina for passing the nullification ordinance, and for his threat to use force. It passed ninety to twenty-four, with Smith in the affirmative. Immediately afterward they passed a resolution that the nullification ordinance was now a part of the state's constitution and laws, and that henceforth all judges and chancellors and other state officials must take a special oath as a test of allegiance not just to the state, but to its nullification act, as a requisite for holding office. Several days earlier Smith had already voted with the majority to pass a special bill to provide for defense of the state.[14]

It would be his last vote as a legislator. Having delayed his acceptance of the attorney general's portfolio until after he could play his part in seeing nullification safely into law, he ended his service in the house by serving on a joint committee to settle some minor differences in wording between house and senate versions of the ordinance on December 17, and the next day he resigned his seat and submitted a letter accepting the new position. "I trust that I shall bring to the service of the State, a zeal surpassed by none, an ability only limited to my faculties, and a devotion to her holy cause," he wrote, "in this her time of trial." His only regret at leaving now might have been missing the vote on December 20 that further condemned Jackson for his December 10 proclamation declaring their action treasonous, unconstitutional, and destructive; denying the doctrine of state sovereignty; asserting that the Union was perpetual and could not be sundered by secession; and making it clear that he would have no choice but to enforce all of the laws by any means necessary.[15]

The new job made it possible for Smith to move his family to Charleston, where he would spend most of his official time as attorney general, since the local bar was, in his view, the most able and learned in the state, its star being Petigru, whom Smith regarded as the greatest lawyer in the Union.[16] There he would be able to provide a better education for his young sons when they grew old enough, and there certainly he would be closer to the most influential men in the state. There, too, he could come closer to his roots, to those earliest ancestors whose memory he revered and whose names sometimes sprang up in his public addresses as reminders to constituents of his prominent blood. He visited St. Philip's Episcopal Church on Church Street and could not help but wander the churchyard where so many of his forebears lay buried. "This Church you know is our old family Church," he told William Barnwell. "It was built chiefly by one of my Ancestors William Rhett." Lamentably the Rhett pew was sold out of the family only a few days before Smith's arrival, and he hoped to purchase another one to maintain the family presence. Looking at Rhett's family vault on the grounds, he already began to think that he should be placed there himself when the time came, completing the link with those founding fathers he so admired.[17]

He actually started attending St. Paul's Episcopal Church but found that the service there left him entirely disgusted, complaining that "it is out of the case for me to believe that the Spirit of God can be in such heartless and sluggish form." It was dull, too cold and aloof, too unlike the personal and passionate religion of Baker. Men were imitative, he lamented, and dull services made dull people. Even there he felt the need to overturn the existing regime. Sitting through a service in February 1833, he thought to himself: "Can I not make these dry-bones live?" They needed a true minister of the gospel in Charleston, he concluded, "or before long we may be no better than these people, unless a Revolution can be effected."[18] He began working to arrange for his cousin William Barnwell to come to the city and found St. Peter's Episcopal Church on Logan Street the next year.[19]

Smith scarcely gave more attention to his practice in Charleston than he had in Walterborough, however, for politics ravenously consumed his time, and he left running the law office to his brother Edmund, now admitted to the bar and a partner.[20] Jackson's December 10 proclamation, which Smith erroneously believed was actually written by Daniel Webster, represented a presidential denial of everything Smith conceived of as underpinning republican government.[21] "The interests which hold people together are negative," he believed, revealing his conviction of the intrinsic evil of men. Governments "exist chiefly by the prevention of wrong; but they can be preserved only by active intervention, with practical checks on power, which defeat despotism." Removal of such checks was consolidationism; "preserving them is liberty." All of his study of history convinced him that free government could not survive consolidated central power, whether in the hands of one man as a dictator or many men as a congress. The Constitution itself, he believed, was a protest against consolidated government. If Congress was omnipotent, then there was no protection in the ballot box. The tariff, passed by a majority against the wishes and interest of the South, was evidence of that.

As for Jackson's assertion that the states had transferred their sovereignty in such matters to the central government when they joined the Union, he observed that the Constitution said not a word on it, and the predominantly Northern idea of such a transfer could only be inferred. Impishly he remarked that "inference with a Yankee, like 'instinct' with Falstaff, 'is a great matter.'" The states, having been independent prior to the ratification of the Constitution, could be the only source of whatever sovereignty the central government enjoyed, and the Constitution explicitly said that such powers were granted for "the general welfare." Moreover, in a federation power resided not in the people as a whole but in the people of the states acting as citizens of those states. There was "no such people as the people of the United States," he maintained. The Constitution made no such reference except in its Preamble, which in his view was not a part of the general law and spoke only of the will of the states and not of the people as a whole. From that he argued that there was no such thing as a citizen of the United States, but rather each person was a citizen of his respective state. Thus one had precisely the same rights before the federal government as citizens of any other state, but he had no sovereignty over them, nor had he the right to give anyone else sovereignty over himself.

Thus again the idea of congressional sovereignty became absurd. Power might belong to a sovereign, but it did not constitute the sovereignty itself. The Constitution did not specifically grant a single power, he maintained, but rather provided for the several states to use their power together, and the government was simply the agency by which they were to do so. In fact, it was impossible for such a government to have sovereignty because of its very impermanence. A state was everlasting as a physical, territorial, and populated entity. The federal government was ephemeral, subject to elections, even to reformation through amendments, and there was no supreme authority within it since each branch could veto the actions of the others. It could hardly be supreme, then, or "self-existing," but must inevitably be subordinate to the will of the people. As it could be altered by the states meeting in convention, so logically it could be abolished by them.[22]

Seeing all of this threatened by Jackson's December 10 proclamation, Smith felt chagrined to find throughout the state a hesitation, a taking of the breath in the full realization of what they had done. Acting alone, they found themselves still alone, for no other state joined them in nullification. Some people were even rumored to be leaving South Carolina before the bloodshed began. At Beaufort the nullifiers called a meeting late in January, and Petigru found them crying like spoiled children in rage at the proclamation.[23] Suddenly to many the more temperate counsels of Calhoun looked better and better, and a rump meeting of the State Rights and Free Trade Party met in Charleston on January 21, 1833 and proposed without authority to postpone enforcing nullification while attempts in Congress to modify the 1832 tariff were under way. It was a retreat at the very moment that they needed to be most resolute, but there was nothing Smith could do to stop it.[24]

Calhoun worked with Henry Clay and others to avert a crisis as the February 1 deadline came and passed, and Smith closely watched the debate in Congress, especially the protectionist Clay's efforts.[25] Late that month they reported a new tariff that gave something to everyone and allowed all parties to emerge honorably from the fray. Duties were removed from many more items, while the balance of the tariff on everything else that was currently above 20 percent was to be reduced to that level over the next nine years, thus meeting Southern objections while still saving face for the protectionists. The compromise tariff passed Congress on March 1, and Jackson signed it the next day, ironically at the same time that he signed the Force Act authorizing him to use the armed forces if necessary to collect duties in South Carolina.

Smith saw the Force Act as only the natural consequence of the earlier proclamation and concluded that it and the compromise tariff finally demoralized the State Rights and Free Trade Party completely.[26] Coming as they did on the very eve of the March 11 reconvening of the state convention, they almost entirely undercut those, like him, who wanted to press forward and establish their principle. Some nullifier hotheads responded to the Force Act with a plan to cross the Savannah River to Augusta, Georgia, and forcibly seize the federal arsenal there. Smith probably was not involved in the scheme, but he knew of it and yet said nothing of an intention to take an offensive action against the federal government—and violate the sovereignty of another state in the process. Fortunately the foolish notion dissolved in embryo, but he could only see it as another instance that, from having been on the offensive a few months before, his forces were on the defensive now, following rather than leading events.[27] Smith took his seat on the opening day of the convention, when the body formally received both the compromise tariff and the Force Act, and there was no mistaking his anger and frustration at being thwarted so close to the goal.[28]

From the outset the convention leaders realized that they had no course left them but to amend the original nullification ordinance, since the primary cause for it had been removed. They created the Committee to Reconsider, on which Robert Barnwell sat, and when the committee delivered its report with an amended ordinance, he spoke eloquently in favor of accepting the new tariff. Their choice was either compliance or violence. "I am bound, however, to declare to you, that the question will now be of civil war, not the Tariff or Secession."

The time for the "mock-heroic bravery" of the radicals was over. If the compromise did not deliver them a victory on the principles of protectionism, internal improvements, and state sovereignty, still their immediate goal of tariff reduction was accomplished.[29]

No doubt it only made Smith's ire greater to hear his cousin and closest friend, who always stood more with the moderates, seemingly condemn his own actions as imprudent and foolish. When the report called the compromise tariff a cause for "congratulation and triumph," Smith fumed all the more. After Barnwell finished, he took the floor. He agreed that they had no option but to change the ordinance in the prevailing mood but insisted on reminding them yet again of their history with protests and federal usurpation. Even the compromise tariff before them did not lower duties as much or as immediately as they had demanded, nor did it lessen the inequality of the tariff system to the South. He asked how, then, this was cause for congratulation. "Greet each other with congratulations, when our rights are not obtained!" he shouted. Even when the duties expired in 1842, the South would still be in the minority in Washington and could expect a new measure to replace the old. In treating the immediate symptom of nullification, the compromise did nothing to cure the disease of protectionism. "We may sing peans of triumph if we will," he told them, "but I tell you, Sir, the People of this State would rather have taken the Coercion Bill with the battle-field, than accept of this modification." Volunteers had mustered to their companies and sold their stock, and they had sent their children to safety to prepare for what might come, he claimed. This was the sentiment of the people, not a craven retreat to hide behind a compromise that gave them crumbs and still kept them slaves.

On top of that, the committee's report struck him as "ostentatious, beyond all necessity," when it affirmed their attachment to the Union. It was an attachment that certainly he could not profess. "Our State, injured, reviled, insulted, threatened, is, at this very instant in arms. Her cry of defiance is scarcely yet appeased. Troops are mustering upon her borders; her chief town is half beleaguered. Do you tell me of 'Union,' when I have seen the cannon of ships and fortresses pointed at your towns, and the insolent soldiery of an angry tyrant lording it in your streets?" He had seen all that in Charleston, and in the memory of that vision he declared, "I cannot love, I will not praise that which, under the abused names of Union and Liberty, attempts to inflict upon us every thing that can curse and enslave the land."

Make no mistake, he told them—he opposed accepting the tariff compromise. They could accept it and withdraw nullification, but he urged that at least they still stand against the principles embodied in the new tariff. Meanwhile he advised that the state continue to prepare for war. "Let her make herself one general camp," he said. "Let her not lie down, except in arms. The enemy is, for the moment, beaten back. He has given way, not fled; but it is only that he may presently pour upon you, with thicker numbers, and redoubled fury." Could they ignore the Force Act, also delivered to them that very day? Was that a cure for their oppression? "No sir; the disease is still there, and formidable as is this new feature in it, the enforcement bill, it is but a symptom. The true disorder is that pest of our system, Consolidation." If they accepted the compromise, they betrayed their people at the moment that South Carolinians were ready to go to arms "in a contest which even this compromise can but for a little while avert." Giving way now, he warned, would unnerve the people "of all that strength on which our hopes, in this struggle, must ultimately rest."[30]

When he was young his own pulse had beat high for the Union, he said. Those days were past. "The star-spangled banner no longer waves in triumph and glory for me." He had seen it over federal warships in Charleston harbor and flying above forts being manned to put down their rights. In the face of this they were supposed to affirm their ardent attachment to the Union? "Sir, if a Confederacy of the Southern States could now be obtained, should we not deem it a happy termination—happy beyond expectation, of our long struggle for our rights against oppression?" There was no more freedom for them in the Union, and "a people, owning slaves, are mad, or worse than mad, who do not hold their destinies in their own hands." Not just the North but the world criticized them for their system of labor. Every action the government took brought it a step closer to "your peculiar policy," he warned. That is what awaited them from this Union to which they were to assert their attachment. "Let slaves adore and love a despotism," he concluded. "It is the part of freemen to detest and to resist it."[31]

He moved to table the report, saying that left to his own preference, he would simply repeal the nullification ordinance without any statement of cause, and without making any endorsement of the compromise. Thus the state would not be contradicting any pledge in the future should it try to assert her principles once again. "We are not yet vanquished and fallen," he pleaded, but they would have no rights under this government that they were not ready to fight for by arms if necessary. "And if driven to the last alternative of the sword, by which alone all the liberty which man has ever enjoyed, has been acquired, or maintained,—let her conquer fairly, or fall nobly, with her brow unsullied by the damp of timidity, and her free arm, striking home to the last, for her usurped and trampled rights."

Those present found Smith's manner "warm and high" as he spoke, the old temper overcoming him once more. His exclamation "I ask the gentlemen upon this floor, whether they can lay their hands upon their hearts, and say, that they are 'ardently attached to the Union'" outraged some. As soon as he sat down, an aged Revolutionary War colonel who lost a leg in service rose and declared that he could lay his hand on his heart and did.[32] Others quickly followed. Hamilton stood and demanded to know what specifically in the committee report Smith objected to, and Smith replied that he objected to the entire document. It might represent the feelings of Hamilton and others but certainly not his own, and he said it warmly enough that the two began to exchange increasingly intemperate words until others calmed them. Franklin H. Elmore stood, trying to cool tempers, and observed that perhaps Smith "in the ardor of debate" had spoken too strongly. Unwisely, though, he asked his friend to just what extent he thought South Carolina compromised its honor by accepting the compromise. The government, replied Smith, was now nothing but "a mere despotism—a purely consolidated Government." He and his constituents loved the Constitution but not this government "under the corrupt, perverted, tyrannical form, in which it at present subsists."[33]

Hamilton moved committing the report to a committee for modification to suit Smith but withdrew the motion upon objection, though the report went back to committee anyhow and at least the offensive word *triumph* was omitted. The next day Hamilton introduced another resolution asserting that if the state did not approve of the condition of things by the time of the tariff reductions in 1842, she would reserve the right to resist it once more by an assertion of her sovereignty—no use of the word *nullification*—and Smith attached a resolution that the military preparations already commenced should be continued "and that effectual measures should be adopted and completed, for putting the State in a firm attitude of defence." When it came time for a vote on adoption of an ordinance repealing nullification, he voted with the majority. However, at the end of the convention he voted to kill an amendment calling for an oath of allegiance and supported instead an amendment to their report saying that they owed "obedience" to the Union but allegiance only to South Carolina. Further he supported the majority that affirmed the power of the legislature to enforce the test oath recently passed and specifying that it should require all state officers and even citizens to take such an oath upon demand. On the last day, by a vote of 132 to 19, he and the majority hurled a small piece of defiance at Jackson by passing an ordinance nullifying the Force Act.[34]

Despite his belligerent posture, Smith knew he had gone too far and was unable to control himself. A few days after the close of the convention he issued a revised text of his speech in which he added a paragraph to soften his condemnation of the Union, asserting that he damned only the Union as it was now, and not as it had been or originally intended. For the original Union and the Constitution, he said, "I will yield to no one in my devotion and attachment." Even then, quite possibly after pressure from some friends of Calhoun, he sent the revised version to the *Mercury* for the information of the people in his old district who elected him to the convention, and in the accompanying communication he explicitly said that his views in the speech were his alone and not to be understood as representing those of the state rights and nullification party with which he had been associated for several years. "The responsibility, and the whole responsibility, of the opinions and views this speech contains, should rest therefore upon me, and me alone," he said. For the sake of accuracy he maintained that he had not altered a word to soften his tone, "however reprehensible, even in my own estimation." Now that he had moved to Charleston, resigned his legislative seat, and taken the attorney generalship, his connection with them was severed.[35]

For the first time Smith revealed just how personal politics was to him, and how ill-suited he was to bear defeat with equanimity. "I have found public life, a life of bitterness and unhappiness," he complained. He was leaving politics and retiring to private life "for that peace of mind, which the world can neither give nor take away." He was being in a measure disingenuous, since he had "retired" three months earlier when he accepted his new position, and the attorney general's portfolio was still highly political, though removed from the forum of debate. Beneath the veneer, however, lay an underlying character trait that helped to explain why he so easily went too far in the heat of argument and could become personally antagonistic and insulting even to friends, so much so that even he afterward would find his own words "reprehensible." He could not lose with grace. Politics was not a matter of difference of opinion to him, but one of him being right and those who disagreed being wrong, even malicious. "Madam Modesty" may have died in him, but a strong measure of adolescent peevishness remained and always would.

Moreover, he had spoken things that were better left unsaid. He raised again the specter of the threat to slavery, now becoming a fixture in his speeches, and of course secession as a remedy was by now an ever-present theme. He was hardly alone in this, for others raised the same issue, but none spoke so readily of violence, of the resort to war, though still only in defense of Carolinian rights if attacked. He was romanticizing warfare now, more and more looking back fondly and reverently to what their fathers had done in the Revolution and preaching a doctrine of struggle and sacrifice, even the martyrdom of annihilation rather than submission. It was well in keeping with his newfound evangelical faith and was in fact probably in some degree enhanced by his rigid and uncompromising concept of the relationship of man and god. From this point on the language of revivalism often filled his political discourse.[36]

Yet still there was something more. For the first time a nullifier had spoken publicly in advocacy of secession not as a remedy to a dispute with Washington but as a prelude to a next step, a new government, a "Southern Confederacy." He still was not advocating disunion as a positive policy in its own right. It was a means, not an end in itself. But now he had taken it farther by suggesting something to come after secession and proclaiming it "happy beyond expectation." He had never spoken of that before. Was it a spur-of-the-moment sentiment with no forethought? Had it been on his mind awhile, since the Force Act or the 1832 tariff or even earlier? More to the point, was it on his mind hereafter as a positive eventuality? He continued to argue in public that he wanted a return to the Union of old and that secession was only a last resort as a means to force Washington into honoring Southern rights so that South Carolina could remain happily in the federation. So saying, he could maintain that he was a disunionist only as an expedient to save the Union. But if or when the moment came that he looked upon secession as a means to create something in place of the Union, from that instant onward he crossed an unseen line as wide as an ocean. When that moment came—and if it had not come already—he was a disunionist.

Smith remained hot for some time to come. Two months after the convention adjourned, a visitor found him bright and promising, "a man of great energy of mind [who] was very explicit in his views and opinions" and yet still a "fierce Nullifier." Smith now spoke bitterly of the plan to seize the Augusta arsenal. Had it gone ahead rather than being injudiciously compromised by loose talk, the issue might have been forced to arms before the convention met in March to yield when they had been so close.[37] He had already said that once South Carolinians struck a blow they would not retreat, and that must inevitably bring other Southern states to her cause.

Whatever he now saw that cause as being, his unhappiness did not keep him out of events for long. Smith became more active that fall, showing that he had recovered from his funk after the convention and was once more on the march. Not for nothing had he made his motto "perseverance will ensure success." With the benefit of a little distance and perspective he could see that the convention result was a battle lost but not the war. Nullification had been a short-term goal for him, an attempt to strike with a burning iron, and its failure showed that the people of the state were not hot enough yet. He needed a long-range strategy, more broadly based on careful planning, that might take many years to achieve. Always industrious, with the instincts of a grassroots organizer and strategist and the fixation on detail that often differentiated the political functionary from the inspired statesman, he began to build, setting his foundations deeper this time and wider.

He started in June. Robert Turnbull, whose writing had much influence on his early political thinking, died in June, and Smith was active in a meeting of the State Rights and Free Trade Party in Charleston that memorialized his death as one of the heroes of the state rights movement.[38] Much more significantly, in September his brother-in-law John Stuart took over the editorship of the *Mercury* when Henry L. Pinckney won election to Congress. There would be rumors that Smith bought the paper for him, which was hardly likely given his recent financial straits, but from that moment onward Smith exerted increasing influence on the paper's course. Already the leading Calhoun sheet in the state, it soon became Smith's organ as well.[39] Then he set about purifying a reformed new state rights party. The recent defeat seemed to offer further proof of the lessons of the religious revival still under way. Smith and the nullifiers lost because too many in the state and the convention, even among their friends, lacked sufficient faith in their political religion to stand for truth and their rights. This was how he saw men fall spiritually as well, and he and other leaders turned their attention to those among them whose spiritual unsoundness might well infect the party. Cleansing their ranks of the impure in religion would make them that much stronger for the secular fights ahead.

Smith discussed this very issue with William D. Martin, former congressman and more recently circuit judge, a few days before Martin died suddenly in Charleston on November 17. Smith and others hurriedly formed a committee to organize a funeral procession to his grave the following day, and that evening they held a meeting of the State Rights Party at which Smith introduced resolutions praising the late Martin and providing for party members to wear crepe on their left arms for the next month. Then he got to the principal reason for the meeting. In his last conversation with Martin, Smith had been told that it was imperative that they secure the removal of Dr. Thomas Cooper as president of the college in Columbia, and in fact Martin had planned to go to the capital to persuade the trustees to do just that before he died.[40]

Cooper had been a problem for some time. His political views were sound as an antiprotectionist and nullifier, and he wrote a pamphlet published in 1832 that had supported the nullifiers' efforts.[41] The trouble was that he had an antagonistic and combative personality and was believed to hold "heterodoxical" religious views.[42] Smith had investigated Cooper's opinions two years before in the legislature, reading his pamphlets on the clergy and the nature of the soul. Certainly Cooper's Unitarian beliefs put him at odds with the growing Calvinist mood. At the time Smith somewhat defended him, however, saying that "every friend of his country must feel the importance of preserving the Christian Religion, in a glowing and animated style."[43] Now, however, he had changed his mind. Martin had expressed worries about educating his children, having the choice of sending them out of state to college where they would get an anti-Southern education or else to South Carolina College where Cooper's "principles hostile to Christianity" would infect them. In Martin's words—as reported by Smith—the State Rights Party, "which in fact was now the State, from holding all its powers in their hands, owed it to themselves and to the people, to see the evil, which was rapidly sinking this institution, rectified."

Now, in giving a warm eulogy on Martin, Smith declared that if they honored his memory, they would honor his last wish. Even though Cooper's own earlier political writings must have been a strong influence on his own thinking, Smith called on Carolinians now to "wipe off the aspersion from the party & from the State of being governed by infidel principles." It was time for the legislature to take action. The next evening much the same sentiments were discussed at a meeting of the Charleston Bar with Smith as chairman and Memminger as secretary, and where Petigru offered resolutions in praise of Martin.[44]

The people at the memorial meeting of the party had been surprised by what Smith said, but Petigru saw well enough that "they wish to purify their party." Smith, his cousin Robert Barnwell, Grayson, William C. Pinckney, and many more of the recent converts saw Cooper as the leader of an infidel faction within the State Rights Party ranks that had to go. Moreover, it was evident that the differences between what Petigru called "the Revival and the atheist party" were such that they could shatter the discipline needed now more than ever. Cooper was the leader of the latter, and if Smith could get rid of him, then he and his faction would have full sway and power to expel the rest or force them to fall into line with state rights orthodoxy. Petigru suspected that they would be severe and merciless in forcing conformity, for "very few of our Religionists have any charity for those who are blind to the light of Calhoun & McDuffie's revelations."[45] Perhaps it was no coincidence that Calhoun was announced as coming to Charleston the very day of the Martin memorial. Cooper's head would make a fine adornment for the figurative platter.[46]

In fact Cooper would stay on a few months, resigning in 1834, perhaps under pressure resulting from "the Revivalists." Meanwhile Smith continued his religio-political cleansing. He joined the Charleston Bible Society, becoming one of its managers, and soon served as a vice president of the Young Men's Christian Association and secretary of the Charleston Port Society for promoting the gospel among seamen. Certainly the goals of all were laudable and his motives sincerely pious, but just as certainly, too, they all represented means of using religion to establish control. The people who looked up to him as a pillar of faith might follow him on the political platform.[47] Serving on the board of the French Protestant Church, the principal meetinghouse of the Huguenot families including his wife's DeSaussure relations, he sponsored resolutions to allow the building to be used for his cousin William Barnwell when he came to Charleston to start preaching, prior to formation of the new St. Peter's congregation. When St. Peter's commenced soon thereafter, Smith could hear the Bible read as he wanted it, impressively and with majesty, and hear sermons that carried the fire and earnestness both to admonish and inspire not only himself but also those whom he would have follow him.[48]

The Smiths had moved into a house on Green Street just across from the College of Charleston in an old section of the city known as Harleston Village. There, the day after the State rights meeting that started the campaign against the Cooper faction, Elizabeth gave birth to a fourth son, Edmund Smith.[49] Fortunately her husband's new position, and the law practice getting more attention from brother Edmund, could provide for the growing brood. The newest boy was scarcely able to open his eyes, however, when duty and party combined to pull his father into the political light once again. The original nullification ordinance had required an oath of allegiance swearing civil and military officers to support state interposition. The repeal also repealed that oath, but at the same time the convention had enacted that a new oath to the state should be taken in addition to the usual oath already provided for in the state constitution. It affirmed allegiance to the state and by implication placed that before any to the United States. Unionists in the state declined to take it, Smith's friend Perry among them.[50] Two months later, in February 1834, Edward McCrady refused to swear that oath when he applied in Charleston for a commission in a local militia company, and his application was denied. He took his case to the court of appeals on the grounds that such an oath violated the state constitution and at the same time was "repugnant" to the United States Constitution. Then a second case arose when James McDaniel, elected colonel of a state regiment, refused to take the oath and lost his commission. A lower court upheld him and declared the oath unconstitutional, and thus both of them wound up in the court of appeals. It fell to Barnwell Smith, as attorney general, to represent the state and the oath.[51]

Smith's opponents, ironically, were his mentors Petigru and Grimké, in his opinion and that of many others the most capable lawyers in the state. The arguments took place on April 3, and since McCrady and McDaniel were the plaintiffs, Grimké opened with a three-hour address making it clear that he and

Petigru would seek to take this issue beyond the case in hand, arguing the constitutionality of the oath and even the question of how the Constitution ought to be interpreted. He especially addressed the issue of sovereignty, likening it to power and illustrating how everyone from the despot to the marooned seaman on a desert isle had sovereignty but could divide it at will. If power and sovereignty were the same and it was admitted that a sovereignty could divide its power, then what did that do to the state rights idea that sovereignty was indivisible and that in joining the Union the states had not divided theirs? "Power is the test of sovereignty," he said, and if sovereignty was divisible, then so was allegiance to sovereignty, and thus a man could not be required to take an oath to the state alone when that state had yielded some of its sovereignty to the Union, nor could allegiance to the one be preeminent over that due to the other.[52]

"What is Allegiance?" asked Smith in opening his response. "Words are things, and often the most important things." He gave a lengthy history of the concept of fealty to sovereignty and then addressed the subject in South Carolina, establishing what everyone already acknowledged, which was that for at least those years between 1776 and the adoption of the Articles of Confederation, South Carolina had been indeed independent and sovereign unto itself. Such sovereignty lay with the people of the state and then with their state government, but only as representatives of the people to do their will. The representatives had no sovereignty of their own and could be turned out of office at pleasure. The same was true of the Constitution, he said. The states created it as the instrument of their will, but it had no inherent sovereignty of its own, nor did its Congress. Otherwise they faced the ridiculous prospect that the central government, as agent of the states, was supreme to them. The Constitution, he said, was "a mere power of Attorney." Thus he concluded that allegiance is only due to a sovereign and that the only sovereignty in the Union was to the individual states.

As to whether or not South Carolina had yielded sovereignty to the Union, he declared that if so, it must have been all or none. To Grimké's cogent argument that power and sovereignty were and always had been in practice divisible, he replied effectively that while a sovereign despot or a congress could delegate power to an agent, be it a general or a diplomat, the ultimate power remained always with the sovereign, as in medieval times when a tenant owed fealty to his lord—who held delegated power from the king—but was always ultimately subject to the king. "No man can serve two masters," he said and then raised a prophetic hypothetical as proof. If a collision came between the states and the general government over disputed powers and it went to a contest of arms, each side claiming title to the allegiance of a man, then a man was doomed to be a traitor to one of them no matter which side he chose to obey, thus putting his head in the traitor's noose of the other. "No principle can be correct which leads to an alternative so unjust and desperate," he declared. One or the other of the two authorities must be supreme and "alone the sovereign."

The question then remained of whether or not South Carolina had alienated her sovereignty, to which he responded with the statement from the Articles of Confederation that "Each State retains its sovereignty" not specifically delegated to the central government. As for the Constitution, certainly there was no express renunciation of total sovereignty. It could only be inferred, and in the inevitable history lesson that followed he could find no acts of the individual states or the constitutional convention that indicated such an intent. Some had seized on the phrase "we the people" in the Preamble as a statement of intent that the people now constituted a national sovereignty, but he showed convincingly that the expression was merely a literary convenience used in place of naming all the states severally in the phrase, requiring constant amendment as more states were admitted. A better argument was the constitutional clause dealing with treason against the United States. He admitted some plausibility to this, at least originally, but maintained that the intent was merely to use the penalties of treason to suppress certain crimes, such as counterfeiting, and that it did not reflect any intent to confer upon the Union such sovereignty that it would be treasonous to deny allegiance, nor could he find any indictment for treason in the federal courts that charged the defendant on the basis of allegiance.

Thus he concluded—by inference—that sovereignty and allegiance being inseparable and indivisible, and allegiance really playing no role in the practical use of the treason clause in the Constitution, that therefore there had been no intent to imply a transfer of sovereignty to the central government. Smith may not have seen it—or might not have admitted it—but he was using precisely the same rational grounds as his political foes used. They argued that the absence of specific limitations to power in the Constitution meant that that which was not prohibited expressly was permissible through inference. Smith was arguing that the absence of express evidence to the contrary meant that the framers had no intention of conferring any sovereignty on the new government.

On the main point that the states had ceded sovereignty, as evidenced in the powers they undeniably granted to the central government, he argued once again that power was not sovereignty; the one could be delegated, and the other could not. Those powers belonged to the states before there was a Union and would belong to them again if the Union dissolved. The Union was only "a general agency" to apply those powers for the common good in a means more efficient than they could do it individually. "There is no sovereignty in the General Government on account of the powers it possesses," he asserted. Nor was it intended that the will of the majority should prevail, for he cited the mode of amendment that required three-fourths of the states to ratify. The smallest seven states—just over one-fourth of the current Union—comprised only 1,000,000 people, one-twelfth of the people, yet they could stop an amendment passed by the other seventeen whose population totaled 11,600,000. Further, this argued that the founders did not conceive of the people of the Union as one sovereign mass, for if they did, then the will of the majority would prevail absolutely.

Thus South Carolina had been a sovereign, had never renounced that sovereignty, and therefore was still sovereign within her borders, and thus all of her citizens owed allegiance solely to the state, making the test oath constitutional. Smith went on to admit that the wording of the oath was ambiguous and should have said that in addition to pledging allegiance to the state, the deponent in doing so repudiated any allegiance "to any other power." Though he failed to say so, and it would give the Unionists the opportunity to point to the attorney general himself admitting a fault with the oath, his intent was that the repudiation clause would have made it impossible for the Unionists to argue that allegiance could be divided.[53] As to whether the legislature had the power to enact a bill requiring the test oath, since there was already an oath required by the state constitution, he examined the oaths of several other states, and of Congress itself, and found that in every branch of civil and military government there were numerous oaths imposed for varying purposes. Since opponents of the test oath had claimed it was unconstitutional since it repeated one already provided, he asked them rhetorically if they thought all the other oaths required in the federal government were unconstitutional because there was already a basic oath contained in the Constitution itself. That said, he then maintained that the last named oath was "foully unconstitutional" because it called for "allegiance," whereas he had just shown to his own satisfaction, if not theirs, that the only allegiance could be to a sovereign, and that was the state.

There he closed his argument. He had shown that the state had the right to the exclusive allegiance of its citizens and the right to pass the bill requiring the oath, thus refuting the two grounds of complaint by the plaintiffs.[54] Petigru rebutted, highlighting the essential intent of the oath as a suppression of any opposition to nullification—which was, of course, its unspecified purpose from the first—and therefore a violation of the basic freedoms of thought and speech, denouncing it as "a *political test.*" Other lesser counsel for both sides followed, but the arguments essentially ended with Petigru's relatively brief rejoinder to Smith.[55]

The attorney general's effort had been an unusual one for him. Absent were the impassioned and intemperate rhetoric, the aspersions on his opponents and their motives. It was a lawyer's argument, laced with Blackstone and Kent and other authorities for precedent. Being before his infinitely more experienced former teachers Petigru and Grimké may have restrained him. The fact that he was in a court before judges, and not on the stump in front of an emotional audience, may also have kept him restrained, as might, too, a sense of the dignity required in his office as chief legal counsel of the state. And he must have been sensible of the necessity of maintaining decorum, for what he said had wider import than just this case. In fact, Smith knew going into the hearing that he was going to lose. There were three judges on the court of appeals bench, two of them ardent Unionists and opponents of the test oath, and quite predictably they decided in favor of McCrady and McDaniel. But state rights men in the state at large would be looking at the case. While the proceedings as a whole were soon published, his own party reprinted and widely distributed Smith's address by itself, comprising as it did yet one more compactly stated defense of their position and refutation of their Unionist opposition. Thus, though a tactical defeat—that in fact cost the state rights men nothing of consequence—his argument provided another block in that broader foundation as they sought to organizationally rebuild and morally rearm their party for the battle ahead.[56]

The arguments attracted considerable attention and revealed the particular bias of the editors, as the Unionist press proclaimed Grimké's remarks while the *Mercury* and others offered mild praise for Smith's, only complaining at his admission of ambiguity in the wording of the oath. It was a setback, even if predictable, for a state court had rejected their ideology that a citizen of the state could owe allegiance only to the state itself, and not to the general government. Meanwhile the legislature had been at work in its last session on the proper constitutional amendment to adopt the oath. If the fall elections lost the State Rights Party their two-thirds majority, that amendment would fail.

Thus in the coming legislative elections the test oath became the leading issue. During the balance of the year there were more meetings to reorganize the State Rights Party, including one in Smith's old power center at Walterborough.[57] By narrow margins the nullifiers just held on to their two-thirds majority and that fall were able to pass their oath amendment, even seeking to abolish the court of appeals to further secure their hold by ousting the judges who decided against the test oath. Such a move was so blatantly an attempt to tamper with judicial independence—for which Smith had been a champion—in the interest of party, that finally the state rights men backed away from it and even softened the allegiance amendment by interpreting it to include fealty to the United States as well as to South Carolina.[58] Barnwell Smith did not comment publicly on the oath when it was finally adopted, but his younger brother Albert did.

Described by one acquaintance as a "hot headed nullifier," Albert had already been briefly expelled from Yale College for beating a fellow student with a cane after the fellow had insulted him. Elected to his own first term in the legislature in 1834, he made it quite clear that so far as he was concerned, the oath meant not only obedience to the Union but allegiance to South Carolina.[59] There sounded the echo of his oldest brother.

FIVE

The Union Must Be Dissolved
1834-1837

THE NEXT TWO YEARS AFTER the test oath case passed quickly, and Smith devoted himself primarily to his work as attorney general and to his family and fortunes. The routine official duties of his office attracted little notice, which was just as well since his personal life needed more time than ever before. In January 1835 he borrowed $9,260.79 on a ten-year note, with his brother Thomas and cousin Barnwell signing as sureties, and then moved the family to a larger house on Church Street, where on February 19, 1836 Elizabeth gave birth to their first daughter, Mary Burnet.[1] There was loss too. His mentor, friend, and erstwhile opponent Grimké died just six months after the court of appeals arguments. Smith appeared in his official role as attorney general at the memorial service in Charleston, lavishing high praise on the deceased. "Lawyers have seldom proved able statesmen," he said in eulogizing Grimké, something that could be said of many attorneys in South Carolina just then. His late friend had been an exception.[2] This was one of the first manifestations of a trait in Smith's character increasingly in evidence as the years advanced. His bitterest attacks were often on men whose differences with him in principle were only slight, who agreed with him but not entirely. His greatest praise was often bestowed upon those, such as Grimké, Petigru, and John Quincy Adams, who stood completely in opposition to him. He could see and respect an enemy as a man of principle even if he thought him wrong, but someone on his own side who withheld total agreement could become an apostate in his eyes.

The winter brought a greater loss. James Smith, now seventy-three, visited his son Barnwell in Charleston and in March 1835 came down with a severe cold. The family soon saw that he would not recover, and Barnwell Smith summoned all of the other siblings. On March 10 six brothers and four sisters stood at their father's bedside, as did Marianna Smith, to whom James gave his assurance that he had always been a faithful husband to her. To the children he made a protestation of his faith and then asked them all to sing "Rock of Ages" with him. While they sang his voice stopped, and with their own verses still filling the room he died. True to his determination to regain his connection with his distinguished ancestors, Barnwell buried his father in the Rhett vault at St. Philip's.[3]

Barnwell Smith gave few hints of what he felt about his father. Certainly theirs had been an affectionate and warm household, if the attention he gave his own children is any measurement. Not a word of jealousy or resentment ever appeared from him over the fact that James Smith somehow managed to send his younger sons to Harvard and Yale, while Barnwell got only Beaufort College and self-instruction. Nor did Barnwell ever criticize his father for his failures as a planter and lawyer or for being the first of his line in South Carolina to achieve less than prosperity and social distinction, less than their forebears would have expected. Yet there must have been some unspoken, perhaps even unconscious, sensitivity about his father's lack of achievement. In later years, while Smith always spoke reverently of his father as a good man, almost one too good for this terrestrial life, he also repeatedly described James Smith as too simple, too trusting, too lacking in guile, "a mere child in the practical means of life."[4] While praising James Smith's depth of faith, Barnwell consciously or unconsciously determined not to repeat his failings. During the years to come Smith set out deliberately to achieve everything that his father did not, even if it meant compromising simplicity, trust, and guile.

Smith was almost thirty-five now. His once light brown hair had receded so dramatically that he was almost entirely bald on top of his head, which he concealed as best he could by combing the prematurely graying remnant up from the side and over the top. His smooth-shaved face was well formed and intelligent, softened in the stern set of his features by a sensitive mouth and his pale eyes. Beneath his chin he wore a short set of whiskers, largely hidden by his high starched collar.[5] His friends and family knew him as a man of an open and confiding nature, like his father, and as a result they thought that now and then others took advantage of him. "His temperament was mercurial," a daughter would recall. "He was quick in movement, & quick tempered, but entirely self-controled" with his family. "We knew no pleasure so great as that of having him play with us—all sorts of games which he would make for us & played as tho' he was a boy." Rhett admitted, "I like to laugh." He seemed to show tenderness of feeling toward all children and all women, not just his wife. Moreover, both through the church and in private life he demonstrated the same tenderness and sympathy for the weak and the poor. "No man ever had a more tender, loving heart," the daughter remembered. "To us," she said, "his tenderness consideration & courtesy was most beautiful & unfailing."[6]

Events elsewhere in the world made possible a major change in Smith's life now. In 1833 Great Britain had outlawed slavery in the empire, further requiring that British subjects living outside the empire could not lawfully hold slaves. Col. John Stapleton, a wealthy and influential planter in the Beaufort district, thus had no choice but to sell his slaves and the plantations they worked and move back to England.[7] Grimké had been his attorney, and it was probably through him that Smith first learned that Stapleton's property was for sale. Sometime in the summer of 1834 Smith took ship for England to see Stapleton, and the result was his purchase of much of the Englishman's holdings.[8] In January 1836 the acquisition was completed with the transfer of title to Smith, and the next month he paid $22,333.35 in cash as the down payment of a total of $88,000, the balance due in three payments of $19,555.55 each, for which he gave his bond secured by his brothers Thomas and Benjamin. What he acquired was Blue House plantation on the Ashepoo River, another adjacent plot called Bugby, one more known as the Oaks, and also Lavington. In all it amounted to several hundred acres of rice land and with it more than one hundred slaves.[9]

Immediately the word spread that Smith had done well. Even Stapleton's Charleston agents for the sale told him that "Mr Smith has been fortunate in his purchase from you," estimating the market value of the deal at nearly $100,000 thanks to a substantial rise in the price for slaves in the past year.[10] A few weeks later Petigru declared that "Barnwell Smith has made a fortune by an advantageous purchase."[11] Indeed Smith had done well. The four plantations—he would rename Blue House to Drainfield—sat at the junction of the Ashepoo and Deer Creek in Colleton District. The land rose from the lowland on the river to a somewhat higher elevation covered with timber, affording plenty of room both for the rice cash crops and also fields for raising provisions for the slaves.[12] Two plantations were already cleared of timber and either under cultivation or else ready for it, and Stapleton wrote to Smith after the sale, "you were fortunate in the purchase upon the whole." That was fine with Stapleton, for he said, "I am far from grudging you your good fortune."[13]

But there was one proviso, a gentleman's agreement along with the legal transfer. When Smith visited him in England, they had repeated conversations about the slaves. Like many masters, Stapleton felt a considerable personal affection for his blacks, and a grave responsibility. In the turmoil and fear that followed the Vesey and Turner uprisings, a number of South Carolina planters had sold their Negroes to traders who moved them to the lower Mississippi, where masters and overseers were believed to be more demanding and harsh on their slaves. Stapleton told Smith of his "horror at the possibility of their being sold to slave dealers & transferred to New Orleans or other countries where neither compassion nor mercy is practiced towards that unfortunate race of human beings, more than belongs to the brute creature." One of the reasons, then, that he felt good about selling to Smith was that the Carolinian impressed him as a man of "benevolent & religious disposition" who would care lovingly for the blacks. He was so pleased that he did not even charge interest on the notes that remained outstanding from the purchase.[14]

Certainly Smith shared Stapleton's concern, and always would, though of his notion of the place of the black in society there was never any doubt either. "Of all the races of man," he declared, "the negro race is the most inferior."[15] It was a place ordained by God, justified by the verdict of history, and sanctioned in the laws of nations. Nevertheless, that only placed a greater burden on the superior white race to show charity and humanity to a race that he believed could not take care of itself if left alone. The frequent cruelty of owners to their slaves appalled him, and on one occasion he actually stepped in to stop a master who was flogging his slave more than Smith thought was deserved—which implied, however, that there were things for which some flogging was appropriate.[16] Stapleton's appeals met a receptive ear, then, "corresponding as they did, with my own sense of humanity and Christian duty," Smith told him. He said, "I am responsible to God for their temporal & spiritual welfare and were I capable of swerving from my engagements express or implied, to man, the accounting, the appalling account over which my heart sometimes almost sinks, which I must render to him who has sanctified us and washed us in his own blood, would terrify me into the path of rectitude. God helping me, I am determined, that every soul he has committed in my care shall have the considerations of the Gospel brought home to its bearer, and whilst I administer to the necessities of these Slaves in this world, the great and one thing needful for eternity shall not be neglected."[17]

Thus Barnwell Smith had become in a stroke what his father had not been in the end, a planter. The law was a profession; planting was a way of life more suitable for one of the old aristocratic families, one that been a part of the oligarchy and that should be again. Smith firmly believed the old family story about his forebear Thomas Smith first introducing rice cultivation to the Carolinas, and thus it was the more fitting that he should himself plant the crop that had made the state great.[18] Moreover, despite his residence in Charleston, he preferred living in the country, and the house on the Oaks plantation would allow him to indulge his preference, especially if he could afford to resign the attorney generalship and devote himself entirely to the congenial gentlemanly business of planting.[19] Rice cultivation was essentially simple, a technique originally taught to whites by slaves. His brother Edmund explained it as hoeing, planting the seed, watering, hoeing when the plants emerged, then watering and weeding until harvest.[20]

Of course there was more to it than that. In the Lowcountry they grew long-grain gold seed rice that required a tidal flow of fresh water to replenish the soil and keep down the weeds. That, in turn, required digging ditches and canals, a year-round and laborious process. Early in 1836 Smith put his slaves to work clearing the stubble from the last year's crop, cleaning the drainage ditches, and plowing the ground. Then they dug the trenches and sowed the seed. During the growing season that followed, Smith's slaves four times flooded the fields with water built up in the ditches and held back by dikes. That controlled insects and weeds, and then the fields had to be drained and weeded again. When time came for the harvest later in the year, it would all be by hand too, the rice on stalks bound in sheaves and floated down the canals to waiting flatboats and then transported to barns for threshing in the winter. When he had his first crop of "paddy rice," as they called it, he would send it to Charleston to market and, he hoped, begin to realize his fortune.

Smith liked to tell friends that he wanted nothing more than to spend his winters working his plantations and his summers in the mountains to the west, like so many other planters, but he little knew himself it he ever seriously believed that he could enjoy or maintain such a life.[21] With a wonderful irony, Smith no sooner acquired title to his plantations in January 1836 than events outside the state forced him to consider out of self-interest doing what his heart must have been longing for anyhow ever since he left the legislature. As he had predicted—though for other reasons—once the tariff issue calmed after the 1833 compromise, the agitation over slavery quickly took its place. Indeed, the American Anti-Slavery Society commenced that same year, and thereafter a trickle of petitions to Congress demanding abolition in the District of Columbia steadily grew until, as with Smith's fields, a dike was needed to hold them back. In the Senate, Calhoun denied that Congress had the authority to abolish slavery in the capital and worked effectively to table all such petitions. Vice President Martin Van Buren, anticipating a run for the presidency in the fall, had Democratic managers in the House who worked to halt the agitation there too but stopped short of Calhoun's position. They came up with a less rigid policy, and Henry L. Pinckney, founder of the *Mercury* and now a congressman from Charleston, presented it in the House on February 4.

He introduced a resolution denying that Congress had any authority over slavery in the states, which was a sovereign matter for them alone. As for the District of Columbia, which had no sovereignty of its own, he proposed that all petitions for abolition of slavery there should be referred to a select committee instructed that Congress had no power to interfere with it in the states and therefore should not in the district either, virtually a "gag rule." In doing so, however, Pinckney unwittingly implied that Congress *might* have constitutional authority for abolition in the district, whereas Calhoun and others maintained that Congress should not even receive such petitions, let alone refer them to a committee. The outrage in South Carolina was immediate and intense. His own old paper the *Mercury* charged him with disloyalty to Calhoun, and Calhoun's lieutenants in the state denounced Pinckney in the press and on the stump, saying he was unfit to represent Charleston in Congress. Calhoun put out the word that in the fall elections his followers should support Legaré in Pinckney's place.[22] That effectively killed Pinckney's chances, for now no one challenged Calhoun in the state and survived.

One of those outraged was Barnwell Smith, who soon took up his pen to add to the chorus of denunciations. Only a few months earlier, he noted, Pinckney had written a pamphlet saying that a Van Buren presidency posed no danger to the nation and the South. Yet now he was consorting with and being used by the Van Buren men. "Our *honour* was assailed, and—you *surrendered it,*" Smith railed in a letter for the press. "The very foundations of our social and political existence have been shaken, and *you,* the sentinel at the gate, *have passed the countersign of our ruin.*" He declared that he regarded Pinckney as "*a public enemy*" whose continuation in office was incompatible with the public safety. "South Carolina would be *dishonoured,* after what has occurred, by your representing her in the national councils." There were still men in the state who, despite the surrender to the compromise tariff, were weary of submitting and ready to rally to the banner cry of resistance. "A 'living cloud of war' shall stretch from the Potomac to the Gulf of Mexico," Smith promised, if slavery were assailed, and all thanks to Pinckney, who argued that his measure would actually calm agitation thanks to gagging abolition discussion in Congress. "Would you have me calm while the assassins knife is at my throat?" Smith demanded.[23]

Not only had Pinckney sent South Carolina into an uproar against him, but he had also wrought the return of the old Barnwell Smith, fiery, passionate, threatening, only now with a new issue. Anything that threatened slavery posed a threat to Smith's newfound status as a planter and slaveholder. To Pinckney's complaints of his attacks, Smith responded that "the world, be assured, is large enough for us both, and if it were not, I do not know *you* are the man whose overshadowing fame need offend my just ambition."[24] There was the other fuse Pinckney had touched off in Smith: ambition. With the prospect of his plantations relieving him of the financial straits that forced him to leave the legislature, he could think of returning to public life once more, and now Pinckney had

given him an issue that not only imperiled him personally but excited him politically. Smith told Petigru just days after Pinckney's disastrous resolution in the
House that he was beginning to feel "anxious to play a part at Washington."[25]
The part he clearly had in mind was a bid for Pinckney's congressional seat that
fall, since he still had a home in Charleston and thus could run as a legal resident. Moreover, some of his friends urged him to run. However, it appeared that
Pinckney did not intend to step down, and Smith told his friends that he felt an
"utter aversion to any contest for any political position" against one of his own
party.[26] But then Calhoun's endorsement of Legaré quickly put that out of the
question, just as another opportunity appeared.

When Stapleton sold his plantations to Smith, he sold another to William
Grayson, and in the ensuing negotiations Smith and his old mentor exchanged
between themselves some of their new property.[27] Grayson won the Beaufort and
Colleton area seat in Congress in 1832 as a member of a still-coalescing group
of old disillusioned Republicans and others united in opposition to the tariff
and to Jackson as well, groups that in other slave states were becoming a part
of the new Whig Party. Thus his party affiliation nominally put him at odds
with Smith, but in fact they were in agreement on most issues other than nullification. Grayson attracted little notice in his first term in the House, Petigru
describing him as "a silent member," but he ran unopposed for reelection in
1834 and won handily, with only a few of the harder State Rights Party men
voting against him.[28]

But now Grayson was tired of Congress, whose constant controversies did
not suit his moderate temperament, and domestic difficulties required him at
home on his plantation. During the previous winter Grayson more than once
told Smith that he wanted to retire from the House, and he suggested that
Smith make a run to succeed him. He knew that many would support such a
candidacy, for during the past two or three years some had spoken of running
Smith against Grayson in 1834 or 1836. When the subject had been broached
earlier to Smith, he had declined, saying that he had no wish to humiliate "an
honourable man" by beating him at the polls—Smith assuming somewhat
smugly that the result would be a foregone conclusion.[29] For his part, Grayson
had mixed feelings toward Smith. Interestingly, he did not regard him as one of
the leading nullifiers in 1832, though at the same time Smith was certainly far
more radical than Grayson.[30] Still, they had shared concerns, differing only in
the means of addressing them, and Grayson thought well enough of Smith to
be willing to withdraw in his favor.

Smith declined the offer at first, having his newly acquired plantations to
put in order, but Grayson kept renewing it, adding persuasion and argument to

convince his former pupil to accept the seat and taking it for granted that whomever he chose to succeed him would automatically be accepted by the voters. Apparently Grayson actually suggested that he resign his seat before serving the final session to convene in December, which would have called for a special election for Smith to fill his unexpired term. Then came the furor aroused by Pinckney's action, and Smith's blood pulsed more politically. Sometime that spring Smith changed his mind and wrote to Grayson, then in Washington, saying that he would accept the seat if Grayson retired. At the same time, though, Smith suggested that he was not entirely certain that he could arrange all of his plantation and financial affairs in time to be able to take the seat the next year, and he at least hinted that it might be better for him to wait until 1838 to make the run. The old "Madam Modesty" in him phrased his letter in such diffident terms that Grayson believed Smith was more acquiescing to persuasion than moved by genuine desire for the seat. Nevertheless, he wrote back in June that as soon as Congress adjourned on July 4 he would return home and publish in the *Mercury* an announcement of his retirement. At the same time Grayson wrote to friends in Beaufort authorizing them to announce his retirement, and they in turn learned that Smith was willing to serve and began to hear from Smith's friends in the district asking them to nominate him.[31]

Meanwhile Smith looked to other issues showing his determination to retake political initiative. That winter he went to Columbia to help organize the Society for the Advancement of Learning with a capitalization of twenty thousand dollars to found a state literary journal. He and his brother Albert, as well as Elmore and Petigru, were among the first subscribers, and Smith chaired the committee to oversee the fund-raising. Such a journal, no one needed to say, could provide a forum for advancing resistance views and perhaps replace the *Southern Quarterly Review,* which then seemed in decline as the leading journal of Southern opinion. Unfortunately the journal never saw print. He also submitted resolutions to a meeting calling for volunteers to go to Florida to put down an uprising by the Seminoles, and through his brother Edmund, whom he briefly had in his place as acting attorney general, he prosecuted a New York man for publishing critical comments about slavery, which was a crime in South Carolina.[32]

For some time Calhoun had been trying to encourage railroad interests in South Carolina to tie the state into a wider Southern commercial network. Now he favored a proposed rail line from Cincinnati, Ohio, to Charleston, and soon there was a charter for the Louisville, Cincinnati & Charleston Railroad. With the precise route of the line still to be settled, the organizers called a convention at Knoxville, Tennessee, for July 4, and Smith was to attend, making it part of a tour that would take him all the way to Cincinnati and Louisville. He was also ailing and thought a trip to the mountain springs of southwest Virginia would do him good, combining it with the Knoxville trip. He left before Grayson could return from Washington and in fact did not expect to return himself before the election, which would be left entirely in the hands of his friends to manage and which, in any event, should be a mere formality as he did not expect to be opposed. Well before reaching Knoxville, while stopping in Aiken, South Caro-lina, Smith received a letter from Grayson's manager saying that he had been informed that Grayson would not run again and that he was going to ask Gray-son if he intended to resign at the end of the current session. Smith immediately wrote back directly to Grayson that he hoped he would not resign before the end of the term, because it would be impossible for him to be ready to go to Washington to serve the remaining winter session in Grayson's place. Smith said nothing, however, about not wishing to run for election for the next term. At the Knoxville convention he merely observed, then traveled on north across Kentucky to Cincinnati, arriving in mid-August. Awaiting him was a letter from his brother Thomas, and it stunned him. Grayson was announced as a candi-date for reelection after all.

All this was the result of a classic case of confusion and missed communica-tions. When Grayson, already thinking that Smith was only lukewarm on run-ning that fall anyhow, received the letter from Aiken declining to replace him in the winter term, he concluded that it was best for him to change his mind, and late in July he decided to run again himself, his reason being not that he felt a desire to serve another term but that his wife, whom he had not previously con-sulted in the matter, preferred living in Washington in order to be near their sons in college. "I can give you no better reason for re-considering my desire to withdraw," he confessed in informing Smith. Unfortunately, Grayson's letter went to South Carolina sometime after Smith had already left, and there it sat unopened. Meanwhile Grayson's friends announced his candidacy, and now Thomas Smith had finally gotten the news to his brother.

Barnwell Smith felt chagrined and embarrassed. At Grayson's behest he had put himself in a position that now left him compromised, announced as a can-didate in opposition to a man he had repeatedly in the past promised not to oppose. Smith immediately wrote to Grayson demanding an explanation. The only choices facing him appeared to be to run against Grayson and seem to be duplicitous or else to back out, which he feared would give the impression that he felt himself "subordinate to your will," which was unthinkable. At first he simply refused to believe that Grayson would be so seemingly disingenuous. At the same time he wrote to Grayson's manager explaining what had happened and asking if there were some honorable way he could get out of running if Grayson persisted, but adding defiantly, "I will be puppet of no man." Being so far from home, he had to leave the matter to his friends but added, "if my name can be withdrawn with honour from the canvass I prefer it to a contested election."

Once Grayson found out about the mix-up, he immediately declared that he would withdraw, feeling honor bound to observe his original commitment to Smith, whom he saw clearly as an innocent party. On September 1 he published his withdrawal in the *Mercury*. That ended the confusion, and three days later he issued a statement absolving Smith of any blame in the affair.[33] It did not end the controversy, however. Smith's brother Thomas and some of his other friends were hard on Grayson in the press for his vacillating position and apparent double-dealing, and even some of Grayson's own friends regarded his reason for wanting to remain in Washington as so frivolous that they determined to support Smith as a matter of honor. On September 19, even while the affair was being resolved, some Grayson supporters, apparently without his permission, held a sudden unannounced meeting at Coosawhatchie, and there one of them said that the congressman would serve another term if elected. Four days later a handbill went up in several places stating that Grayson would not make himself a candidate for reelection but would accept it if the people chose to vote for him. Then one of Grayson's chief defenders and one of Smith's boyhood acquaintances from Beaufort, Richard DeTreville, with whom for some reason Smith already shared bad blood, published an inflammatory defense of Grayson that struck hard at the Smith brothers, saying that "as a candidate for Congress, Mr. R. B. Smith's position is not too lofty for his ambition." He pointed out the difference between Grayson being an announced candidate and merely being willing to acquiesce in the verdict of the people should they go ahead and elect him anyhow. In fact, it was largely DeTreville and other Grayson managers who were responsible for the announcement that Grayson would serve if elected, which may well have resulted from DeTreville's antipathy for the Smiths. He even declared that if Barnwell Smith were elected in the end, it would only be due to a low voter turnout, and that only a minority of the eligible voters in the district would select him.[34]

Through no real fault either of his or of Grayson's, what Smith had hoped to avoid was occurring. The idea of two men of similar principles opposing each other rightly filled him with dread, for anything that promoted dissension in the state rights ranks weakened the party that he strove to strengthen. Moreover, as he knew as well as anyone, there were more than enough divisions in their following already. Falling out among themselves only gave their opponents more ammunition to use against them. Even if he had not already expected to be away until after the election, Smith may well have decided to keep out of South Carolina so as not to be drawn into the fray himself, especially understanding as he did how easily he could lose self-control and the damage that could do. Grayson, too, remained in the North that fall, and consequently the election was conducted entirely by their friends in their absence.

Smith's backers, faced with a contest after all, organized a public meeting in Beaufort on September 23 to nominate him formally and were themselves the most active participants, though no more than twenty-five of them attended. In the end Grayson's followers outnumbered them and nominated their man instead. A formal press announcement of Smith's candidacy went out in early October, and all of the correspondence over the recent confusion appeared in the *Mercury*, no doubt in the hope of strengthening Smith's candidacy and embarrassing Grayson's supporters, if not Grayson himself.[35] There was no campaign beyond that, for no issues really separated the candidates, and there were no candidates present in any case. It was no wonder that the election attracted little interest or attention, and DeTreville proved to be a prophet when the voter turnout was the lowest in recent memory. Where 3,200 came to the polls in 1834, barely more than 1,000 showed up this season, and through several days in mid-October the results steadily came in. Smith opened with a lead of 148 votes, but then Grayson took Prince William Parish by a majority of 138 and St. Helena the next day by another 73. By October 18, Grayson had captured five parishes and Smith only St. Bartholomew and St. Paul. With three parishes still to be counted, Grayson led by 67. Then a few days later St. George's came in for Smith by 80 and St. Peters by 120, and that decided it. On 26 October the *Mercury* announced Smith's election by a majority overall of 133.[36]

This was not the way Smith would have preferred to win the seat. His relations with Grayson had been cordial, and beyond question this controversy strained them, though Grayson always thereafter repeated his absolution of Smith for any wrongdoing. But though they would be cordial again, they would never be close, and political differences in coming years separated them even more. Grayson published a magnanimous declaration the following March when he left office, showing that his own feelings had calmed. However, he may never have forgiven Thomas Smith for publishing his correspondence without his permission, which certainly made him look indecisive at best.[37]

Smith learned of his election while he was still traveling. On his way home he stopped in Greenville, South Carolina, and visited with his friend Benjamin Perry. He was considering buying property in the area, probably to add a cotton plantation to his holdings and perhaps as a summer home as well to escape the heat of the Lowcountry, since he had brought his family with him. He engaged Perry to negotiate for him but in the end bought nothing because he could not get access to water. "There were no two men who were more antipodes of each other," Perry said of himself and Smith, "and yet our social relations were always kind, courteous and cordial." While Smith was in Greenville, Perry introduced him to Judge Augustin S. Clayton, an ardent state rights advocate and former congressman from Georgia, thinking the two would have much in common. Instead, they got into a political argument, and Smith lost his temper. "His manner was most passionate, and his language strong and unguarded," Perry recalled. Clearly the old Barnwell Smith was back in form for his reentry into politics. After the South Carolinian left, Clayton remarked to Perry that Smith "would have to moderate his tone and language when he took his seat in Congress."[38]

It is just as well that Smith did not buy land at Greenville, for a catastrophe lay ahead. Land speculation had been rampant everywhere in a climate of easy credit, Smith himself being an example. But in July 1836 Jackson tried to clamp down on the injudicious boom by requiring all payments for public lands to be made in hard cash and not credit. He also brought down the United States Bank, setting off a credit crisis that in turn caused state banks to withdraw credit, which had already been dramatically reduced in June when Congress distributed surplus money in the U.S. Treasury to the states. On top of it all, a financial crisis in England led British creditors to start calling in debts owed them by Americans, and many planters, unlike Smith, suffered crop failures.

Smith found the beginnings of the crunch awaiting him at home. Debts had piled up thanks to his plantation purchases and his usual inattention to his practice. His crop came in fine, realizing nearly twenty-seven thousand dollars on the Charleston market in the spring of 1837 just before the crash really hit. However, soon the financial panic was well under way, and he could already see that the future looked grim. "How can we sell for the ensuing year," he wondered. "The price of produce may for years be affected by the present state of things." As the price for staple crops fell, so would the value of his property. Slaves had already plummeted from one thousand dollars or more each to a mere three hundred dollars. Although the panic was hitting the western regions and the Gulf South harder, and South Carolina looked likely to weather the crisis better, there was no putting a gloss on the situation.[39]

Faced with heavy debt, Smith toyed with the idea of selling some of his slaves, but their lower value and his promise to Stapleton put that out of his mind. He approached his friends in the crisis. Early in the year he took Perry to dinner and perhaps asked for a loan, and soon thereafter he approached Petigru and told him his situation. "I have no money," said his old teacher. "You know I cannot keep money: but my credit is yours, in any manner you choose to use it, to the last dollar of the property I possess." Smith decided against accepting, for fear of ruining Petigru's credit as well as his own, but he never forgot the act of generosity.[40] Finally he turned to his cousin Robert W. Barnwell, borrowing $12,682 from him in April. He also mortgaged 1,100 acres of his timberland and 260 more of the rice fields. It would take him eighteen years to redeem the mortgage.[41]

Even these acts did not answer all his needs. "I thought I was ruined," he recalled later.[42] He had already expected that his income would be contracted substantially for the next year or so as the plantations required further investment. When he managed to get away for a few weeks in the summer of 1837, he returned to find crop prices falling dramatically and a letter from Stapleton asking about his money, not to mention notices from many other creditors, all of them calling in accounts payable in the growing panic. Legal business had piled up in his absence, and he had to confess, "I cannot but expect a portion of the embarrassment which has fallen upon me." He was about to leave his law practice to go to Washington, thus further reducing his professional income, and it would cost him money to maintain his family with him in the capital. "In times of such sudden and overwhelming commercial disaster," he told Stapleton, "I fear I have been unwise in assenting to go to Congress with the debts I owe." But go he would. It was too late to back out now; besides, he believed he knew much of the cause of the current panic and much of the solution, both of which lay in Congress, where he had not only his own interests to defend but those of the South.[43]

The new president, Martin Van Buren, called a special session of Congress to convene on September 4 to address the crisis, and after borrowing what he could and setting his affairs in some order, Smith prepared for the trip north. At the annual July 4 celebration his friends gave him a sendoff with a toast from his brother Edmund to "R. Barnwell Smith—May his course in Congress be distinguished by the zeal and ability which have rendered his past services honorable to himself, and useful to his country." Smith responded with a toast of his own to the people of his home parish—few, if any, of whom realized that they had delivered their last accolade to R. Barnwell Smith.[44]

There was one more step to take to complete his attempt to reclaim the prominence and stature of his ancestors, and it was one that numerous others had been taking for the past twenty years. In 1804 the legislature enacted laws that considerably lessened the difficulty in effecting a legal change of surname, and as a result a small wave of applications came forward from South Carolinians seeking to assert pride in their forebears by changing their names to something more distinguished or more redolent of the early magnates of the colony.[45] None in the family would agree where the idea came from, but either Thomas or Albert, the oldest and the youngest of the Smith brothers, proposed that they should do the same.[46] Several of them had political aspirations now. James sought a seat in the legislature as early as 1828 and won one in 1832, and Albert won his in 1834, while Benjamin and Edmund were active in State Rights Party affairs. That was a lot of Smiths in public life in one place, and even though theirs had the most distinguished of histories in the state, it was still among the most ordinary of names. Barnwell may even have commented to his friend Perry that it "was so common a name that he and all his family, except his unmarried sister, changed it."[47]

Either Thomas or Alfred or both suggested to all of the brothers that summer that they change their name to honor one of their ancestors. The choice could have come from any one of them, and certainly from Barnwell, who was already fond of alluding to one in particular. The family name of William Rhett had died out completely at his death, yet was still honorably remembered, and Barnwell Smith had plans to be buried in the Rhett vault at St. Philip's. The idea may even have come to them after their father died, as they placed him in the Rhett vault, and they could well have discussed the subject sometime earlier and postponed taking action while their father, James Smith, lived. At the close of the spring term of the court of common pleas for the Beaufort District at Coosawhatchie, Thomas and Albert, acting for all the brothers, filed a petition Ex Parte Thomas Smith et al. before Judge Richard Gantt of the court of common law, stating as their reason, "particularly that the name Rhett, in the grand Maternal line, and now extinct, may be revived and preserved, a name held dear by the Petitioners, and consecrated by natural regard and affection."[48]

Barnwell Smith would tell people that he was indifferent to the change but acquiesced at the urging of his brothers, and that the action had no motive other than honoring William Rhett, who seemed to be the general favorite among their ancestors.[49] More probably he was fully aware of the political and social benefit of discarding the Smith surname in favor of one more distinctive and distinguished. He was away during the summer while the proceedings went through but returned late in August to find them completed, or nearly so. While the rest of the brothers waited until September 26 to assume their new name, he wisely realized that if he were going to have a new name, he had better start using it before he took his seat in the special session on September 4. Consequently, on August 24, 1837, on the eve of his departure for Washington, he assumed his new identity: Robert Barnwell Rhett. It was a good name and a good armor to wear as he went off to fight for the rights of South Carolina.[50]

The new Rhett arrived in Washington in the midst of a dramatically changing political landscape, in the center of which, as had been the case for some time, was Calhoun. The political parties had been in flux for years, and Calhoun had tried to remain aloof, being suspicious of parties in principle and unwilling to commit himself to one or another. The Whigs had emerged in 1832, and by now South Carolina was among their strongholds, bound to them chiefly by opposition to Jackson and the Democrats on nullification and the Force Act. Clay's alliance with the nullifiers in bringing about the compromise tariff in 1833 further enlisted many in the Whig ranks. When Old Hickory all but forced Martin Van Buren on his party as his successor, it drove even more in the South into Whig ranks. Calhoun could hardly side with them, though, since most of the interests in opposition to the South centered in the new party, and Henry Clay was its chieftain. Calhoun also faced problems if he identified with the still-coalescing Democratic Party, since for the past several years he had been one of the leading critics of the Jackson administration, which was itself the foundation of the new Democrats. Moreover, by committing to neither side, Calhoun avoided alienating followers at home from either party, since his platform was and had been essentially South Carolina itself. Yet gravity inexorably pulled him more and more toward the Democrats by 1837, even after another Democrat, Van Buren, captured the presidency.

All across the South the old Jeffersonian Republicans had been gradually falling in line behind Jackson, especially after the 1833 compromise lessened tensions on the tariff and more recently with his killing the national bank and opposition to further internal improvements. As Rhett saw it, Jackson had defeated at last the two great Northern money power principles of protection and the national bank, with its paper money that encouraged speculation, and had returned to the party principles that characterized the old Republicans and now the Democrats. Rhett distrusted political parties and tended to form his associations on individual issues and personal relationships, though essentially he had always regarded himself as a Jeffersonian Republican. Jackson's return to principle and Calhoun's gradual shift to the Democrats now made his own move in that direction a possibility, especially as Calhoun led the way for all conservative South Carolinians to follow. Rhett was sufficiently astute to realize that in national politics, more than in state affairs, power was concentrating in the two great parties, and to have any effect or influence at all a man had to identify himself with one or the other, or else hold the power as an independent to decide the majority. Though some colleagues assumed that he was a Whig, when he took his seat he was still a Republican at heart, though already a man in a position to change more than his name.[51]

When Rhett reached the capital he probably joined with the rest of the South Carolina delegation in meeting with Calhoun. They were a distinguished group with Calhoun and William C. Preston as senators and Elmore, Legaré, Francis W. Pickens, John P. Richardson, and Waddy Thompson among the representatives. There was scarcely any question that they would take their lead from Calhoun on any issue, and any inclined to act otherwise had the example of Henry L. Pinckney before them, for it was Calhoun personally who exiled him from South Carolina politics. Though Rhett and Calhoun certainly met a few times prior to September 1837, as yet no real friendship or intimacy seemed to have arisen between them. That would begin here and now as Rhett showed for the first time that he could be a loyal lieutenant even when others balked.

The House came to order on September 4, its first order of business being the election of a Speaker for the special session, and Rhett demonstrated at the outset that he had no intention of observing the custom of freshman silence. Pending the formal organization of the House, he rose and proposed the selection of Lewis Williams of North Carolina, the oldest member present, as chairman pro temp—and possibly at Calhoun's prompting. The action showed a spirit of assertion, certainly, but also reflected ignorance of customary procedure, for in the past the clerk from the past term read the roll and performed the other formalities until they chose a Speaker. Williams rose to observe that this was the proper procedure and recommended that Rhett's motion be tabled, as it was. Still, in so doing he gave notice that he intended to be heard in this chamber.[52]

As soon as Congress assembled, Van Buren sent a special message dealing with the financial crisis. He proposed to face the immediate money shortage by issuing several million dollars in U.S. Treasury notes, putting off the further distribution of the U.S. Treasury surplus to the states, and most of all by a daring new policy of complete separation of the federal government from the nation's banking system. Rather than charter a new national bank, as most expected, he would instead locate independent "subtreasuries" in the major cities of the nation and allow them to take in and pay out government revenue. Until then there had been far too much unsecured paper money from state banks in circulation and far too little specie. The result had been wild speculation and uncontrolled inflation. In the financial crisis those opposed to the inflation caused by the paper money issued by state banks saw that the concentration of specie in the now-defunct national bank only encouraged the collapse. Proponents of a "hard money" system welcomed Van Buren's plan because the regional banks would have more specie on hand to meet payments, while at the same time the U.S. Treasury, no longer hampered by the national bank, could keep a tighter control on credit.

Calhoun, whom everyone expected to oppose the independent treasury scheme, saw in it rather a chance to free the South from vassalage to the New York bankers who held most of Southern credit. He did, however, want one change. Van Buren was silent on whether the regional banks would accept notes from banks that backed their paper with gold or silver in payment for public lands, duties, and so forth. Despite the storm Calhoun knew it would create, he wanted the measure to provide for the government to take increasing proportions of its debts in paper for the first three years, after which, the crisis being presumably over, it should switch to specie payments exclusively. It was a sharp curb on credit but the best thing for an out-of-control economy in collapse.

Calhoun got a postponement of debate until he could present his proposed amendment, but already everyone in the South Carolina delegation knew what he was going to do. They were shocked. "Nothing can be more monstrous than to support a scheme for doing away with bank paper and of course with credit, and ruining all who are in debt," railed Petigru, who was then in Washington. "It is awful—it is so sudden—and of Mr. Calhoun so unexpected," he said. Soon it was known that only two members of the entire delegation in Congress would support Calhoun. One was his cousin Pickens, which was predictable. The other was Rhett. And when Calhoun delivered his speech on September 18, some saw more in it than a divorce of the government from the banking system. It was Calhoun divorcing himself from the coalition that had backed him to date, and it implied a first step toward alliance with the administration and the Democrats. His speech disappointed many, but another one taking the same ground was expected in the House from Rhett.[53]

Just what allied Rhett with Calhoun is unclear, though certainly his own experience pushed him in that direction.[54] He seems always to have been suspicious of too much reliance on unsecured paper currency, recognizing the speculation and inflation that inevitably followed in train. He had also seen firsthand how easy credit based on paper left many in South Carolina seriously indebted to Yankee creditors. Calhoun and Van Buren might very well dry up credit, but in the end that would lead to a sound money policy. Rhett still relied on the previous century's policy of borrowing from friends and family rather than banks, which had no inflationary influence and little or no impact or reliance on specie or the economy at large. In short, in his own financial dealings the only parties at risk were Rhett himself and those individuals who backed him. If he could do so, then so should others, without making themselves subject to Northern bankers and endangering the prosperity of the whole nation with their personal speculations. Rhett was not a "hard money" man, a stance that he regarded "as wicked as it would be impracticable."[55] There was a need and a place for paper money, especially in such a vast country as the United States, still expanding, still building its capital in the land and manufacturing, still needing credit to keep growing. Moreover, there is nothing to suggest that in backing Calhoun now Rhett was enlisting himself wholeheartedly to the service of the great Carolinian's policy. Barnwell Smith had never supported Calhoun's nullification ideas in 1828–30, preferring his own more radical solution and only accepting nullification as next best when his own scheme was rejected. His backing of Calhoun now came chiefly from the simple fact that, on this issue, he shared the same principles and goals, and always had.[56]

When Van Buren's message came before the House, Rhett initially confessed that he was "in a mist" on some aspects of the business, but he soon made himself familiar enough with it to take the floor in the House on September 29 during the debate on the U.S. Treasury note portion of Van Buren's message.[57] He made it clear from the first that he supported the issuing of Treasury notes in the current currency crisis for use in paying debts to the government repositories and the utter divorce of the government from the banking system itself. He opposed making the Treasury notes bear interest, for that would make them a source of revenue, which was not their intent, and would encourage people to hold them for profit, whereas they were to be created in order to give people a medium of exchange for circulation. Rhett went on to expound in his usual fashion with a lot of history, and an impressive array of facts, showing the depth of his application in preparing for this maiden speech as well as his considerable grasp of banking theory and currency. Indeed, he went considerably beyond Calhoun's recent address in laying out the case for following Van Buren now, suggesting still more that Rhett spoke for himself here and did not just ride on Calhoun's coattails.

In fact, though willing to accept U.S. Treasury notes in the crisis, he proposed a solution of his own that he thought superior: the issuance of bills receivable in payment of public debts. A simple statement of a promise to receive a debt, it required no specie to back it, yet could be exchanged and circulated like a Treasury note. It would have the benefit of being received at virtually the same value everywhere in the country, no more subject to fluctuating value and discounts at acceptance than Treasury notes, yet without tying up specie as a reserve. Nothing would come of his proposal, but it revealed that he was thinking independently and as less of a "hard money" man than Calhoun appeared to have become.

To the proposals to recharter the national bank instead, he turned with scorn. Time had set its mark on that system. Twice it had been tried, and twice it had failed, both times floundering in political corruption and ineptitude that had visited financial ruin on the nation as well, he said. To the argument that a national bank imposed, under congressional mandate, some uniformity and system over the hundreds of state banks, he responded that in the Southern states nine of ten dollars owed was not to a bank but to an individual on a personal note backed not by specie or stockholders' deposits but by land and slaves. Logically, then, should not Congress assume authority over the management of that financial system too? To him it seemed an absurdity. For Congress to charter a special bank, whose benefit would go to a particular class of its investors, was just as unconscionable as a protective tariff, both of which involved the national revenue for the benefit of private interests. Above all, he objected to the power a national bank gave to the government. "I am a nullifier," he declared, "and will never consent that more power should be given to this Government than strictly belongs to it." History had shown a tendency to consolidationism that was already strong enough without giving Washington a hand in the monetary control of the country. A national bank would not solve their problems. Neither would his own proposal, he confessed, though it would alleviate the difficulty. "The remedy is in time and the people themselves," he stated.

That said, Rhett could not resist in this, his first House speech, making his position known in broader terms, establishing a benchmark by which all his future actions on the floor might be judged, whether members wanted to hear it or not. He closed by devoting fully one-third of his address, not to Treasury bills or Van Buren's message, but to a statement of his credo and grievances against the central government. Jackson had been a tyrant; the national bank had been unconstitutional; and the protective tariff had created the surplus revenue that spawned corruption and fueled the unbridled speculation that brought on the collapse. He damned it all, especially "the American system—that poison still lingering in the veins of the body politic—that unhallowed and corrupt combination," he charged, "by which one section of the Union was plundered for the benefit of another." Had it not been for the usurpations of Congress, he said, the current crisis would not have occurred, and even that was only after South Carolina nullified the tariff and thus brought on the compromise of 1833. How much worse would it have been without nullification, if the surpluses built up under the earlier tariff law had continued, fueling unimaginably greater speculation? He suggested that it would have been three times as bad as it was. He asked, "Could the liberties of the country have survived such a state of things?"

In short, he implied that, far from endangering the Union, South Carolina and nullification had saved it from a far worse situation than they faced now. And as thanks, they had been called traitors and disunionists. "South Carolina met the emergency in which you placed her as it became her," he declared. "She nullified your tariff laws. And did you then enforce them? No! and why? Sir, I will tell you: you dared not. It is one thing to sit here upon well stuffed hair-seated chairs, and legislate the property of the South into the pockets of more favored sections; and it is another to collect your black mail by the sword." To those who claimed that the compromise of 1833 had saved South Carolina from being crushed for treason, he contemptuously responded that only a bigot or a slave could suppose that his state needed such salvation. "Had South Carolina been invaded, upon the first gleam of the bayonet along our mountain passes, he would have seen and known what the chivalry of the South really was, not in bloodless tropes and metaphors, but in the stern realities of the tented field. Not only Carolinians, but thousands of volunteers from the whole South, whose names are upon the file, would have met you in that fierce contest," he promised. The passes of the Saluda mountains would have been a Thermopylae for Jackson and his minions, the plains of the state's heartland would have become a vast cemetery for Yankee dead, or else Carolina would have been laid waste by fire and sword with not a living soul left. "In her fall liberty would have been avenged; and, like the mighty Nazarite of old, grasping the pillars of the Constitution, the Union would have perished in her ruins." They had won their land by the sword, and they were prepared to keep it thus or die. Yet whether they died in battle defending their state or hanged on the gallows as traitors for resisting tyranny, "it is the cause which makes death glorious," he said.

His distant cousin John Quincy Adams still sat in the House, and as he watched Rhett's address he saw the old passion rise, the old intemperance come out once more. The two acknowledged their relationship and were respectful, but they would never be friends, which was not surprising. Rhett's manner so struck Adams that he wrote in his diary of how his cousin "literally howled a nullification speech." He continued, "I say howled, for his enunciations were so rapid, inarticulate, and vociferous that his head hung back as he spoke, with his face upward, like that of a howling dog."[58]

"Shall things come to this in the administration of affairs in this Union?" he asked. If differences of opinion must be regarded as crimes, and threats of the scaffold used to measure truth, then "we had better separate at once, for the Union must be dissolved." He hoped it would endure, even though the South must continue to bear an unfair share of the burden of the government. All she demanded was that Congress take what was needed for its legitimate purposes, "but in all other things leave her alone to her own resources and destiny." Honor the Constitution rather than using it as an instrument of bigotry and oppression, he said. That done, they could forget the past and start anew. South Carolina would be "too generous to remember wrongs, too proud to resent them—too great to practice them."[59]

Rhett left no mistake of where he stood, and only the brief appeal for Union at the close showed any moderation of his old attitude. Coming as it did after an extended resort to the sword-rattling threats that had been a part of his repertoire for a decade now, it was hardly convincing as evidence that Calhoun had exerted any influence in moderating his stand and bringing him into line. And as well, there had been that easy appeal to disunion if they could not agree. When the House voted to postpone action on the subtreasury bill, it passed 120 to 107, with Rhett and Pickens standing alone in trying to keep it alive.[60] The measure would not pass during the special session, though Van Buren's other proposals did. More significantly for Rhett, however, Calhoun had found himself opposed by almost everyone in the delegation and was stunned to learn that many of his most influential friends at home also stood against him in the matter. That made Rhett's support stand out all the more and probably for the first time really attracted Calhoun's attention to the freshman congressman as a potent ally. Calhoun never forgot those who opposed him, and in this one speech Rhett supplanted many who had once been higher in the great statesman's estimation. In an alliance between the two there were ends to be served for each, and in the success of such an alliance might be measured much of the future of South Carolina and the Union.

SIX

Like Rotten Fruit, You Are Only Fit to Fall
1837–1838

AS A MEASURE OF THE NOTICE Rhett had attracted even outside South Carolina with his extremist speeches, it was not only friends back home who were surprised by his support of Van Buren's independent treasury initiative. Adams sarcastically remarked that he saw Rhett "passing from the chrysalis state of a late voracious nullifier to a painted Administration butterfly."[1] For the balance of the month-long session Rhett kept hammering away, fighting those who wanted to charter a new national bank, repeatedly declaring himself a nullifier in principle, and proposing amendments to prevent any association between the government and banking. This continued right up to the last day of the session, when proposals had either been defeated or tabled, until he admitted himself that they were wasting the people's time. When the final U.S. Treasury note bill passed, incorporating none of Rhett's proposals, he still voted with the majority in passage.[2] Despite his reservations, Rhett regarded the larger measure as "eminently conservative and democratic," and after the fact there were hints that he came to his support of it entirely independent of Calhoun, though he confessed that in the rush to prepare he did allow some opinions of others on the act to influence him.[3]

Rhett scarcely had time to get back to South Carolina before he faced another family loss. His mother, Marianna Smith, had been nursing her youngest daughter, Elizabeth, through a cold when she herself came down with it, and she died on October 20, 1837. In an act that showed some of the tender sensibilities of sentiment that characterized Rhett and his family, they buried her not in the vault with her husband James, but in the cemetery at Beaufort beside her mother, Elizabeth Gough, for whom Marianna had been a lifetime companion.[4]

There was a fight at home now over the independent treasury bill, for if Calhoun could not get his own state behind him, he could hardly hope to rally supporters elsewhere to carry the measure. Moreover, it was becoming a test of loyalty to Calhoun and a measure of the slow shift of the State Rights Party men toward the Democrats. In the legislature both Hayne and Hamilton, old allies of Calhoun, were ready to revolt, but again Rhett came to his aid. For a start, his brother-in-law Stuart made an abrupt turnaround in the editorial pages of the *Mercury* and got behind Calhoun, though no one but Stuart knew whether Rhett or Calhoun was the more influential in this or whether it was Stuart acting unilaterally. Meanwhile in the legislature Alfred Rhett, undoubtedly guided and advised by his brother, sat with Memminger on a special committee to consider Van Buren's proposals and produced a report that precisely echoed Barnwell Rhett's expressions in Congress.[5] Even Unionist brother James Rhett stood with them, and the influence of Franklin and Benjamin Elmore, the former soon to be president of the Bank of South Carolina, added further weight. In fact, some accused the Rhett-Elmore family clique of bullying the legislature into supporting Calhoun, but that was an overstatement. Calhoun probably won most of the legislators to his side by presenting a case that the subtreasury system represented an initial step in the reversal of power consolidation in Washington, as indeed it was. Echoing Rhett's declaration in the House, he said that nullification had won the day because the Democrats now admitted that national banks and currency management were not in the province of the central government. In short, the administration and its party had changed course, not Calhoun. If his argument, like Rhett's before him, smacked of expediency and rationalization, still it was persuasive, and added to the Rhett-Elmore-Stuart efforts, it turned the tide. Calhoun was in Columbia when the legislature came to vote on resolutions supporting the subtreasury, and they carried both houses by enormous majorities.[6]

Undoubtedly the success further cemented Barnwell Rhett to Calhoun, having demonstrated that he and his brothers and the Elmores who were so tied to them could help to deliver results, though outsiders mistakenly assumed that Rhett had acted at Calhoun's instructions rather than following his own predilection. Still, with only one brief session in Congress behind him, Rhett returned to Washington with a standing and clout in the Calhoun forces that placed him far above any other freshman congressman, virtually repeating his experience in the legislature. The lesson was not lost on him that taking a bold, independent, even strident stand risked much but if timed properly could reap enormous gains. Henceforward he would speak with an authority and confidence far beyond the merits of his station, significantly on the verge of a major redefinition of the Democratic Party that, as one of Calhoun's chief lieutenants, he would have an opportunity to help shape.

When Rhett returned to Washington for the next session in December he found slavery awaiting him. The infant Republic of Texas, which had only just won its independence from Mexico, applied for annexation to the United States

and set off an immediate furor. At the moment the slave and free states stood
slightly out of balance, when the admission of Arkansas in 1836 gave the slave
states a majority of one. Texas, already a slave nation, would naturally come in
as a slave state as well, throwing the balance even more to the South, and the
antislavery forces, led by Adams, mounted an immediate and rigorous opposition. Several memorials and resolutions against annexation were introduced,
and Adams tried to steer all of them around the proslave Foreign Relations
Committee to a select committee that he could hope to dominate. Rhett and
others demanded an opportunity to speak in opposition, and he found Rhett in
particular "ferocious for battle," but Adams's motions failed.[7] When Adams's
talk on Texas shifted subtly into an antislavery diatribe, one member called him
to order, for Pinckney's gag resolution had actually passed in May 1836, making Adams's comments out of order, but Rhett rose and asked that his cousin be
allowed to proceed.

In fact, Rhett objected to motions from fellow Southerners who would have
cut off debate. Clearly he wanted this issue addressed fully and openly in the
House there and then. Cutting off debate, he complained, meant that Southerners could not reply and try to demolish the antislavery men's arguments. It was
entirely in keeping with Rhett's instinct to make a fight as early as possible on
any issue, and make it strongly. "It is in vain to deny, that the authority to interfere with our institutions, is claimed entirely because of the Union," he wrote
the day after the debate with Adams. "And from what I see here, my opinion is,
that now, and forever after, so long as this Union endures, agitation, harassment,
and insult, upon this vital question, in Congress and out of Congress, is the
fixed destiny of the South." He saw as evident, too, that if they did not secure
some new guarantees of noninterference with slavery, then they must secede. He
told South Carolinians that they must stand up again and threaten now as they
had before with nullification. "If you do not admit Texas," he would warn the
North, "we will dissolve the Union."[8]

That was only the beginning. Adams started chafing the slavery wound on
December 13 and got away with it because the gag rule of 1836 had just expired.
Almost immediately he introduced anew the petitions for abolition of slavery in
the District of Columbia, and on December 20 the debate exploded. A member complained that anytime anyone made a reference to slavery and abolition,
he was called to order and attacked, though there was no gag in effect. William
Slade of Vermont rose and began to make reference to slavery in Virginia half a
century before, which prompted Rhett to leap to his feet to ask, "impertinently"
thought one observer, what opinions in Virginia fifty years earlier had to do with
slavery in the district today. Henry Wise of Virginia then stood and indignantly

pronounced that he would walk out of the hall and called on his colleagues from the Old Dominion to follow him. As they rose a Georgian stood and asked his colleagues to do the same, and pandemonium broke out. Amid noise, confusion, and angry words as one after another of the slave-state delegates began to move, Rhett's voice cut through the din, shouting that if a man from Vermont had a right to talk about slavery on the floor of the House, he called for every Southern delegation to join in the walkout, telling them to gather immediately in the rooms of the committee for the District of Columbia.[9]

Spur of the moment as it may have seemed, there was nothing spontaneous about their act. Surely all of the Southern delegates expected a renewal of abolition petitions, and Rhett announced that the South Carolinians had previously signed an agreement to walk out in such a circumstance. Clearly Rhett, and perhaps Wise and the rest, were ready for this moment and were prepared even to the point of having chosen where to gather afterward. They met that afternoon at 3 P.M. in the committee chamber, meanwhile sending a member back to the now-disrupted House to invite any remaining slave-state men to join them, while the House itself adjourned.[10] In all, sixty-four Southern representatives and senators assembled, and they soon appointed a committee of three from each house of Congress to present a report when they reassembled that evening.

When they gathered again the ensuing discussion, some of it angry, revealed how much division there was among them on how to confront the issue. Rhett and Calhoun declared that they should demand that a Southern convention be called to formulate a final and permanent settlement of the slavery issue, but more moderate men easily outvoted them. Significantly, though, in the argument that lasted well past midnight it was Rhett from the House, and not Calhoun's cousin Pickens, who led the elder statesman's supporters, and Pickens did not miss the fact. Rhett was starting to stand between him and Calhoun's sun, and Pickens did not like the shade. It was the beginning of a lifelong enmity between them founded on the jealousy of the one and the ambitions of both.[11]

In the end, with the moderates fully in control, the meeting agreed simply upon a renewal of the old gag rule, with a resolution to convene again if the House failed to adopt. It was only the fact of the threat to slavery itself that at this stage led to any united action, for still a significant number of Whig members from the South, and consequent party divisions, continued to divide them. Yet in the end slavery overcame party.[12] It was not enough for Rhett, however. On December 21 when the resolutions for a gag renewal were introduced in the House, they made no statement of principle, though Rhett had pushed hard for it during the meeting. He wanted the battle fought out then and there, not merely postponed by a parliamentary gambit that only forestalled the problem rather than solving it. As a result, Rhett refused to vote for or against the gag resolutions. "I will not long sit here, liable myself to continual insult, and the people I represent, to the grossest abuse, and the most open contumely," he wrote back to the *Mercury* after the passage of the new gag rule. "As a man, as a gentleman, I cannot bear it." He wanted the antislave men to continue their campaign on the floor or make them stop of their own accord, and he believed that sufficient force or threat might have accomplished the task. Of the nature of the threat, of course, there was no doubt. They must have constitutional guarantees of slavery protection, he demanded, "or the Union must be dissolved."[13] Indeed, while the rump meeting did appoint a committee of one member from each state to devise some plan for permanent settlement of the slavery problem, Rhett had gone further. He drafted a resolution to be introduced in the House declaring that "the constitution of the United States having proved inadequate to protect the southern States in the peaceable enjoyment of their rights and property, it is expedient that the said constitution should be amended, or the Union of the States be dissolved," and a companion resolution calling for the appointment of a committee of two members from each slave state to report on the "best means of peacefully dissolving it."[14]

Rhett and Calhoun were not to give up, however. In the Senate, Calhoun presented resolutions calling for a final definition of the Union and its authority, at the same time condemning antislavery agitation. Meanwhile Rhett took the case to the people of South Carolina. In addition to writing letters to the *Mercury,* he responded to a January meeting in Beaufort that called on representatives to demand additional constitutional guarantees on slavery protection. His brother Albert had been instrumental in the meeting and may even have engineered it in order to give Rhett a forum for the address that he sent to his constituents on January 15, 1838.[15]

He freely acknowledged authorship of the proposition for peaceful disunion and averred that he was ready to introduce it from his seat in the House but had not as yet, though he did show it to a number of friends. Of course he had no expectation of seeing the resolutions pass, or of their even coming to a vote. He simply hoped to use them to get the subject of slavery onto the floor and thus to lay before the public his own opinions of the true issues before them and the policy that ought to be followed to settle the matter. He was tired of all the insulting abolition petitions. Southerners were accused of being murderers and arsonists, fearful of truth, enemies of humanity. Worse, fifteen hundred or more abolition societies in the North, he believed, lay bent on inciting insurrection among their slaves and the destruction of slavery itself. A new one formed every day, he exaggerated. States in the North refused to surrender fugitive slaves.

"Here is a subject in which passion, and feeling, and religion, are all involved," he added perceptively. "All the inexperienced emotions of the heart are against us; all the abstractions concerning human rights can be perverted against us; all the theories of political dreamers, atheistic utilitarians, self-exalting and self-righteous religionists, who would reform or expunge the bible,—in short, enthusiasts and fanatics of all sorts, are against us." Only those who really understood the nature of the black race and had seen the practice of slavery firsthand in the South could understand them, he maintained. Not just the North was against them on this, he added, and acknowledged their condemnation by "the whole civilized world." There were even antislave inroads in sister states such as Kentucky, where movements for voluntary emancipation and repatriation of slaves to Africa were taking root, and as a result such people stood by rather than helping when South Carolina's institutions were assailed.

Rhett felt that emancipation was part and parcel of the evil that emerged in France the previous century, for the Enlightenment was not the only evil it helped to visit upon the world. The misguided push for universal rights and against slavery was "born in atheism, and baptized in the blood of revolutionary France," and it accomplished its purpose. "It has never failed," he said, "and never will fail, in accomplishing its purpose, *where the slaveholder does not control his destinies.*" Again appealing to the still-lingering echoes of the revival that swept him and his district a few years before, he claimed that abolition was gaining adherents faster than the gospel itself, while his allusion to the "atheism" of slavery opponents referred to the fact that slavery was acknowledged and accepted in the Bible. "The institution is sanctioned by christianity and best for the race over whom it prevails," he declared, thus portraying their opponents as not only power-mad and grasping, but godless.

His message was clear. The Constitution had failed to protect Southerners. If an independent nation had treated another as the North had treated the South, it would justify a declaration of war, he claimed. He then asked the root question: In their situation, should the Constitution be amended to provide guarantees to protect them, or should they leave the Union? "The evil must be arrested," he demanded. "It is vain, utterly vain to suppose, that the south will submit to the present state of things." Southerners must have peace, either in or out of the Union. Duty required them to seek relief first through the Constitution, by amendments abolishing any right to tamper with slavery in the District of Columbia or in any of the western territories south of the Missouri Compromise line. They must "shut the subject of slavery forever out of the halls of Congress." If introduced in time, before the abolition infection spread too far, he believed that such amendments might pass, or at least so he claimed, and again he made the argument that if Southerners presented a threat of secession to back up their demand for rights, the North would acquiesce. More than that, the direction of Northern society would make it anxious to preserve its union with the South. The North grew rapidly in numbers from European immigration, and competition for daily bread might increase dramatically. Worse, "universal suffrage, will give to those who have no property, the absolute control of the property and legislation of the country." Then the Yankees would learn the truth, "in all its horrors, that the despotism of numbers may be the most terrible that can scourge a fallen people." Having labor in control of the destiny of a nation would spell disaster. In the South, thanks to slavery, that could not happen. "Every white man is a privileged being," he said, and "selfishness and honor alike impels him to an alliance with his race; and (whether he possesses property or not) to uphold the institutions in which, in fact, chiefly exist the property of the country; whilst the very existence of slavery around him, gives him a loftier tone of independence, and a higher estimate of liberty." Slavery, in short, gave even the lowest white on the social scale a claim to some status, he being at least better than a black, and at the same time could make him grateful even in poverty that at least he had his freedom. Moreover, they must all remember that "*no republic has ever yet been long maintained without the institution of slavery,*" though he did not name a single example of one that had. Indeed, he asserted that it was the South, because of the need to defend slavery, that had preserved the Constitution this far, for in protecting the one she naturally guarded the other.

He could not help but revert to the tariff, if only briefly. The South produced three-fourths of the nation's exports, he said, but paid three-fourths of the government's revenue in indirect taxes as import duty. His solution to that was an idea mooted by Thomas Cooper years before, direct taxation by which every citizen paid a share of taxes equal to his property. In 1827 in his Walterborough memorial to Congress, Rhett and the committee he headed referred to direct taxation as a "desperate alternative," but now he felt the situation called for desperate measures. This was the first time Rhett proposed it publicly as his own preferred solution to tariffs. Though he stood alone, it would not be the last time. Meanwhile, the government had spent $290 million in revenue in the past two decades, but only $80 million went to the South, while $210 million was spent in the North and the "middle States" of Maryland, Kentucky, Delaware, and others. Rhett was playing a game here, heavily loading his argument to give it undue strength, a technique that did not trouble him now and never would in the future. Without question the spending on internal improvements had been unduly balanced in favor of the North, but by separating out the middle states—all of them slave states—Rhett exaggerated the imbalance against what for convenience of this argument he was calling the South, meaning really only the southern Atlantic and Gulf states. Moreover, in his complaint that of the $480 million in revenue raised in the past twenty years, $360 million had been "collected upon the imports" to the South, he made no attempt to differentiate between tariff paid *in* the South and tariff paid *by* Southerners. The Northern coastline possessed but few ports of entry, principally New York, Philadelphia, and Boston. By contrast, there were a dozen entry points and customshouses from Baltimore to Charleston and Savannah, and around to Mobile and New Orleans on the Gulf. More to the point, the fact that duty was paid at those ports did not mean that it was a Southerner paying. Baltimore was the chief port of entry for substantial goods that actually went to purchasers in central and western Pennsylvania, and New Orleans was the only source for imports traveling all the way up the Mississippi and Ohio Rivers to Illinois, Indiana, Ohio, and even western Pennsylvania, not to mention the territory north of Missouri. Not a cent of duty for anything shipped to such destinations came out of a Southern pocket, but Rhett conveniently omitted mention of this, for any such subtlety in evaluating the basis of his arguments would only weaken them.

He had even more interesting rationalizations to offer as evidence that the North could not afford to let the South go and therefore would respond to the threat of secession. The South was the North's greatest market, which was true. Disunion would cost Northerners the Southern carrying trade (though only a few paragraphs earlier he complained that the North already monopolized shipping). Assuming that independent Southerners would decline to sell to Northerners, he averred that Yankees would lose access to Southern staple crops that were the bases of their textile industry. Producing nothing that European nations wanted, the North would be thrown into commercial, manufacturing, and shipping competition with England and France, which would only create a hostile environment, "and contention, and war, would be the natural relation which would spring up between them." In his imagination Rhett managed to parlay Northern repudiation of constitutional amendments protecting slavery into a future Yankee war with Europe.

If those amendments were rejected, he said, it would "conclusively prove to the south that the Union ought to be dissolved," and what would be the condition of an independent South? She would enjoy universal peace because her cotton provided employment for the looms of the industrialized nations, and her citizens a fine market for foreign products. Mutual interests would bind nations to the South by cords stronger than the force of armies or navies, and without onerous tariffs. The South could practice free trade, buying at the lowest rates available and selling at the highest it could secure, a guarantee of endless prosperity.

Division did not need to happen, he urged, and would not, for he was certain the North would back down at the threat of secession and concede the necessary guarantees. But Northerners must stop their wanton attempts to break down slavery, for that was in his eyes equivalent to a Northern demand for disunion, casting the fragments of the Union "upon the wide ocean of new and untried experiments." He did not say what those experiments might be, but he had already suggested years before the idea of a Southern confederacy. As for the necessary amendments, they would not be easily won. Individual action by the Southern states could not accomplish their end. He wanted the congressional delegations from all the slave states to unite in calling for the amendments, for then they might be adopted, but he frankly confessed that this would not happen for there was too much dissent among even the slave states. Congress certainly would not act for them. The only hope, in the end, would be a convention of all the Southern states. A meeting in itself must show unity and determination, and that was all they needed to win. Implicit in his argument now as ever was the belief that a weak-willed North could be intimidated into compliance. Threats and ultimata worked, and he had the year 1833 as proof. But they must act now and not wait until the distraction of the coming 1840 presidential contest was out of the way or until Southerners coalesced more fully into a single party. Delay was fatal, for the abolitionists were ever moving. Already Maryland, Kentucky, and Virginia, "once powerful slave states," were weakened by the decline of their cash crop tobacco and the migration of their slaves to the deeper south cotton fields. Someday they might have few slaves left and be that much the weaker as allies. It was up to South Carolina and the other states that depended for their existence upon slavery to make the fight now. "The southern states, are destined to no common fate in the history of nations," he closed. "They will be amongst the greatest and freest, or the most abject of nations. History presents no such combination for republican liberty, as that which exists amongst them. The African for the laborer,—the Anglo-Saxon for the master and ruler. Both races will be exalted." Ahead lay either glory or infamy, defense or destruction.[16]

Though there was much in the address that he had said before, there was much that was new too, and with variations this would be his platform argument for the next decade. Gone was the focus on the tariff, though not the old resentment or the old exaggerations. Now slavery was his issue, and he made his case on every front—political, economic, and social. He played to the poorer whites on preservation of a class and labor system that gave them at least some status and protected them from competition in the labor force. He related slavery to the preservation of republican government and indirectly credited it with protecting the South from the mobocracy of universal suffrage that threatened the oligarchy in South Carolina especially. Free labor and slave labor must inevitably be in opposition to each other.[17]

The address was an instant success in his district, where more public meetings were held as soon as it was published, the slaveowners backing Rhett unreservedly with resolutions calling for adoption of Rhett's plan for a congressional walkout and a Southern convention if constitutional protection were not forthcoming.[18] Moreover, the address was widely republished, including in the influential *Niles' National Register* with its nationwide circulation. Once more Rhett went further than Calhoun, for the senator stopped short of the threat of disunion and always would, his attachment to the Union being deep and sincere. Certainly Rhett toned down his rhetoric of earlier years, but all the resorts to threat were still there, just not the exhortation to blood and martyrdom. Nothing would come of his resolutions, as with his similar call in 1830, and he may never have expected any such result, for he knew as well as anyone how fragmented was regional sentiment on resistance. He had stated his position, stood against the odds, and risked provoking a heated reaction, and that may have been enough for him. With his longer-range vision he had to know that only by keeping alive the fear and the resentment could he hope in the end to persuade others to rally to him. If he allied himself with Calhoun's more moderate stance, it did not mean that he had accepted the senator's policy but only that so long as they were in substantial agreement up to Rhett's point of departure there was strength in working together. South Carolinians had no confusion as to the differences between the two. A few weeks after the address to the constituents, Petigru described them to Legaré as "our politic townsman Mr Secretary and our impolitic countryman Mr Rhett."[19]

The impolitic congressman continued the fight at his seat. In late February he was still complaining of the new gag measure in the House, called "the 21st Rule" for failing to meet the matter squarely. Pinckney's resolution of 1836 had done immeasurable harm to the South, Rhett protested, and warned that as the abolition controversy continued there was danger even of South Carolina polarizing into opposing parties on the issue. "If you do," he warned sternly, "it will only prove, that like rotten fruit, you are only fit to fall. When all agree upon the wantonness and wickedness of the aggression, will you quarrel about the time or manner of resistance or redress? Surely upon so vital and delicate a question, the impulse of every true Southern heart ought to be, any time, any method of redress rather than submission?"[20]

Ironically, while breathing the fire of resistance and possible war domestically, Rhett came out vehemently in opposition to talk of international war that erupted briefly in January after an incident with Canada in which some New

Yorkers were incited to cross the border to participate in a local rebellion and English authorities seized an American steamboat involved. It was the duty of the government to control its citizens, he argued, even praising the British soldiers who took the boat, his approval no doubt augmented by the fact that here was an incident of one people meddling in the affairs of another that was redolent of Yankee interference with Southern slavery.[21]

In the less controversial business of the House, Rhett took an immediate and active part just as he had when starting out in the legislature, and his efforts so consumed his time that he had to apologize to people for tardiness in his personal affairs.[22] Yet he could make almost any business controversial by his approach. Since the very opening of this Congress there had been seats contested due to irregularities in elections, the most glaring case being two delegates from Mississippi, John F. H. Claiborne and Samuel J. Gholson. Both were Jacksonian Democrats and thus now loyal Van Buren men, and their elections were questioned by two Whigs, Sergeant S. Prentiss and Thomas J. Word. In his first overt alliance with the Democrats, Rhett backed those who opposed unseating Claiborne and Gholson, and took the floor for what Adams, hardly an impartial observer, thought "a ranting declamation" against decreeing the seats vacant. During the speech, on February 3, he for the first time spoke of "my party predilections," seemingly placing himself with the Democrats and the administration, though at the same time pointing out that in the early sparring over the seats he had actually voted against that party until he became convinced that Claiborne and Gholson were entitled to their seats. In the end they lost them. Moreover, when the Whig John Bell of Tennessee implied on the floor that Legaré, himself a Whig, had influenced some in the South Carolina delegation to support the claims of Prentiss and Word, Rhett quickly asserted his own independence from Whig counsel. Though he continued somewhat ostentatiously to proclaim his personal independence from time to time, he was gradually—and conditionally—positioning himself in Washington as a Democrat.[23]

Rhett further aligned with the administration when a bill came up in April to finish the Cumberland Road, sometimes called the National Road. Commenced westward from Wheeling, Virginia, its completion through Indiana and Illinois required one last appropriation. For the first time on the floor of Congress, Rhett had an opportunity to oppose an internal improvement, and he did so energetically during two days of debate, even trying to get an adjournment to prevent a vote and using another parliamentary tactic to delay passage. The vote proved close, ninety-six to eighty, as the appropriation passed against administration wishes, but Rhett had attracted the attention of Van Buren men in his declarations, not only upholding state rights but also admitting that the states did have obligations to the Union.[24] If the president and his managers took offense at Rhett's February 19 proposal for a constitutional amendment limiting a president to only one term, they gave no sign. It was hardly a strike at Van Buren, anyhow, but more a reaction to Jackson staying in office long enough to become a tyrant. As his reward for backing the party and the administration through the session thus far, Rhett got a seat on the important Ways and Means Committee in April, once more revealing just how much influence he had achieved beyond that of the average freshman congressman. No doubt it helped that back in December, shortly after they had convened the session, Rhett had spoken in defense of the committee when a Massachusetts Whig accused its chairman of being Van Buren's tool and the administration majority on the committee of doing nothing for the country.[25]

Certainly the South Carolinian gave a little attention to the less controversial and more parochial affairs of state and regional interests. He called for an inquiry into the need for buoys and lighthouses off Port Royal and supported a bill to restore an express mail from Europe to the South. Some attacked the latter as a ruse to gain Southerners early news of foreign affairs to benefit financial speculation, while Rhett argued that it would merely put his section on an equal footing with the North. Ever-mindful of what the spread of immigration was doing to the Northern electorate and society, he strongly opposed a naturalization bill that would have allowed foreign paupers into the country.[26]

By far the greatest test of administration loyalty came in May with the return of the independent treasury legislation, held over from the previous session. The South Carolina delegation stood divided almost evenly on the measure, as did the House as a whole, the administration being only a couple of votes away from the thinnest of majorities. Rhett, Pickens, and Elmore supported the legislation, of course, but it was believed that they might be able to switch a couple of the wavering Whig members, which could just turn the House to an administration majority. They decided on a two-front offensive. In the House, Rhett would use his new prominence to take a leading role in managing the legislation, while his brothers Albert and James, and Elmore's brother Benjamin, worked on the legislature to pressure Legaré and one other in Washington to side with Calhoun and Van Buren.

The fight started when Waddy Thompson, definitely in the opposing camp, stood to speak and after denouncing the treasury bill used his time to distance himself from Calhoun's sudden and apostatical shift to the Democrats. That set Rhett off, and as soon as he could get the floor he replied in what Richard Menefee of Kentucky called "a volcanic eruption."[27] He started by defending again the temporary need for government paper until the federal revenues could pick up again as the economy improved, but he then attacked Thompson's criticism that Calhoun's call for payments in gold and silver to the subtreasuries implied distrust of the state banks and a desire to ruin them. He accused Thompson and the opposition of trying to embarrass the administration by denying the printing of treasury notes and thus crippling the money supply in a time of crisis. The people needed to suffer more, he supposed, and the banks to fail, so that the Whigs might declare the administration a failure. If the Whigs intended to bring the government to a halt, let them do it then and there and adjourn, and then they could all go home to their constituencies and put the case to the people. He warned them that they would be committing political suicide, and that the people would take the Constitution into their own hands. The war between the banks and the government had gone on long enough. He accused opponents of the bill of a "the more distress the better" policy that they thought would lead to the charter of another national bank to concentrate credit and money power in the North, and he warned that the people would bring them down. He appealed to the House to support Van Buren for the benefit of the country. His remarks prompted ruffled responses from Menefee and others as the debate carried over to the next day when Rhett was on the schedule to take the floor.[28]

On May 13, Rhett launched into a lengthy speech reminiscent of his defense in the test oath case, devoid of the usual fire and passion, empty of threats, and crammed with statistics and historical precedents to support the constitutionality and efficacy of the treasury note bill. He emphasized that the crisis was short-term, no more than six months before the economy picked up to the point that the many state banks that had suspended payments could resume them and the currency crunch be alleviated. Declaring "I am a State Rights man," he said he would not support the measure if government borrowing in the form of promissory treasury notes were not constitutional, and he cited the provision in the Constitution allowing the government to borrow. When opponents argued that treasury notes constituted the creation of a de facto government bank, he pointed out that the notes were all to be redeemable in six months, at which time, there being no notes outstanding and no capital remaining that would have backed them, there could hardly be a bank. To those who argued that the government should simply take out a conventional loan of the necessary $10 million, he pointed out that there was nowhere in the country in its current financial state where such a loan could be found, especially in specie. "We must pass this bill, or disgrace and dishonor the country," he argued, and he charged opponents with using the crisis in the country to try to bring down Van Buren. Ironically, he seemed to have forgotten his own declaration just two months earlier, which stated, "my inference in debate is, that every gentleman upon this floor acts

conscientiously." Now he took it for granted that there was no basis for principled opposition, "no higher motives than those of a corrupt party nature."[29] It all
came down to the insistence of the Whigs on a national bank, even though they
should be able to see that it was the mismanagement and corruption of such an
institution that helped get them into their current mess.

The business of government, he said, was to stay out of business and leave
banks to operate on their own in response to the market, and the government
should conduct its affairs uncomplicated by interference from the moneyed
interests. This was a war between the capitalists and the people, and in their
attempts to restrict or stop the supply of money in a crisis he accused capitalists
of revolution, "justifiable only when we are prepared to dissolve the Government." Unable to pay civil servants or the military, what could they expect? "I
bid gentlemen beware," he said. "They may sow the wind, and reap the whirl-
wind." He considered himself a friend to the banks—though not to the national
bank—and as a property owner he felt friendly to the interests of capital. Both
were the natural allies of sound government. But for the opposition to array the
banks against the government in the interest of party politics was infamous.
That said, he made his own declaration that he approved nearly all of the Van
Buren administration measures to date and confessed that the more embattled
it became, "the nearer I have found myself to its destinies." Should the administration fall, he was willing that he should fall with it.[29]

If that were not enough of a statement of adherence, Rhett helped to coordinate the campaign in South Carolina to sway votes in his delegation. A few days
after his speech in the House he met with Pickens, who showed him drafts of
resolutions supporting the subtreasury to be introduced in the state legislature
when it convened on May 28. Rhett approved, and he wrote to his brother Albert
in support of them.[30] He further advised his brother that two members of the
congressional delegation in particular, Legaré and John Campbell, needed to be
pressured, for their votes might make the difference.[31] James Rhett immediately
made a long address in the legislature supporting the administration measures,
and meanwhile he turned up the heat by writing a number of editorials for the
Mercury and elsewhere against Legaré and supporting Memminger as a candidate for his seat in the next election. The message to Legaré was clear—fall in
line or risk losing office with the weight of the Mercury and the extended Rhett-
Elmore connection against him. At the same time, in the legislature Albert
secured passage of a resolution that any elected official who opposed the independent treasury legislation was defying the will and welfare of the people.[32]

The maneuvers in South Carolina did not go unnoticed and, combined with
Rhett's speeches in the House, attracted no little attention. The support of the

Mercury for the administration led some to conclude that Rhett himself owned the paper, which was untrue, though he certainly exerted no ordinary influence with its editor, his brother-in-law Stuart. The *Mercury* actually had to publish denials of Rhett ownership and similar disclaimers when the opposition press accused Rhett of being the unsigned correspondent in Washington who wrote a series of well-informed and inflammatory letters to the editor. In fact he almost certainly was their author—as he certainly would be again more than two decades in the future—but it was inexpedient to say so, and so he wrote a denial—as he would in the future—maintaining that he did not even know who the *Mercury's* correspondent was by name or sight, a statement scarcely credible given his closeness to Stuart and the paper. And in the most pointed accusation of all, a Baltimore editor called Rhett "the most notorious Van Buren man of the day."[33]

Hyperbolic or not, Rhett was going down to the last vote for Van Buren on the legislation. On June 25 he took the floor one more time and spoke at almost painful length, first in defense of the State Rights Party—he had not yet called himself a Democrat, but the alliance appeared nearly secure now—and denied that he had changed his allegiance or affiliation. "I came here allied to no party," he said, explaining that, not knowing Van Buren's proposed course, he had at first felt wary and reminding them that he had voted for the Whig John Bell for Speaker. He claimed that when he saw Van Buren's message and found himself in agreement with it, he came to the administration side at once. He also realized attacks on him as a political changeling were only echoes of the attacks suffered by Calhoun across the lobby. In response he reiterated his arguments that separating the government from the banks by the independent treasury bill was in every way a state rights measure, "and that the State Rights party, unless they were prepared to abandon their principles, could not have acted otherwise than they have done." The Independent Treasury was constitutional. It was first proposed by Calhoun and other state rights men years before to separate the government from control of credit. Moreover, the opponents of the bill were incestuously intertwined with the abolitionists, and that alone compelled state rights men to this bill. "I prefer my position," he said, "identified with neither the Whig nor the Administration party, but prepared to act zealously with either."[34]

That said, he entered into a prolonged discussion of the ancient struggle between labor and capital, and for the first time he developed his ideas publicly. He denied the assertion of some that the two were synonymous, the interest of one identical to the interest of the other. "There are different and opposing interests in society, and especially between those two great elements of industry—

capital and labor," he argued, and government interference invariably favored the former unfairly. Most of all, population always increased faster than production, which meant inevitably greater competition among labor just for subsistence, while in the labor glut wages declined. Capital automatically gained the better of the equation, and Rhett did not question this, for the capitalist was "far more intelligent and independent." But if he stopped employing labor, all he lost was profit, while the laborer starved. "There can be no equality in competition under such circumstances," he argued. As population increased, labor competed with itself for work, driving wages lower, out of all relation to the profits of the employer. As a result, "where there is the most capital there may be the most want," and that in the most civilized nations on the globe. "When a man has to work, as in England, eighteen hours a day for bread, and is worn out in eight years, and it is forbidden by statute, that children shall be worked beyond ten hours a day, it is vain to talk of labor competing with capital," he believed. Capital, rather, benefited from the competition within labor to earn mere existence. Moreover he observed that it was far easier for capitalists to combine among themselves to keep wages down than it was for laborers to unite to force wages upward.

There were but two solutions for labor, other than death, to alleviate the inevitable effects of overpopulation. One was sexual abstinence, which he freely confessed did not work, pointing to the rampant licentiousness that he saw among the laboring class who, working long hours from childhood on, never had time to learn or acquire moral and mental cultivation. The laborer "works and sleeps, lives and dies," and that was all he had to life. "Hence the laborer growing up to manhood, possessed of neither moral nor intellectual discipline, turns to the only means of gratification in his power,—that which the senses afford," and hence overpopulation. The other solution, of course, which was all around them, was emigration, "labor flying from its own competition, which crowds our shores with paupers and emigrants from the old world." Now it pressed steadily westward, and so long as the western territories could continue to absorb this overflow, Northern capital could continue flourishing and Free Government endure. But when the West was full and there was nowhere for labor to go to escape its own competition, the laborer would be stuck in place, his degradation into poverty commenced, and finally he would have neither means nor intellectual will to try to escape. "He will stay and propagate," said Rhett, and he asked what then would happen in the Northern states with their universal suffrage? By their sheer numbers alone ignorant, immoral laborers would hold the government in their hands with their votes and use it to take the wealth of capital, by corruption if possible, by revolution if necessary. He did not need to mention, as he had before, what had taken place in France just half a century before.

There was only one place in the world, Rhett concluded, where labor and capital shared an identical interest and thus were not in competition, and that was "where domestic slavery exists; and under this form of society alone, have Republics hitherto ever been maintained." With slavery, labor *was* capital and capital *was* labor. The great principle of capital in a slave society is not to degrade and destroy labor in search of profit, but to preserve and foster labor, thereby ensuring profit. "Overworking, starvation and cold, and worse than all these, the heart-sickening fears of their horrors, which often make life one long agony, cannot be the fate of the laborer." Even discounting humanity, simple self-interest compelled capital to cultivate the happiness and well-being of the slave. "In such a form of society, there is no collision between capital and labor," he concluded, "and a free Government may exist so long as the intelligence and virtue of the most enlightened and cultivated portion of the population will permit."

"In all the advanced stages of society, where domestic slavery does not exist," he maintained, "there is a continual contest between" labor and capital. In such a situation capital naturally looked for an advantage and invariably found it in government. The national bank had been one such device and the tariff another. "The contest between labor and capital is already sufficiently unequal," he argued, "without the aid of the Government, designed for the common benefit of all, being used to increase it." Inflation of the currency, oversupply of notes, and banking expansion did nothing for labor and everything for capital, he protested. And how could the government be truly independent, in order to transact its business with impartiality, when all its money was in the hands of a national bank allied with the moneyed interests of the nation and subject to their control, favoritism, and speculation? The independent treasury bill solved that problem, leaving each section free to pursue its own capital enterprises, and with equal access to the capital resources of the Union that were constitutionally available to all. Moreover, Rhett favored the growth of a Southern carrying trade, so that the South might trade with Europe on its own bottoms rather than through Yankee shippers, and thus even the field yet more.

Rhett thought it incredible that some could actually accuse supporters of the measure of posing a threat to the Union itself by their opposition to a national bank, yet some did. The bank robbed the South, and they were traitors to complain? The tariff plundered the South, yet they were disunionists to resist? Abolitionists attacked slavery, and remonstrance in return was treasonous? "Hard names have but few terrors for me," he declared. "My hair will not stand on end at the appellation of 'disunionist' or 'traitor.' I was born, sir, of disunionists and traitors." Proud of his revolutionary ancestry in England, in colonial South Carolina, and in 1776, he promised that there would be revolution again if the Whigs succeeded in their policy of stopping the supply of money, for an unpaid army and civil service would cease to function, and rebellion be the inevitable result. And when his adversaries attacked him as a disunionist and, worse, attacked South Carolina for its lawlessness, he responded with scorn. Stating his utter disdain for others who would sully the House with personal aspersions, he went right ahead and did it himself, saying that their acts showed "neither genius, nor patriotism, nor honor" and that their comments were more fit for "the oyster-cellar or pot-house in the blind alleys of our cities."

He defended South Carolina's nullification of the tariff as not lawless but rightful protest against the lawless enactments of Congress and the capitalists of the North. Moreover, he promised that Congress would encounter that sort of "lawlessness" from South Carolina again and again, "so long as this Government presides over the destinies of a free and enlightened people," for they were defending their liberty. And how could his state have been lawless in its protest, when the result was an acknowledgment of victory by the money power. "You gave way," he gloated. "You proposed a compromise," he taunted, that was more advantageous than the one Hayne had suggested in the Senate in 1831. "And why, sir, did you yield? Was it because the resistance of the State was so very contemptible as to be likened to a company of boys with cornstalks, marching against fifty thousand grenadiers six feet high?" Far from it, he charged. They yielded because they could see "the resistance of the State was formidable" and that the peace of the country and the Union itself was threatened if they did not back down. It had long been clear to Rhett that South Carolina's threats had worked, and he was suggesting that his opponents in the House draw the same lesson.

Combined with his address to his constituents in January, this House speech virtually completed Rhett's statement of his political and social credos. The independent treasury bill was defeated, the efforts of the Rhett-Elmore-Stuart bloc in South Carolina proving of no avail in changing the votes of Campbell and Legaré, but still Rhett achieved something. He had stated a bedrock state rights position in the House, just as Calhoun had been doing the same in debates in the Senate, and knowing that the vote on Van Buren's measures might be lost, he may have had a greater purpose in mind for elaborating so much on principle while straying from the issue at hand. Just days after his speech a caucus was called for Democrat members of the House and those leaning toward that party, and Rhett attended. Rhett made a long address to the caucus and offered resolutions presenting the grounds on which the party ought to stand

and on which all would-be adherents should commit themselves. Rhett wanted "to justify future Party affinity" between Northerners who may have supported Jackson on the nullification issue but who returned to sound principles with the 1833 compromise and in killing the national bank, and those from the South who had been nullifiers in fact or in spirit but who currently supported the independent treasury bill. What they needed to bring them together, he said, was "a re-affirmation of the fundamental principles of the Democratic Party." When the caucus appointed Rhett and Francis Johnson of Maryland and James McCoy of North Carolina as a committee to draft an address to the people stating and defending Democratic principles, that reaffirmation is what they produced. In their *Address to the People of the United States* they looked back to the Virginia and Kentucky Resolutions, and submitted a document that Rhett said resettled the Democratic Party "on its ancient principles and policy," which happened also to be the Southern position of opposition to protective tariff, and condemnation of any and all agitation or interference on slavery. It was, in its way, a new test oath.[35]

It was a seemingly dramatic turn of events. When Barnwell Rhett arrived in Congress just nine months earlier, he came with—by his own admission—no party affiliation, and some actually thought him probably a Whig. Now, thanks to the independent treasury legislation and the conservative demeanor of Van Buren in general, and certainly the influence of Calhoun, with whom he was becoming almost daily better acquainted, Rhett had made what to outward appearances looked to be a complete shift. And yet the appearance was deceptive, for he was still pursuing precisely the same course that he always had, and toward the same end. Circumstances and events had simply turned much of the Democratic Party in the same direction, and he was content for them to travel with him. More than that, in just his freshman term in Congress he was making bids on the House floor and now in the *Address* to define the terms of allegiance, and set the course, for the party itself—if it could keep up with him.

SEVEN

A Compound of Wild Democracy
1838–1840

ONCE ON THE OFFENSIVE, Rhett could be tireless. On July 1, only a few days before the end of the session, Elizabeth, now living with him in the capital, presented him with another son, Robert Woodward.[1] It was their sixth child in eleven years of marriage, but Rhett gave no indication that he saw any inconsistency between his own fecundity and that of the ignorant laboring class that he so recently stigmatized in the House. Happy as he always was at the birth of a child, and though reluctant to leave Elizabeth, the newborn, and the other children behind while she recuperated, he could not stay in Washington with them for long. In mid-August he returned by himself to South Carolina to leap into the campaign for the fall congressional elections.[2]

In his own district he ran virtually unopposed, assured of reelection from the start, though he still spent most of his time with his brother Edmund in Beaufort planning a campaign beyond just their own district. They wanted to defeat Waddy Thompson and Campbell and Legaré for their refusal to fall in line with the Calhoun forces, and to that end Rhett stated and restated the principles that were now acceptable in a Southern representative. On August 21 his constituents invited him to attend a dinner in his honor at Coosawhatchie two weeks later, and even before then, on August 29, Beaufort held an all-day dinner for him with the usual rounds of toasts and reading of letters of support from those who could not attend. Rhett discussed what was happening in Washington, the intrigues he saw and the dangers mounting against Southern institutions, and proudly avowed his authorship of the resolutions relative to dissolving the Union, "rather than suffer the discussion of the Abolition question in Congress."[3]

He told them something else that he elaborated upon at more length a few days later at Coosawhatchie. Even as he recently attempted to erect the boundaries within which all Democrats in the future must stand, he now sought a way around the recalcitrant Legaré and Campbell by coordinating through his brother Albert the introduction of an act in the South Carolina legislature that would obligate her congressional delegation to walk out if antislavery discussion continued taking place in Congress under the faulty gag rule. Of course it was a blow at further abolition discussion, and that is how he presented it, leaving unsaid the fact that in the larger picture it represented an effort to establish firm Calhoun-Rhett control over all the state's representatives by imposing their will through the medium of Columbia. Then there was a renewal of his support for the subtreasury and Van Buren's fiscal policy, and the usual attack on internal improvements, which he now portrayed as a conspiracy between the North and the West, using Congress as a means for what he called—in a rare public flash of wit—relieving the U.S. Treasury of the "embarrassment of surplus revenues." But he could not stray for long from the rhetoric of confrontation now. The South would not stand united for its rights, he warned. Virginia and Kentucky were especially apathetic. South Carolina could seek remedy nowhere but in herself by independent action. One of the toasts at the dinner had been to the abolitionists, who should be met not in legislative halls but on the battlefield, and not with words but with swords. To that Rhett's assent was hearty, with a renewal of his declaration that the legislature should withdraw their delegation in Congress if abolition talk there continued.[4]

Calhoun had been invited to attend the Beaufort dinner but could not, or perhaps thought it politic not to appear too close yet to his more radical and explosive ally. In declining he sent a letter to be read on his behalf, however, expressing "my very high regard for one, who, on the great question of the day, has so nobly stood up for the cause of the people and the Constitution, and who, high as my regard for him was previously, has grown in my esteem on a more intimate personal acquaintance."[5] It was the great man's first public avowal of support and approbation of Rhett, and it meant a lot, but what the audiences at Beaufort and Coosawhatchie were not to know was that Calhoun's praise was not unqualified. Rhett seemed to him to be positioning himself rather too close to Van Buren for comfort. After all, there was a presidential election coming in two years, and Calhoun as a perennial hopeful needed to keep some distance between himself and the current administration in case he had to run against Van Buren in 1840. At the same time there were Calhoun friends such as Pickens and James Henry Hammond who distrusted the Rhetts and their faction as "third rate—trading politicians going for self alone," fearing that Rhett was actually ready to sell out the state rights and nullification party—even Calhoun— in order to bring themselves closer to the unionists in South Carolina and thus cement absolute control over the state in the legislature.[6]

That Rhett wanted control was certain, nor did he deny the ambition. With Albert and James both in the legislature they covered unionist and state rights bases, and Albert may have been the most influential single legislator in Columbia.

Rhett and now Elmore were in Congress, and Elmore's brother sat in the legislature, while Elmore's ties to state banking were augmented by Benjamin Rhett's directorship of the Bank of South Carolina. Add Rhett's brother-in-law Stuart running the *Mercury*, and they had by 1838 easily the most powerful political machine in the state.[7] That Rhett, in charge, genuinely hoped to promote Calhoun as well as his own agendum did not obviate the fact that he had an agendum that did not in all respects harmonize, and now Calhoun felt the necessity of discreetly nudging Rhett back into line. Rhett's recent speeches, and the toasts they prompted, seemed to him rather too supportive of Van Buren. He warned Rhett that the state rights men should stand by their old principles, remaining aloof from parties and presidential politics. They might support Van Buren issue by issue, but if they seemed to offer too much general adherence too early, it would weaken them in 1840 when it came time to try to influence platforms and nominees. Calhoun's self-interest was transparent, though his argument was sound enough. "*Position* is everything in politics as well as war," he told Rhett, and asked him to rein in Stuart and the *Mercury*. Indeed, Calhoun seemed to believe that Rhett lay behind Stuart's editorials, which had been running rather too strongly in favor of Van Buren.[8] Calhoun even warned against calling themselves Democrats as yet. Not only did that imply a liaison with the administration party, but it also implied to him favoring "a government of the absolute numerical majority." There he agreed with Rhett that such a form of rule would destroy the South. He preferred that they call themselves the "State Rights and Republican Party," which stated their position but left them free to make alliances where they wished.[9]

Rhett may have been slightly miffed at Calhoun's gentle exertion of authority, especially since Calhoun had been largely behind the recent movement to narrow the gulf between unionists and state rights men in South Carolina by adopting a more cooperative and conciliatory attitude toward Van Buren and the Democrats.[10] But he hardly needed any hints about standing for their old principles. Through Albert he saw introduced in the legislature his motion for a walk-out in Washington in the event of further antislavery discussion in Congress, and though it failed in spite of the backing of the Rhett-Elmore machine, still there was no mistaking that Rhett had not budged from his hard-line stance.[11]

Meanwhile, in spite of Calhoun's admonition to stay clear of outright affiliation with the Democratic Party, Rhett chose instead to continue his efforts to force that party into his own mold, which would achieve both his ends and Calhoun's. Rhett by now accepted that the state rights men needed a national party if they were to achieve their goals short of disunion, but Calhoun could not risk being tarred with the current administration brush. The solution to Rhett was not to join with the Democrats but to make the Democrats conform to Calhoun. He had already made a start on that with his role in preparing the *Address* during the last session. Even though some thought it placed him too close to Van Buren, still he got into it the state rights stands on abolition and internal improvements. Now, with his reelection accomplished, he returned to the winter session in Washington prepared to press his cause.

Shortly before the House convened on December 3 the assembling Democrats met in caucus to take up the *Address* once more and to plot their course. Rhett gained the floor at the meeting and outlined for them a series of resolutions that he had obviously been working on during the recess, and perhaps in consultation with Calhoun. These were the grounds on which the South stood and to which the party must commit itself to gain Southern adherence, he told them. First, Congress had no constitutional jurisdiction over slavery in the states. Second, to undo the harm done by Pinckney, he affirmed that petitions for abolition in the District of Columbia or in the territories were intended indirectly to interfere with slavery in the states, and since Congress could not do indirectly what it was prohibited from doing directly, all such proposals were equally unconstitutional. Moreover, since the Constitution was founded on the equality of the states, any attempt to discriminate against the institutions of some of the states constituted an assumption of inequality, again making any attempts at congressional abolition in the district or the states or the territories unlawful. Consequently, in the coming session they should affirm that no petitions discussing abolition in any form, at any place, ought to be considered.[12]

The session opened while the caucus continued to meet, and only on December 8 did the Democrats concur in adopting Rhett's resolutions. Wisely, he chose not to try to introduce the new gag rule in the House himself. It would have more impact, and appear to be a party rather than a sectional measure, if proposed by a Northerner, so Rhett suggested that Charles Atherton, a Democrat from New Hampshire, propose it on December 10.[13] But on the appointed day they postponed the introduction when some of the New England Democrats balked at the stridence of Rhett's wording. That evening in another caucus Rhett found himself forced to give way by sacrificing the statement that abolition agitation was unconstitutional, settling for the weaker declaration that it went against the spirit of the Constitution. Far worse was the removal of his final and uncompromising resolution that no petitions whatever were to be received or discussed by the House. Instead, the Atherton resolutions would conclude now with the old statement that such petitions could be introduced but were to be tabled immediately without debate. It was a point lost, a return to the old Pinckney resolutions that he had so castigated, for Rhett saw their mere introduction not only as a thin edge of a wedge, but also as an unceasing opportunity to win publicity for abolitionists by their being denied debate. Far better to deny any right to submit such petitions. Outvoted, Rhett had to yield, and the next day Atherton presented the resolutions, which passed with a Democratic majority. The party had come into line, at least, and with Northern and even New England support, but still Rhett did not trust the North to abide by the gag. He wrote immediately to his old friend Huger in the legislature at Columbia to introduce once more a resolution demanding that the state's congressional delegation walk out if the gag rule were ever overturned.[14]

Though that failed, as did Albert Rhett's earlier effort, still Rhett was making progress. The Democratic Party had adopted the modified gag rule as party doctrine, in addition to what he had already carried in the *Address*. Seemingly Rhett had removed slavery from the floor of Congress once more, and at the same time taken the only major party that could counter the consolidationists effectively on the national stage and helped shift its center of gravity southward. Having done so, he continued his support of Van Buren's fiscal policy from his perch on the Ways and Means Committee, defending the U.S. Treasury against charges of blunders and ignorance, and coming to its side when the annual report delivered in January 1839 made reference to the tariff and protectionism as evils. When Van Buren opponents rose in the House to attack the report, Rhett stood to reply, more restrained than usual but still confrontational. The opposition party in the North and the western region fought the administration's economy and voted time after time for more protection, taking with them even the administration men from those areas who had to go along out of regional sentiment. Yet now those Northerners complained that the administration was profligate, ignoring the fact that the money it spent was what they had appropriated, and that the flurry of patronage jobs Van Buren filled were ones created by his very critics.

Only the South had stood up forthrightly and consistently against waste and protectionism, Rhett asserted. If the Republican Party were to survive at all—regardless of whether as Democrats or state rights men or under any other appellation—their day of reckoning was at hand, and the U.S. Treasury report outlined their true course as conservative, restrained, constitutional. "Be true to the people," he said to those on his side of the issue, "and they will be true to you." Moreover, in the straightened climate after the panic of 1837, appropriations only meant debt now, with the Treasury exhausted and not enough currency in circulation. And in that he thought he saw their real purpose. By spending more than they had in the Treasury, the opposition would create such a debt that there would be no way to repay but to maintain or increase the current level of revenue, and that would mean abrogating the 1833 tariff compromise and retaining the old rates after 1842, which is what he had expected all along. In part that was why his Ways and Means Committee had tried to preempt the opposition with a report the previous month that started the process of establishing the new lower rates to take effect in 1842. Despite that, however, he said on the floor now that he would welcome a violation of the 1833 compromise, for then he and South Carolina would act to meet the occasion, which he predicted could not be far off in any case. He said nothing about either nullification or secession, but he did not have to, for his past views were well enough known. In the crisis he would be found "striving, although feebly, against privilege and monopoly—contending for the rights of the many against the oppression of the few." No one pointed out to him that as a member of South Carolina's oligarchy— its privileged few—he had spent years striving to prevent just the opposite, to keep "the many" from oppressing "the few" of his class.[15]

Toward the end of the session, as the debate continued and became a bit more heated, he could not restrain himself when the Whig George Briggs of Massachusetts inconveniently pointed out that one of the early proponents of protection had been Calhoun, back in 1816. William Lowndes, too, and even Jefferson and Jackson had supported it. No, he admonished Rhett, the protective tariff was not a Northern idea, but of Southern origin. Rhett would never learn to appreciate others highlighting inconvenient inconsistencies in his arguments. He tossed aside Briggs's assertion, admitting it to be true, but added that he did not care a farthing for what anyone before him from the South might have said. He had his own opinions, and he would continue to hold them "though Mr. Jefferson, and Mr. Lowndes, and Mr. Calhoun, and all the South Carolina delegation, ay, and Andrew Jackson to boot, had held opinions diametrically opposite."[16] Once again Rhett made it clear, probably unintentionally in the heat of the moment, that he was not adjusting his views or principles for the sake of the administration or building a stronger Democratic Party, or for any other reason, but expected that they would adjust themselves to suit him.

When the session closed and the Rhett family returned to South Carolina, he still felt uneasy over the prospects for the new tariff rates to come. With the bit in his teeth, he hoped to be able to force the administration to honor the compromise, which would at the same time further cement the Van Buren Democrats to the state rights ground he was staking out for the party. For Rhett, the strongest means of persuasion was always a threat, and he only ever had one in his arsenal: secession. At the annual July 4 celebration on the Salt Ketcher River in his district, he made his appeal.[17]

Tariff opponents must not wait until 1842 to see the new duties, he said, for then it could be too late, besides which merchants needed in fairness to have some advance warning of the rates they faced. Since the sitting of Congress in 1841 would be a short session, only the coming seven-month session to start in December would allow time to do the job properly. They were free to adjust the tariff in any way they chose, for the 1833 legislation placed no legal constraints upon them. They could abolish the tariff entirely and resort to another form of taxation to fund the government, or they could create a new tariff structure. Rhett made it clear that he favored the former, a direct tax upon each citizen, by which that citizen knew what he paid and had an interest in how the government spent it. Rhett had concluded that direct taxation was a solution sometime before, no doubt influenced by his early mentors such as Cooper. The fact that it was an idea with no widespread appeal would not stop him from advocating it again and again.

The tariff was an indirect tax that fell only on consumers, but he attempted to show that it fell disproportionately on the South. In so doing he revealed that old convenient disregard for facts and consistent logic that often infected his arguments. The rice and cotton regions of the South—which for his purposes included all of the slave states except Virginia, Maryland, and Kentucky—constituted just one-third of the nation's population, he said, and he went on to maintain that since the population as a whole consumed imports equally—an unwarranted assumption—therefore the South purchased one-third of all imported goods. That meant that the South paid one-third of the $21 million in indirect taxes that went to Washington. There alone he was in error, for the bulk of all imports went to urban buyers, and of the fifteen largest cities in the nation the slave states had only three. He went on to state quite correctly that the majority of federal revenue was spent outside the South, citing 1834 when only $1,958,000 went to the cotton states, a figure that he thereafter rounded *down* to $1.9 million to sweeten his argument. Theoretically, if they were to receive back tax expenditures in proportion to their contribution, those states should have received $7 million and thus were being cheated of $5.1 million of their equitable share.

Instead, that was going to the North and western region, meaning that instead of the $14 million that ought to be due those regions, they were receiving $19.1 million. By his reckoning, this meant that after paying $14 million in import duties and receiving back $19.1 million in federal expenditure, the actual tax burden of the North and the western region was only $8.9 million. In fact, of course, it meant that they would have had no tax burden at all but would finish the year with all import taxes paid returned to them, along with an $8.9

million surplus, but Rhett somehow missed making this telling point in his favor. Perhaps he overlooked it in his anxiety to go ahead to an even greater mathematical error that supported his case just as well. The cotton states paid $7 million in import duties, he said, and got back $1.9 million in federal expenditures, meaning a net loss of $5.1 million they spent that went to the North and the western sector. Now he took that same shortfall and *added* it to the cotton states' original presumed $7 million in import duties, subtracted the $1.9 million received, and wondrously concluded that the Southern tax burden was not the $7 million he said they paid at the beginning, but actually over $10 million. It was a blatant sophistry—or a crude and uncharacteristic error in math—that the merest schoolboy at his slate could disprove, an eloquent example of Rhett's attitude toward facts when it came to supporting his arguments. Now he employed it to make the argument that, in fact, under the current tariff system the cotton states bore more of the burden of the federal government's expenses than did all the other sections of the Union combined.

He employed the same sophistical line of argument in addressing revenue from exports as well, starting with the unsupported assumption that since the cotton states exported $65 million worth of goods every year, "of course, these exports, must have purchased at least their equivalent in value, and been the instrument of bringing into the United States, sixty-five millions of importations."[18] He thereby completely ignored the enormous annual expenditure in purchase of domestic slaves, new lands, home construction, and all the machinery and other articles purchased from the North. Having done so, however, he could then conclude that at current tariff rates, the cotton states in fact were paying $14 million in duties on that presumed $65 million worth of imports, virtually double the fair share of $7 million that would be theirs based on population.

Of course his object was transparent. "I think I have shewn," he said, "that through the unequal disbursements of the Government, and the manner in which the taxes it imposes on importations, effect the Southern Producer, the Southern States are most unequally burdened by our system of indirect taxation." This abuse would be rectified under a system of direct taxation, he argued, first because everyone would pay tax individually on the same basis, and secondly because the taxpayer, knowing what he was paying, would take a more active interest in controlling government expenditure of its revenue. But having devoted almost two-thirds of his speech to advocating direct taxation, he then freely admitted that it stood no chance at all of being adopted. That said, a reformed tariff was the only option, and he said what he had said so many times before, that he would accept only a revenue tariff and that all items ought to be taxed the same on a flat rate. That too, however, he confessed to be all but impossible. There was no escaping some measure of protectionism in any new rates for 1842 without a hard fight. Most of all, however, tariff reformers had to be united in their stand or they would lose. "Unfortunately for our interests or honor," he lamented, "upon what subject in these latter times has the South been united?" Even on abolition they were divided. As for the rest of the Union, the Whigs were their foes for sure, and only the "Administration or Democratic party of the North"—perhaps in deference to Calhoun this was his only use of the term *Democrats*—could win the day if it followed the principles Rhett had been laying out for it recently and stood with the South.

Interestingly, Rhett suggested that if the administration did as he hoped, it might "once more plant the Republican party on the broad foundations of equality and the Constitution," thus revealing yet again that he was not moving toward the Democrats so much as trying to move them toward the Jeffersonian Republicanism that spawned them and which he had espoused since youth. If they did, he said, the South would rise and stand beside them. Yet could the South trust the Democrats? He did not forget that under Jackson they repudiated nullification and passed the Force Bill, on the one hand professing Republican principles while on the other betraying state rights. Only the tariff divided them now, he believed. Bridge that gap and the South could unite with the administration party—calling themselves Democrats or Republicans, it did not matter—and safely rule in Washington and at home. Under Van Buren, whom Rhett called a remarkable man of grace and dignity, the Democrats had stood sound on all the great issues of the past two years, and he paid special notice to their rejection of abolition and support for Southern slavery. Despite Calhoun's urging not to get too close to the administration, Rhett proudly averred that he had supported almost every Van Buren measure. They were so close to unity that if only the tariff could be settled on Southern ground, they would solidify. Until then, however, "neither your interest, nor my honor will allow me to identify myself with any party, which will not join me in redressing its oppressions." There it was in a sentence. It was up to the Democrats to join Barnwell Rhett, and not the other way around. If they did not, then there would be no unity; there would be renewed strife. There must be either direct taxation or an equal ad valorem tariff without protectionism. "There is yet another alternative," he added inevitably—"the sword." Yet as if to blunt the edge of the weapon just invoked, he expressed confidence in Southern unity and reliance on the Northern Democrats to see the right.

Rhett's Salt Ketcher speech was not to be for his constituents' ears alone. He had it printed and distributed inside South Carolina and without, and he sent

copies to influential Democrats such as James K. Polk, newly elected governor
of Tennessee, Jackson's successor to influence in the Volunteer State, and a probable future presidential contender. Possibly in response to renewed urgings from
Calhoun, Rhett tried to back away somewhat from his apparent endorsement of
Van Buren. In all but an outright lie, and even when acknowledging that some
now called him Van Buren's adjutant in South Carolina, he claimed, "I have
never been able to identify myself entirely with the administration Party," despite
having said only months before that he would stand or fall by Van Buren. He
confessed his personal esteem for Van Buren but argued that his own relations
with Calhoun put him in such a position that he could not approach the president personally to argue his tariff case since it might put him in an awkward
posture should Calhoun subsequently have to challenge Van Buren in 1840.

Instead he asked Polk and others to use their influence with the president to
get him to accept the Southern position on the tariff. "For Gods sake My Dear
Sir," he said to Polk, "let us have no more strife upon this subject." The South
asked only for justice, but he averred that South Carolina would take nothing
less either. She would resist any new tariff plan that recognized in any degree
the principle of protectionism. If divided on the issue, Southerners faced oblivion, but if their states could unite, they must prevail. He felt certain that Van
Buren was not far from them in his own ideas on the tariff. If Southern men
approached him properly, surely he would take their side, the constitutional
side, in preference to mean and narrow Northern interests. Moreover, it was important to act now. Van Buren would leave office in March 1841, if not reelected,
and Rhett seemed to be assuming that he would not. That meant that the 1833
tariff would expire under whomever his successor might be, and it just could be
a Whig. Thus all the more reason for the administration to pass a new tariff bill
in 1840 while a friendly Van Buren was still in office to provide backing. "Heal
up the division in our Party," Rhett pleaded of Polk, "and give the South repose
with her rights." Despite having declared on the Salt Ketcher that he could not
yet ally himself with any political organization, he spoke urgently now to Polk
of "our Party," yet for Rhett, as for other Southern extremists, even Calhoun, party
loyalty would always be an expedient rather than a principle.[19]

Before the coming session of Congress, Rhett strove all the harder to secure
the hold of his own faction on state politics. Elmore, whose term in Congress
expired in March and did not seek reelection, now controlled the *Columbia
South Carolinian,* which added a second sheet to the machine's press, and also
became president of the Bank of South Carolina. James Rhett, meanwhile, married Elmore's sister, further binding the two influential families, and Elmore
handled some of Rhett's personal business in Charleston while his friend was

away in Congress.[20] Beyond strengthening the internal and external ties of the Rhett-Elmore faction, Rhett also did not let pass any opportunity to advance his cause, even when in questionable taste.

Robert Hayne, the revered opponent of the tariff and champion of nullification, whose epic debates with Daniel Webster had electrified the nation in years past, died unexpectedly in North Carolina on September 24, and when his body came back to Charleston for interment at St. Michael's, Rhett saw a chance to capitalize on the widely attended funeral. Petigru was present and regarded it as "a very disgusting affair." The state rights people all but hijacked the event, delivering eulogies that were only thinly disguised party speeches and adopting resolutions that Petigru described being "as little connected with any sympathy for Hayne, as with any sentiment of Religion." In trying to sanctify Hayne as one of the gods of nullification, the Rhetts and Stuart and the rest of what some called the "*Mercury* set" fooled very few. "Many of them had long ceased to think of him as a friend," said Petigru, "and the Rhetts were never his friends further than party." They would all have abandoned him in a minute if in life he had voted or spoken against the subtreasury. Petigru did not attempt to hide his disgust at the cynical opportunism of his old friend and pupil. "If they had had a particle of respect for the man, they would not have been willing to convert his funeral into a caucus wh[ich] put his grave in a place of amusement," he grumbled. "The truth is that from mere egoism it came into their heads to erect a monument to nullification."[21]

There was more to it than ego, however, and more even than party-building, though certainly Rhett understood that the more they could co-opt distinguished past as well as present South Carolinians into their ranks, the stronger their voice in the state and the greater his influence in trying to shape the Democratic Party. There had been talk of electing him to fill a vacant seat in the state senate in Columbia, but Rhett had his eyes on a much greater prize.[22] Calhoun sat securely in the Senate in Washington as long as he wanted the position, but if he won the presidency in 1840, and even if he just won a nomination, he would certainly resign. Moreover, Rhett learned shortly before the Hayne funeral that the state's other senator, William Campbell Preston, intended to resign his seat at the end of the long session in 1840. Though once an ardent state rights man, Preston had come around to the Whig position on most issues by this time. His resignation would mean that within a few months at least one and perhaps both of South Carolina's Senate seats would be open, affording the additional opportunity to get two state rights men in the Senate. Just at the time that Rhett was managing the Hayne funeral event, he also sounded out leading state rights men to gauge support for his candidacy to succeed Preston. Calhoun's cousin and

protégé Pickens seemed the most likely potential rival, but Pickens assured
Rhett that he would not oppose him, his sights being fixed on the Speakership
when Congress reassembled in December. Indeed, Pickens offered Rhett his
backing, further observing that with both himself and Calhoun hailing from the
Upcountry, the Lowcountryman Rhett was a better candidate anyhow, to preserve the traditional division of the state's senators between the two great regions.[23]

Another potential rival appeared to be James Henry Hammond, who perpetually complained that he was weary of politics and yet ever tried to gain
office. Hammond and Pickens were much closer to each other than either ever
would be to Rhett, and that same summer Hammond warned Pickens to beware
Rhett's motives and actions. "I know them thoroughly," he said of the Rhett-
Elmore group. "A viler association never attempted to rule in South Carolina:—
they are without talents, without principle & without courage." The Hayne
funeral circus was just one example of how Rhett attempted to prostitute influential men in the state—even after death—into connecting themselves with him
"for the most utterly selfish purposes." Hammond, who was just as intemperate
and blinkered when it came to opponents as was Rhett, believed that he could
cite half a dozen recent instances when Rhett had intrigued against his own
ambitions. He may have been right, or it may as well have been his own vivid
suspicion bordering on paranoia, but through his cloud of prejudice Hammond
still saw clearly enough that neither he nor Pickens should trust Rhett or any of
his clique. "I do & always have defied them," he grumbled; "God damn them."[24]

Despite his own affection for Barnwell Rhett, Petigru saw his weaknesses well
enough, and others in his family noted that Rhett and his associates "were
exceedingly envious of every So[uth] C[arolinia]n more distinguished than they."[25]
Moreover, Rhett, Pickens, and Hammond were all locked in a continuing dance
for which Calhoun supplied the tune. They were the great man's three foremost
acolytes now, everyone in his way useful, and yet their very closeness resulted in
a natural friction among them as each sought to be first among equals. Calhoun
knowingly used this at times, favoring first one, then another, and occasionally
profiting from their internal squabbles. Among other things, it meant that none
of the three was ever likely to rise to challenge Calhoun for preeminence in
South Carolina, though unlike the other two, Rhett had already shown himself
willful and headstrong and quite capable of slipping Calhoun's reins on occasion.[26] One way to stand free of that control entirely would be to stand beside
Calhoun as an equal in the Senate, and there is every indication that in these last
months of 1839, with the taste for higher office in his mouth, Rhett took counsel of his own ambition to help ensure that neither of his rivals dined on the coveted fruit first.

He showed his hand when he returned to Washington several days before the opening of the first session of the Twenty-sixth Congress on December 2. The Democrats had to decide upon a candidate to back for the Speakership. The administration would surely propose its own candidate, supporters of Van Buren's chief Democratic rival Thomas Hart Benton of Missouri might put up another, and naturally Calhoun's state rights followers—who would meet in caucus with the Democrats—would offer their own. Pickens, as Calhoun's kinsman and protégé, wanted and expected the state rights men to propose him, as Rhett had indeed pledged to do. Yet that posed two problems for Rhett, the one tactical and the other personal. Identified as he was as a nullifier, Pickens might be too extreme for the administration Democrats to accept, whereas they needed a candidate who would bring together the administration and Calhoun forces. The other problem for Rhett was the conventional wisdom that regarded the Speakership as one of the stepping stones to higher office, Henry Clay having moved from it to the Senate. Far from sidelining Pickens as a rival by supporting him for speaker, Rhett might actually be advancing him at his own expense.

Pickens reached Washington on Saturday, November 30, a day or two after the other state rights men, having advised Rhett of when he would be there. He should have come earlier. Knowing when Pickens would arrive, Rhett brought the state rights men together in caucus on Friday evening, November 29, and effectively withdrew Pickens's name from contention, saying that he would not "get on" with the House at large. Instead, after consulting with him, Rhett put forward Dixon H. Lewis of Alabama, a state rights Democrat who shared his views on the Van Buren administration and who just happened to be Elmore's brother-in-law. It was an act that must have been coordinated by correspondence for some time before, and at one stroke it diminished Pickens as a rival and also raised the potentiality of the Rhett-Elmore faction holding a favored connection with arguably the second most powerful man in the land, next to the president, and as part of a South Carolina–Alabama alliance that would be useful in future resistance when needed. Moreover, Rhett must have done it without consulting Calhoun first, or even Elmore, for if the great man had known of and sanctioned the move, then Pickens could not have reacted as he did when the next morning Rhett presented the shocked Carolinian with the fait accompli. Elmore denied any complicity or foreknowledge, refused thereafter to support Lewis, and began collecting testimony from others to whom he had earlier confided that he had always preferred Pickens to his brother-in-law, whose health he feared might not be up to the rigors of the job. That did little good for Pickens now, though, who angrily told Rhett to his face that he would see him dead before he would support Lewis in the general caucus. That same afternoon Pickens complained bitterly to Hammond, "I have been the victim of the vilest intrigue ever known."[27]

It was also an intrigue that narrowly failed. When the state rights men met with the Democrats in general caucus, the administration and Benton supporters united on John W. Jones of Virginia. As Rhett would have predicted, the Lewis nomination attracted a number of the Van Buren men and most of the Calhoun supporters. They could see that with a foot in both the Calhoun and the administration camps, Lewis as Speaker could be an important bridge in Rhett's effort to shift the mainstream of the Democratic Party toward the Calhoun position. Unfortunately, some of the state rights faction thought Rhett was "truckling" to the Van Buren men disgracefully with the Lewis nomination and reacted accordingly. Several votes from Georgia and even Pennsylvania that Rhett thought secure for Lewis went elsewhere, and most South Carolinians went against Lewis, some in disgust at Rhett's action, or so thought Pickens. As a result, Jones became the caucus nominee by one vote. Certainly no one blamed Calhoun, who stayed out of the whole mess and seemed completely undisturbed by the imbroglio among his leading courtiers, perhaps because it resulted in keeping both of them in their place.[28]

Events made things uncomfortable at Hill's boardinghouse on Capitol Hill, where not only Calhoun lodged but also Pickens and Rhett, both in third-floor rooms, no doubt making for stiff accidental meetings on the stairs. Indeed, both moved to other lodgings within days, each citing the poor food at Hill's, though it is more likely that it was each other they found unpalatable.[29] Certainly it was a poisoned atmosphere when Congress assembled on December 2 and began trying to elect a Speaker. The problem was five contested seats from New Jersey, where, neither for the first nor the last time, there were charges of corruption and mismanagement. The state had six seats in the House, but eleven men were there asserting claim to admission. Unfortunately the Democrats and state rights men on one side stood so evenly divided with the Whigs on the other that those five seats would decide the majority and the Speakership. Being Whigs, if their credentials were recognized, they would defeat the administration candidate.

From the sound of the first gavel the House was hamstrung by its own procedure. Pending election of a Speaker, the clerk presided, but Hugh Garland refused to allow a vote on any motions from the floor except those to adjourn, maintaining that until a Speaker was chosen, the House had no constitutional authority to transact any other business. Yet without a decision in the New Jersey case, no Speaker could be elected. It was a classic parliamentary logjam that led the always sarcastic Henry Wise of Virginia to declare that they were not a Congress but a mob. For two days they argued and postured to no avail, and then it was Rhett, who so recently failed at one maneuver, who found the way out. On December 5 he moved that they call John Quincy Adams to the chair on a pro temp basis and empower him to conduct business pending the election of a Speaker. At the same time he declared his own conviction that Adams would act impartially, a rare compliment from Rhett for any opponent. There was never a closeness or any socialization between Rhett and Adams, though they acknowledged their distant kinship. Yet Rhett always respected "Old Man Eloquent" and described Adams as "a most extraordinary man." The clerk allowed Rhett's motion, and the House concurred. Rhett went to Adams's seat and escorted him to the chair to preside.[30]

Well before this Rhett had leaped into the fray over the New Jersey seats, appearing to Adams, at least, as very much a party man now, "frothy with the rights of the people, technicalities, and frauds."[31] But they were largely in agreement on the idea of a call of the roll of those present and that if they were sufficient for a quorum, then the House should proceed to vote on the acceptance or rejection of the disputed credentials from New Jersey. For the next several days the House wrangled inconclusively, with Rhett sometimes playing the role of parliamentarian and generally arguing that the House should hear the cases of all of the disputed Whig delegates from New Jersey, even though if they won their case the administration lost the Speakership. Rhett's insistence on what he saw as fairness in the matter cost him temporarily the goodwill of a few of the administration and state rights members who found this adherence to principle incompatible with immediate party interests. However, in the main he conducted himself in such a fashion as to stand by the administration, even pitting himself against Adams when the chair attempted to enter the debate and Rhett introduced an amendment to the resolution that made Adams chairman, stating that he was only to preside and not to speak on debated topics.

After ten days they still had neither a Speaker nor a solution to the New Jersey problem, and on December 12, Rhett again moved that they try and settle the New Jersey question first. Clearly the House was having none of that. Meanwhile, Rhett and others worked behind the scenes to secure election of a friendly Speaker. Jones was unacceptable to the Whigs, but Robert M. T. Hunter of Virginia, an avowed independent who actually stood closely aligned with Calhoun, proved to be a man who could command almost all of Jones's following even though he had been siding with the Whigs in the New Jersey case. At the same time Rhett worked on one of South Carolina's Whig members to come on board, with Pickens laying aside his sulk to aid in the cause. Adams likened them to a "flying squadron, who subsist by passing from side to side, with the perpetual prostration of all honest principle." That may have been hyperbolic, and Adams of course was a Whig himself, but still there must have been some hard dealing off the House floor, some pressure, and maybe even some promises. In the end it worked, and Hunter finally won the Speakership on December 16, although in a bizarre finale, on the last ballot, when Hunter already safely had enough support otherwise to win, Rhett turned about and voted for Pickens. If it was meant to mend a fence, it failed.

The wrangle frayed nerves. As the immediate battle over the New Jersey delegates proceeded following Hunter's election, the Whigs contesting for their seats were finally rejected, and then in a post mortem debate Rhett smugly charged that Whig Henry Wise, through parliamentary ineptitude, had thrown away the chance to seat them. Wise rose to the challenge, and an acrimonious exchange ensued, Adams remarking on "Rhett having the address to shield his own gross prevarications by retorting upon Wise, and charging him with the loss of the battle by bad management." It was ungracious, at the least, but Rhett made up for it a few days later when, calmed, he refused to permit his angry interchanges with Wise to be printed in the *Congressional Globe.* The gesture immediately erased any ill will with Wise.[32]

Others, such as Pickens, were not to be so easily assuaged, and he avowed to Hammond after it was all over that while Rhett might have betrayed him once, "let him try it again."[33] Indeed, Rhett's flirtations back and forth between the administration and the state rights men raised doubt in a number of minds and confirmed it in others, for Adams was not the only one to perceive Rhett "passing from side to side." Pickens, still smarting from the "great treachery and selfishness" of his pretended friend, charged that "Rhett acted an unmanly part and his conduct this session has shaken my confidence in his sincerity or generosity."[34] Hunter, who knew Rhett's efforts for him behind the scenes and held no grudge over that last pointless vote, was warned by friends to beware his new ally. "I have no faith in the soundness of his head or the honesty of his heart," wrote Congressman Francis Mallory of Virginia, who had known Rhett for several years and admitted that "he is no favorite of mine." Rhett was a reformer, he thought, and like most of that sort a selfish changeling. "As sure as you live he will deceive some of those who now confidently calculate on his services," Mallory warned Hunter. "Rhett aspires to be a leader and will some day or other set up for himself."[35]

Though there was a lot of business before the House, especially with the weeks lost on the Speakership impasse, Rhett left Washington at the end of the month and made a brief trip to Charleston on another mission of his own, though he probably had at least the sanction of Calhoun. For one thing, he needed to heal—or at least patch over—the breach with Pickens, though still Calhoun gave no sign of rebuke for Rhett's treatment of his cousin. Lewis probably had been the wiser choice from a strategic vantage, and however much Calhoun might have wished to see his kinsman's fortunes advanced, his own program came first. Now Rhett sought to do in South Carolina what he had been trying to do in Washington, bringing the state rights and union factions together behind him, and perhaps incidentally to sideline another rival in the offing.

The method he chose was the coming gubernatorial election. Leading men regarded the governorship as an all but powerless position, more ceremonial than political, and yet it carried some symbolic significance. The current incumbent was a nullifier, and many expected Hammond to seek the post in the coming election in the legislature. The governorship, too, was seen as a prelude to the Senate. For some time now Rhett and Elmore and their friends had been suggesting that handing the post to a unionist in 1840 would go far toward achieving their and Calhoun's aims for Carolinian unity. If it also made even stronger Rhett's own power in the state and removed a senatorial rival in the process, so much the better. As soon as he got to Charleston, Rhett held final consultations with John P. Richardson, a unionist with whom Rhett's followers found they could work, and on January 10, Stuart's *Mercury* announced Richardson's nomination by an unnamed meeting in Columbia, to run on a reconciliation platform of Rhett's devising.[36]

Hammond was just as shocked as Pickens. Everyone knew that Richardson's nomination was the reason Rhett made his lightning visit to Charleston, and few would believe that it was anything but another plot by the Rhett-Elmore cabal or that Calhoun had any role in it.[37] "Their clique aim [is] to rally the union men & with their state right squad that they can carry over," Hammond ranted to Pickens, "to defy you over Calhoun & all." This was not just a blow at Hammond, but an attempt to challenge Calhoun for power. "The gauntlet is thrown down," Hammond postured. "The war is begun." It would be infamous if Richardson were to win and thus put a union man over the state. Hammond pleaded with Pickens to go to his cousin and persuade Calhoun to repudiate the Richardson nomination and support his own. The people at large mistakenly accorded influence to Rhett because of the assumption that he acted in the shadow of Calhoun's mantle, and thus few would oppose Rhett unless Calhoun spoke up, even though he risked losing Rhett's support in the process. Once the people knew the true condition of things, however, they must abandon Rhett instantly. "The State is galled & cross at the dominion of such people," groused Hammond, and would gladly chuck them aside if once repudiated by Calhoun.[38]

Pickens did start consulting with men in Washington, and probably Calhoun, as well as writing to others to start a movement for Hammond. By now he was convinced that his handling and Hammond's were part of a single conspiracy hatched by Rhett the previous fall in Columbia and involving the Elmores and even Richardson at that early date.[39] Certainly Rhett was capable of such a complex undertaking. Moreover, as one of Hammond's friends observed, the Rhett-Elmore state rights machine now influenced most of the major corporations in the state thanks to domination of the state bank, and by adding the unionists to their ranks with the Richardson nomination they were now the dominant group in Carolina, "with everything in the state ordered for the good of the state, that is, for the good of Honl F. H. Elmore, R. B. Rhett & Co." In fact, he said, they hated Calhoun for his recent vacillation from their hard line and would denounce him if they dared. Some claimed to know that Calhoun did not agree with Rhett's actions but feared to make a break with him on the eve of the 1840 election.[40]

Calhoun said not a word either to distance himself from Rhett or to support a Hammond candidacy. Instead he remained above the squabble in South Carolina and to Hammond's pleas for support responded only that he must be neutral, and that his strength in Washington depended on a union of factions at home.[41] If anyone needed proof that Calhoun at least sanctioned Rhett's action with Richardson—if he was not in fact behind it in the first place—there it lay. The *Mercury* nomination soon gained support through the state's press, and though Hammond continued to try to ignite a movement for himself, it never took fire. The ensuing campaign proved to be bitter and divisive, precisely what Calhoun had hoped to avoid. Yet in some degree Calhoun had achieved the coalition of his old party with a significant number of unionists, and Rhett meanwhile saw his two chief rivals for Calhoun's favor, and a seat in the Senate, derailed. Late in the campaign Calhoun actually asked Hammond to withdraw for the sake of unity, and when Hammond refused he lost his standing in Calhoun's inner circle for a time.[42] Even Pickens eventually came to agree with Calhoun that the Richardson nomination was the right one, and in so doing he may have come to accept the wisdom of nominating the more moderate Lewis in his stead for the Speakership. Rhett managed to persuade Pickens that Elmore had no part in that affair, thus renewing the friendly relations between those two at least, and even suggested that if Hunter were elevated to the Senate from the Speakership—as he would be in a few years—then Rhett would use his influence to put Pickens in his place. It was cold comfort, even if believed. For the rest of their lives their relations never rose above a truce, and that was intermittent.[43]

It had all been very messy, but by late spring unity at home was well under way, and the prospects for an amalgamation of the state rights and Democratic parties in Washington looked promising. As for Rhett, with Pickens and

Hammond out of the way, he now took it for granted that when Preston or Cal-houn resigned, a seat in the Senate was his for the asking. There were even rumors that with Andrew Stevenson, minister to Great Britain, in poor health, Van Buren might reward Rhett for his support of the administration by giving him the ambassadorship. By June, Rhett felt so certain of the Senate seat that he wor-ried that family and financial affairs in South Carolina might actually force him to turn it down.[44]

Against such a backdrop the actual proceedings of the session of the House were anticlimactic, and the rigid parliamentarian's distraction showed when Rhett found himself called to order at least once for failure to follow House rules. On another occasion the Speaker fined him when the sergeant at arms had to bring him and others from Rhett's lodgings to the House so that there would be a quorum for a vote on the treasury bill that Rhett himself had been advocating. At least he finally saw the independent treasury legislation passed, but on the preeminent issue of revenue his repeated pleas on the floor for a direct tax met no response, and no one would lift a finger for an advance revision of the tariff in a presidential election year.[45] Of course Rhett did not stay out of the heat of debate. He brushed against the crusty Wise yet again and earned Adams's con-demnation during final debate on renewal of the national bank. Adams regarded his cousin as "a compound of wild democracy and iron-bound slavery com-bined with the feudal cramp of State sovereignty—the mongrel blood of doc-trinal nullification," and pronounced his fulminations absurd.[46]

Meanwhile there were financial problems at home, for as usual Rhett largely ignored his practice and rice plantations in his fever for politics. Without rec-ognizing the fact, he had also compromised his promise to Stapleton to look after the welfare of his slaves. Two years earlier he had finally sold some of the slaves he bought from Stapleton to his old mentor Grayson, and he passed the bonds that Grayson gave him on to Stapleton to relieve some of his own debt. He also sold another slave, one whom he found "turbulent," yet felt he honored his promise to be kindly toward his slaves by also selling the offender's mother and sisters along with him so that the family might be kept together. However, he did not realize enough to match the needed investment in improvement of the rice plantations, and in February 1840 he missed the next installment due to Stapleton. His solution was to propose paying just the interest and postpone paying the principal for two years, but even then he could not promise to meet all of the interest, making it all conditional upon his fall crop. Still Stapleton remained remarkably patient with Rhett, offering him almost fatherly advice on financial responsibility.[47] Rhett also missed a twenty-three-hundred-dollar install-ment on a loan from the Planters' and Mechanics' Bank of South Carolina that was due in July, and eight months later still had not made the payment. Just as bad, two years before he and Pickens and Calhoun had borrowed three thousand dollars from the Charleston Insurance and Trust Company to help support the *Washington Chronicle*, the Calhoun organ in the Capital, and now the payment on that, too, was long overdue.[48] What Rhett would not see, of course, was that just as his obsession with politics led him to ignore his plantations—as his father had done—that neglect led directly to his being forced to sell slaves into an uncertain future. Ultimately it was only by attending to his business that Rhett could be certain of honoring his pledge to Stapleton to be a humanitarian master, but as with everything else, politics and personal ambition claimed his first and greatest allegiance.

Only his family exerted a pull on him as great as that of public life. The absence of his sons "Barny," Edmund, and Alfred also told on Rhett, for he had left them staying at the Ashepoo plantation for schooling in nearby Beaufort. "It is a grievous thing to be separated," he confessed, even while chastising the boys for spending all their time living outdoors riding their horses and shooting rabbits and birds, and not enough at study. "Too much pleasure makes Boys stupid," he warned, showing a little streak of the puritan. Still the ever-indulgent father could rarely refuse them anything, and in the spring he gave in to their pleas to leave school for the Ashepoo plantation for a few days, even encouraging them to enjoy "some glorious egg-nog frolics" while there and enclosing a $2.50 gold piece under the seal on his letter to add to their fun.[49]

Even the relief of the end of the session on July 21 and his return home was blunted by his financial straits. He contemplated taking Elizabeth, once more pregnant, on a voyage to England to rearrange his affairs with Stapleton, though he decided against the trip, and he also toyed with converting some of his crops from rice to cotton, which was less rigorous for the slaves and commanded better prices than rice at that time.[50] Then there were the twin distractions of the gubernatorial campaign in the state and the presidential contest nationally. Even Calhoun could see that if Richardson won, it might come at the price of the unionists in the legislature, with his backing, giving the vacant senate seat to a more moderate man such as Daniel Huger, disappointing Rhett "& the whole host of nullifiers who have been designated for the office."[51] There is the possibility that this is what Calhoun foresaw all along, thus having used Rhett to keep Pickens and Hammond in their places and even indirectly through the Richardson nomination to prevent Rhett from rising too high too soon. Hammond actually expected that the machinations of Rhett and Richardson's supporters would offend legislators and cost Richardson votes when the time came, and was convinced that what many in what men were calling "Mr. Rhett's Party" were panicking when they approached Hammond and promised to support him for the governorship or a Senate seat in 1842 if he would back out now.[52] By August, Hammond believed that Elmore and Rhett had fallen out over the fact that Rhett would reap all the profits from their schemes, leaving none of the spoils for his associate. "They have I presume the common virtue of thieves and will not cheat each other," Hammond crowed in August. "I am greatly deceived if *their* schemes of self-aggrandisement do not turn to ashes and bitterness."[53]

Hammond was deceived, and badly, for in the end Richardson defeated him overwhelmingly. Yet he was not the only one disappointed. Calhoun had months before given up any idea of challenging the incumbent Van Buren for the presidency in November, for it would have ruined all that he and Rhett had done to try to create a new coalition based on Southern conservative principles. The president was entitled to seek a new term, and after all the support Calhoun had given him recently it would have cast him as a hypocrite to challenge the nomination. Besides, he could wait for 1844 when it would logically be his turn. Calhoun may just as well, however, have seen that in the depressed economic climate Van Buren and the Democrats were too weak to win, even with state rights support. This they got, with Rhett going on record saying that the new Democratic Party, "reformed" by its realignment toward state rights, offered the South's best hope for protection of its interests.[54]

In November the Whig candidate William Henry Harrison sent Van Buren back to New York. Of course Rhett had realized long since that Calhoun would not now be resigning his seat, but on top of the defeat in the polls there came word that Preston had changed his mind. With a Whig administration about to take power, his voice would be more useful in the Senate than before. He would not resign. The certain seat in the Senate, for some time now Rhett's greatest political ambition, virtually evaporated overnight. All the planning, all the scheming, and even the possible deceit and cross-purposes had come to nothing in the end. To cap his personal misfortunes, Elizabeth gave birth on October 13 to a daughter, Caroline, who only lived a day. Rhett swallowed his disappointment and his hurt, buried his daughter, and began to rebuild.[55]

EIGHT

We Are Something of *Lucifers*
1840–1843

AT LEAST RHETT WON REELECTION to his own House seat, but there was no challenge to him in his district. The short winter session in Congress produced nothing of interest or import, and after the personal and political losses of the past year Rhett simply may not have had the heart for a while to engage in debate. He remained unaccustomedly quiet and rose only to defend the administration's treasury note bill in what Adams described as a "senseless" speech, and he once again got into a brief exchange with Henry Wise, who this time taunted Rhett with proposing dissolution of the Union during the 1832 South Carolina nullification convention. This elicited from Rhett the declaration that neither he nor any other member of that body "ever proposed a dissolution of the Union, nor was any such proposition ever made or discussed in the convention." It was a hair-splitting response at best. Rhett may not have proposed actual secession at the time, but he suggested and backed measures designed to lead eventually to secession, and outside the convention his rhetoric was unmistakably that of disunion rather than acquiescence.[1]

In poor health and low spirits, he was anxious to get back to South Carolina. Barnwell saw the strain he was under, and it did not help that some of Rhett's companions even in the state's delegation were cool and uncommunicative with him after his recent actions. His cousin begged him to moderate his tone in debate, admitting his own ardor in the cause of South Carolina and nullification but still criticizing them both for allowing their often intemperate natures to overcome grace and decorum. "I regret very much that you are without a confidential religious friend surrounded as you are by cares & temptations," he had written Rhett late in January 1841. "Let some pious author of the old time be your companion & you will not feel the want of personal converse."[2] Worse, Rhett was unwell and had renewed fears for Elizabeth's health after the last season's fevers and her loss of Caroline. At the same time there came confirmation of what he had suspected for some time. From several sources he learned that his brother-in-law Stuart had become an alcoholic, neglecting his wife—Rhett's favorite sister, Claudia—and endangering the *Mercury*.[3]

He learned that his eleven-year-old son Alfred was being bullied in school, and that at last proved too much. Rhett was always an indulgent father, never severe with his children, but he required strict obedience to his wishes.[4] Despite a decade now of devout religion and the resolution he had formed never to engage in physical violence himself, he made it clear to his son that he expected him to fight his tormentor or make him apologize. Rhett was so upset in the matter that he did not tell Alfred directly but rather communicated his views through Elizabeth, directly penning but a single sentence to the boy. She quailed from telling her boy to fight, but his father expected it. Moreover, he made it clear that Alfred would not be allowed to come home at the end of his term unless he had fought, not for the sake of revenge, but to "clear yourself from the charge of dishonorable cowardice." She could only remind the boy of his father's motto, "perseverance will ensure success."[5] Having resorted to intemperate verbal violence all his public life, Rhett seemingly encouraged his sons to take the next logical step in escalation of their own affairs, though he quailed on presumed principle from doing so himself. In years to come the lesson would come back to torment them all tragically.

Rhett needed to practice his motto more himself where it applied to his private affairs, for when he got back to Beaufort and the plantations he found his finances in even greater disarray. Contrary to his expectations, his last rice crop was a poor one, and his monetary straits were compounded by his generosity, not only with his family but also toward outsiders. For example, he had been funding a profligate young man's education at South Carolina College, but that money would be wasted when the fellow later dropped out without graduating.[6] He fell even farther behind in his payments to Stapleton, and the patient Englishman began to stiffen. Rhett wrote to him in January, putting something of a gloss on the situation by claiming that in fact his recent crop had been a good one, then proposing yet another delayed repayment scheme. "This is all I can promise you," he said, then loaded his argument by saying that his only alternative would be to mortgage his remaining slaves to someone else to secure the debt. That, of course, was the last thing Stapleton wanted, since the kindly treatment and welfare of the slaves had been his principal concern in selling them to Rhett a decade earlier.

"I am not one of those who regard slaves, merely as property, to be sold at any time upon the principle of pecuniary loss or gain," Rhett said, and everything in his demeanor with those blacks bore out his declaration. Even when the market price rose in past years he refrained from selling, when he could have used the money badly. In buying them he had accepted responsibility for their spiritual and temporal welfare, and it was an obligation that he felt at heart. At considerable expense he built frame houses for the field hands on raised foundations to free them of damp and with cypress shingles to keep out the wind and rain. At yet more expense he paid a preacher to come and hold services for them on Sundays. They were settled on two plantations that Rhett had cleared and put under rice cultivation, erecting barns and other outbuildings, and one had been producing for some years now, while the other was almost ready to begin.

It would all be for naught if now he had to part with the blacks to pay the debt he owed for them and the plantations. Rhett laid the matter in Stapleton's hands with a shameless plea to sentiment and guilt. "Do you think it reasonable under these circumstances to expect me to sell these negroes," he asked, "scatter them abroad from their home and friends and relatives, and sacrifice all the labour I have expended on these lands, and the cost of settling these plantations?" He would do so if Stapleton insisted on payment now, but made it clear that "the loss will be mine, but the *responsibility* yours." With the same self-serving illogic that he used occasionally in political arguments, Rhett now somehow cast Stapleton in the role of villain as a result of what had been his own mismanagement and inattention. "This pushing of points with you, in affairs of interest, is very revolting to me," Rhett told him. There was nothing disingenuous in that, for whatever his faults, Barnwell Rhett always recoiled from sharp business practice, or indeed from discussing money at all, which was part of his problem. He had adopted the planter ethic that a gentleman should be above trifling with money and that it was unseemly to be concerned with finance, something to which only Yankee capitalists and monopolists resorted. Stapleton saw through Rhett's argument well enough and did not let him get away with it, but still the debt went unpaid and the slaves unsold. Indeed, by now the Englishman almost preferred to see them emancipated, and he regretted that he had not done so himself, for increasingly he saw the pall that slavery cast over America. He told Rhett that the institution was a curse on the Union. "It will be a long time, I fear, and occasion much distress before she can extricate herself," he predicted.[7]

Then came a bombshell. Rhett had not been home a month when word arrived from Washington that President Harrison was dead of pneumonia and Vice President John Tyler of Virginia would succeed him. Far more inclined toward the Southern state rights and nullification camp, and like his fellow Virginian Robert M. T. Hunter a Democrat in almost all but name, Tyler found himself saddled with a cabinet dominated by Henry Clay supporters. His first inclination was to replace the lot, and revealing his true sympathies he turned to Calhoun. In an incredible surrender of executive prerogative, he offered Calhoun the portfolio as secretary of state and then carte blanche to fill the rest of the cabinet posts as he saw fit. In one stroke a Whig victory would be over-turned, leaving the Democrats and Calhoun forces in almost full control of the executive branch of the government. It seemed too good to be true, and yet it was. Calhoun never made a move without careful calculation, however, and he asked Rhett and Hunter and perhaps others their views of what he should do. Rhett and Hunter agreed that he should accept, but in the end Calhoun decided oth-erwise. Tyler had been elected by the Whigs. If Calhoun associated himself in such a prominent way with him, then he would be assuming responsibility for an administration that was still basically Whig. If it failed or betrayed state rights principles, then he would inevitably share the odium, and that could ruin his chances for a presidential run in 1844, which was now his settled intent. Rhett thought Calhoun was making one of the greatest mistakes of his career, assum-ing like so many others that Tyler would be a mere caretaker and that the sec-retary of state's portfolio would lead inevitably to the Executive Mansion, but Calhoun was not to be moved.[8]

Calhoun's refusal only highlighted another effort, however, one that had been under way since the election. In December 1840 Calhoun met with Rhett and Pickens individually and persuaded them to meet with each other independ-ently to make peace. The great man needed his subordinates to stop feuding with each other—in the House, Pickens had referred contemptuously to Rhett as being factious and a "disappointed politician"—so that they could start work-ing to put him in place for a run in 1844, and Rhett and Pickens both fell in line. Each was no doubt encouraged by renewed hopes for Calhoun's Senate seat, should he be elected. It was common knowledge that spring that Rhett's imme-diate Senate hopes were dead, yet always willing to risk a short-term liaison with someone distasteful when a long-term gain beckoned, he apparently made the first overture, and Pickens acquiesced. With peace in their own house Calhoun and his lieutenants could turn their sights on that other house on Pennsylvania Avenue, and Rhett still continued his close relations with the new governor Richardson, advising him on appointments, and all the while trying to maintain the hold on the state. Robert Barnwell, meanwhile, tired of seeing South Caro-lina perpetually in turmoil and hostage to Calhoun's ambition, confessed to Rhett that he wished they could find someone better as a presidential candidate.[9]

Thus Rhett was once more planning for the future when the first session of the Twenty-seventh Congress sat on May 31, 1841, in an atmosphere of uncer-tainty over the direction of the new administration. This time Rhett brought most of his family with him to a rented house in Georgetown, feeling it to be the only way he could meet his obligation to educate his sons and still attend to public business. He had seen the effect long absences from home had on the children of other congressmen and had experienced some problems himself, and thus he determined that he could only fulfill his duties as a parent and as a legislator by having his family with him. His ideas on his obligation as a father were strong, and fixed. "If your service, and parental duty conflict," he said, "it is plain, the former must yield to the latter." He either had to leave Congress—another reason he had feared he might not be able to accept the now-evaporated Senate seat—or move his family to Washington, though it was expensive and stretched his already flimsy finances.[10] He thought of sending Robert Jr. and Alfred to Georgetown University, but Barnwell and others persuaded him against exposing them to the "soul destroying influence" of a Roman Catholic school. Instead he enrolled them in the Georgetown Classical and Mathematical Academy. Their mother, incredibly, was pregnant yet again, and this time Rhett would be certain to be with her when her time came due in December.[11]

Rhett commenced the session with a personal distrust of Tyler. He predicted to Petigru that the new president would not get along with the Whigs but hesitate to come across the line entirely to the Democrats either, while his cousin Barnwell advised—erroneously as it happened—that Tyler would become Henry Clay's puppet.[12] Clay did have a secure hold on the Whigs in both the House and the Senate, however, and it was apparent that they were going to have their own way unless Tyler used his veto. Rhett expected the national bank to be renewed once more and Van Buren's independent treasury to be scrapped, while the prospects for reformation in the next year's tariff seemed bleak now. All he could do was outline for himself what he hoped could be accomplished in 1842. The South would want protection for cotton, sugar, tobacco, and Virginia's coal, while other regions would want their wool and manufactured goods covered. Those mutual wants just might lead to a give-and-take that would end in an adjustment of rates beneficial to all, while still continuing the general downward trend of duty. Accepting that protection did at least buy domestic arts and industry the time to gain sufficient market strength to fairly combat imports, he expected that all across the Union in 1842 there would still be assent to continuation of protection on at least a few articles still in need.[13] Of course it all depended on how determined the ascendant Whigs would be to have their own way.

With the Whigs in power in the House and a new Speaker handing out committee assignments, Rhett lost his coveted seat on the Ways and Means Committee and was assigned instead to the Foreign Affairs Committee and the Committee on Currency, both chaired by his foe Adams. Still the Carolinian entered into the fray with all the old vigor seemingly renewed. Within two weeks of the first gavel he was already in the thick of action over an attempt to renew the gag rule on abolition petitions, this time trying to get it settled not just for that session but for the term of this Congress. Far more important, however, was the tariff question, and Rhett did not wait long to start the debate. Again he proposed his direct tax alternative, prompting one man to compliment him as the only person in Congress daring enough to advocate such a revolutionary measure, and Rhett confessed that he was its only Southern advocate. The seemingly sectional implications of a direct land tax, which naturally would fall harder on the North than the South since there were many more Northern landowners, even involved him briefly in a polite exchange with the great Daniel Webster, to whom Rhett denied that he would seek "as a legislator of the whole Union, the oppression of any section of it."[14]

From the start he made it clear that he wanted the tariff issue faced squarely and not avoided, as some preferred. He was for debating it day after day for the entire session if need be, though he predicted that the Whigs would evade the issue. Worse, early in July the Whig majority amended the customary House rules requiring a two-thirds majority to suspend the rules, so that a simple majority— which is what they had—could move the House into and out of committee of the whole, and proceeded to use the device to close off debate at will. On July 6, Rhett characterized it as a new gag rule, and an uproar broke out in the House when it was used to cut him off in the middle of what Adams called a "nullification trumpeting." Almost at once Rhett became identified as the champion of a new and downtrodden Democratic minority, a role that he could use effectively given the opportunity.[15]

Two days later he was back on his feet when Pickens sparred intemperately with the Whigs over a loan bill in a debate that quickly degenerated into North versus South and accusations of disunionism. Rhett declared that he was not one of those who thought the Union was destined to be dissolved, but he then went on to make it clear that his conviction did not grow out of a feeling that it *should not,* but that the history of confederacies showed him that rather than breaking up, they inevitably grew more and more centralized and despotic. Disunion held no terrors for him and never had, and there would be no fear of it for them so long as Congress observed the Constitution. The patriotism and common sense of the people could ensure that, so long as the growing agitation over slavery and the continuing injustice of the tariff and protection did not fatally pit North and South against each other. The sections were not naturally antagonistic; it was only their politicians who sought to make them so. He seemed surprisingly moderate, even Adams commenting that his cousin spoke "in a tone much subdued from that of his usual swaggering."[16] Rhett also took time to comment on a current diplomatic eruption with England that had some talking of war, though he certainly never thought it would come to that nor that it should. But when Whigs asked for a loan to bolster defense, the U.S. Treasury being inadequate just then, he was quick to charge them with irresponsibility when only weeks earlier they had appropriated millions from the Treasury to distribute to the states for improvements.[17]

He continued his drive at Whig fiscal policy from his perch on the Commerce Committee, chiefly by opposing a majority resolution to appoint a subcommittee to investigate the current operation of the tariff, with a view to making recommendations for its revision in 1842. He distrusted the composition of the proposed group, more so since he now had in his hands resolutions passed in recent years by the legislatures of Rhode Island and Massachusetts that opposed any reduction of the tariff in spite of the 1833 compromise, even underlining the passages that most outraged him. Since the investigating committee would be appointed by the Whig chairman, Adams, Rhett anticipated that its findings would be skewed against the South and that its recommendations would abrogate the obligations of the compromise. The Constitution was a bargain between the states, and protective tariffs violated that pact, he declared. Now would the Whigs break yet another bargain by ignoring the explicit provisions for reduction in the 1833 agreement? "Do you expect us to trust you after breaking two bargains solemnly made?" he asked. He returned, as he now did again and again, to what had become a mantra. He asked for nothing more than the Constitution, but he would accept nothing less. If that cast him as an extremist, so be it. In passing, he more than once returned to his own preference for direct taxation, though he confessed that he did not expect it would come in his lifetime unless the country was at war. Chairman Adams concluded that Rhett and one or two others on his committee were as dangerous as eels. "Hold them by the tail if you can," he advised.[18]

Through it all Rhett did in fact rein back his usual vehement rhetoric, for Calhoun's program of conciliation with the union men in South Carolina and in the broad Democratic Party was still in effect. If Rhett could not in conscience simply adopt the tone of those unionists who were still sympathetic to a strict construction of the Constitution, nevertheless he sailed close to their wind. To make his points in more restrained fashion he even tried the—for him—new tactic of asking to be excused from voting on an objectionable fiscal bill for which the new Whig gag restricted debate. Though the majority denied his request, still he saw read into the record his enumeration of reasons for not wishing to vote, which comprised essentially all of the points that he would have made in a normal extended speech in debate. Cleverly he thus got around the gag by not seeking to speak directly against the bill.[19]

Not a few reminded Rhett of his seeming hypocrisy in complaining about the Whig gag rule when he had himself been one of the principle authors of the old 21st Rule. His response, of course, was that whereas abolition was a subject that Congress constitutionally had no power to consider or act upon, the Whig gag was a parliamentary device that interfered with debate on a number of topics whose constitutionality no one challenged. On the latter point at least he was certainly right, but it was small comfort. Increasingly he found that the speeches he did make were inaccurately reported in the *Congressional Globe*, and he probably suspected the Whig reporters of interfering with his remarks.[20] Rhett would always be sensitive to the right of the people to see what their elected men were saying, as much so they could judge for themselves how they was being represented as to make certain that Rhett himself got credit for his efforts. The gag was making that impossible, and toward the end of the session he decided to take his case to the people in a series of three open letters rather daringly addressed to the leading Whig organ in the capital, the *National Intelligencer.*

He attacked the gag as being an assault upon the rules of the House and upon the minority, whom he maintained that rules were originally established to protect from the majority. The Whigs were using the gag to attack the independent treasury bill and other measures not on constitutional grounds but for partisan purposes. During one debate not a single Democrat was able to obtain the floor. Not even in discussing the tariff could they be heard, which thus effectively removed from the people themselves the right to be heard through their representatives on the means and manner of their taxation. "Tyranny, in the shape of a majority, is erected in the Capitol," he declared. Silencing a minority in a democracy meant essentially the end of liberty. "The new reign of terror is begun." Of course he could not stay away from violent images; he complained, "It were easier to have deluged the Hall of Representatives in blood, than to have submitted to this imposition." Yet the Democrats—and throughout these letters he spoke only of Democrats when he mentioned the minority—determined to submit, leaving it to the people at large to recoil in disgust and take action with their ballots. What he did not say was that he was doing exactly the same thing Adams and the abolitionists had done for years, turning a gag rule to his advantage by howling loudly about it and taking every opportunity to generate publicity, just as Rhett was doing now. Even without the gag the Whig majority in Congress this term made it impossible for the Democrats and state rights men to defeat their program with or without chicanery in the House rules, but the gag allowed Rhett and the opposition to elevate their position on partisan issues to a seemingly higher constitutional plain.

While maintaining the injustice of the change in House rules, Rhett also returned repeatedly to a broader and older theme, the inherent tyranny of majority rule. It was the old Calhoun doctrine, and even here in his protest at the gag he combined a defense of the rights of the Democratic minority with renewed assertion of the state rights viewpoint toward which he had been trying with some success to persuade the party for some time. Given that for the first time in twelve years the Democrats were the minority now, the Calhoun position took on a new attraction it previously lacked, lending added weight to Rhett's protest. "The majority have shown the people, by their use of their power, how worthy they are of possessing it," he declared. The Democrats had submitted long enough. Now it was time for the people to react, ostensibly by the ballot box as special elections occurred and in preparing for the congressional election the following year. He warned that there might even be violence in the House in the future, though he added that "liberty has ever been the result of conflict."[21]

Rhett was wise enough not to expect the *National Intelligencer* to publish an attack on its own party, and indeed he probably counted all along on its refusal to print them, as refuse it did. This only added more weight to his argument against Whig censorship. As he wrote each letter, one a week, he sent copies to the editors of the Democratic *Washington Globe,* and to the *Mercury* at home, along with full particulars of the refusal of the *National Intelligencer.*[22] At the same time the *Globe* editors compiled them into a pamphlet that they printed and distributed widely in Democratic circles. The letters attracted considerable notice, much of it from conservative Northern Democrats who did not overlook that a state rights and Calhoun man was standing up for them. Across the Capitol, Sen. James Buchanan of Pennsylvania spoke of Rhett's letters on the floor in debate, declaring, "This question soars far above all mere party distinctions." With Rhett's able letter in his hand, he believed that he could enter any district in the land and obtain a condemnation of the gag.[23]

Granted the temporarily helpless condition of the Calhoun-Democratic forces, Rhett had done good work. Before the end of the session Rhett met with Calhoun and Pickens to plan their next moves. Rhett was to make a brief visit back to South Carolina, and Calhoun wanted him to see to some reorganization among their forces in the state and adopt a policy of remaining quiet for the next year or two in order not to frighten other Southern states away from a possible combination of the state rights and Democratic forces behind Calhoun in 1844.[24] Rhett fully shared his views. State rights men needed to rally behind a man who shared their principles fully, and Calhoun had to be the man for 1844. They could bide their time until then. "Let us prepare and wait," Rhett agreed. At this meeting Calhoun may also have suggested that he might resign his Senate seat in 1842 in order to concentrate on his presidential run, or Rhett may have presented the suggestion to him. In either case, it was an idea that Rhett would find intriguing, for his own purposes.[25]

Rhett had several things to do during his brief trip south. Not surprisingly, one of the first was an address to his constituents. It lacked much of the vigor and fire of his earlier efforts, but that was in keeping with the plan not to excite passions more than could be helped. He warned them that though Tyler had successfully vetoed a renewal of the national bank twice, they should expect years of redoubled Whig efforts, as well as an attack upon the presidential veto power itself, as the Whig majority in Congress sought to overrule its unruly president. Then, too, they had better be prepared for battle over formulating the new tariff now imminently due, and also a renewal of unconstitutional raids upon the Treasury in the guise of internal improvements. The Whigs were recklessly spending far more than the Treasury was taking in, which left only the alternatives of loans or abandonment of the 1833 compromise and continuation of high protective rates. He could point out the huge expenditure on fortifications as an example of fiscal irresponsibility, for with white settlement moving ever westward stationary forts could hardly move with the frontier and would be left behind, obsolete. He even foretold that advances in naval technology were making their seacoast fortifications useless, yet congressmen vied for appropriations to be spent in their states on useless defenses that created jobs and temporary prosperity. Their only salvation from such fiscal irresponsibility—not to say tyranny—lay with the people themselves. He denounced even a distribution act to allocate money from the sale of public lands to the several states. It was neither the government's to give nor theirs to take, and he promised to fight for its repeal.[26]

In the short time remaining to him before returning for the start of the next session on December 6, Rhett met with Elmore and his other associates, including Stuart, with whom personal relations would be somewhat strained now. He told them of the conference with Calhoun and what was expected, and also expressed some concern over the wavering loyalty of some of his followers during the recent gubernatorial campaign. It became clear that he did, indeed, intend to back Hammond for the office in 1842, pursuing a policy of alternating governors between the unionists and state rights parties. Unfortunately, some of the former balked at swallowing Hammond, and Rhett feared that he might not be able to manage them.[27] He also tried to mollify state rights men such as Andrew P. Butler, whose personal hostility to Calhoun had led him to oppose Richardson, which had led in turn to a brief break in Butler and Rhett's personal friendship of many years. Rhett even heard a new rumor suggesting that Preston might be appointed ambassador to France, making his seat potentially available before long after all. Even as Rhett put out feelers for his own support again, he learned that his old friend and sometime rival Huger was also interested.[28]

There was not time to do more before he had to return to Washington. Rhett arrived to find a small family crisis when his son Edmund's school report charged him with pulling other students' hair when the instructor's back was turned and, more appropriately for a Rhett, talking too much in class. Of far greater moment, however, Elizabeth, who had stayed behind in Georgetown to avoid the fever season in South Carolina, safely gave birth to a healthy baby girl named Elise on December 2, bringing the number of Rhett children to seven.[29] The distraction made him miss an opening meeting of the Foreign Affairs Committee on which he sat, but he was on the spot when the tariff debate commenced a few days later.[30]

On December 22 he rose repeatedly on the floor and delivered one of his longest House speeches to date, more than ten thousand words that he must have rushed to finish within the one-hour limitation. It contained all the old arguments against protection, and added to them he limned the tariff as an issue of class, for the duties were most applied on the articles predominantly bought by the working classes who could least afford them, making the indirect tax especially inequitable. In closing he even introduced the subject of the collision between free labor and slavery, though he denied that such an issue existed or could exist. "If it is true that the interests of the North and the interests of the South are incompatible under our form of government, then the Union not only will, but ought to fall; and if it is not true, it can only be an appeal to prejudices, to sustain a cause whose rottenness can find no support in truth," he stated. As he saw it, the protective policy naturally pitted one section against another, and this growing agitation over slavery was one of its natural manifestations as it sought other congenial issues to achieve its fell purpose.

"Nothing keeps the Union together but an abiding sense of a common and reciprocal interest," he argued. Raising the issue of slavery only told the North that it must prosper by destroying the South and warned the South that slavery was the real target behind the protectionist legions. "How long will the Union last?" he asked, when this was the message his opponents sent broadcast. The doctrine of equal rights was the doctrine of free trade, he argued, and free trade was the doctrine of Christianity, which was itself the doctrine of peace. Standing them one behind the other like dominoes, he implied that the fall of one would bring down all the rest, and with them freedom. If the South ever abandoned the Union, he said, "it will be because the Union will be incompatible with liberty." Darker still, in returning to his earlier dire predictions, he warned that in such a calamity, "war must come, and with it oceans of blood."[31]

Rhett kept his temper on the floor these days and adjusted his approach to the extent of ceasing to use disunion and violence as an overt threat. However, he used them all the same, only now as predictions of consequences to be deplored but still inevitable if the majority persisted on its course. Occasionally he lost his composure, as in April when, according to Adams, "in hatred of internal industry," Rhett "blazed out for free trade and the rights of the citizen."[32] For the next several months, however, he lowered his profile in the House, though once he sparred with Adams when Rhett was apparently a part of a Democratic movement to shift power on several House committees to chairmen more sympathetic to the Southern viewpoint. Adams himself introduced a Georgia petition that he be removed as chairman, which allowed him under the rules to defend himself. He made his defense an occasion to attack slaveholders for their efforts to force Texas into the Union as a slave state, and when that led to motions of censure, his continuing defense of himself became only more excoriation of the South. Then Adams introduced a petition from a Massachusetts community for a dissolution of the Union, a thinly disguised satire on Southern complaints, by arguing that too much tax money from the free states was being spent to support the South. Rhett and other state rights men did not see the joke—he would never show much of a sense of humor when he was the object of the jest—and he began trying to oust Adams from the chairmanship. Adams saw what was happening and brought it out on the House floor, forcing Rhett to admit his tampering. In characteristic fashion, Rhett did so by asserting his conviction that Old Man Eloquent was unfit for the post, a jibe that Adams accepted by ignoring it, though privately he wrote of Rhett being "insidious" and utterly untrustworthy. Unable to depose Adams, Rhett asked to be taken off the Foreign Affairs Committee.[33]

There were other affairs to occupy Rhett's attention that spring. On a small scale the new baby, Elise, needed a crib and mattress. On a larger scale, his family's medical bills for babies and repeated illnesses had risen to $540, all of it yet unpaid. He still had not paid Stapleton, who finally agreed to a further extension on the installment overdue. In South Carolina it was rumored that Rhett's debts to creditors and banks amounted now to well over $70,000 on which he could not even pay the interest, with a $3,000 payment to Stapleton alone now due. Soon there would be stories that he was on the verge of bankruptcy.[34] A friend on whose mortgage he had signed as surety was about to default, which would only add to his debts, and he was borrowing now from a bank in Georgetown too, just to get living money while awaiting the next crop. In addition friends he had helped in years before were not forthcoming now when he was in great need. The ingratitude of some offended his closest friends, but Rhett simply responded that kind acts should not look for their reward in this life.[35] When finally his sister Claudia left Stuart and took their children with her, he gave her his hearty approval, saying that the preservation of the youngsters' morals and souls was of transcendent importance to their being raised by a father who was a drunkard. Opposed as he was to divorce, which was all but impossible in South Carolina, he told her to resign herself to spending the rest of her life separated and alone, and he briefly left Washington in late spring to visit with her in Charleston and help her settle on her own.[36]

His own home in Georgetown in the District of Columbia—with his debts, teeming children, and all—proved a haven that he treasured from "yon dark dome, where burns contentious fire," as he called the Capitol. Every night he left the House almost joyfully as he mounted his horse and pointed it toward Elizabeth and the children, fixing his eyes on the growing steeple of Christ Church as he got closer. To him that spire was an

> Emblem of peace, of bliss without alloy!
> I come where kind affection spreads her bowers
> And heart to heart, can tell its silent joy,
> And childrens smiles, renew my wasted powers[37]

Friends and foes alike would have been shocked to find Rhett writing verses, and his brother Albert was equally amazed that anyone could read "the Harum-scarum" scrawl of Rhett's calligraphy.[38] Yet no one who ever knew Barnwell Rhett could doubt that his greatest living happiness, his solace in trial and the only true release for the softer emotions that a man as contained as he kept restrained, were the smiles of those children and the heart of their mother, his first and always his greatest love. Few of men's shortcomings earned greater condemnation from him than being an abusive or inattentive husband and father. "The slaveries, the corruptions, the cruelties which are daily practised in the parental and connubial relations, cry aloud to heaven—and to heaven alone—for vengeance," he would say. Home, he said, afforded "all those tender affections and charities which create all of happiness we can hope for in life."[39]

Elizabeth's only rivals, of course, were politics and her husband's ambitions, and both occupied most of his attention during the otherwise dull session. During that visit to Charleston he spoke again with his brothers and the Elmores and the rest of the machine, and he reported to Calhoun in May that everything seemed under control. Certainly the pliant Governor Richardson was well in hand. "I must depend on some one to *think* for me on matters not pertaining to Office," he told Rhett, "and there is no one I am sure that I would sooner depend on than yourself."[40] Elsewhere in the clique, Rhett thought that Elmore had a good chance of being put in public office again, while his own brother Albert was ready to seek brother Barnwell's seat in Congress if Preston did indeed resign and Rhett could garner his Senate desk. Just to be safe, however, Rhett let it be known that he would be seeking reelection all the same, even as signs multiplied that Preston might soon create a vacancy. Heeding the signs, Rhett avoided any contact with Preston, the more to distance himself. Once again the clique seemed on its way to even greater power in the state and in Congress.[41]

There was the session to finish first, however, and inevitably it became heated when finally they dealt with the tariff. Tyler had already earned the opprobrium of the Whig majority in Congress with his numerous vetoes of party legislation, and back in February, Henry Clay had introduced a bill to make legislation virtually veto-proof by a constitutional amendment allowing a simple majority to override. Though that failed thanks to Calhoun, now when Tyler vetoed a first tariff bill in June because it included the odious disbursement of public lands proceeds to the states, the Whigs rose up in indignation, accusing him of collusion with the Democrats. On July 1, Rhett stood to defend Tyler from charges of tyranny by veto and accused the Whigs of starting just one more battle in their war on the Constitution. In terms almost as glowing as those he had applied earlier to Van Buren when he was in office, Rhett called Tyler "the pride of his country," even though he asserted that personally he had never been a follower of Tyler and had scarcely more than met the president. Moreover Tyler was "a Virginian—a name never coupled with dishonor." That would play well in the Old Dominion, where men such as Hunter could wield large influence for Calhoun.

In a much more extended speech on July 1, Rhett expanded on the veto power in one of his finest speeches yet, making it at the same time a defense of the Democratic Party for its firmness and uniformity. He laid out the sordid history of the antecedents of current Whig bargaining as he saw it, all the way back to 1824, and defended Tyler even more warmly than before. He challenged the Whigs that their attempts to subvert the Constitution in the end would fail. If nothing else, the people of his own district, at least, had not forgotten the lesson of the Revolution. He did not have to say what that lesson was; he had said it often enough before.[42]

It was an approach suited ideally to his purpose and to Calhoun's. He had supported Tyler not as a Whig but as an embattled president defending the Constitution, and on principles rather than partisanship. At the same time he spoke not for the state rights faction but repeatedly in defense of the Democratic Party, leaving it implicit that he saw them on the same side of the issue here and united in all but open declaration. The fact is, the Whigs had achieved in their war with their own president the culmination of Calhoun and Rhett's campaign of the last two years by helping shape the state rights and Democratic positions, stances in which each could make common cause with the other. That was the sort of unity that could retake the Executive Mansion for them in 1844, especially behind a Calhoun candidacy. When word of Rhett's July 1 speech reached South Carolina, it won wide compliments, his sister Claudia hoping that he had the wisdom not to let all the praise addle him with vanity. Even Henry Wise, often at odds with Rhett, so admired his defense of Tyler that he said, "it ought to be printed in letters of gold and hung up in the White House."[43]

Throughout July, Congress worked on another tariff bill, but Rhett did not much enter the fight other than to protest one of the clauses on cotton manufactures stating that any item valued at between six and twenty cents ought to be taxed on the basis of twenty, part of a general policy of minimums that seemed to lay the heaviest percentage duties on the cheapest items. He still protested the overall bill, of course, maintaining that the country would never submit to the hurriedly assembled patchwork that generally stopped the downward trend toward 20 percent maximums under the 1833 compromise and revised them upward toward 30 percent instead.[44] But he knew that the Whigs had the votes to pass it, and with the disbursement measure removed, Tyler would not veto this time. Just days before the close of the session in late August the revised bill was finished, and though no one seemed pleased with it, Tyler signed. Significantly, it had passed with the support of some of the Van Buren Democrats in the North. This, to Calhoun, signaled that with Southern state rights men and the conservative bulk of the Democratic Party now welded together, Van Buren had no hope of carrying the South in 1844, and thus the Democrats would need to turn to someone untainted by the new tariff who could. In short, the tariff looked sure to be a pyrrhic victory for the Whigs, a battle won in a war they would lose two years hence.[45]

Apparently Rhett agreed, though smarting at one more betrayal by the Northern money interests. In fact, years later his son Robert Jr. would maintain that it was this treachery in 1842 that finally made Rhett a confirmed secessionist.[46] He was wrong. Rhett had been a secessionist in principle for years, no doubt for some time even before that first Colleton speech when he brought it out in public, but always he had advocated secession as a remedy to a problem rather than as a desirable end in itself. This new tariff simply pushed him farther toward that invisible line between the two, although not over it, not yet, for it was a defeat that could be turned around completely with a Calhoun and Democratic victory in 1844, and now more than ever that was to be his goal.

Of course there were a few who thought the response to the new tariff ought to be renewed nullification, but Calhoun discouraged them, and Rhett agreed, counseling people to postpone any nullification talk and concentrate instead on the presidential contest. Prophetically his cousin Barnwell warned him that if they did so and Calhoun was defeated, then any subsequent state action would appear to be out of spite and resentment rather than principled policy. Yet the fact was that at the moment even most of the old nullifiers of 1832 were not prepared to act, making Rhett and Calhoun's more prudent course the only one immediately available.[47]

Rhett devoted almost the entire recess to organization for Calhoun and monitoring the mood in South Carolina and the nation. He returned to his pen, writing articles for the *Globe* denouncing the Whig tariff and Henry Clay, the certain Whig candidate in 1844. At the same time Rhett encouraged the friends of Hunter of Virginia to nudge their man toward Calhoun, and in September he went to New York to meet with Northern supporters and encourage them to come out more in the open. He came away convinced that Calhoun's strength was growing with the Northern Democracy while Van Buren's waned, suggesting even that Old Kinderhook would pull out of the race before the Democratic convention. Soon it appeared that Tammany Hall would go for Calhoun, that Pennsylvania's Democrats were favorably disposed, and that even the party in New England could fall in line. Adding to this the assumption that Calhoun would carry the South and split the northwestern states, he advised his candidate-in-waiting that "our prospects are bright and growing brighter."[48]

Rhett's own prospects looked brighter as well. At the close of the session in August, Calhoun had told him that he had decided to resign his seat at the end of the current Congress in March 1843. At the time Rhett advised him against such a move, thinking that no public questions were likely to arise that posed a conflict of interest for him as a sitting senator and a presidential candidate. Now, however, he anticipated that an 1834 Senate resolution expunging an 1832 censure of Andrew Jackson would soon come to vote to be rescinded. The Whigs would vote to rescind, thus restoring the censure, while the Democrats would oppose them. If Calhoun voted with the Democrats, he would be reversing his own highly public former support of the censure, but to remain consistent with his earlier views he would have to vote with the Whigs. Either way he lost, forfeiting Democratic support by one vote and the still largely anti-Jackson Southern Whigs by the other. "Your prospects for the Presidency will utterly expire under the question," Rhett warned him. "It is impolitic, and will probably be fatal, for you to expose yourself." Rhett overstated the importance of the Jackson issue, if it ever even got to the Senate floor, but once having gotten a strategic issue or problem in his mind he usually magnified its meaning, subconsciously enlarging himself in the offing. He admitted that Calhoun's other advisers might have greater wisdom in general matters yet told him frankly that "without disparaging them, or exalting myself, I think I may assert, that with one half their sagacity I may be a far better judge of the effect of political questions, and the temper of the People of the Union." He felt that Calhoun definitely should resign. "Act how you may, I will strive to support you," he said, "and where I cannot commend, I will try not to blame."[49]

If Calhoun found Rhett getting just a bit above himself, he said nothing, but he made his own decision in any case, basing it not on the Jackson censure business but rather on the accepted convention that it was best not to be currently in office, nor even to be perceived as seeking office, when a presidential nomination was proffered. Henry Clay would also resign his seat in the Senate, and on that basis Calhoun determined to do the same, but not until the following March. That meant that there would be at least one South Carolina seat open, and if Calhoun did not actually tell Rhett he would support him for the post, certainly many widely assumed that such was Calhoun's wish.

Thus Rhett decided that he would not seek reelection to his House seat. There had been a recent reapportionment in South Carolina, as a result of which the ordinary fall election was postponed until January 1843, and Rhett's old constituency of Beaufort and Colleton had been combined with Orangeburg and Barnwell. Moreover, the incumbent from the other district, Samuel Trotti, had just been appointed to replace a resigned predecessor and did not feel like standing aside before he had even taken a seat in the House. As a result, for the first time there would be a serious contest, but Albert Rhett seemed more than up to the challenge. Indeed, it was time for a shift in the Rhett power holdings in keeping with their rising public fortunes, and their aspirations. With Rhett going to the Senate and Albert taking his brother's seat in Congress, they also planned now to elect James Rhett to the congressional seat from Charleston, and brother Edmund would leave the Charleston practice for the legislature to assume Albert's leadership role in Columbia.

The Rhetts were reaching farther than ever before, and beyond their grasp as it happened, for they reckoned without the substantial store of resentment that their increasingly high-handed attitudes had produced. They were all quick tempered, and all except James impressed people as high-handed and arrogant, Barnwell and Albert most of all. Their very clannishness offended, for they seemingly looked out for each other in everything, attracting accusations of selfishness and rank dynastism—some called them "The Regency." Albert told brother Robert that summer that they resembled matchsticks bundled together. "We are something of *Lucifers*—dipped one end in Sulphur, and extremely apt, if any one or two ignite," he said, "the whole to flame up in sympathetic conflagration."[50] When Albert, described as a "pestilent demagogue" by at least one opponent, commenced running for reelection to his legislature seat that fall, he became quickly aware of just how extensive was the resentment against them.[51] "*Down with the Rhetts,*" he heard people cry. At one of his earliest appearances in August he found his opponents concocting stories against him. "Everything known or remembered, and a great deal more neither known nor remembered, not only against myself, but the whole Rhett blood, was brought up in judgment against me," he complained. "Professional rivalry—Social jealousy—personal envy— political rancour—all threw in their devilish ingredients to fill the boiling cauldron." During Edmund's stump campaign Richard deTreville, never a friend of the family despite having been a childhood playmate of Robert at Beaufort, said something insulting. The hotheaded Edmund leaped up to demand an explanation from deTreville until Memminger and Barnwell Rhett, who was present, pulled him back to his seat.[52]

That was only a prelude to what awaited Barnwell Rhett. Albert and Edmund won their seats in the legislature, and Calhoun announced on November 26 that he would resign at the end of the next session. Two days later the *Mercury* raised his name to its editorial banner and supported him for the presidency. The day after Calhoun's resignation William Campbell Preston also finally resigned, making both seats available. Filling them depended on the legislature, and it quickly became evident that the Rhetts' control there was seriously threatened. When it convened in Columbia, Calhoun was easily nominated for consideration by the coming Democratic convention, and the promise to back Hammond for the governorship was redeemed successfully on December 8. But only four votes decided the issue, and many attributed the closeness of the race to the open anti-Rhett sentiment and Hammond as the Rhett clique's candidate.[53]

That brought them to filling Calhoun's and Preston's seats, and immediately it all went wrong. Calhoun's own support for Rhett, to the extent that it ever existed, may have been eroded by a resurgence of the feud with Pickens, who warned his cousin that Rhett was virtually bankrupt and would do anything to win office, as he was dependent on his salary for support. He might be energetic but was now "*entirely* selfish" and not to be trusted.[54] Of course, Pickens coveted the office again, as did William R. Davie and Daniel Huger, and Calhoun had experience enough in the past of the conflicting ambitions of his subordinates to see beneath the surface. What support he promised, if he ever promised any, he may well have quietly directed away from Rhett and Pickens.[55]

Rhett spent early November in Charleston with Stuart writing a sketch of the life of Calhoun for the *Mercury* to run after making the nomination, but he had intended to go on to Columbia before returning to Washington, in order to be on the scene to impress the legislature with his standing as Calhoun's anointed successor and pull whatever strings were necessary.[56] In any event, he changed his mind, and perhaps it was just as well that he did not see firsthand the animosity he and his brothers had garnered. It started when the *Mercury,* which everyone knew spoke for Rhett even if he did not own it, smeared his friend Andrew P. Butler for his unionism and "anti-Calhounism." Preston and others saw another motive for the attack, however, "no other provocation than a rumor that he might be a candidate for the Senate in Calhoun's place, for which Rhett was designed." The assault was "indecent and savage," and though unjust, it effectively ruined Butler as a candidate.[57] More to the point, though, the blatantly self-serving attack outraged all but the most ardent state rights and Calhoun-Rhett supporters in the legislature, who were fed up with the Rhett-Elmore machine's behavior. Even Robert Barnwell believed that it hurt Rhett's support.[58] This also worked against Hammond in his run, and now when the Senate elections came up, all that resentment was directed at Rhett.[59]

When Calhoun's letter of resignation was announced by state senator Ker Boyce, to whom it had been addressed, Boyce kept the actual letter in his pocket, hoping that by not showing it he might prevent the resignation being accepted or, if it were, that any expression of support from Calhoun for Rhett would be unknown and Pickens might then get the place instead. Ignorant of the letter's content, Rhett's opponents and even some supporters on the floor interpreted it to suggest that Rhett himself was responsible for the action—and indeed he had counseled it—inducing Calhoun to resign in order that Rhett could succeed him. The accusation took fire, and soon it was generally bandied about that he had acted in the most blatant self-serving manner and in the offing helped to remove South Carolina's most distinguished son from a high position of influence. Stuart thought that Rhett should have been in Columbia in person to counter such accusations, enlisting Richardson's aid, and moreover that he ought to have asked Calhoun to write letters of support to influential legislators. That done, "your success was certain," he thought.[60]

What happened instead was that Preston's seat went to George McDuffie, and when Calhoun's successor came up for consideration, there were four names in nomination: Rhett, Huger, Davie, and Pickens. Then all of the accumulated anger came out. The first ballot showed the tenor of the body, Rhett with forty-six votes finishing second to Huger with fifty-six, thirty for Pickens, and twenty-nine for Davie. Almost three-fourths of the assembly had voted against Rhett. Though it was to be expected that Calhoun's loyal supporters Pickens and Davie would then transfer their votes to Rhett, if Calhoun had indeed let it be known that he wanted Rhett in his place, they did not. Instead, he appears to have left them free to do as they pleased, while Pickens may well have taken his final revenge by actively urging his support to Huger. By the third and final ballot the Pickens-Davie votes had divided themselves almost evenly between the two leading candidates, leaving Rhett with seventy-one and Huger with eighty-two and the Senate seat.

The anti-Rhett forces were exultant. "This is the *denouement* of the plot formed here 3 years ago by the Rhetts," said Hammond, "to rule the state." Despite the junction with the union men in 1840 in electing Richardson, the unionists had abandoned Rhett now, or so it seemed, and Hammond believed that even Richardson had betrayed the clique. Indeed, Hammond thought that he had himself "broke them down," though at the same time he confessed that Rhett had stood by the bargain to support him for the governorship, and most of his own friends voted for Rhett against Huger, while Hammond managed Pickens's bid. "I shall act fairly and kindly to them," he resolved, "but take care not to link my fate with theirs. They have talent and energy, but are incredibly indiscrete."[61] Preston was similarly delighted. He told Waddy Thompson, "You cant imagine a gang more utterly drubbed and dismayed." The defeat automatically ended Albert's congressional run, for Rhett would have to seek last-minute reelection if he were to stay in Washington at all, and there were signs that he might not beat Trotti. James Rhett's bid in Charleston looked equally doomed. "Thus has dissolved the dynasty," trumpeted Preston.[62]

Rhett felt mortified and betrayed. Three years later he was still angry, blaming it all on the widespread belief that he had persuaded—some actually said forced—Calhoun to resign to suit his own ambition. Only Rhett himself could know how much truth, if any, there was in the charge, but that hardly mattered now. "His friends in hot indignation rallied against me," he moaned to James Buchanan. "If you would believe some people in this State I am the D——l himself."[63] Stuart in the *Mercury* engaged in undisguised sarcasm when he editorialized that Calhoun's bid for the presidency "was of the greatest service to Mr. Rhett *before the legislature*," with the apparent suggestion that Calhoun had abandoned his protégé. "It is certainly a *superior tub* that stands (not on its own bottom) but on the bottom of another!"[64] Brother Edmund rather naively suggested that somehow the family actually benefited, from having themselves identified more clearly than ever before as the head of the Calhoun party in the state, "with all the necessary advantages of such a station," but that was a futile attempt to put a gloss on the defeat.[65]

Nor did the disaster stop there. Isaac E. Holmes handed James Rhett a humiliating defeat in their congressional race, outpolling him five to one, and Petigru observed that "his disgrace is very popular with the public."[66] Robert Barnwell saw the scale of the rejection well enough and advised Rhett that he should retire. Indeed, seeing that he had been rebuffed in the public arena, Barnwell actually suggested that Rhett join with him and that they move to Beaufort and take up the ministry. "You perhaps are too contentious and ardent & bold to promote the law of peace & love without a drag," he said, and Barnwell with his self-confessed indolence would be that drag. Together they would be "laboring directly for the advancement of Christ's glory, with the zeal and boldness and sincerity, with which I believe that you now labour for your country."[67]

Barnwell Rhett had no intention either of retiring or of taking the cloth, nor did he have much time to chew over his bitterness, more than to learn the lesson that he had made a bargain with unionists in the state and kept his end but they not theirs. Only the advice of Elmore and Stuart kept him from attacking Huger in the press.[68] Of course he knew he was disliked, despised even by some, yet his was the sort of temperament that wore the antipathy of others as a crown. To Rhett it was proof of his unyielding rectitude, that he was the true statesman who refused to pander his principles for mere popularity with the small-minded and easily misled multitude. Like unpopular people throughout the millennia who seemed to go out of their way to abrade others, he would argue that his great and eternal cause was far more important than transient public opinion. And the fault, of course, lay with others, not in himself.

Now, with only weeks to go before the polling, he had to scramble for reelection to his House seat, and against a real competitor for the first time since 1836. At last Calhoun openly supported him. Pickens and Rhett were the two most experienced South Carolinians in the House, and Pickens was retiring, which made it all the more important to reelect Rhett. "I hope he is in no danger," Calhoun told Hammond. "I would regard his defeat as a great misfortune at the present time." Breaking his own rule not to interfere in congressional races, Calhoun actually asked Hammond to use his influence for Rhett, who would be the senior man in the House delegation if returned.[69] Elmore encouraged Rhett, saying that now he could show the state its mistake in rejecting him for the Senate. "The next year sees you our Great Gun," he said. "You cannot fail to contrast with your colleagues & the late defeat will inure to your benefit in the Congress."[70]

It was not going to be a walkover. In the first place, the next session of Congress started on 5 December, and once he took his seat he would have to seek election from afar. Some in his old Beaufort and Colleton Districts complained that they were tired of only hearing of him through the press because he was too busy elsewhere to address them. "Why can't Mr. Rhett come among our people?" one asked. Then someone, perhaps one of Trotti's supporters, circulated a story that Rhett had actually emigrated from South Carolina and that now he lived in Georgetown and therefore was no longer suitable as their representative. Thrown on the defensive for the first time, Rhett answered the charge in a long open letter in the *Mercury*. He pointed out that thanks to extra long sessions during the current term he would be in Washington fifteen out of twenty months. He pleaded his parental duty to have his children with him and stated that when the first and second sessions both ended in the fever season, it was not safe to take his weak wife and children back to Charleston.[71]

When Rhett did leave Congress briefly late in January in order to meet the appeals to speak in the district, one wag responded to his *Mercury* letter by assailing him anew for neglecting his public duties and coming home to make stump speeches, suggesting that he had returned home to convince the voters that he had not left home. Worse, when Rhett got home he found that Trotti refused to meet him on the stump in spite of calls for the candidates to give their views to the voters in person. In such a case, he said, "I have felt myself, although unwillingly, bound to pursue the same course," and consequently he made no public appearances. Trotti's people still accused him of making speeches while there and also circulated allegations that Rhett was the author of some unsigned letters in the *Mercury* that promoted his candidacy. Whether he wrote them or not, there is no question that there were several writing for the *Mercury* who advanced his cause.

Such campaigning as there was turned heavily on Rhett personally, reactions for and against his clique, and the more telling argument put forth by Calhoun— and the author of those letters in the *Mercury*—that the continuing crisis over the tariff and Calhoun's election campaign required Rhett in Washington, for now he would be senior to all the other South Carolina senators and representatives alike. That and the old loyalty of the Beaufort and Colleton Districts probably won it for him in the end. Unable to debate Trotti, Rhett left Charleston for Washington on February 15, and a few days later the polling began. Early returns showed Trotti trouncing him soundly in Barnwell three to one and by a slim majority in Orangeburg. Everywhere else, however, Rhett came through with a huge majority, and overall in the new district he outpolled Trotti by nearly eight hundred out of just over three thousand votes cast.[72]

It was a fine majority, though not the sort he had enjoyed in previous elections, but it was the only good news for the old Rhett-Elmore faction that year.

Indeed, the clique and its plans were almost wholly disrupted. Elmore was no longer in office, though his banking and mining interests remained strong. His brother in the legislature had died the year before. James Rhett was severely beaten; Albert's congressional hopes were dashed; and Stuart's alcoholism increasingly jeopardized his usefulness and made his continued tenure uncertain. Some saw it all as an overdue comeuppance, even Rhett's forgiving old friend Petigru. Paradoxically, the unionist was delighted at James's defeat yet immediately after Barnwell Rhett's victory declared his satisfaction in the result, especially that the win came "with such difficulties as will be a lesson to him."[73]

If he thought any of the experience of the past few months would be chastening, however, Petigru was sadly mistaken. Barnwell Rhett did not learn lessons; he taught them. And in the year ahead he would teach everyone, even Calhoun.

NINE

There Is Policy in Quarrelling

1843-1844

BETWEEN HIS ABSENCE IN SOUTH CAROLINA and the distractions of the recent disasters, Rhett scarcely opened his mouth in the last session of the term that ended March 3, 1843. There hardly would have been time in any case, for Calhoun's campaign preempted Rhett's every moment from now on, and his work began even before he made the brief electioneering trip home. The first and most important task before Calhoun was securing a regular party nomination, and although the Democratic convention scheduled for Baltimore would not come for months, he and Rhett started laying their strategy now.

The Democratic Party system for nominations presented an immediate problem. Delegates were chosen by state conventions, which sent them pledged unanimously for a candidate. Thus, despite the probability of large minorities for other candidates in a state, only one man would get its delegate vote, thus leaving the minorities unheard. That virtually loaded the Baltimore convention in favor of Van Buren, who to everyone's surprise had emerged from the tariff debacle almost unscathed. Despite considerable support for Calhoun among a number of likely Northern delegates to state conventions, Van Buren would probably carry most of them and thus come to Baltimore with more than enough commitments to take the nomination. What Calhoun needed to do was change the system of nomination. That would give him a better chance of capturing the prize and carry out his long crusade to prevent the majority from stifling a minority.

He gave the job to Rhett, who certainly started working on the matter even while still smarting from the defeat in Columbia. On January 25 he revealed the result in the *Mercury*, titled "An Appeal to the Democratic Party on the Principles of a National Convention for the Nomination of President and Vice President of the United States." In cogent, unimpassioned sentences he argued that the relatively new phenomenon of the nominating convention had taken over a part of the constitutional function of electing a president, by reducing the field of candidates to just one per party. The whole system favored the larger states and reduced the power of the electoral college. Admitting that general sentiment seemed to favor a general convention, and the abandonment of all subsidiary candidates after such a convention had made its choice—he did not argue the practicality of such a system—it was but just that the convention be conducted in the spirit of the Constitution itself, especially the Baltimore meeting, which would be the first in Democratic history to have more than one contender for the nomination. If Democrats were successful in November, then practically the convention was the election, which made it imperative that it be conducted in the spirit of the Constitution. If the candidate chosen were to manifest the will of the people, then "the *people* must rule in the convention," he said. "If it is a convention of politicians and personal partisans—if it is a machinery for putting up men, and grasping the offices of the country . . . it will be vain." He argued that delegates ought to be chosen locally in their communities to give the broadest possible expression of popular sentiment, and that state conventions should not have the power to pledge or encumber their entire delegations, thus denying minorities their rights. "The voice of the people must be taken in parts," he argued, "to obtain the whole." The current system saw townships choose delegates to county meetings, which in turn sent delegates to the state conventions, and they to the national, recognizing the will of the majority at each step. Yet it also meant that at every decision point the minority got left out. What Rhett proposed was proportional representation at the meeting in Baltimore instead, even though in so doing he was essentially arguing against Calhoun's famous doctrine of concurrent majorities by favoring something close to pure popular election of the nominee. He also argued that in order to give the people the fullest opportunity to make up their minds, the traditional timing of the convention more than a year before the election ought to be moved back as late as possible, to the summer of 1844.[1]

They were persuasive and reasonable arguments. How much of the "Appeal" originated entirely with Rhett and how much was suggested to him by Calhoun is uncertain, but it immediately caught fire. At the same time that he sent the document to the *Mercury,* Rhett recast his arguments into a pamphlet titled *The Compromises of the Constitution Considered in the Organization of a National Convention* and handed it to printers, who produced thousands of copies to distribute to the Democratic press and leaders across the nation, Calhoun and Hunter helping with the distribution.[2] Within a month party sheets were declaring themselves in favor of Rhett's reforms, and by late February, Democrats in Annapolis came out for a later convention and Virginia seemed on the verge of doing the same. Hunter told a colleague, "our prospects are bright," forecasting that at the moment eight of the slave states' delegations would be behind Calhoun for the nomination, along with Michigan and New England.[3]

Immediately after promulgating the "Appeal," and while waiting to see its results, Rhett gave some assistance to an equally important task. Calhoun may have been a household name in the South and much of the nation, but he needed now to be presented in the freshest and most positive light possible to all of the Democrats who would be voting, by whatever means, to choose the final nominee. Calhoun had commenced preparations for a biography the previous fall, and on his trip to New York in September 1842 Rhett visited with Joseph A. Scoville, Calhoun's choice for editing and publishing the text when written.[4]

Calhoun wrote roughly half the text himself by the time he reached Washington in December, and he determined to have one of his supporters finish and polish the work based on sources he would supply. Well-known for his facility with the pen—if not for his handwriting—Rhett might have seemed a likely choice, but faced as he was at the time with the disaster in Columbia and the need to win his House seat again, he may have been too busy. And, as well, Calhoun may have been unwilling to trust his public image just now to his least controllable lieutenant. Instead, at a meeting of Calhoun and his friends that month, probably before Rhett arrived from Charleston for the session, they chose Hunter.

Rhett, meanwhile, had already written a sketch of Calhoun for the *Mercury* in December, later issued as a pamphlet titled *John C. Calhoun in his Personal, Moral and Intellectual Traits of Character,* and no doubt a copy of this was furnished to Hunter for his use.[5] The Virginian quickly finished the job and took it to Rhett's Georgetown house in January where they read through it together. On the spot Hunter added a couple of pages of additional material, possibly at Rhett's suggestion, and by the end of the month it had gone to press. Years later, when authorship of the biography was attributed to Rhett, he disclaimed any part, believing—or at least suggesting—that it was all Calhoun's work except for the insertions made by Hunter in front of him.[6]

South Carolina generally accepted the "Appeal," and the *Mercury* of course endorsed it immediately. In April, Albert Rhett ran a meeting in Beaufort calling for a state Democratic convention in May and the nomination of Calhoun, with the proportional representation scheme his brother proposed. Rhett, meanwhile, wanted to push beyond that and had already chaired a meeting in Beaufort on March 20 at which those present resolved that participation in a Democratic convention ought to be conditioned on a pledge by the party to reform the 1842 tariff when a Democratic majority took over in Congress in December.[7] As so often before, Rhett was getting caught in the groundswell of initial success and the promise of more, setting himself up for disappointment.

It came quickly enough. Van Buren forces across the country naturally came out in opposition to the "Appeal," and quickly made their power manifest. In Democratic conventions in New York, Tennessee, Missouri, and Virginia they rejected Rhett's reform and stood solidly behind the current system. Calhoun was shocked, especially over Virginia, where he had placed high expectations, and Rhett was despondent, admitting his misery to Hunter. "What am I to think of your people," he asked. That alone put him into what he called "a plantation lethargy," but then came equally disturbing news. In a special election Hunter was defeated for reelection. That electrified Rhett. "Is your defeat any indication of Mr. Calhoun's fate in Virginia?" he wondered. The news did what disaster always did to Rhett. It roused him from his despondency, made him restless, and set him thinking again, "as if there might be some thing to do."[8]

Rhett renewed distribution of the "Appeal," trying to get friends to republish it in their local press as well. "We go for a convention of the People—and a convention where the People have made up their minds," he declared boldly. "To that we will bow, but we neither intend to be driven nor cheated."[9] He worked hard to ensure that South Carolina's state Democratic convention on May 22 came in behind the reform, as it did, though not without some dissent over the conflicts between proportional representation and Calhoun's well-known theories. It adopted as well Rhett's Beaufort resolutions about tariff reform by the coming Congress, though Pickens feared that being too tied to the tariff just now could hurt Calhoun. Yet some detected other currents at the state convention. Van Buren still had good support in the state among the union men such as William Preston, and some thought they saw Rhett and his friends softening their attacks on Van Buren, seeing his strength and cynically realizing that they should not distance themselves from him overmuch should he win the election. Preston even suggested that Rhett was beginning to "turn a cold shoulder towards Mr. Calhoun."[10]

That was nonsense, and yet Petigru decided that the convention was a tame affair, with Rhett and Pickens and Elmore talking a lot, Pickens stressing unity with Northern Democrats, and Rhett speaking more and more favorably of Van Buren. Petigru suspected that Rhett was playing it safe, laying "an anchor to windward against the probable accession of V. B.," and avoiding a confrontation over policy differences between the two leading candidates. "The impression it made on me was certainly not of Mr. Calhoun's power," said Petigru.[11] Pickens, selected by the convention along with Elmore as delegates at large to the national convention, seemed to agree and warned Calhoun that his support in South Carolina seemed to be slipping. He accused Rhett of trimming in the hope of winning a high appointment from whichever candidate took the nomination and the White House.[12]

Such doubts about Rhett's loyalty said less about him than his accusers, especially Pickens, who now never lost an opportunity to attempt to undercut Rhett in Calhoun's trust. As his own efforts over the next several months made abundantly clear, Rhett was as committed to Calhoun as ever. Far more likely, having seen the dwindling chances of convention reform after the setbacks in Virginia and elsewhere, and being ever the political tactician, he was adjusting his approach. In the short run, despite Van Buren's strength, there was still the chance that he would wrong-foot himself before the convention. If the Calhoun men went too far in attacking him and his followers now, they might alienate themselves and their candidate when the convention sought an alternative to Old Kinderhook. In the long run, if Van Buren won in 1844, Calhoun would still be the logical candidate for 1848, but to succeed then they must keep the still-shaky coalition of Democrats and Southern state rights men together now. In either case, it would be self-defeating to allow attacks on Van Buren to undo all the work invested in the past years to achieving sufficient unity to drive Calhoun to the White House. Rhett was as capable as the next politician of being self-serving, but he was not stupid, and even his enemies credited him with long-range vision.

Demonstrating his commitment to Calhoun, after the state convention Rhett spent the rest of the summer and fall working tirelessly, chiefly with his pen. The death of Hugh Legaré in June removed one impediment, although typically, for all their being on opposite sides where Calhoun was concerned, Rhett much liked and admired Legaré, thought his literary works outstanding, and Legaré himself "very much of a Cicero."[13] Now Rhett started writing Calhoun articles for the *Mercury* under the nom de plume "South Carolina," pressing the convention reform theme, and he continued writing three to five editorials a week for the paper through August, assisted only by his brother Albert. As he could, he also sent a piece to the *Washington Spectator,* the Calhoun organ in the capital now edited by his old mentor Virgil Maxcy. He would have gone to Washington himself, where he thought he could have made "the 'fur fly'" in the sheet, but sickness in the family and paucity of funds kept him at home. "I have been keeping up a pretty steady fire," he assured Calhoun in August, "and I think the enemy seems to feel it."[14]

No sooner did he say that than Calhoun's other managers decided that they needed to get Rhett to make the "fur fly" in Washington and elsewhere. Calhoun's campaign had always suffered from the inexperience and disorganization of his people.[15] The previous winter Rhett had urged men in Charleston and elsewhere to start raising money for a campaign fund in Washington and the North. "To act would have been to conquer," he believed, but others would not stir themselves and his calls went unheeded.[16] To Calhoun, Rhett criticized the indolence and apathy that he thought squandered their opportunity in Virginia, despite Hunter's promises back in February that they were organizing efficiently. Hunter was supposed to be getting out a triweekly Calhoun paper in the state, yet as late as August nothing had been done. Even in South Carolina, Rhett told Calhoun, he thought that "the little energy they appeared to possess seemed to be employed to injure you," no doubt his own return blast at Pickens.[17] In Washington everything had been left too late, and it was only in March that friends bought the miserable little *Spectator* to turn it into a campaign organ. It then went through Scoville and Maxcy as editors, to little effect.

Elmore and others in Charleston turned to Rhett to remedy the chaos. They raised several thousand dollars, with pledges of more, and asked Rhett to go to Washington to take over publishing the *Spectator*. Mindful of his unheeded admonitions months before, he lamented to Calhoun, "I fear now, it is too late for success—but it is never too late to strive in a good cause." Meeting with a large funding committee that included Elmore, Rhett accepted the charge, pledging five hundred dollars of his own, though where it was to come from he probably did not know at the time. Rhett said that his immediate idea would be to get Hunter to take over editing the paper, while he remained in Washington for a time to help. He also undertook on their behalf a trip to New York to solicit contributions matching South Carolina money for starting a journal there as well, all the while trying to get a general Calhoun organization going in Washington. It was precisely the sort of crisis that called for Rhett's peculiar abilities and energy. The "plantation lethargy" evaporated at once.[18]

Rhett stopped in Richmond for a couple of days on the journey to meet with Hunter and other Calhoun supporters. Hunter refused to take the editorship of the *Spectator,* which only added to Rhett's second thoughts about Hunter's effectiveness as a supporter after the convention debacle. Washington Greenhow, the editor of the *Petersburg Republican,* attracted his attention during the visit, although he was doing a good job for Calhoun where he was. Rhett went on to Washington determined that he would have to edit the *Spectator* himself. After meeting with Maxcy he decided to return to Richmond to hire Greenhow, who could not leave until they found someone to take over his place on the *Republican.* Until then Rhett would have to handle the *Spectator* in Washington, including writing the editorials, buying the paper, hiring out the printing or buying a press, and more—tasks made doubly strenuous by the determination to turn the paper into a daily. Eventually they had to settle for its being a triweekly, with Rhett as its sole writer for the moment. Fortunately that lessened the expense of the sheet and freed some one thousand dollars of the money Rhett had brought with him to start the newspaper in New York.[19]

At the same time he learned that Charleston could now definitely commit five thousand dollars for the New York sheet. His response was that it would take twice that and that twenty thousand dollars was needed to do an effective job, but Hunter suggested that in fact all the money necessary could be raised among supporters in the Empire State. Barely three weeks after reaching Washington, Rhett went to New York, where he found that absolutely nothing had been done in advance to start a Calhoun press. Within ten days he had things in place to get one operating. He was still fearful that it would be so underfunded as not to effect much, even though his brother Albert warned Calhoun that "everything now depends on what can be done in New York."[20] The challenge was daunting and the drain on his energies profound, but Rhett found it exhilarating all the same. "I am here, amongst other things, setting up the Spectator on a proper footing," he told Buchanan, and he appealed to the Pennsylvanian for aid in getting the House printing contract shifted from the Van Buren–dominated *Globe*. "In politics I have ever been disappointed," he confessed to Calhoun after his trip to New York, "but there is great enjoyment, in mere intellectual gladiatorship."[21]

The gladiator had to fight more battles than journalistic contests, for at the same time he was to try to get a Calhoun campaign committee organized in Washington, even though some thought that impossible in the face of Van Buren strength.[22] Rhett felt some optimism, having become convinced that the Northern states alone could not elect Van Buren. Polk had been making presidential noises in Tennessee, but his recent defeat in a gubernatorial bid seemed to put him out of the way. Rhett also had held out hope of a junction of forces between Calhoun and Tyler, but Calhoun himself discouraged that, and now Rhett believed that Tyler was choosing his executive appointees with a view to building a base of political debts to help him win the nomination himself. Nevertheless, even while complaining that "the cringing servility and personal canvassing of ambitious and low-minded individuals" was fast destroying the dignity of the presidency, Rhett was happy to exhaust himself advancing Calhoun's ambitions.[23]

Rhett worked in the pages of the *Spectator* to lay the groundwork for a South Carolina protest over the rules at the Democratic national convention, and a possible boycott or even walkout. He told Buchanan that the South could not possibly submit to a convention based on the current rules. "It must come to this at last," he told Calhoun, "that they will give up, their method of approving in the Convention, or we will blow up the whole concern." To be effective, however, a walkout had to have other states following South Carolina, and so Rhett continued to hammer at the unfairness of the unit rule of nomination.

He wanted Calhoun to stay quiet, so as not to draw criticism and harm his chances beforehand, but Rhett kept up the battle throughout the fall. "There is policy in quarrelling as in every thing else," he declared, "and we must endeavor first to let our grounds be understood in the Country, if we hope to be sustained in standing on them."[24]

Early in October he went to New York again and returned in high spirits after what he saw. Van Buren appeared to be losing ground in the city and also in New England. In fact, what friends told him convinced Rhett now that Van Buren could not be nominated after all, and that if he made a fight of it in the convention to retain the unit rule, he would defeat himself. Nevertheless, though Calhoun may have been rising at Van Buren's expense, still he was not strong enough to win. "Van Buren cannot succeed without us," Rhett told him, "& we cannot succeed without his friends." For that reason he counseled Calhoun not to proceed with some recent discussions on running an independent third-party candidacy. What he saw in the North also convinced him even more that they should remain uncommitted about participation in the Baltimore convention right to the last minute. They must lay low, repel attacks but make none themselves, in order to present a defensive posture, and they should let their demeanor rather than their declarations speak for them. And they must hold off splitting away from the convention to the very last. That way if they did walk out, the move would be the more dramatic, being unexpected, and they could make it look as if it was the consequence of Van Buren's attempts to control the convention. Then "when we move off we may move with power."[25]

Rhett's views oscillated between optimism and pessimism and back again through the fall, changing in response to continued developments, and by mid-October he felt less sanguine. Now he suspected that even if united on the same ticket, Calhoun and Van Buren might not beat the likely Whig combination of Clay and Webster. Moreover, he now suspected that if Calhoun got the Baltimore nomination, the venal Van Buren would not support him in spite of party unity. In fact, he began to think that the main factions were in such disarray that they might well see a "dark horse" capture the nomination, Lewis Cass of Michigan perhaps or even Buchanan. The only way for the Democrats to win now, he thought, was for each section of the country to run its most popular man. Doing so might just throw the election into the House of Representatives, and assuming that the Democrats would control the next Congress, Calhoun might gain a victory in the House if Van Buren could be sufficiently discredited in the meantime and if enough Calhoun supporters were in the right places in Congress.[26] It was more than bold; it was a reckless scheme. Rhett approached leading men such as Buchanan to see if they would back the effort, though none did.[27]

Still he did not yield. When New York fell in line behind Virginia in support of the old nominating process, it became quite evident that there was almost no hope of reform unless in a floor fight at the Baltimore convention itself, and no chance at all of postponing its convening. That only raised another congressional option. He held little hope for the composition of the next Congress, at the same time expecting an agitated session. If Calhoun were the nominee of the party, then his prestige would bolster a daring stand for free trade and support of the annexation of Texas, but without that Rhett gloomily expected that "the probability is, dissension and defeat."[28] Thus the Democratic leadership in the House would have to be reshaped when it convened in December. While still trying the delicate task of keeping Calhoun from striking out on an independent candidacy, he conceived the idea of persuading anti–Van Buren Democratic congressmen to avoid party caucuses before the opening of the next session on December 4 and instead to bargain with Southern Whigs for their support in keeping Van Buren men out of the Speakership and the posts of clerk, sergeant at arms, doorkeeper, and others. Installed in those positions of power, Calhoun Democrats ought to be able to sufficiently embarrass Van Buren on those issues in the months leading up to the election that he would be completely unviable by November 1844.

Amid all this Rhett consciously neglected the nurturing of his own constituents, and complaints came from his district that he had not been seen in far too long and that if he did not come before the people soon he might face opposition if he sought reelection the next year. In September he had expected to go back, but by early October, with the newspapers getting started, and before the New York setback, he decided he was accomplishing too much for the good of the cause to leave Washington. If his constituents did not like it, he told Calhoun, "they may turn me out, if they please."[29] But then he learned that a yellow fever epidemic had broken out in Charleston, and he decided at once to return home long enough to bring Elizabeth and the children back to Washington for safety. He put John Heart in charge of running the *Spectator*, with Hunter and Maxcy to help him, and on October 20 boarded a ship for home.[30]

It was a short two-day passage, and on a Sunday morning, October 22, Rhett stepped off the ship and went straight to his brother Albert's house in Charleston in time for breakfast. Albert and Elmore had been out feasting on oysters the night before, and that morning Albert felt unwell, but he still went to church while Rhett napped away the weariness of the voyage. When he awoke, Albert had returned, feeling worse, and either because of his illness or else despondency over Calhoun's faltering fortunes, he declared that he was through with politics and would not take his seat in the next legislature. It was just one more blow to the Rhett-Elmore faction's dreams of dynasty, but Barnwell Rhett had no time to argue now, for the next morning he had to go to Barnwell to meet with some constituents and consult with Pickens and others over the confused signals of his intentions coming from Calhoun.[31]

Rhett returned on Wednesday with a mild fever but found Albert even sicker than before. All through that night in the house he could hear his brother being repeatedly ill. By the following Sunday, October 29, when Rhett took his younger children to St. Peter's to be baptized, Albert was clearly in a dangerous condition. Rhett returned from church to find his brother vomiting yellow bile, and he immediately borrowed a carriage to fetch a physician. The doctor found nothing particularly wrong and suggested that it was all just an upset stomach, perhaps still outraged by some problem with last week's oysters. But then Albert threw up black bile, and another doctor hastily summoned pronounced his condition serious, and almost certainly yellow fever. Though it was not automatically hopeless, the situation was perilous, and Rhett quietly told Albert of his condition. Albert had been seeking a religious conversion like his brother's for some time, but his family had opposed him. Now his brother promised that Christ would save him and at the bedside began a long discourse on Christianity.

After a time Albert tried to rise from his bed and kneel to pray, but he could only manage to get on his knees on the mattress. Asking the rest of his family to leave the room for a few minutes, he prayed privately with his brother. "Is it possible that I have got religion at length so cheap?" he asked almost teasingly. Rhett said yes, then read to him from the Psalms. For a while after that Albert slept, his brother at his bedside, then he suddenly reached out and grabbed Rhett's collar and pulled his ear down to his lips. He asked if he should pray until he died. Yes, said Rhett.

"Do you look to Jesus?" Rhett whispered in his brother's ear.

"Yes," Albert replied.

They prayed on into the night, and then the next morning at dawn Albert once more grabbed Rhett and tried to say something incoherently, then lay back with a look of contentment. On and off through the rest of the day he slept, then raved occasionally, and finally at ten o'clock that evening he stopped breathing. With his own hand Rhett closed his brother's sightless eyes.[32]

The loss devastated Rhett, for Albert had been clearly his favorite brother and certainly his most able ally in the legislature. Temperamentally they had much in common, including their impetuosity and hot tempers, and Rhett had hoped to see him rise in politics and the world. More than a month later he was still depressed by the loss. "In him is gone the chief personal reward I looked to in my public labours," he lamented to Calhoun, "lifting up this great and virtuous mind to a sphere of usefulness congenial to its powers."[33] No doubt he held Elizabeth and the younger children to him all the closer when he got them back to Washington and out of the path of the epidemic, while acting ever more the protective parent with the older boys, especially Edmund and Burnet, who had taken up the habit of "filthy and wicked conversation." He left the eldest, Robert, with strict instructions to correct their behavior. "My sons ought to act always as if in the sight and hearing of their parents," he admonished.[34]

No wonder Rhett threw himself all the more into his editorials and the plan to capture the House leadership in the next session, if only to keep his mind occupied and away from dwelling on his loss. All through November he worked at building an organization of Democrats and Whigs opposed to Van Buren to challenge the House offices. "I thought this would give us a pretty good test of their mettle and character," he thought. First he approached William Wilkins of Pennsylvania and Richard M. Johnson of Kentucky, both of whom agreed to the plan. They would stay out of the general party caucus and run Wilkins for the Speakership. With the large Pennsylvania delegation in tow thanks to the Wilkins candidacy, and with Johnson running the Southern adherents, they should succeed, and Wilkins promised to stand behind continuation of the abolition gag and to hand out the committee chair appointments to Calhoun supporters. But then Jared Ingersoll and James Buchanan of Pennsylvania reached Washington and immediately balked at the plan, the former thinking it unstatesmanlike and Buchanan from what Rhett called his "good for nothingness." They took the rest of the state delegation with them. Two days before the opening of the session on December 2 the Pennsylvanians met and decided to go into the general party caucus after all, and immediately after that Johnson lost control of the nervous Southern congressmen who were to go along with the scheme. "What can we do with soldiers who will not fight?" Rhett moaned to Calhoun.

Though he continued his resolve to boycott the caucus, it would be pointless, and he confidently predicted that Van Buren men would be put forward for all the important offices. That evening Dixon Lewis sent a carriage to Rhett's Georgetown home to beg him to come to the Capitol to meet with remaining stalwarts and try to find some new means of effecting their aims. When Rhett arrived they discussed and agreed on a last-minute idea to attend the party caucus the next day and try to force through a rule requiring a two-thirds majority to carry nominations for House offices, in the full expectation that there was still more than sufficient Van Buren opposition to prevent its carrying. When that happened, they would then walk out of the caucus in hopes of disrupting it entirely, which would mean that when the House convened the next day it could be an open fight with no endorsed Democratic nominees, and the Calhoun slate might still have a chance. It was a desperate last-minute ploy, and it backfired, for when Rhett proposed the two-thirds rule in the caucus, to his chagrin it carried. Since it was his own rule that had been adopted, he then had no choice but to stay in the caucus and accept the nominees, who were all Van Buren men as he predicted. Almost as bad, when he introduced a resolution to commit the party to tariff reform, believing the New York delegation behind him, they would not stand up. Worst of all he learned that it was the avowed policy of the Van Buren leaders to keep the tariff where it was, table the whole issue of Texas annexation, and repeal the gag rule.[35]

There was no way to put a gloss on the disaster, nor to conceal the fact that it symbolized the whole Calhoun campaign. The newspaper efforts had been inconsequential, and the *Daily Gazette* that Rhett started in New York was starving for want of funds, including the five hundred dollars that Rhett pledged but still had not paid, and without which it could not continue.[36] Supporters outside the South had always been skittish, fearful of the Van Buren power and possible reprisals, and with the issue of annexation of Texas due to come before this Congress and an escalation of the slavery question, too few were willing to take risks. In the end all they had gotten so far was an agreement from the Van Buren people to postpone the Baltimore convention from November 1843 to May 1844, but in the current climate that availed them nothing.[37]

All Rhett could do was write to Calhoun and suggest the obvious. Even if the Carolinian could get the nomination now, in the current climate he could not possibly win, and unless tariff revision were adopted by the Democratic Party as a whole, Van Buren would be defeated too. Still, he did not counsel giving up entirely. For the time being they should stick to their principles, keep pushing for convention reform and a change in the 1842 tariff, and be ready to capitalize on any Van Buren misstep. "Our policy at present is, to keep things as they are." They must exert such influence on events as they could and strive to keep Calhoun always in place to assume the party leadership if it was defeated in 1844. This should be done even if the party should succeed, for if Van Buren could not be elected, then likely it would be some dark horse who, as a last-minute compromise, would not have the political authority to command the party the way Calhoun could. Of one thing Rhett was sure. Van Buren would be decisively beaten if nominated, and at least there was some good in that, for it would knell the "end of the cursed and cursing influence of the old Jackson Clique."[38]

Yet another problem was the perception that in attending the party caucus after all, Rhett and the others in his scheme had given up on Calhoun as a candidate.

Rhett tried immediately in the *Spectator* to counter that misconception put about by the Van Buren people, but then Democratic managers seized on this as an excuse to suggest that Calhoun ought now to withdraw in such a way that he would be free to make a run in 1848.[39] Yet Calhoun held out, awaiting actual events, but if he thought Congress would do anything to encourage him, he was mistaken. After the first week of the session Rhett reported that they should expect nothing on the tariff, that South Carolina had been shunted aside in party circles, and that he had no hope of the House doing anything beneficial. The new Speaker, John W. Jones of Virginia, appointed a Rules Committee that made it clear that the 21st Rule was to be repealed.[40] Rhett had hoped for appointment to the chair of the powerful Ways and Means Committee, but even this peace offering to the South was not forthcoming. Instead he got only the second spot on the Foreign Affairs Committee, chaired by Adams.[41] Two weeks later, on December 21, Calhoun withdrew himself as a presidential candidate for the Democratic nomination, though still holding out the option of making an independent third party bid.[42] Rhett even began to suspect that Jones and other Van Buren Democrats were in collusion with old John Quincy Adams and the Whigs over abolition, but he caught himself in the unlikelihood of such an idea and confessed to Hunter, "I have become so enraged of the toothlessness and rascality of this Northern Democracy, that I am probably no judge of policy." In a moment of near-despair he even declared, "I know not which will be the greater calamity, the election of Clay or the rotten clique who rule the Democratic Party."[43]

The only immediate course he saw open to them was for the South to take its stand on principles, which was the only way that a minority could exert any control in the months ahead. He did not suggest nullification or secession, though it was implicit in any discussion of a minority controlling, but no doubt hoped that if the South stood united on the tariff and Texas and other issues, then the majority would be wise enough to grant concessions rather than risk pushing them to that logical next step. Otherwise, said Rhett, "we must take the fate of Numbers, and these being against us, we are forever subject."[44]

Now for a time Rhett considered a different tack for the Baltimore convention, one that would make good use of Southern unity if it could be achieved. Those delegations that would have been for Calhoun should instead go to the meeting as neutrals, taking no side, and using their possibly decisive bloc of votes in a bargain to get the platform committed to tariff reform and Texas annexation.[45] Calhoun disrupted that plan when he allowed some of his advisers to persuade him to stay in the race after all but bolt from the party and make an independent run. After months of negotiations an agreement with the

Republic of Texas for its annexation was concluded in December, which meant that it would be the dominant topic of debate in 1844 and could be a president-maker if Calhoun pressed the issue. At least it might give him enough support to throw the election into the House. Calhoun began readying his announcement, and soon there was talk of a rump convention in Richmond to challenge Baltimore. But then Rhett and Elmore and others used every persuasion to change his mind. Once more they pressed their conviction that Van Buren would be beaten if nominated and that Calhoun's effort would only split the Democrats and alienate important men whose support he would need in 1848 when the prize could easily be his, but only if he remained within the party. Yet again Calhoun allowed himself to be persuaded. Finally on January 27, 1844 the *Mercury* removed his name from its banner, and a few days later the paper published his letter withdrawing himself from the contest entirely.[46]

The only good news on the horizon was the arrival of another Rhett daughter, Sarah Taylor, born in Georgetown on February 3, just as Calhoun's letter was in the press.[47] Yet even the birth of another child to be loved probably did not sway Rhett's mind for long from the disaster before them. In the embarrassing disarray now even a few South Carolina Democrats such as Henry L. Pinckney came out for Van Buren, destroying hope of state solidarity. Even his hope of a neutral bloc at the Baltimore convention was dashed when Pickens and others persuaded Calhoun to back a boycott instead, and when the party committee in Charleston went along, Rhett found he would have no choice but to acquiesce or else bolt himself from the very party he had been trying to unify.[48]

As for affairs in Congress, Rhett saw little but gloom. "Matters here are pretty bad," he told Calhoun in mid-February. He saw the Ways and Means Committee start work on a tariff reform that simply did not meet the case, reducing some rates to 30 percent and even lower on a few items, but without any system or logic. When the House got the bill, he believed that all the duties lowered would be run right back up by the protectionists, while at the same time the huge list of items left free of duty in 1842 to please manufacturers were to remain free. Neither did the bill hold out any schedule of progressive reduction in the years ahead. Rhett told the chairman of his committee that he would denounce it as no reform at all and merely an added betrayal of the compromise of 1833. If the Democrats took a protective tariff passed by the Whigs and only slightly modified it without striking at the spirit of the document, then both parties would explicitly have adopted the principle of protection, knelling the end of free trade forever. Behind it he saw the Van Buren men's machinations. They were taking the 1842 protective tariff and by some reductions trying to pass it off as a revenue measure instead. Having demanded a revenue tariff for so long, the Calhoun men would be thrown on the defensive if they did not support it, for then they could be portrayed not only as going back on their own goals but also as spitefully breaking ranks with the party. Rhett thought that he and his friends should not vote for any bill not clearly for revenue only and, seeing what a mess it all was, could only lament anew the caucus debacle in December. "Had we all stood firm," he told Calhoun, "we would have commanded."[49]

The same day that he unburdened himself to Calhoun, Rhett did something seemingly most out of character. He wrote to Van Buren. Any store of trust or goodwill that his support for the New Yorker might have earned him when Van Buren was in the White House had surely disappeared in the ensuing years as Rhett's challenges to him, and even more to his wing of the party, became more commonplace. Still he took it on himself to inform Van Buren of the dangers facing the party from the action of his minions in Congress, and it was worth a try, for if Van Buren had any lingering gratitude for Rhett's support in earlier times, it might come to some avail. In the offing, he clearly dissembled and even resorted to flattery, something he had done with no one else except Calhoun on occasion.

Rhett reminded Van Buren that he had supported him when he ran for the presidency in 1836, "not merely from public considerations and party associations, but also from personal esteem," ignoring the facts that his support had not been all that warm, that he had called Van Buren a part of Jackson's rotten set, and that in 1836 Rhett had no associations at all with the Democratic Party. He even averred that the previous fall, while actually in Virginia working for Calhoun, he told men that if the Democrats in Congress this session stood firm on Southern principles, then South Carolina would support Van Buren in November if he got the nomination. If in fact he did so, then he was speaking on behalf of Calhoun and a large faction without authority to do so. Now that Calhoun had pulled out, Rhett approached Van Buren, "not merely that our Party should be [united] but that South Carolina might sincerely offer her testimony before the whole Union of her confidence and esteem for you." That was a far cry from the "cursed and cursing influence" Rhett had charged Van Buren with only a few weeks before.

He asserted—disingenuously, as it happened—that he had not anticipated any problem with the gag rule in the House except from the Whigs, and now that some Northern Democrats were joining forces with the opposition to attack the rule, the South felt betrayed. Indeed, now he expected that the gag would be dropped, though it would not if its retention were made an official party issue and Northerners were forced to toe the line. "But let that pass," he said, for the tariff was the greater issue. Rhett outlined the same problems with the tariff legislation that he described to Calhoun but then said he blamed not the party, but only those individuals in it who were betraying the revenue principle. He hinted that condemnation from him and the Calhoun faction could be targeted just on those apostates, and "the Party will be saved." If the Democrats could only show themselves united for a revenue tariff and the retention of the gag rule, he asserted that Calhoun's people would get in line. "We dare not, if we had the disposition, advocate a further support of the Democratic Party or the candidate, if these pledges are not redeemed." The South and West were right in their minds, but the Northern Democrats were the problem. Without the treachery at the North, "the whole South would have been moving cordially and energetically against our common enemy," he said. Instead, he told Van Buren of the seeming avalanche of letters he received every day from Southerners protesting Calhoun's withdrawal from the race. "My wish is to keep him withdrawn," Rhett wrote, and to unite the party on the presidency and a platform of sound principles. Now he invited Van Buren's "cooperation" in achieving those ends, but to do so the candidate must "arrest and settle this adverse state of things," and that meant forcing his people into line on principles acceptable to the South. "I am not only serving the country and our Party, but looking to the interest of both of us—you, in being supported for the presidency, and I in having the satisfaction of supporting you." Writing that last bit of hypocrisy must nearly have made Rhett's ink curdle in his pen. That he could write it at all, as he would do in the future with others, revealed how conditional was his integrity in dealing with men from whom he wanted something. He always thought of himself as a high-toned statesman who looked down upon the low resorts of mere politicians, yet he was himself a politician through and through.[50]

Rhett's scheme was plain enough, and surely Van Buren saw through it easily. In the guise of striving for party unity and the promise—which he was not empowered to make—of South Carolina support in November, Rhett was trying to make a deal with Old Kinderhook to have his people in the House take a stand in support of continuing the 21st Rule and rejection of protectionism. Against that he offered the implicit threat of a Southern break with the party as a whole rather than just condemnation of individual protectionists, and that Calhoun was only being restrained from making an independent run by Rhett's influence, a separate bid that would ruin Van Buren in November. He was offering a deal. If Van Buren would either repudiate or control some of his managers in Congress and meet Southern objections on the tariff and the gag, then the South would join Van Buren at the polls to defeat the Whigs. Fail the South, he warned, and "the consequence must be the Party must go to pieces." There is no indication that Rhett had discussed this with Calhoun beforehand, nor with anyone else. Apparently he acted on his own, making yet another bold gamble with no authority but his confidence in himself.

Van Buren showed Rhett's amazing letter to some of his principal advisers in Congress to sound their reactions, but of course most saw it as an attempt to alienate them from their leader. "I do not know what to think about Mr. Rhett's letter," responded Sen. Silas Wright of New York, whom Rhett had character-ized to Calhoun as the head of "the rotten portion of the Party."[51] But he knew well enough not to be taken in. "He has no faith, as I am compelled to believe," Wright counseled, "and should not be trusted at all." In fact, in the House, Rhett had implied to the Ways and Means Committee chairman that he actu-ally approved the new tariff bill, making it appear that he was covering both sides of the issue. In fact, Wright doubted that Rhett ever understood the dif-ference between principles and mere expedients, and certainly in his boldness, or his desperation, Rhett was trading some of his long-proclaimed principles in his offer to Van Buren in order to get at least something in return.[52] Sensing his own strength, unwilling to put himself in the position of having dictated to him a bargain that could explode in his face, and probably aware that in any case Rhett—who had failed to achieve Southern unanimity on any issue previously —was hardly likely to be able to deliver on his assurances, Van Buren wisely kept his distance. He sent him a politician's response, grateful for good wishes but promising nothing, making no deals, and taking no positions. It was as good as a refusal, and Rhett knew it.[53]

Tragedy intervened to change the direction of affairs dramatically. Just a week after Rhett wrote to Van Buren, an accident aboard the USS *Princeton* killed Secretary of State Abel P. Upshur and Secretary of the Navy Thomas W. Gilmer, along with Calhoun's friend and Rhett's old mentor Virgil Maxcy. It was a critical moment, for the Texas annexation treaty sat all but ready for signature, and there were other pending questions equally as vital. President Tyler sent one of his confidants to meet with the South Carolina delegation in Congress and suggest that the president would offer the state portfolio to Calhoun, at least hinting that in return they might expect Calhoun's friends to support Tyler at Baltimore if he made a bid for the nomination. Rhett immediately wrote to Calhoun at his home at Fort Hill, South Carolina, but not to advise acceptance. The Texas question and the boundary dispute over Oregon with Great Britain were vital questions to the South, and only days before his death Upshur had told Rhett that he anticipated great difficulty with both. If they went wrong and Calhoun was associated with them as Tyler's premier minister, it would be dis-astrous for his chances of election in 1848. At best, Calhoun should only take the portfolio on an admittedly temporary basis to settle those two issues alone.[54]

Others such as Lewis of Alabama and Armistead L. Burt of South Carolina disagreed and strongly backed Calhoun's acceptance without qualifications.[55] Significantly, Calhoun now chose to listen to them instead of to Rhett. Calhoun was not a man to accept personal responsibility for failure, and the embarrassing ineptitude and repeated about-faces in his campaign over the past year were not about to be laid at his door. He certainly valued Rhett's unflagging energy, but by now he had cause to doubt his efficiency and certainly his judgment in some matters. Moreover, thanks to Pickens and others, he may even have come to doubt Rhett's loyalty. Pickens declared that Rhett had ruined Calhoun by persuading him to resign his Senate seat, and when Calhoun had left Rhett in charge of trying to effect the support of Virginia for convention reform the previous fall, Rhett exclaimed that "the game was up."[56] Rhett was a schemer and a liar, Pickens told his cousin directly, and had always been working really for himself, whatever he pretended to do for the candidate.[57] Pickens even overcame Rhett's influence in persuading Calhoun not to mount an independent campaign and pushed through the Charleston committee a resolution to be prepared to vote for Calhoun after all after their boycott of Baltimore.[58]

Even allowing for Pickens's peculiar animosity toward Rhett, undeniably there were others of Calhoun's confidants who also distrusted him, or at least doubted his abilities, even if he was the best of an inept bunch.[59] Then there was the matter of the sudden correspondence with Van Buren, done without Calhoun's knowledge and making promises without his approval. Few secrets were kept in Washington, and even if news of the correspondence did not reach South Carolina in the normal course of rumor, it would have been much to the purpose of Van Buren men such as Wright to ensure that Calhoun did learn of it, further disrupting harmony in the ranks of the opposition. Rhett also apparently published an unsigned article some months earlier urging unity between Calhoun and Van Buren supporters, even arguing that both men should be on the Democratic ticket and neither should object to second place. Then Sen. George McDuffie learned of Rhett's opposition to the proposed tariff revision and his attempt to win Calhoun to his position, and he exploded. In fact, of all the South Carolina delegation, Rhett was the only one who opposed it, imperfect though it was. Yet had they followed Rhett's lead and threatened the Van Buren men instead of working with them, they would have gotten no concessions at all. "Frankness requires me to say to you that I now regret as I have long done, that you have made such a man as Rhett your confidential adviser. You could not have selected a worse. . . . He is vain, self-conceited, impracticable & *selfish in the extreme,* & by his ridiculous ambition to lead & dictate in everything, has rendered himself odious both in Congress & in the State. I know of no man who is injuring you so much. Every thing he does in Congress & writes in the Spectator is ascribed to you."[60] If they lost what little they had gained in the new tariff proposal, he would lay the blame squarely on Rhett.

McDuffie had neatly captured in a few sentences virtually all of the worst aspects of Rhett's personality: the ambition, the arrogance, the inability to follow others and compulsion to enforce his own will, his unwillingness or inability to countenance any ideas but his own, and his constant scheming. Of course as a shrewder judge of politicians than most, Calhoun knew all of that already but had determined that it was worth putting up with because of the obverse: Rhett's indefatigability, his determination, his adherence to principle, his fertile imagination. Certainly he was hard to control, harder than any of Calhoun's other lieutenants, and there was always the sense that Rhett regarded himself as Calhoun's ally rather than subordinate, with all the independence that might imply. But even if turbulent, Rhett had always been loyal, for which Calhoun would forgive much. Now, however, at last he seemed to have concluded—or been persuaded—that that loyalty was suspect after all. Certainly with Rhett as his chief strategist, affairs had gone from crisis to disaster. It was time for a change. Though Calhoun did not openly separate himself from Rhett, he rapidly backed away from him after February. There would be a dramatic decline in their correspondence, and henceforward for a time Pickens supplanted Rhett as the great man's principal confidant and adviser.[61] Rhett could hardly fail to notice the chilliness in the air coming from Fort Hill, not to mention his own near-isolation in the state's delegation in Washington. Typically, rather than feeling chastened, he only regarded it as giving him more independence.

With all the time spent editing the *Spectator*—which continued to operate to advance Rhett's ideas even after Calhoun pulled out of the race—the distractions of the new baby, and of course the disarray in the state rights house, Rhett was only marginally less active on the House floor during the session. Just a week after they convened he was on the floor asking a suspension of the rules so that he might propose a resolution calling for repeal of the 1842 tariff, putting in its place a straight ad valorem tax of 20 percent maximum, with reduced rates on some items "on the principle of producing revenue only." It was the first actual demonstration of how little support the Democratic majority was going to offer, for his motion to suspend lost substantially. A month later he tried again, this time with a resolution that would reduce all tariffs to a maximum of 30 percent and staging an overall reduction to 20 percent within two years. Yet when Adams called for the previous question to shut off debate, it carried easily, and in the vote on the resolution Rhett lost by almost three to one.[62]

Tied with his tariff opposition, of course, was the continuing fight against internal improvements, and in April, even though unwell, he rose to deliver an assault on a bill for expenditures on western harbors and rivers. In fact, he had been ill for some time now though still able to hold the floor, the *Mercury* correspondent averring that on occasion Rhett was "one restless stream of eloquence." Now, however, the rivers and harbors measure brought him out "in all his fury," according to Adams.[63] If the government could spent tax dollars improving the navigation of certain rivers, why not do so for all rivers, and if it was for promoting commerce, then did not the power extend to railroads as well? He had heard some of those present declare themselves opposed to protectionism and at the same time bring forward enormous schemes for regional and local spending programs on improvements that could only be funded by the kind of revenues produced by a protective tariff. Worse, he saw them trading bills, one section saying it would not support another's unless reciprocated, and all of it a raid on a U.S. Treasury fattened by unjust indirect taxation. He did not even bother to go into his arguments for direct taxation instead, accepting the fact that he was the only man in Congress to favor such a scheme and was likely to remain so.

Where would it end but in Congress having absolute power over every form of public expenditure in the land, and with the ultimate money power came omnipotence in all things. This brought him back to the tariff. He asked if forming a government granted the right to take property. Not ordinarily given to parables, he posited three men, independent, one of whom killed a raccoon and skinned it. Did either of the others have a right to the pelt? Certainly not. But what if they then formed themselves into a government? Would a majority of two of those three then have the right to take away the pelt of the third and hand it to another for his benefit? Again no, and the Constitution embodied this simple principle. Yet this is what protection and internal improvements accomplished. If protection was a laudable policy between the United States and other nations, then why not between the states themselves?[64]

Then in an opening round of the escalating battle over slavery that he expected, Massachusetts submitted to Congress resolutions calling for an amendment to the Constitution to abolish the inclusion of slaves in the census for purposes of determining apportionment and representation from the slave states. Rhett was appointed to the select committee chaired by Adams to consider the resolutions, but he publicly refused to be a party to any discussion entertaining such a scandalous and unconstitutional proposal, which he believed amounted to a dissolution of the Union. Later in the session he also asked to be excused from voting on a resolution declaring that Congress had no power to interfere with slavery in the states. Though certainly he agreed with the resolution, he did not recognize that Congress even had authority to consider such a question, and he would not have his vote involved in a discussion that might, if it failed, seem to imply that such jurisdiction existed. And when his Foreign Affairs Committee received a petition from the American Colonization Society seeking an appropriation to advance its cause of relocating freed slaves in Africa, he delivered the unfavorable decision to the House himself. Congress must have nothing at all to do with slavery, he stated, even in the most indirect fashion.[65]

His greatest fire, however, he spent early in the session when the inevitable challenge to the gag rule arose. House managers held off the debate for more than a month after convening, but on January 11, 1844 they began, and when Rhett rose to speak he made it clear from the outset that he knew he was beaten. He spoke, he said, not to try to reverse a foregone conclusion, but only to vindicate those others like himself who stood firm on the principle of keeping slavery agitation out of Congress. Having said that, he laid out his principles and in the process revealed the degree of logical contortion he could summon when necessary to back an argument. Discussing the right of petition, which was what was being infringed, he averred that the whole concept was an absurdity if there were no hope for the petitioner to derive some benefit from the act, and the framers of the Constitution would not have left such a subject in doubt. Where was the infringement? Was it in not receiving petitions at all, or in receiving and then tabling them without debate? Where, in fact, was the difference? He argued that the right of petition included the right to have such an appeal received, referred to committee, reported on, and perhaps debated, and that right derived from the First Amendment. But then he pointed out that this amendment dealt entirely with personal rights of the people to seek redress of grievances. The amendment did not give the people the right to introduce unconstitutional subjects onto the House floor, however. If Congress had an obligation to receive such unconstitutional petitions, that implicitly implied a right to act on them, thus subverting the Constitution itself. Even if Congress merely lifted the gag so far as to receive the petitions, without taking any action on them, the abolitionists of course would not be satisfied. Debate on the House floor would be their next goal. "If you have not the right to legislate," he said, "you have not the right to receive." The fact of a petitioner asking them to do an unconstitutional act imposed no obligation upon them to debate the issue. "We cannot entertain it because we have not the power," he declared.

Unusually for Rhett, he spoke in low tones, so low that the House reporters could not hear much of what he said, but they got the message that he believed any discussion of slavery there was dangerous and that they must not yield an inch now or the agitation would only escalate. Did anyone suppose that if slavery were abolished in the District of Columbia it would all stop there? Certainly not, no more than a man setting fire to his own field could do so without danger of the fire spreading to those of his neighbors. And disunion was the goal of the abolitionists, he charged. They had but to look at the Massachusetts petition presented by Adams. Rhett warned them to think carefully before they acted. "In the South dissatisfaction is increasing every day," he said, "and, if not stopped, it will end with a dissolution of the Union." It would happen the minute Congress started to act against slavery, and nothing would then be able to halt the breakup. He prayed that they could stop short of that calamity and that retaining the gag rule would curb the evil before it could start. But he hoped even more that the South would maintain its integrity by standing firm, declaring at the finish that "neither for the Constitution, nor for those who had gone before them, would they permit themselves to be degraded, or surrender their rights, Union or no Union." Even Adams admitted that Rhett's appeal had been eloquent, but he added that he also found it "pathetic, and full of absurdities."[66]

Much to Rhett's delighted surprise, when the rescinding of the rule came up at last for a vote in March, it failed by a close margin. It was the only state rights victory of the past year, and now he held out hope for another presented unexpectedly by Texas. Both Clay and Van Buren came out opposing annexation just at the moment the treaty was before the Senate for ratification, which alienated the slavery men in both Whig and Democrat camps, and wounded Old Kinderhook's hope of a nomination at Baltimore, perhaps mortally. Suddenly for a brief time it looked as if Calhoun might have a chance at the nomination after all, for there were no other strong contenders, and even Tyler was going to try to hold a competing convention to renominate himself, which no one took seriously. Unfortunately, neither Calhoun nor Pickens had made any real effort to maintain their organization after Calhoun pulled out in February, and thus there was no machinery in place to capitalize on the opportunity. Worse, Pickens had engineered the decision to boycott the Baltimore convention and went only as an observer when it convened on May 27. Thus South Carolina would not be represented at the very moment it needed to be there to put Calhoun's name in nomination. As if entirely unaware of his own role in the debacle, Pickens complained to Calhoun that "there has been something wrong somewhere," but he could not tell where.[67] For a change he could not blame it on Rhett, for Rhett had since March been out of the Calhoun circle's confidences and during the convention itself was at home attending to personal business.

When news of the convention result reached him, it came as mixed. The platform called for annexation of Texas and settlement of the Oregon boundary

above the fifty-fourth parallel, and that was fine. But there were no planks supporting the gag rule or calling for tariff reform to a revenue basis, and no condemnation of the abolitionists. It was half a loaf or less and was made worse by
the fact that the convention did not turn to Calhoun in a draft or even to Lewis
Cass, who might have been Rhett's next choice. Instead, and as he had predicted
might happen months before, the delegates settled on a dark horse once Van
Buren was clearly out of the running. "Unwarrantedly," Rhett would later complain, they nominated James K. Polk of Tennessee.[68] Part of the deal for support
from Van Buren men was that Polk would not retain Calhoun in his cabinet.
When he learned that, Rhett lamented all the more Calhoun's rejection of a
coalition with Tyler and his declining Tyler's earlier offer to head and form his
cabinet. Calhoun surely would have made that administration so successful that
no one would have made such a demand, and Polk would not have had to
accept it.[69] All Rhett could do now was take at least a little pride in believing that
his editorials in the *Spectator* had helped defeat Van Buren's nomination, though
just three months earlier he had told Van Buren how much he wanted to support him.[70] Politics may have coupled Rhett with a few unusual bedfellows of
late, but regardless of the company he seemed unable to sleep comfortably with
any of them for long.

TEN

We Must Slaughter or Be Slaughtered
1844

IF ANYTHING, THE LAST WEEKS of the session only added to Rhett's insomnia. With the Calhoun campaign now history, its shambles became even more embarrassingly public, and Rhett soon became the object of rumors of considerable personal unpaid debt growing out of the *Spectator*. Worse, everything that had looked promising fell apart. Vengeful Van Buren supporters, angered at their man's loss of support after he came out against Texas, blamed South Carolina, even though Rhett and the rest of his delegation publicly disclaimed any part in the stampede that led to the candidate's failure in Baltimore. To get even, those Northern Democrats joined with the Whigs in tabling the new tariff bill that, unsatisfactory though Rhett found it, at least afforded a beginning. He had finally spoken ably in its favor on the floor in late May, yet now the Van Buren press somehow blamed Rhett for the defeat, citing his vocal opposition.[1]

Just as bad, if not worse, was the fate of Texas. Ratification of the treaty being solely a matter for the Senate, Rhett did not address the subject on the House floor, but in the editorials in the *Spectator* he hammered it home issue after issue, sounding an increasingly expansionist chord and inevitably resorting to threats and ultimatums that keeping Texas—which naturally would be a slave state not only because slavery existed there already but also because it lay below the Missouri Compromise line—out of the Union was only another attempt to marginalize the South and further reduce its power in Washington. In fact, it would amount to an attack on the future of slavery where it already existed. Rhett did not have to suggest calling a convention of all the slave states if the treaty were rejected, for some Alabamians had already done that, but it was clear that he would support such a move. They must have Texas in the Union or no Union at all.[2] That strident stance only gave the opposition ammunition against Calhoun and annexation, and they used it. In the last days just before the adjournment on June 17 they managed to defeat the treaty in the Senate.

Rhett felt shock and outrage, and had for some time. Every article of trust or faith he had put in the Democratic Party had been shaken. Much of it had stood behind internal improvements, helping Whigs to pass two rivers and harbors bills. It did not stand solid for the gag rule, and as a result they almost lost it and surely would at the next session. Rhett and other Southern members had even agreed on an unofficial protest gag of their own, boycotting debate by refusing to speak or vote on any measures connected with slavery. Then the Van Buren Democrats furthered their treachery with the tariff, in spite of the bargain that he at least thought had been made that South Carolina and the Calhoun people would support the Baltimore nominee as a quid pro quo for party support in reducing the tariff. Now those same Northern Democrats had joined the enemies of slavery in defeating the Texas treaty.[3]

It was more than Rhett could take, his always fragile equanimity shattered by disappointment and continued ill health. He managed to call the delegation together and declared that they could no longer trust the Democratic Party for fair protection of their interests, proposed that they promulgate an address to their state on the crisis—one that would hint implicitly at attempting nullification of the 1842 tariff by a state convention the next spring—and also demanded Texas's annexation. McDuffie was to write it but pleaded poor health and suggested Rhett instead, who may actually have had a draft ready in advance anyhow. Rhett soon submitted the document to the delegation, who approved. McDuffie signed off on it, and then Rhett ran it past Senator Huger, with whom his relations had remained socially cordial despite their political differences. Up to this time Rhett had said nothing to Calhoun about the document. He explained this to the others by noting that as secretary of state Calhoun was an officer of the government they were about to challenge, and any involvement with the address would compromise Calhoun with a conflict of interest. Privately, Rhett no doubt knew that Calhoun would not approve, especially with their currently strained—or at least constrained—relations. The address went too far from Calhoun's continuing reluctance to try nullification or confrontation again. Huger, despite his sympathy in the crisis, refused to sign before Calhoun had a look, and needing unanimity from the state's delegation, Rhett had no choice but to approach him. The result was as he might have predicted, for Calhoun positively refused to sanction the address. The South still expected redress and reform if Polk were elected, and Calhoun would countenance nothing that imperiled a Democratic victory in the fall. Ironically, having been largely led by Rhett into an alliance with the party, Calhoun now based all his own future hopes on it at the same moment that Rhett was prepared to jump ship. Still the delegates acquiesced and decided to withhold the address. All they could do was sign a joint statement with other House members saying that they had not given up on Texas and would promote annexation when they went back to their constituencies and then go home.[4]

That was not good enough for Rhett. He had given in to Calhoun's will too often, to no avail. He had backed his seemingly timid approach, his vacillation, his constant measuring of his current positions against his future presidential aspirations, and he had had enough. For the past year he had worked himself feverishly, perhaps endangering his own health and certainly imperiling his already precarious finances. "Five years of agitation like these five last years, will cost you your life," Barnwell warned him.[5] During that hasty visit home in May he found that he faced virtual bankruptcy, for a note for $10,800 was coming overdue and Rhett had no money to make payment. Worse, if he defaulted, Barnwell and Thomas Rhett had endorsed the note, meaning that he might injure his brother and bankrupt his closest friend in the offing. When Rhett approached another friend who owed him money, the man took offense but no action to pay, only adding to Rhett's chagrin and embarrassment. Worst of all, as security for the loan he had pledged thirty of his slaves purchased from Stapleton. If they had to be sold to meet the debt, he feared it would start a run of suits from his other creditors that would end in the loss of all his property. "Unless I can obtain aid, which will give me time to meet these debts, the entire liquidation of my debts by a forced sale of property seems to me inevitable," he confessed.[6]

He had lost too much already, and now possibly his plantations—with all the hardship that must entail for his family and the social humiliation of his fall from the perch he had made for himself in the oligarchy. Most of it he could trace to his years of adherence and obedience to Calhoun, only to find himself without reward and now even excluded from the inner circle. "I spent more ink in defending him personally and politically, than any man living," Rhett would say of his efforts for Calhoun, perhaps with a hint of bitterness at the absence of reward. So great was his peril that he feared it could cost him the one thing in life he valued above all else, excepting Elizabeth. Indeed, it was out of love for her and the children, and the need to support them, that he might have to sacrifice that other great love, politics. Barnwell was urging him to abandon it anyhow, and now the financial crisis meant that if he lost his property he would have no choice but to quit public life and chain himself to rebuilding his law practice. Worse, he would be ending his political efforts in failure. "I confess that to myself," he lamented in May, "altho arduous they seem to have contributed but little to arrest the fatal tendency of things for the South." In his current frame of mind he believed that "it would be a great relief to leave an arena where we but fight to fail," and yet it would tear him apart to quit. It had nothing to do with honor or ambition, or so he told others. "Our property and existence itself, to us and our children are involved." The issues were too great, the risks too high. "Under such impressions of the state of public affairs for the South," he concluded, "I will not voluntarily leave my post." Yet it seemed inevitable unless he found relief. "As things are tending, they may soon end with me, by closing my public life." So dejected was he at the possible end of his dreams in South Carolina, that he actually considered the possibility of emigrating to England to start over.[7]

Happily, Rhett did find some temporary relief to get him past the financial crisis of the moment, but the accumulated weight of his personal misfortunes certainly only added to the velocity with which his political disappointments now propelled him. The other South Carolinians might yet again slavishly yield to Calhoun's will, but Barnwell Rhett had had enough. He had differed publicly with the great man before, and at least twice he declared forthrightly that he held his own independence and principles to be above his allegiance to any man, even Calhoun. The time had come to show that he meant what he said.

He would send a letter of his own to his constituents, as was his right and his duty, and Calhoun could do nothing about that. The letter he sent, however, was nothing but the recently rejected address to South Carolina somewhat modified. He warned of the danger to the gag rule, excoriated the Democrats for treachery on the tariff, and proclaimed the danger from abolitionists posed by rejection of the Texas treaty, along with all the old grievances against protection and internal improvements. They ought to have a Southern convention to meet the crisis, but the excitement of the pending presidential contest would divert too much attention and tug too many loyalties. However, South Carolina was already on record by a resolution of the legislature on December 20, 1842 that if the Democratic Party, once in power, did not remedy the 1842 tariff, then the people of the state "must, in accordance with their principles and recorded pledges, adopt such measures to redress their wrongs, and restore the Constitution, as in their opinion may be due to themselves and their property." That, of course, meant nullification, or worse. He reminded them forcibly of that resolution, including it verbatim at the end of his letter.

"The South is driven back, before the anti-slavery influences of the North," he declared. "She must make her own position." Of one thing he assured them. They must not stand still. "I think the State should move on, slowly and deliberately if you please, and in any form you please," but she must move on. "We must neither stop, nor recede." He called for the people, through their legislature, to "place the State in an attitude of sovereignty, so that she may be able to act next spring, meaning that they should schedule a convention to follow the presidential election and the winter session of Congress. If the actions of Congress, or the attitude of a new administration, offered any tangible hope of redress, then the convention could adjourn or dissolve. But if not, then the state would be ready to act for herself. "My voice to you now," he concluded, "is—on! on!"[8]

Rhett sent the letter to the *Mercury*, which published it June 27, and also had it printed as a pamphlet to distribute, and he would not have been surprised at the furor it sparked. Hammond chided that Rhett had "rather imprudently, because unnecessarily, commenced agitation." With Stuart away from Charleston and his desk at the moment, in poor health and no doubt fighting his alcoholism, even the *Mercury* criticized Rhett for breaking ranks with the state's avowed support of the Democratic Party in the election by attacking Northern Democrats. The Whigs capitalized fully on his letter by accusing him of seeking a breakup of the nation and contrasting that with Calhoun's continuing avowal of the Union, their goal being of course to fragment the Democrats not only in South Carolina but throughout the country.[9] Calhoun and his counselors kept quiet, refusing to take the bait and risk enhancing the embarrassing division in their ranks, but they discovered that Rhett's call struck a resonant tone with the younger men in Charleston. Weary of Calhoun's continual temporizing and apparent passivity, their warmer blood and less mature judgment wanted action and resistance.[10]

Ironically, the split with Calhoun suddenly found Rhett a most unlikely ally in Hammond, who had made his own break with Calhoun sometime before and who at the same time was now estranged from Pickens, in whom he saw a treacherous rival for his own future Senate hopes. Then, too, Hammond just then was suffering greatly from widespread—and true—rumors of his sexual dalliances with two of his nieces, the daughters of Wade Hampton, and he needed friends.[11] He had himself come around to seeing nullification as the only alternative to continued betrayal in Washington and was beginning as well to regard it as only a prelude to secession and the formation of a new slaveholding nation, and not just as a curb on the excesses of the existing Union.[12] Repelled as he surely was by the stories of Hammond's licentious escapades, Rhett too needed friends, and in the months to come he and Hammond managed to put aside, on the surface at least, much of their previous antipathy.

Governor Hammond, too, demanded action, and soon Rhett's constituents called for him to come home from Washington in spite of the unhealthy season. They needed leadership now, and Calhoun was not providing it, nor were they in a mood to follow his cautious dictates. Coincidentally, in an attempt to stop the breach between Northern and Southern Democrats from widening after Rhett's letter and pamphlet appeared, candidate Polk wrote an open letter in which he said that he favored a tariff for revenue only yet hedged about still maintaining some protective rates. It sounded like trimming, reminiscent of

Van Buren in earlier days, and only seemed to confirm Rhett's declaration that the Democrats were not to be trusted to protect Southern interests. Calhoun accepted Polk's letter with equanimity, regarding the Tennessean as the least of evils come November. Besides, Polk was still solidly behind Texas annexation and settlement of the Oregon boundary, and he had also committed himself to serving only one term as president. Even if the South lost ground on the tariff under Polk, it would gain with Texas, and Calhoun would gain with it if he stayed in the party and backed Polk.[13]

But Rhett no longer took counsel of Calhoun. He had already accepted the invitation of men at Bluffton, in his district, to meet with them on July 31 for a dinner. "My Constituents have sent for me; and I go in a few days to meet them, and tell them a story of wrongs which their Fathers would have died rather than bear," he told a friend. Of course he went prepared, expecting to address them more than once on the controversy he had started. He knew that he was break-ing not just with Calhoun but with some of his closest friends and allies, includ-ing Elmore, who was trying his best to discourage in Charleston the very furor Rhett created. At the same time Rhett was finding a new constituency in the generation born after him, bred in the agitation of the last fourteen years, flam-mable, and demanding not just words but action. "They are raging," he declared, "and if the rest of the South was of their temper we would soon bring the Govt. straight both as to Texas and the Tariff."[14]

They were there to hear him at Bluffton that Wednesday, the attendance depressed somewhat by several days of rain and the inability to get an extra steamboat run to bring more people from Charleston and Beaufort. Still several hundred came, the ladies in their carriages drawn up in a large semi-circle around the platform that had been erected in the shade of a huge oak on John Verdier's plantation. Most of the great planters were there, all of them wearing badges of palmetto leaves as symbols of resistance. Rhett's brother Edmund, just as ardent for resistance, brought a contingent of friends from his home in Beau-fort, and as Rhett was escorted forward at 2 P.M. there were cheers, handshakes, and introductions as he passed through the crowd. Then after an introduction on the platform he rose to speak. Many knew him. Those who did not saw a man slim and ramrod straight, nearly six feet tall, balding but for graying wisps at the fringes, with a tuft of whiskers beneath his chin. His pale blue eyes had the sparkle of an inner fire, and when he began to speak in his clear, high-pitched voice, he scorched them with his flames for the next ninety minutes.[15]

He first attacked the abolitionists who felt contempt for their rights, with their "jubilee songs" from the free states anticipating the downfall of the insti-tution in the South, painting them as incendiary fanatics. This made annexing

Texas all the more important, the great question of the moment he said, and he did not downplay the calamity that would come with rejection of the treaty. The North hated the South, he said, and regarded them with contempt. The ultimate aim was abolition of slavery everywhere and with it the destruction of their economy and society, and an eternity of vassalage. The tariff, too, was part of the plan for their subjugation, and he detailed for them how the protectionists had tried to conceal their purpose behind pretended reforms, and then how the Democrats had broken faith with them in killing even the poor bill just defeated. "They falsified their most solemn pledges," he declared. As for any good coming of the presidential election, that was futile, for Polk had revealed himself to be no better than Van Buren, or Clay for that matter.

There were only four routes for their defense, he said. One was the hope that as president Polk would uproot the whole protective conspiracy, but he had already dismissed that summarily. Another was a Southern convention to present Washington with a united and defiant opposition, but that, too, he damned as a futile hope. There were two remaining defense routes, nullification or secession. Either, he said, could be effective in the right conditions, and both he preferred to continued submission, and though he did not mention Calhoun once, it was apparent that now Calhoun was a submissionist in Rhett's eyes. South Carolina had been great, he said, and could be again. Indeed, she could be what he called "a light upon a hill"—borrowing ironically from John Winthrop's description of the Massachusetts Bay Colony two centuries before—a beacon for lovers of the Constitution and the rights of the people to follow, but she must act. Then he echoed his recent letter in calling for a state convention to be gathered immediately after the end of the next session of Congress in March 1845. When he finished, thunderous applause and cheering rewarded his effort. "We never witnessed any scene that surpassed the enthusiasm created on this occasion," wrote Stuart, present in the audience and now back at the *Mercury*, whose criticism of Rhett had ceased. Again, the youth of much of the audience won note, and accounted for much of the enthusiasm.

The dinner followed, all of the edibles homegrown and none of them imported with odious duties paid. Rhett, perhaps already attracting attention for his gargantuan appetite, had pork and chicken and everything else in abundance, but there was little in the way of strong drink present except wine for the many toasts, including one even to Calhoun. At a final toast to Rhett he arose and raised his glass to propose one of his own to the 1845 convention he had just demanded: "May it be as useful as the Convention of 1776." The allusion to revolution, whether accidental or intentional, was hardly lost on the crowd, and the toasts that followed became increasingly militant, calling for secession if the Union could not be freed of corruption and for the federal government to be either reformed or abolished. A letter from Robert W. Barnwell was read that supported Rhett's call, and then came more toasts endorsing the convention call, including a pledge to resist the tariff or "*perish* in the attempt," calling all who dallied "dastards." They invoked the shades of Francis Marion and revolutionary heroes of old and drank to "native swords" and "*resistance*—constant, *energetic resistance.*" One actually toasted secession.[16]

Hot to his theme, Rhett spoke at Orangeburg Court House five days later and was even more fiery. "The only hope of the South," he declared, "is in resistance." If South Carolina took the first step, other slave states would join her. The Democrats could not be trusted, and Polk was a humbug. "There is no redress to be expected from him," charged Rhett. They needed a state convention where "those who advocate Nullification" could decide what to do, for now the issue was down to submission or resistance. If they could arrest the progress of federal usurpation on just one issue such as the tariff, that would halt its aggressions everywhere, he believed. Even to try and fail was better than to risk submitting to abolition demons, and he left no doubt that ultimately that was their greatest danger. For years he had maintained that the battle for Southern rights should be fought for the tariff, because he wanted to stop Northern aggression there, for if the South lost or yielded, then inevitably slavery would be the ultimate target of their enemies. "Should the present attacks upon us prove successful," he said, "a firebrand would be thrown into our midst." They would lose not just civil rights but their social identity. "If Abolition prove triumphant," he promised, "we must slaughter or be slaughtered." He knew he stood alone in Congress in advocating such a course, but he despaired of all others. "If you value your rights," he concluded, "you must resist."[17]

There were more dinners and more addresses, all in the same vein, and meanwhile the reaction to Rhett's Bluffton declaration of resistance erupted all around him. The *Mercury* endorsed him wholeheartedly, and as well his policy of making the battle "on the outer walls of the tariff if we would successfully defend our slaveholding institutions."[18] Soon many of the Democratic newspapers in the state took up the Bluffton message. The hotheaded youngsters and old nullifiers such as Hammond cheered his declaration and came out in favor of calling a convention. More young men in Charleston organized themselves into what they called the Young Democracy, and carrying on the theme of the youth of his supporters, Rhett's adherents adopted for themselves a title first thrown at them in derision by their foes, "Bluffton Boys." At last someone was for doing *something,* exulted James Gadsden. "Our people are like a 'Stifled volcano.'"[19]

For some, however, it was too much or too early. One of the men in the audience at Bluffton spotted what he felt was the fatal weakness in Rhett's call for
action, and Rhett himself had pinpointed it. "The whole South must go together
or we can do nothing," R. W. Singleton wrote a week after Bluffton. "The whole
South will not go together, except upon the slave question, and this will never
be put in such shape by the Government, as to be so clear as to unite the
South."[20] Only some dire action would convince the South that slavery itself was
threatened, and the tariff would not suffice. After the first flush of enthusiasm
other, calmer voices were heard. From Columbia there came counsels for patience
and discretion, in spite of sympathy for Rhett's views. James Hamilton, a onetime
proponent of separate action by South Carolina who once represented Rhett's
district in Congress and had favored it in 1832, argued now that Rhett's movement was premature and harmful, "for it is quite obvious that he has neither the
sympathy nor support of the other portions even of South Carolina, in his ill
timed move." It was only rash blustering that risked alienating the rest of the
state and the South.[21]

The criticism quickly mounted and became more pointed. Rhett's course
was "embarrassing in the extreme & in all respects singularly unfortunate at this
time," one Calhoun confidant told him. Other than the Young Democracy and
their association, most of Charleston opposed Bluffton, and the Young Men's
Democratic Association in the city regarded Bluffton as "rash & uncalled for."
Elmore had to confess that he did not know what Rhett was doing, character-
izing Bluffton as "hasty and unadvised, attributable to the imprudent zeal of
Rhett." Another Carolinian called Rhett "useful as a whipper in, but fit for
nothing else. . . . too hot-headed, too rash, too hasty, and too heedless." Wise
men should hope that Rhett remained always in a subordinate capacity in which
he might stimulate action but never direct it. Another blasted Rhett's wildness
at Bluffton and felt alarm when he saw "how blindly the movement was conducted, how it stumbled and groped along." The *Charleston Courier* derisively
called him the new Joshua, and Stuart had to come repeatedly to his defense in
the *Mercury.* That only resurrected the old charges that Rhett in fact owned the
Mercury, and denials of that almost got Stuart into a personal affair with another
journalist. Some even questioned his right to make the speech, until defenders
pointed out that his constituents had asked him to come and demanded his views.[22]

Pickens, of course, could be counted on to weigh in and did not wait long,
choosing the tack that most of Rhett's South Carolina critics would use, namely
that Rhett had broken with Calhoun and even insulted him. Certainly there
was a general feeling that the "Rhett clique" had removed itself from Calhoun's
authority. Now Pickens told Calhoun that Rhett was accusing him of being

bought off on the tariff by the promise of the presidency in 1848, and others such as Louis T. Wigfall repeated the charge. Hammond believed that Pickens was merely using Bluffton to further lower Rhett in Calhoun's esteem, thus making his own position more preeminent, and he was right.[23] "The only difficulty in our position is the mad & reckless moves made by Mr. Rhett," Pickens told Calhoun's brother-in-law. "I seriously believe they are made deliberately to injure Mr. Calhoun."[24] Soon Rhett found himself charged with declaring at Bluffton that Calhoun was failing their cause and that he was breaking with him to chart his own course, even aspiring to supplant Calhoun in leadership in the state. However much Rhett might have felt that, he issued through the *Mercury* a clarification that all he said was that he and Calhoun differed over whether South Carolina ought to resist now, and privately he doubted that Calhoun was sincerely against him.[25] Affidavits appeared from Bluffton citizens affirming Rhett's denial, supported by William F. Colcock and others who were present though allowing that it was an occasion for deep sorrow to have to differ with Calhoun. Even the old accusation that Rhett had engineered Calhoun's withdrawal from the presidential race came up again, and with it the charge that Rhett controlled the *Mercury* when it took Calhoun's name down from its masthead. Pickens's private comment to Calhoun about Rhett's near-bankruptcy somehow got into the press, with the charge that he fomented all of this fuss cynically to revive his "shattered fortune" by agitation that he hoped would gain him leadership. Though it was untrue as to Rhett's motives, still the charge looked plausible enough that Stuart had to lie to counter it, arguing that such could not have been Rhett's intent since "he enjoys a substantial and honorable competency, the fruit of his own industry."[26]

Moderates and Calhoun supporters moved quickly to stop Bluffton before it built any momentum, even as Rhett continued his speeches throughout August. Besides the renewed castigation over Calhoun's presidential withdrawal, some even dredged up the circumstances of Rhett's first election to Congress in 1836 and the confusion with Grayson, the *Charleston Courier* charging that Rhett's "public life began in social treachery" and now he was ending it by betraying Calhoun. Grayson came out to repudiate that charge.[27] In Charleston some Democrats set out further to isolate Rhett and his faction from the party and Calhoun, in order to hamper any attempt at a state convention, and Memminger discussed trying to force Rhett into a public declaration of union or disunion.[28] Soon Rhett, even while maintaining that Calhoun was not himself condemning Bluffton, complained, "not only the weight of Mr Calhouns name, but that of the whole Delegation has been brought to bear, to crush me." He began to complain of feeling persecuted.[29]

Calhoun had his own way of dealing with the problem. Quietly he met with Hamilton and others to make certain their loyalty to him transcended any possible sympathy with Rhett. Then, probably at his behest, a meeting of Charleston Democrats declared its support for Polk and the party, and continuing faith in Calhoun, while denouncing a call for a convention.[30] Meanwhile Polk had called a party mass meeting in Nashville for August 15, and Calhoun now sent Pickens to represent him there, his mission being to promise Polk that nothing would come of the Bluffton episode, especially if Polk would promise to bring in a lower tariff. When Pickens returned with Polk's pledge to go back to the 1833 tariff and also to ensure the annexation of Texas, Calhoun had all he needed. The old Rhett-Elmore machine was finally defunct with Elmore's refusal to countenance Bluffton, and the years of resentment in the state at the clique's frequent arrogance and high-handedness had only Rhett now as its focus. He soon discovered that he really just had support in his own district, more especially in Beaufort and Colleton. Polk's pledges, Calhoun's opposition, and the attacks of the Whigs and unionists of all stripes were enough to stop Bluffton dead by late August.[31] "Through the influence of calmer counselors they have for the present time been quieted," Elmore told friends in Virginia.[32]

Rhett resolved not to respond to the attacks but rather to let his opponents say anything they wished about him, probably under the assumption that even adverse publicity worked to his advantage by keeping the issue alive and constantly before the public.[33] Instead he kept spreading his message—at Robertville (in Beaufort District) on August 22 and again at Barnwell on September 7.[34] Pleading that he was only meeting his obligation to give "free and independent expression of opinion" to his constituents, he denied any desire to lead the state, which was at best a half-truth. If not to lead, his intent was to propel, which was much the same, and he added to his exhortation now a call for other Southern states to meet in convention as well.[35] At Barnwell Court House on September 9 he also took the controversy into the personal lives of his audience by showing how the abolition poison had infected the Methodist Church and was even then starting to divide the Baptists. So far as the Democrats were concerned, he averred that South Carolina was pledged to support Polk in November, but nothing more, and was free to act as she chose on the issues.

While favoring state conventions, he dismissed a regional convention as impractical and destined to break up in a row because not all of the states felt the same threat or urgency. "One State must make the issue," he said. "South Carolina must be that State, or it will not be done at all." If she acted, then perhaps a Southern convention could follow. While there had been hints at such an approach before, it was Rhett's first public declaration of his policy of separate state action, his conviction that others would follow if South Carolina led but that the states would never act together first. South Carolina must resist abolition. At the same time he professed as well his continuing attachment to "the Union of the Constitution," which was his way of saying the Union as he believed it had been intended, not as it was. The best way to reclaim and perpetuate that Union was for the state to act at once to "restore the Constitution upon which it rightfully rests, through the people in Convention, and support the decision of the Convention."[36]

Significantly, while Rhett called again and again for state action, for the convention to meet, he never explicitly declared precisely what he wanted that convention to do. That in fact was one of the problems with his sudden Bluffton movement, for he had no avowed policy beyond the call for a convention, or so it seemed.[37] A month after the Bluffton speech Rhett tried to explain his motives to Hunter and as well deflect the charges being laid against him. "As to all the outcry that I am seeking to destroy the Union," he said, "you know very well that there is no truth in it." He protested that he wanted to return the Union to its "true basis" on the Constitution, that was all. "I hold the Constitution in politics as I do the Bible in religion," he continued. "My object is not to destroy the Union, but to maintain the Constitution, and the Union too, as the Constitution has made it." Convinced that the reform would never come from Washington, he felt it had to come from the states and that as a result, "we will probably have to risk the Union itself to save it." Only the threat of disunion would swerve the government from its course. He did not mind being called a traitor and disunionist in the process, for such charges had been the lot of all men who attempted to reform evil. "They do not much disturb my equanimity, being satisfied the liberty and safety of the South requires the strong policy I propose."

It perhaps hurt him a bit that friends such as Elmore were not with him in this movement, "and that I alone must bear all the 'anathemas' of my Democratic friends in and out of this little State." That could not be helped. It hurt him, too, that Calhoun's name and prestige were being used against him. He had exhausted himself trying to advance their cause within the Democratic Party and said, "but I am done with it." The betrayals of the past session convinced him that "we of the South have no hope in their assertions." The party would do nothing. "They have given way and have given way forever to the foul and insulting interference of the Fanatics on the floor of Congress, and will go on plundering us to the end." He was sick and disgusted with a party that he constantly had to turn around and oppose. He would continue to associate with it but would not follow it. "We of the South will be ruined, unless we will act independently of both parties, against supporting what both parties of the North and South join to put upon us." Even if miraculously something happened to put Calhoun in the White House now—and it could not happen without Calhoun surrendering all his principles and agreeing to become a mere tool of the party—it would avail nothing. As for Polk, he would be the mere puppet of the protectionists and consolidationists, and his equivocating letter on the tariff had "rendered him too despicable in my estimation, to regard him in the least in my course." Despairing of everyone and everything else, "I turn to this little State, and am striving at least to save her honour." South Carolina had declared in 1833 and again in 1841 and 1842 that she would resist the tariff. "I say let her go on."[38]

Thus, Rhett suggested, he was only proposing some saber rattling, and probably another nullification, in order to bring Congress and the Democrats to their senses. But this is what he was saying to Hunter, who did not himself back the Bluffton move and who, though sympathetic, was still in the mainstream of the Democratic Party. That being the case, Rhett could well be hedging on his real goals, for here, too, as in his speeches, he made no specific statement of what he thought a state convention ought to do. That did not mean he did not have something specific in mind, however, only that he felt it unwise to confide it to those who were a part of the establishment with which he had broken and which he now attacked, even if they were friends. In addresses after he wrote to Hunter he continued his strident call to action, and with it his ambiguity as to what final action should be. Having started the religious theme at Barnwell, he continued it, perhaps hoping to revive some of the old fervor of the 1830s and affix it to his cause. "I call Heaven and Earth to record this day against you," he said on the Salt Ketcher on 5 September, "that I have set before you life and death, blessing and cursing, therefore choose life that both you and your seed may live."[39]

But if he did not openly declare his own preference, the real policy driving his Bluffton movement, still it was there in his speeches, communicated not in direct words but by his manner of speech, and quite certainly by intent. What he would not say openly to Hunter he readily confessed to his friend and Bluffton supporter Armistead Burt of Abbeville. In his speeches he was calling for "that mode of action, which in the convention, would be *at once the most efficient & at the same time most unite the people.*" Saying that, he laid out for his audiences three proposed courses: nullification by the convention as attempted in 1832; nullification by act of the legislature; and secession. "I so spoke as I think pretty plainly to intimate in what mode my preference lay," he went on to confide. When he mentioned the two forms of nullification, the audiences remained silent. However, he said, "when I spoke of Secession, the people often cheered."

There it was at last. Like any skilled speaker, and Rhett was more able than most, he knew how to convey his intent by means other than words. Just when he came to his epiphany is unclear, but the logic behind it for him was not hard to trace. South Carolina had tried nullification once before, and a combination of apathy, lack of unity, apprehension, and being bought off by a tariff that was still protective ended it all in a whimper. What reason was there not to expect such an outcome if it were tried again, especially since Polk had already promised what sounded like another equivocal tariff reform that was no reform at all? Nullification was useless now, for it would not unite the people at home and it would not intimidate Washington. Indeed, Old Hickory had told Rhett recently that if the nullifiers of 1832 had not backed away after the compromise and the force bill, he would have raised fifty thousand volunteers and invaded the state.[40] Was there any reason to suppose that Jackson's protégé Polk would not do the same, or that he might not be forced to do so by a strong anti-Southern Whig minority in Congress and a Democratic majority seemingly hostile to South Carolina's interests?

In short, there was no point in nullification, and even if they did try it, the outcome might well be the same as that for an even stronger measure such as secession. Yet secession offered strengths that nullification did not. Seemingly incongruously, Rhett argued that secession would actually unite the old nullifiers with the unionists in the state, presumably because in the constitutional crisis that secession would bring about, no one, not even the unionists, could stand in opposition without branding themselves disloyal to the state. He had support for such a notion, for a number of unionists echoed his call for a convention and even secession, though he may have misread their action and some at least may have wanted secession to be tried only so it could be defeated and forever removed as a source of agitation.[41] They could oppose nullification as an inexpedient measure, but in the face of a prosecession majority in convention, facing the ultimate question of loyalty to the state or the Union, choosing the latter would be political and social suicide. Moreover, Rhett believed that in practice secession would differ little from nullification, both requiring a call by the legislature and the same election of delegates. Thus, if they were to go in for the penny, why not the pound?

Rhett, who like Calhoun fully accepted the compact theory of the government, had always believed in the abstract right of secession. Of that there was never any question, as he made clear in the old days of nullification. All that had changed now was simply that in the immediate event he advocated bypassing the intermediary step of nullifying, which had been demonstrated to be a paper tiger. Yet he still declared his devotion to the Union and denied the accusations

that he sought to break up the nation, and outwardly there was nothing contradictory in his claims, for his objective in secession was identical with his earlier
aims in nullification. He did not declare secession to be necessarily a permanent
act, an end in itself, or a step on the way to forming a new union with other
seceding states that might follow South Carolina. Rather he implied that it was
simply a stronger demonstration of commitment to equal justice under the Constitution, and an escalation of the danger to the permanence of the Union if
South Carolina's rights were not recognized. He fully expected Polk, the Whigs,
and the Democrats to back down and give them a revenue tariff, Texas, and an
end to abolition agitation, and in return South Carolina would rescind its secession ordinance and return to the Union. That was what he had meant by risking the Union to save it, and if it was a rash and dangerous policy that said much
for Rhett's own penchant for bombast and confrontation, still it had the merit
of a certain logic and method if one accepted, as Rhett did, that Washington
and his opponents could always be intimidated into backing down if the threat
were great enough. He was a secessionist and a constitutional unionist at one
and the same time, and he saw nothing at all contradictory in the combination.
Rather, the one in the short term could guarantee the longevity of the other. But
being Barnwell Rhett, he could very well have been saying this just for public
consumption while harboring a deeper motive for Carolinian independence, a
motive that he may not have admitted even to himself.[42]

Rhett did try to shift some of the responsibility for the Bluffton outcry from
himself to "the people in my district, [who] have spoken out their indignation
and determination," and he rather disingenuously cast himself merely as one
who took his lead from them. "I cannot, altho suffering in your opinion or that
of others, shrink from any effect on myself, their voices have produced," he
protested to Burt. "They had a right to speak—they, I believe, thought they
ought to speak." They did as they should, he believed, yet he disclaimed any
responsibility for the radical or incendiary expressions those people made at
Bluffton and elsewhere, because after he delivered his addresses he invariably
stayed only long enough to politely hear a toast to himself and thus did not hear
what came after he left. Since most of those occasions were dinners given in his
honor, such repeated disappearances from the festivities would have been
ungrateful at best if done once or twice. That Rhett made it a policy to leave at
a certain point on every occasion, however, suggests method and a purpose.
That he later used his absence as an excuse to claim that the Bluffton Boys' and
others' calls for a convention and even secession were spontaneous reveals his
motive. If he hoped to see a convention called, Bluffton had to be perceived as
a grassroots movement and not as Rhett trying to persuade the people to mount

his own hobby horse with him. He confessed that if he had advised his audiences, whom he described as being as high-toned and independent as he was, not to express such sentiments after he laid out their wrongs for them, he would have been ignored. "Yet because *they* have spoken out their opinions," he complained to Burt, "I am a breeder of mischief."

As September wore on, however, Rhett could no longer maintain the pose that his had been a spontaneous movement of the people, nor could he help but sense that the Bluffton momentum was wearing down, defeated by Calhoun's silence and his supporters' active opposition, Polk's promises, and the inactivity even of some of those in most harmony with Rhett's ideas. Even his friend Burt only gave encouragement from the comfort of his study and would do nothing active. "Your silence has nearly killed our party in Charleston," Rhett complained to him. "My constituents have marched out into the open field, and placed themselves and me, in open line for battle. You and your constituents are in the woods, and lying so still and concealed that they are claimed as a part of our enemies." If Burt and McDuffie and others whom he knew to be in accord with him had only found the courage to stand up, then others such as Elmore would not have been forced into the position of trying to dampen Bluffton for the sake of ill-advised Democratic unity. As for Calhoun, Rhett predicted that if he continued to stand by and watch the erosion of their rights by the protectionists, he would live to rue his inactivity. Worse, Rhett had to admit to himself that he had misjudged the sentiment of the state. "I was totally mistaken, in supposing that the people are prepared to act," he lamented. "A new generation has arisen in the state since 1833, who know but little of the Tariff," and knowing little they could hardly be excited on the issue or stimulated to action, though he had seen enough to realize that this new generation could be aroused over slavery, and that might prove useful. He saw the Calhoun and unionist forces working hard to elect William Aiken governor in December, over the state rights candidate Whitemarsh Seabrook, and feared that everyone who was for taking action now would be shunted aside. His opponents were acting on the fears and ignorance of the people, he declared, and he sadly confessed, "we will be put down."

While Rhett cared nothing about the assaults on him, or protested that he did not, his family did, and from Washington came pleas from Elizabeth for him to return. His sons smarted under the attacks on him that they read in the press, and they, too, wanted their father back. By 9 September he had already been away twice as long as he expected or prepared for, and it was clear that Bluffton was about played out. So in a somewhat dispirited mood he left South Carolina, considering possible resignation of his seat in the House, for he resolved that "if South Carolina does not redeem her pledges, and submits to the Protection system, humble as I trust I am, I shall be too proud to serve her." But he would see Calhoun first, and immediately on reaching Washington. For now, on leaving the state in the wake of all the furor, he could not help making a last appeal, though he all but despaired. "I have made my Congressional District safe," he claimed. "Having done this, I leave the State, satisfied that I have done my duty."[43]

In a strange twist, no sooner was Rhett en route to Washington than the support he had longed for from leading men in South Carolina began to appear, starting with Langdon Cheves, a war hawk in 1812 and later president of the United States Bank. Well-known as a secessionist himself, he remained quiet during the Bluffton controversy but came out on 11 September with a public letter that went far beyond Rhett. He declared that the danger from abolition was so great that it called for secession throughout the South, with the aim not of forcing redress from the North but of separating permanently and forming a new Southern nation. They should support Polk in November, but only while planning their ultimate independence. Significantly, Cheves played far more on the slavery string than the tariff, recognizing, as did Rhett, that this was the only issue that had a hope of getting the South united in action.[44]

Suddenly Rhett felt reinvigorated, for Cheves carried considerable prestige in the state. Knowing that Huger intended to resign his Senate seat to make a place for Calhoun, yet still expecting that Polk would retain Calhoun as secretary of state, Rhett immediately suggested through the *Mercury* that Cheves should be appointed in Huger's place. Of course it was a position that Rhett himself ordinarily would have coveted, but he was realistic enough to know that in the current climate, and with relations with Calhoun strained as they were, he would have no support in the legislature for the succession. Cheves in the Senate would be a powerful ally, even though he differed on the matter of coordinated action by several states. It would never come, Rhett repeated, until South Carolina acted first and alone. "It is the stand-still policy which I condemn as fatal to all redress," he said. It was impossible for several of the slave states to act in concert, but if only one would move first, the others would follow, and thus their risk was minimal at best. He reminded them that before the Revolution there was little unanimity or cooperation among the colonies until one—he could not bring himself to mention Massachusetts by name—acted in the Boston Tea Party. "All we want is, that the tea shall be thrown overboard—that the issue shall be made," he declared. Whatever Jackson's reaction to nullification might have been, if an array of seceded Southern states presented themselves and their demands to Washington, there would be no attempt at coercion; of that he was sure, for "coercion will simply dissolve the union." And thus, again, without having publicly called for secession, he reiterated that its result would actually be reunification, for the North would never knowingly make secession permanent by attempting to curtail it with a force that could only achieve the opposite.[45] As for Cheves, he would learn the folly of hoping for cooperation. "The Southern Delegation has always been the meanest and most spiritless on the floor of Congress," he declared. "They are the merest coteries for power, without regard to principles, and when Cheves finds them so, I cannot but hope he will help us to unite the State in a bold effort to recover our rights." Cheves would never accept submission," Rhett told Burt; "he will at length go with us—for secession."[46]

Then McDuffie, whom Rhett had assumed to be in sympathy with him all along, came out at a public dinner late in September and called for a state convention, though he differed on the method. Abhorring more controversy, he wanted the legislature to issue the convention call without debating the subject first, for more speeches would only aggravate the situation. He wanted South Carolina to declare no further submission to the 1842 tariff nor any acceptance of antislavery discussion, and if either demand was not met, then to issue a call for a convention of all the slave states in May 1845. Should those states decline to act in concert, then he wanted his own state to hold a convention on July 4, 1845 and decide on submission or secession.[47] It was a middle ground between Rhett's Bluffton aims and Cheves's dependence on cooperation or nothing, but Rhett saw that it made McDuffie, too, a public ally at last, and he predicted that McDuffie and Cheves side-by-side in the Senate would be a potent team.[48] Then to Rhett's disappointment Cheves protested that he had no wish to take public office again and politely but firmly refused the suggestion that he draft a public address that would advance his candidacy.[49]

Meanwhile, Rhett resigned his editorship of the faltering *Spectator,* which was pointless for Calhoun's presidential hopes for now and perhaps somewhat embarrassing, given his current standing with the Calhoun people.[50] "I am here kicking up my heels," he wrote Burt, "feeling very much I suppose as a loon does on a winters day in his hollow." With ten weeks until Congress reconvened, he hoped to relax and step out of the eye of controversy. In fact, his unpopularity at the moment was such that "some vindictive devil in our neighborhood" poisoned his son Alfred's Irish setter, and Rhett had immediate fears that the culprit would kill the other family pets as well. Such an act could only further convince him of the fanaticism and fiendishness of his foes, whom more and more now he associated with abolition. This was soon to be confirmed when men such as John Quincy Adams determined to condemn him in their Yankee constituencies for his "disunion schemes," as Adams called Bluffton.[51]

Despite the small bursts of life that the Cheves and McDuffie declarations gave to Bluffton, the enthusiasm virtually disappeared by October, as the elections approached. The Democrats were everywhere triumphant, not a Whig being elected to the state legislature, and Rhett won unopposed. However, Beaufort and Colleton sent to the legislature substantially more Calhoun men than Bluffton supporters, and Edmund Rhett was defeated. The ever-vengeful Pickens gleefully spread the rumor that more than half of the voters in Rhett's district returned blank ballots rather than vote for him.[52] If Calhoun did not aid in Rhett's bid—and of course there was no need—still he did not put up a Democrat from his own coterie to chasten and challenge Rhett, as he had done with Henry L. Pinckney when he defied him. In fact, Calhoun made no effort at all to discipline Rhett for his recent rebellion, perhaps recognizing that the rejection of Bluffton and the further loss of influence in the state with the collapse of the old clique was punishment enough. Calhoun was once more firmly in control, had other recalcitrants to discipline, and thus could afford to leave Rhett alone to fall back in line. Besides, Rhett could still be useful for his ability to arouse emotions, and now that Hammond had broken with Calhoun, Rhett provided what might be a useful bridge to the more extreme elements in the state.[53]

Beyond question Rhett felt the effects of his fall from favor and influence, and he told Barnwell that he was exhausted and dispirited from the emotional stress of the dramatic rise and fall of Bluffton. Despondently he blamed himself for Edmund's defeat and no doubt dwelled again on the loss of his brightest hope, Albert. Even Stuart had been won over to Calhoun in October, which meant the loss of the *Mercury* for a state convention and secession. "Our State is true and ready for action I am sure, when the time comes," Stuart wrote his brother-in-law, "but I do not agree with you that the time *is* come." Rhett had made his statement with Bluffton, and there were men such as Seabrook and others who agreed with him, but now it was time to abandon the movement. "It has been *made*. It has had its effect. It can have no better effect—prolong we the same trumpet note ever so loudly on the same key."[54]

Rhett confessed to feeling persecuted, and even Memminger agreed, though frankly telling him, "I think you are answerable for much of the trouble which we have now on our hands." One moment Rhett considered retiring to Beaufort. The next he toyed with the idea of going to Columbia when the legislature convened, still hoping that his presence might exert some influence for calling a state convention, or at least to rebuild his now-shattered base there, but Barnwell, Stuart, Elmore, and other friends advised him not to go, fearing that it might be taken as campaigning for Huger's seat, which was clearly an impossibility now. Memminger—no friend—warned him in what may have been a threat to stay away from Columbia or that his financial difficulties might just be paraded publicly before the legislature. "Look to your private affairs," he counseled. "Had your energy been directed to them for the last five years, how very different they would have been." Worse, his children were growing up in Washington rather than in South Carolina where they belonged.[55] Calhoun's shadow and the state's own timidity had put the legislature in a condition not to take any advice that Barnwell Rhett had to offer at the moment, and in the current state of divided opinion, it would be foolish to try to mount a convention movement and fail.

Barnwell told him to bide his time. "If South Carolina rekindles her old Beacon fires of resistance, you will not fail her at the finish," he said. As for giving up his office and going back to his childhood home in Beaufort, Barnwell reminded him of Petigru's advice those many years ago, that their social relations there did not match their political views. The older generation at Beaufort had mellowed and were far less sympathetic to Rhett's radicalism than were their sons, the Bluffton Boys and their ilk now largely moved to Charleston. If Rhett tried to start his political career anew when the time came, he might find himself with no base in Beaufort, and the rumored blank ballots in the recent election may well have been his proof.[56] Even Stuart encouraged him not to resign, despite his current low ebb. "In *six months* you will begin to find all your old and added political strength coming back to you, without an effort," he predicted, and Elmore thoughtfully sent equal comfort to his old friend.[57] "I know *the respect* in which your talents *are* held by your colleagues," he assured Rhett, "but I also *know* that some of them have little love for you—and that it is *in your power* to do much *very* much to change that feeling." He should keep his seat in the House and try to cultivate his fellow members of the state delegation rather more.[58]

Only Memminger advised him to resign. Given his opposition to Rhett and Calhoun, his counsel could hardly be disinterested, and yet he made some sense nevertheless. Several times over the years he had suggested to Rhett that the pulpit, and not politics, was his true calling. Besides the hardship inflicted on Rhett's family, Memminger asked him to take a look at the toll on himself. "Consider all this my dear Rhett and see whether the good you are doing is at all commensurate to all this." What a price he had paid for his compulsion for the public life. "I will rejoice in seeing you sheltered from these many rude storms which I have seen break over your head," he went on. Then he finished with a prophecy of his own. If Rhett persisted in his reckless course of threats and agitation and confrontation, there would one day be even ruder storms, "which I fear will at last overwhelm you."[59]

ELEVEN

I Would Rather Talk Treason Than Not

1844–1846

POLK WON IN NOVEMBER AS part of a general Democratic victory, though Rhett met the news with despondence.[1] Practically his first utterance when the House convened in December was that thankfully they would have no more presidential elections for four years.[2] His only comfort in these dark weeks as he struggled to regain his equilibrium came from the legislature in Columbia where Governor Hammond, in one of his last acts, delivered a message that fell right in line with Rhett on the tariff and a convention call. Rhett even wrote to Hammond to offer his congratulations, and then McDuffie issued another statement of his own. Hammond spoke of arming the state to resist the tariff, and there was a last gasp of Blufftonism in Columbia. Calhoun's friends feared that if it persisted it could still split the state into two parties, Calhoun's and Rhett's, but Pickens, now in the state senate, was able to contain the outbreak, denouncing it as foolish and too ultra. Hammond believed that Pickens simply sought to disintegrate further what little following Rhett still enjoyed, and to complete Rhett's isolation, state senator Ker Boyce urged Calhoun to make certain that Rhett would not be able to secure any patronage appointments for his friends from the new president. William Gilmore Simms, popular Charleston novelist and proslavery advocate, told Burt that Carolinians were no longer willing to be led "by *Bluffton*."[3]

Hammond would never be in Calhoun's confidence again, and his call for a convention was easily defeated in the legislature, though Rhett still sent him compliments when he ended his term as governor, bitter and disillusioned with Calhoun. Despite Stuart's conversion to Calhoun, even the *Mercury* was to be reprimanded as now people in Charleston began to investigate starting a new Calhoun journal in the city. It would have ruined the *Mercury*, and the move's objective clearly enough was to force Stuart to step down. "He is a man of great and original genius," thought Hammond, "one of the Lions." But he was also drinking himself to death and was still too close to Rhett. In January Stuart gave way to his assistant editor, John Milton Clapp, an Ohioan with few apparent ties to Rhett, who complimented him on his independence and ability. Calhoun may not have chastised his unruly lieutenant directly, but Rhett was still to be punished. His isolation in the state and his own delegation in Congress were soon such that some of the Whigs began calling him the "lone star of disunion."[4]

Rhett's expectations for the session were few, and cynically he told Burt, "I should not be surprised at a vehement outbreak of futility." He hoped that with the Democrats carrying a majority of the seats just elected for the new Congress to convene in December 1845, they should resist any revision of the tariff now by this lame duck Congress in its short session.[5] As he expected, the Whigs and Northern Democrats launched their assault on the gag rule on the opening day of the session, and there was never any doubt of success. It was rescinded 108 to 80, and Rhett did not even enter the debate, despite having accumulated a considerable file of abstracts of antislavery arguments that he might have used.[6] In response the state senate in Columbia declared the House's action to be in effect a dissolution of the Union, and then Hammond issued his call for defense, but the House postponed consideration of the resolutions. Hammond and the Bluffton Boys blamed Calhoun.[7]

With news like this, so disinterested and disgusted was Rhett that he abandoned his usual punctuality, sometimes missed committee meetings, and could only occasionally muster enthusiasm to spar with his old antagonist Adams. He did, however, make a new friend. His old associate Dixon Lewis of Alabama had resigned his seat, and replacing him this session was a thirty-year-old lawyer and sometime editor from Wetumpka named William Lowndes Yancey. Rhett found a kindred spirit in him from the first, for Yancey was just as fiery and intemperate as he. After only a month in the House his maiden speech on the floor so infuriated a North Carolina delegate that challenges to a duel ensued in January 1845, and Yancey already felt spiritually close enough to Rhett to ask him to act as his second and handle the ensuing correspondence. Declaring his sympathy with Yancey in the affair, still Rhett declined, pleading that his religious scruples prevented him from taking any part in dueling. Nevertheless, there was the sure beginning of a political bond between them.[8]

Only Texas presented either stimulation or hope, and Rhett put himself in the middle of that battle from the outset. He had been involved peripherally as far back as 1843 when he called on then secretary of state Abel Upshur to discuss annexation. At the close of the last session Rhett asked friends to let him know the sentiment on Texas in their constituencies, urging them that delay might well cost them the slave state and all that went with it.[9] Now McDuffie in the Senate and Pennsylvanian Jared Ingersoll in the House introduced an unprecedented joint resolution to annex. Quite apparently it seemed to violate the Constitution, which clearly stated that such treaties were the exclusive province of the Senate. On the other hand there was the plain parliamentary fact that while Senate ratification required a two-thirds majority—and the votes were not there—passage of a joint resolution needed only a simple majority, which was a certainty. There was an immediate outcry, and several amended resolutions were introduced in its place. Then Stephen A. Douglas of Illinois offered the House a substitute that split hairs neatly by pointing out that the United States had taken the position in 1803 that the Louisiana Purchase included Texas; therefore annexation of Texas now was not a treaty with a foreign sovereignty that required Senate approval but was merely the admission of what had always been a lawful territory of the nation—even if not pressed for the past forty years—and thus a simple joint resolution was all that was required, as in any admission of a territory to statehood. It was an ingenious plan, and it also settled the slavery problem simply by the automatic operation of the Missouri Compromise line on any American territory acquired in the Louisiana Purchase.[10]

Rhett was immediately enamored of the Douglas plan, and his first action was to recommend that Douglas withdraw a preamble specifying the details of the annexation that would itself have required debate. By so doing he hoped to bring the House immediately to a vote on a resolution declaring simply that Texas should be annexed. If that passed, then the other details would follow in train. Rhett's proposal took the Whigs by surprise, but it did not achieve the quick results for which he might have hoped.[11] The debate dragged on for three weeks, and in the course of them Milton Brown of Tennessee introduced a substitute that was even simpler than Douglas's resolutions, with none of the shady areas that could act like barbs to catch opposition debate and waste time. Douglas quickly shifted his support to the Brown resolutions, and Rhett delivered a major address on them on January 21, 1845.

He opened with a reference to the Battle of San Jacinto in 1836, when the Texans held their fire until their Mexican foes were well in their sights, than mowed them down quickly with heavy volleys. He promised, like them, to be "as brief, as dense, and as pointed" as possible, and for a change he stayed straight on target throughout. He dismissed peripheral arguments against annexation, such as the assumption of the debt of the Republic of Texas or the possibility of war with Mexico, which still failed to recognize Texan independence. His only interest was the Brown proposal, which provided simply for admission to statehood, and for leaving to Texas itself the decision of whether or not to include slavery as allowed by the Missouri Compromise. Brown was a Whig, and yet Rhett backed him completely, saying that Brown's resolution gave him "more unfeigned gratification than any which had been offered." It showed that even though a Whig and opposed to him on many of the great issues of the day, still Brown and Whigs like him were true Southerners first "when questions arose vitally affecting their peculiar section," meaning slavery.

Rhett dispensed with the argument of usurpation of Senate treaty power. Nothing in the Constitution gave the president and the Senate the power to admit new states, he argued. Rather, it specifically stated that "Congress may admit new states into the Union." It was only by the doctrine of implied power that authority for annexation could be vested in the Senate. Moreover, bringing in a new state was the business of all the people, and the House was universally regarded to be the place where the people's views were represented, whereas the Senate was where the states in their sovereign capacity spoke their will, reflecting the fact that senators were elected not by the people but by the legislatures. His arguments were well laid, logically presented, and entirely cogent. Absent was any of the emotion or invective that characterized most of his addresses now, for he knew that he was trying to win not just Democratic or even Whig votes but *Southern* votes regardless of party. As for the other principal argument that Texas was an independent sovereignty, and that no foreign nation could be admitted into the Union, he had only to point out that in 1787 every one of the thirteen colonies was an independent entity and thus "foreign" to all the others, and this same argument also countered the protests that all states had to pass through a territorial phase before admission. In fact, he said, "to be a foreign State, so far as the Union is concerned, is, therefore, a necessary state of things, for the admission of a State into the Union."

There was another argument, of course, that annexation was about more than Texas—it was a sectional issue tied with slavery. He hardly denied that, nor did he wish to. Texas by geography would be a part of the South, and by the presence there already of slavery it would be a slave state. But by the same token, the pending settlement of a boundary dispute with Britain promised that the Oregon territory would one day belong to the United States, and by terms of the Missouri Compromise it would be a Northern state and a free state, and was that not a sectional and slave issue too? No territory for admission could be at once in all parts of the Union, and thus not have sectional ramifications, and no territory could equally impact the balance of slave and free states at admission. It must be one or the other, but still the South and the slave states were the smaller part of the Union and always would be. Was it fair for other sections to try to expand themselves while at the same time restricting the South? "This will not do," he declared, and he warned that it would be the death of the spirit of Union. Besides, add Texas or any other territory to the South, and was there any danger of her ruling the country? "You of the North and West," he said, "to you the empire of this Union belongs—to you the population and the dominion of this continent." The South could participate in the spread of that empire and all that came with it, "but we will not rule the mighty progress," he stated. But did they not have a right to be participants? "We must too advance, or we must be destroyed by its march," he warned.

Rhett felt that the tread of their advance must be to the beat of slavery. For more than a decade organizations in the North and now the West assailed their institutions, seeking to interfere with the very "domestic tranquility" that the Constitution was formed to preserve. He decried the shouts of "slavery—slavery—slavery—falling from the lips of every opponent" of the Texas resolution. Once the South was indifferent to annexation, for it did not immediately serve her interests. "But you have disturbed our 'domestic tranquility,'" he charged. "You have rendered Texas, in the southern mind, necessary to insure it; and now, after creating the necessity for her annexation, will you deny us the acquisition?"[12]

It was a brilliant appeal not just for Texas but for equity. After years of threats of what the South would do to the Union, Rhett portrayed it now as a poor underdog that could hardly pose a threat to the bigger and stronger regions arrayed against it. There was not a single mention of secession or disunion, or bloodbaths in the wake of Southern wrongs. But there was the constant appeal to Southern loyalties in the chamber, be they Whig or Democrat, with the plea that slavery was more threatened than ever, a peril that cut across party lines to endanger the "domestic tranquility" of all who lived in the South. Having given up on the Democratic Party, Barnwell Rhett was trying to assemble a new constituency.

It was probably the only time in his House career to date that Rhett found himself applauded from all sides.[13] Within four days all the other variations in annexation resolutions had been abandoned, and the Brown measure passed and was sent to the Senate. A month later that body also passed it, and on March 3, as one of his last acts, President Tyler signed the act for annexation. Never before had Rhett exerted such a dynamic influence in passing a piece of legislation. Indeed, few knew just how great his influence had been, for a decade later Rhett suggested that in fact it was he who first approached Brown and gave him the idea for the simple joint resolution. Knowing that at the moment nothing that came from him would meet a welcome, and being ever the tactician, Rhett planted the seed where it would do the most good, with the result that it was a Whig offering a solution to draw Democrats to him and appealing as well to Southern unity. It must have galled Rhett, always anxious to receive credit for his actions, to see the kudos go elsewhere. All the same, the "lone star of disunion" had done as much as any man in Congress to add the Lone Star to the Union.[14]

The triumph in gaining Texas and another slave state helped make up some-what for the disappointments elsewhere, though Rhett would not have been human had he not felt at least a twinge of satisfaction when Calhoun's rejection suddenly rivaled his own. Even before the Texas question arose in the House, Rhett found Calhoun despondent and disgusted. Calhoun had heard nothing from Polk. There were no offers of continued tenure at the State Department, nor even solicitations for his views on issues.[15] And when Polk took office in March, it was Buchanan who got the State Department portfolio. To Calhoun he offered instead the appointment as minister to Great Britain. It was a serious blow, for if he accepted it would remove Calhoun from the scene just when he needed to be influencing the Polk administration, which was exactly what Polk had in mind. Calhoun turned it down. Meanwhile, an angry Rhett wrote an anonymous letter in the *Mercury* criticizing Polk's appointments and his abro-gation of the presumed bargain to retain Calhoun in his cabinet. Then, in what must have come as a surprise, word came that Polk intended to offer the ambas-sadorship to Rhett. However, Rhett scarcely had time to get excited before the ministerial post evaporated after Polk learned of the *Mercury* letter and its authorship. Regarding the position as due to South Carolina, Polk then offered it first to Elmore and next to Pickens, and both of them also declined to be asso-ciated with the administration.[16]

Calhoun's forces were in disarray, and he himself was feeling betrayed, the more so after they heard Polk's equivocal inaugural in which he made no con-crete promises on the tariff and other important issues. A dejected Barnwell told his cousin that he feared "the Southern civilization must go out in blood."[17] But as Rhett returned to South Carolina in March at the end of the brief but event-ful session, he found yet another surprise. He was back in the inner circle. The letter to the *Mercury* may have helped, but mainly Calhoun needed all the help he could get to start building anew his base for a presidential run in 1848. On May 8, Rhett was invited to a meeting at Elmore's home in the city. It may have been a bit chilly, for besides friends such as his brother James and Dixon Lewis, there were also Hamilton and Ker Boyce, both of whom had rebuffed him over Bluffton. Their mission transcended personal rivalries, however, for they had to plan Calhoun's best course for the next three years.

Out of the discussion came agreement that he and his supporters should all adopt a conciliatory posture with Polk, though they agreed that by not being in the administration, Calhoun now would be spared any criticism that might attach to Polk. At the same time—and this could well have come from Rhett—they suggested that they get their press active in promoting opposition to any general nominating convention "which put the Party in the hands of the office holders and seekers." There must be no repetition of the Van Buren–dominated convention of 1844. Calhoun needed to make himself better known in the North too, and they asked him to make a northern tour as a private citizen, making no speeches and eschewing politics but allowing himself to be seen. It was also possible that South Carolina might need to call him to the Senate, since Huger had resigned his seat at the end of March to create a vacancy should Calhoun want it. As of the meeting date Pickens had not yet declined the British mission, and they decided that if he did, and it should be offered to Calhoun again, then he ought to accept only if given absolute negotiating power to settle the Oregon dispute, something with which Rhett stood in full agreement. That way credit for any success would be his alone.[18]

Being included in the committee meeting brought Rhett out of his funk, if the Texas victory did not, and soon he was acting himself again, though observing the agreement not to take on the administration. He returned to the pages of the *Spectator* and wrote more for the *Mercury*, starting again the tariff agitation though refraining from attacking Polk. Moreover he made certain that Calhoun knew what he was writing and, in the case of one *Mercury* article, actually included a disclaimer of any position for or against a state convention or a Southern convention, dictated to him by Calhoun. Still Rhett felt sure that his articles would leave the public "not in the dark as to my opinions as to the disease of the times or the remedy."

As for the recent actions of what he called "the rebellious proceedings of my constituents," so far as he was concerned they were the only ones who upset the Whigs and Northern Democrats, so Calhoun would be safe from being damaged by their actions. Privately he showed that he still seethed at the denouement of Bluffton. "I was so mad at their sickly delicacy concerning the Union," he told Burt, "that I believe I would rather talk treason than not." It all reminded him of an incident years before when he accosted an overseer near Beaufort whom he caught brutally whipping a slave. Rhett tried to stop the flogging, and the brute agreed that there had been punishment enough for the actual offense committed but claimed that now he was beating the slave because the slave would not stop "hollowing." So it was with himself, Rhett declared. "We are not allowed to hollow." He still wanted South Carolina to resist, though every day his fears that it would never happen mounted. If it did, however, his constituents and Burt's in the Abbeville district in the western part of the state would be most prepared. "Mine are ready," he said. "I know that there is no danger in our people being too hot. The danger is the other way. I will keep up the fire, if like a lost hunter in a prairie, I have to kindle it alone, with my gun flint, and watch by the blaze, rifle in hand to keep off the wolves."[19] Rhett liked the image of himself standing alone against all odds and would use it again and again in the years ahead. Unpopularity could be to him a badge of courage, proof that he was right.

Rhett kept up the fire through June and July, first from home and then from Washington, and a few friends did as well, their letters generally written under the fitting nom de plume "Bluffton." A year had passed since the inauguration of the movement, he charged, and still nothing had been done. Calhoun was turned out of the cabinet, the gag rule was gone, offices were offered to South Carolinians that they could not in conscience accept, and the 1842 tariff remained in effect. Supinely South Carolina waited on Congress to act, but it was a false hope. However, they promised that "the Bluffton Boys have been silenced, not subdued. . . . The fire is not extinguished; it smolders beneath, and will burst forth in another glorious flame that shall overrun the State and place her light again as of old, upon the watch tower of freedom."[20] There was Rhett's old "light upon a hill" again, the blaze he would kindle alone if need be and tend with rifle in hand. Clapp turned out not to be preferable to Stuart for Calhoun after all, as he let his pages keep the heat up on the tariff, with Rhett assumed to be behind most of it but Hammond, and some even thought Pickens, in the wings. It all worked against Calhoun and played to the strain of sentiment against him, with meetings soon adopting resolutions condemning him for his failure to speak out on the tariff.[21] The old uproar, quieted by Calhoun but not quelled, rose once more. Indomitable, unrepentant, and unstoppable, the old Rhett was back.

He left the scene of action for several weeks in August and early September, but only to shift the battle line to England. A group of merchants and importers of Southern rice had commissioned him to represent them in a dispute over rice duties overcharged by Her Majesty's custom and excise, despite a long-standing agreement with the United States. For some time Whitehall admitted that refunds were due, but no one seemed to do anything about it, thanks to confusion over who really owed the money, whether an act of Congress would be required to appropriate funds, and whose currency the refunds should be paid in and whether to shippers in America or receivers in England. It was exactly the sort of confused documentary mess that needed Rhett's special talents, and he in turn needed the fat commission he stood to make, since his fee would be 5 percent or more of the sixty thousand to eighty thousand pounds due, which could amount to as much as twenty thousand dollars and go a long way toward solving his financial woes. He learned what he could of the circumstances, called on responsible people to establish the case law involved, and then worked out a solution, in the process doing far more work than his employers anticipated and earning some extravagant compliments along with the promise of an enhanced fee for his "most instrumental" services when finally the refunds were paid.[22]

While serving his own interests in London, however, Rhett tried to advance the cause of tariff reform at the same time. He chanced to meet Reverdy Johnson, recently elected Whig senator from Maryland, and Johnson told him that from his own conversations with Polk he believed the president preferred a revenue tariff but also favored moderate protection duties at the same time. Rhett hardly found this equivocation disquieting, but it was what he had expected all along. They would get nothing more than a modified tariff out of Polk.[23] However, that did not prevent him from gaining an audience with the foreign secretary, George Gordon, Lord Aberdeen, under the pretext of arguing that the rice duty case was interfering with efforts in the United States to reform the tariff. While arguing that settlement of the case would make reform easier, Rhett told the foreign secretary that when Congress convened in December he was going to attack the 1842 tariff vigorously, and if he failed to shift Polk he was determined "to renew the *Nullification* vote in South Carolina which he had formerly proposed, and which had produced such serious consequences."

Rhett was acting unilaterally again, with no authority from Calhoun to invoke nullification nor any authority from anyone to be holding out the prospect of reduced import duties on British goods as a consequence of a favorable decision on the rice business. At the same time he was resorting to his old habit of threats—quite veiled this time—to suggest to Aberdeen that a quick settlement of the rice difficulty would in some way help forestall nullification by making tariff reform easier. Aberdeen concluded that Rhett was certainly a clever fellow and ended the meeting having been impressed that the Carolinian was "an influential man." He was neither the first nor the last to be taken in by Rhett's assumed air of authority and importance, when in fact he represented no power but himself.[24]

On his return in mid-September, Rhett carried dispatches from the ambassador in London and stopped in Washington first, where he immediately called on Polk, Buchanan, and U.S. Treasury secretary Robert J. Walker to deliver the dispatches and tell them what he had learned in London, no doubt also hoping to see if Reverdy Johnson had been right about Polk. Rhett said plainly that he wanted to know what Polk intended to do over the tariff, but the president was evasive, declaring that he wanted a reduction but without outlining any prevailing principle. Buchanan argued that a revenue tariff was all they needed, though he spoke only vaguely about a possible 25 percent maximum, and then suggested that the tariff bill killed in the last Congress should perhaps be the goal. Walker at least spoke in detail, but he made it clear that he stood completely on the bill defeated in 1844. "I am satisfied that the Bill substantially is all the administration will propose," Rhett hurried to report to Calhoun, "and that is all we will get, from the Democratic Party, if we get that." Polk and Walker were not sincere on reform, and Buchanan was weak and vacillating, as always.

Rhett advised Calhoun that they needed to decide their course on the tariff before Congress met in December, and also to decide some vital points. Ought they to proceed as if assuming that Polk and his party would honor his tariff pledge and therefore participate in the party caucus for organizing the House, or should they assume they were betrayed and boycott the caucus? "You know my opinions of the Democratic Party," he reminded Calhoun. Should they make a bid in the Senate through McDuffie and Huger, aided by other trusty supporters, to secure the public printing for the *Washington Constitution,* which was about to supersede the *Spectator* as Calhoun's organ and would desperately need the contract? Most of all, what should Rhett do? He did not wish to be "found again as at the opening of the last Congress attempting what our friends have not courage to execute." If Polk gave them a protective bill, should he support it, fight it on the floor and denounce it, or come home to fight it there? He did not say anything of nullification or secession, but his meaning was clear enough. All these questions should be settled now, he argued, "for they must shape our line of policy from the beginning." Whatever Rhett was to do, he stated, "I must be sure of my game before I attempt it."[25]

It certainly sounded, to Calhoun at least, as if Rhett were being the good subordinate at last and awaiting orders. Yet his declaration to Aberdeen suggested otherwise, and then within just days of arriving back in Charleston and without hearing Calhoun's reply, Rhett spoke to some of his Blufftonites at the Salt Ketcher. Quickly rumors reached Calhoun that Rhett declared there that if the tariff were not brought down to a strictly revenue basis South Carolina would nullify, and that if Calhoun did not acquiesce "they would throw you overboard."[26] Two weeks later, now with a response from Calhoun in his hand, Rhett learned that Calhoun rejected forming a separate organization and wanted to work with the Democrats, which meant joining them in caucus, but he wanted Rhett to coordinate sympathetic senators to secure the printing for the *Constitution.* Rhett, however, was acting on his own again. He met with state legislator James Walker in early October and told him that he had no intention of getting involved in the public printing issue and then disparaged his friend Elmore for his continuing timidity on resistance. Walker was guarded with Rhett, having been warned to take care by Hammond, yet came away with the conviction that Rhett was dropping a lot of names of influential men in South Carolina and Congress, suggesting as he had to Aberdeen that he spoke with powerful backing.

"He need not have volunteered his confidence had he not had some motive," Walker concluded, and when Rhett mentioned that he intended to visit Columbia during the next session of the legislature in December, Walker spotted the motive well enough. "He still has his eyes fixed upon the Senatorship." At the same time Rhett complained to Buchanan that too many people held him responsible for Calhoun's actions, suggesting at least a disposition to distance himself from the great Carolinian.[27]

Then Calhoun did something that outraged Rhett and to many Carolinians seemed to break the unanimity with which they had opposed internal improvements for so long. Barely had Rhett returned to Charleston before Calhoun went west to Memphis in November to chair a commercial convention to promote river transportation. The West had always been Henry Clay's great base of support, and transportation improvement for commerce was one of his primary issues. In a clear attempt to co-opt some of Clay's constituency, Calhoun made an address at Memphis in which he came out for a vast scheme of river improvements, a canal connecting the Mississippi with the Great Lakes, railroad links, and more, much of it to be funded by federal land grants to the private enterprise that would carry out the work. The Mississippi was a vast internal sea, he said, and therefore its improvement was not a local matter but a national one and thus just as constitutional as the maintenance and improvement of harbors and other navigational aids. It was a clear rationalization that blatantly served Calhoun's presidential aspirations, and many at home saw it so. If not quite governmental internal improvements, it was virtually the same thing by another name. South Carolina reacted dramatically, and when Calhoun did finally allow his name to be used in the legislature for election to replace Huger—thus ending yet again any hope Rhett may have had—he nearly met defeat as a result.

Rhett went to Columbia for the opening of the legislature, even though he knew by then that Calhoun would take the Huger seat and so did not enter the contest. He was there when the report of Calhoun's Memphis performance arrived. His old Bluffton crowd immediately stood on the floor and introduced resolutions condemning Calhoun's action, in spite of the fact that Rhett advised them not to, and soon it was assumed that Rhett was the author. Calhoun even heard rumors that Rhett was trying to poison old McDuffie's mind against his program, thus dividing the state's congressional delegation that would be vital to passage of the legislation for Calhoun's new program in the next Congress. Rhett's enemies reminded Calhoun of similar rumors that Rhett had condemned Calhoun during the Bluffton summer.[28] The *Mercury* charged Calhoun with inconsistency, and Pickens was in Rhett's camp, for a change, and began writing an anonymous attack on Calhoun's Memphis declaration to appear in the

Southern Quarterly Review. Calhoun quickly spotted his cousin's writing style in the unsigned assault and all but ended their personal and political association for the rest of his life. Yet again tremors were leading to shifts in the tectonic plates of Carolinian politics.

Amid all this Rhett left for Washington, stopping with McDuffie and Burt in Richmond where they found that many old Calhoun supporters in Virginia were shocked by Memphis. Presumably feeling uneasy about contacting Calhoun directly himself, Rhett asked Elmore to warn Calhoun that he needed to come to Richmond to clarify things and mend fences. He also wanted to meet with Calhoun as soon as they were both in Washington in order to have a frank discussion and learn his views, promising to reserve decision as to his own course until then.[29]

Rhett arrived to take his seat in the first session of the Twenty-ninth Congress only to find even more excitement. Polk sent a message to Congress that sounded ominously warlike toward Mexico, which was refusing to acknowledge the annexation of Texas and yield its claims. The message was equally belligerent toward Britain over the Oregon question, demanding all of the territory. Calhoun preferred a policy that he called "masterly inactivity," counting on time to achieve Polk's ends rather than resorting to confrontation. As for Rhett, perhaps after the face-to-face discussion that he asked for he felt inclined to side with Calhoun, at least where Oregon was concerned, in part perhaps because the settlement of the rice duty question, and a handsome commission to himself, would be disrupted or even quashed if war broke out. He complained to Buchanan that "the whole question has been so bedevilled by diplomatists, that a plain man might well fire at any delay," but he realized that firing now could be ruinous.[30]

Beyond his personal interests, Rhett felt the general Southern opposition to a war over Oregon, which the United States had shared in a joint occupancy with Britain that Polk wanted now to terminate with one year's notice. Resolutions came on the floor of the House to start raising troops and building forts for defense, and there were demands for the whole of Oregon being undisputed American property or they should fight. Even old Adams, sensing additional free states in the offing, voted for preparations, and when Rhett charged him with inconsistency in voting against the War of 1812 but favoring conflict with Britain now, Adams rather embarrassed him with the reminder that in 1812 he was serving as minister to Russia and had no vote at all.[31] The move for all of Oregon became a Democratic Party measure and gained rapidly in popularity, which only isolated Rhett more when he continued his opposition even though friends advised that it might ruin him. To Rhett, of course, such a warning was only encouragement.[32]

He took his opposition to the floor repeatedly, first on January 5, 1846, resting his case on the assumption that in all her wars the United States ought always to be in the posture of defending herself, not of aggressing on another nation. "We must have strong and imperious reasons to justify us in entering upon any war," he declared, "still more an aggressive war." Britain had violated no American rights nor made any act of aggression. Moreover, in the race for joint settlement the United States stood way ahead of Britain, and inevitably the mere direction of things would bring them most or all of Oregon in time. Giving notice of the termination of joint occupancy would not in itself give them all or even a square inch of Oregon exclusively. They would have to fight for it, and he warned that it would mean meeting Britain virtually on a global front. "Does any one believe that we can get Oregon without first achieving the utter destruction of the British empire?" he asked. They were talking a greater war than they imagined. "I am not afraid of a war with England, nor with any other nation," he averred. "No nation can conquer us." But to defeat Britain would require such concentrated and sustained effort over so long a period that inevitably it must alter Americans' very form of government, leading eventually to a military dictatorship. "I have ever been what has been called a Jeffersonian Republican," he said, even if he had never actually affiliated officially with that now-dead party, and to him the idea of such a consolidation of power was anathema. "As a Democrat, as I might be called in the North, or as a Republican, as I would be termed in the South, I demand that you give us good reasons for urging us to a war." A man who killed one fellowman they called a murderer; a man who killed millions in war became a hero. "War is always an enormous crime," he warned, "often on both sides—always on one." He did not want that crime on their heads, and they should think well before putting it there.[33]

Rhett was on the floor daily thereafter, in one instance defending Calhoun against charges that as secretary of state he had a secret bargain with Britain to trade part of Oregon for Whitehall's promise not to interfere with Texas. In another instance he engaged in a pointless contest with Adams for the last word over matters irrelevant to the Oregon debate, though it showed the temperaments of the two men well enough. He also used the same sectional argument accusing the North of wanting Oregon to expand its power that others had used against the South and Texas, and which he had freely admitted.[34] In the end Rhett could not stop the administration, of course, even with Calhoun now taking the same stance in the Senate, and Congress authorized Polk to give notice of the termination of joint occupancy in April. Yet Rhett later believed—or chose to claim—that his pleas for patience and forbearance made the debate less belligerent, in the end avoiding a confrontation, and in June the two governments worked out an amicable settlement with a boundary on the forty-ninth parallel.[35]

Rhett's "masterly inactivity" policy and defending Calhoun against attacks may have cooled Calhoun's dissatisfaction with him somewhat, but the problem of the Memphis declaration proved harder to surmount, for Rhett remained immovable against internal improvements, voting against every such act, even one that would spend federal money for improvements to Charleston harbor. When a bill growing out of the Memphis convention came on the floor, he opposed it unconditionally, along with several others in his delegation, and bent only on the point of allowing that the government could contribute public land to some extent to canal builders and river improvements, as was already the policy with railroad companies. The western rivers were no different than any other rivers and harbors, and he pointed out that the Supreme Court itself had declared such bodies of water constitutionally ineligible for government appropriations. He made it clear that on the basic issue of improvements he would not budge, and without naming Calhoun, he still assailed him for the fact that the great Republican principle against improvements was to be buried, not by its ancient enemies "but by those who profess to be its friends." Besides, if they were to engage in the business of encouraging transportation, it ought to be the railroads, which were faster and more efficient, and could go anywhere.[36] Nevertheless, a rivers and harbors bill did pass Congress, only to be vetoed by Polk, an action that began to give Rhett hope for this administration and the Democratic Party after all, a hope furthered by the passage of a new tariff pushed by Polk and framed by Walker. It was not much different from the earlier failed tariff bill, but at least this tariff reduced maximum rates to 30 percent on imports of special concern to the South. Rhett was not enthusiastic over it, and Calhoun fought it in the Senate, but it was better than it might have been and bore the promise of later reductions. When the new tariff bill passed in July and was signed by Polk, at least the tariff agitation was over.[37]

Now Rhett finally came to an accommodation with Calhoun. Despite any estrangement between them, Rhett still regarded Calhoun's election to the presidency as the South's, and South Carolina's, best hope for achieving more definitive safeguards within the Union and for defeating protectionism and abolition definitively. If Calhoun hoped to take the White House he would have to have support in the West, and that might just require some compromise of principles, though for Rhett such a thing came hard and only after tortured rationalization. Thus when Pickens's anonymous attack came out, Rhett defended Calhoun against its strictures—though no doubt taking some pleasure in being able to help alienate Pickens from the great man for a change.[38] In July, Calhoun reported in the Senate a memorial from the Memphis convention in which he presented his own rationalization. Federal appropriations had always been perfectly lawful for lighthouses, buoys, and other aids to navigation, under constitutional authority to oversee interstate commerce. Therefore that same authority extended to regulation of rivers that ran through more than one state and thus conferred the power to appropriate federal funds for their improvement and development.

Several people saw the merit of accepting Calhoun's rationale, and Polk's veto of the rivers and harbors bill helped, for with the administration apparently hostile to internal improvements it could be safe now to yield a thin margin on the issue if in return it bought Calhoun the West in 1848. J. Milton Clapp changed direction with the *Mercury*, and if he did not outright back Calhoun's position, at least he stopped his criticism. Rhett soon followed. Calhoun's rationalizations were sufficient for him now, and when asked to contribute an article of his own in the *Southern Quarterly Review*, he agreed.[39] Though uneasy with the approach, he based his argument on eminent practicality. Polk successfully vetoed the recent bill only because there was not the two-thirds majority in Congress to override. Two new Whig Northern states would come into the Union soon, however, and their four additional senators would give internal improvements the necessary majority in the Senate. As for the House, there would be a new census and resultant reapportionment in 1850, and the prevailing population trends showed the North growing much faster than the South, which would mean more Whig representatives. In short, after 1850 no veto of internal improvements would be secure, and therefore any constitutional arguments against such legislation would be mere abstractions. That meant facing "the practical business of statesmanship," the first time in his career that Rhett proposed practicality over principle.

"The question is not then, how shall we rightly think," he suggested, "but it is, what shall we do?" There was always the last resort, "state interposition or secession," but he had seen that the South was not ready for that. Such being the case, Calhoun's proposal, limiting appropriations and including as it did the expedient of separating the West from the North and binding it to the South, remained the only practical alternative. "We must yield a part," said Rhett, "divide the interests, and thus deprive the policy of its fatal effect on the whole constitution." Calhoun's plan was accused of being unconstitutional but could be defended at least on moral grounds, though Rhett now made a case for its constitutionality as well. While he still dissented from a few of Calhoun's arguments, his article presented on the whole a ringing endorsement.[40]

The future of the Union could ride on this alliance of South and West, he seemed to say, though in reality what he implied was that without it the South might be forced to secede, which was rather a different matter.[41] Rhett did not feel entirely at ease with his article, confessing that he feared it would brand him as subservient to Calhoun. "If I were a greater coward than I am, I would not write this article," he told Elmore in September.[42] Yet he felt he had done an effective job of explaining what he called "Mr Calhouns move around," thinking it a better argument for Calhoun's report than the report itself.[43] Rhett believed that the *Review* article would be important to Calhoun's future prospects, yet he had several concerns of his own, and not just Calhoun's ambitions, before him.[44] McDuffie was ailing and feeble and had resigned in August. When the legislature met in the fall it choose his successor, and healing his breach with Calhoun would make Rhett a more acceptable candidate, especially now that he regarded Pickens as dead in the water.[45] Certainly others spoke of him as a possibility, and Elmore, also being considered, urged Rhett to come home at the recess to test the waters. "That there are difficulties in your path I know—the same that you have met heretofore," he confessed. Still, he continued, "it seems to me that if you can be elected you should run." Elmore would happily stand aside and had said so to others whom, he said, "would generally, if they do not prefer you, be as well satisfied with you as myself." If not hearty encouragement, still it looked promising, and even Hunter in Virginia heard rumblings that Rhett's prospects for a Senate seat were on the rise.[46]

Thus Rhett, like Calhoun, could dance to the tune of expedience if need be, and in that mood he began to extend his new attitude elsewhere. At the beginning of the summer he criticized cousin Barnwell and others for being too easy on the Polk administration.[47] By the end of the session on August 10, however, the Oregon question was peacefully settled, the rivers and harbors bill had been vetoed, and the Walker Tariff had been signed into law. Polk was showing signs of at least moderate loyalty to Southern interests, and Rhett considerably softened his attitude. Suddenly Rhett was making social calls at the Executive Mansion, and at a time when both Rhett and Polk needed allies, for the president had gone to war with Mexico.[48]

The first skirmishes along the Rio Grande came back in May. Rhett, however much he opposed going to war over Oregon to add Northern free states, was wholeheartedly in favor of fighting Mexico, especially with the prospect of California and much of the Southwest that might be acquired, most of it below the Missouri Compromise line. Despite his recent rapprochement with Calhoun, Rhett broke with him here—one of only two such occasions that he actually acknowledged, though there had been several—for with Mexico, Calhoun favored "masterly inactivity" as with Britain.[49] In fact, Rhett had felt concerned for readiness to fight Mexico as far back as February, though he apprehended no

real danger of a conflict.[50] As soon as word of the opening skirmishes reached
Washington, Polk sent a request to Congress for $2 million in appropriations to
"repel invasion." Rhett defied Calhoun by standing behind the administration
on the floor even though privately he dismissed Polk's claim that Mexico precipitated the conflict. "I knew better," he told Hammond later.[51] Still he declared
himself willing to vote "money to any amount, and men in any numbers."[52]
After that he found himself even more welcome at the White House and began
to find—or so persuaded himself—that he was beginning to acquire influence
with the president.[53]

With the country going to war, his relations with Calhoun thawed if not
warmed, and with his stock with the administration growing, Rhett felt his fortunes rising again. Moreover, on June 27, Elizabeth gave him another daughter,
Claudine. An addition to the family was always buoying, but the child was sickly
from the first and soon contracted whooping cough. Though she survived, her
father found her "utterly prostrated, a living skeleton with all its organs of life
deranged."[54] And she was also another mouth to feed. Much to his impatient
chagrin, after nearly a year his commission from the British rice duty affair still
had not been forthcoming. His financial situation had seen no improvement in
the past year. His mortgage holders were bent on foreclosure, especially deTreville, and Barnwell had warned him the year before that a sheriff's seizure and
sale was imminent. The pressure to sell his slaves became all the greater as a
result, and to forestall that extremity he used the recess to return to London to
press for collection.[55] He had involved Secretary of State Buchanan in his efforts
to bring a resolution the past winter, then waited patiently through the Oregon
crisis, and afterward reminded Buchanan, "I have proved my faith by my work,"
suggesting that Rhett's arguments for calm and against war may have been part
of a bargain for assistance in the rice matter. Now he wanted Buchanan to prove
his faith, and the secretary began correspondence with British authorities.[56]

Rhett made the trip in October, only to find that now that he had done all
he was asked and more, the parties who hired him began to argue about who
owed him what, the result being that they were only prepared to pay him about
seventeen thousand dollars instead of the more than twenty thousand dollars he
was due. Never adept in financial transactions, he admitted defeat in this one
and agreed to accept what they offered, though it would not all be forthcoming
even then. However, on his return to Georgetown in November, weary and suffering from a cold, he found the good news that after several years of poor crops
his rice yield for the present year ought to bring in another eighteen thousand
dollars or more. Taken all together, the money now in hand or forthcoming
would be enough to retire the mortgage that endangered ownership of thirty of

his slaves, so that he could now use them to substitute for Elmore's security for a debt he owed the bank. "My prospects are decidedly brightening," he told Elmore with relief.[57]

They seemed to be improving in South Carolina, too, though his full rehabilitation was still a way off. There had been a small movement to find a candidate to oust him from his House seat late that spring, in revenge for the false rumors of his being behind the legislature's attack on Calhoun, but it never took fire.[58] Even though Stuart was gone from the *Mercury,* Clapp proved just as congenial, and now there was some talk of Rhett for McDuffie's seat. Several were spoken of, in fact, including Elmore, Hammond, Cheves, and even Barnwell, though none had come out yet to seek the post.[59] Simms thought none of them except Hammond worthy to wear the mantle of Calhoun in the Senate and dismissed Rhett's chances, thinking he had not "the slightest claim to wisdom," but Hammond believed that "Rhett is stronger than we think."[60]

Rhett himself regarded his chances more reservedly and decided not to return to South Carolina until after the election. Friends meanwhile told him that Elmore actually expected to be elected and had his business affairs in order so that he could afford to accept, where formerly he would have declined. Elmore's plan was that after being chosen he would move to live in the Upcountry near an ironworks he owned, and that would leave the Lowcountry seat to Rhett, assuming Calhoun was elected president in 1848. That was a lot of assuming, and it included the assumption that Elmore would have Rhett's support. Friends though they were, Rhett had not forgotten that Elmore abandoned him during Bluffton and took side with Calhoun instead. "I always endeavor to act upon the divine precept of doing unto others, as I would others to do towards me," he wrote Elmore now, "and am now about to give you, after painful deliberation, an instance of the application of this precept." He would not support any of Elmore's potential rivals, but he would not support Elmore either, despite the promises of making way for him in the future. He would take no part in the election whatsoever.[61]

Of course Rhett knew that without Calhoun's backing he had no chance, and after the past two years the trust between them remained strained. Rhett took pains to maintain communication with the senator and in fact wrote to him immediately on returning from England, talking strategy as always. The North would never unite on a presidential candidate in 1848, he said. "If we can only unite the South, it seems to me we must prevail." The war with Mexico and the tariff were the winning issues, and he advised Calhoun to lay aside his continuing opposition to the war and help instead to push it to a quick and triumphant conclusion, at the same time offering some initial thoughts for campaign organization.[62]

When the legislature met, Elmore had not the support he expected, and in the end it came down to Hammond and Andrew P. Butler, with the latter taking the prize. As for Rhett, despite the earlier talk of turning him out of his seat, he ran unopposed and went back to Congress in December. He did not realize that an awaiting issue would reunite him with Calhoun once again—a threat so powerful that the need for unity all but erased past differences, an issue greater than the tariff or internal improvements or even foreign conflict. What he was to find was the first serious attack in Congress on slavery.

William Rhett, whose name his descendants would borrow (South Carolina Historical Society, Charleston)

The only known likeness of Elizabeth Burnet, first wife of Robert Barnwell Rhett, painted by "King" of Washington, D.C., ca. 1840, with their daughter Elise added in 1846 (South Carolina Historical Society, Charleston)

J. L. PETIGRU.

Barnwell Smith's mentor James L. Petigru, whom he always loved but whose devotion to the Union never rubbed off on Rhett (Library of Congress, Washington, D.C.)

The grave of John C.
Calhoun in St. Philip's
churchyard in Charleston,
South Carolina. Only
with the death of his
sometime friend and
mentor, and sometime
antagonist, could Rhett
reach unfettered for full
power in South Carolina
and the South. (U.S.
Army Military History
Institute, Carlisle, Pa.)

Rhett's rival for Calhoun's
favor, Francis W. Pickens,
for whom he maintained
at best a lifelong contempt
(Library of Congress,
Washington, D.C.)

The interior of Institute Hall in Charleston, South Carolina, sometime in the 1850s but surely much as it appeared as "Secession Hall" on December 20, 1860 when Rhett reached the zenith of his career by kneeling in thanks before signing the secession ordinance (Library of Congress, Washington, D.C.)

Robert Barnwell Rhett, the so-called "Father of Secession," photographed by George S. Cook in Charleston, South Carolina, in January 1861 just days after signing the secession ordinance (South Carolina Historical Society, Charleston)

The man Rhett hated more than any other on earth and considered the "Judas" who betrayed his dream and his Confederacy: Jefferson Davis, photographed in Montgomery, Alabama, in 1861, about the time he was inaugurated as president (Alabama Department of Archives and History, Montgomery)

Robert Barnwell Rhett Jr., ca. 1860, when he was editor of the *Charleston Mercury.* "Barny" was the son most like his father, the one who carried Rhett's crusade for vindication and the last word on into the next century. (South Carolina Historical Society, Charleston)

TWELVE

A Rash and Ultra Man
1846–1848

RHETT SHOULD HAVE KNOWN THE battle was coming. Just before the close of the last session, when he supported Polk's $2 million appropriation, he had no choice but to take with it an amendment proposed by David Wilmot of Pennsylvania. It specified that as a condition of acquisition of any territory from Mexico in the war, slavery should not be reintroduced into such territory, since Mexico had abolished slavery in 1824. In the rush to pass the appropriation before the House adjourned a week later, the so-called Wilmot Proviso got through, for without it Polk could not have financed the campaigns then under way and about to be launched. It was a bad bargain for the administration but one they made for the moment, no doubt hoping to effect its repeal later.

Now that fight in the House began early, with Rhett in the thick of it, and since Polk himself opposed the Proviso, the Carolinian was soon seen more and more as a champion of the administration. He defended the actions of Polk's military commanders occupying California and New Mexico, and then on January 15, 1847 delivered a major address attacking the power of Congress to enact any legislation affecting slavery in the prospective new territories.[1] He deplored the introduction of the subject of slavery onto the floor, where it should never be allowed to intrude and would not but for the repeal of the gag rule. Now it was introduced again as the provisions of the Wilmot amendment were proposed as an attachment to a new $3 million appropriation. Such a prohibition of slavery amounted to a refusal to recognize the Missouri Compromise, he argued. In an apparent inconsistency, Rhett, who had regarded admitting Texas to statehood with its preexisting slavery intact as undeniable, chose not to recognize the preexisting prohibition of slavery in Mexico and its provinces. "The South is compelled to defend herself, or stand mute and inactive under aggression and insult," he thundered. He reminded them that in 1837, when he first came to the House, he had proposed a constitutional amendment prohibiting all discussion of slavery, and had it been enacted then, they would be spared this continuing and growing controversy. Worse, Democrats and Whigs were joined in the Wilmot movement, making it not a party measure but a sectional one.

The issue turned upon whether Congress had the power to exclude the people of one region from entering the commonly held territories with all their property of whatever description. "There cannot be a higher act of sovereignty than determining the persons who shall constitute members of the body politic, or be excluded from the territory," he argued. If in principle Congress did have such sovereignty, then he confessed the right of Congress to exclude slavery. But of course he did not recognize the principle and proceeded to show why. He resorted once more to history to define just what sovereignty meant, then looked at its use in the Constitution, and of course concluded that the document did not confer such power over the territories. Quite clearly the framers intended that territories acquired were the property of all the states equally, and since sovereignty resided in the states according to his reading of the Constitution, Congress had no authority not specifically granted to it by those sovereign entities. He denied the assertion of the inherent sovereignty of a nation's central government and as well the notion that any nation acquiring territory automatically assumed full authority.

The states were joint proprietors of the territories, "co-sovereigns" he called them. Every foot of land acquired in the war would be bought with their joint blood and at the cost of their common treasure. If a Northern majority could prohibit introducing slavery into California and New Mexico, then it established the tyrannical principle that sovereignty actually belonged to one section only of the Union. If that were so, then what was to stop that same majority from next prohibiting slavery in the actual states where it existed? The one did not logically follow from the other, but Rhett rarely let logic interfere with making a good argument. And was not power the ultimate goal? "Political power, the power of the different sections of the Union, seeking the mastery, is undoubtedly a strong element in the proposed exclusion of slavery," he stated. It would determine the political makeup of any new states by excluding Southern men who could not emigrate and take their slaves with them. That guaranteed that such new states would come in as free states, and thus the Wilmot Proviso was a de facto regulation of the future political majority of the nation, perhaps for the rest of time. Where, he asked, did the Constitution grant anyone, even a temporal majority, the right or the power to legislate future party domination? "What have we done to elicit it?" he asked. "What have our people done to merit it?" If the North actually wanted disunion, it could not have crafted a better tool to bring it about, for this measure would enflame the South in righteous indignation. "Pride often masters reason," he reminded them in admonition. "Passions lead to revolutions; and to dare, is to awake them."[2]

It was the finest address he ever made as a congressman—it was logical, pointed, and most of all rational, with the right amount of passion but well short of his usual posturing and threats. Moreover, he had introduced his one and only original contribution to constitutional theory, the motif that the territories were "common property" of the states and that the central government was only the agent of the states in administering such territory and therefore bore the responsibility of doing so for the benefit of all the states jointly. Thus no right that any citizen enjoyed at home in his state could be denied him in the territory. It was a persuasive enough doctrine that a month later when Calhoun proposed resolutions condemning the Wilmot Proviso in the Senate, he adopted Rhett's approach almost entirely, especially as it accorded with his own private views.[3]

The bill with the proviso passed by a close vote in spite of Rhett, but the Senate rejected it and substituted one of its own without the offending amendment, and finally the House accepted it, putting an end to the Wilmot threat for the moment. But it had raised the slavery debate to a new level and virtually overshadowed everything else that short session. More, it proved to Rhett's mind that he had been a prophet all along in his declarations that if the South gave way on the tariff, then slavery would be the next target of the consolidationists, further evidence of their concerted policy all along to dominate the South, reduce it to servility, and run the government to profit their own ends. Fired by that realization, he did not stop at his House address. Calhoun urged him to write an exposition of the issue for the *Southern Quarterly Review*, and though at first Rhett thought he could not meet the hurried deadline, he spent his mornings for six days in a row working on it before attending the House debates.[4]

The article appeared in the April number. The issue before them was as great as the Missouri Compromise itself, he declared, and once more the South was under attack. This time it was not the extension of slavery that Congress threatened but the establishment of a free state majority that could extinguish it where it already existed, for such, he declared, was clearly the ultimate objective of the policy Wilmot commenced. He rehearsed all the "common property" arguments he had made in the House, and at greater length. Though the proviso had been defeated in this Congress, he expected it would rise again in the next, and meanwhile an abolition press was commencing in Washington. Where would it end but in encouraging servile insurrection and devastation? And where was the Democratic Party but helpless or fawning for favor from Northern interests? "The spirit which yields one position will yield another," he warned, "until at length, self-respect and self-confidence is gone, and a conscious degradation prepares the people to be the victims of corrupt and traitorous demagogues." The Yankees argued that opposition to slavery was based not on the constitution but on sentiment, and Rhett rightly recognized that any ideal founded in emotion or personal values would never yield to dispassionate reasoning.

That being the case, what was the course for the South? "We have the right," he maintained, "but how shall we use it?" They had to have power that they could make "felt and dreaded." They had tried this power once before on the tariff, though he did not say its name. Perhaps Southern representatives in Congress could halt the war by opposing further appropriations or defeat the acquisition of any territory in treaty proceedings following a victory, which they were certainly strong enough to do in the Senate. But should they not begin preparing for an even greater assertion of their power? It had been said in the last session that there were no traitors in the South, but he disagreed. There were always traitors in every body politic. "Every cause, the holiest, has found its traitors," he warned, and they must make allowances for the men in their own midst who would be too frail or corrupt to stand with them. "The South, should this contest arise, must be prepared to meet not only her enemies of the North, but her worst enemies within her own bosom; and with a stern relentless arm, to repel or crush both." He never mentioned secession directly as the cause that would so test their unity, but he made his notion of their true course evident when he concluded by observing that the North had too much at stake to risk its profitable union with the South. That could only mean one thing.[5]

"It was written in great haste, but I hope will do me no discredit," he told his eldest son, but when the essay did not at first generate much press notice, he grumbled to Calhoun, "I suppose it must be pretty poor."[6] Even before the appearance of his article, however, Rhett's stand against Wilmot renewed the passions of his old Bluffton Boys at home, and they began to speak out anew, especially in the *Mercury*, which had gone through even more changes in February. Though Stuart had left the editor's chair, he still shared ownership with Clapp, and now they sold the paper. John E. Carew, a friend of Rhett though he had opposed Bluffton, replaced Clapp, making him the first editor in twenty years who would be entirely independent of the Rhett family financially. Stuart's portion of the proceeds went into trust with Benjamin Rhett for Claudia and his children. Benjamin, however, thinking it a sound investment, turned the money over to his brother in Washington, and Rhett used it to retire his debt to the bank for which a mortgage on his slaves had been security. Instead, he now mortgaged those slaves as guarantee for repayment of the money due the Stuarts. Slaves were safer than land as an investment, so the debt appeared to be secure, and it also meant that though there was no longer any Rhett ownership in the *Mercury*, still their fortunes were inextricably intertwined.[7]

Just days after the sale, one of Rhett's constituents sent an open letter to Rhett to the editor. "It has been our custom in times past to look to you for the signal of danger," he wrote, and Rhett had given the signal in his House speech. He should resign from Congress at once and come home. "If the doctrine of State Rights and Secession, formerly advocated by the party here, was ever correct, *now is the time* to give an example to us, and mankind abroad, of their propriety and force." If South Carolina faced the possibility of the war and desolation that might follow secession, then Rhett should be "present and perish with your fellow citizens."[8] Similar calls came from others as well, leading a cynical William Gilmore Simms to complain to Hammond, "Who is it that calls upon Barnwell Rhett from Barnwell C. H. to rescue & become saviour of the State?"[9] Quite clearly he believed that such letters were mere plants by Rhett himself or his close friends, creating an excuse for him to come home and stir trouble on the pretext of answering the call of his constituents.

Certainly the invitations were forthcoming, and Rhett and his family did return in April to South Carolina, where he expounded his doctrine of resistance in several meetings throughout his district. Moreover, in his Senate speech echoing Rhett's "common property" approach to the territories, Calhoun, too, had called for Southern unity. More than that, he proposed a cross-party affiliation of all true Southerners to resist future aggressions against slavery, the implication being obvious that he would be at its head as a presidential contender in 1848. That suited Rhett perfectly, and in his public statements now he echoed Calhoun's call. Wilmot had brought them back together.

In addition to alluding passionately to all the old wounds of 1832 and 1842 and now the Proviso, Rhett gave his listeners something new. He announced that he would not seek reelection in 1848, which meant that he would leave Congress in March 1849. Despite entreaties in the toasts that followed his addresses, he remained immutable in his determination, promising, however, that should a crisis arise that required his services he would cheerfully take his station "at any post where duty called."[10] Rhett explained his motives publicly to no one, but they were easily discerned. The recent sale of the *Mercury* and the transfer of much of his debt from the bank to his sister's family greatly eased the financial burden that almost constantly threatened his ability to stay in politics. Calhoun would need his services in the renewed efforts at organization and promotion required by the new Southern movement. Most of all, if Calhoun won the White House in 1848, and if Rhett played an important role in putting him there, then this time there would be no denying him Calhoun's vacant desk in the Senate. Anticipating the rebuilding of his own power base in the state, Rhett had apparently already made an agreement with one of his Bluffton Boys, William F. Colcock, to succeed him representing this district.[11]

Certainly Rhett was ready to go to work for Calhoun. There had been talk of trying to buy the *Southern Quarterly Review* and turning it into a Calhoun organ, but the movement needed something much more immediate and reactive than a magazine appearing only once every three months. Rhett had sometime before suggested the need for a new Calhoun paper in Washington, and now the idea was revived. Elmore quite logically suggested Rhett for the editorship, and Calhoun approved. After only a few weeks in South Carolina, Rhett gave up the house he had been renting in Charleston and returned to Washington. As part of his determination not to seek reelection, he had also given up the place in Georgetown, but now with the prospect of almost permanent residence in the capital for the next several months, he took new lodgings. As soon as he did, however, there came disturbing news. After word got out that Calhoun would have Rhett oversee the anticipated new newspaper, some who were close to him reacted strongly, and those who were pledged to fund the paper bolted. "He is considered to be a rash & ultra man in his politicks," complained one, "frequently bent upon extreme & desperate courses—very excitable & unstable—& intolerant & contemptuous of all about him—with neither tact nor discretion & without sympathy or popularity with the great mass of men." Worse, after Bluffton and the accusations of Rhett's role in Calhoun's earlier resignation from the Senate, too many men simply did not trust Rhett's loyalty to their man, and Calhoun supporters in Charleston were almost unanimous in their distrust. "His ambition is of so exceedingly selfish a character as to leave no doubt in my mind that he would without hesitation sacrifice you & all the world besides," complained Henry Conner, "if the least in the way to his own advancement." Conner admitted Rhett's talents as a publicist, "his energy—industry & elevated private character," but everything else about the man disqualified him for the post. "If it be known that it is in contemplation to get up this paper for Mr. Rhett, his name kills it dead on the spot—but if it did not, he & his paper would kill the party as sure as fate."[12]

As one of Rhett's more ardent opponents, Conner and others like him could hardly be regarded as objective, and thus comments such as his were certainly hyperbolic. Yet Calhoun had seen for himself enough episodes in Rhett's public life so far to know the truth underlying Conner's exaggerations. Rhett was arrogant and impulsive. He did arouse intense dislike. Certainly he did hold his own opinions above those of all others, and he had shown at Bluffton and on support for the war with Mexico, as on other occasions, that he could not be counted on always to stay in line. Choosing such a man to edit what would be Calhoun's most important public vehicle for influencing his presidential hopes simply posed too great a risk, and Calhoun had to agree. As Rhett reached Washington, Calhoun diplomatically told him not that he was being relieved of the job but that the anticipated funds were not forthcoming and therefore there was no job at all.[13]

Rhett kept his frustration in control, only complaining to Calhoun that it was now too late to return to Charleston and hire lodgings for the season. Yet he quickly put his time in Washington to good use on Calhoun's and his own behalf. Taking advantage of his increasingly good relations with Polk, he became a frequent visitor at the White House and an occasional caller at the homes and offices of some in the cabinet, gathering information for Calhoun and ingratiating himself at the same time. He found that though the war was going well, the end was not yet in sight, and that Polk was determined to conquer a peace by taking Mexico City. As for the Wilmot problem, Polk appeared to be trying to settle the slavery issue back on the Missouri Compromise line, which was what Calhoun and Rhett wanted all along, and with some prominent Northern Democrats such as Buchanan and Cass in support. That was good, for it divided them and would drive the antislave men among them to the Whigs. If they could keep the South united, said Rhett, then "our triumph is certain."[14]

Rhett suspected that Polk would not support the current move to annex all of Mexico after a victory, and neither did Calhoun. However, Rhett feared that the Whigs and Northern Democrats would try to string out the war as long as possible in order to amass such a huge war debt that the continuation of high tariffs would be necessary. It was a baseless fear, saying more about Rhett's almost paranoiac distrust of the opposition and his ready credulity for theories of conspiracy. Still he repeatedly advised Polk to make every effort for a speedy peace as a result. Of course, as soon as the war ended, there would be a renewal of the Wilmot Proviso spirit that they must battle, for it would surely be attached to approval of any peace treaty in the Senate. If Polk could end the war and defeat the proviso, then the Democrats would win in 1848. If the war and slavery in the territories questions were not settled by the end of the next session, however—that is, by August 1848—then the Democrats would be beaten. Rhett foresaw a new party rising to replace them, and that of course would be Calhoun's Southern party. Such being the case, all the South had to do was stand united in the Senate and it would have the votes to defeat the treaty and the proviso, and withhold ratification until the Missouri Compromise line was recognized in the new territory. That would disgrace the administration, fracture the Democratic Party, and force Polk to fall back on Calhoun for support, ensuring that finally in 1848 the Carolinian would be bound for the White House.[15]

The mere suggestion of such an active strategy went a long way toward justifying the doubts of Conner and others about Rhett's idea of loyalty. At one and the same time he was posing a potential plot against Polk, for whom he had been showing rather ostentatious friendship this season, and also cynically posing the idea of making political capital out of prolonging a war for his own and

Calhoun's ends. At the same time he condemned the opposition when he thought they would do the same to achieve their ends. For a man who lately categorized all warfare as a crime, it was, in the kindest light possible, a contradictory pose to adopt. It also revealed, as had so much before, that Rhett's deep suspicions of conspiratorial motives in others really mirrored failings in himself that he could not, or would not, see.

Meanwhile, Rhett did what he could for Calhoun, managing to get a few articles in the capital press defending him against attacks, but his main energies he expended in investigating Calhoun's potential opposition for the presidency in 1848. Polk had declared that he would not be a candidate, but even as that took him out of the running, the war created two heroes in generals Zachary Taylor and Winfield Scott, whom both Whigs and Democrats found enticing as possible candidates. There were others as well, among them Cass, Levi Woodbury, and Gen. John Quitman of Mississippi—all of whom might seek to fill the vacuum. Even the weakling Buchanan had his hopes, though Rhett dismissed him and most of the rest.

Within only days of arriving in Washington, Rhett became convinced that the most promising contender would be Taylor, whose political views were not well-known. Indeed, at the outset he predicted that the Whigs would nominate him and defeat the Democrats in 1848, but that could prove to be a premature judgment. At first he asked Calhoun what he might know of the forty-year army veteran's positions. "I have not seen any one, nor anything from him that is at all satisfactory," Rhett complained, though Taylor was a Southerner and a slaveholder. Both parties courted him, but Rhett felt uncertain whether he could support "Old Rough and Ready" should he capture the Democratic nomination, and Calhoun choose not to make a third-party bid. Rhett rather thought that Taylor, as a military man who never dabbled in politics, might have no fixed ideas in fact, but also believed that Taylor's social ties linked him with the Whigs, as indeed they did. Still, Rhett at least floated the idea of trying to establish some controlling influence over Taylor, reasoning that if he were not experienced at politics, then he might be led or dominated by more sophisticated and presumably more intelligent men. If Taylor would support them on free trade and against the corrupt nominating convention system, then he thought that Southern men could take his side. Still the whole idea of Taylor troubled Rhett, making him reluctant to support him and at the same time fearful that he would be elected. "To be afloat as to principles, with a successful General at the Head of the Government, without a safe and steady and strong counsellor in his cabinet to keep him straight," feared Rhett, "is to exchange the corruptions of party usage as a present exercise, for almost if not quite as dangerous a condition."[16]

Calhoun could not answer Rhett's queries but suggested that he get in touch with others known to be close to the general, which Rhett did immediately, writing to several including Taylor's onetime son-in-law Jefferson Davis. Rhett and Davis did not know each other socially and to date had only met in the last Congress when Davis briefly served in the House before leaving to command a volunteer regiment in Mexico under Taylor. On one occasion in February of the previous year during the Oregon debate, Davis offered to yield the floor to Rhett, yet other than that there seems to have been no association between them.[17] Yet Rhett felt comfortable enough to consult him, and Davis's reply was at best equivocal. In fact, Davis marked his response "private," which Rhett found bound him to keep its contents secret even from Calhoun, although it hardly mattered, for Davis's response was no more illuminating than any of the other rumors about Taylor's politics. Rhett did hear through other channels that Davis had said Taylor supported free trade and opposed revival of the national bank, however, which meant that if the general got a Democratic nomination, then "we may be driven to support Taylor." Rhett feared, however, that the Whigs would nominate Taylor first, making it impossible to support him regardless of his views.[18]

In this state of uncertainty many wanted Calhoun to take the lead by choosing one of the myriad candidates, whereas Calhoun repeatedly advised that they should make no moves for the presidency until the candidates had weeded each other out and South Carolina could then see where lay her best interests with the remainder. Of course that posture also left Calhoun free to make a run himself, by not being previously committed. In fact, he decided that he and South Carolina should boycott the Democratic convention to come, ostensibly because there would be an antislavery contingent from the North there and this would alert the South to the dangers from that source. Rhett, meanwhile, more and more attracted to the potential candidacy of Supreme Court justice Woodbury of New Hampshire, who stood right on all the chief Southern issues, could not endorse another boycott. He had seen the disaster the last time South Carolina tried that, and quietly he suggested to Woodbury's managers that despite Calhoun's wishes, the state would be in the convention.[19]

Was Rhett once more earning his reputation for disloyalty? Probably not, for by the end of the summer Calhoun had all but taken himself out of contention, from lack of funds and organization. The newspaper in Washington never materialized, and neither had the Northern support among conservatives that he knew he needed, which was why he was sounding views on Taylor and Scott and others. Of course he would hold himself ready to run if drafted, but with the popularity of Taylor especially, a successful campaign looked improbable at best.

Calhoun agreed with Rhett that Taylor would probably be the Whig nominee, and his standing on vital Southern issues would command so much support in the slave states across party lines that it must certainly siphon away much of the support for Calhoun's hoped-for new sectional party. At the same time there was no way Calhoun could stand on a Democratic platform with the Wilmot crowd, and in any event it looked likely that the Democrats would split in 1848. Thus, once again, circumstances outside his control kept the presidential ring beyond his grasp.

If Calhoun sat remote in South Carolina and watched his strength ebb that summer, Rhett rejoiced that his own seemed to be ascending dramatically. Shortly after reaching Washington he concluded that he had little influence if any with Polk and the administration, but by late summer he dramatically revised his opinion. "I cannot doubt that I have influence with the administration," he boasted, "for they have granted me almost every thing I have ever asked of them."[20] When he took an interest in establishing a mail-line steamer route between Charleston and Havana, Rhett managed to get Secretary of State Buchanan to start diplomatic endeavors to clear the path. He also began to enjoy some patronage, securing appointments for friends to federal jobs including the superintendence of the construction of the new customhouse in Charleston and finding appointments in the navy and army for constituents.[21] "This influence I cannot suppose to be partisan," Rhett thought, "for I have done nothing which can induce them to think me a partisan." Somewhat smugly he concluded that it must be "the result of a personal respect for me."

In fact, Rhett had been one of Polk's best supporters on all but minor issues and especially on internal improvements, beginning with support of Polk's rivers and harbors bill veto in 1846. Through much of the spring and summer of 1847 Rhett continued to advise the president on his approach when the issue would surely be revived at the next session, and he probably consulted with him on an explanation of the veto that Polk was preparing in case it should be needed. More than that, Rhett could not or did not see that it served Polk's interests to coddle some of Calhoun's people. The president, a political pragmatist and dedicated Democrat, never entirely trusted Calhoun, especially as he threatened to ruin the party. Thus if Polk could tempt the loyalties of men such as Rhett, it diminished the threat from Calhoun, and certainly he succeeded in flattering Rhett's vanity. Rhett was able to act as Elmore's power of attorney in securing him valuable government contracts for iron shot for the war from Elmore's South Carolina works. As a favor to Hammond, Rhett even interceded on behalf of Simms for a diplomatic appointment to Naples, despite Simms's antipathy, and believed that he almost had influence to guarantee it, ranking his clout with the

White House just below that of the cabinet. "I shall thank Rhett for his zeal," Simms told Hammond, "though *inter nos,* he is about the last man in the world to obtain any favor for himself or others."[22]

In fact, Rhett may just have been trying to get a favor for himself. With Calhoun's presidential hopes looking dimmer, so did the likelihood of a Senate vacancy, which meant that after March 1849 Rhett would be politically unemployed. He had been offered the diplomatic posting to Great Britain once—or nearly so—and now that he had redeemed himself with Polk and stood in such good repute with the administration, might he not expect such a post now in reward for his support? In late September he made a hasty trip to London and Liverpool once again to collect some of the money due him from the rice duty affair. Perhaps he also tried to muster some support in Whitehall, for when he returned to Washington late in October there were suddenly rumors that Rhett was doing so much to endear himself to the administration that a friend warned Calhoun that Rhett was ready "to barter all the South for a foreign mission."[23]

Even with the portion of the rice commission that he collected, Rhett was still hard-pressed financially when he returned to Washington, despite the fact that he was also receiving a 1 percent commission on the contracts he got for Elmore's foundry. In fact, he had to withhold part of the money that he collected for Elmore that month in order to meet his rent, promising that it was only a loan for a few weeks "until my prudence should overtake my expenses." He had also managed to borrow a..other ten thousand dollars from the Charleston Bank, having just retired his debt there the previous winter, and already hoped that Elmore could get him more, making it evident to his old friend—as if it had not been transparent for years—that Rhett would never succumb to financial prudence.[24] Thus a foreign appointment would have been fortuitous indeed just then. In the event, no appointment was forthcoming, but perhaps only because Polk and Rhett had something else in mind when Congress reconvened in December.

The first session of the new Congress, Rhett's last, convened December 6, and the favor in which Rhett stood became immediately apparent. There were three parties represented now, for the war and the Wilmot Proviso had precipitated the appearance of a new American Party, precursor to a later vehement nativist organization some of whose adherents opposed slavery. The administration put Rhett's name forward for the Speakership, evidence indeed of the position he enjoyed with Polk, and if the Democrats had not been split he would have won. The Whigs put up their own candidate, Robert Winthrop of Massachusetts, but just as the Whigs did not have the votes to elect their man, neither did the administration party. The House went through two ballots with neither side polling a majority, and Rhett hoped that at that point the proslavery Southern Whigs would come over to the conservative Democrats and give him the victory. Instead one antislavery American Party member voted for Winthrop, and Isaac Holmes of Charleston, a close friend of Calhoun, simply did not vote. That was enough to make Winthrop Speaker. Rhett took the defeat well enough, though he would not soon forgive Holmes, concluding that he was a Whig in all but name. Worse was that now there would be "a violent Wilmot Proviso—anti Slavery—Southern hater—Speaker of the House."[25]

Four days prior to the opening of the session Rhett had called on Polk, and the president showed him a draft of his annual message. Rhett took it into a room to read privately and returned with his approval except for a few minor suggestions, one of which Polk incorporated. Rhett objected particularly to establishing territorial governments in New Mexico and California though agreed that they should not be returned to Mexico. Rhett suggested waiting until there was a peace treaty before establishing territorial governments, though his real concern was that they not be organized until the spirit of the Wilmot Proviso had been defeated.[26] Almost all of the territory would be below the Missouri Compromise line and thus should be a future province for slavery. Better yet, he found that thanks in part to his own efforts, Polk was prepared a few days later when the internal improvements forces renewed their attack with a proposal to restrict the duties of the commerce committee to interstate commerce and create a new committee to handle commerce with foreign nations. Then they attached a proviso that the interstate commerce committee would consider all of the petitions for improvements of rivers, harbors, lakes, and the like on the coastline and in the interior.

Rhett was immediately on the floor, no doubt prepared to speak on behalf of the administration, and quickly charged that this was only a new way of promoting internal improvements. As he had argued for years, there was no constitutional authority for appropriations for such works. However, the same document did allow Congress to permit the individual states to levy taxes on imports by tonnage in order to finance maintaining harbors and such. There, then, was the only lawful mode for financing improvements. Why should Congress attempt to accomplish something by unconstitutional means "when the States themselves have the power of doing it?" he asked.[27] That Rhett spoke for the administration was eloquently confirmed when Polk submitted to the House the message he had been preparing to explain his veto of the rivers and harbors bill the previous session, and it took precisely the same ground as Rhett had. Soon thereafter Rhett introduced on behalf of the administration a bill to accomplish just what he had proposed for financing such improvements for commerce, obviously having prepared it in advance and in conference with the president. At first a competing resolution recognizing the policy of internal improvement appropriations shunted Rhett's bill aside by nearly a three-to-one majority, and Whigs rather sneeringly pointed out the pitiful strength of the administration party "with R. Barnwell Rhett at its head." Yet neither bill passed for the moment, and Polk and Rhett at least held their ground.[28]

Rhett defended the president from Whig attacks that the war with Mexico was unconstitutional and repudiated their assertions that only Congress had the war-making power, once again turning his wonderful—if often misused—skills at rationalization and parliamentary interpretation to the task. The Constitution may have said that Congress had the power to declare war, which he said did not mean it had the authority to "begin" or to "conduct" war. But first he gave them a definition of war as a condition of utter confrontation between two nations involving every man, woman, and child, all property, and all life itself in hostilities that were political, social, cultural even, and certainly military. He was describing, of course, what later generations would call "total war." But then he went on to aver that the current conflict did not fit this definition and really amounted only to "the mere fighting of soldiers on our frontier." The simple collision of arms with another nation did not constitute war, he declared, for if it did, then any petty military commander could start a war by initiating a skirmish or battle, and as example he cited a number of past collisions with other countries that no one regarded as declarations of war.

Thus they were not truly "at war," and thus Polk had done nothing unconstitutional. It was as neat an example of his skill at splitting hairs in an argument as any he ever made, and then he frosted it with yet another interpretation in pointing out that the wording of the Constitution empowered Congress to "declare" war but not to "make" it. That meant, of course, that Congress had the power only to make official a state of things already in place, virtually to recognize that a state of war existed. That being the case, then only the president could have the power to "make" war—that is, to oversee its conduct, the selection of commanders, and the planning of strategy and military goals.

As for the charge that Polk provoked the conflict by ordering troops to the Rio Grande—which Rhett believed to be the case—he dodged the issue by standing on the constitutional ground that as commander-in-chief Polk had full authority to order United States soldiers anywhere he wished within the borders of the nation, and as of 1845 that included the state of Texas. In broader scope, Rhett was defending executive power as defined by the Constitution against an attempt by the Whigs to circumscribe Polk's authority. It helped, of course, that he fully agreed with Polk's policies. Not likely would he have made the same defense for Andrew Jackson a dozen years before, and certainly he would take a different view of constitutional executive power a few years hence.

In his defense of Polk, Rhett accused the Whigs of seeking to draw out the conflict and the current peace negotiations through the fall, in order to draw strength from war weariness in the presidential election in November. In this argument he had some sound reasoning, though he seemed untroubled in making it after recently proposing almost the same thing to Calhoun, and for much the same motives. The charge got him into an extended and heated personal explanation the next day that rapidly degenerated into attacks on Rhett himself and put him on the defensive over his actions during nullification. Still he emerged unscathed, and even the Whigs acknowledged his closeness to the administration in their sarcastic remarks about his being "initiated into the secrets of the Cabinet."[29] In the event, the peace treaty was concluded the very day Rhett made his personal explanations and was ratified by the Senate in March, largely removing the now-concluded war from the presidential discussion in the coming campaign.

Certainly Polk made known his appreciation, and Rhett endeared himself further when he assured the president that if he actually chose to run again, South Carolina would support him despite what Calhoun chose to do.[30] He did not reveal on what basis he made such a promise, and most likely it was just another case of Rhett presuming to speak for others out of self-importance or a desire to impress. In either case, at the same time he applied his efforts toward whomever really would be the candidate of the Democrats that fall. By the end of March, Rhett came around to Calhoun's view on boycotting the convention, and in a meeting with Calhoun and Senator Butler he expressed his view that the delegation in Washington should make no official declaration in favor of any candidate prior to the convention meeting in June. Thus all options would remain available, the state would not be committed to supporting *any* Democrat if none proved acceptable, and discord among their people in South Carolina might then be kept to a minimum. The next day the whole state delegation met again, and all but one concurred in staying out of the convention, particularly on slavery grounds, for with Northern antislave men sure to be there in a large bloc, and with highly publicized strife over abolition in French and Spanish colonial possessions in the hemisphere at the moment, the whole subject would be too volatile. Just as their position remained that it was unconstitutional for slavery to be discussed in Congress, so did they maintain that it was an issue beyond the mandate of any political party or convention, other than to uphold the undeniable rights of slaveholders in their own states and in the territories.[31]

Rhett's own choice of candidate wavered. At first he favored Woodbury or Quitman and joined in the general condemnation of Lewis Cass when the

Michigander proposed that as a solution for all the Wilmot hubbub the people who actually inhabited any new territories acquired from Mexico should be allowed to settle the subject of slavery for themselves. That was unthinkable— "squatter sovereignty," the Southerners called it. Sovereignty lay only with a state, and not with a territory. Moreover, it was clear that all the free states had to do was ensure that they sent more settlers into the new territories than the South, and as a result when it came time for any referendum, slaveholders would always lose. Indeed, the prospect of this happening must in itself deter Southerners from even trying to settle the new lands, and thus the South would be denied its constitutional rights to share in the "common property" newly acquired. At the same time that he told Polk that South Carolina would happily support him, he declared that she could never stomach Cass.[32]

The Democratic convention met on May 22 in Baltimore and split predictably over slavery. That same day Rhett called on Polk at the White House, where they discussed the convention, Rhett telling the president that he would have preferred him over any other candidate and that he could not support Cass and neither would South Carolina. Indeed, his state, he believed, would have supported a Polk candidacy in spite of Calhoun's recent course. Rhett did not attend the convention officially, but he was absent from Washington for a few days that month and may well have gone to Baltimore to watch from the wings.[33] Rhett's new friend Yancey was there and had introduced a platform plank pledging the party to noninterference with slavery everywhere, but it fell to an overwhelming majority that convinced Van Buren supporters that slavery had killed the Democratic Party. His antislave men bolted and nominated him on a separate ticket for their new Free Soil Party. That ended forever any lingering respect Rhett might have had for his onetime champion. "He defeated and cast down the Democratic Party at a most critical period," charged the Carolinian. The remainder settled for Cass after all and then nominated him on a platform that reaffirmed strict construction of the Constitution, repudiation of internal improvements, opposition to the national bank, and most of all a statement that Congress had no power to interfere with slavery in the states. There was conspicuous silence on the whole territorial issue. Van Buren had claimed that slavery would dissolve the Whigs too, but Rhett believed him mistaken simply because they had nominated Taylor after all, and Van Buren, by splitting the Democrats and running a third-party candidacy, virtually guaranteed victory for Taylor. Winning the presidency was hardly the act of a ruined party, he thought.[34]

The reaction in South Carolina was agitated, helped along by a Yancey visit to Charleston that included a speech at city hall and excellent coverage in the *Mercury*, suggesting that Rhett may have had something to do with it. Shouting an angry protest at the nomination of Cass, and denunciation of the Wilmot Proviso, Yancey echoed Lewis of Alabama in calling for the South to put its own nominee in the field on a platform of strict construction of the Constitution. The futility of further dividing anti-Whig votes had to occur to Yancey, for it would only guarantee even more Taylor's election, though in the context of Yancey's actions twelve years in the future it may only have demonstrated his early realization that losing a battle could help win a war.[35]

Certainly Calhoun recognized it, and there was nothing more said about his already moribund chances for running that year. Indeed, as more was learned about Taylor's position he became somewhat more acceptable to state rights men, and soon it was rumored that Calhoun himself would support him in preference to Cass, whom a public meeting of Democrats in Charleston refused to back. Shortly after Cass's nomination Rhett attended a party in Georgetown and spoke with several leading Whigs about the coming election. He told them his conviction that Cass would be beaten and that squatter sovereignty would kill him in the South. Most thus took it for granted that Rhett would follow Calhoun's lead along with the rest of his lieutenants. The first indication of his position on the Cass nomination came when he took the floor in the House on June 1 after failing to gain the floor a few days earlier when Cass supporters ruled him out of order, chiefly from fear of what he would say about their candidate's position on the territorial issue.[36]

He delivered one last blast at the spirit of the Wilmot Proviso, which though dead in itself continued to live on in other proposed legislation over the territories. He also condemned a new approach by the antislave people, who pointed out that Mexico had abolished slavery in the 1820s and that therefore the preexisting laws of California and New Mexico prohibited its introduction. Then he came to squatter sovereignty. Territories, as dependencies, could not be sovereign, he argued, and since all power in the Union derived from the states, then these states had authority over the territories. Thus, to allow that the people in the territories had sovereignty themselves over slavery in their borders would mean that the settlers' sovereignty overrode that of the states that owned them—a clear absurdity.

Moreover, if a white majority in a territory could decide to exclude Negroes by excluding slavery, he posed the interesting prospect that the majority of the population in California and New Mexico would likely for some time be of Mexican birth. Since they must be citizens as free men, could they not then use their "sovereignty" to frame state constitutions excluding *white men* from immigrating? It was, he said, a "beautiful consequence" of the fallacious doctrine, for thus white Americans "after all the whipping of the Mexicans, can only enter *their* country by permission." Of course he glossed over the fallacy in his own analogy, there being a great difference between excluding by law a domestic institution and banning a specific race of individuals. As for those who argued that a territory could have a limited or qualified sovereignty sufficient to decide the slavery issue, Rhett returned to his old argument that sovereignty was indivisible. Southern blood as well as Northern blood won these new territories, he argued. "We ask that our rights, as joint proprietors in the common property, shall not be outraged. He demanded that Congress repudiate what was only another attack on the South and its institutions. "We ask to be let alone," he said. Let this attitude of aggression and contempt of one section for the other continue longer, he warned, "and it is not in the power of man to prevent the downfall of our system of government." The Union would be "torn to pieces by the hand of desperate resistance." He harkened back twenty years to his Colleton address and his first premonitions of the doom slavery agitation would bring on the land. Now he was speaking probably for the last time in Congress on the subject. "I desire it to be remembered," he declared, "that here and elsewhere, I have counselled but one policy to the South; yield not one inch, but meet the question here and elsewhere with firm, uncompromising, and unflinching resistance." They must settle this matter, and soon. "There is no other course to save the Union."[37]

His speech certainly appeared as a repudiation of Cass and his platform, though Rhett mentioned neither the candidate nor his party specifically. He thought his words so important that he took pains to get them distributed through the press as quickly as possible.[38] And yet there were soon suggestions that Rhett was not so far away from the nominee after all and that once more he was not going to take his lead from Calhoun, who in the end backed no nominee in 1848. Rhett seized upon an expression by Cass that slavery should be left to "the People of the Confederacy in their respective local Governments" and interpreted this to mean that Cass avowed that neither Congress nor territorial populations could decide in the issue and that only those "People of the Confederacy" could do that. Who were they but the people of the states, which meant that Cass believed—or Rhett assumed—that the slavery issue could only be decided by the people of a territory at the time of their becoming a state. That made all the difference, for that gave Southern men ample and equal opportunity to settle in a territory and thus affect the decision. Moreover, with Van Buren and his crowd now off in their own party, the Democrats had been cleansed of the infection of abolition, making it possible to stand with them again and support their ticket.[39]

Meanwhile Rhett also considered Quitman, a much safer candidate since he followed virtually the same rigid stance on Southern issues as Rhett, but he soon found no enthusiasm among others in the South Carolina delegation. What quickly became apparent, however, is that regardless of whom else he consulted, Rhett was not asking Calhoun for advice, and not just about the election but about anything it seemed. Burt thought Rhett's speech against squatter sovereignty "remarkable" for the absence of any condemnation of the Democratic platform, and by early July it was rumored that Rhett had finally come around to supporting Cass and the regular party. Meanwhile he mistakenly read that to mean that Rhett would not support the Democratic nominee, and when Polk heard that Rhett had predicted Cass's defeat, he met with the Carolinian one morning to ask for an explanation. Rhett soon cleared the misunderstanding and promised Polk that he fully intended to back Cass and expected that South Carolina would do likewise. He may have been telling Polk what he wanted to hear, though, for Rhett continued to keep his opinions generally obscure and thus his options free awhile longer. Privately he regarded Cass as simply the least of evils.[40]

The remainder of the session only drove Rhett more determinedly away from any union with Southern Whigs behind Taylor when a compromise bill on slavery in the territories came on the floor. Rhett and his delegation quite approved of the measure, which entirely dodged slavery and provided for organization of Oregon, California, and New Mexico into territorial status, leaving slavery to be decided later by the local courts, with right of appeal to the Supreme Court if necessary. Though not perfect from Southerners' point of view, still it eliminated both squatter sovereignty and the Wilmot question from the equation, and the Supreme Court was safe enough on the slavery issue that they could live with it, so it passed the Senate, though only by one vote. In the House, however, the Whigs killed it by a tabling motion, eight Southern Whigs joining in the vote. Rhett believed that they did so in the expectation that leaving the slavery question unsettled would help Taylor carry Southern states, his position on slavery being preferable to squatter sovereignty. Then the last day of the session during debate on a bill organizing Oregon as a territory, he tried to delay until adjournment by a call for the yeas and nays. If successful, the issue would remain undecided when the election came and might well be turned to their advantage in future bargaining over New Mexico and California. But again the Southern Whigs refused to remain solid with their section.[41] All it did for Rhett, however, was to convince him that Calhoun's notion of Southern solidarity between Whigs and Democrats was an illusion. With Taylor in most other respects now seen as too much in the hands of the Northern protectionists, the only possible course was to back Cass.

Soon the perception that Rhett supported Cass was echoed in a change of editorial tone in the *Mercury,* which now began to warm toward Cass. Some such as Simms lay the responsibility for that with Rhett, who he thought "has too prevailing an influence," placing the paper "in the hands of the enemy."[42] Finally when Rhett came home at the end of the session in August, no doubt remained. He met with the Democratic committee in Charleston and persuaded them to come out for Cass in a public meeting on August 21. It proved to be an unruly affair, someone throwing a burning lamp on the stage during one speech, but still Rhett and Cass emerged clearly on top, and no one doubted that Rhett now headed the Cass backing in the state. Though he was in the city, Calhoun did not attend, but neither did he condemn Rhett's action. The likelihood of a Taylor victory in the face of a divided opposition made any repudiation of Cass unnecessary.[43]

Rhett took an important role in the local campaigning, although it was limited because, as usual, his finances plagued him. All that spring he worked at capitalizing on his contacts with Polk's Navy Department in selling more of Elmore's shot and cannon balls, and as each payment arrived he asked Elmore to let him keep some of it for himself as an additional loan. He owed five thousand dollars to one creditor that was to come due soon and warned of "heavy consequences" if he could not pay. "You know my situation and the *immediate* means it demands," he told his friend. "Let nothing but a *severe extremity*, prevent you loaning me this money." When he reached Charleston he found his debt crisis deepening, no doubt distracting him from the campaign, but apparently Elmore made the loans in the end. He had hopes at least of a good rice crop and found the harvest going well on his return, promising two good years in a row on the plantations.[44]

But of course Rhett could never attend to plantation business when politics beckoned, and he privately admitted that his real reason for returning to South Carolina now was "political matters." By late summer Rhett clearly took the forefront in stumping for Cass, and elsewhere in the state his friends Burt and even Benjamin Perry did the same.[45] Their efforts took on renewed energy when a rump convention of Whigs and Democrats in Charleston tried to nominate its own ticket of Taylor and Kentucky's William O. Butler, currently Cass's vice-presidential running mate. Rhett came out in a speech in Charleston on September 21, his first political address in the state outside his district, explaining his backing of Cass and defending the Polk administration as well, attempting, as some thought, to reconcile supporters of the president into backing Cass.[46]

Rhett followed that with a major speech at Hibernian Hall on Meeting Street just two days later before a large and enthusiastic crowd of Democrats from St. Michael's and St. Philip's parishes. He began with warnings, rather than condemnation, for those who were changing their party affiliation and going for

Taylor. He mentioned the fate of Henry L. Pinckney, for one, and then reminded them of the many victories the state rights men of South Carolina had achieved in partnership with the Democrats. Contrasting that and what the current platform affirmed with what the Whigs offered, he asked how there could be any difficulty in making a choice. To defuse lingering distrust over Cass and his squatter sovereignty flirtation, Rhett declared that "the personal or even political character or opinions of the Presidential candidates, are comparatively nothing in this great issue." The party was now their hope, especially purged as it was of the Free Soilers. Taylor would not veto the Wilmot Proviso or a similar piece of legislation; of that he was sure, and that alone made Taylor unacceptable. Cass would use the veto. As for squatter sovereignty, Rhett asserted that linking Cass with the policy was a misconception based upon faulty interpretation of one of Cass's letters, and he concluded, "I have no alarm for any thing that Gen. Cass's administration may do towards the South."

Having said that, however, he went on to declare that he put no reliance on presidential elections for the protection of their state and section. For that, as always, they must look to themselves. Indeed, as evidenced elsewhere in the world, slaveholding communities were under threat universally. "We are surrounded by dangers in the Union," he warned. Congress was becoming nothing more than a debating center for abolition, and slavery had become, as he always feared, the dominant issue in the nation's politics. The only way to stop it going further was for them to act, and at once. Talk and threats had accomplished nothing but delay, and now the Northerners despised them and declared openly that Southerners would never make good on their threats and thus could be ignored. If they convinced the North that passage of even one measure striking at slavery would lead to the instant dissolution of the Union, then no such measure would ever be proposed, much less enacted. Soon they would be forced to choose "between the alternatives of a dissolution of the Union—or your own salvation."

They could have both, and that had been his object for two decades in public life. He reminded them of his Colleton speech in 1828 and how he warned that if they gave in on the tariff slavery would be next, and here it had come. His counsel now was the same as it had been then: "Meet the question at once, and forever." Forget debates in Congress and forget, too, a Southern convention. It would never happen, and even if it did, his own experience showed all too well that Southerners would not stand united—not yet. They and their sister slave states should demand that their delegations leave Congress the moment any legislation such as Wilmot or squatter sovereignty, or anything else touching slavery, was passed. It needed only two states to resist, and the South would be safe. And if not, "if driven to action by the aggressions of the North in Congress, all other steps which the honor and interests of the South shall demand will be easily assumed." If not even one other state would stand with her, still South Carolina should do it on her own. "She can force every State in the Union to take sides, for or against her," he declared. "She can compel the alternative— that the rights of the South be respected, or the Union be dissolved."[47]

The address was electrifying and was emotionally received and widely reprinted in the weeks ahead, though Rhett refrained from using the word *secession* even once. He did not need to, of course. The Hibernian Hall speech served as the centerpiece of his efforts for the balance of the campaign, and it also brought forward once more some clear differences between himself and Calhoun, who seemed almost forgotten. In fact, this was the first major public speech Rhett ever made in South Carolina in which Calhoun played virtually no role, being mentioned but once in passing. Forthrightly he rejected Calhoun's continuing reliance on a Southern convention to achieve their aims, and the *Mercury* was backing Rhett's call on this. In fact, it was believed that the entire South Carolina delegation in Congress was following Rhett's lead for Cass, and just days after the speeches Hammond felt that the sentiment in the state had well shifted from Calhoun's position. "Rhett has out generalled him fairly," Hammond told Simms; "the State goes for Cass."[48] At the same time Rhett's foes such as Simms—who showed little if any gratitude for the diplomatic effort Rhett made on his behalf—made no secret of their belief that Rhett supported Cass in the hope of receiving a high appointment, perhaps even a cabinet portfolio, in return.[49] Granted that Rhett always suspected the motives of others, it is no wonder, for South Carolina's ruling oligarchy in which he was raised and functioned was a nest of vipers continually hissing at one another and often willing to strike if to their own advantage.

In the middle of the campaign Rhett took time to explain the great issue to his sons Robert Jr., now starting his final year at Harvard, and Alfred, who was commencing his sophomore year there. Like many Southern planters and aristocrats, Rhett recognized that the best education for his boys was in the North, but as did other parents, he ran the risk of having them contaminated by Yankee political doctrine. "You are among . . . haters of the Slave institutions of the South," he warned. A year earlier when abolitionists attempted to capitalize on the Wilmot controversy by trying to enroll a free black student at Harvard, Rhett was outraged. "Allowing the negro into Cambridge, is to insult the South," he declared, "and to compel an acknowledgment of equality, between the Races." The black did not get in, but Rhett instructed Barny that if he were to be admitted, then his son must immediately leave Harvard and finish his college in South Carolina. As a preventive against foul ideas contaminating his sons, he sent them a pamphlet that collected all of the portions of the Bible that explicitly or implicitly supported or endorsed slavery. "If Slavery is contrary to Christianity," he told them, "undoubtedly it should be abolished." If holding slaves was a sin, they should be freed. However, "reviewing the word of God in all reverence, I cannot but believe, that I am sinless, so far as my Slaves are concerned—serving in my moral & religious accountability, in ministering properly to their physical and spiritual necessities." He had always held the Bible up to his children as the one true measure of right and wrong, "the sole criterion of truth," in all things.[50] Certainly there was no doubt in his mind that slavery was the most humane condition for blacks in Western society, for beyond question, having been introduced into the white world, they could not be responsible for themselves. He declared:

> Slavery has existed in all ages, and Negro slavery was common in Egypt 5,000 years ago, & has existed there ever since. The history of the Negro race is simply a page of natural history, it has no intellectual history, because God has not endowed it with the faculties necessary. From the "Great Desert" to the "Cape of Good Hope" the true land of the Negro, not a vestige of civilization [is] to be found. Egypt is the oldest country of which we have any authentic record, and is the cradle of art, sciences & civilization. The brain of a race as with it the intellect cannot be enlarged or developed by education nor [can] that capacity of an inferior race even through successive generations be brought up to the highest standard. The intellectual & physical characters of the different races were the same five thousand years ago as they are now.[51]

In such a time of turmoil over slavery his sons needed to understand the full ramifications of the institution and the issues at stake with the rise of the Free Soil Party.

Though he asked his boys to read the pamphlet and absorb its truths, he also admonished them not to use the contents to indulge any controversy with fellow students, "for this you should disdain." Nevertheless, when Robert Jr. got in trouble for refusing to attend a campus chapel where sermons attacked slavery, his father fully supported him for not suffering "a church where your country & her institutions are reviled and abused," and he wrote to the faculty endorsing his son's action.[52] That demonstrated but one of the contradictions in Rhett the father. Though his whole public life had been spent in controversy of his own making, he told his sons to avoid—disdain—such confrontations. Similarly, he maintained that his religious convictions prevented him from engaging in any act of physical violence, and yet he condoned, and even encouraged it in his sons. On the one hand he asked them to rise above the passions he could not control in himself; yet on the other he allowed them to give way to the outcome of such emotions, whereas he could stop himself short of coming to blows, or pistols. They were conflicting examples, to say the least, and went a long way toward explaining how his older boys grew up to be just as volatile as he, and less restrained.

Certainly no one could fault his efforts to get them the best education, and from the moment that his eldest entered Harvard in 1845, and Alfred two years later, Rhett took a keen and proactive interest in their studies and progress, writing to his eldest almost daily with advice. Both had shown some interest in going to Mexico with the volunteers—especially Alfred, who wanted to leave Harvard in March 1848 and join a regiment of mounted rifles. Rhett forbade him, noting for one thing that the war was all but over by then but more significantly that this war did not afford sufficient possibility for distinction on the battlefield for his father to be willing to send him. "I have told you all," he said to Alfred, "that I will give you education for the business & duties of life, but that I can promise no more." Indeed, he warned more than once that this might be all he could give them, yet even then he feared that they might become so absorbed in the rigor of their worldly studies that they would forget their attachment to a higher wisdom. More than once he asked them to attend the authorized campus church until its preachings against slavery became intolerable to the boys, and throughout their school years he offered advice on which classes would best serve them later in life.[53]

While Rhett expected much from his boys, he yet understood that they had their limitations academically, just as he had recognized his own. "Tell me frankly of your difficulties and trials," he urged his eldest toward the end of his junior year when his class standing began to slip. "If I cannot relieve them, you can always be sure of my sympathy. A parent should be resorted to, not only in times of success and prosperity, but in discomfiture and adversity. I would rather hear of your failing from you, than from any other person, and if I am first to hear of your success, I shall not be the last in rejoicing in it." He always told his sons that he hoped they might do better, but he rarely found cause to censure. "God forbid, that I should blame any one for not being stronger than it has pleased God to make him, and thus impugn Providence himself," he assured them in July 1848, though blaming others for the weaknesses that he perceived in them was what he did almost daily in politics. "We can never get any thing by deceiving ourselves," he went on. "To know our deficiencies is the first step to reform them"—certainly an apt aphorism but a strange one coming from a man who seldom recognized deficiencies in himself, and from whom reforming even those received scant effort. He encouraged the boys when their grades slipped, and he showed unbounded pride when they excelled. Indeed, he went farther than a father should in trying to help, and at the end of Robert's junior year, when the boy was asked to prepare and deliver an address on "moral heroism" before a club to which he belonged, the father actually took time from his congressional duties to write it for him.

Rhett made it clear that so long as the boys studied hard, he would be content, "for it ought to be enough to know that one does his duty." He also advised them on their demeanor in class, instructing them at "high recitation" never to hesitate in their speech. Barny did not yet have the gift of smooth declamation, while Alfred had what his father called "a wretched way of stammering." He expected the older brother to work at least two hours a day with the younger in practicing debate before Alfred's actual entrance examination, for fear the boy would fail. They must also not make themselves liable to being corrected by their professors, for just as their father could not tolerate being corrected by others, neither should they. "Your mind like mine is not quick," he encouraged his favorite son, "but you will find it, by due exercise, capable I trust of great improvement." He especially wanted them to cultivate good relations with influential men, as he had tried to do. He recommended them to two of his friends, distinguished Massachusetts publisher Orestes Brownson and Amos Lawrence, admonishing them that "friends are very few in this world, and after they meet us, they ought to be cherished." He also urged them to secure the good opinion of Harvard's president and his old acquaintance from Congress, Edward Everett. Though Rhett would think many of Everett's political opinions mistaken or even foolish, he still entertained high regard for him as an educator and a man of character. He even encouraged Robert to show special attention to Everett's daughter as a means of endearing himself to the president, a species of sycophancy that Rhett would have condemned when done by others yet which he had practiced more than once with Van Buren, Calhoun, and others.[54]

Of course, part of the father's concern for his boys' performance grew out of the considerable strain that Harvard put on his precarious finances, especially since he was also undertaking to pay for the education there of Julius Stuart, his dead sister Claudia's son, though doing so without the boy's knowledge. It cost him $800 a year for Robert, and he sent money whenever he could—$50 here, $150 there—although having less confidence in Alfred, he allowed less for the younger boy and funneled all of that through the elder. At that, he had constantly to remonstrate against Alfred's extravagance. In fact, Alfred would always be a greater concern to Rhett because of his willfulness and irresponsibility, his father complaining that he always wanted too much too soon and spent it too quickly and frivolously. When he first sent Alfred to Harvard, he frankly confessed to

Barny that he did not expect great things from his second-born but confided that of course he could not share that feeling with Alfred. Rhett wanted Robert to become a lawyer and hoped Alfred could study medicine, perhaps later completing such studies in Paris. "He will I fear be a great annoyance, but you must bear it patiently," he advised Barny, with whom Alfred would live and for whom Alfred felt the adulation of a younger brother for an older one. Alfred shared his father's impatience and would be difficult. "He is a good youth, of a frank bold and honorable disposition," said Rhett, "but not strong intellectually, and lacking in patient enduring labour." He also knew that Alfred would likely be profligate with the money their father sent for expenses. "You had better look sharp to your expenditures," he warned, reminding both that "the best remedy against expenditure is hard study." Still, complaining was hard for him, and so instead of remonstrating Alfred directly Rhett usually spoke of it to his older brother, asking him to take Alfred in hand. "I dislike to say any thing on this subject," the father confessed, "implying as it does, that any of my sons have not acted in the best way."

He also felt that it was important to develop responsibility in both of the boys, and after this year he would send college money to each of them separately instead of having the eldest handle it all, even at the risk of Alfred continuing to squander his share. By late 1848 Rhett was reduced to enlisting the help of the despised Speaker of the House Robert Winthrop to endorse Massachusetts bonds necessary to finance Barny's final year of school. He repeatedly begged both boys to ask for money when needed. "You must neither be troubled or mortified on this score," he reminded them, as in the end and always he was a father too loving and indulgent to deny them anything it was in his power to supply. Rhett had even made what was for him an extremely rare joke during the summer past when he heard again that the boys were out of funds. "Your money-bag, seems pretty much like that [story] of the clown, who was asked by a Gentleman on horseback, whether the bottom [in a marsh] was hard," Rhett reminded them. Told yes, the gentleman rode past the clown into the bog and immediately sank deep into mire that all but swallowed him. Remonstrating with the clown that the bottom was not hard after all, the clown replied that yes it was but the gentleman had not sunk down far enough to reach it. Rhett sent the boys more money "to make another plunge at the bottom."

Rhett especially chafed at Alfred's failure to write to his parents and report his life and progress at school. Not only did his facility at writing suffer, but also the father feared he was allowing a distance to grow between himself and his parents and was failing to show the interest in and appreciation of their affections for him that ought to signify his own affection for them. "Be assured,"

Rhett admonished him, "the last thing you ought to slight or trifle with, is the love of friends." On a more practical level, the father teased that Alfred "may depend upon it, that he will not learn to spell or write English, by *not* writing." It pained Rhett particularly to see his beloved wife Elizabeth pine for news from Alfred. Their latest baby exhausted her now-failing constitution, especially when the girl's near-death from whooping cough forced Elizabeth to sit up night after night. "Claudia has made sad ravages on her health and looks," said Rhett, and he then reminded Alfred, "you too have aided in enfeebling a frame once robust—and you ought to endeavor all in your power, to please cheer and support her. Do what you may, you can never repay the debt of gratitude you owe to this devoted and wonderful mother."

Only rarely did Rhett allow chagrin over Alfred's behavior to propel him to serious complaint, but when the boy failed to improve his grades at the end of his freshman year, his father dismissed his excuses as "most absurd" and chastised the boy for trying to fend off his parents' concern for his progress. Alfred even spoke of leaving college at the end of the spring term, and finally Rhett scolded him directly for his lack of steadiness and purpose. "It seems, that you think that whether you stand high or low in your class, you can abuse the opportunity afforded to you for an education—[that it] is your own look out—and concerns nobody else, and nobody else has a right to complain or interfere," an angry father wrote him. God gave Alfred life, and his parents were raising and educating him, but they had a right to expect him to make use of the advantages given him. If he quit, he failed not only himself but those who loved him. "Push on with your education," Rhett said, and that seemed to mollify Alfred for the time being. Their father encouraged both boys to study hard even during their Christmas and summer vacations. "All other matters must yield to this duty," he told them. "Take care you do not allow company to interfere with your studies," he counseled. "Bow an untimely visitor out, without hesitation telling him frankly, that you cannot then see company." Rhett even told Robert Jr. that if Alfred distracted him from his own work, then he was to move out of the room they shared rather than allow Alfred's influence to impair his studies. He advised, "*Rise up and cast off from you, every thing which impedes you.*" He applied the same dicta that fall when he sent his younger son Burnet off to South Carolina College in Columbia, for he was shocked to hear that almost every student there smoked or chewed tobacco. "I send Burnet with great reluctance," he confessed, but he could not afford a third son at Harvard and had instead to rely on persuading the boy to put from him temptations and evil associations.[55]

Despite the expense and in spite of Alfred's frequent selfishness, Rhett wanted them to enjoy their college experiences. He encouraged the boys to take whatever classes they wanted so long as they met the core curriculum. He compared girls their age to "wild geese" and hoped they would wait until after college before entering the battle of the sexes, trying to cut off even his wife's efforts at matchmaking for young Barny. "When a young mans brain is once fairly addled by their charms, he is defunct as a scholar," Rhett warned Robert, "and may not recover his senses under 30." He wanted his boys to keep their acquaintances with young women few and discriminating, and after some girls visited them at Cambridge late the year before, their father detected a sudden dip in their class standing and feared that the visit had seriously distracted the boys and that Barny especially was about to be made a fool of by one calculating female. "Do not let this occur again," he scolded. Still he urged them to engage otherwise in the full range of extracurricular activities. Rhett persuaded Robert Jr. to take up boxing and fencing to strengthen his body and keep himself in good physical condition to sustain the mental exertion of college. "They are in fact the only means by which a gentleman, can acquire the strength and agility of a labourer," he advised. When Alfred showed interest in joining one of Harvard's rowing clubs, Rhett encouraged him to do so, promising somehow to find the money to cover the expense, and he also encouraged Barny to go rowing often. "I wish you whilst improving your mind, and obtaining a mental education, to educate the Body too," he told his son, adding, "it will always give me pleasure to minister in any way to your happiness in any innocent enjoyments." He even sent the boy some sixteen-year-old wine for Christmas, affirming it to be very good and asking only that "it will be *well* used, and not abused," which suggested either that the family table in South Carolina was off-limits only to hard spirits or that Rhett did not demand that his grown boys adopt his own abstinence of alcohol.

In all things he constantly urged Robert Jr., ever his favorite, to be a good example to his brother and help him with his studies. As Robert Jr. commenced his crucial senior year, Rhett warned him that "*this will be your trying winter*" and that he must take care of himself above all. His class standing was slipping again, as was his resolve, and now even the favorite son spoke of leaving school in discouragement with only one semester to go. His father sternly admonished him in terms that echoed his own resolution in finishing his education years before: "Observe this rule, however disagreeable; and do not allow little things to stand in the way of success in your career. Sacrifices are necessary to all high attainments; and little things sometimes show the difference between a weak & a strong mind more than great ones. Look high, and step over all minor objects, in reaching your end. Be prudent & ready for any required duty, for it is astonishing, how some men, for the sake of a few minutes unresolve, will forfeit the esteem & confidence of more determined and conscientious men. The truth is, a man who cannot conquer little difficulties, cannot be expected to conquer great ones." Above all, he wanted his sons at Harvard to "show the Yankees what a Southern Gentleman of real character really is; and that in all that becomes a man, you will acknowledge no inferiority." More than that, they needed to understand that "no influence of mine shall be used to support them in any course other than one of duty & honor."[56]

Rhett himself had obstacles to conquer. His sons could not vote in November, of course, but while trying to mold their opinions into the proper shape he continued efforts to do the same to South Carolina. As the Democratic meetings continued through October, some thought they saw an effort by the old Blufftonites to revive their movement, with Rhett fully in agreement, and suspected that his real motive now, as then, was ultimately secession.[57] Yet if his Hibernian Hall declaration was at all sincere, then Rhett still felt it was possible—if not likely—that the South could win its point short of disunion. Just which side was Rhett on?

As far as what Cass could do as president, Rhett at the very least had to regard him as a stopgap, for his veto could halt abolition measures in Congress and there were enough Southern votes in the Senate to prevent an override. Then in 1852 a revival of Calhoun's fortunes might yet put a true and affirmative state rights man in the White House, though the sixty-six-year-old Carolinian was in failing health and spirits now and might not have another four years left to him. Could Rhett's recent influence with Polk and the party have turned his head, making him see himself as a successor to Calhoun not just in the state but in the nation? If so, then Cass could keep the lid on the Union until then, and though Oregon would be lost to the free state people, if California and New Mexico should be brought in as slave states there might just be enough votes to halt further antislavery legislation. What they really needed, of course, was that constitutional amendment he had proposed back in 1837, but that was practically unattainable now.

Could Cass even be elected? That, at least, was a practical possibility and indeed a certainty if only a few of the Southern states stood behind him. But everything that might come after a Cass victory was only a series of slim chances, each building upon the last, and cumulatively their weight overwhelmingly discounts any sincere expectation on Rhett's part that a win for Cass would eventuate in Southern security and no cause for secession. All of the circumstances now, let alone his own past history, make it clear that Barnwell Rhett *hoped* for a Cass victory and *wanted* secession. Nor were the two incompatible, for with Cass in the White House and a Democratic administration there was all that much more chance that an accomplished secession would result in exactly what

Southerners wanted. Secession would have to *force* a Whig administration to back away from interfering with slavery; a Democratic government in power could be expected to work *willingly* to preserve the Union on an acceptable basis and equally to strengthen the party with a return of satisfied Southern Democrats who were now defecting to Taylor.

Certainly South Carolina, at least, could be won for Cass. It was the only state in the Union in which presidential electors were still chosen by the legislature and not the people, and when they assembled in Columbia they showed that Rhett's influence had been considerable, if not decisive, for 129 out of 156 voted for Cass.[58] Certainly Simms regarded it as Rhett's victory, as he claimed, "He has been the mover of wires in this instance." And it was the only time in his career to date when Rhett managed to wield decisive influence outside his own district. Ironically, it came at a time when his old machine was completely defunct, even his brother James having retired from the legislature.[59] Unfortunately Rhett's wires did not stretch to Georgia, Tennessee, Louisiana, North Carolina, Maryland, Kentucky, Florida, or Delaware, for any two of the larger or just four of the smaller of them would have been enough to defeat Taylor. In the end the slave states, and Van Buren's defection from the party, elected the Whig candidate, and Rhett would not forget or forgive. "The election of General Taylor, was a pregnant calamity," he later declared, "which led directly to all the future complicities and contests, which eventuated in the dissolution of the Party."[60]

The disappointment was palpable but not unexpected. Those more cynical about Rhett's motivations suspected that his real dismay was not at Cass's defeat but at the loss of what Rhett might have expected from him as reward. First Pickens had stabbed Calhoun in the back to side with the party, and then Rhett had sold himself, so they charged. "Their failure now stabs themselves," Simms gleefully concluded after the election. "Neither Rhett nor Pickens can possibly now realize their 30 pieces of silver."[61] Yet others saw something else: the shadow of the passing of power. It had been Rhett's year in spite of the defeat. Calhoun scarcely made himself felt, nor did he try overmuch. The Virginian novelist Nathaniel Beverley Tucker called the South Carolina state rights party now "that mischievous faction of which C[alhoun] is the head, and Rhett the tail." It reminded him of a mythical sea serpent, the amphisbeana, of which it was said that one could not tell head from tail and sometimes the tail could lead.[62]

THIRTEEN

Into a Circle of Fire
1849–1850

EXPECTING LITTLE ACTIVITY DURING the Christmas recess, Rhett left on December 19 to go to the Ashepoo plantation for the holidays and stayed through the New Year, his time home marred by a fresh round of debt problems thanks to a short crop that season and low rice prices.[1] When he returned to Washington there was soon no doubt that the head of the "great serpent" was ill. Calhoun fainted on the floor shortly after Congress reconvened and then again on January 24, 1849. Friends carried him to the vice president's office and laid him on a sofa in the chilly room. Word of the collapse spread through the Capitol quickly, and Rhett immediately hastened to the room to find Calhoun sitting up, his coat and waistcoat removed, and clearly burning with high fever. Calhoun held out his hand.

"Ah, Mr. Rhett, my career is nearly done," he said. "The great battle must be fought by you younger men."

"I hope not, sir," Rhett replied. He told Calhoun that they needed him and that the South needed him.

"There indeed, is my only regret at going," he said, eyes welling with tears. "The South—the poor South! God knows what will become of her!"

Rhett tried to get Calhoun to put his coat back on against the chill, but with his fever he would not. Others got him to his lodgings, and gradually over the next few days he improved, but the root causes of tuberculosis and heart disease remained. Many feared that this would be the great man's last session.[2] As for Rhett, whose account of the episode may well have been colored by personal and political motivations, it was more evident than ever that a time was coming, and perhaps very soon, when Calhoun's mantle would be laid down for someone else to don. Had Calhoun not said that it was "you younger men" who must carry on his work? If he did not say specifically that he wanted Rhett to be his successor, certainly he had not named anyone else. Maybe before long the tail would be the head.

The two ends were already in conflict when Calhoun fell ill, for they disagreed on what course to pursue in the wake of the Taylor victory. Several days before, on the evening of January 15, a caucus of Southern members from all parties met in the Senate chamber to discuss their course. It turned into a miniature Southern convention, and as Rhett reported to the *Mercury,* "this debate disclosed the fact, that it was *impossible to unite Southern politicians in defense of Southern rights.*" Instead they divided along the old party lines and demonstrated tragically what could be expected to happen at any true convention of delegates from all the Southern states. "Cooperation was an impossibility," Rhett concluded. "The States able to act will have to act separately." A sectional convention would only work as a consequence of separate state action, he declared, and moreover it would have to be a convention composed entirely of men propelled to leadership "on the great issue of slavery."

Calhoun submitted a document titled *Address of the Southern Delegates in Congress to Their Constituents* in which he called for Southern unity to force concessions from the North, and the disagreement was such that in spite of Rhett's opposition, the Whigs tried to get it redrafted and then submitted a substitute address. Tempers ran hot at a second meeting to discuss the issue, with the three Georgians Howell Cobb, Alexander H. Stephens, and Robert Toombs in support of resubmitting the address for Whig revision, and Rhett and Jefferson Davis strongly opposed. Then the Whigs simply declined to vote at all, leaving it to be a contest among Democrats, and Calhoun's original version finally won. Rhett dutifully reported the proceedings to Polk, no doubt including his own conclusion about the futility of cooperation.[3]

The address laid out their grievances, concentrating especially now on Northern refusals to give up fugitive slaves to their Southern owners, the territorial question, and the flood of new abolition petitions placed on the floor since the opening of the session. Calhoun contemplated the effect of abolition or emancipation on society, declaring that black and white could not live peacefully together. Worse, he predicted that emancipation would only be a first step. The North would then lift blacks to political equality and use them as allies in the subjugation of the white South. In short, white Southerners would trade places with their slaves. To fight this, the South must unite. After the Whig rewrite, anything more specific than that disappeared from the document, though clearly the logical next step was a Southern convention. It was the most incendiary thing to come from Calhoun's pen yet. Though nothing approaching some of Rhett's declarations, for Calhoun it was strong stuff indeed and would have been stronger.[4]

Yet the flaw in the address and Rhett's own justification for differing with Calhoun became immediately evident when he circulated it to the other delegations for signature. Of 121 Southerners in Congress, only 45 signed. Not one of them was a Whig, and South Carolina and Mississippi were the only states whose entire delegations approved the address. Rhett had been saying for some time that Southern unity was an illusory hope, and the fate of Calhoun's *Address* proved his point. He had loyally signed it himself, but he knew as he did so that it was a pointless gesture.

Much to Rhett's surprise, the reaction in the South at large was strong enough to give some hope, most likely spurred by Calhoun's newer and stronger appeal to racial and social fears. In the legislature in Columbia, Whigs and Democrats came together to issue a call for a Southern convention, and when they did that Rhett found himself forced by his signature to the *Address* to go along. Thus for the balance of the year he subordinated his own views and loyally stood behind Calhoun's plan, once again the faithful lieutenant. He began writing again for the *Mercury*, and in a more moderate tone differing little from the Calhoun line—especially after September when John Heart, once editor of the *Spectator*, took over from Carew. Rhett's only digressions from Calhoun's calls for unity were his repeated condemnations of the Whigs. If those in the South could be brought down and replaced by Democrats elected "on the great issue of slavery," as he had suggested, then the chances of unity in a convention would improve tenfold.[5]

The brief second session produced little for Rhett to do other than follow the appearance of the inflammatory *Address* with an argument in the House after a comment criticized South Carolina's law allowing the arrest and incarceration of free black seamen on Northern ships entering the port of Charleston and their release only when their ships sailed. The city had to protect herself, Rhett protested, and declared his conviction that the Denmark Vesey plot in 1822 was the result of free blacks and Northern instigation. How could the city be secure if she allowed free blacks from Yankee ships to walk her streets, since each was a potential outside agitator?[6] The reference to an alliance of Northern whites and free Southern blacks, and what they had done and presumably might do in the future, was too close to Calhoun's message to be coincidence.

Back at home after the adjournment Rhett remained active but unaccustomedly out of public view, which was part of the Calhoun strategy. They wanted other states to take the lead in the Southern convention program, so that the undecided could not complain that it was only South Carolina making trouble again. To do so, however, Carolinians had to stay in the shadows using their pens instead of their mouths, though Calhoun did far more than Rhett in that line. It gave Rhett time to attend to his long-ignored private affairs now that he had before him the prospect of an indefinite period out of office. His plantations, managed for him by his brother Thomas, harvested only two bushels of rice to the acre, and the summer crop came in at $10,418, well below usual expectations, which would not have helped. The notices of interest due on loans and payments required on bonds came in month after month, and in August, having seen Elmore's success with his ironworks, Rhett briefly looked into becoming a partner and sales agent for a new patented process for smelting copper.[7] Making no public appearances himself, Rhett did write a speech for Elmore to deliver at a small dinner for the ailing John Stuart, but that was small glory now.[8]

He also worried even more about Robert Jr., whose health had set back his studies, and now feared he would have to leave Harvard. Perhaps just as bad, having earned membership in Phi Beta Kappa, the son now failed to maintain sufficient marks to remain a member. Rhett arranged with Everett for his son to go back after recuperating for a time, and even though the boy lost his high standing in his class, his father still encouraged him that he could secure a respectable place by renewed application. "It is a folly through indolence or any other course to trifle with ones progress of reputation," he told his son, more likely thinking of Alfred, "but it is a greater folly to shrink from the consequences our folly has brought upon us." He then turned immediately from mild scolding to encouragement and advice, including telling Barny to practice his recitation for at least an hour a day and to try to recast the ideas found in his readings into his own words. It worked, for Robert Jr. would graduate that spring. His father had hoped to send him to Niagara Falls, Canada, and Newport, Rhode Island, on a vacation tour to celebrate completing his education, but there simply was not the money. Even then, however, Rhett was still not entirely satisfied with his boys' deportment. Barny had an offensive habit of wrinkling his nose "like a pin-cushion" when he laughed, and Alfred had a habit that he found "exceedingly vulgar"—he laughed too loud. "It might be pardonable in a college student, but now that you are a *man*," the father would tell him, "and are to perform the part of *a gentleman,* overcome this vulgar habit." They must both stop slapping their hands on their knees in mirth too. "So give up laughing, any how," he told them, "but be quiet and always pleased."[9]

Albert, always the greater difficulty, began suggesting now that he did not want a profession such as medicine after all. Instead he proposed to his father that he quit Harvard and become a planter, attracted by romantic notions of what seemed to him to be a life of indolence and pleasure. Rhett immediately quashed that notion, saying that to quit school would be to return home in disgrace. He related the tribulations of his own recent crops, long droughts, brackish water ruining his seed, and then rain turning to sleet and snow to kill the shoots. He had suffered six frosts in a row and a drought after each. As of May 1849 one-third of Rhett's anticipated crop had been destroyed, and unless the weather improved, he could not replant enough that summer to do more than break even. Pointing out that he had three sons at college and an enormous load of debt, the father hoped the lesson to Alfred would be self-evident. "A profession is after all the surest means of support, besides being more improving to the mind and elevating to the character," he said. Alfred would have to stay at Harvard, and moreover his father insisted that he apply himself to a more challenging curriculum, including Latin, Greek, and especially French. "No man can go to school with any advantage to himself without writing and speaking French," he advised, for it was the language of successful men of the world. It was also time for him to reform his extravagance with money, as he quickly spent all his father sent and then ran up bills for more. With Robert Jr. graduating that summer Alfred would be on his own, choosing new associates, and his father admonished him to be careful of his friends. "The world may overlook our virtues, but never our failings or vices," he said, telling his son that schoolmates exert a powerful influence on the formation of virtue and vice alike. Already Alfred was smoking, of which his father did not approve because it is "very nearly akin to positive vice and generally leads to it." Told by his haughty son that the other Southern boys in his class were not worthy of associating with a Rhett, his father chided him to "depend upon it nothing is more silly than an affected superiority to others in little things, when we are not superior in great ones." He even asked Robert to find new associates for his brother, hearing that Alfred was in danger of being "ruined" by two friends who habituated saloons and gambling dens. "I anticipate no such course for Alfred, from the evil influence of any one," the father admitted, "but for any success in obtaining his education, he must be with a studious and virtuous chum." Rhett directly admonished Alfred to raise his grades, reform his spending, and get himself closer to God, with the result that then Alfred would genuinely be superior. Meanwhile he should seek companions among the Northern students. Even though Rhett believed that "the Yanks no doubt endeavor to delude the students of Harvard, to support the plunder of Yankeedom," still he expected that "there must be some gentlemen amongst those who are the best scholars.."[10]

In the meantime their father watched events from the peace of his study but found the retirement hardly restful in the continuing crisis before the South. The enthusiasm that immediately followed the appearance of the *Address* seemed, for a change, to hold, and he could see evidence in his own old district. The Fourth of July had long been an annual political and patriotic ritual, with dinners and addresses and innumerable defiant toasts. For the celebration this year the state rights men had arranged a considerable celebration at three of the parishes in the district, and when the day arrived, one meeting at Walterborough saw the real passion of the Bluffton days manifest when its toasts included ones to secession.[11]

Then came an assault seemingly from within that further inflamed many. Thomas Hart Benton of Missouri made a public attack on Calhoun's convention plan, accusing him of being a disunionist. Calhoun had to respond quickly, for Missouri was an important slave state, and if his scheme could be successfully labeled a disunion convention, then more moderate Southerners whom he needed could well balk. Calhoun responded in print, defending not only himself but the convention idea and restating Rhett's position on the "common property" of the territories as justification for a Southern stand. Benton's attack destroyed his political career, while Calhoun's defense saw wide publication and delighted Rhett. "Benton as a Southern statesman is killed," he predicted to Calhoun.

From his vantage Rhett thought he saw the course the fight was going to take in the next year or two. Despite endless antislavery proposals to come, he did not believe that the Wilmot Proviso or any legislation of like kind would be passed, since even Taylor seemed safe on that point. Instead he anticipated that now the Free Soil people would make their stand territory by territory, as they applied for statehood. The enemy would encourage bringing in Oregon as a free state and try for California, while attempting to prevent turning any of the New Mexico territory into slave states. Wisconsin had come in the past year as the thirtieth state, making the split between free and slave states exactly even at fifteen each. Oregon or California would tilt the balance. He expected the opposition to act within the Constitution in bringing them in but would argue that Taylor was using the military occupying California to force it toward a territorial constitution outlawing slavery. He felt that for this Taylor ought to be impeached but that Southern Whig support would help him get away with the usurpation. If they succeeded it would be fatal to the South. "On the present issues the South will triumph," he told Calhoun in July, "but all such victories only shift the ground of battle, with increased strength to our foes, and increased weakness to us." In fact, he felt chagrined that on Wilmot and abolition in the District of Columbia they would defeat the Yankees. "Would to God, they would do both, and let us have the contest, and end it once and forever," he complained to Calhoun. "It would then accomplish our emancipation, instead of that of our slaves." Yet he feared that the Yankees were too smart to do something that provocative now that constitutional measures could achieve their dominion instead. Thus, he feared, "we are put off to another and more formidable contest."[12]

As the year closed, Rhett saw the possibility of returning to the public stage, as Calhoun's continuing poor health made it apparent that he would probably have to resign, perhaps even before the new Congress convened in December. His old ambition rekindled—if indeed it had ever stopped smoldering—Rhett considered his most likely Senate rivals to be Elmore and Hammond. Yet Elmore was in poor health and protested that he did not want the seat, and Rhett wrote discreetly, or so he thought, to Hammond's friends asking about support in their districts. The replies were noncommittal, and of course Rhett's inquiry reached Hammond's ears, seriously compromising the personal truce between them in recent years. Still each faced serious obstacles, for Hammond's indiscretions with Wade Hampton's nieces had made a formidable enemy, while Rhett's reputation as an arrogant hothead did him no good. The mystery was which of them Calhoun would endorse, if either, since both had defied him at one time or another.[13] On this score, however, Rhett at least appeared to stand closer. Years later Nathan Clifford, until recently Polk's attorney general, maintained that in Washington now Rhett was believed to be Calhoun's "next friend," closer to him than any other.[14] But what if Calhoun did not resign or endorsed no successor?

In the weeks before the meeting of the legislature in Columbia, Rhett began to sense that, in spite of his earlier pessimism, Calhoun's call for a Southern convention might actually come to fruition. At the beginning of December Rhett even good-naturedly threatened his Whig friend Amos Lawrence, one of the largest textile manufacturers in Massachusetts, that if unity could be achieved and it held, in a decade's time the South would be weaving its cotton on its own looms, thus defeating Yankee capitalists by industrializing itself.[15] Then Calhoun's campaign culminated a few days later when the Mississippi legislature issued a cross-party call for such a meeting, to be held in Nashville in June 1850. While governors in several other states came out in support, in Columbia the legislature immediately turned to selecting four delegates at large. Calhoun probably did not interfere with the choice, or else Hammond would not have been named, and if he did let his preferences be known, then Rhett was not among his choices, for at the end of the first ballot that selected Cheves and Elmore, Rhett ranked seventh, followed by Pickens and five others. Clearly neither enjoyed active backing from Calhoun. On the second ballot Rhett moved up to fifth place, but that was as far as it got, as even most of his previous votes had rushed elsewhere to Hammond and Robert W. Barnwell, who were thus selected. Possibly, Rhett's rather crude feelers about succeeding Calhoun while he was still living put some of the legislators off him and spoiled his chances of being chosen, assuming he even wished to attend, for despite his comments to Lawrence, still nothing suggests that he actually expected anything positive to come out of Nashville.[16]

Besides, there were domestic concerns, not least being the appearance of Ann Barnwell Rhett, his eleventh child with Elizabeth. While Thomas ran the rice planting, Rhett lived in new lodgings in Charleston and practiced law again to put the older boys through their colleges. He found time, for a change, to return to community involvement too, serving as vestryman at St. Bartholomew's Episcopal Church when he was out on his principal plantations in Colleton. There were his slaves to look after too, and he took seriously the duties toward them that he professed to his sons. With more than three hundred slaves just on his Colleton plantations, Rhett was one of the largest slaveowners in a parish in which blacks outnumbered whites three to one, and he had more than twice as much invested in them as he did in the fields they worked. Their care, of course, only added to the drain on his cash in years like this when the crop yield was short and the prices low.[17]

Discord could find him even in the tranquil surroundings of his fields, for he and his neighbor William Elliott still had unresolved a long-standing dispute over the boundary in some swampland between their holdings. By now Elliott threatened legal proceedings, but they had already been to court more than once in the past, so that held no terror for Rhett. Yet he did fear something. "Some things are worse than litigation," he told Elliott. "Amongst them is a teasing, harassing, and dangerous difference as to the rights between neighbors." Their argument ran deeper than a property line, for Elliott was an old and ardent unionist, one of the most vocal opponents of nullification in 1832, and he and his family staunchly opposed all that Rhett represented. The added dimension of political hostility combined with the aggravation of their land conflict threatened consequences that Rhett found troubling. "We are both of us heads of families," he warned, "surrounded with inflammable materials which may not be hard to kindle."[18] The message was unmistakable. They both had grown sons now, and Rhett recognized that in his own boys' temperaments there was much of himself, and without his self-imposed restraints on violence. In such a charged atmosphere of animosity and resentment, and a threat to property rights and all that implied for the invasion of family domain, flaring tempers could erupt in tragedy. An impartial observer might have seen in it a metaphor for what was happening between North and South.[19]

Other affairs in a larger world than Colleton fortunately took Rhett away from neighborhood feuds, though they were no happier. His old constituents determined that in spite of the legislature they wanted him to represent them, even if in an unofficial capacity, at the coming Nashville convention. In early February the people of Orangeburg nominated him as their delegate, but not to be outdone, Colleton residents immediately afterward pointed out that his plantations were within that district's borders. "We claim him as our man," they said, and so he would be.[20] What they did not anticipate was that when he went in June he would also be, at last and unequivocally, his own man. Calhoun was dead.

From the opening of the session the previous December, it was apparent that the great Carolinian was dying, making his appearances in the Senate only through sheer will power. Yet the issue was so great that he had to be there. Just as Rhett had predicted, the administration tried to push through statehood for California, bypassing entirely the customary territorial phase. California had come up the year before, with considerable debate over the slavery issue, and it was Polk who suggested omitting the territorial condition, and with good cause. Gold had been discovered, and it seemed that all the world was rushing to the West Coast. Soon the population of California would be greater than that of half a dozen of the established eastern states, and without the immediate implementation of a strong local government, anarchy threatened. Polk even feared, so he said, that the settlers might declare their own independence and try to form a new western nation with Oregon. Yet the issue of whether California should be slave or free, and with it the problem of the rest of the New Mexico territory, remained unsettled. Calhoun fought that battle in the Senate as late as March 4, when James Mason of Virginia read for him a stirring speech that was to be his last. On the final day of the month, racked by tuberculosis, fears for the South and the Union, and a lifetime of unrealized presidential ambitions, he calmly gave instructions for his effects and said, "I am now perfectly comfortable."[21]

He covered all of his physical legacy, but among those last words there were none about who should take up his work, whom South Carolina should follow now, and apparently no mention at all of Barnwell Rhett. No doubt, like all of South Carolina, Rhett felt shocked, though not surprised, when the news reached him on the plantation. Calhoun had been the dominating presence in his and all Carolinians' lives for most of his generation. Theirs had been a singular and tortuous relationship. Personality, character, and even ideology divided them, yet they could not or would not separate. Calhoun always recognized in Rhett a useful laborer in the field, one whose almost excessive zeal could be capitalized upon so long as he could be kept in rein, but one not to be trusted without reservation. Rhett found in Calhoun the corridor to personal political ascent and entree to the councils of power in South Carolina, but a flawed champion nevertheless who was too soft on the Union to take the steps that needed to be taken and too besotted with presidential ambitions to remain always true to principle. Of all his lieutenants, Rhett was the only one who ever defied Calhoun—and more than once—yet still enjoyed his favor, if not his complete confidence. Calhoun was the only man in his entire adult life to whom Rhett would defer and subordinate his own pride, if not always.

Rhett might have expected something in return for that rather qualified loyalty, but if public perceptions were any guide, Calhoun had excluded him from his thinking, on the national scale at least, sometime earlier. In fact, for the past two years Calhoun had grown more and more publicly close to Jefferson Davis of Mississippi, sent to the Senate in 1847 as a war hero and almost the mirror image of Calhoun's own genuine attachment to the Union combined with determination to stand up for Southern rights. The two were much together. Calhoun adored Davis's wife, Varina, and even on Calhoun's last day in the Senate, Davis sat at his side and helped him to his lodging when he was too weak to remain longer. Now the perception in Washington and the South at large was that Calhoun's mantle passed to the Mississippian.

Rhett remained silent about that, but he would not have been human—he would not have been Rhett—had he not felt that he should have been the one at Calhoun's side at the end, where he had been for much of the past two decades, and not a cold, aloof upstart who never set foot on the political stage until 1846. Just as bad, now that the crisis was greater than ever, Calhoun's sword was to be taken up by a man who would be far too reluctant to use it, as Calhoun had been. There was too much Union love in Jefferson Davis.[22] Certainly Rhett saw himself as the spiritual successor. Acknowledging that he had broken with Calhoun over the Mexican war and the election of Taylor—and there were other occasions he later chose not to mention—in the last months Rhett still declared, "we came together again." He said, "We fought for the South. . . . Had he lived we would together have conquered."[23] His use of "we" suggested that he saw himself as being able in the future to work with Calhoun with a unanimity that certainly he had not in the past; the "together" apparently indicated that he saw himself not as subordinate but partner.

More immediately, in the smaller world of South Carolina, Rhett entertained heightened expectations of a succession, but his first rebuff came when Gov. Whitemarsh Seabrook appointed a committee of twenty-five to go to Washington to escort Calhoun's body home. He placed on the list both unionists and nullifiers but not Rhett, an omission that glared and can only be explained by the governor's ardent wish to avoid any controversy in the prevailing tension. Thus Rhett was only one of the crowd when the statesman's remains came home escorted not only by Seabrook's delegation but also by a guard of honor appointed by the Senate, and including Jefferson Davis.[24] The next rebuff came just days later. In the crisis the state could not leave Calhoun's seat vacant for long. The three men regarded on all sides as the leading contenders were Elmore, Hammond, and Rhett, and it was up to the governor to make an interim appointment until the legislature met in the fall to elect a replacement. Appointing

any of the three would be to give him an advantage as incumbent come the subsequent election. Seabrook dodged the problem by offering the appointment to
Hamilton instead, but he was no longer an official resident of the state. Then
Cheves declined when it was offered to him. On April 10, at a loss, Seabrook
finally gave the appointment to Elmore, whose health made it increasingly apparent that he would probably not allow his name to be used in the fall anyhow.[25]

If Rhett felt any chagrin at being immediately denied his longtime dream of
a Senate seat, it did not prevent him from leaping back into the political fray. In
fact, he probably regarded himself as the best contender come the election, and
even Hammond said he thought Rhett should have gotten the appointment, since
Elmore and Hammond had been elected to the Nashville convention. Moreover, Hammond seemed content that the legislature should elect Rhett when it
met, and certainly this appeared to be Seabrook's preference, for even as he gave
the temporary appointment to Elmore, he invited Rhett to deliver the principal
oration before the legislature. The placement of Rhett eulogizing Calhoun in
front of those who would choose Calhoun's successor was hardly coincidental.[26]

Rhett worked to assume direction of state rights affairs even before Elmore's
appointment. He all but took control of the *Mercury's* editorial policy now,
with Heart happy to oblige, and began seeking financing for the Southern press
in Washington.[27] Yet his greatest bid for leadership was to all but take over
Calhoun's dreamed-of convention. Having been passed over by the legislature as
a delegate at large, and with his selection by Colleton being only informal, Rhett
was a candidate in early May when the state held a general election of delegates
from the several congressional districts, and his own old constituents quickly chose
him. He would be going in good company, with Hammond, Cheves, Barnwell,
Pickens, Maxcy Gregg, James Chesnut, and more slated to attend. Elmore was
to go too, though he had only just reached Washington to take Calhoun's seat.
But then in a sad twist of fate, word came on May 29 as they were about to leave
for Nashville that Elmore had fallen dangerously ill. He died that same day.
Seabrook, still trying to steer clear of the leading candidates, persuaded Barnwell
to accept his seat on the condition that it would be only temporary. South Carolina, it seemed, was having trouble finding and keeping a senator.[28]

Rhett reached Nashville to find that there was less realization of Calhoun's
expectation than most hoped. In spite of declaring in 1849 that passage of anything like the Wilmot Proviso would result in its secession, Virginia did not even
send a full delegation, and there was rather an air of trepidation now that they
were actually attempting to meet. Delaware, Maryland, Kentucky, Missouri,
North Carolina, and even Louisiana sent no delegations at all; and Florida, Alabama, Arkansas, and Tennessee sent only informal delegates with no official

state sanction. It bore out what Rhett had been saying for years about the illusion of Southern unity on action, for once proving him right and Calhoun wrong. In such a ticklish atmosphere Rhett and Pickens argued that their delegation should speak up and take the lead, but the rest of the South Carolinians wisely decided to stay calm and as quiet as possible in the deliberations, for fear of being too ultra and frightening the others into abandoning the effort.[29] They convened on June 3 at the Odd Fellows Hall but soon found it too small and adjourned to a nearby church, and they promptly set about dropping so much cigar ash and tobacco juice that they would have to replace the carpet when they adjourned.[30]

Rhett and the rest of the South Carolinians sat in the front pew on one side of the aisle, and the Mississippi delegation sat on the other, with W. L. Sharkey of Mississippi in the chair. A short session that afternoon settled only procedural business, and the next day saw propositions from the several delegations, South Carolina all the time remaining silent. Hammond spoke only once to answer Sharkey on a point at the insistence of his colleagues, but otherwise they kept their vow of quiet. No progress was made for several days, and then on the evening of June 7, apparently with no prior warning, Rhett was asked to write an address to place before the convention the next day. Sitting in his hotel room, he apparently drafted it extemporaneously, amazing his roommate Henry Young, who marveled at the speed with which Rhett produced the document. "I had supposed it was carefully prepared at home and taken with him to the convention," Young recalled.[31] The fact is, it probably was. This was neither the first nor the last time that Rhett would show up with just the right document to serve his purposes if he got the chance to use it. Having already made it clear that he, at least, wanted to be heard on this floor, he certainly thought out carefully and well in advance what he wanted to get across. Following the plan to stay in the background, however, Rhett decided not to introduce the document himself. Wisely an Alabama delegate was chosen to present the address, since several other Alabamians were showing reluctance to take any action. Wisely, too, there was to be no mention as to its authorship. That, at least, should get it a hearing from those who might otherwise have closed their ears to anything they knew to come from Rhett.

The next morning Pickens presented resolutions calling for governmental noninterference with slavery, the sort of thing expected by most of the moderates present. Then the Alabamian stood and presented Rhett's address, which made clear that the issue before them was slavery and its place in the relations between North and South. The address rehearsed yet again all of the past agitations and indignities and pointed out that now, added to that, Southerners found themselves reviled in Congress and daily insulted, as slavery was dragged into every debate. Now the North wanted to abolish slavery in the District of Columbia, restrict the movement of slaves between states where it was lawful, use the courts to prevent the return of runaways, and deny them their share of the new territories. "These are all means aiming at one great end," the address warned, "the abolition of slavery in the States." If they surrendered on even one point, it would only inflame the fanaticism of their opponents the more, and in twenty years' time the course of growth guaranteed that there would be so many free states arrayed against them that resistance would be futile.

"Our past policy of non-action and submission to aggression cannot bring us peace and safety," Rhett had written. Moreover, their passive stance for so long had wasted any chance they might once have had to halt the progress of this evil, but now it was with them and they had to confront the danger. Worse, their supine stance had allowed those Democrats in the North who would have stood by them to be marginalized and overcome. On top of that, geography and economy dictated no commonality of interest between North and South, thus naturally setting them at odds and making it inevitable, in Rhett's view of history, that one or the other must become subject. Slavery in the South made it worse. Almost every colony in the world where African slavery once existed had seen it overthrown by rulers in the home country, and from that Rhett derived the lesson that a society with slavery "must rule themselves or perish." The Yankees did not realize the inferiority of the blacks nor the impossibility of social amalgamation of the two races on any basis of equality. Thus the Yankees would press and press until finally they destroyed what they did not understand.

Like all free minorities, the South must protect itself from the majority—which is what the Constitution was designed to do before the North began to override that charter. The South, therefore, had the dual duty of self-protection and of preservation of the Constitution that their opponents sought to trample. They could not do it by election now that they were a minority. "The ballot-box in the South is powerless for its protection," the address pointed out. There was no likelihood of a change of heart by the North, for even the few statesmen there who spoke for adherence to the Constitution were shouted down by the abolition fanatics. And now a report had just appeared in the Senate proposing the admission of California without slavery and granting territorial status to Utah and New Mexico and the transfer of half of Texas to the latter, prohibition of the sale of slaves in the District of Columbia, and provisions for apprehension of fugitive slaves in the North.

This, of course, was the Omnibus Bill introduced on May 9 and based on proposals from Henry Clay for settling the troubled territorial question, and

Rhett condemned them every one. The proposals excluded the South from any of California, which was large enough for two new states, by prohibiting slavery, violating Rhett's common property doctrine and incorporating the spirit of Wilmot. Taking territory from Texas was just as heinous, for the annexation treaty with Texas provided for the future possibility of its being divided into as many as five smaller states, all of which would naturally have been slave states. Now territory large enough for two states was to be added to New Mexico, and Rhett felt no doubt that soon the North would force New Mexico, too, into statehood without slavery. The effect was to add two new free states while at the same time eliminating the possibility of two slave states being calved by Texas to maintain parity in the Senate. It was only a matter of time after that before the so-called Indian Territory, set aside for the removed Cherokee and other tribes by Jackson, would be forced through the same process, excluding the slavery currently practiced there, and it was large enough for two states. Rhett considered the proposals and their repercussions all but diabolical, for ultimately the South was to be denied potentially eight new slave states—two from California, two from Texas, two from the Indian Territory, plus Utah and New Mexico.

Add to that the abolition of slave sales in the District of Columbia, which had been slave country long before Virginia and Maryland ceded it to the government. Any slave introduced there for the purpose of being sold would be automatically free. Could that be anything but the first step to a general abolition in the District? In return for all this loss, the South was offered a new fugitive slave law, conceding in fact nothing more than what the Constitution had required all along, and with no guarantees that Northern authorities would obey—while some made it clear that they would not. Worse, the bill allowed a runaway to take his owner to court to demand proof of ownership before his return, thus allowing state and federal courts to insert themselves between master and slave. "If Congress can legislate at all between the master and slave in a State, where can its power be stayed?" he asked. The answer, of course, was nowhere. And this was being hailed as a compromise, when the South was yielding everything.

What was the South to do? They had proposed the simple expedient of extending the Missouri Compromise line to the Pacific before, allowing it to settle where there should be slavery, and it had been rejected in the past. Rhett had proposed it in 1838 in his Atherton resolutions. Should the North be willing to accept that line now, they ought to take it, but nothing less and certainly not the Omnibus Bill. Of course Rhett knew full well that the Yankees would never go for the Missouri line extension and apparently actually said so to the Tennessee delegates in Nashville in order to persuade them that they could support the address, since they would never face the question in actuality.[32] That said, Rhett said no more, nor could he if there were to be any hope of the convention adopting his address, and that was what mattered. He had stated the basis of Southern opposition to the compromise, and if the convention ratified that, then he had established a fundamental, and apparently sectionwide, base of opposition. That was important because he acknowledged disagreement among them even on the proposed compromise.[33]

Mild though the address was, Rhett's authorship, an open secret, may not have helped when it came to consideration. The convention did not meet on Sunday, June 9, but there was considerable informal discussion as advocates, especially Hammond, wheedled and cajoled. On Monday when the debate resumed, a few amendments were offered, and predictably several of the Alabama delegation still expressed opposition, as did Sharkey, who favored the Omnibus Bill. Expecting this, Hammond had urged Rhett to be ready to reply, but now that he saw how visibly angry Rhett became at the Mississippian's opposition, Hammond, who managed the address debate, stood instead and met the objections. Striving all the while to overcome the prejudice against South Carolina as a bed of hotheads, he had also to try to control Rhett's impatience and intolerance.[34] Still a few feared that Rhett was serving his own ends rather than theirs, and one Georgian took the floor and reported that in the past two days it had been "whispered that a little infant president was quickening in some portions of the Address." Nevertheless Hammond, who all along pleaded for moderation, got it through safely, avoided a feared split over its content, and saw it to unanimous adoption.[35] The content of the address mattered much less than the fact of this rather illusory unanimity, for it was the first time that delegates from Southern states—even if six of them were entirely unrepresented—had ever done anything together. The next step must wait until they reassembled in the fall to consider the actual outcome of the deliberations in Congress.

Rhett may well have learned some things to his advantage at Nashville, for this was the first time outside Congress that he was thrown together with a substantial number of leading men from several of the slave states. All his career Calhoun had seen Virginia as the natural ally of South Carolina in the struggle for state rights, influenced by her historic role of leadership and mother of statesmen, and also by her size and importance in the Southern economy and society. But for several years now Rhett had seen that Virginia's influence waned so far as state rights, as her slave population declined, and at Nashville she did not even field a full delegation. Moreover, it was Mississippi that issued the call for the convention in the first place, her governor now being Rhett's spiritual brother John A. Quitman, and in the actual deliberations Rhett found the most kindred sentiments in men such as Henry Benning of Georgia. Rhett concluded that Calhoun had been misled in casting his gaze always northward to the Old Dominion for support. Hereafter, when he contemplated any concert of action, Rhett would look west.

The delegates returned home to rounds of praise, and along the way Rhett learned that one of the Upcountry districts had given up on the Nashville convention achieving anything and was already calling for secession, an encouraging sign of resistance to counter the submissive posture of so many at the gathering. It emboldened him when he reached Charleston. Quickly the supposed secret of Rhett's authorship of the address became common knowledge.[36] Not surprisingly many of his friends organized a dinner in his honor at Hibernian Hall on June 21, and naturally at its end they called on him to speak to them about Nashville and the state of the Union. Though he later argued, as he often did, that his remarks were "quite extempore" and "almost entirely unpremeditated," the fact is that he well knew he could not appear before any group at home without being expected to speak, and indeed without wanting to speak. The fact that he was later able to furnish a lengthy text of his speech, supposedly from memory, is evidence enough that if he did not have something written beforehand, still he knew perfectly well what he expected to say.[37]

He also showed the frustration at his enforced silence in Nashville. However much that mild address and the semblance of unanimity in its adoption may have done to serve the temporary purpose of getting the other states to do *something* together, it fell far short of what needed to be done and what he knew that only South Carolina and perhaps Georgia and Mississippi now were willing to do. He praised the convention all the same. "It counselled, it united," he proclaimed. He pointed out how their host delegation from Tennessee, at first in favor of the Omnibus Bill, came around to accept the extension of the Missouri line instead, while saying nothing of his private assurances made to them. But having said that, he told them that the North would neither recognize their rights in the territories nor go along with extending the Missouri line. Nor would the current so-called compromise pass the Senate; and if it did, it would not get through the House in any case, for the abolitionists must have the Wilmot provision or nothing now. "If, then, all these expedients of adjustment fail in Congress, where are we?" he asked. He knew well enough. "We are in the beginning of a revolution!"

The political air lay hot and thick on the ground now, with little hope of the sun of reason coming through. Bigotry and stupidity drove Northern politicians, according to Rhett, while party allegiance was breaking down in the South to make way for a spirit of independence and "the gathering resolve to be equal in the Union, or independent without it." They were moving now, and Nashville had been that first step. "One step leads to another by inevitable consequence," he said. "To begin is to go on; and to go on, is to go on to the end." Now the South must have justice or revolution, and the convention had set it in motion. It was time for the people to change their government to a free one that taxed them fairly and recognized their rights. He denied that he had been a disunionist in 1828 when he spoke out in Colleton, or in 1833 during the nullification fight. His desire had been to reform the existing government until 1844 when the repeal of the gag rule convinced him that it was impossible. Even Calhoun, in his last days, realized the impossibility, or so Rhett maintained. The South might still for a few years longer stave off utter subjugation by parliamentary skill in Congress, and chiefly by her strength in the Senate, but inevitably that must wane. Now, he told his audience, "I see but one course left, for the peace and salvation of the South,—a dissolution of the Union."

Did disunion present such a frightful prospect? Southerners would be free of onerous taxes. They would be loosed from the constant insult and assault on their institutions. Certainly they had within their own section all the tools and materials for continued and advancing prosperity. "By our physical power, we can protect ourselves against foreign nations; whilst by our productions we can command their peace or support." The South held in its hands the key to the prosperity of the industrial nations of Europe and by free trade would make it available. He all but said that cotton was king. Their cities would grow again, and their people would stop the tide of emigration westward that economic hardship had commenced. "Wealth, honor, and power, and one of the most glorious destinies which ever crowned a great and happy people await the South, if she but controll her own fate."

Some might call him traitor for what he had said. Let them, he thought, for where lay his treason, and to whom? There was no longer a Constitution for them, and without it there was no Union to betray. "But let it be that I am a Traitor. The word has no terrors for me," he went on. All of those ancestors he so admired—the Thomas Smith who helped bring down a king, another who aided in the overthrow of the Lords Proprietors, the Thomas Smith of the Revolution—had been traitors in their own time. "I have been born of Traitors, but thank God, they have ever been Traitors in the great cause of liberty," he stated. And from what he saw and heard, he was no longer alone as he had been in 1844. All around him now he saw the signs that others were ready for patriotic treason as well, and as his audience now interrupted him over and over with cheers, he thought he saw his kind of traitors there too. South Carolina would happily join with any other Southern states in efforts at redress, he concluded.

But she would never submit to subjugation, and even if all the others forsook her, she would stand alone to "make one brave, long, last, desperate struggle, for our rights and honor, ere the black pall of tyranny is stretched over the bier of our dead liberties." They must all die, and how much better to do it sooner rather than later if in the cause of freedom.[38]

It was a sophomoric speech, overblown, bathetic, inflammatory, and therefore perfect for his audience, many of them his old Bluffton and Young Democrat followers. It had been six years since anyone spoke to them this way, six years of the aging Calhoun's pleas for calm and sectional unity, and six years of consequent inactivity, while in Washington the abolitionists were gaining in power every season. His followers wanted to hear this sort of call to arms, and that is what he gave them. For Rhett, of course, it also presented the chance to speak his mind, unmuffled by foolish concerns for unity as in Nashville. The convention had served its purpose, such as it was. Indeed, from Rhett's point of view he could not lose regardless of the consequences at Nashville. If true sectional unity had been achieved, so much the better for his ends. If not, or only equivocally as happened to be the case, it only advanced further his argument that it would never come and that separate state action was the only alternative. Now he had simply concluded, as he probably intended all along, not to await events in Washington to decide what to do next. More to the point, with Calhoun gone and no anointed successor, it was his bid to take the leadership in the state and carry it with him in a new and dramatic direction.

Others did not feel so inclined to be led. Hammond, for one, was shocked. "Altho' I concur in every sentiment of Rhett's, I regret exceedingly that he gave utterance to them just now," he complained a few days later. They had just succeeded in convincing the others at Nashville that South Carolina was not an asylum of reckless hotheads. "This speech will destroy all the effect of our policy, and destroy all confidence in Rhett as people may view the matter," according to Hammond. It only helped their foes in the West and here at home. Worse, Rhett had called even the Nashville convention a revolutionary step, which would not play well in the legislatures of those states that felt uneasy about participating in the first place. "Rhett has overthrown it all," Hammond grumbled. "Such men spoil all movements." Yet it would not do to come out and oppose Rhett's policy publicly, for that would only cause internal discord and weaken them further.

Simms had predicted that Rhett would act to suit his own ambitions and motives, and now Hammond agreed. "It was criminal. He was led to it partly to vent himself after his restraint at Nashville, partly from love of notoriety and ambition to go further than any one, but mainly to draw down on himself denunciations for expressing what are believed to be the sentiments of the State, in the expectation that the sympathy, indignation, and defiant spirit of the State would in return send him to the Senate. He must have had more sense than to suppose such a speech could do any *public good,*" Hammond told Simms. "As you say it is self," he lamented. "He wants to be ahead."[39]

Rhett was more than pleased with his Charleston speech. "It exacted more applause & enthusiasm here than any speech I have delivered," he boasted. Inaccurate reporting of it in the opposition *Courier* gave him an excuse to prepare a full written version "to let my true position and grounds be known" for the *Mercury,* and the very day it appeared he began sending it to friends such as Benning, hoping to see it published out of state. Cleverly, he told such friends to have it quoted as coming from the *Courier,* thus anticipating and defusing criticism that some would level at anything that came from the *Mercury.*[40]

Regardless of the source, there were some who found much to applaud in Rhett's speech. An editorial writer in the *Southern Quarterly Review,* which always stood spiritually in the resistance camp, called it a "truthful and forcible performance" and asserted that when Rhett referred to secession, he did so only as a last resort, choosing to ignore the Speaker's lengthy comments on the positive good to come from disunion and a new confederation in the South. Although many might criticize, and indeed in the Senate, Henry Clay had accused Rhett of treason for his remarks, the editorial predicted, "he will survive them."[41]

Perhaps, but he would need to survive more than just the one speech. He was toasted throughout his old district, and many declared their hope that he would return to public office, and soon. On July 24 he spoke at St. Helena Island on his old mentor William Grayson's property, with partitions from Grayson's house taken down to build a stand beneath a banner that declared, "The Hon. R. B. Rhett, 1850. Oh that we were all such traitors." The flag showed nine stars— one for each state represented at Nashville—and on the other side carried a motto: "Southern Rights and Southern Wrongs, we will maintain the one and resist the other." Though Rhett was ninety minutes late in arriving, after he spoke for fully an hour the crowd felt delighted, especially that he went beyond his declaration for secession in Charleston and speculated not just on the future after disunion but on "the probable destinies of a Southern Confederacy." At last, for the first time, he spoke of the step to follow secession, the step that truly defined the difference between being a secessionist and being a disunionist. From this point onward there could be no pretending that he wanted to save the Union, and hereafter he would stop pretending.[42]

Events came swiftly that summer. Quite unexpectedly President Taylor died on July 9, which actually came as a blow to Southern hopes, for he opposed much that was in the Omnibus Bill, and his successor Millard Fillmore of New York felt no such opposition. At the same time Rhett learned that the state rights people in Georgia were mounting a series of Southern rights meetings, and at all of them resolutions condemning the compromise proceedings in Washington were passed along with demands for the Missouri line extension as the only acceptable solution—the solution that men such as Benning and Rhett knew would be impossible. "I congratulate you on the way Georgia is moving up," Rhett wrote Benning in July. "God bless you! Go ahead! We will follow."[43] Meanwhile Governor Seabrook sent Congressman Daniel Wallace on a mission to Mississippi to promote cooperation of the two states. Thus between them the governor and Rhett, a private citizen, worked to promote not Southern unity but a league between South Carolina, Mississippi, and Georgia, the three states seemingly most disposed to take radical action.[44]

It was only a short step to Rhett taking his work outside the state in person, and as the foremost exponent of radical action now, he inevitably received an invitation to speak at one of the meetings in neighboring Georgia. It came from Macon, and on August 22 he appeared there in company not only with leading Georgian secession advocates but also with Yancey of Alabama, unaware of the suddenly conspiratorial shadow this cast on his appearance. Yancey, once a unionist, freely confessed that he had made Rhett his model now and patterned his course after his mentor.[45] With a crowd variously estimated at five hundred to fifteen thousand, depending on the views of the reporters, Rhett probably spoke to no more than fifteen hundred.[46] Speaking for the first time in his life to a popular audience outside his native state, he came with a carefully prepared text that gave them variations on his Charleston theme, condemning the compromise measures being debated in Washington and asking them, "Why should we wait?"[47] It was time for secession, though now he qualified his Charleston declaration by calling for a "temporary secession" until the North amended the Constitution to guarantee their rights not only to their slaves and the opportunity to take them to the territories and form new slave states, but also to end internal improvements. Surely the free states would yield this, rather than have a permanent split in the Union, he said, but did he really mean it? Surely Rhett knew that the enormity of the conditions he demanded were impossible of achievement, guaranteeing that temporary secession must be permanent. And if the North did not accept, that only proved that the two sections could never have lived amicably together after all. That being the case, he told them, "let the Union be permanently dissolved."

He should have stopped there. Indeed, as he was about to discover, he had gone too far already, but now he went even farther. He asserted that once seceded, the Southern states would "appropriate all our Territories." They would exclude Yankees from them instead, and New Mexico and Utah would become slave states. And how could anyone keep California out of a Southern confederacy? There was more. "As portions of it shall become fit to be added to our Union," they would annex Mexico and take as much as it pleased them to take, until they were as great as the Roman Empire of old. It was all theirs if they acted, but they must act now, for delay was fatal. Move immediately and Virginia, Kentucky, and Maryland would be forced to choose sides and must come with them. Moreover, they could secede now and accomplish it without bloodshed, for the North was not yet strong enough to dare to face them on the battlefield, whereas if they waited another twenty years their freedom would have to be won at a terrible blood price. He called on them to strike now. Indeed, he called on them to be the first to secede, promising that South Carolina would rush to her side if Georgia but moved to save the honor of the South.[48]

It was a clever gambit, of course. If either Georgia or Mississippi seceded first, then gone would be the old complaint that all the furor was just firebrand South Carolina. In the interests of the great movement Rhett would sacrifice the honor of being the first to secede if another state doing so instead raised the likelihood of more following, and surely states such as Alabama that might not follow South Carolina would be more amenable to taking their lead from Georgia. But he reckoned without some things that he even alluded to in his address. There were old animosities between Georgia and South Carolina, going back to colonial disputes and aggravated more recently by trade problems. He alluded to them in closing when he spoke of "whatever in the past has occurred to breed alienation" between the states.[49] Then there was the fact that he and Yancey were both there, bringing the scent of plotting with them. Two days after the meeting a person present wrote in disgust that "it was a stupendous failure" and said disdainfully that "the godlike Rhett and his adjutant Yancey preached most eloquently in behalf of treason."[50] Now Rhett was the outside agitator, and how dare he come into Georgia to try to tell her citizens what they should do. "Has such a man no respect for the intelligence and patriotism of the people?" one Georgia editor complained. And Howell Cobb thought it just possible that the state would side with the Union just to spite Rhett and his incendiary calls for disunion.[51] In fact that is almost what happened. This was the first time in the state that ultra men called openly for secession, and the reaction to Rhett's interference helped drive the more mainstream Democrats away from the incipient disunion movement so that, by the fall, Georgia rushed right back toward the Union and embraced the Omnibus Bill when it passed in September.[52]

One thing did come out of Rhett's visit that would last, however. There had been an old term in use for a generation or more applied first to hotheaded duelists, but now in the aftermath of the Macon speech a unionist Georgia editor applied it to Rhett and Yancey and their followers. He wrote satirically of a proclamation by fictional governor "Absalom Trickum" proposing the motto "United we fall—Divided we stand," and he sounded the secession call to arms when "Col. Hydrogen Gass will take command with Rhett-orical flourish" and lead a campaign in which every man would kill twenty Yankees apiece. The call was to all the "Invincibles" and to the "Chivalry" of Georgia. And it was to one other group, not so named before but to be so ever afterward, whom he called "Fire-eaters."[53]

It would be a few weeks before Rhett saw the real outcome of his Macon speech. Immediately afterward he returned to South Carolina, only to hear that on September 9 the Utah territorial government was established with squatter sovereignty, as was New Mexico the same day and on the same terms, and California was admitted as a free state. Nine days later came the new Fugitive Slave Act. Instead of ending the battle, the now so-called Compromise of 1850 only accelerated it, and the fight was on. Mississippi, Georgia, and South Carolina would all call for conventions to address a response, inevitably secession, and Rhett began speaking even more urgently, demanding a new Southern nation. In fact, he declared, soon Northern states would be trying to join their confederacy. To make the issue just as vital to nonslaveholders, he also raised the specter of racial interbreeding as an inevitable concomitant to emancipation. "Shall the African rule here?" he demanded. He predicted that Georgia would be first to go out, South Carolina at her side, then Alabama and Mississippi not far behind. Eighteen months would see the whole South out of the Union, and then they would reach out and take the territories and Mexico too, "as much of her as we want." The North would do nothing to stop them either. "I tell you my friends," he said, "there will be no fight, but when our Southern Confederacy is formed, it will not be long before these Northern men will crawl to us and beg to be admitted into our Union."[54]

In October, Rhett and his fellow radical John Means attended "Anti-Submission" meetings for those who preferred secession to submission. A new Southern Rights Association formed in Beaufort, and Hammond sadly concluded that there would be no point in the Nashville convention reconvening because the furor was such that they would split fatally; as he saw it, this was thanks entirely to Rhett.[55] That did not matter to Rhett, for he never expected any real action from the convention anyhow. His program was in South Carolina, and though passage of the Compromise of 1850 slowed the pace of secession sentiment in most other states, his agitation, with the aid of Means and Seabrook and others, bore fruit in his home state in the fall when the disunion faction came out of the state elections with majorities in both houses of the legislature.⁵⁶ That could only make him stronger when it came time for that same legislature to choose a senator to replace the temporary Barnwell.

First would come the second session of the Nashville convention, and Rhett determined early to attend. He may not have expected much, but he would at least give the other states an opportunity to seriously address secession. Just before leaving he declared that South Carolina should hold secession and wait on other states out of courtesy, but he felt that if they decided to submit, then she would go out alone.⁵⁷ Being committed now to separate state action by Georgia or Mississippi, followed by South Carolina, he regarded the pitiful attempts at general Southern unity that would occupy the convention as meaningless. Yet if the debates could exert any additional influence on Mississippi or Georgia they would be useful, and in the mood of increased hostility created in the South by the compromise, they might even persuade more states to join the fold. He did not expect Hammond to attend. Indeed Hammond did not, pleading sickness, but Elizabeth Rhett rather suspected that it was an excuse so that he could remain in the state to be on hand for the senatorial election as Rhett's chief rival.⁵⁸

After all the uproar the moderates who attended the June session did not travel to Nashville now, and only South Carolina and Tennessee had full delegations, with the former fully in control. "God grant you wisdom, and might, in the trying hour," Elizabeth told him, "and may your united counsels save our unfortunate country." But Rhett was quiet once more, and any unanimity was a sham given the limited turnout. Worse, all the news coming to them was gloomy. In Georgia the fall elections had gone to the unionists. In North Carolina the legislature decided that it would adopt a policy of nonintercourse with the North as its mode of resistance, while in state after state in the South the legislatures were clearly on their way to accepting the compromise despite all their recent outrage. They simply were not yet ready for the alternative of secession and disunion. Elizabeth wrote to her husband at the convention, "Where are the true, & brave, & enlightened, who are to carry through, so mighty a revolution?"⁵⁹

Certainly they were not in Nashville. Rhett left it to Cheves to make a stirring secession speech, and after that resolutions were introduced asserting the right of secession and issuing a call for the slave states to send delegates to a Southern congress, though without naming a time or place. Rhett, seeing the uselessness of it all, wrote from Nashville to Quitman urging him to get his legislature to call a convention to consider secession, and Quitman was all in favor, though it would take time. Rhett also proposed that they set the time for the proposed Southern congress for as early as possible in 1852 and locate it in Montgomery, Alabama, which happened to be Yancey's residence and the geographical center of the Deep South. Soon Quitman agreed and asked Rhett for advice on their proper course leading up to the congress. For the first time Rhett attempted to coordinate secession efforts outside his own state.[60]

The convention did not even come to a vote on the resolutions introduced and broke up in failure. Rhett returned immediately to Charleston, coincidentally or by design on the same afternoon that the city council held a public dinner in honor of Hammond. When his hosts called on him for a speech, Hammond suggested that Rhett talk to them instead and reveal what had happened in Nashville, and he obliged. Hammond may have hoped that Rhett would say something—as he had in his earlier Charleston speech—that might rebound against him, and some did think remarks by Rhett, Colcock, and Memminger were "all pretty much failures." Hammond still came away feeling that his magnanimous gesture had done him as much good as if he had made a speech himself.[61]

The news on Rhett's return was disquieting, helping account for the convention's decision not to set a date and place for the anticipated congress, for it appeared increasingly probable that it would never take place after the growing defections. By early December only South Carolina and Mississippi still held out against accepting the compromise, and the regional movement that Rhett so suddenly started to lead was faltering, perhaps fatally. Even leadership in South Carolina looked uncertain, for many saw Rhett's assertive leap forward as a grab for Calhoun's legacy. While Rhett was in Nashville, Hamilton came out and declared that the state did not have a leader worthy of filling Calhoun's shoes, a direct slap at Rhett, while his neighbor Elliott condemned Rhett as "a bellowing mooncalf" and "a mountebank with his puppets."[62] Even the unionists, though still a minority, were gaining strength, but cooperationists—those wanting South Carolina to act only in concert with other states rather than unilaterally—were also gathering power, Barnwell and Grayson among them, and soon it looked as if once again Rhett might stand alone.[63]

That made Calhoun all the more important, not for his life but in death, for the official state funeral ceremonies were set for late November, only days before the legislature chose the new senator. Hammond spoke in Charleston on November 21 and delivered a long and academic biographical account of the great man's life that was devoid of passion and eschewing current political ferment. A week later Rhett stood in the statehouse in Columbia and delivered his own oration. The perception was universal that not only were these two men the chief contenders for the succession but these eulogies were campaign speeches, breaking the tradition that one did not publicly campaign for a post to be chosen by the legislature. Hammond recoiled at the appearance; it bothered Rhett not a whit. As for his address, it proved to be one of the best of his career. The dignity of the occasion kept him from indulging in the overblown hyperbole and incendiary rhetoric of which he was ordinarily so fond, and constrained him to a level of decorum unusual in his speeches. He kept it simple and appropriate, and most of all reverential of Calhoun. Of course he realized its potential to influence the coming election and did not neglect to connect himself with Calhoun as an intimate friend and adviser. Absent was any mention of his own serious differences and occasional breaks with the great man, yet he did reassert his own and Calhoun's conviction of the inequality of the two races in the nation just then and what their proper relation must be.[64]

To whatever extent the eulogies had any influence on the legislature, there is no doubt that they favored Rhett, who not only spoke closer to the voting time but also in Columbia. Hammond was hampered by not attending the second session at Nashville, while Rhett, of course, continued to suffer from the imputation of rashness and blind ambition.[65] Pickens had so waned in the public confidence that he was hardly considered. As the legislators assembled, Hammond was considered as a moderate and Rhett, obviously, as the radical. Thanks to the fall elections, the legislature sat firmly in the hands of those favoring Rhett's separate state action posture, and so the outcome was never really in doubt. The legislators first deliberated a bill to call a state convention but fell short of the two-thirds majority needed and would not go on to call for the Southern congress without a convention first sitting. A compromise was reached at last on calling for an election in October 1851 to send delegates to the proposed congress in Montgomery now timed for January 1852, and a state convention to follow would consider the congress's proposals. It was certainly less than Rhett wanted or expected but still showed that the spirit to follow a more direct act by Mississippi was there given the opportunity.[66]

Then came the election. At first there were garbled rumors that Rhett had been elected governor, but they were false. John Means got the position. Rhett would not have wanted it in any event, and Hammond could not help speculating on how toothless he would be in the governor's mansion where he could only fume. "Whether he will usurp any power I cannot tell," Hammond mused. "In *some* things he is scrupulous." But Rhett's eye was fixed on the other election that followed. On the first ballot Rhett led with fifty-six to Hammond's fifty votes, with Barnwell a distant third with twenty-seven, James Chesnut with fifteen, and four others lagging far behind. The movement after that was slow but inexorable. Rhett stood at sixty-five atop Hammond's forty-eight on the next ballot, with Barnwell and Chesnut virtually unchanged and the others out. Another ballot added twelve to Rhett's total and only six to Hammond's, with Barnwell and Chesnut both losing ground. When the fourth and final ballot was counted, Rhett at last achieved the simple majority needed with ninety-seven, though at least ten legislators—probably unionists who had no acceptable candidate before them—chose not to vote on the last ballot.[67]

And so at last he was to be Senator Rhett. Former senator Andrew P. Butler saw great significance in the outcome for South Carolina. "She has in reality passed the Rubicon," he told a friend.[68] Others were less jubilant. Among the unionists the reaction was equivocal. Petigru watched the election from the gallery in the capitol and wondered that, even though the majority of the legislature were disunionists, still so many resisted voting for Rhett "because he is so violent." That gave him hope that the assemblymen were not as mad as he feared, "and that with a great deal of real malice there is a good deal of acting." The fact that it took four ballots from such a body to get a majority for Rhett suggested to the old unionist that his friend and onetime student "has his cup dashed with a bitter taste even in the act of raising it to his lips."[69]

Hammond expected that Rhett would mistake the act of the legislature for the voice of the people, and that he and his hotheads would push for immediate secession now, capitalizing on the wave that brought them to office. There would be a renewed test oath, and Rhett would make the mistake of thinking the public was roused for any action. Rhett had told Hammond a few weeks earlier that unless they were pushed—or driven—onward, the ardor of the public would calm as it had in other states and that his policy would be to keep them excited. "The Legislature have given *their approbation to abortive violence,*" Hammond complained at the selection of Rhett and Means. "They are both of the violent bugle blast section and neither of them capable of effecting any thing." All he feared from them was rashness and wind.[70]

But Hammond predicted that secession would only result in putting their own necks in nooses. South Carolina "could never be any thing *under Rhett.*" Indeed, in two years' time when Calhoun's unexpired term ended, he expected someone else would defeat Rhett and his program, for Rhett could not survive except in crisis. "On the least calm he must sink," he believed. "He will therefore have but one object in view—to keep the waters troubled as long and to the utmost extent he can." Moreover, if Rhett tried to push the policy of those who elected him, he would be seen as a blustering bully and bring odium on the state; if he did not, and showed the decorum and statesmanship that his new position required, he would lose their support, while if the crisis passed, the absence of controversy would consume him. "I am curious to see the result," Hammond confided to his diary. "He has got himself into a circle of fire."[71]

FOURTEEN

Such a Fire-Eater
1850–1851

"RHETT IS YOUR DICTATOR AT LAST," Hammond warned his friend Simms after the election. "It is line of march—the route of 'Joshua' is apparently right into the Jordan."[1] Simms was no happier than Hammond, believing that the voting showed that the legislature really would have preferred not to elect Rhett. "They do not like him, & he will soon lose his rank," he predicted.[2] Hammond was less sanguine. "An effort will be made by Rhett & Co to precipitate the State into secession, which will probably prove so abortive a movement as to be regarded as an insurrection only," and that would provoke the federal government into enforcing its authority.[3] In short, Rhett could wind up bringing down on them exactly what he was loudly trying to prevent.

The past season had taken a toll on Rhett. His frequently fragile health took a beating, and on New Year's day as he left for Washington he confessed to having trouble keeping warm. Elizabeth, too, was ill, and both of them had been nursing their sick year-old daughter Ann, whom they called "Nannie." Elizabeth had not been well for some time now, growing thin and pale—no wonder having given birth to eleven children, and with six still at home. She was only forty-one but looked older, worn out by years of pregnancy and labor. She begged her husband to lay aside his prejudice that all French were "infidels & imposters" and hire a French governess to help her raise the smaller children. She could not sleep and felt too weak to take any exercise. Rhett told her to spend more time outside and eat to fatten herself if she could, but she complained that it was too late for her now. "Oh! If you had bestowed upon me the loving tenderness & gentle fostering which I really required, & my nature yearned for, when we were first married," she chided him good-naturedly, "I might now have had some of her grace and softness." She was not so much reproachful of him as afflicted with disgust with herself. Of course he had loved her, yet beneath her banter there may have lurked a lingering resentment that he had loved politics more.[4]

Rhett turned fifty just days after his election and, surprisingly after his years of confrontational rhetoric and denunciations of opponents, decided before leaving for Washington to change his ways. Perhaps it was the realization that the dignity of the Senate would not be served, nor would his cause, by his old style. Perhaps it was the calming influence of Elizabeth, or maybe even a sense that now at half a century old he should behave differently. In leaving he told Elizabeth that on reflection he had adopted a "holy state of mind" with regard to those who would stand against him. "I intend to assail no one," he wrote his son Alfred, especially those Elizabeth called "those poor old men (Clay & Webster)." He would take no animosity and no spirit of revenge with him to the capital. This pleased his wife, who encouraged him "to preserve a dignified & patient course towards them, without stooping as a *Senator* of South Carolina to compliment or conciliate them."[5]

The new Barnwell Rhett walked into the Senate on Monday, January 6, 1851, escorted forward by his colleague Senator Butler, who presented his credentials. Rhett took his oath and sat for the first time in Calhoun's seat, a moment he had coveted for a generation.[6] Not a few there and at home looked expectantly to see what he would do. Some in South Carolina expected him to revenge the state against Clay for his role in the compromise, and others certainly awaited verbal sparks when Rhett responded to Clay's accusations of treason.[7] Surprisingly, however, Rhett kept to his seat and was largely quiet during this short session, trying no doubt to adhere to his recent resolution. More importantly, however, his attention was focused elsewhere, showing that even if he intended to be pacific in the Senate, he was preparing—quite literally—for war.

He kept his eyes on South Carolina and the legislature. Before he left home he saw signs of that creeping apathy that he dreaded, and he repeatedly wrote to find the prospects for the election in February for delegates to the convention. The responses were depressing. By the end of the month Elizabeth told him that to all appearances Charleston would be lost to the submissionists, though she expected that he would be elected to the convention if he let his name go on the ballot.[8] Worse was the news that apathy was taking over everywhere, which could only mean a general rise of submission. It appears that the people were waiting in hopes that two or more of the other states would take action first in their own conventions, with Barnwell and even Cheves advancing this policy. The legislature backed away from radicalism, with the minority controlling the majority. One friend doubted that the convention would ever meet at all, even after a Southern congress took place. People had found too much time to think, especially the merchants of Charleston who began to tally their potential losses from secession, and statewide the hesitance might prove fatal.[9]

It was what Rhett always warned of. The iron had been allowed to cool before they struck, and now he was in Washington when he needed to be in

South Carolina putting his bellows again to the coals. Still he did not despair. In fact, he was so confident that the state would secede after the convention that he wrote to his son Alfred, now at the college in Columbia, to warn that there might well be fighting in the state if the Yankees tried to apply coercion after South Carolina seceded. The college had a militia company that paraded from time to time, and Rhett wanted Alfred, as its captain, to lead it to Charleston if conflict came. "Of course you will volunteer, if there is any prospect of the Govt. coercing South Carolina," he told him. He also wanted to make certain that his son Edmund, though just turned seventeen, was in Alfred's company. It was unthinkable that a Rhett son would stay out of the fight, even though the father all his life assiduously avoided participating in any violence himself. But then, he had always encouraged his boys to fight. After asking if his sons were ready to go to war, he also thought to inquire after their school grades.[10]

In the face of South Carolina's faltering Rhett based his continuing expectation for secession and confrontation on his hopes for Mississippi. Georgia was lost to the submissionists for now, but Quitman was his sort of man, and Rhett wrote to him to see what prospects were for the Magnolia State. But there, too, the news proved bad. The legislature had called in November 1850 for the election of a convention, but it could not take place until the coming fall, which postponed convening the secession meeting until at least November 1851, the same time the South Carolina convention would be meeting. That might have seemed good coordination, but with the course of affairs in South Carolina, Rhett needed some action in Mississippi first in order to spur his own state to action in November. Quitman had told Rhett that Mississippi would be prepared to secede on her own, and now Rhett was counting on it. But then in January, Quitman began to see his state, too, faltering. He also had expected that secession would risk war with the North, and now he told Rhett that it was simply too premature to take the chance of bringing on such a conflict with his legislature and people not yet hot enough for the fight. At the same time a personal crisis suddenly engulfed the Mississippi governor. He had flirted with involvement in a filibustering expedition to Cuba, in violation of federal law, and now he was confronted with being arrested and charged, or resigning his office. He chose to resign, and at a signature Rhett lost his greatest ally for immediate action. He did not give up immediately, however, for Quitman might rebound, and Mississippi in any event could go out with or without this governor. Slavery was going to split the Union; of that Rhett felt certain now. He still promised Quitman that if only Mississippi and Georgia would secede, South Carolina would follow, and the three states arrayed together would forestall any attempt at coercion. Secession did not have to mean war, though his advice to Alfred certainly suggested that Rhett was ready to accept war as the price for realizing his dream.[11]

He had done all he could from his position in Washington for the moment. He had to turn his attention when he could to his senatorial duties. Fortunately quiet held the floor this session. His first act was simply presenting a memorial for the Ravenel family of Charleston for compensation for property they lost as a result of the Revolution, one of the myriad mundane chores of any representative. He and Clay did participate in a general debate on the credentials of a fellow senator from another state appointed to fill an unexpired term, but they were entirely civil. He also found himself on a couple of occasions involved in discussion with Jefferson Davis, whom he referred to on the floor as "my friend from Mississippi," though they were on opposite sides of minor issues. Davis was a friend to the Smithsonian Institution, and Rhett ardently opposed any government expenditure on its behalf. They disagreed more strongly over a resolution to promote Winfield Scott to the rank of lieutenant general. Ironically it was Scott whom Jackson would have ordered to lead troops against South Carolina if nullification had led to secession in 1833, but now Rhett thought Scott deserved the compliment in reward for his performance in the war with Mexico. Davis, on the other hand, who disliked Scott for trying to undermine rival General Taylor in the war, opposed the new grade. During the discussion Davis may have embarrassed Rhett slightly over a minor point of military knowledge, but still their relations, such as they were, appeared cordial. James Chesnut's wife Mary Boykin Chesnut observed that Rhett certainly acknowledged Davis as a Southern spokesman in the Senate. Toward the end of the brief session Rhett assisted Davis with a filibuster that killed a rivers and harbors bill, in the process seeing Davis lose his temper in debate with Clay and others just as Rhett had in the House in years past. Yet just possibly Rhett harbored some distrust for Davis all the same, for the senator had been far less ardent than Quitman about bringing Mississippi to secession and seemed to share the old Calhoun disease of too much Union feeling.[12]

Rhett could not help keeping an eye on events in his old chamber across the Capitol as well, and he was delighted when an effort to increase the tariff failed in late January, especially since, as he saw it, "the South stood more united than ever against all increase of the duties." Indeed, the tariff issue was so quiet now that he did not think any increases would pass in this or the next Congress to come. But then that was only because the North had a different issue now for subjugating the South. "The Slavery question is still festering in the body politic North & South," he warned a friend in early February, "and in my opinion, will dissolve the Union."[13]

Events in South Carolina could decide when or if that dissolution were to come. Elizabeth told him that by early February the signs for the coming convention election were improving after all. "The country is coming out bravely for secession," she said, even though Charleston still lagged behind.[14] Thinking to capitalize on what he still felt to be the prevailing mood of the people at large, Rhett published in the *Mercury* a demand that every candidate ought to pledge himself as for or against secession so the people would know how to choose. Hammond only scoffed at the move. "His game from the first has been to commit the State as early & as deeply as possible," he told his confidant Simms, stating that cooling emotions would terrify Rhett. "But what statesmanship! What Patriotism! He copies Mirabeau with neither his talents nor his provocations & will open the way for Danton & Robespierre—if he does not play their parts himself also."[15] Hammond probably did not know how utterly insulted Rhett would have been, not at the accusation itself but at being compared to a bunch of Frenchmen.

Rhett's name did not appear on any convention ballot after all, perhaps because he had recently moved back to Charleston. Thus those who would have elected him, his old constituents of Beaufort and Colleton, could not, while the less radical voters of Charleston simply would not. Besides, in his new position he may have felt above being an actual participant, just as Calhoun always preferred to pull the wires without actually mingling with the puppets. A far greater concern was the course of the campaign, however. Many of Hammond's friends refused even to run, boycotting what they saw as being Rhett's show all along. When election day came on February 10, Rhett also felt chagrined to see an appallingly low voter turnout, less than half of those eligible actually casting ballots. It betokened apathy, which was death to action, and an apparent rejection of Rhett's attempt to push the state ahead, just as deadly. "Believing that God is in all our ways, I shall be content by any result," he said on the day of the voting. That result was still a fine majority of 127 out of 169 elected delegates pledged to separate state action when the convention met in April 1852, but there was no concealing that the excitement of the previous fall had gone, and a few even questioned if the vaunted convention would ever really convene. "The policy of Rhett & Co has been to commit the State and commit the Members as *irrevocably as possible while the* excitement was up," Hammond repeated after the vote, and he was delighted to see it coming undone.[16]

Rhett would have to attend to the mood in South Carolina as soon as he could get home, but first there would be one major stand to take in the Senate before the adjournment. He continued to observe perfect decorum on the floor, with the help of Elizabeth, who constantly wrote to him from home praising his determination to stay calm and serene. She asked him how he coped with the cold outside the Capitol and "the heat within, mentally and physically in the Senate," and inquired how he got along with Clay and the ardent Mississippi unionist Henry S. Foote, confessing, "I fear they will annoy you excessively this winter." She and Rhett even feared that his foes had gotten hold of a letter he wrote her that went missing and that they would make its contents public. "It really does alarm me to think what those ill-disposed yankees may do with our missing letter," she confessed. "They would like prodigiously, to make you appear ridiculous if they could." She put it down to "impertinent yankee curiosity" to see "what such a fire-eater, as yourself had to say to your wife."[17]

In mid-February he rose, however, and incredibly found himself siding with the abolitionists in questioning the constitutionality of the new Fugitive Slave Law, though for very different reasons. The Northerners objected to being required by law to assist in the capture and return of runaways to bondage. Rhett, of course, maintained that the whole issue had already been settled quite sufficiently in the Constitution, which he saw as a compact between the states that required the states themselves, and not the federal government, to enforce the clause. Thus Rhett found himself in what he called "co-alition" with abolitionists for a change and actually expected attacks on himself not so much from the North as from Southern unionists such as Foote. Sen. Salmon P. Chase of Ohio stood firmly opposed to the law as a Whig antislavery man, and thus despite their differences, Rhett found himself on the same side of the issue as Chase after one vote. Rhett actually walked over to Chase's desk to say, "I agree with you in the views you have expressed, they are the true States' Rights doctrine," which no doubt surprised Chase. Certainly it surprised many others in the chamber.[18]

On February 17 he first entered the debate merely to observe that he thought the opposition to the enforcement of the law was strong in the North, but then a week later he rose to contribute substantially to the debate.[19] A week later the debate arose over the rescue of a fugitive slave in Boston from the grasp of slave catchers, and soon Rhett, Davis, Clay, and others were all involved. Rhett declared that the law would never be enforced to any extent to make it a real guarantee of Southern rights. If he thought otherwise, regardless of his constitutional objections to the law, he would keep silent. However, he felt that "by the action of the States, and the States alone" could the rights of the South be protected. "The law is not always a law," he said. "There is no lawyer who does not know that." To be effective a law had to be consonant with the opinion and values of the community it was to serve. He granted that the whole North was opposed to slavery, and that included opposition to returning runaways to their masters.

Would a law really make them do otherwise? With no basis in actual fact, he argued now that at the moment there were at least fifteen thousand fugitive slaves in the North—perhaps twice that. Yet in the months since the passage of the new law, he pointed out, only fifteen had been captured and not one of them returned to slavery before the owner incurred court fees and other costs greater than the value of the slave.

"I am a State-rights man," he told them. "I abhor constructions." He took the Constitution literally, as he took the scriptures. He considered the human mind so subtle that it could find any desired meaning when resorting to interpretation. The Constitution contained no specific grant of power to the government to interfere in any way with slavery, and that included the matter of runaways. Rather, in speaking of fugitives from justice in general, it provided the requirement for extradition as strictly a matter between the two states involved, the one where the fugitive was captured and the one where the crime had been committed. The very same clause specified that runaway slaves were to be delivered upon claim from the owner. It was solely a matter between states, and thus the new law that inserted the federal government into the equation in place of state authorities was unconstitutional. "I protest against this doctrine," he declared. Acknowledging that his remarks might be taken as supporting the abolitionists, and that he might even be attacked by some in the South, still he argued that he would stay immune to criticism on this issue. Any man who attained his age and could not listen to aspersions on his opinions and character without maintaining "coolness and self-possession" was unfit for public office. "Public life, in all free countries," he said, "is not a life of quietude and repose."

A handful of people opposed to a law could stymie its enforcement in any town in the land, he argued, a natural expression of his own deep faith in the power of a determined minority. And that minority could be in the North or South, he implied. South Carolina and Mississippi had not yet accepted the Compromise of 1850 that included the fugitive law, and in his thinking, as long as they held out they could form a nucleus for growing resistance. Yet now he charged that, unlawful though he agreed the law to be, were they not all the more pernicious in opposing it themselves in the North? They had already plundered the South of the territories; was not that enough? And then, despite all his pledges, he could not resist accusing someone. It was the Democrats, he said, whose party he had tried for thirteen years to save, who went over to the Whigs to follow Clay into this compromise. They had abandoned the South and their own credo, and as a result they were in disarray, their principles destroyed. He feared they would never rise from the ashes they had created for themselves, and thus the Whigs and their consolidation would reign indefinitely, trampling the rights of the South. He said that as a result, "this Union will soon come to an end." Clay's people and principles would roll on, crushing "all faith, all brotherhood, and peace, until the whole fabric falls a vast pile of ruin and desolation."

Clay was in the chamber and took the floor next. He remained calm but still chided Rhett for wasting so much of their time with his customary history of the Constitution and its interpretation, as if he were telling the Senate something it did not already know, likening him to a lawyer who began every argument by starting at Noah's Flood and working forward. "The whole difficulty with the Senator and his school is," said Clay, "that they undertake to say what are the granted powers, and what is and is not necessary to carry into effect the granted powers. And if all others do not concur with them they are consolidationists, Federalists, Whigs, precipitating the country into ruin." Of course, he had put his finger on Rhett's personality precisely. He went on to show his frustration at those who, like Rhett, argued endlessly for strict adherence to the Constitution but fled from the Constitution and took refuge in the manner of its origins rather than its literal content when it was pointed out that nowhere did that document sanction nullification or secession. Rhett interrupted to ask for time to rebut, and Clay made no objection but continued his remarks, trying to get the body back onto the issue at hand, the Boston problem.[20]

Rhett was not prepared to reply just then, but he fully meant to, for Clay had not only made fun of him—no more than was common in Congress—but had also tied him with Chase and ridiculed them together. So little time remained in the short session that he would not have time to prepare and make his response now, but he resolved that when they reconvened in the fall he would give Clay the raking he deserved. Indeed, the Senate became so backed up with business now that it had to go into a special session of an extra week. Rhett became so frustrated at continuing delays that he declared two days before it closed, "I have done what my duty requires of me . . . I shall stay here no longer." It did not help that a colleague immediately pointed out that Rhett himself had wasted some of the previous morning in a pointless complaint about a letter in the local press that he thought reflected on South Carolina. Rhett did not like being found to be inconsistent.[21]

Rhett left Washington on March 12, 1852 for the return to his home, unaware that he would never have the satisfaction of replying to Clay, for within four months the Great Compromiser was dead, victim of the tuberculosis that had killed Calhoun a year before. Rhett's anxiety to get back must have been due to Elizabeth's continuing poor health. Just days before his Fugitive Slave Law speech he received a letter from her that had to be disturbing. "Do not expect dear Husband, to see me look *pretty*," she warned. "That is forever past,

—I am in truth *very* ugly, and will never be any thing else again in *this* world. Pray try & reconcile yourself to this state of things—in fact I have grown old suddenly, & take but little interest in any thing or any body, besides yourself & our children." She feared that the past four or five years of poor health and continuing childbearing had hurt her more than she thought. The children, too, were sick. Burnet and Robert Woodward—called "Robin"—had nearly died the previous year, and she believed that the house on their Oakland plantation where she was staying was unhealthy, though he disagreed. "You are never long out of my mind, & almost every thing I do, is done with reference to you," she told him. "I might be worse than I am," she said to put the best face on her condition. "For your sake I will try & grow young again."[22]

In the excitement and preoccupation of politics and his continuing flights of strategy and forecast, Rhett frequently let public affairs force thoughts of his family from his mind temporarily, just as with his plantations, his responsibilities to his slaves, his supposed aversion to controversy, and even his self-proclaimed dedication to truth. But such appeals from Elizabeth had to bring him back abruptly. He needed to look to his family again now. He inquired after the progress of Alfred and Edmund at South Carolina College in Columbia, sent what little money he could—he was still trying to collect his fees from the British rice settlement—and encouraged Alfred to try to achieve first honors in his class. "You can if you make up your mind to do it," he advised, paraphrasing his old motto. Mindful of the temptations before young men away from home, he also admonished them to pray and read the Bible at least once a day. "Get Gods favor," he encouraged, "and you need no more for this life or the life to come." To his eldest he confessed, "My success in life, as well as nearly all its future happiness; so far as this world is concerned, depends upon my sons." He wanted his younger boys to learn Latin and Greek, and he desired all of them, the girls included, to ride as often as possible for their health. One daughter, Mary, was now fifteen and wanted to be allowed to go to parties, though her father thought her too young. Elizabeth wisely overruled him, however. In all her pitiful dejection at her own early loss of youth and health, she still remembered what it had been like when she and Barnwell courted. "Old people are too apt to forget the feelings of youth," she told him, and she allowed Mary to go.[23]

Even before his return to South Carolina and his family, Rhett had sent ahead his speech on the Fugitive Slave Law for publication in the *Mercury*, which complimented him—perhaps inaccurately—on being the first to question its constitutionality. He came home to find the state floundering even more on the problem of separate state action in the absence of real leadership, and with a continued reluctance to follow him. "Rhett is vain, self-conceited, impracticable,"

Simms complained, "and by his ridiculous ambition to lead and dictate every-thing, has rendered himself odious in Congress and in the State." Simms, of course, could be expected to indulge in hyperbole, but more reasonable state rights men such as Cheves also complained that they did not want to be linked to Rhett, however much they approved his basic position. Worse, some believed that he dangerously misled the people in proclaiming that they could achieve secession and a new Southern nation with no fear of forcible resistance from the Union. When Rhett arrived back from Washington, he expressed this view to an officer in the state militia, only to be told, "No fighting, well, that is the worst news I have heard for a long time! How in the name of heaven, are we to get the Southern Confederacy?" Rhett's answer was that it would come with the prom-ise of liberty and justice. "This is mere imbecility," grumbled Simms. "Rhett is really our ruler, and he is rash, arrogant and a surface man, with one idea only—a good idea doubtless had it companionship."[24]

Rhett threw himself into the campaign for delegates to the anticipated Southern congress in Montgomery, as the election would be in October. No sooner did he get home than he was asked to speak at Hibernian Hall on April 7 before a meeting of the Southern Rights Association. He told them that the state must maintain its rights regardless of the consequences. If she seceded, it would force the issue and other states would have to follow. He made it clear that he expected nothing from the proposed congress and declared, "A South-ern Congress now would be our ruin." Sensing the sentiment throughout the region, he told them confidently that "it would counsel submission." They had only two real alternatives: submit or secede. In so saying he attempted to polar-ize his audience into an either/or choice by denying the legitimacy of any other alternatives. Since the secessionists had "heartily labored" with those who wanted to wait for cooperation until now, when cooperation was clearly impossible, should not they now join forces with Rhett and his supporters to achieve the only other option?

"Secession, then—secession by South Carolina alone—is to be our policy," he declared. With it would come free trade, and there would be no blockade of their ports as some feared, for that would mean war. "If war is made upon us we will fight," he asserted. But he did not believe that the North would assail them, and if it did, South Carolina would resist until the last man. Long before that time her sister slave states would have joined her. Should the free states assail them, it would only guarantee the formation of a new Southern confederacy. If South Carolina seceded, which she must do during the next congress, "she will go without a single hostile gun being fired, or a single tombstone being erected." There would be no fighting, and for proof he offered the fact that two recent bills to increase the United States Army had failed in Congress. The reason, according to Rhett, was that South Carolina had just held her election for delegates to the coming state convention, and clearly the victory of the secession majority gave proof of her determination, frightening the Yankees away from putting themselves in a condition to fight. Rhett was implying that the Union was afraid of South Carolina. This was about the most foolish argument he would ever make, yet it illustrated perfectly his underlying belief that politics consisted essentially in the balance of fear and threats. For the first time now in Hibernian Hall he actually encapsulated his philosophy: "We will have no fighting, not because you are loved, nor from any principle, which restrains from shedding your blood. You are hated, no doubt, quite enough to bring on you, any calamity, which unscrupulous power, avarice or fanaticism can inflict. But there is policy in power. There is policy in avarice. There is policy in fanaticism; and all these perceive, that to attempt to coerce South Carolina in any way, is to secure their own defeat, and our speedy deliverance from their degrading thraldom. They acquiesce only in the necessity of things." Every consideration pointed in the same direction, he promised—toward the union of all the South. He had been fighting in this cause for a quarter-century now, he said, though he did not say when he crossed the line from protest and redress to disunion. "As a citizen of South Carolina, I demand that she makes me free." If he were to draw his last breath that moment, he said, his final syllables would be "secede." The coming convention would declare for secession, he promised, and when it did the rest of the South would rally to them.[25]

It was a renewed call to arms to infuse new vigor into the lagging secession sympathy of the state, and it worked at least for the Southern Rights people who had been inclined to follow him all along. He sent copies of his address to his sons for them to circulate and asked Alfred to call a meeting of his Southern Rights Association at college to read the exhortation.[26] The very day of his speech his audience nominated Rhett and Butler to serve as delegates to a Southern Rights Association convention scheduled for May 4 in Charleston, and when it met, Rhett and his faction predictably triumphed. The delegates were overwhelmingly secessionist, and for four days some 430 of them deliberated, in the end producing a report and resolutions that took it for granted that the convention to come would call for secession.[27]

In their hubris, the meeting's managers and Rhett blundered, for instead of bringing everyone in line behind separate state action, it only further divided the state's secessionist leadership. Just as Rhett's earlier ultimatum called for individuals to choose sides, now these resolutions polarized instead of uniting those who wanted South Carolina to act alone and those willing to secede but only in concert with other states. Colcock came out for separate action and Barnwell for cooperation, and so they split everywhere, even Senator Butler doubting that Rhett's approach would work.[28] To far too many it appeared now that Rhett took secession for granted and was trying to take command of the convention even before it met. The unionist press in the state, especially the *Courier*, began a counterattack, especially against Rhett's promises of abundance and prosperity after secession, and soon an opposition among the cooperationists started to gain strength. In the meantime outside the state in Georgia, Rhett's extremism had the effect of driving some state rights people back toward the regular Democrats.[29]

Within a few weeks even ardent Southern rights men such as Maxcy Gregg, a delegate-elect to the coming convention, found it expedient publicly to try to distance themselves from Rhett. "But he leads them & the State & they have anointed him leader," observed Hammond. Of course Hammond was critical of the meeting, since he had before it a more conservative plan of his own similar to North Carolina's nonintercourse policy. He thought the state could pursue that until the rest of the South came up to the right heat, but Rhett's call for immediate action completely overrode his plan. Hammond also felt mortified that his and Rhett's Calhoun eulogies were being published in the same pamphlet, with the effect that his words were appearing in literature being used to advance his rival's cause. "Do I belong to Rhett?" he railed. "He had crushed me it is true so far [as] my present & future political prospects & moral character are concerned," he told Simms. "What is there between us & associating us but that he has been my conqueror and destroyer?"[30] Hammond may have been a man greatly motivated by jealousy and animosity toward Rhett, yet he was more than objective enough to delineate perfectly the nature of the radical leader in any movement, and Rhett in particular. "He will continue to lead while he has cunning to foresee where their passions will carry them & impudence to run ahead of them."[31]

While those passions ran high, Rhett stayed in the forefront, especially with the spread of cooperation sentiment at his heels. "The truce nearly killed us," he told friends, "but under discussion, the People are recovering from the terrors, and false impressions." He accused opponents of purchasing votes and tried to counter by urging all in favor of resistance to some out on the hustings. Already he spoke in terms of war. "Can you not come over to the conflict?" he asked one. The issue before them was simply submission or resistance, and he was confident of victory. "The discussion I believe will do us good," after which "our majority will then be an unchangeable fighting majority."[32] The *Mercury* ran editorials, some no doubt written or approved by him, proclaiming, "Secession is at once liberty and prosperity." Meanwhile, when not speaking, he kept an eye focused constantly on anything that might further inflame those passions to his purpose, and in June the commander of the United States forts in Charleston harbor, Fort Moultrie and Castle Pinckney, gave him the issue. Already there had been an announcement that President Fillmore intended to reinforce the tiny garrisons, which the *Mercury* denounced as an undisguised threat. Then the local commander, fearing the excited state of the people, declined to let Charlestonians hold their traditional anniversary celebration of the Revolutionary War battle for Fort Moultrie inside the fort on June 28. Rhett could easily portray both acts as provocation, and when the anniversary celebration went on elsewhere on Sullivan's Island, he offered a toast to cooperation, defining it as South Carolina seceding and forcing Georgia to follow. He then added that their ancestors had achieved that sort of cooperation in the 1770s by seizing the tax stamps and firing the guns of Moultrie at their oppressors. When their ancestors gained their independence it was not by eating and drinking as they were this day, he said, but by fighting. South Carolina did not want to begin the conflict, but if anyone in the Union wanted a fight with them, he said, "in God's name, let them come on." One of Rhett's friends had already claimed the honor of being in the foremost rank in the battle, but Rhett pledged that if he were himself behind, it would only be by a little. It was all but a call to arms, and then when someone offered a toast to the Union, another proposed one to Quitman as the future first president of a new Southern nation.[33]

There seemed no stopping Rhett now, as happily he started trying to export his revolution to other states He vocally espoused the candidacy of secessionist Charles McDonald for Georgia's governorship that fall and came out at the same time for Quitman, who was free of his legal problems and seeking Mississippi's governorship once more. In fact, Rhett even mentioned in a speech on July 4 that he and Quitman were in some way cooperating, the implicit suggestion being that Mississippi and South Carolina were coordinated in their march to the brink.[34] He renewed his earlier correspondence with Quitman as well, warning him not to be misled by South Carolina cooperationists who might try to get him to support their policy and declaring to him, "If we can carry you in Mississippi and McDonald in Georgia, the game is up, and the South will be redeemed without a blow."[35]

Yet even while saying that, Rhett, incredibly, considered the political efficacy of striking that blow himself. At the inevitable July 4 celebrations, especially at Walterborough, with the largest turnout of slaveowners yet seen, the toasts were to "separate secession." In St. Peter's Parish one toast came out to "Hon. R. B. Rhett—May he be the first President of South Carolina," leading one cooperationist editor to ask, seizing upon this evidence of Rhett using his movement presumably to feed his own ambition, "sits the wind in that quarter?"[36] Rhett addressed the new Auxiliary Southern Rights Association, a splinter from the older one that atrophied from too much cooperationist membership, and told them they could wait no longer for new issues to arise to spur Southern unity and that if other states did not join them quickly, they must act alone. He spoke again at Hibernian Hall on July 31, proclaiming that now only secession offered them salvation.[37]

It was increasingly evident that Rhett felt the movement stalled somehow. His followers were ready, and even the cooperationists had many in their ranks who would act if provoked, but they needed that new issue, that act that would suddenly carry them all beyond restraint to action. Somehow someone needed to throw the tea overboard. The reinforcement of the Charleston forts probably gave him the idea, and he outlined it to Governor Means. He would manufacture an incident by having South Carolina state forces attack Fort Moultrie and Castle Pinckney without prior warning to Washington, seizing them from their little garrisons. The pretext could be anything—perhaps a claim that reinforcing the forts posed a threat to state sovereignty, or in retaliation for denying the anniversary celebration access to Fort Moultrie. The important point was not the reason behind the attack, but the reaction it must create, and the fact that such an attack prior to secession was undeniably treason did not concern him. It would galvanize the state and precipitate the rest of the South to action. It was the same rationale that lay behind the botched plan to capture the Augusta arsenal many years before, of which Rhett certainly had foreknowledge if he were not actually directly involved.

Even Means, as much a secessionist as Rhett, was shocked. As governor he could not possibly countenance such an act, arguing that the state could only take such a step after secession if the Union refused to recognize her independence. Besides, if they failed they would be ruined, and their cause with them. He warned Rhett of the "unnatural state of excitement" in Charleston and asked him to use his influence to bring calm. What he really wanted, of course, was for Rhett to allay himself, but calm now was not a part of Rhett's program.[38] Though Rhett did not press the plan with Means, the *Mercury* continued to complain over the reinforcement of the forts well through August, and just possibly he hoped that a spontaneous public eruption of some kind would take place. Rhett even warned in a reference to Napoleon's pyrrhic victory in Russia that they might have to make Charleston a Moscow to defend their rights.[39]

The only spontaneity that fall, however, was the growing reaction against precipitate action. The campaign became more heated and bitter through August and September, with an endless round of dinners, rallies, and public meetings. Cooperationists were damned as cowards and immediate secessionists as self-seeking demagogues. Rhett moved and spoke constantly on all his old themes and was so overtaxed and badly coordinated that he started to miss meetings, and even double-booked himself at two different places at the same time. He exhausted himself in the process, complaining on August 23 that he had traveled one hundred miles to make one poorly attended rally.[40] He sometimes spoke for ninety minutes or even two hours at a time, and the strain showed. He contradicted himself, now saying that Mississippi would not secede unless South Carolina went first, speculating wildly that soon there would be sixty-four free states arrayed against their fifteen, and promising that if South Carolina did not secede, then he would secede himself. He became short-tempered. When Perry's *Southern Patriot* mistakenly said that Rhett had been born in North Carolina and declared that if the state should be sacrificed to folly and madness at least it should be at the hands of a native, he fired off a petulant correction that promenaded all of his distinguished ancestors and prompted a cooperationist editor to call it "a jackday exhibition of vanity."[41]

There was worse ahead. In September, with Quitman's gubernatorial campaign heating up in Mississippi, someone discovered his correspondence with Rhett, and it all became public. Already cooperationists in Georgia were backing away from any leanings toward secession after Rhett's intemperate declarations about forcing their state to secede and his backing of McDonald. Now Quitman's enemies attacked him for making promises about the course of Mississippi and encouraging South Carolina's secession. It smacked of conspiracy and meddling in the affairs of another state, clear violations of the sovereignty doctrine that they were all supposedly fighting to uphold and an attempt to compromise the public will to suit their selfish ends. Quitman denied ever having corresponded with the Carolinian, and now, forced to the wall, Rhett lied as well, denying any transactions between them. "Gen. Quitman never, that I know of, wrote to me a letter in his life," Rhett declared publicly, despite having received at least one letter from Quitman just the previous January and having written at least two of his own to the Mississippian.[42]

The attacks on Rhett mounted as the election approached, and he became the focus symbolizing all that the cooperationists opposed. Simms ridiculed his "feverish suspicions," and Hammond charged him with leading a party that knew nothing more than that it wanted to do *something*. "Rhett is the great leader of this Party," he maintained, "tho' strange to say no one is willing to own him." Old William C. Preston saw fools rushing to a precipice under his lead. "Our Senator Rhett a light unmeritable man puts himself at the head of the movement," Preston complained. "He has neither property, principle or sense, and no impulse but for notoriety." William Elliott, no friend to be sure, damned him now as a "mountebank player with his puppets." Rhett had convinced some people that they could secede and be a separate sovereignty, which Elliott regarded as absurd. "They believe it and prostrate themselves before this bellowing mooncalf and swallow all his fatuities as oracles," he grumbled. "One who has gulp for this would swallow a haystack."[43]

Certainly Rhett had his defenders too, and they were worried for him by the time the Quitman matter became public. "Our great leader, Mr *Rhett*, is *dangerously ill*," wrote one. He had what some called a "country fever" that superstition believed he could catch in the rural districts. More likely it was simple exhaustion, added to a respiratory and occasional intestinal problem that he had encountered intermittently for years. He admitted that he found the campaigning "constant & engrossing occupation," especially after what he thought the brilliant opening of the effort in Charleston back in May. Now he was all but prostrated, and on September 25, practically the eve of the election, he had to cancel all his remaining speaking engagements. His nomination two days later as a representative from his old congressional district to attend the Southern congress in 1852 hardly improved his condition, deprecating its prospects as he did.[44]

For the remaining two weeks of the campaign Rhett remained largely an observer, and what he saw was depressing. South Carolinians, remembering how they had tried to act independently back in 1832–33, only to find themselves isolated and unsupported by other slave states, ultimately feared too much the same thing happening again. Chesnut's wife Mary would perfectly capture their mood when she wrote that though they "are wonderful for a spurt," South Carolina's planters were "impulsive but hard to keep moving."[45] By October 6, a week before the polling, Rhett felt able to attend a meeting in Sumter County where the cooperationists, headed by Preston and Chesnut, set up at the courthouse while the secessionists held forth at the local academy. It was his last campaign declaration, and he defiantly told the audience still that "*the State would secede alone.*"[46] Yet others everywhere saw the sudden and dramatic collapse of the secession party, and it was not helped when an abnormally southerly display of the aurora borealis in the night sky panicked some of the more ignorant who saw it as a sign of fiery retribution from the North.[47]

Rhett did not stay for the election. His rice crop had been bad again that year, the third in a row. His employers for the rice duty affair in England still delayed in paying his commission, and as well he may have had some railroad bonds he hoped to sell overseas. Financially strapped as always, he left shortly after his last campaign appearance, having done all he could and no doubt anxious not to be in the state for the disaster that he probably knew was to come.[48] It is just as well, for it was shocking. Overall, secessionist candidates for the convention garnered 17,710 votes, while the cooperationists and unionists, who had combined, took 25,045. They won Charleston and all of the backcountry, twenty-five of the forty-four legislative districts, and six of the seven congressional districts, with only Rhett's old constituents standing by him. Rhett was elected as a delegate from Charleston, but that was cold comfort now. The election had been a clear referendum on secession, and it lost.[49]

The victors felt entitled to gloat. One editor called for Rhett and his followers to "hang up their fiddles," while Petigru wrote to Daniel Webster that the unionists had "taken the state from Rhett and broken as I think the spell that Calhoun left." Cooperationists felt equally relieved. Elliott damned the secessionists for "their factious conduct and their subserviency to the despised Rhett," expressing the hope that at last "these would-be pettifogging tyrants, will be put down." Certainly it was not a victory for unionism, of course, for all that was defeated was separate action, not secession itself. The vote also showed that the Lowcountry parishes where the slave population predominated all went with Rhett, while those districts with a majority of whites all went with the cooperationists. It was the planters against the yeomen, a bad harbinger for days ahead if ever there were secession and a truly critical need for unity.[50]

Elizabeth wrote her husband a letter with the news, and it caught up to him somewhere on his journey, though he may have seen the result in a newspaper before then. "I declare to you, the shock has been so great to me, that I feel giddy, as if I had received a blow," she told him. "I cannot think at all & am bewildered." She feared that their god had forsaken them, but most of all she worried for the effect on her husband. "What you must suffer, I cannot bear to think of—after all your noble exertions, your generous self-sacrificing devotion to this ungrateful, cowardly, stupid state." No one seemed to know what to say or do; they were all stupefied, and the submissionists ruled the day. Robert W. Barnwell had deserted them. Of course Rhett always knew of the essential difference with his cousin, and though no rancor rose between them, Elizabeth could not help wishing that he might suffer for his apostasy. If there were no change, and if current predictions that the forthcoming convention would accomplish nothing proved correct, she assumed that Rhett would resign his Senate seat, even though it would leave his enemies in triumph. How could he do otherwise, if the state so clearly repudiated the position he took in Washington? "I am willing to go with you any where from this dishonored state," she lamented. The shame of South Carolina was too great to bear. "We shall indeed be a by-word among the nations."[51]

Rhett would only say that the defeat was "mortifying."[52] Hammond accused him of fleeing to Europe in anticipation of the result, and there may have been some truth mingled with his undeniable prejudice.[53] Some of the secessionists recognized that Rhett was a part of their problem by the very hostility he generated, even among those who favored the cause. "If Rhett takes any part in a movement it is half dead the moment he touches it & whole dead when he embraces it," one protested. "Rhett's leadership cannot give it success," said another after the defeat, and some started to turn to Hammond, whose nonintercourse plan was still on the table and appeared more achievable. "I will not consent to act with any party having Mr Rhett as its leader and the Mercury as its exponent," declared Hammond's supporter Alfred Aldrich. "I am informed that he is now so unpopular with his own party that they are anxious to get rid of him." Maxcy Gregg now said that Rhett and Butler ought to resign from the Senate at the beginning of the next session and that the legislature should decline to replace them as a first act of nonintercourse.[54]

Rhett stayed in England no more than a couple of weeks and by early November was already on his way back home, landing first at New York. It had been a fruitless trip, and he brought little or no money back with him but only the promise of future payment, hardly what he needed to cast a glow on his return home. As soon as he got to South Carolina he went to Columbia, probably to confer with Governor Means and others and most likely about the very issue of his resigning. The probability that all separate action and cooperationist secessionists would rally on Hammond's plan if Rhett resigned and left the leadership to his old rival was certainly presented to him, and just as certainly he refused to give up his seat and rejected Hammond's plan out of hand. Acting on Hammond's plan would make South Carolina "a conquered province" dependent upon change from the North or assistance from the South, with no expectation of either.[55]

Besides, he still had a mission, he said, and that was to make his answer to Clay, even though the Kentuckian was five months dead now. Hammond could scarcely contain his contempt. "With this puerility our poor pitiful legislature is perfectly satisfied," he ranted. He predicted that Rhett now planned to fall back from his defeat, taking his followers with him in order to kill nonintercourse. "In due time I shall not be surprised to see Rhett re-appear," he wrote, even suspecting that if all else failed, one day Rhett would rejoin the Democrats in order to return to power. "Nothing from him would surprise me," Hammond told Virginia secessionist Edmund Ruffin. "I have long thought he was not sincere in his Revolutionary tactics. They were too wild & *insured defeat.*"[56]

Rhett's friends confessed their despondency at the recent outcome. "The late recreancy of South Carolina has discouraged the friends of the institution [of slavery] every where," wrote one. "She put herself in the situation to be regarded as the *Vanguard* of Southern Rights, and, when the war-cry was about to [be] made 'ingloriously fled.'" That was not exactly true, of course. It was Rhett who put his state in the vanguard, not the state itself, and that is much of what defeated him. Now the friends of slavery worried that their only remaining protection might be in reuniting with the Democratic Party, to "let slavery take its fate" and stay in and support the Union in order to protect slavery from national legislation. "If there is no reliance to be placed in So Ca, slavery is doomed," one feared.[57]

Yet there were still those who encouraged the dejected but determined Carolinian. "The majority may talk at you and against you," wrote one friend on Rhett's return, "but nevertheless you are on the side of Constitutional Rights, of Political Justice, of Republican Equality."[58] So he was, and bloodied though he might be, he was not ready to give up—not yet. At the very least he would sit in the Senate and state his position, and await the outcome of the convention in the spring. There might still be a turnaround in sentiment in the state. If he had been one to give up in the face of defeat, he never would have come this far after all the setbacks of the past.

Besides, there was still an enemy to fight. An ever-growing antislavery party threatened like a fell North wind. Men who formed parties were despots by nature, he believed, "self-willed men, without principle; and entrusted with power, they spread contention and misery around them." They were "the ambitious, who aspire to place and power to enhance their consequence." Such types often combined with "the weak and indifferent, who are usually led by the boldest—and we have a mass of dissentients or malcontents, ready at all times to form a Party to assail, pervert and overthrow a Free Government." Such groups were made of those who would "destroy the Government—of those who appeal to assent, and those who rely on force to maintain it, creating a never-ending struggle between despotism and liberty."[59] This was what he had to remain on the stage awhile yet to fight.

Rhett's words constituted an apt, if bleak, assessment of a certain political animal and certainly delineated perfectly his foes as he saw them, as he always saw them, regardless of who they were or on what matter they opposed him. Yet there were troubling resonances in his portrait of the enemy. Some would have said that they were not reflections from others at all, but rather radiations from the artist himself.

FIFTEEN

The South Must Be Free

1851–1852

WHEN THE "FIRE-EATER" WENT to Washington for the opening of the new Congress in December, he took with him a peculiar set of motives and intentions. He meant to reply to a senator who was all but dead. He came to represent a people who had repudiated his policy of immediate separate secession. He sought to claim the mantle of leadership of the Southern rights people that Calhoun had already bestowed on another. Yet there was nothing contradictory or out of the ordinary in this, for he was only doing what Barnwell Rhett had always done in reality. He was representing himself. His idea of representative government had never been that elected officials ought to reflect the feelings of their constituents. This statesman was no mere steward. He was responsible to South Carolina as her agent, "bound to inform her and to counsel her in all matters affecting her interests or honor," he would say. "Such is my view of the duty of a Senator."[1] Yet he implicitly drew a line between representing her people's views and their interests. The former meant nothing to him, or certainly so little as not to merit acknowledgment in his definition of his mandate. Only the latter bound him, but it was essentially *his* notion of South Carolina's interests that he was there to defend, and not those of the people. And when he spoke of South Carolina, he meant in fact only the planter elite who ruled. Rather, he chose to assume that the fact that Carolinians elected him after he declared to them his principles signaled that they approved and wanted him to pursue those principles on their behalf. But, of course, it was not the people who had elected him but rather their legislature, a body that he and his friends had cultivated and tried to mold for a generation. Their sending him to replace Calhoun was no more a true vox populi than the choice of governors was. Moreover, even in the legislature Rhett was only chosen as the second or third choice of a fourth of the members, while nearly half never voted for him at all. In reality, when he took his seat in the Senate for this session Rhett represented a minority within a minority. But that would not have troubled him; he would have been perfectly willing to represent a constituency of only one—himself.

As he settled that constituency from his desk he could take stock of those around him—some old acquaintances and others men he would come to know all too well in the days ahead. There was fiery Jeremiah Clemens of Alabama; Stephen Douglas from Illinois; the swarthy Hannibal Hamlin of Maine, whom Rhett had heard rumored to be in fact a mulatto; the abolitionist Charles Sumner of Massachusetts; and Lewis Cass of Michigan. Jefferson Davis represented Mississippi and wore as well the cloak as Calhoun's approved successor, the garment Rhett felt should have been his. Beside Davis sat Henry S. Foote, a born controversialist—one minute ardent Southern rights man and the next a Unionist, his present incarnation. William Seward sat as a Whig from New York and was ironically one of Rhett's closer friends in Washington—yet another example of his peculiarity of getting along much better with political foes such as Petigru and Perry than with those on his own side of the aisle, probably because the compulsion to lead that so alienated men in his own party naturally did not come into play with the opposition. Sam Houston held a seat from Texas, while James Mason and Robert M. T. Hunter, two old comrades in Calhoun's cause, sat for Virginia.

Rhett arrived on December 8, a week late for the opening, and drew his first committee assignment, ironically the one most likely to deal with internal improvements, the Roads and Canals Committee. He did only a little constituency business, introducing his one and only Senate bill to indemnify South Carolina for money spent on behalf of the government during the war with the Seminoles and presenting a memorial for relief of Revolutionary War claims for the Ravenel family.[2] Indeed, he may not have intended to do much real business. The issue of whether or not he should even continue to hold his seat after the repudiation the past fall may not have been entirely resolved in his mind, though, ever the optimist, he still hoped to regain control when the state convention met in April.

Matters unanticipated by Rhett immediately conspired to put him on the defensive. First, Clay was not in the Senate. He had arrived and attended for a day or two before Rhett arrived but now lay confined to his hotel, clearly dying of his tuberculosis. On December 17 he would resign, and thus Rhett would never get to respond to his face. Worse, Rhett found himself under attack on the floor for his actions of the past two years. His attempted interference in Mississippi especially brought forth denunciation from Foote, who went out of his way on December 15, during debate with Butler of South Carolina on the 1850 compromise, to disassociate his state from South Carolina in the call for a Southern congress. He referred to Rhett, without naming him, as one of "certain intriguing politicians" who tried "in bad faith" to use the Nashville convention to foment disunion, "a very ingenious plan having been adopted, under the advice of certain persons who have openly avowed themselves subsequently to have been secret disunionists in heart and design." Then he referred to Rhett specifically, citing his declaration after Nashville that he never expected the North to acquiesce in the demand for extending the Missouri Compromise line—the demand in the convention address that he had himself written—as proof that his real intent had been to present an unachievable ultimatum that would lead to secession as an alternative.

Butler rose as soon as Foote finished and noted that the references to Rhett could not be mistaken nor ignored, and in justice to him he yielded the floor to his colleague.[3] When Rhett stood, he complained at first that he had not yet been able to make his reply to Clay, repeating the circumstances from the previous session and then promising that he still intended to do so as soon as Clay could appear on the floor. None of them at that moment knew that Clay would never again set foot in the Senate. Rhett next turned on Foote's attack. "There is not much force in epithets," he said, then resorted to his own and declared, "they are generally the resorts of silly weakness or malignant rage." He would respond to no insults thrown at himself, he protested, but Foote had insulted South Carolina. He maintained that the majority of South Carolinians were secessionists and favored disunion, though how he could say that in the face of the unionist-cooperationist forces' victory in the recent convention election he did not explain, for it made his declaration now at least equivocal. "I am a secessionist— I am a disunionist," he continued, and there was the constituency for which he really spoke.

Naturally there had to follow the lengthy justification of secession and explanation of all the South's wrongs, now more specifically based on the inequities of the recent compromise. For the first time he presented an integrated catalog of wrongs from tariff and antislave action to defend his position. Now he said he had despaired of saving the Union ever since 1845, not 1844 as he said previously, or even years before as in other addresses. "There is nothing wrong in upturning governments," he declared. Some needed to be overthrown, and it had become manifest that this in Washington was one such. The compromise made clear in its effects that the settled policy of the majority now was to end slavery everywhere; of that he felt certain. And the Fugitive Slave Law was only a futile and insincere gesture, easily made and even more easily ignored.

Rhett spoke from a prepared text filled with his usual myriad figures and statistics, and he was ready with a printed text of one of Foote's earlier speeches, making it evident that this response to Foote was not at all spontaneous. He had been preparing this speech for some time, awaiting only the opportunity to use it. Much of it may have been intended, in fact, for the reply to Clay that now he could not make. As with most of his speeches, Rhett had folded a sheet of foolscap vertically and then written his outline in eight numbered columns, two on each face of the four-page document, listing only catchphrases and key words, and relying on his well-proven powers of extemporization to fill out the address.[4] From it all—none of it new, though it had never before been stated at this extended length—he defied any Southern man to conclude that there would ever be any true conciliation. "The South must be free, or the South must perish," he protested. It was impossible now, he said, "to avoid the conflict that must come." That being the case, the South gained nothing by delay. As it was they in South Carolina were nothing but a degraded colony, not sovereign freemen. "I am for meeting the difficulty now," he said, "the sooner, in my estimation, the better."

Now, to all his old litanies he added a new and tortuously long justification for the right of secession. It did not derive from the Constitution—that he admitted—but neither were any other rights of the state governments. They, like secession, were part of the reserved rights. One state could not give to another state the right to secede any more than a group of states could give to another that right, for it always lay inherent in the sovereignty of the state itself. He went on at much length on the matter, he said, because "it is a question upon which bayonets may be crossed and blood may be spilled." After citing Thomas Jefferson and James Madison and a host of others with arguments supporting his claim, Rhett even mentioned a speech by Foote from the previous March in which the Mississippian had quoted Andrew Jackson and others as recognizing the right. Foote made no denial that he was a secessionist, which lessened somewhat Rhett's point, but Foote had made it clear that he believed that the recent compromise removed any cause for secession talk.

Rhett went after Millard Fillmore as well, not forgetting the refusal to allow Carolinians to celebrate the Moultrie anniversary on the grounds of the fort. Worse, the president had just complained that he had sent every available soldier to face threats from hostile natives on their western frontier, and yet he kept a large garrison at Moultrie and the other Charleston forts, along with cannons aimed at the city. "He has thus, openly held forth the sword as the instrument of our obedience," and this insult would never be forgiven. "I will secede, if I can, from this Union," declared Rhett. "I will test, for myself and for my children, whether South Carolina is a State or an humbled and degraded province."

During the course of Rhett's remarks Foote stood once to ask leave to make a brief explanation, but Rhett declined. "The Senator has not a good temper," he said, "and mine is not much better." As his remarks proceeded, Rhett even resorted to bathos. He depicted Calhoun's last appearance in the Senate, in which, too weak to speak, he had Mason read his speech, only to be attacked by Foote at its conclusion. Then Rhett portrayed a pathetic scene of Calhoun's agitation charging that Foote "hurried him into his grave." Worse, Rhett depicted Foote now as trying to exhume Calhoun only to heap more scorn upon his remains. "I leave him to his own thoughts," Rhett said in closing, "his own conscience."[5]

Of course Foote had to respond, and three days later he gained the floor during continuing debate on his own resolution declaring the recent compromise measures to be a definitive settlement of the issues aggravating the sections. After some discussion of the need for his resolution, he referred to "the treasonable doctrine of secession" that had been "so pompously expounded in our hearing during the last day or two." Rhett was the leader of a "school of extremists," he said, and his recent speech a "noisome tirade of factious declamation." As for what he called Rhett's "affected and semi-dramatic" account of his hurrying Calhoun to his grave, Foote made clear that he held the dead statesman in just as high repute as "any of those who now make such ostentatious parade of their sympathy and admiration for him." Moreover, Foote also demonstrated that Rhett had gotten the episode completely wrong and was merely repeating a two-year-old slander that had been effectively exploded in the press by other witnesses sometime since. He did not explicitly say that Rhett knowingly charged what he knew not to be true, but the suggestion was there by inference, and it was almost certainly correct. Rhett had already demonstrated more than once, as in denying the Quitman correspondence, that he would not allow inconvenient truths to obstruct his path in argument, and hereafter this tendency would become only more pronounced. In spite of his no doubt sincere professions of piety and Christian virtue, Rhett was well on the way to his eventual assumption that no exaggeration, half-truth, or unequivocal untruth could be a lie if it supported one of his great truths.

Foote renewed the charge against Rhett of attempting to subvert the Nashville convention, which Foote himself attended, in order to advance secession. As added evidence of Rhett's disloyalty, he mentioned Rhett's presence at public meetings earlier that year when Quitman and Davis were both toasted as future military commanders of Southern armies in any civil war and even as presidents of a new Southern confederacy. Rhett stood at once to issue a denial of being present at any such occasion, which was manifestly untrue, for he heard such toasts at the dislocated Fort Moultrie anniversary, if not elsewhere, and obviously still remembered that occasion well enough to have complained of it three days earlier. When Foote also charged Rhett with arguing that Utah would become a slave state one day and would unite with the fortunes of the other slave states,

Rhett again issued a denial, despite his having said just that in his Macon speech and elsewhere only months before. Rhett was starting to evidence the ancient human phenomenon that after the first compromise with the truth, thereafter the lies become easier, more frequent, and more numerous.

Foote showed himself just as adept as Rhett at pettifogging over his opponent's statements and positions. At one time he actually tried to make Rhett's Nashville declaration supporting the Missouri Compromise line into an antislavery effort because it would have excluded northern California from ever embracing slavery, whereas even though California had come into the Union now as a free state, there was nothing to prohibit it from deciding to embrace slavery in the future. That was just one of many blunders at the Nashville convention, and some were worse, he charged, willful offenses, and his manner left no doubt as to who made them. By reading extracts of Rhett's speeches in the legislature in 1833 protesting against remaining in the Union any longer, Foote took on Rhett's claim that he only became a disunionist in 1845, and Rhett dodged the issue when asked by Foote to state just when he really came over to secession as a policy and not an alternative. Foote especially went after Rhett for his opposition to the Fugitive Slave Law, even hinting that he might be in secret collusion with its Northern abolitionist opponents. He traced what he saw as Rhett's course as a secessionist, all to demonstrate the breach of his oath as a senator by harboring such aspirations while being sworn to uphold the Constitution and the Union. Foote was all his career a chancer and opportunist, and the fact that he had been Quitman's successful opponent for the governorship that fall—he would resign to assume his office in a few weeks—no doubt lent added vigor to his assault. While there were several palpable hits in his attack on Rhett, there were also some charges to which he was just as susceptible himself. Yet Rhett certainly felt the wound when Foote proclaimed that all in Mississippi who had favored separate secession six months before now repudiated both Rhett and his program. He had attended nearly two hundred public meetings in his state in the past nine months, and at not one of them did anyone mention Rhett's name "with even the ordinary indications of respect."

Rhett was a dangerous man, Foote implied, noting especially his frequent invocations of revolutionary days when Charlestonians seized British muskets and fired their artillery on the English fleet in the harbor. "The gentleman wishes to incite his fellow-citizens of South Carolina," charged Foote, "to an immediate attack upon the forts of the General Government in South Carolina, and thus to bring about a regular struggle of arms between that State and the General Government." He quoted Rhett's "gusty language" on Sullivan's Island the previous June when he called for fighting instead of eating and drinking, accusing

Rhett of apparently forgetting his religious vows against active violence. Foote went on to question whether "bluster and bravado gentlemen" like Rhett really had as much stomach for a fight as they pretended. "He thunders forth with that magnificent voice of his, and in that imposing oratorical manner which has given him so much distinction as a speaker—'Let us Fight.'" Foote could not have captured Rhett's efforts and intentions more accurately if he had in his hand Rhett's letter to Means proposing an attack on the forts, of which he may have heard something. But he did have disturbing documents detailing South Carolina's recent expenditures on military goods, including eighty cannons, nine thousand muskets and pistols, and two thousand swords. What could this be but a buildup for confrontation, and an example of Rhett's disunion plans in action?

Foote held the floor for much of two days, and then on December 20, Rhett rose in reply, though at first it was only to backtrack and hedge. He equivocated on when he had really come over to secession and now corrected his claim of 1845 from a few days earlier and said it came in 1842 with the passage of the new tariff. He also maintained now that his remark about Foote hastening Calhoun to his grave was only metaphorical, as everyone surely knew, but then went on to try to establish that Calhoun really had been weakened in spirit and body after Foote challenged him. After that he showed some inconsistencies in much of Foote's argument against him and provided an able refutation of a portion at least of the Mississippian's attack. "Whenever he is very violent in impugning any course, only watch him a little while," said Rhett, "and you will find that it is because he has practiced it before himself."

Yet Rhett closed the exchange with another untruth after Foote asserted that the rumor was common that Rhett had counseled Calhoun to resign from the Senate years before in order to make a place for himself. Rhett would never have admitted the latter portion to be true after the political damage he suffered from the perception in South Carolina that he had done precisely that. Yet in spite of the undeniable fact that Calhoun did consult him about resignation and that at one point Rhett advised him to resign, he now declared, "Mr. Calhoun resigned his seat without consulting me" and only informed him of the resignation after the fact "without asking my opinion." Rhett could hardly hurt himself by admitting that he had once counseled Calhoun *not* to resign. In lying now about being consulted at all, especially after telling several other half-truths and outright lies in the past three days, he was trying to distance himself from the much more damaging truth that he really did advise Calhoun to resign.

Finally in the battle for the last word even the chair became weary and called them to order. Almost miraculously they had not come to blows. Foote admitted that his had been a somewhat stormy career with its share of confrontations, while Rhett claimed to pride himself on almost a quarter-century in public office without one such altercation, conveniently forgetting the exchange and challenge with Huger many years before, as he had seemed to forget so many other facts of his history during the debate.[6] Inevitably South Carolinians who read the exchanges in the *Mercury* regarded them as a contest, and most proclaimed Rhett the victor. Some who thought he should have resigned his seat after the repudiation of his policy in the recent election for convention delegates now changed their minds, thanking him for telling the North in the Senate what the South thought of it. One thanked him for his rebuke of "the Grand Lama of political Idolatry" and his rejection of the 1850 compromise, while even an Alabamian wrote to praise his effort as "the most conclusive, truthful, and dignified exposition, which the occasion has drawn forth." Requests for copies of his addresses, in quantities up to five hundred, came in from secessionists throughout South Carolina, and the volume of requests for his autograph experienced a marked increase as well.[7]

Many lost sight of Foote's resolution approving the Compromise of 1850, which began the debate and was the focus of much of it, as all were attracted instead to the personal exchanges. Perhaps the only critical comment from home came, predictably, from Hammond, who thought that in declaring openly for secession on the Senate floor Rhett may have been the first ever to do so but that it was undignified, "about as bold as to shoot at a man and then run away." Worse, Foote had ridiculed him and thereby insulted South Carolina, and yet Rhett answered only with mere words. Hammond would have preferred a challenge.[8] Among the moderates, cooperationists and conditional unionists, reaction matched Hammond's, though for different reasons. "As to the Rhetts, Yanceys, &c., the sooner and more effectively we get rid of them the better," John Slidell of Louisiana told Howell Cobb. He, like many moderates, still believed the South could actually control events better by staying in the Union, and he feared the influence that radicals such as Rhett could have on the coming 1852 Democratic nominating convention. He felt that extremists, both antislave and secessionist, must be isolated in order that Democrats could unite on a pro-Southern unionist candidate. "I would infinitely prefer defeat to a victory purchased by truckling to the abolitionists or disunionists," Slidell complained, warning that Rhett and his ilk could ruin it for them all.[9]

Just after the exchange with Foote, Rhett returned to the Oaks Plantation on the Ashepoo, both to recover his once-more fragile health and to take Elizabeth and the smaller children back to Washington. Instead he found the usual chaos with his personal affairs. Awaiting him was a letter from England from one of the eight principals in the rice duty business, who now questioned that he owed

Rhett anything at all and stated that if he ever did, Rhett had forfeited his right to expect payment when he made public their correspondence to the other seven who had paid him in an attempt to get them to influence his payment. At stake was a fee of eight hundred pounds, or around thirty-two hundred dollars, which Rhett could hardly afford to let pass, and now he would have no alternative but to pursue the matter in the courts.[10] "I am dreadfully pressed for money," he lamented to his oldest son in February 1852, and he found several of his creditors threatening suit. He could not even afford to move furniture from his Charleston house to the Oaks Plantation for Elizabeth when he left her there, because he could not afford to replace what he moved. Meanwhile the Charleston house needed painting, which he could not afford unless the painter waited until June to be paid; shade trees needed planting on the lawn; and he was especially concerned about installing strong locks on all the doors, perhaps fearing retribution from the rabble in the wake of the coming convention and its hoped-for result.[11] Then there was trouble with a neighbor Henry Gourdin, one of the directors of the Bank of Charleston, over the attentions paid to his daughter by Rhett's headstrong son Alfred, who had graduated from Harvard in 1851 and was spending his time at Ashepoo hunting turkeys and deer instead of attending to his new profession of planting. Rhett continued to be unhappy with Alfred's behavior. The young man, having actually finished at college, valued his achievement so little that he did not even want his diploma. His father begged him to take a productive interest in something, even if just in gardening.[12] Now rumors of his behavior with the Gourdin girl circulated in the Lowcountry, and Rhett brought them to Gourdin's attention, warning the girl that people were bound to talk if she received unchaperoned visits from single men, even his son. Gourdin took affront, accused Rhett of slandering his daughter, and threatened legal action, though nothing came of it. There was concern, too, for young Andrew Burnet Rhett, now at South Carolina College and due to graduate in the spring. Rhett believed that through a combination of excessive nighttime study and apparently too much liquor the boy was ruining his sight, and he counseled him to "stick exclusively to cold water or milk."[13]

Political affairs intruded as well on his recuperation. It appeared likely that the people of Walterborough would elect Rhett as their representative to the hoped-for Southern congress if it ever materialized, though it looked as if the district where their plantations on the Ashepoo lay would decline to send anyone at all. Robert W. Barnwell had gone into a funk, convinced more than ever that the state would have to secede or face degradation but disillusioned with his own efforts as a cooperationist while yet unable to cross the line to separate action. More of the leading secessionists now backed Hammond's plan for South

Carolina to cut all ties with the federal government and wait for other states to catch up, and Rhett told Maxcy Gregg that at the moment it was the state's best hope of resistance, suggesting that Hammond prepare resolutions to that effect for the coming convention in April. The plan still fell far short of secession but was at least a step on the way. However, Rhett may have been at his old game of telling different people different things, for to others he declared that the convention should not meet at all if it were going to give up the idea of secession. He was putting a foot in each camp, cooperationist and secessionist, clearly preserving the option to try to lead whichever way the convention jumped.[14]

In the last days before he left for Washington, Rhett finished editing and correcting the text of his reply to Foote for publication, expecting to make capital of its popularity. He also learned that his nephew William Taber had joined with Heart to buy out Carew on the *Mercury*. He may not have welcomed the news, for Rhett's opinion of his nephew had not improved in the years since he warned his sons not to emulate their cousin's behavior. As early as 1846 Rhett concluded that Taber was "a low-reckless debaucher" unworthy to associate with his sons. Already the father had warned Robert Jr. to cut off all correspondence with him and was worried when the boy gave evasive answers to his father's repeated inquiries wanting to know if Taber was "addicted to low dissipation." With his own mother dying in January 1848, Taber only made her last days more burdened by heavy drinking, and when Alfred invited his cousin to spend some time with him on the Ashepoo, Rhett admonished that Alfred impress on young Taber that "we are cold-Water People" with an abhorrence of liquor. It did nothing for Rhett's opinion of his nephew when Taber left college in order to pursue a wealthy young woman in hopes of marrying a fortune. By the end of 1848 any association at all with Taber was intolerable to the father. "I have no faith in his morals and pride of character," Rhett told Robert Jr. in December.

The past year Taber had been caught more than once indulging his sexual appetites with slave women belonging to friends and associates, once even in the kitchen of a house where he was a guest and quite possibly forcing his attentions on the hapless victims. Being caught apparently brought from him a promise to reform his behavior, but Rhett doubted his sincerity. "He is not restrained from licentiousness from convictions of its degradation meanness & wickedness," he charged, "but merely from a sense of self-interest and expediency." He thought his oldest son mature enough not to be contaminated, but Rhett worried about his other children being exposed to Taber, especially Alfred, who was himself willful and irresponsible, and far too fond and admiring of his older cousin. "Such a person cannot be a fit associate," said Rhett. "Be he son or nephew, no Debauch associates with my family, nor shall William Taber enter my House or associate with my sons or Daughters under my roof until I learn that he has reformed his habits and character." Rhett had decided in December 1848 not to have any personal communication of any kind with Taber, either directly or indirectly. "The baser passions must be controlled," he warned his boys. "The beast must be suppressed within us." He would have no compromise with vice in any of his relations. "If my right arm or right eye offends in this particular, I shall cut it off," he said.[15] Yet now Taber would have considerable influence with the *Mercury*, a right arm for Rhett if ever there was one. Rhett could not help but wonder if the tongue that he found too free and foul a few years before might not make even the *Mercury* itself offensive, although the paper could be counted on now more than ever with a member of the family as coeditor—even if he was a relation Rhett preferred not to countenance.[16]

In the latter part of January, Rhett finally left for Washington. The disappointment in his expected income from the rice duty business meant that he could not afford to rent a larger lodging in the Capitol, so he had no choice but to leave Elizabeth and the children at the Oaks after all. Though he was fearful of an outbreak of measles, thankfully his young ones passed through safely.[17] Rhett had already gleaned annoying news from the press while at home and may have learned more during a brief visit with Hunter in Virginia on his way north.[18] His response to Foote, his repudiation of the 1850 compromise and the resolution of acceptance, and his declaration of disunionism had brought Clemens of Alabama out in bitter and very personal denunciation. Cass did the same, though in milder tone. Clemens had portrayed Rhett as being in treasonous league with the abolitionists Sumner, Chase, and Seward—all with the design of destroying the Union, though for different purposes—and seemingly denounced him as a knave.[19] Rhett thought he saw in this a design to unite Southern unionists and cooperationists and conservative Northern Democrats to assail and isolate South Carolina through systematic personal attacks on him, no doubt thus to achieve Slidell's hope of uniting Northern and Southern Democrats for the coming party convention. As a result he was probably already at work on his reply to Clemens as he traveled north once again to resume his seat.[20]

By February 20, Rhett was back on the floor again attending to minor business, introducing a resolution to raise the salary of federal judges, and opposing special appropriations for those suffering damages due to the impact of tax laws for the general good. But this was all prelude to his reply to Clemens. As soon as he reached Washington he read the full reports of the debates containing Clemens's assaults, and for several days he waited in hopes that the compromise resolution might come up again as justification for his taking the floor. Meanwhile friends such as Daniel Wallace and John McQueen urged him not to reply to Clemens, arguing that to notice Clemens at all would be beneath Rhett's dignity. At first he felt undecided. Clemens had already destroyed much of his small stock of respect in the Senate, being drunk now almost every day, and Rhett believed that politically the man was dead now in his home state, Alabama. But in the end it simply was not in Rhett to turn another cheek. By February 18 he made up his mind to respond should the resolution come on the floor. When it had not by February 26, he stood to announce his intention of answering Clemens on the morrow, even sending notification to the absent Alabamian, as Rhett wanted his opponent there to hear him. "I am on the watch for Old Cass & Clemens," he wrote his eldest son, and Clemens especially "must come up to the scratch." It was time to strike back, though he fully expected it might result in a tumult. "I am in for it," he confided.[21]

The next morning Rhett took his seat early, before the Senate formally convened. He had his response to Clemens fully prepared in front of him yet felt uneasy all the same, knowing his own temper and having seen and heard of Clemens's. Moreover, he knew just how inflammatory what he was going to say would be. He confessed to a nearby colleague that he expected Clemens would respond heatedly and that serious unpleasantness would ensue. Taking a few minutes now to scribble in his hieroglyphic hand brief letters to his sons Robert Jr. and Burnet, he admitted that what lay before him was "a very disagreeable task to me." He abhorred and feared contention of any kind, he claimed, "for my temper is I fear far from being moderate or good." Still he had to defend himself and his principles. "I am at my desk—the Senate will meet in a few minutes," he told them. "I intend that the severity of what I shall say, shall consist in making Clemens destroy himself; he shall be self-convicted." He hoped to conduct himself "so as not to forfeit my character as a Christian, whilst, I perform my duty as a man, and a Senator." At that moment the gavel sounded, and he set aside the letters to face what lay ahead.[22]

After an opening prayer the body agreed on motion to set aside its normal business of private bills to allow Rhett to speak for an hour, though his first words were a warning that he might need more time. And then, echoing what he had written to his son only moments before, he declared, "I deprecate all such contention from the bottom of my heart." In his twenty years in deliberative bodies he had never engaged in a serious conflict with anyone, he said, once more forgetting or ignoring the near-duel with Huger. Now he remained calm as he began to lay out his case, starting with Clemens's accusation that Rhett's Northern coconspirators had cheered and applauded his attack on the compromise resolution. From Sumner and Chase he elicited denials that they had applauded or even approved of what he said in response to Foote, and he then asked if anyone present heard any signs of approval, which they had not. That alone made Clemens a liar, and from that the country might well conclude "how far he is fit to stand up here and arraign others for a want of integrity, truthfulness, or consistency."

Rhett might have stopped there, he said, but of course he could not. Pleading that "the cause of the South" required that he continue, he went ahead in a typical point-by-point attack on Clemens, which was methodically prepared and more detailed than any of his previous lectures. He was not only getting even with Clemens for his personal attack but also clearly trying to display publicly the Alabamian's hypocrisy, for if he could break down Alabama's most noted Unionist, then he might hope to wound unionism itself in Yancey's state. "I propose to show what kind of man he is," Rhett declared.

Rhett formed his assault exactly as a lawyer presenting a brief, laying out in advance nine points he intended to make against Clemens. Then at length he used extracts from Clemens's speeches to demonstrate his overall contention that Clemens had been just as opposed to the compromise as Rhett, and on largely the same grounds, and moreover that he had been an avowed secessionist out of his own mouth. It was long, tedious, but effective, as all Rhett's preparation and study of Clemens's record convinced him it would be. He showed that Clemens had opposed admitting California directly to statehood as a free state, that in 1850 he had denounced both abolitionists and Southern submissionists as traitors, and that he had declared that disunion was preferable to the admission of California on such terms. Furthermore, Clemens had denounced the compromise measures in 1850, calling secession a sharp and severe remedy, and protested contemptuously the advice from many that the compromise should be accepted by the South as the best it could get. Rhett even charged Clemens with saying that the states were sovereign and claiming his first allegiance to Alabama, not the Union, but then in 1851 presenting himself as a submissionist and even a consolidationist, an ardent Unionist defending the compromise against those with whom he had stood in agreement just a year before.

The speech was lengthy but not uninteresting, and Clemens stayed surprisingly quiet, even as Rhett gradually abandoned—perhaps unconsciously—his pose of the impartial prosecutor. More and more he began using satirical or sarcastic adjectives and adverbs when he mentioned Clemens by name or described his acts as "brave" and "gallant." Despite his continuing poor health, Rhett still managed to produce one of his best oratorical efforts. Perry always regarded him as an eloquent speaker, "bold frank and manly," and certainly he was so this day. Among the fire-eaters Yancey was regarded as the better orator—less emotional, less prone to mixed metaphors, his cadence more measured than Rhett's rapid-fire delivery, and without the frequent rather sophomoric declarations and images. Yet today Rhett combined boldness with calm, spoke carefully and deliberately, and showed more than the usual restraint in his imagery—all of which served to make his presentation all the more effective.[23]

Having presented his case, Rhett did not stop there but went on to add one more thing. Clemens had been elected in 1849 to fill a vacancy, but when his own Democratic Party caucused to choose a nominee, Clemens got no more than a dozen votes. Seeing his only chance for a Senate seat to lie with a combination of Whigs and Democrats in the Alabama legislature, Clemens sent a verbal pledge to a Whig caucus the night before the balloting that he would support Taylor's administration in return for their votes.[24] Since some did not trust him, on demand he followed up his verbal promise with a written pledge. Rhett charged that the conclusion was inescapable that Clemens, an avowed state rights man and antisubmissionist, had sold himself to the Whigs in order to win election and was paying them back with his support of the compromise.

Now Clemens could not stay quiet. Angrily he rose and, first, accused Rhett of trying to notify the whole world of his address in order to obtain maximum publicity and charged him with "vain self-conceit" in thinking his effort so newsworthy. Then he accused Rhett of ignorance of the compromises's history and Clemens's course toward it. He declared Rhett's conclusions so false that they could only come from "that blind and rapid spirit of disunion which prevents him from seeing things, that, to other men, are as apparent as the noonday sun." He denied calling Rhett a knave or traitor, saying that those were only "illustrations," rather like Rhett's plea of metaphor in accusing Foote of hurrying Calhoun to his grave. But he said that if he had called Rhett such things, "the subsequent career of that Senator justifies me in adding the epithet of coward, to that of knave and traitor."

At once the chair called Clemens to order, but the Alabamian, severely embarrassed, was not about to be stopped. Two months had passed since Clemens attacked Rhett in the Senate, and yet the Carolinian waited until now to answer and did so in a speech. "He does not deserve the character of a man," Clemens declared. "No man, with the feeling of a man in his bosom, who believed such a charge was pending against him would have sought redress here." He would have issued a challenge instead. Clemens went on to repeat the charge that Rhett was in league with abolitionists and tried to discredit Chase's denial of congratulating Rhett on his response to Foote. When Chase substantively repeated it, however, Clemens ignored the words of his denial and tried to find support in the context of what Chase said, without effect. He denied, too, that he had actually insulted Rhett in calling him a traitor. Had not Rhett called himself that

time after time, and if so, how could it be offensive for another to call the Carolinian by the epithet he applied freely to himself? "He is a man for whom I never
had any fancy," said Clemens. "I never sought his acquaintance," he went on,
and averred that he refused to show Rhett the customary courtesy when he first
took his seat and refused to be introduced to him. Moreover he never intended
to discuss Rhett's character or conduct in the Senate, protesting contemptuously
that "the subject is too small." As for Rhett's charge of a "corrupt bargain" by
which he won his Senate seat, Clemens denounced it as "a foul lie" and one that
many could and would refute.

Of course it could not end there, for Clemens took the floor the next day to
reply officially. Again he averred that Rhett should have challenged him privately
if he felt insulted and pointed out that he would have satisfied Rhett one way
or another. He repeated, too, his charge that the Whig bargain was a falsehood
and then began his lengthy defense against Rhett's nine points of inconsistency.
His arguments were not convincing, turning heavily upon interpretations of
words and claims that regardless of what he said, his meaning had been misunderstood. He even concluded that Rhett was conspiring with Sumner and Chase
and others by the fact that their seats were close to his, though in this Clemens
was ignoring the fact that, as everyone knew, seating was determined by long tradition and not the choice of the senators themselves.

Rhett responded only briefly, further refuting Clemens's exaggerations. He
said that he had not brooded two months over Clemens's attack, for he only
learned of it late in January. He was ready to respond as soon as he reached Washington and only waited for the debate to return to the compromise resolutions
which had been the context for the original attack. Rhett knew, too, that having
insulted him gratuitously in his absence in December, Clemens would answer
with nothing more than renewed insults now, adding with some satisfaction
that "he has come up precisely to the estimate I had put upon his character."

As for the business of issuing a challenge instead, Rhett confessed that it was
the custom in South Carolina for men to seek redress in that fashion. "But, sir,
I am a professor of the religion of Christ," he said. "I did not think it proper to
challenge the Senator." He feared neither Clemens's insults nor public opinion
that thought he ought to seek redress on the field of honor, and certainly not
enough to force him to violate his religious principles. "I profess the possession of
no extraordinary courage," he said, "but I trust I have the courage to support the
right and defy the wrong," regardless of who opposed him, be it a senator from
Alabama or the entire North. "I am here alone; but, I trust, alone without fear."

Besides vindicating himself on the floor of the Senate, Rhett also vindicated
the South and the cause of her rights, he believed, and it was part of that to

expose Clemens as a hypocrite or worse. He returned to Clemens's election to the Senate and actually engaged Clemens in some debate that produced in the Alabamian equivocation, a distinct reluctance to provide more detail, and in the end a refusal to answer any questions at all, creating at least the impression that he was unwilling or afraid to say more. When Rhett finished, Clemens could only add that he still assumed Rhett should have challenged him, and he protested that he had never heard of this profound religion that prevented Rhett from doing so. Upon learning of it, he concluded that such piety ought to have prevented Rhett from attacking him at all rather than being an excuse for avoiding a more manly resolution. He accused Rhett again of cold-blooded assault and "malignant bitterness which would have done credit to a fiend." As for the manner of his own election, it was a matter between Clemens and his constituents, and he would say no more about it.[25]

The impartial observer would have had to give the exchange some study to determine who got the better of it, for in fact each had been guilty of the same transgressions with which he charged the other. Certainly Clemens started it all with his attack back in December, though it had been scarcely any more severe than many others hurled at Rhett over the years, and to many of which Rhett never bothered to reply. This time, however, the assault came within just a few months of the meeting of the South Carolina convention, and if there were to be any hope of wooing the skittish cooperationists and unionists into supporting even Hammond's nonintercourse plan, let alone entertaining actual secession, then Rhett had to answer Clemens.

His manner of doing so was well calculated to do the maximum damage to his opposition's cause too. By portraying Clemens, one of the leading Southern submissionists, as a senator for hire, Rhett thus by association demonstrated that Carolinians could not trust their professed friends in other states—more evidence that they must act for themselves. To be sure, Rhett used some of Clemens's statements out of context in trying to show his apostasy from the state rights cause, and he applied literal interpretations to some clearly rhetorical expressions. His use of Clemens's supposed bargain with the Whigs may have been even more questionable since Clemens's refutation of the charge may have been known to him already, even if Rhett, like some others, did not believe it. And if Rhett did not directly hurl ad hominem insults at Clemens, still his language was well chosen throughout to convey the maximum in disdain and contempt. In reply, Clemens had of course been far more intemperate, even intentionally goading, while his defense mixed genuine refutation with a lot of equivocation and taking refuge behind pettifogging over definitions. Still, in the end it was Rhett who deservedly emerged slightly ahead. He had made Clemens look the bully and blowhard—with Clemens's help—and succeeded in raising questions about the Alabamian's allegiance and reliability, as well as his integrity. In return Clemens said nothing about Rhett that had not been said before, and though he exposed some of the flaws in his opponent's brief, he did not quite manage to cripple the overall case. In the end Clemens simply subsided weakly and ineffectively from the debate, and it appeared as if he were attempting to avoid further exposure.

Rhett felt that he had acquitted himself well. "There is an end of him," he crowed. "The fangs of the viper are drawn, and a heavy blow I trust has been given to the traitors." Two days after his February 27 assault he boasted to his eldest son, "I buried politically Jere Clemens, or rather I made him bury himself." As for Clemens's insults and provocations in response, they were only what Rhett expected and only sank Clemens lower in general esteem. Rhett stated, "I think that this is the last time I shall perform the part of executioner, on Southern Traitors, but in performing this office, I hope I have aided in some degree the course of the States and the Constitution."[26] Rhett sent press reports of his speeches to his sons as soon as they appeared and told his eldest to get them printed in the *Mercury* as soon as possible, while soon others would distribute his remarks throughout the South. He especially wanted his words to appear in the Huntsville, Alabama, paper where they could do maximum damage to Clemens, even offering to pay for their insertion if the editor did not want to run them otherwise.[27] He may have thought he had let Clemens bury himself, but Rhett was anxious to shovel as much earth on top of him as possible.

Generally most observers gave the victory to Rhett, the *Mercury* predictably being most ebullient in bestowing laurels as it printed letters of praise from men in Washington as well as several other Southern presses. Almost everyone focused on the provocation for a duel and Rhett's refusal. A Macon paper condemned Clemens as "an unmitigated poltroon and coward" for trying to goad into a duel a man known to have religious scruples against dueling, while another averred that the audience in the Senate gave the victory to Rhett in spite of not wishing to sympathize with a secessionist. The *Montgomery Advertiser*, while refusing to endorse Rhett's attacks on the compromise, still complained that Clemens had disgraced his state by his behavior and vulgarity. Even while admitting that Rhett was "perhaps the most unpopular public man, out of South Carolina, in the United States," the paper accused Clemens of cowardice in attacking someone whom he thought no one would defend because of "his odiousness." Granting that Rhett may have overstepped proper etiquette under Clemens's assault, one man in Washington still believed that the provocation extenuated his actions.[28] Even Lorenzo Sabine of Massachusetts, soon to sit as a Whig in this Congress, praised the Carolinian's "lofty stand" against dueling.[29]

Not everyone agreed, however, and Rhett's reluctance to issue a challenge hurt him with some in South Carolina. Paul Hayne complimented Rhett's verbal response but still longed to hear that "R. has blown out his brains." Granting that Rhett was a Christian, Hayne still felt that "*such* an affront is beyond all codes, civil or religious." He felt that Rhett owed it to his state and to his own family name to meet Clemens on the field of honor, and that failure to do so would damage the secessionist cause in the state. "If Rhett *does* not resent this insult he is not the man I take him for," Hayne complained. "Some quarrels are sacred."[30] An editor in Washington, while disparaging dueling, still argued that pleas of Christianity came with bad grace from such a man as Rhett, "who has probably done more to provoke public and personal difficulties, and to disgrace the discipline of a christian church, than any other of our living public men." Apparently Rhett had forgotten that the convictions that would keep him from killing another man on the dueling ground "should also restrain him from a course of conduct calculated to kindle the worst passions, and to embroil whole States in the horrors of civil war."[31]

Hammond, of course, could be expected to be critical. "This is very disgusting," he said of the whole affair. Rhett's assertion that he only spoke to defend the South was "egotistical in the last degree," while his plea of religion to eschew dueling, Hammond found nothing but hypocritical. "He has talked more of shedding blood and fomented quarrels, both political and personal, more than almost any man living for all these twenty years." Hammond had long since left behind any impartiality where Rhett was concerned, and yet through his bias there still shone glimmers of truth. "Rhett's object simply is notoriety," he concluded. "He is willing to be spurned, to be called a traitor and a windy demagogue to his face, and by his tame truckling to bring Disunionism into disgrace, that he might have the distinction of first avowing himself a Disunionist in the Senate." Hammond regarded him now as nothing more than "one of those morbid lovers of public attention, who would commit murder, and suffer on the gibbet to produce a sensation." As for the quarrel with Clemens, and Foote before him, Hammond condemned Rhett's performance as "a striking example of the Eunuch Spirit which now rules in SoCa and of which he had proved himself a faithful representative *in undertaking what he could not perform* and *ignominiously backing out*." Thinking that Rhett's shirking a duel completed the humiliation begun with the convention elections the previous fall, Hammond concluded that at last "I am quite revenged on him."[32]

Rhett's critics, even Hammond, were entitled to doubts as to his sincerity about dueling and about violence in general, for during most of the past two decades he had made incessant appeals to resistance even to bloodshed in defense of his concept of state rights. No one spoke more often of the resort to war, even of the utter devastation of the South in a self-immolation preferable to subjugation. Had he not appealed to Means just the past summer actually to start hostile action, knowing that it could possibly lead to war? And had he not told others that if a conflict ever came, he would be in the forefront? Did he not urge, even demand, that his son Alfred meet violence with violence in dealing with a childhood bully? In years to come three of his sons, Barnwell, Alfred, and Edmund, would all be principals in duels or in some way involved in such affrays, and yet not a word of reproach appears to have come from their father, and it is difficult not to see their adult behavior—arrogant, intemperate, even violent— as reflections of his influence on them, if nothing more than sons' natural tendency to emulate and exaggerate a parent's behavior. His Christianity was strong enough to keep him out of duels but not sufficient to restrain his invocations of violence in his speeches, and for all his protestations that he deplored confrontations, he rarely waited long to leap for the jugular in debating his enemies. At the very least, his public posture and private demeanor were dramatically inconsistent, and though surely he maintained some rationalization that explained the anomaly, it is difficult not to see at best a double standard operating. Few went one step farther in accusing him of simple personal cowardice, though one who could condemn war as a crime, as he often had, yet blithely speak glowingly of sending hundreds of thousands—even his own sons—to risk their lives on battlefields, while pleading Christian scruples to prevent hazarding his own life, might well have invited the epithet that Clemens applied to him. Certainly Rhett felt sensitive to suggestions of cowardice. His greatest fear was that his sons Robert Jr. and Alfred might think him craven for accepting Clemens's taunts and insults without a challenge. "I must confess, they threw me into a prodigious tumult, altho I expected them," he told his oldest son. "It is the first time since I have been a man that I have been insulted," he said, "but by Gods grace, I was able to command myself and do as I have done." Any matter affecting his own honor affected theirs, he told them, and he promised that they should always be consulted as he determined his own course. "I have certainly lived to little purpose, if after a life of 50 years, in prominent political positions, my courage is doubted. My folly I thought was the other way—but I must say with St Paul 'by Gods grace, I am what I am.'"[33]

Everything Rhett said in the Senate after the Clemens debate was anticlimax. He presented a few petitions from South Carolina, opposed granting land concessions to builders of a proposed transcontinental railroad, and pursued again his desire for a pay raise for judges. On Friday, April 9, he spoke for the last time, now in advocacy of a revision of the apportionment legislation governing representatives in the House of Representatives, for South Carolina was in danger of losing one that she could scarcely afford now. At the same time he also argued for recognition of California's right to two representatives under the terms of her admission, even though there was question as to whether or not her population warranted this. Doctrinaire though he might be, he could still speak for fairness and honoring of agreements, even though he violently objected to California even being represented on the floor.[34]

Rhett's attention was naturally elsewhere during those weeks. As late as March 8 he still did not know the precise day when the state convention would convene and urgently asked Robert Jr. in South Carolina to let him know as soon as a date was set. Finally notified that it was due to meet on April 27 in Columbia, Rhett feared that the issue still remained very much in doubt. As a secessionist leader he would have to be there even though he was not an elected delegate, but to what end he could not entirely see. The effort to get delegates to commit themselves for or against secession beforehand had failed. Indeed Rhett complained bitterly that the policy even of the secession party was to make no public declaration of position for fear of spooking moderates, a prudent course that, of course, could not suit him. Hammond was refusing to take any lead in putting forward his nonintercourse plan, though he was taking perverse pleasure that "even Rhett at last, in his extreme, comes to me." When the *Mercury* would not risk printing Rhett's call to arms for secession, even with his name removed in order not to prejudice moderate readers, he sent it instead to his friend Maxcy Gregg while Gregg took over trying to promote Hammond's scheme as something on which separate state action and cooperationists could unite. Rhett had approved the effort, but there were signs that the cooperationists would not go along unless Rhett's forces abandoned separate action as a policy entirely. In such a state of confusion South Carolina faced grave danger, and Rhett left late on April 10 to be where he was needed.[35]

He reached home to find that no one knew what was likely to happen in Columbia. Some so despaired of any action being taken that all they could do was counsel that everyone should capitalize on the moment and profit as much as possible from remaining in the Union. The *Mercury* offered no real leadership, and Means, slated to chair the convention, could see no direction other than to try somehow to achieve some degree of unanimity on *any* course that would cease the divisiveness.[36] As for Rhett, he kept a low profile in the days prior to going to Columbia, giving no sign of what he expected to do there or even if he would attempt to make his usual bid for leadership.

On Monday night, April 26, Rhett and the other secessionist delegates met at Hunt's Hotel in a private caucus to try to determine their policy, but their disruption by the previous fall's election result clearly showed in a want of resolution. One old secessionist even walked in and then turned around and walked back out, thinking he had come to the wrong meeting.[37] Edward Bellinger offered a strong resolution stating that though the people by their vote for convention delegates had declared against immediate secession, this did not mean they had abandoned any other means of redress of grievances, and it was therefore the duty of the convention to adopt some strong measures. The discussion that ensued revealed, however, wide division on what such measures could be, and Rhett felt that the whole tone of the affair was low and discouraged. Seeking to infuse some animation into the proceeding, and quite possibly by prior arrangement between them, Maxcy Gregg then suggested that Rhett, though not a delegate, should be asked to offer his views on what policy the convention ought to follow. But instead of the acclamation that secessionists once would have given in response, Drayton Nance responded to the suggestion by saying, "I hope not, we are twenty-one years old and capable of making up our own minds." He and others who followed him were tired of being told what to do by Barnwell Rhett.[38]

It was a stinging repudiation, and as Gregg withdrew his proposal, Rhett felt humiliated. "Thus the party refused to hear my views or to be counselled by me," he lamented. He suspected that the majority of those present knew there was no consensus among them and wanted it that way, preferring inaction, "and therefore did not wish to hear reasons which might embarrass their policy." In the end the caucus could only agree on a bizarre proposal to defer to the cooperationists the appointment of a general committee to prepare measures for the convention to adopt. It seemed to Rhett a complete surrender of the convention, even though the immediate secessionists and cooperationists combined still made up two-thirds of those present. The intent was not surrender, however, but rather to give their opponents enough rope to hang themselves. Once the submissionists put forward their policy, the disunited prosecession forces would then be able to come together in assailing and repudiating them, and presumably use that momentum to take control of the convention once more and come to some definite plan of action that now seemed to elude unanimity. Rhett thought the whole idea incomprehensible, for as elected delegates they had no right to forfeit their majority power and shirk responsibility. "It was certainly a new thing under the Sun, to give up to your antagonists the whole game of making issues with us," he concluded, and all founded on the notion that the submissionists were so foolish that they could not come up with any proposals that would attract widespread support.[39]

The idea carried the majority of the caucus, and they so informed Means. As a result the next day at noon when the convention first convened, Means appointed Cheves to head the proposed committee of twenty-one, and the convention adjourned for an hour while Cheves chose the members. They included Cheves, Richardson, Seabrook, Butler, Huger, Barnwell, Perry, Gregg, Pickens, Hayne, and others, in all twelve cooperationists, eight secessionists, and Perry the solitary Unionist.[40] That done, the convention adjourned to allow the committee to meet. Predictably, given its composition, the committee showed no disposition to do anything other than assert the abstract right of secession—perhaps even amending the state constitution to declare the principle—and then justify not exercising the prerogative at the moment.[41]

That evening the secessionists again met in caucus, and their representative on the committee reported that the cooperationists were up to nothing but words. Rhett felt incensed. "Having cajoled and deceived a noble people, having crushed the vindication of State sovereignty by the bold exercise of a reserved right, having prostrated her spirit, and made South Carolina the butt and jeer of the world, cooperation bursts at last like some wind-bubble, at the first test of its solidity," he thundered in an unsigned letter to the *Mercury*. The rumor that they would countenance amending the state constitution was good but did not go nearly far enough. "I think that the secession party will insist on some more explicit and practical measures," Rhett wrote afterward, though now he gave up on his other hopes for a withdrawal of the state's congressional delegation and rescinding the act providing for appointment of presidential electors in the state as part of nonintercourse. But at last he thought he could see that others realized the hopelessness of sustaining any spirit of resistance through all the months it took to elect a secession convention.[42]

Bellinger proposed appointing a committee to meet with a committee from the cooperationists to see if they could find some common ground for action, and Rhett was appointed as its head. For the next day and more there were meetings and deliberations by the joint committee, and all the while the committee of twenty-one continued to meet on its own, with clear cross-purposes at work. Finally on Thursday evening Rhett's committee met in the senate chamber to hear a general report from Cheves's group. It was a general resolution declaring that the state should not secede now, along with an ordinance affirming its right to do so. Rhett regarded the one as submission and the other as pointless. That evening in their caucus the secessionists adopted a motion by Bellinger that they propose an amendment to any convention report that would allow the legislature to enact secession by a two-thirds vote without the call of a special convention. Richardson actually authored the proposal, and after a lengthy debate the secessionist caucus finally adopted it at 1:30 in the morning, with all but seven present in favor.[43]

An exhausted Rhett returned to his hotel, satisfied at least that by their amendment the secessionists had once more taken control of the state's destiny. There was a much better chance of secessionists controlling the legislature, as they had in the past, and if a crisis came and the legislature voted for secession, then the cooperationists would have no choice but to go along since they affirmed continually their own belief in the right to secede and this amendment made it state law. It would take only a crisis to bring them over and leave the submissionists isolated and shattered, and Rhett knew how to supply a crisis if need be. Just as he reached his room, however, one of his roommates told him that some secessionists felt unhappy with the caucus decision and that Bellinger had second thoughts. Rhett went to bed but half an hour later heard an urgent knocking on his door. Bellinger came in and told him that there would be another caucus the next morning to reconsider their decision, after which he and the other secessionists on the committee of twenty-one would present their plan at the final meeting of Cheves's group and press its adoption. Rhett was content with that, though he warned that if they could not pass this amendment, given the full backing of the secessionist caucus in the face of a puny and indecisive opposition, then it meant the end of the state rights party.[44]

He spoke prophetically. Friday morning, April 30, Rhett was surprised to learn that a hastily assembled meeting of those opposed to the caucus amendment had been called at ten o'clock. Their numbers had grown, with Bellinger among them, and they determined not to support the measure after all. Astonished, Rhett spoke with John F. Richardson, who told him that the secessionists on the committee of twenty-one had met that morning and that W. F. Colcock, not even a member of the convention, appeared before them and "bullied" them into abandoning the measure. Reeling from this, Rhett went on to the statehouse and learned that the secessionists on the committee of twenty-one had agreed to support the policy of the opposition, and even to assist in stifling debate by fellow secessionists on the final report.

The general session opened with Edmund Rhett proposing that people from Massachusetts and Vermont, states that had passed measures nullifying the Fugitive Slave Law protecting the property of slaveholders in their borders, be prohibited by law from owning property in South Carolina. Then Edward Bellinger's brother John proposed as an amendment the secession caucus resolution of the night before, in spite of that morning's decision. He made a stirring speech in its favor, asserting that agitation on secession now was the very thing they needed, but immediately afterward Cheves moved that it be tabled. Edmund Rhett, among other delegates, protested that such action stopped the very discussion for which they had been sent there, but Cheves went ahead and called up instead the report of the committee of twenty-one. When another protest was made, Cheves explained that he was acting on the suggestion of his committee and then took a vote on the tabling motion. It passed 96 to 59, with about 55 secessionists joining the majority and only Gregg and Richardson among the secessionists on the committee of twenty-one opposing. Then Edmund Rhett's motion, too, was consigned to oblivion on the table by a vote of 112 to 44.[45]

Then came a minority report from Perry, as the sole unionist, that in fact showed more spirit and determination than anything else done by the convention, for it affirmed that the right of the people to defend their lives and property and liberty stood paramount even to constitutions and compacts. Knowing it to be pointless, he declined to make a speech, contenting himself with having put forward the amendment. Afterward Rhett came over to him and sat down to tell his old unionist friend that his resolution put to shame the rest of the proceedings from both secessionists and cooperationists. There was irony indeed.[46]

After that Cheves called up again the report of his own committee, which offered nothing more than ten lines of what Rhett styled "solemn and vapid truisms" and the mere assertion of their having cause to secede and the right to do so, but a determination not to. The report accomplished nothing either in resisting their enemies or in justifying their submission, but it was adopted. Most of the secessionists voted for it in the absence of anything else, though Rhett denied that it was an endorsement. Even Perry thought it "dastardly," calling it a case of a mountain going into labor and delivering a mouse.[47] Putting the best face on a disaster, Rhett told the *Mercury* that "it was the will of the Secession party, that the subject matter should not be made an issue before the people," and he made sure to repeat that the report was not the work of the secessionists, but only something in which they had acquiesced.[48]

Rhett regarded the result as a complete surrender of the secession party to the cooperationists and submission men. Worse, they had refused even to hear him, and many joined their old opponents. Had he been a sitting member of the convention, or if he had been allowed into their deliberations, with his old optimism in the face of disaster he believed that he could have prevented the debacle, for he was confident he could have divided the cooperationists and triumphed with the ordinance allowing secession by the legislature. As it was, the course of his friends in the convention was suicidal for them, and for him. "I was left without a party in the State," he complained, "and thus disrobed of all moral power." Even before the convention adjourned he decided that "there was no other action left to me." His son Barnwell was there as an aide to Means, and now Rhett sat down and put pen to paper. "In consequence of the proceedings of the

Convention which has just adjourned, I deem myself no longer a proper representative of the position and policy of the people of South Carolina with respect to the aggressions of the General Government," he wrote. "I therefore resign into the hands of your Excellency the office I now hold as a Senator in the Congress of the United States from the State of South Carolina." Giving the message to Barnwell to deliver, Rhett left for home to face oblivion.[49]

SIXTEEN

Profound Retirement
1852–1856

IRONICALLY, NO ONE PRAISED RHETT'S ACT more than one of his firmest political opponents. "This is the brightest feather in his cap, and evinces the true spirit of the Chevalier and Patriot," Benjamin F. Perry declared. "He has honestly and sedulously tried to break up the Union, and the people and Convention have decided against him. Now he says to them, you have no further need of my services." Differ with him though he did, Perry called Rhett's act one of nobility. "Nothing so became Barnwell Rhett as his abdicating the chair he coveted all his political life."[1]

Hammond disagreed entirely. He regarded Rhett's resignation as the only incident of note in the entire convention, gloating that when the caucus refused to let him speak, in essence "he was literally kicked out in disgrace and infamy." Two years earlier Hammond had thought there was a good chance of forming a united disunion party in South Carolina, one that with prudence would grow in time. "But Rhett snatched the helm," he grumbled, "and in less than twelve months he scattered the party to the four winds—prostrated it in every Southern State, even in this, and reduced it to a mere faction, about to dwindle into a conspiracy." It was a hyperbolic assertion, surely, yet only an exaggeration of undeniable truths. Rhett's interference had embarrassed the movement in Mississippi, crippling Quitman and giving rise to Foote while helping drive the Unionists to power in Georgia, which "recoiled from his violence," Hammond said. At home his Charleston speech all but repudiating the Nashville convention, his rabid calls for action through the past summer, and his well-known appeals to arms—the suggestion to Means of attacking the forts may have been a poorly kept secret—alarmed all but his most radical followers. When he then preached separate action throughout the state, it was finally too much, and the reaction by the cooperationists and submissionists was too great. Hammond thought that the cause was probably ruined in the South for the next ten years and said, "Rhett has done it."

> He is morbidly ambitious of notoriety. He may be a good patriot, but with such propensities no man can be a good Statesman or Party Leader. Rhett has

other glaring disqualifications besides his impatient and reckless ambitions. He is narrow minded, ignorant, and excessively rude and assuming in his manners. Personally he is extremely unpopular, and the Party in this State, which has implicitly followed his dictation and enabled him to ruin the cause, have all the time openly and indignantly disavowed him as a Leader. But he cunningly placed himself just before them on every step that they seemed inclined to take and managed to decide them to that movement. He has sense enough—just enough for this, and manages very adroitly to promote himself. He is now crushed however, I think, and it will be clear soon. Still he is so cunning and managing that I should not be surprised if he is re-elected to the Senate, though everybody hoots at that idea now.[2]

Hammond was the last man to have an objective opinion of his old enemy, yet through his bitterness and resentment and even envy, still he struck at the true heart of Rhett the radical politician and captured ably his situation now. Henry Clay had described Rhett and his fellow fire-eaters as "men who live by agitation" and for whom sowing discord was "their meat, their bread, the air which they breathe." Calhoun had ruled the state by the mere expression of his opinion, but though he thought himself Calhoun's heir, Rhett could not command that obedience, and the mass of people finally recoiled at what appeared to be his attempts to hurl them into a crisis, perhaps only to suit his own prejudices and ambitions. With no little satisfaction, Hammond concluded, "so terminates the career of the man they used to destroy me." His friend Simms saw all around him evidence of repudiation of Rhett's doctrine. Regarding the Union as "that which he would exultingly destroy at every hazard," Simms gloated that Rhett had instead destroyed himself.[3]

The *Mercury* and some of the other state press tried to put the best face on the debacle. The convention was at least something of a victory, it reported, interpreting the resolution recognizing the right of secession as a repudiation of the cooperationists and submissionists and claiming that the votes of Cheves and Barnwell now placed them in the right line. Another paper argued that the convention had healed the division between the secessionists and the cooperationists by placing them on a common platform. They were feeble arguments at best, since virtually all cooperationists and most submissionists had averred all along that a state had the right to secede, with Cheves and Barnwell most of all, objecting only to South Carolina doing so on her own. Having said that, the *Mercury* fatuously complimented the secessionist party on their forbearance when they presumably had the majority. As for Rhett's resignation, the paper said that, of course, it was necessary. He stood for redress of past wrongs, by secession preferably, and by Hammond's or Bellinger's plan otherwise, but the convention took no such action. "A proud and independent man, who has sought and used distinction only for the defense and advancement of his State, finds office without an attraction or an object, when he can no longer use it for these purposes," read an editorial.

Unconsciously the *Mercury* had reaffirmed Rhett's own notion of his role as senator, which was to "use" the office to defend South Carolina according to his own dictates, not to represent the preferences of his people. He gave up his office not because he no longer represented his constituents, for he never truly represented them. He resigned because they had decided to stop following him. Even friendly editors out of state agreed that he had to go. "Mr. Rhett is the most consistent of politicians," said a Virginia editor; "he pushes his doctrines to their legitimate conclusions." Certainly he was logical, "but remarkable impracticable" and "something of a fanatic withal," traits of character that "combined with his proud independence and incorruptible integrity, do in fact, render him an 'unfit representative.'"[4]

Not unexpectedly, immediately after receiving Rhett's resignation, Governor Means asked him to reconsider, arguing that the convention report was not a complete repudiation, but Rhett refused to change his mind. He had known for months that the people would not go for immediate separate secession, but he had not expected that they would accept total submission instead, and that is what he saw in the report. "I have all my life been a supporter of State-rights and State sovereignty," he wrote in his reply. "Co-operation repudiates both as practical entities, and instead of enforcing them, for the protection of the citizen of South Carolina, casts him on the aid and strength of the other States." A lawfully elected convention of the state had determined its policy, even if it was no policy at all. As a loyal son of South Carolina, Rhett would have to be bound by that policy if he continued in office, and that he could not do.[5]

Rhett did not give Means all the reasons that impelled his resignation.[6] There was the stinging personal humiliation of being ignored and told that his views were not wanted. The past year had also brought inescapable confirmation that the Southern states would never act together, as he had all along predicted. It was evident to him that no other state was going to take the lead, for the secessionists were at bay everywhere. Quitman had resigned his governorship; Yancey had resigned from Congress; the Georgia secessionists stood humbled by unionists; and there was not even a movement to speak of in the other slave states.[7] Moreover, hard as it was to accept, Rhett had learned that he did not have power of persuasion sufficient in himself to move South Carolina as Calhoun had done. At best he could only hope to influence its course when and if it should ever start again to move in his general direction.[8] Until such a time, his efforts were pointless. Disillusioned, disappointed, bitter at rejection, and undeniably petulant at not having his way, he would leave South Carolina and the South to their own devices for a time. Let them see how they got along without him, he thought. He had put himself ahead of them, as Hammond said, and they would not follow. Well, he was smarter than Hammond thought, and he knew beyond doubt that there would be new crises ahead. When they came, the people would need someone daring to lead them. He had been up and down too many times before not to know that he could rise again.

The mood around him only seemed to reaffirm his decision, for even in St. Bartholomew's the people appeared to lose interest in secession, as if the tension of the last years had exhausted them and burned out their once bright resistance flame. At the usual July 4 celebration there were still a few toasts to secession, but others expressed a desire for a change in the state's attitude. In some future years there would be no secession toasts at all.[9] There were family affairs to attend to as well. His son Burnet's eyes seemed to be getting worse, and he might need to see a specialist. The financial woes never went away either. Rhett briefly ran out of money entirely upon his return to Congress in February and found himself unable to send enough to his sons in school and at home. "The only *trouble* your ever applying to me for money produces is that I may not have it to give you," he lamented to Burnet. "When I have it and am at liberty to give it to any of you, the bestowment imparts to me unmitigated gratification."[10]

He also worried about his oldest son. Since his 1849 graduation from Harvard, Robert Jr. had vacillated as to his future. At first he stayed home and undertook tutoring his younger siblings. Then he spoke of going to graduate school at Columbia University in New York. Then he talked of settling in California and even of selling some slaves he was due to inherit from his mother to buy land out there, while sending the rest to work property for him. In spite of the Compromise of 1850, the elder Rhett thought it still possible that the legislature of California might somehow admit slavery, but he persuaded the boy to wait all the same, since the value of slaves was bound to go up dramatically. Instead, beside pressing his son to become an attorney, he also began advising him on the purchase of a small plantation of his own, at first trying to find a way to buy one for him from his cousin Robert W. Barnwell. He thought that the slow and steady work necessary to improve a home and rice land would be good for the son's character, and when Barny hinted that he might sell his slaves instead, his father strongly advised against it. He preferred that his son learn to work and manage the slaves, who were his responsibility as well as his property, admonishing him to "let there be no neglect of the little negroes."

Meanwhile Robert Jr. took an appointment as military aide on the staff of the governor, though his father advised him against it initially. Rhett then paid for his son's horse, saddle, and uniform and arms, but soon the boy showed no interest in attending the required drills of the militia in his district. His father had to chide him to participate. "You may depend upon it, a man loses nothing by an earnest effort to learn or do," he advised. "Energy altho useless, is better than slowth." The boy must attend the evening drills regularly. It was only moderate exercise such as his constitution could stand, he could still study law in the mornings as his father wished him to do, and it would give evidence of diligence of purpose. Part of the son's lack of interest was because he had fallen in love, but his father assured him that he could study law, meet his militia obligations, "and carry on a Love affair besides." The only real problem was the occasional need to travel through the country with the governor to review the several militia companies. It took the boy away from his young lady and forced him to incur some expense that the state did not reimburse, and which his father could not afford. Young Barny did, however, show some promise at writing articles for the press, and his father encouraged him in that line. "Write for the papers," he said. "It will improve your style and habituate you to think on public affairs."[11]

The only really good news on the horizon was that Elizabeth was expecting another baby in November, their twelfth, but then there came personal sadness that summer when John Stuart died on August 7 in Beaufort. Even though he and Claudia were estranged, and he given up to drink, still he had been a good friend and a loyal supporter, and the loss had to hurt.[12] Then the last of the great lights of the Senate winked out when Daniel Webster died on October 24. Though he and Rhett were political opponents, Rhett had always admired the great statesman. They sometimes attended the same church in Washington, and he had received some kindnesses from him. He thought Webster had been perhaps the finest secretary of state in the nation's history and even leaped to Webster's defense when an editorial in the *Mercury* was less than charitable in its obituary. Rhett praised him as an "unrivalled intellectual leader" and advocate of the Whig policy, while as an orator he stood unsurpassed. "No man ever had a more free and generous nature," he said, and he pointed out that as a public man Webster had lived for his country. It was stunning that all the great triumvirate had passed within two years. "The Presidential laurel has not adorned the brows of Webster, Clay, or Calhoun," he said, "but as each of them, has dropped from amongst us, thousands have felt as if the fabric of the Confederacy shook to its foundations."[13]

Rhett sang no such songs of praise for Webster's Whig Party, which suffered a severe beating that fall and lost the White House and the Congress to resurgent

Democrats led by Franklin Pierce, a New Englander whose views were much in accord with state rights doctrine. That was good news for the slave states but bad news for any hopes of rekindling secession fever, for the combination of the calming effect of the 1850 compromise and Pierce's victory only spread more balm over an emotionally weary South. For Rhett, still actively watching affairs in Washington though now from afar, the happiest effect of the fall was that neither Foote nor Clemens won reelection, and he flattered himself that his debates with them played no small part in their repudiation.[14]

Whether or not Rhett held any hopes of an immediate political resurrection of his own, he seems to have made no efforts in that direction. When the legislature met in early December they had to choose a new senator to take office when the Calhoun term that Rhett had been filling expired. Some suggested Rhett and others Hammond, but neither aroused any enthusiasm, nor did Rhett apparently make any attempt to put himself forward. In the balloting he came in seventh with only 7 of 156 votes, and on subsequent ballots he got not a vote. Colcock, Chesnut, and even Pickens all started way ahead of him, and in the end the prize went to Josiah Evans, a cooperationist promoted by Perry and James L. Orr, an Upcountry cooperationist now capitalizing on the recent convention to seek unity and strength behind a policy of accepting the 1850 compromise, and proceeding to build and strengthen the state economically and politically within the Union. Nothing could more harshly signal Rhett's all but total eclipse.[15]

Yet it was nothing to the darkness in his Charleston home. On November 28, Elizabeth gave birth to another son, but the infant lived only for a day, not even long enough for them to give him a name. Worse, Elizabeth did not spring back from her labor as she had so many times before. She had been married for twenty-five years and had given birth to twelve children. Of 310 months of marriage, she had spent at least 108 of them pregnant, and all told, nearly half her married life she had been either expecting, giving birth, or recovering. She was not yet forty-three but ravaged and wasted by motherhood. For three weeks she lay ill in her bed. Then on December 14, with Rhett by her side, she repeated the words to the song "Rock of Ages," just as his father had done years before, and died.[16]

The family kept their grief private, and Rhett scarcely ever spoke of it except to his children. Twelve years later he told his daughter Elizabeth—called "Elise"— that the shadow of her mother's "presence and love still rests upon me, and will I believe mingle with my last pulsation of life."[17] She ever remained to him "dearer still than all else," the greatest love of this very loving man.[18] Indeed, quite literally he had loved her too much, and it had left him with an abundant crop of children and a wrenching emptiness within that no one else would ever be able to fill. Even the most perverse of those French philosophers he so detested could not have devised a more tragically apt coda to 1852, his *annus horribilis*. He had lost, it seemed, everything.

For now he would adopt what he called "profound retirement."[19] There were his plantations and his deplorable finances to look to, and for the first time in his life he gave them almost undivided attention. He had three plantations now, having deeded Drainfield to his brother Thomas back in 1831 for a mere five dollars as a token of affection and reward for Thomas's management of that and his other plantations. The Oaks was mostly planted in rice and sat on the west bank of the Ashepoo River, and Lavington and Bugby sat immediately upstream of the Oaks. Rhett bought Lavington in 1841, it once having belonged to the great Carolina patriot Charles Pinckney, and it too grew rice, while Bugby sat on higher ground and held staple crops for the family and the 380 or more slaves who worked all of his holdings.[20]

But there were serious problems. His best plantation, Lavington, had been mortgaged for years to the Bank of South Carolina in Rhett's perpetual race with debt. In three years he would be forced to try to sell it to his brother James for thirty thousand dollars and Bugby outright to his brother-in-law Nathaniel Heyward. His brother Thomas had managed the Oaks ever since 1837, while for some time now his son Barnwell had managed all the other plantations and in 1850 produced a crop of 1,350,000 pounds of rice. With the price averaging about three and one-half cents a pound, that crop had yielded forty-seven thousand dollars or more, but it all went to retire debt, and not all of that. Competition from Asian rice was working to keep the price down, and it would rarely climb above four cents in the years to come. When Barnwell Rhett moved back to Charleston to work in his father's law practice, Rhett would turn over management of all the plantations to his brother Thomas, though he often conferred with him in matters relating to their running, especially management and care of the slaves.[21] Rhett's unfortunate history with money was a subject that none could ignore. For all that he craved the social and economic standing it brought, he simply never valued wealth for its own sake enough to apply himself to its acquisition, and he passed his attitude on to his children. More than thirty years later young Barnwell Rhett confessed that neither he nor his father had ever been mercenary when it came to money, "but, if we had each of us attached more importance to money, we should have been much more potent, successful and happier and done much more good in the world."[22]

Rhett even looked outside South Carolina. Having heard glowing reports of Florida when in the Senate, he now briefly investigated buying land there, but then in 1853 he bought a plantation called Cedar Hill on the Altamaha River just outside the coastal community of Darien, Georgia. For years Rhett had spent his winters in Washington and summers either in a handsome house on Thomas Street in Charleston, which he had bought for ten thousand dollars from Thomas Legaré, or else at Beaufort, though every other spring, at the end of the short session of Congress, he would stay at the Oaks. Now he all but moved to Darien, perhaps attempting to escape his grief, and he would remain there for much of the next four or five years until 1857.[23] By 1854 he had nearly seventy slaves working the place, including a full complement of artisans and mechanics as well as house servants. Soon there were even the luxuries of life again, including pecans, sardines, ale, porter, wine, and French bitters, along with any quantity of cheroots, though the liquor and tobacco may only have been for his overseer. All but a teetotaler, Rhett may not have been completely abstinent, since he did not object to sweetmeats containing brandy and allowed his sons to have wine, but now he drank almost nothing but cold water and milk. Besides, by 1854 he had found something to soften his grief, though never to replace Elizabeth in his heart, and there was cause for more gaiety at Darien. He was in love.[24]

Rhett bought Cedar Hill and another property from the family of Comdr. John H. Dent, United States Navy, formerly of Maryland. In the natural course of things he met the rest of Dent's family, including his thirty-two-year-old daughter Katherine, a distant cousin of his dead wife, Elizabeth. She was getting well past prime matrimonial age now, but Rhett, at twenty years her senior, was not a youngster either. An interest developed and then blossomed, though the Dents were not at all pleased. They did not care overmuch for Rhett and liked even less what they saw of his children, especially the arrogant older boys. Then, too, they knew all too well of his continual financial straits, and Katherine's brother Edward knew the most, since he had gotten into an embarrassing predicament when he handled the sale of some of his father's land to the Carolinian and was forced to demand some kind of security that he would be able to pay, considering what Dent called "the indebted state of your property."[25] There was also the matter of Rhett's health. For some time now his face had been red, no doubt inflamed by exposure to sunlight, and an aggravating growth appeared on his nose; it was no larger than a pimple, but it would not go away and seemed gradually to grow larger. Rhett joked that his complexion was florid because, "the truth is, the Englishman is not out of me yet." The Dents were also fearful that Rhett's continuing poor health was a sign of consumption, perhaps even that same tuberculosis that killed Clay and Calhoun, and they did not relish their daughter marrying only to become a nurse or a widow.[26]

But their affection was not to be denied, and for her part Katherine seemed to have more spirit and independence than the always-subservient Elizabeth. She would stand up to Rhett, even scold him, and when they argued it was often as not he who gave way, and with an affectionate good grace that no political antagonists ever saw in him in defeat. When he was away in South Carolina he wrote her almost adolescent love letters. "Ah! Mon petite ami! You have not in vain wielded your cunning scepter over our sex," he acknowledged after one apparent disagreement. "You know that the best way for woman to defend herself is to avail herself from marrying, make men crazed, and then what have we to do, but to be sorry." He teased, "Don't you know that I am very much fond of you?"[27] Theirs would never be the deep-felt love of youth that he had shared with Elizabeth, who would remain first in his heart to the end of his days, but with Katherine he would form an abiding affection and friendship that in the years ahead would find her his most devoted helpmate, providing him a strength and foundation that Elizabeth probably never had. With or without the Dent family's blessing they were married at Darien on April 25, 1854, and Rhett immediately demonstrated that neither age nor misfortune had dimmed his ability in at least one realm where he had always been supremely successful. Even family members such as his nephew Barnwell Heyward commented that Rhett was a man subject to "the temptations of strong passions," though he had been ever faithful to Elizabeth and so would be to Katherine. On January 29, 1855, exactly nine months and four days after the wedding, Katherine gave birth to their first child, Herbert.[28]

Katherine inherited six children at her marriage, three of them teenagers and little Ann scarcely out of diapers, not to mention her own Herbert when he came along. Inevitably, along with the plantations Rhett had his family much on his mind. In the fall of 1854, when yellow fever appeared again, he took them all to Sullivan's Island, which seemed more healthful than the mainland. That same year Edmund graduated from Harvard, where he had transferred from South Carolina College, and began to study law in Petigru's office.[29] As for Rhett, perhaps Katherine's urgings made him take the little problem on his nose more seriously than he had before being married. In the summer of 1855 he went abroad once more, this time to Paris in spite of his Francophobia, and there consulted with a distinguished physician who comforted him by deducing that the problem was nothing more than a lesion of the skin and removed the affected tissue surgically. Paris was full of people that summer, with Queen Victoria visiting briefly, and Rhett was forced to stay in meager but expensive lodgings, his embarrassment at the appearance of his swollen and bandaged nose keeping him from enjoying much of the excitement and bustle. He returned home in October, hoping that he came back a well man.[30]

He returned to a Union that was once more approaching the boil over slavery in the territories, just as Rhett always knew it must. Despite his retirement, he hardly took his eyes off public affairs. He still read the debates in Washington in the *Congressional Globe,* occasionally wrote letters of reference for old acquaintances from the Capitol, and even asked a favor from his former Senate colleague Jefferson Davis, now Pierce's secretary of war.[31] He also happily contributed to the perpetuation of the memory of Calhoun by helping an editor locate Calhoun documents for an edition of his public papers and addresses, insisting upon absolute accuracy and disclaiming any authorship in the campaign biography written by Calhoun and Hunter. He could not help but muse on his course with Calhoun, recalling that they only differed on the Mexican War and the election of Zachary Taylor but were united in the cause of the South. "He fell dead in the cause—I, living," Rhett added. "Had he lived we would together have conquered. As it is—neither of us will be able to vindicate ourselves. But time will do it for us." Looking back on his own career, Rhett dejectedly concluded, "My who[le] public-life seems to me to have been a failure and to have ended in vanity," but at least he could proudly say that he had spent much of it in company with Calhoun. Flattered that the editor thought him the last remaining faithful exponent of Calhoun's principles, Rhett's old fire flickered when he predicted in October 1854 that "the Southern people have but one alternative—Independence, or ruin."[32]

He could say that with renewed certainty a year later after his overseas trip. He had spent some of his idle time the previous year reflecting on the nature of government, and in April 1854 he contributed to the *Southern Quarterly Review* a review of a new book on the subject, though the review was only an excuse for Rhett to air his own ideas.[33] He vented all his old ideas about free government and civic virtue, of the need for the public to be informed in order to preserve their liberty and their prosperity. He returned to Calhoun's discourse on government and his inventive concept of concurrent majorities, and he declared that government had no jurisdiction over those social interests such as slavery for which Calhoun had sought to set up separate majorities for protection. Government only existed because men were naturally unjust, and one must be protected from another. "We want it for no other purpose," he argued, and it was inherently powerless to be of any good or effect in their homes or social relations where it had no right to intrude except by brute force. Government had no business stepping across the threshold of the home whatever, nor could government purify society or inspire religion or enforce morality. Indeed, he firmly believed in separation of church and state, for the latter could do nothing for the former.

Yet he saw Americans now not as the masters of their ruling bodies but as the ruled instead. "Men are naturally adventurers and quacks," he said, "and the grandest quackery in the world, has been in government." Nowhere was this more true than in taxation and the tariff, and he denied that government's purpose in such levies was the general welfare. It was impossible, for the good of all could not be served when some met with injustice for the benefit of others. That was mere protectionism, no better than what he called "Red Republicanism or Communism," the supposition that every citizen was entitled to the support of the government, even the layabout and the willfully lazy who refused to work. Nor was government merely supposed to be an instrument of restraint, the policy adopted by the late South Carolina convention. Rather, it was government's duty actively to prevent injustice, which included not committing such transgressions itself. Schools and prisons were places of restraint, but they also served higher goals.

Most of all he denounced the notion that as men grew more enlightened and improved their ability to govern themselves, the restraints on that government should lessen. The world abounded with countries in which restraints had been loosened, and they were all despotisms, he argued, asking how then the people could improve their lot and gain a more liberal government. History revealed only one means, he said, and that was "*by fighting.*" He had come back, as always, to revolution. He felt that there was no such thing as a peaceful revolution against despotism and said, "The people must resort to force—to fighting," he went on. "The truth is attested by oceans of blood, that liberty is won only by force." Every people had a right to be free, and if they were not it was because they had submitted through fear or policy. There was South Carolina and the South now, as he saw them, shamed and oppressed. "Certainly it is better far, to fight, and to fight on forever."

Inevitably he got to the tariff and slavery in the territories, and the failure of the government to prevent injustice to the South. By the pressure to make all of the new territories into free states, the equilibrium in the Senate must be upset forever, casting the South into a hopeless minority unable to ensure justice for itself on any issue in the face of the corrupt majority will. The South could only survive within the Union by playing "between the parties at the north," shifting its smaller but deciding strength from one faction to another according to which promised best to defend Southern interests. Thus did Pierce go to victory in 1852, and they could expect the same sort of result in 1856. Yet this could only be a temporary resort, a stage in the Southern progression to what must be inevitable, absolute subjugation. Calhoun had foretold such for years, and indeed Rhett told his readers that they had but to look at the printed portraits of the dead statesman made in his last years to see in his face his stern determination, and the look of despair. The nation, the South, had been false to Calhoun in life, and so would the future if the people of the slave states did not make that manly resistance to tyranny that was ever the right and obligation of free men.

One reader took Rhett to task for an inconsistency in his article when he maintained that no government could be just that was not free. "Does he mean that the government of the whites over their slaves, is not a just government because the negroes are not free?" asked the critic.[34] Rhett meant nothing of the kind, of course, for blacks had no more right to freedom or self-government than squatters had to determine the destiny of the new territories. Rhett wrote his review amid the political explosion that occurred over the organization of the Kansas and Nebraska territories and expressed all of the renewed emotions aroused by this new controversy. Inevitably it turned on slavery. For several years midwestern representatives had been trying to get the region formally organized as a territory in order to push schemes for a transcontinental railroad to compete with a proposed Southern route being pushed now by Jefferson Davis. What stopped them was Southern opposition, for the territory lay above the Missouri Compromise line and would thus automatically be free and ultimately make free states that would destroy the precarious balance of power in the Senate. Then on January 4, 1854 Douglas reported a new bill that implicitly abrogated the Missouri Compromise and would leave it to the settlers of the territory to decide for themselves prior to statehood. It was Cass's old popular sovereignty, "squatter sovereignty" to Rhett and its other opponents, and still Douglas met Southern opposition until he included an explicit repeal of the Missouri Compromise, for that would mean that all future territories everywhere would be potential slave states. With the aid of Davis, President Pierce was pressured to make the repeal an administration measure, and after bitter and divisive debate it passed in May.

Rhett heartily approved of the Missouri line repeal, since he had always regarded any impediment to the spread of slavery to any territory as unconstitutional. Though his own influence had waned dramatically, still letters from fellow Carolinians sitting in Congress kept him abreast of the progress of the Kansas bill. While some warned that they were still at the mercy of unscrupulous Yankee plunderers, at least the Kansas debate had aroused some strong Southern feeling again. Foote was now an outcast gone to California, and Howell Cobb seemed about to be abandoned by fellow Georgians for his opportunistic unionism of 1850.[35]

But Rhett was not at all sanguine about the Kansas bill even with the Missouri repeal, for the hated squatter sovereignty could achieve what the Missouri Compromise had not—the elimination of slavery from all future states. "The People of a Territory can have not one single element of supremacy," he argued.

"They are dependents." Thus they could have no sovereignty sufficient to decide issues such as slavery. That could only come when they became a state, yet Douglas would allow them to form constitutions and organize themselves as if they had full sovereignty at any time they chose prior to admission as states, "one of those queer intellectual and moral exhibitions, which no other Country than the Northern United States could have produced," he said contemptuously. The result was predictable, for soon Rhett saw the abolitionists of the North sending what he called "armed Emigrants" into Kansas, clearly intent on intimidation to keep slaveholders out and thus determine that whenever territorial government was formed, it would be by an antislave majority. That Southerners also began sending settlers, fully armed with guns and slaves, into Kansas did not trouble him. They were only defending their rights.[36]

Douglas's repeal split the Democratic Party badly, driving its antislave elements into the arms of the old Free Soilers and the bulk of the Northern Whigs to form the new Republican Party that same season. In its formation Rhett could see at last the realization of his long-voiced predictions about the opponents of the South. Now at least there was a major political party, exclusively Northern, whose single overriding issue was opposition to slavery, first to its expansion but ultimately and inevitably to its existence everywhere. The Republicans were not a threat yet, though they might be in 1856 at the presidential election; yet it was evident that as long as the slavery question remained agitated, they would have the issue they needed to keep them alive. Ironically, Rhett needed that same issue and agitation to keep his own hopes for Southern independence alive. The turmoil that ensued the following year, as Kansas began to bleed from increased confrontations between armed slavery and abolition settlers, served his ends well. It was not the true crisis needed to galvanize South Carolina into action—not yet. But with the looming cloud of Republicans in the North and the actual shooting between Northerners and Southerners on the western frontier, the gathering thunder must eventually spread to the South, and then people would act. Looking at the Republican menace in October 1854, he insisted to Jefferson Davis that "the Union must go down, or the South be destroyed." For himself, as always, he preferred "*resistance.*" If they had done their duty as men and as Southerners, a friend told him at the same time, "we can rightfully claim the sympathy of angels." For Rhett there was never any doubt that *he* had done *his* duty.[37]

For the next two years, while the Kansas controversy smoldered on without erupting into an outright crisis, Rhett attended to his family and his fortunes as best he could. There were some cases for the law practice to bring in fees, enough to keep him tied to Charleston and unable to handle more distant matters, for which he engaged Armistead Burt on Upcountry business. Together they acted as agents of heirs for the sale of several plantations, including one from his wife's Dent relations, with the fees from executing one estate coming to as much as six thousand to ten thousand dollars, which he desperately needed.[38] He also took an interesting case that became *Rhett and Robson* vs. *Henry L. Pinckney, Tax Collector,* over the state charging taxes on produce from other states brought into South Carolina under an 1854 act of the legislature. As a free trader Rhett opposed the notion, even when applied to Northern goods. Rhett argued the case before the court against his old friend Isaac Hayne, who was representing the state, and Rhett eventually won.[39]

Most of his attention went to his landholdings, however, when a painful and embarrassing falling out over suspicions of misconduct by his brother Thomas led Rhett to take over direction of his plantations in 1855, and he engaged Alfred to assist him. "God is his judge," Rhett said of Thomas, though he never discussed the disagreement otherwise.[40] James Rhett did not buy Lavington after all, but in January 1856 Rhett sold it, along with Bugby, to Nathaniel Heyward not long after ordering his slaves to dig an irrigation canal between the two plantations to the Ashepoo for flooding the lower rice fields of Drainfield and the Oaks in the dry season. He had also made a canal through Thomas Rhett's Drainfield in order to irrigate the back portions of Lavington and Bugby but still feared that he would lose half of his 1856 crop to drought.

The problem with Thomas, in fact, may have had something to do with water rights from those canals, for before long an ugly difficulty arose with his former brother-in-law Nathaniel Heyward over rights. It led to a legal battle that continued until 1858, when as the result of a suit a court ruled that the canal through Drainfield was properly the Rhetts', thus cutting Heyward off from water. It was all mortifying to Rhett, who as ever recoiled from any sort of difficulty with neighbors or family. Moreover, he believed that he had included an easement allowing Heyward access to the canal when he originally sold him the plantations. As soon as the suit concluded, Rhett took Drainfield back from Thomas and gave an easement to Heyward in an attempt to return to harmony.[41] "He was always liberal with money, affording considerable assistance to relatives and friends," Heyward's son and Rhett's nephew Barnwell Rhett Heyward would recall after this generosity. More often than not it was a generosity he could ill afford.[42]

Meanwhile there was work to be done on the Darien plantation too, where he continued to spend much time, and he shipped a considerable quantity of goods from Charleston to get in operation. In fact, the sale of Lavington and Bugby may have been in part to finance the work at Darien. Rhett engaged workmen to construct a canal and clear ditches in preparation for rice planting, and by early 1857 he had eighty-eight slaves on the Altamaha, most of them field hands, while some of the women worked on building earthen dams on the canals. They were sowing rice by the spring, when Rhett engaged a local manager to oversee the plantation. The first crop was a poor one, however. Early frost stunted it at the start, then caterpillars and maggots attacked the shoots, and inattentive hoeing let weeds do their work.[43]

"I am a diligent Planter—driving negroes & doctoring them," he wrote goodnaturedly to his friend Burt in the summer of 1856. The more slaves he acquired, the more solicitude Rhett seems to have felt for them. Beyond any doubt regarding them as helpless inferiors, he took all the more seriously his responsibility to care for them physically and spiritually. On at least one occasion he personally stopped an enraged master from brutally flogging a slave.[44] Whenever finances allowed, he had bacon sent to his Ashepoo slaves, no doubt accepting the common wisdom that pork was the best meat for blacks and kept them happy. At Darien he insisted that his overseer carefully record all clothing, blankets, fabric, and even needles and thread given to the slaves there to ensure that they received what they needed.[45] Especially he turned his attention to religion. In 1845, along with William and Robert Barnwell, Rhett attended a meeting of the Episcopal diocese of South Carolina from which came the declaration that it should be the fixed policy and responsibility of the South to give proper spiritual instruction to its slaves.[46] He became involved in the work of the Reverend William Capers of St. Thomas's Parish, an eminent Methodist who devoted much of his time ministering to plantation blacks, and built a large church on one of his own plantations for the slaves from all the neighborhood to attend. Once a month a white preacher came to hold services, and Rhett and his own family often attended.[47] At Darien, too, Rhett erected a church on his property for his slaves, and more than half of them became regular members, leading one local Methodist to declare that "there is a most delightful state of things among the colored people."[48] Rhett's nephew later recalled that he "contributed largely to churches and charities," and the expenditure on religion for his slaves only added to his constant near-impoverishment.[49]

There was always the comfort of family. With little Herbert just over a year old, Katherine was pregnant again and expecting in December 1856. The other children, especially Rhett's favorite daughter, Elise, had him more to themselves for their sport and games than ever before, and Elise thought she could see a spark of the child come out in his enthusiasm for their play "as tho' he was a boy." Of her father she said, "No man ever had a more tender, loving heart." Moreover, seemingly they never saw him show or express any anger in the home.[50] Yet surely now there was cause.

Inevitably, having given an example of willfulness, independence, and even arrogance, Rhett was bound to be challenged eventually by that same spirit in at least some of his sons, and now it came from two of them at the same time. He had sent his son Robert Woodward Rhett to Germany in 1856 for further education, but the boy seemed to be wasting his money on fast living instead. Worse, against his father's wishes, Edmund stopped reading law with Petigru, probably the first time that one of the children actually defied him. Somehow Edmund managed to afford to go to Paris in the summer of 1855 instead and while there continued to show his independence by writing back letters that Rhett found dictatorial and not at all properly deferential. On Edmund's return in the fall Rhett renewed his wish for his son to continue legal studies, even if he had no interest in the subject, for at least it offered the promise of a secure living. But the young man, now in his twenty-third year, could not find a taste for any calling as yet, and with his father already financially strapped, he pleaded reluctance to add further expense for law school. Neither did he find business attractive, and in any case his family's money embarrassment precluded any assistance to get him started. It all made for a tense atmosphere at the Oaks that fall. "Disagreement of opinion, money harrassments, contrary views and conflicting wills, seemed to have produced a general misunderstanding and unpleasantness of feeling" in the Rhett household, Edmund believed. "We were all," he told his father, "and each of us thoroughly dissatisfied with our respective positions, and restless under the circumstances we found ourselves in, none more so than yourself."[51]

Edmund was a perceptive young man, even if headstrong. By the spring of 1856 Rhett had been in his "profound retirement" for four years. After the loss of Elizabeth, he had personal equilibrium once more in a happy marriage with Katherine. His finances were chaotic as always, yet he seemed at least to be maintaining headway with his debts, and his legal practice brought in good money when he gave it his full attention. Indeed, his suggestion that Edmund practice law even if not much interested in it probably reflected his own diffidence toward his profession. "I think Mr. Rhett was more of a politician than a lawyer," his old friend Perry observed. "He certainly acquired more reputation as a member of Congress than he ever did at the Bar."[52] Perry was right. Rhett's heart was in the political arena where it had always been, and his absence from the fray produced that restlessness and dissatisfaction that Edmund saw in him. This was to be an election year, and now it was between the badly weakened Democrats and the new and frighteningly strong Republicans. Southern votes would likely decide the outcome, just as James Orr and others had predicted that they could rule from within the Union. It was a chance for bold Southern leaders to exact strong guarantees of their rights from the Democrats, or for even more daring men to let the election go to the Republicans in the hope that a resultant wave of shock and fear in the South would finally lead to action. The frustration of being sidelined and ignored at such a moment must have been overwhelming, and perhaps as early as that spring Rhett began to turn his thoughts to making a reentry into the political world.

Fatefully, it was Edmund who first brought the name back before the public. With the penchant for editorializing that beset all of the Rhett men, he settled his professional indecision that spring by taking a job at the *Mercury,* working for Heart and his new co-owner William R. Taber Jr., Edmund's cousin and Barnwell Rhett's nephew through his sister Emma. Almost at once Edmund entered into the year's political battle, especially at first writing editorials lambasting Sen. Andrew P. Butler. Most readers assumed that he was only speaking for his father, especially when he condemned Butler for any thought of participating in the forthcoming Democratic national convention.[53]

It was all a part of Orr's program of realigning South Carolina away from the extremism of the Rhetts and toward integration into the nation as a whole politically and socially, as well as economically. They must be a part of the mainstream of the Democratic Party, thought Orr, and there they would find security, whereas all Rhett's experience had told him that no party could be trusted and that the Democrats would only take them for granted, use them, and betray them in the end. Worse, it was parties and their corrupting influences that had divided the South at times when it most needed unity to act.[54] Opposition to national conventions had been an article of faith with Rhett for years, as with Calhoun before him, and especially this year. If the Southern states attended, they would be bound by their participation to support the party nominees, whereas if they remained aloof, they could drive a harder bargain for their support.

Orr was having his way, nevertheless, and despite the opposition of the *Mercury,* the Democrats of the state held a convention of their own and selected delegates to the national convention to be held in Cincinnati in June. The state convention took no position on the pending matter of Dred Scott, a slave who tried to sue for his freedom when his master took him to a free state but whose case would go before the Supreme Court and involve a decision of the power of Congress over slavery in the territories. Barnwell Rhett Jr. attended and derisively called the meeting "an Orr affair" and its acts those of "a packed Jury trimming to keep in with Douglas."[55] Meanwhile, in their editorials Rhett, Heart, and Taber tried relentlessly to cast the issue of the election that year as one of union or disunion, despite the fact that most in the state were simply sick of hearing the argument and equally weary of the *Mercury* trying to keep the banner of secession flying. In fact, the paper's dramatically declining circulation revealed that few even wanted to read it any longer, which seemed only to make it howl the louder. When the Democrats met in convention, Douglas's popular sovereignty stand virtually killed him with the Southern delegations attending. The nomination went instead to James Buchanan, another so-called "doughface" like Pierce, who could be expected to be sympathetic to Southern interests. That in itself effectively ruined disunion as an issue, for no one saw the need of it. A united Democratic Party had more than enough votes North and South to defeat the Republican nominee John C. Frémont and a last gasp of nativism from the so-called Know-Nothing Party nominee Fillmore. But that did not stop the *Mercury.*

Late in August, Congressman William Aiken resigned his seat from Charleston, and that being the *Mercury's* bailiwick, the paper immediately started pressing for the nomination of a secessionist as a replacement. Some of the editorials were by Edmund Rhett, and it is quite possible that the nominee he had in mind was his father. Of course a Senate seat would be more fitting, but neither of South Carolina's two positions was up for filling that year. At least a return to the House of Representatives would get Barnwell Rhett out of the doldrums and put him back in the middle of the fray, and at a vital moment. Rhett neither said nor did anything to advance a candidacy himself, but then the state party nominated Andrew G. Magrath, an old-line cooperationist whom the late Albert Rhett defeated for the attorney generalship in 1840 and who had opposed Bluffton in 1844 and defied Rhett and secession in 1852. Rhett's reaction was contemptuous. "It is plain that the element of discord can not be composed by submission," he told Burt, yet that was what could be expected from Magrath. "The state is now in the hands of wretched self-seekers and charlatans."[56]

All it took was the political bad blood already existing between the Magraths and the Rhetts, strained through the family streak of verbal intemperance in all of the latter, to produce from Edmund some *Mercury* editorials that were scathing even by the paper's own incendiary standards. They depicted Magrath as a traitor to South Carolina and the South who would sell them all to the national party if elected.[57] Robert Barnwell Rhett Jr. encouraged his brother's editorial attacks, in fact expecting that a challenge to a duel would ensue. He even advised his brother to practice with a pistol in anticipation, and Alfred gave encouragement of his own.[58] They were all arrogant, hotheaded, and wanting in both humility and restraint. Somehow their father—and surely their time and place—had communicated to them some of his worst features without the leavening of his better, with Alfred easily the most arrogant of all. One of their female relatives declared of them that "the world, you know, is composed of men, women, and Rhetts," as if they regarded themselves as above the rules that encumbered mere mortals.[59] Twice before Alfred had been involved in challenges, though no duels were fought, yet he was always in love with his pistols. As for Edmund, he was handsome and regarded as being conceited of his looks, a dandy who affected a cool, detached manner but whose vituperation in denouncing someone he disliked was far greater even than his father's.[60] He, too, must have expected a challenge from Magrath. What happened instead is that Magrath's brother Edward issued a challenge to William Taber, holding him responsible as co-owner of the *Mercury*. They met on September 15 at the Washington Race Course, with Alfred Rhett acting as Taber's second, and in the exchange of pistol fire Taber was killed.

The tragedy seemed to take the wind out of the paper and upset Charleston as well. Sensitive to his old friend Rhett's feelings, Petigru counseled his family and friends to say nothing about the affair that might upset him. Magrath resigned his nomination, and soon William Porcher Miles was put forward in his place, ending any discussion of a Rhett candidacy, if there ever had been any. Yet the Rhett ambitions were aroused all the same, and he may have had higher aspirations all the while. "I have been ahead of the times, and have fallen," he wrote to Henry Wise of Virginia on November 7, even while election returns were coming in to show that the aging Buchanan had been elected.[61] Rhett took little pleasure in that, though he and Buchanan had been friendly acquaintances in Washington and the Pennsylvanian's principles were generally good. Still Rhett regarded him as spineless and unreliable after his failure to support the scheme to throw the 1844 election into the House for Calhoun and his backing out of the move that same year to control the election of officers of the House. Worse, the safe rejection of the Republicans seemed to layer even more calm over South Carolina, burying hope of secession beneath a veneer of relief that crisis had been averted yet again. If there were to be any hope for the South ultimately, as Rhett told Davis, there must be resistance. Now with a weakling in the White House, determined Southern states could perhaps reassert their demands for sovereignty with some hope of success, but only if leadership existed to stir their determination again. Better yet, if so aroused they could risk secession with an even greater confidence that Buchanan was not the man to try coercion to hold the Union together.

The whole matter would rest back in the state houses, and as it happened the legislature in Columbia was to elect a new governor when it met late in the fall. It was an office Rhett had not coveted before, but now it could bring him back into politics and at the same time put him in the perfect position from which to engineer South Carolina's reassertion of her rights and independence. In a scarcely disguised appeal for support, he sent an open letter to sitting governor James H. Adams in the first week of November and had it immediately published in the *Mercury*. South Carolina needed to know his views on what its course should be, he thought.

He offered the same old story he had been telling for years. The North was taking control of the government, and its design was the ruin of the South by iniquitous taxes and the destruction of slavery. The tariff and slavery were the glue with which the North would consolidate power in Washington and destroy state sovereignty forever. Northerners were "a great, but essentially a domineering, fanatical and avaricious people." Moreover, they were a different people in pursuits and industry, and those differences were building all the time. Never before in history, he proclaimed, were the rival interests between two sections greater. The natural consequence must be explosion or the tyranny of one over the other, and it was the lust for spoils and booty that now impelled the North to seek to plunder the South as the barbarian hordes of northern Europe had sacked Rome ages before. The Constitution could no longer protect them, for the North no longer honored the compact and felt it had the raw power to subvert it at will. The South might have held its ground in 1820, but instead it compromised over Missouri, and did so again and again. At every step a firm resistance from the South could have halted Yankee aggression, but they had been weak and trusting. There would have been no attempt at coercion, and if there had, then it would only have proved that the two sections could not live together harmoniously.

In a typical example of Rhett's by-now-obsessional fixation on the song he had been singing all those years, he averred that the only honorable course for the Northern majority was for it to adopt an entirely passive stance, backing down in the face of a resisting Southern minority in order to preserve the Union or else meekly letting states secede without attempting to hold the Union together. The South had every right to "resist" to preserve its rights, but the North had no right at all to resist to preserve the nation. He clearly showed, as he had for some time now, that balanced thinking about Southern rights and the nature of the Union was beyond him. The events of 1850–52 especially had pushed him across an invisible line that separated the radical partisan from the fanatic. Now, in fact, he spoke as if the Union were already dissolved, with only legal ordinances needed to ratify what had already happened spiritually.

"We must, practically, rule ourselves," he declared, dismissing the argument that the South's role in the election of Buchanan meant it still had power or that the election had settled anything, for they were still in a Union with people who refused to honor the Fugitive Slave Law. Then in a resort to that distortion and invention that had more and more often characterized his public statements, he portrayed mobs of abolitionists beating and murdering innocent Southerners attempting to reclaim their lawful property in the North. Abolitionists were hiring and arming ignorant immigrants to send into Kansas, and worse, the abolition majority in Washington intended to raise an army to force Southerners out of the territories. He even presented it as an intolerable outrage that an abolitionist majority would have the power to elect a Speaker of the House of Representatives, though how the House was to operate without some kind of majority he did not deign to explain. The election would change none of this, for it brought no guarantee that future aggressions would not try to reclaim the ground temporarily lost in the Republican defeat—and for Rhett, Republican and abolitionist were synonymous, or at least it was expedient for the incendiary impact of his arguments to make them one and the same, which of course they were not. But misrepresentation and demonizing of his opposition had always been an integral part of his style of argument.

Only constitutional guarantees of Southern rights would offer any lasting relief, and he saw nothing in the election to promise that. Indeed, the North, now conscious of its power, would rather risk disunion than offer any security to the South. What course lay open for them to pursue then? There was only one answer, and it surprised no one. "In my humble judgment, all true statesmanship in the South consists in forming combinations, and shaping events, so as to bring about, as speedily as possible, a dissolution of the present Union, and a Southern Confederacy," Rhett stated. Toward that end, the South—a united South, not just South Carolina unilaterally as in earlier days—must demand at the next Congress a return to the 1833 tariff rates, and if it did not get it, then the slave states should withdraw their delegations from Washington. Even if they were not prepared to secede, they should at least pursue nonintercourse, Hammond's old plan. At the same time, the Southern states should propose their own amendments to the Constitution for their own protection, and if the North did not agree to them, then they should secede.

Rhett was being transparently disingenuous, for if there was one thing that everyone in South Carolina knew, it was that he of all people did not believe that the South would ever act together as a unit. It was the very basis of his twenty-year battle with the cooperationists. Thus he really expected nothing either from nonintercourse or Constitutional amendments, but rather counted on their failure as catalysts for the next step of secession. "We can never be known, appreciated or respected," he said, "until we are an independent people," and he made it clear throughout that he saw Southerners as one distinct people, more honest, righteous, religious, humane, and mannered than the North or most other nations. And why should they not be, for after all, he had long subscribed to the fanciful myth that the North had been peopled by the narrow, miserly, Puritan class of England, while the Cavaliers, the descendants of the aristocracy, sent their sons to the South. His own family put the lie to that, for with a few exceptions his immigrant ancestors were solidly middle class, just like those who settled New England.[62] But it was a convenient myth all the same.

Moreover, he declared that Southerners now were "the most important people in the world to its welfare and happiness," thanks to cotton. They had nothing to fear from anyone foreign or domestic. "Eight millions of the white race, raised to the use of arms, and constituting one of the most military people in the world, inhabiting a country intersected all over by railroads, are unconquerable by any power upon earth," he proclaimed. Did not that alone entitle them to independence? And against that he raised the specter of recent events in Haiti and Jamaica and all the ever-present fears of mobs of slaves loosed on the South by abolitionists, who would seize their land and their daughters and hand them to the blacks. "Break from the North," he pleaded, "as you value honor, prosperity, life itself." Men such as he who had yearned for years for an independent Southern nation were taking heart from the sounds of the abolitionists gathering their strength in the North, for these only signaled that at last the time of reckoning was at hand. "On! let the contest come!" he demanded. "If true to ourselves, a glorious destiny awaits us."[63]

Interestingly, nowhere in the letter did he tell Governor Adams just why he was writing it, for it came not in response to any inquiry from the governor nor any demand from the people to know his views. But when the *Mercury* raised Rhett's name on its standard as nominee for the governorship, the purpose became plain enough. Just as plain was the fact that the entire effort fell embarrassingly flat. When the legislature met, it did not consider Rhett seriously as a candidate, and the response in general in the state was silence. They had heard all he had to say before. Moreover, his new level of intemperance bordering on irrationality convinced some critics that he was no longer fit to serve the state in a position of responsibility. Carolinians found that they preferred a Rhett in "profound retirement" and were content to keep him there. At the end of November, as it became obvious to Rhett that his effort had backfired, his old friend Petigru felt rather sorry for him in spite of their radical political differences. "You know how much regard I have always had for Mr. Barnwell Rhett," he reminded his daughter. At the moment it appeared that he was one of few who did.[64]

SEVENTEEN

I Have Already Passed Out of the World
1857–1859

BY NOW RHETT WAS TOO INURED to disappointment to be much surprised by the indifference with which the state met his gubernatorial hints. "I seldom leave the House," he told Burt the following February, "and feel as if I have already passed out of the world."[1] Yet there was compensation in the delivery of another daughter, Anne Elisabeth Constance, on December 2, and challenge in a new family enterprise that could play an important role in reversing his political fortunes.[2] Finally the Rhetts owned the *Mercury.* Somehow they found the money to buy out the late Taber's share in the paper in January 1857. Barnwell Rhett Jr. was officially the new partner with Heart, though the money in fact came from his father, who mortgaged slaves to raise the capital, once again compromising his promise to Stapleton for the sake of his political obsession.[3] It would not be seemly for Rhett himself to be known as the owner of a paper that would advance his ideas, and probably his electoral prospects, but there would never be any question from the outset that his was the controlling ideology behind the editorial policy to come.

Rhett had picked a poor time to make the purchase, for a collapse in cotton prices had hurt the Lowcountry and, in turn, Charleston suffered a severe depression that soon was manifest throughout the nation. As a result, the Rhetts found that the *Mercury* was in even more dire condition than they had thought. More than fifteen thousand dollars in accounts receivable for advertising sat in its files, while it could not collect enough to meet its weekly payroll and expenses. Circulation had been plummeting for some years and now ran scarcely more than six hundred subscribers for the daily at ten dollars a year. Anxiously Rhett appealed to friends such as Burt in Abbeville to find it subscribers to bring in some cash. Editing the paper was a calling, not an enterprise undertaken for profit, but they must at least meet expenses in order to keep it alive and get their message to the people. "In our efforts to continue it, we anxiously are looking to the condition of our country, believing that our efforts to aid it are not entirely in vain," Rhett protested. "We have tried to lay open the way of hope and salvation, amidst the

darkness which environs our destiny."[4] While Heart oversaw the precarious business side of the paper, the younger Rhett took over the editorial pages and quickly
began to emulate his father. His editorials brooked no dissent from Rhett positions, made little effort to present opposing ideas fairly or accurately, and scarcely
gave notice to any sort of objectivity.[5] Rather, theirs was to be a species of advocacy journalism never before seen in its virulence and aggression, revealing that
Edmund was not the only one who saw no lesson to be learned in the price
Taber paid for Rhett editorial intemperance.

As the year wore on, Rhett at least had the satisfaction of seeing the financial crisis hit the North and the West much harder than it hit the South. Cotton prices rebounded and the crops came in full, but for Rhett, as ever, funds
remained low and debt high, especially with the burden of the *Mercury.* Early in
the fall he went one more time to London to try to wring out the remainder of
the rice duty commission owed him, but he now felt such animosity toward
the one debtor that he would not even call on him personally. Instead he turned
the whole matter over to all the others who had paid him and trusted to their
social and business pressure to force the recalcitrant partner to meet his obligation. However, all that did was give the debtor an excuse to complain that Rhett's
behavior canceled any right he might have had to expect payment.[6] In the end
Rhett involved the British minister for foreign affairs, who finally produced a
settlement. Rhett returned to Charleston in October, just in time to see a minor
panic as depositors made a run on the banks, prompting him to come out in
the *Mercury* in favor of suspending specie payments until the panic subsided, an
echo of Van Buren's policy two decades before. Meanwhile he plied his law practice intermittently to bring in what little cash he could, even undertaking a case
of accused rape when a spinster who wanted to be a noted roué's mistress took
revenge in accusations when rebuffed. The man deserved to be ruined, whether
guilty or not, thought Rhett. "A life of pleasure as it is called, is nothing but a
miserable bondage to sin ending in shame and dishonour," Rhett told Edmund.[7]

All through the spring and summer of 1857 Rhett kept his eye on the
national political pool and occasionally put his finger in to stir. To get his views
known abroad, he managed to have his letter to Governor Adams extracted in
the *London Quarterly.* At home he joined most other men of note in Charleston
in subscribing to the Order of Mount Vernon, an organization dedicated to preserving the home of George Washington and his grave. Though seemingly only
philanthropic, the Order quickly attracted Southern rights members all across
the South, including Yancey in Alabama, as a small movement to unite them in
memorializing a Southern hero.[8] When he could, Rhett spoke with prominent
secessionists from other states, including paying a call on the Virginia agriculturist

Edmund Ruffin when he visited Charleston in May, sharing with him his despair at the want of any leaders of will or ability with sufficient influence to guide the Southern states out of the Union. Too many who once stood for secession had given up, while others still in the movement at heart were unwilling to stand up for it now because they were seeking high office and could not risk ruining their careers as Rhett had ruined his.[9] Simms told Hammond that Rhett's great mistake had been in speaking of the Union as "that which he would exultingly destroy at every hazard," and that instead it was Rhett who was destroyed.[10]

As always, an issue was needed to create leaders and arouse the people. Simms told Rhett that if only cotton had come down to five cents a pound in the recent fall, then secession would be easily accomplished in all of the South, for the economic hardship would have been enough to foment discontent. But it was running safely at twelve cents at least, and the enactment of a new tariff that year saw significant reduction in rates, effectively taking the heart out of that issue for secessionists.[11] Rhett continued to watch the squatter sovereignty debate as it unfolded, collecting what press accounts he could get from Kansas. There at least he could find scope for agitation, especially after the March 1857 Supreme Court decision in the Dred Scott case declared the Missouri Compromise unconstitutional. Meanwhile Leonidas W. Spratt, publisher of the *Charleston Southern Standard,* had been raising a ruckus ever since 1853 over reopening the African slave trade. Proclaiming that slavery was a positive moral and social good—with which Rhett certainly agreed—he maintained that it was therefore incongruous for the foreign slave trade to be abolished, implying as it did some stigma on the institution. Moreover, the only way to preserve and protect slavery was in a separate Southern confederation, though Spratt envisioned a social revolution as a result of reopening the African trade, for the influx of millions of new blacks would lower the price so that every white Southerner could afford to become an owner and thus be a stakeholder in a slave society. At its most extreme, Spratt's was a populist crusade that would have blurred or eliminated one of the main distinctions between the oligarchy and the yeomanry, offering at the same time a plan for the salvation of the South while homogenizing the class structure on which Southern society had been based since its foundation.

There was at least something in this new movement, whose adherents were soon dubbed the "slave traders" and pitted in opposition to Orr's so-called National Democrats who represented the traditional oligarchy. Then Governor Adams embraced Spratt's idea in an annual message delivered to the legislature just after the appearance of Rhett's letter to him. That dumped the whole matter in the state house, where Orr's minority could resist but not eliminate the movement for reopening.[12] As for Rhett, Spratt had an interesting idea but was taking it too far, for as Rhett had discovered, the more radical a notion, or the more it threatened any vested interest in the South, the less likely it was that the slave states would ever unite in support. Rather, Spratt's movement only promised to split the already weakened secessionist forces even more, for though almost all of them thought the prohibition of the slave trade abominable, as a practical matter they had no desire to see the value of their blacks drastically reduced by a sudden influx of new Africans. Spratt's was not the issue that would bring secession, concluded Rhett, and the columns of the *Mercury* consequently counseled remaining quiet. They should wait until after secession was an accomplished fact, and then they could consider the advisability of reopening the trade and at the same time have perfect freedom to do so if they chose.[13]

Serendipity seemed to throw an opportunity suddenly in Rhett's way just as he and his son were discouraging the divisiveness of Spratt's program. Senator Butler died unexpectedly in May, and that fall the legislature would have to elect a replacement to fill his term. Here was a battleground for testing the strength of Orr's submissionist party and the secessionist old guard. Orr's people would back Orr or Pickens, now making a new bid for leadership free from the shadow of disapproval of the dead Calhoun. The state rights men had none but their longtime leaders to turn to, and that meant particularly Rhett and Hammond or perhaps Hamilton.

Rhett's own role in seeking the position he kept almost perfectly quiet, but there is no doubt that he took some active steps to position himself favorably before the legislature. His old friend and colleague Daniel Wallace began working on a lengthy biographical essay that clearly had assistance from Rhett, if the Carolinian did not in fact write it himself, merely using Wallace's name as he had Atherton's and others' in the past. Asserting that "the power and influence wielded by Mr. Rhett on the national theatre have never been generally understood," the essay presented him as the intimate of Calhoun, rehearsed his career from his entry into the legislature, and called attention especially to his role in imposing the gag rule in the House and his fight against the tariff and internal improvements, crediting him with keeping the Polk administration out of a war with England. His role in opposing the 1850 compromise and his subsequent battles with Foote and Clemens completed the portrait of one who had ever been the champion of South Carolina and Southern rights, though nowhere did Wallace use the word *secession*. He did aver that the crisis between North and South required either a treaty or a revolution and argued that of all the public men available, Rhett was most fitted to the occasion.[14]

Once more showing prudence, Rhett did not have the biography published in the *Mercury*. Instead it appeared first in the *Laurensville Herald* along with the nomination of Rhett for the Senate vacancy, and then the *Mercury* felt free to reprint it on August 10, along with the comment that it was accurate.[15] But if the Rhetts hoped to see a groundswell emerge as a result, they were rapidly disappointed. As soon as Wallace's biography went into print, voices of dissent appeared. Despite admiring Rhett's frank and impulsive nature, some asserted that the state had seen more than enough agitation already, and the Orr followers declared, "We desire to fight or serve under a more peaceful banner, and one whose folds are large enough to extend beyond the limits of South Carolina." A Spartanburg editor held no punch when noting that Rhett was "notoriously unpopular" even in his own state and would exert neither strength at home nor influence in Washington. Despite his talents he was "a man without influence—and therefore totally unsuited." No such "dogmatist" would be effective at statesmanship, and Rhett in office would do more to prejudice secession than to advance it. "Give us, say we, a man who knows when to advance, when to recede without yielding gained ground, and ready at all times to be governed by circumstances." That definitely was not Robert Barnwell Rhett.[16]

When the legislature met late in November, Rhett's few friends in the chamber found that many members there were new to politics and did not know him personally. Rather than appear to be politicking—and perhaps realizing that it might backfire against him—Rhett did not travel to Columbia, and through the *Mercury* he let it be known that he was not actively seeking the place but that, of course, he was available if asked.[17] In fact, he no longer had a base with which to work even if he had gone. Worse, the course of the *Mercury* in the months leading up to the election alienated far too many with its constant harangues on the Kansas question and its unyielding insistence that only the Rhett line was the proper one for the state to pursue. "The Mercury, from its selfishness & indiscretion does the cause it professes to advocate infinite mischief," complained Isaac Hayne. At a time when South Carolina needed unity, the Rhetts could only preach the gospel of their small clique and thus risked pushing Charleston and the state back toward the old extreme of opposition rather than harmony with the rest of the South.[18]

When the balloting began, the weakness of Rhett's following became immediately apparent. On the first ballot he came in last with only six votes, while Hammond clearly led the pack and Pickens was a distant second. Seeing the hopelessness of any further attempt for their man, Rhett's handful of supporters gave their votes to Hammond on the next ballot, while bravely saying that if Hammond could not get a majority they then expected all the state rights people to turn to Rhett instead. It was a hollow declaration, not just because

Hammond easily won on the third ballot, but because there simply was no depth of support for Rhett in the body.[19] Equally pointless was the attempt of Rhett's people in Columbia and the *Mercury* in Charleston to try to make out of the result a victory for him all the same by implying that their six votes shifted to Hammond represented an alliance of the supporters of the two men under the old Calhoun state rights banner. Once again Barnwell Rhett simply seemed no longer to matter, as if he had indeed already "passed out of the world."

At least he and Katherine timed their children to appear soon enough after such disappointments to soften the sorrow, and now on January 29, 1858 she gave birth to another daughter, Katherine Ethelind, Rhett's fifteenth, and last, child.[20] Robert Woodward was still abroad, and with all the children, plus the *Mercury,* the strain on his purse was greater than ever, and this was not helped by a flare-up of his recurring rheumatism that left him seriously ill for some time.[21] When he could he attended personally to the Darien plantation, still fighting the maggots that had plagued his crop the year before, and Katherine, after recovery from her labor, returned to her task of acting as nurse to the slaves on all their plantations.[22] Sadly now, to meet his obligations and keep the paper going, he had no choice but to put half of those Darien slaves on the market, and he immediately found a buyer in Langdon Cheves. He listed thirty-eight of them, including men, women, and children (one of the women was pregnant) —"some of the best negroes I own," Rhett averred—and hoped to realize about $25,000. Cheves offered $23,750, half then and the balance in one or two years, and Rhett finally accepted without bargaining and sent his son Edmund to meet with Cheves on the Altamaha to examine the blacks before closing the deal. Cheves found a few of the blacks unfit and in the end purchased thirty-one for $20,475, paying just over half in hand on February 19.

Ever unwilling to take advantage in business, when Rhett discovered that one of the men might have syphilis, he immediately suggested a reduction in price. But when Cheves took possession, one of the women was too ill to travel and was left behind under doctor's care, only to die a day or two later, and Rhett then raised the issue of whether or not he owed Cheves a refund, even though Cheves bought the girl after examining her. "If you think on any principle of justice or honour I ought to sustain the loss, I am ready to do so," Rhett told him. "About the law I know and care nothing." He also warned Cheves about the unreliability of some statements from the leader of the slave gang, a man named Moses, who told Cheves that he and some of the others were not entirely fit and were unable to perform strenuous labor. "Moses and the women he patronises, are making the usual experiment of negroes on new masters," Rhett advised him, "that by deprecating their capacity to labour, they might do as little as possible."

It was that sense of absolute fairness in his personal dealings that often bound to Rhett in friendship men otherwise hostile to his public posture.[23]

Unfortunately, it looked like the slave sale would not be enough to relieve his debts. The *Mercury* was in desperate trouble, and typical of Rhett's lifelong preoccupation with politics to the exclusion of more practical personal affairs, he put all of his effort not into his own finances but to the salvation of the paper. In 1850 the *Mercury* had 5,000 subscribers, the same as its Whig competitor the *Courier*. By January 1858 that had dwindled to a mere 656 for the daily edition and 2,311 for the thrice-weekly version. They were paying Simms, one of their contributors, in cigars and wine instead of money. Other Southern newspapers made good profits, but they were not monomaniacal political sheets. The *Mercury* paid almost no attention at all to local news or city affairs, as most papers did. It told its readers only what the Rhetts wanted them to know and think of national events, thereby severely limiting its audience. The younger Rhett insisted that any reporters or stringers writing letters for publication from Washington should follow the strict state rights line of the *Mercury*'s editorial columns, and he would edit them if they did not agree sufficiently.[24]

As a result, by January 1858 the *Mercury* owed $26,293 in line of credit bank debt and another $18,250 in bonded debts. On paper it had assets of $20,500 in office equipment and subscription list, and another $48,113 in advertising and subscription accounts receivable, which meant overall that it had a net worth of $24,070. Operating income for the past four years ran ahead of expenses by about $29,000, and somehow Rhett projected that actual income ran about $10,000 a year. It all looked good on paper, and that is how young Barnwell Rhett presented it to Hammond when he proposed to him that the state rights men in the state, now behind Hammond, should raise a five-year loan of $15,000 to keep the paper afloat and relieve it of its enormous bank debts and at the same time undertake to increase its subscriber list. Now at last he revealed a major part of the motive for the abortive suggestion earlier that the Rhetts and Hammond had joined forces. The *Mercury* needed Hammond and the mainstream state rights men he represented to save it from ruin. But in Barnwell Rhett's presentation, it was the party that needed the *Mercury* as an "independent and influential paper," oblivious of the fact that no one in South Carolina would ever regard a Rhett newspaper as independent of the senior Rhett. Barnwell raised the specter of Orr and his National Democrats handing the state over to nationalists and argued that only a strong *Mercury* promulgating state rights views could save them but that to do so it must be "beyond reach of pecuniary embarrassments."[25]

Hammond had been considering the possibility of buying or starting a newspaper as an organ for his constituency for some time now, having Hayne investigate hiring an editor from the Upcountry, but he concluded that he really did not need a journal of his own. The nationalists were a problem, but Rhett's warning was all too self-serving. Hayne advised him that those whom Rhett condemned were really just those who opposed "the selfish & self-sufficient Journal" itself, and that "the vexatious & silly arrogance of the 'Mercury'" had brought its own just desserts. Hammond was wise enough to see through the Rhetts' proposition, of course, and yet did not want to see the *Mercury* die all the same. "The Rhetts have played the devil with it," he told Simms, but he then cannily added that it would never do to discount them. He had seen Rhett rise and fall to rise again before. "The Rhetts may be in position shortly again," he speculated, with the smoldering issue of Kansas still threatening to split the Union. "A few weeks then you see may bring the Rhetts up."[26]

Rather than raising a loan, then, Hammond's friends began to look into buying out the Rhetts instead. Heart was disillusioned with his partners, complaining that the paper lost ground because of the perception that it was a Rhett organ. "Old Rhett writes an occasional article, always on the one text," said Simms. "Young Rhett's work upon the paper might be done by an ordinary man in 20 minutes per diem." Meanwhile Heart did all the business work of selling advertising and subscriptions, handling the banks, and more. The previous fall he had tried to swing the paper away from extremism, softening its editorial approach and suggesting that South Carolina should only attempt to enunciate the issues before the South but leave it to other states to lead for a change. There would be no more talk of unilateral action, but henceforth the *Mercury* would stand behind cooperation.[27] The young Rhett went along for a while, perhaps even initiating the apparent change, since it came just before the senatorial election and might help make him more palatable.

Now, though, Heart had had enough. In March he proposed to Hammond that they raise funds for him to purchase his partners' share.[28] This was a much more attractive proposition, for it would save the *Mercury* financially, remove the poisoning influence of the Rhetts, allow the paper to reflect more the mainstream of the state rights party, and still give them an organ without all the trouble of starting one of their own. Soon Simms, Miles, Hayne, and others were all involved in investigating the possibility, the idea being to put Simms in the editor's chair, though he felt himself too old now. The immediate problem was all the debt—seventeen thousand dollars to the Bank of South Carolina alone and more than forty thousand dollars to other creditors. The Rhett share of the business was worth about twelve thousand dollars, and that above all would have to be paid first, thought Simms, "so as to get his influence completely away." One idea was for Heart to allow a debt foreclosure, and then to buy it back on the open market with investors' money for probably only half of the outstanding mortgages, but Heart argued that such a course would damage the sheet's prestige. Hammond shared Heart's concern but saw foreclosure as the only way. It was ridiculous to pay twelve thousand dollars to buy half of a paper that had fifty-six thousand dollars or more in liabilities and at best twenty-five thousand dollars in assets, for he rightly discounted all the huge accounts receivable that likely could never be collected. Of one thing Simms was certain. It would take a long time and good luck to return the paper to profitability after years of mismanagement and, worse, editing.[29]

Another idea occurred to Simms instead. Heart and Rhett had a mutual buy-out provision in their agreement, and Simms suggested that Heart should instead sell to Rhett, predicting that "if they do, they are ruined." If the elder Rhett became the sole proprietor he would lose all patronage, get no new business, and lose the patience of the banks who had a long history of unhappiness with him. Forced to support the journal out of his own pocket, he would not last a year before there was a foreclosure, and then Heart or anyone else could buy the *Mercury* for ten thousand dollars or less, a savings in money that had the added bonus of ruining Rhett. Heart was more than sufficiently unhappy with his partners to prefer that option.[30]

The trouble was, however they looked at the *Mercury*, it appeared to be doomed no matter what the cost. Hayne met with the Rhetts and came to his own evaluation, which showed that seventy-six thousand dollars at least was needed to get it out of debt. Anyone acquiring a half-interest short of a foreclosure sale immediately bought half of that debt. The assets were overvalued, the press and equipment not being worth more than five thousand dollars, and the debts due would never come in at more than twenty-five thousand dollars. By April the subscription list was down to only 550 for the daily, worth almost nothing. He suggested that the state rights men should buy the struggling *Charleston Standard* and add its list and advertising to the *Mercury*. They could get it for as little as six thousand dollars, which the owners would contribute to a newly capitalized firm, with another forty thousand dollars to come in subscriptions from leading friends of Hammond. They could raise enough to reduce the *Mercury*'s debt to twenty-six thousand dollars, which, after collecting a realistic proportion of the accounts receivable, should see the burden of debt eliminated or reduced to manageable proportion. Thus the *Mercury* would be reformed on a sound financial footing, with a distinguished new management that could expect to attract significant patronage with the Rhetts out of the picture. "In proper hands," it could still be a force for good.[31]

The plan to find investors ran afoul of the problem that Heart was nearly as much disliked as the Rhetts, and backers did not prove anxious to put their money in any enterprise connected with him. Some thought they could keep Heart in a capacity that would not allow him to interfere with the paper even though he was still a half owner, but by mid-April, Heart started applying heavy pressure for a decision. He had learned that Rhett was about to realize enough money from the slave sale to Cheves to buy him out, and if the Hammond people did not come up with something first, he would be forced to sell. Finally Hayne proposed the scheme he had outlined to Hammond for a share raising. At first Heart refused, but he then changed his mind. Unfortunately only then did he reveal that in all the statements of debts and expenditures, no one had included the salaries that he and young Barnwell Rhett drew for their professional services, which amounted to about six thousand dollars a year. Adding that to his earlier calculations, Hayne saw that even after the reduction of debt, there would be absolutely no operating profit after salaries to further retire debt. As far as building any equity was concerned, the *Mercury* was worthless. Only "patriotism & politics" would induce anyone to invest, he concluded, for there would be no profits now or in the foreseeable future by the best of calculations.[32]

It all came to nothing, for when Rhett received his payment from Cheves, instead of using the money to pay off much of his own debt, he paid it instead to Heart to buy him out. Hammond and his friends learned the news at the end of May, though it amazed all of them to think how Rhett could carry on the paper along with his other all too well-known financial disabilities. Everyone predicted his ruin. On June 7 the *Mercury* announced the dissolution of the Heart-Rhett partnership and the assumption of Barnwell Rhett Jr. as sole proprietor. He published a restatement of the paper's historic principles and pledged to continue to stand for the Constitution as shaped by the Virginia and Kentucky Resolutions and further molded by the philosophy of Calhoun. It would defend the South, expose aggressions, and propose "the best means for repelling" any such assaults on their rights. Confessing that the paper had not been profitable, Rhett went on to aver that its warnings, if not its budgets, had been accurate and that its "ultraism" had proven to be wisdom of a high order. He said that its greatest misfortune had been to be right in its opinions "expressed in advance of the times." It was the old Rhett plea of having been too far ahead of the people and the age.

Significantly, however, young Rhett showed that he was gauging the times carefully now. During the protracted negotiations over the *Mercury,* Hammond confessed grudgingly, "I concur in most things with the Rhetts except that at bottom I prefer—at least to *try* the Union—after the Free States have the ascendancy." Certainly the state rights people needed more than ever to unite the South for its own protection and challenge every aggression on their rights, but that could be done, he thought, without the need for "croaking, for denouncing, for keeping our voices always strained to the highest key & using no language but vituperation as the Rhetts do, & can't help doing."[33] After the brief foray toward the center the previous fall, the Rhetts predictably took the paper back to its old radical stance in response to affairs in Kansas. Proslavery men in 1856 had sacked Lawrence, Kansas, and in retaliation an abolitionist fanatic named John Brown had massacred slaveholders, starting an outbreak of small incidents that kept "Bleeding Kansas" in the headlines. Buchanan appointed a new governor in March 1857 who tried to organize a territorial government and frame a constitution. Antislave men boycotted the proceeding, thus ensuring that slavery would prevail by default. But then that fall the antislave people took control of the new legislature, and in the spring of 1858 they held a referendum on the so-called Lecompton Constitution. This time it was the proslave men who boycotted, thus seeing the constitution and slavery rejected. Buchanan tried to get Kansas admitted as a state under Lecompton in spite of the referendum, but it failed in Congress, which passed a compromise bill in April that essentially offered Kansans a bribe. In a subsequent election, if they approved Lecompton, with slavery, they would receive an enormous grant of land and be admitted as a slave state. If they rejected it, statehood would be postponed until another constitution could be framed. Either way the South won for the moment.

All during the growing controversy the *Mercury* became increasingly inflammatory again, seeing in the rising emotions over Kansas a possible lever to pry South Carolina back toward secession. But passage of the compromise completely defused the situation right on the eve of the Rhett takeover.[34] Robbed of the only issue going at the moment and faced with business realities ahead of them, the Rhetts had virtually no choice but to back away from their old stand. Nowhere in the new statement of policy did the family watchwords of secession or disunion appear. Far to the contrary, he pledged now to use the *Mercury* as a force to unite all parties to the defense of the South. To some it might appear that the Rhetts were changing their tune, moving more to the center of the state rights party and aligning themselves truly with Hammond and others. In reality, of course, they were doing nothing of the kind. They had simply acknowledged the fact that if they and their paper were to have influence, it must survive, and to survive it must attract more readers and advertisers. The way to do that was to soften their tone and broaden their appeal, but it would only be an expedient, not a genuine sea change, and they would always be ready to leap back to the extreme when the moment was ripe.[35]

Within six weeks the Rhetts also bought Spratt's *Southern Standard,* paying just eight hundred dollars but acquiring twelve hundred subscribers, thus overnight tripling the *Mercury*'s circulation and adding seventeen thousand dollars in annual revenue. The Rhetts announced that both papers would follow the same line in supporting the Democratic Party and abandoning separate state action. "This is news," proclaimed a competitor, mindful of the *Mercury*'s long history of opposition to nationalism and consolidation.[36] The change did not immediately improve the atmosphere in the *Mercury* office, however. Heart continued hanging around every day more than a month after the sale, annoying the staff and impressing one of the new editors as a "thief and a liar." Eventually the Rhetts tried to get Heart a civil service appointment in Charleston to provide him support and get him out of their way. Meanwhile the staff were overworked, with one new writer, George Gordon, forced to run around town trying to sell advertising and collect on bills when he had been hired to do editorial work instead. He confronted the younger Rhett over the matter, declaring, "I am not to be sent hither and yon, for all the Rhetts combined," but Barnwell only walked away leaving the matter unsettled.[37]

During the upheaval attendant to the buyout of Heart and Spratt, the elder Rhett remained quiet and above the proceedings, though certainly he was behind every move his son made since it was the father's money and slaves that financed the deal. And tentatively he began to be involved in public occasions again. In 1854 Charleston nominated him as a city representative to a Southern Commercial Convention that it hosted in April, but his attendance was quiet, and in the wake of the Missouri Compromise repeal the meeting remained relatively unpolitical.[38] He had skipped a regional commercial convention in Knoxville in 1857, but early in 1858 Yancey invited him to attend a similar event scheduled for Montgomery in May, and Rhett agreed. By now the conventions revealed dramatic change. Yancey was attempting to exert the sort of leadership that Rhett had tried and failed at, calling the fire-eating secessionists from all across the South to gather and address their future course. The conventions now were thinly disguised political meetings, with increasingly few businessmen present and ever more politicians, and in Montgomery, Yancey hoped to capitalize on the Kansas Lecompton controversy to refuel the secession fire.

When Rhett arrived in Montgomery he joined a band of delegates that a local editor described as including "every form and shape of political malcontent," bound only by their anxiety to "assent in any project having for its end a dissolution of the Union, immediate, unconditional, final."[39] Not surprisingly, fellow delegates asked Rhett to address the convention, but he wisely demurred. He felt unwell and actually missed some of the opening sessions, but in any event, even before he arrived he had determined not to be drawn into speaking publicly. The convention was really Yancey's show anyhow, and Rhett pleaded that he had come only to renew old acquaintances and exchange views with fellow Southerners. He dined with Ruffin and a fellow secessionist from Virginia, Roger Pryor, and listened patiently when Yancey addressed the crowd for hours at a time, at least once visibly all but drunk.[40] The meeting proved a disappointment to Yancey, for the recent Lecompton compromise somewhat defused that issue for the moment, and conservative men from the border states defeated any resolutions on reopening the African slave trade.

Yet the failure to agree on lesser issues may have worked to the fire-eaters' advantage. Rhett was not the only one who came to learn and exchange views. So had many others, and some like Rhett and Ruffin really wanted to sound opinion on how to bind their states closer together on secession. The failure of the slave trade issue suggested that they should abandon it since it divided rather than binding slave states. Secession must be their sole aim; all else could follow easily thereafter. All seemed to agree that the time was not yet at hand, lacking a critical issue to galvanize public opinion. Moreover, long experience still told them that they would never get all of the states, or even a few, to act in unison for secession. There was no hope, then, with the cooperationists. A single state would have to lead, and it would have to be a Deep South state, for the border states, especially the powerful Virginia to which Calhoun had long looked, no longer had the stamina for secession. United States Supreme Court justice John A. Campbell of Alabama, an opponent of secession, believed that at Montgomery the fire-eaters finally settled on what he called a "program of disunion," led by Yancey and Ruffin and no doubt influenced by Rhett's conviction that separate action was the only choice. A few weeks later Yancey would announce a new organization, the League of United Southerners, ostensibly to promote Southern rights, but its real underlying purpose had been set in the discussions at Montgomery. Henceforward the South could not rely on any political parties, national or sectional. The League of United Southerners would therefore be a movement dedicated solely to watch and wait, to choose the right moment, and then to "precipitate the cotton states into revolution."[41]

Rhett certainly had his share of influence in the private discussions that led to the league, though he would not openly embrace the organization. Although the league amounted to nothing, the convention had served a purpose in bringing together the largest assemblage of extreme secessionists since Nashville in 1850, and this time there were no compromises with the cooperationists. He went to Montgomery hoping to meet with Yancey and others "with a view to a policy for the Southern States," as he put it, and if nothing else, he returned with the feeling that he was not so alone after all, his own convictions bolstered by hearing his same sentiments from the mouths of others from all over the South.[42] It had to be heartening, and not coincidentally it was within just two weeks of his return from Montgomery that Rhett finally closed the deal for the purchase of the *Mercury*. Certainly doing so had been on his mind for some time, but now that he saw at least a nucleus for reviving the regional secession sentiment that had come so close in 1850, it was no time to give up his most effective organ for promoting his cause in South Carolina.

Instead, and despite the proclamation of a more pacific policy, the Rhetts almost immediately renewed their pressure in the pages of the *Mercury*, only stopping short of preaching secession itself since, as they confessed, "there is no issue that would warrant it."[43] Rather, they attacked all manifestations of disloyalty to the South or weakening of resistance to Northern aggression. Unity was their watchword, in the state and in the South, heralded by publishing a letter from Yancey on that theme at the same time the League of United Southerners was announced.[44] One of their first targets was Rhett's old colleague from the House and Senate, Jefferson Davis. Rhett's encounter with Foote in 1851 should have bound him and Davis together, for the Mississippian and Foote were all but mortal enemies, but the prickly personalities of both, and no doubt jealousy over Calhoun's seeming endorsement of Davis, seems to have kept Rhett at a cool, if not unfriendly, distance during their few encounters in Washington.

Now, having left office as secretary of war, Davis was back in the Senate, and in July he made a tour through New England that commenced with a celebrated speech on July 4 "at sea" aboard the steamer *Joseph Whitney*, in which he dismissed the "trifling politicians in the South, or in the North," who talked of breaking the Union. Soon afterward he accepted an honorary degree from Bowdoin College in Maine, and both acts outraged the Rhetts.[45] Davis had broken Southern unity. Immediately they loosed their editorial claws, accusing him of treason to Southern rights and outraging the slave states by taking a degree from an abolitionist college. "What a pitiable spectacle of human weakness and political tergiversation!" screamed the editorial. He was a submissionist after all, they charged, scorning the secessionists who were once his companions. He should not only go to Boston, they urged, but he should stay there, for he was no Southerner.[46]

With lesser venom Rhett at least hinted at taking on Hammond, for when he took his seat in the Senate at last, Hammond finally edged toward the Orr position that the South could actually rule by staying in the Union. Some thought that this had been South Carolina's original role in the Union until Calhoun and his nullification began the move toward confrontation. "I think Mr. Rhett the logical consequence of Mr. Calhoun," William Trescot told Hammond, while Hammond offered "the logical correction."[47] To the Rhetts that was nothing but a sellout to the submissionists. The younger Rhett first gingerly approached Hammond that summer to express their disagreement, predicting that in 1860 the Republicans would be strong enough, and the Democrats divided enough, to win the presidency and that having done that the victors would show no charity. The *Mercury* did not want to come out against Hammond, but he was betraying South Carolina. The elder Rhett was urged to issue an anonymous denunciation of Hammond and his position, but he refused to do so. "Agreeing as we do in principle," his son told Hammond, "it would be capricious and wholly without sense to quarrel on a matter of fact that time will decide." For the sake of unity in the state, the paper would not attack Hammond or any other South Carolinian personally, but it would have to open its columns to free discussion, which meant that criticism would still appear.[48]

In fact, the *Mercury*'s new policy of stopping short of secession talk cost it some goodwill among its old disunion constituency. Disillusioned with Hammond's getting into bed with the Orr forces, Maxcy Gregg now repudiated his old friend and sent to the Rhetts a scathing article that called for all state rights men to unite against the Hammond-Orr forces. There would be a Democratic convention to choose nominees in 1860. The *Mercury*, predictably, was for making no commitment to participate by South Carolina, the posture Rhett had always adopted toward national conventions until he could see where the best advantage lay. But Gregg now believed that if they waited, Hammond and Orr would gather all the place-men and weak-willed to them and force the state into the convention behind a national ticket almost certain to be headed by the odious Douglas of squatter sovereignty infamy. Gregg even suggested that the state rights men should nominate their own candidate for the senate seat to be filled that fall, and he rather clumsily hinted at supporting Rhett for the post if he backed their program. When the Rhetts declined to publish his appeal, however, he was outraged, and yet their decision made sense, for Gregg was also Spratt's partner in continuing the divisive slave trade controversy. Committed at least to the semblance of striving for harmony within the state, and still convinced that the slave trade could be a fatal issue for Southern unity, Rhett was right to refuse. Besides, he might have a chance at the senate seat even without Gregg and Spratt.[49]

But the posture of moderation was illusive, for increasingly the letters from readers that the Rhetts published attacked Hammond, even though in their editorials the Rhetts did not. They reserved their broadsides for enemies outside South Carolina, especially Seward, Douglas, and the rising Republican Abraham Lincoln, all of whom they felt free to demonize. They attacked Douglas especially as a betrayer of Democratic principles and virtually the destroyer of the party. On top of that, after Lecompton they attacked the party itself as having abandoned the South, suggesting that even the border slave states were no longer to be trusted, for Rhett had not forgiven Henry Wise of Virginia for coming out in opposition to Lecompton, destroying his credibility and weakening his state.[50]

Even with its weapons aimed at external foes, still the Rhetts drew fire for their vitriol. "Why Miles don't you make those damn fools at the *Mercury* . . . stop their war on Douglas," a friend complained to William Porcher Miles. "It is criminal wickedness."[51] Certainly it worked to weaken any chance that Douglas, almost certainly the Democratic nominee come 1860, would have of carrying the South and thus defeating the Republicans. Even some staff remained unhappy with the journal's course. "The Mercury is not managed to my satisfaction," complained one; "there is too much politics." He missed the point, of course, for the *Mercury* was intended for nothing but politics, and even he had to confess by the fall that people in Charleston were talking about the improvement in the paper with its new, seemingly more moderate tone, and old subscribers were starting to come back.[52] "We have sought to draw together," their editorials proclaimed in November. "We have eschewed all division."

Indeed, the editors condemned arousing any personal antagonisms within the state now just because of possible future divisions, a clear rebuke of Gregg and Spratt. The South was stronger than ever, but that unity came only from an outside threat to all and did not mean that they would ever have strength within the Union. The pages even began to echo some of Orr's call for regional industrialization to achieve self-sufficiency from the North. But still the old radicalism was there, as were all the old Rhett trademarks, only now growing more exaggerated. Critics and dissenters were not principled opponents but traitors, and he crossed party borders in appealing first and only to Southern loyalty. This limited the *Mercury*'s effectiveness, in that it could not elect candidates as could some solid party sheets, but it could hope to galvanize sectional fear into action. It had to achieve that aim by hypocrisy, which had never troubled Rhett otherwise in public life. He closed its columns to all contrary views, and the paper assumed an infallible rectitude, the same arrogance in print that so many had seen in Rhett on the stump. Moreover, in constantly foretelling a crisis Rhett could hardly lose, because the threat to the South was perpetual. Thus when one issue ceased to aggravate, there was always another one, or else the constant underlying perfidy of the North. It may not have been enough to redirect sentiment toward secession, but it constantly ripped the scabs from sectional wounds, keeping them open and festering awaiting the next great infection. In making the *Mercury* a reflection of himself as what some called a "one-idea paper," Rhett and his son constantly harped on wrongs rather than remedies, but of course anyone who knew the Rhetts knew what recourse they really had in mind. In trimming to pander to a broader audience across the state, they fooled few.[53]

Yet the same tensions that they capitalized upon editorially were beginning to show signs of saving the paper. Early in November the younger Rhett complained to Hammond that the debt load was still staggering, fearing that he would either have to sell or watch it fail, though in fact he was really only hinting that Hammond use his influence in the state to help increase sales.[54] In fact, by the end of the year the Rhetts saw the *Mercury* start a steady climb in subscriptions as a combination of its feigned moderation, and advancing sectional tensions made it seem increasingly relevant to Carolinians. Though no match for the financial success of the rival *Courier*, it was beginning to define Southern radical journalism as the crisis pressed on toward 1860.[55] If the Republicans could be defeated in 1860, they would be delighted and South Carolina would stay in the Union happily, but if not, then the editors "assumed" that the state would resist—no call for disunion, and no mention of secession.[56]

Amid all this the United States brig *Dolphin* captured an illegal slave ship called the *Echo* off Cuba on August 21 and brought the vessel into Charleston harbor with a cargo of 306 surviving blacks out of an original 470, whom she was attempting to illegally land in the South. Most suffered from dysentery, and another thirty-eight of them would die in the ensuing month.[57] Charleston was already excited over a new yellow fever epidemic starting to appear, but coming as it did while the debate over the slave trade still divided Carolinians, the *Echo* case produced an even greater sensation. "The great topic of conversation, the great theme of interest," wrote a staffer at the *Mercury*, "are the new niggers." Everyone seemed to be trying to find a way to get them off the *Dolphin* and out of the hands of United States officers.[58]

Rhett's reaction had to be mixed. Just the previous month on July 28 an anonymous correspondent to the *Mercury* argued that the South needed the introduction of a new "slave peasantry" to balance the large foreign immigration to the North and thus by population help preserve a balance of power between free and slave states. The only way to achieve this would appear to be a renewal of the slave trade. This was the Spratt and Gregg argument that he had previously discouraged, and it would appear again in the months to come, and from the same correspondent.[59] It was unlike the Rhetts to open their columns to views dissenting from their own. More likely it was a peace offering to Gregg and the other "slave traders" hoping that Rhett might attract their support in the senatorial contest at the end of the year, for just five days later one of them wrote to the paper nominating him for the office.[60] Thus keeping those slaves in Charleston could serve him politically with one constituency while damaging him with Hammond and many of his followers.

The immediate issue over the *Echo* was the government's intention to try its Yankee crew there in Charleston for piracy in violation of the 1807 law prohibiting the importation of slaves. To Rhett and fellow exponents of slavery, to equate slave trading with piracy was an abominable slur on the institution itself and thus upon the South. A *Mercury* editorial read, "There is not a man in our community who may not ask if it is a crime worthy of death to carry slaves from Africa even to a country which sanctions the slave trade," said a *Mercury* editorial, "what is the moral position of every buyer and seller of slaves in the South?" If the law outlawing the slave trade were constitutional, then "the Constitution lays the whole South under a black cloud of deep, damning moral reprobation."[61] The real pirates, if any, were the officers and crew of the *Dolphin,* for the *Echo* had not entered American waters when captured and was thus presumably beyond the reach of lawful authority of the Union. To convict the *Echo* crew amounted to a conviction of slavery itself.[62]

It had the makings of a landmark case, and touching the very nature of slavery as it did, it might afford the issue needed to reawaken Southern secession sentiment, for Rhett had maintained for some time that only a mortal peril to slavery itself would spur South Carolina to resistance. Here was an opportunity to argue the constitutional issues of whether the clause in the Constitution allowing Congress to regulate commerce meant that it could lawfully prohibit trade in a certain legal commodity and, equally important, whether that law could govern the conduct of American citizens engaging in such a trade between foreign nations and not actually introducing slaves into the United States. However such a case might eventuate, Rhett could make the court a focal point for the eyes of every slaveholder in the South, and that, not the judge or jury's ruling, would matter most to his purpose.

He wrote privately to President Buchanan reminding him of their past friendship, and he offered his own services and those of his old Bluffton Boy William F. Colcock as commissioners to settle the disposition of the slaves then being held at the unfinished Fort Sumter in the middle of the harbor. If he could once get them out of military hands and on the mainland, then they would almost inevitably be sold to local planters. Clearly he saw in it the potential for a test case, and for weeks afterward the *Mercury* kept the issue alive even after Buchanan politely declined his offer and ordered that the slaves be returned to Africa.[63] In the case of the *Echo's* crew, Hayne got the brief to act for the government and Spratt acted for the defense, but in November a grand jury in Columbia refused to return an indictment—some said in revenge for Northern refusal to honor the Fugitive Slave Law. The crew languished in jail until the following April when a jury in Charleston returned a verdict of not guilty. It was a decision that meant many things, but most of all it served notice that no slave trader would be convicted in a Southern court, a moment of resistance that the Rhetts cherished and tried to magnify.[64]

The *Echo* case kept interest and some passions high for months in late 1858 and early 1859, and at exactly the right time to be of some use to Rhett even if he did not get the case, for it furnished the *Mercury* with much fodder for continuing editorials. Where their former opposition to agitation at Montgomery and by Gregg and Spratt had been based on preventing Carolinians from fomenting internally divisive arguments, in this instance the federal government had created the crisis, and thus it only had a unifying effect, bringing all who believed in slavery toward the central position adopted by the *Mercury* that the slave trade prohibition was unlawful. Rhett might have made even more of that had Buchanan inserted him into the proceedings. In the end Rhett might not have been able to act anyhow, for his son Barny came down with the fever late in August, and Rhett took him to the son's home on Sullivan's Island where he nursed him for fully two weeks until the danger passed. Meanwhile he ran the *Mercury* by messages sent across the bay that offended staff with their high-handedness.[65]

The election for the senate seat came up just after the Columbia jury refused to indict the so-called pirates, and now, unlike two years before, Rhett seemed to have serious backing. This was no doubt helped considerably by his relative silence during the past year and his apparent shift toward accommodating the slave trader faction. One friend complimented him on staying true to Southern principles, unlike the "corruption & treachery of Southern Politicians (Jeff Davis in particular)," and the election of his brother Edmund to the legislature signaled that perhaps the antipathy toward the Rhetts in public office was at an end.[66] To help matters along, the *Mercury* republished Rhett's November 1856 letter to Governor Adams in order to put his policy once more in the public mind, and more and more both friends and enemies began to discuss the possibility of his election. When the legislature convened, however, it became quickly apparent just how fractured South Carolina politics was at the moment and how much Rhett's silence and apparent shifts in the *Mercury* had left people confused as to where he stood. Some thought he had embraced the Hammond platform of trying to rule from within the Union. The slave trade men, whom he might have thought to have wooed, backed Adams, who had come out for them in 1856 and had never wavered since, unlike Rhett. Christopher Memminger, John McQueen, and John Manning, cooperationists, were also in the running, and so was James Chesnut, whose views were unclear.

With such a division, only coalitions would produce enough votes to make a winner. Rhett's managers in Columbia stood on the basis of his letter to Adams and hoped thus to take votes from the slave traders, while also asserting that though Rhett differed with Hammond, still the two could harmonize on current issues if sitting together in the Senate.[67] It was a blatant attempt to cover all bases in the likely event that the first ballot produced no winner and the legislators would then be free to start shifting their votes. In fact, Adams led with thirty-six votes on that ballot; Manning got twenty-four; Rhett, McQueen, and Memminger all tied at twenty-three; and Chesnut was just two behind, with twenty-one. The combined opposition to Adams and the slave traders was clearly overwhelming, but they refused to budge, demanding all or nothing and thus betraying Rhett's hopes for their support. By the fourth ballot, in fact, it was Rhett's people who shifted, more than half of them moving to Adams or Memminger, and after four more ballots he was down to a single vote. It went ten ballots in all, and at the end virtually all of the opposition to Adams had coalesced around the uncommitted Chesnut.[68]

It was a bitter loss, reaffirming Rhett's original belief that the slave trade people would make trouble and that it was an issue promising only divisiveness. When it was clear that Adams could not be elected, that left Rhett the man closest to their ideals, and had they shifted to him he would have been in a clear plurality, though not yet a majority. By their intransigence the slave traders in the end drove state rights men supporting other candidates toward Chesnut, whereas if they had shifted to Rhett, then probably the rest would have, too. A friend told Barnwell Rhett Jr. that "if there was any 'gratitude in Republics,'" his father would have been sent to the Senate again. "Those most true to principle are rarely appreciated while living," he lamented. "The next generation will appreciate him."[69] Perhaps so, but for a man just turned fifty-eight, another generation was a long time to wait.

In fact the balloting was scarcely done when talk began of finding another office for Rhett, for despite the defeat, it was a stronger showing than in the last election, and all indications suggested that despite a considerable state of disarray and confusion among the electorate, Carolinians in general were increasingly less content with their own lack of direction. The old Rhett machine was dead, never to resurrect, but still he had a fair base of support. Some spoke now of running him for Hammond's Senate seat when his term expired, it being implicit that a definite choice between the candidates' policies would have to be made.[70] That would be several years off, of course, but meanwhile the young fire-eater Lawrence Keitt, who currently held Rhett's old congressional seat, was rumored to want to resign, and some suggested that Rhett should have the seat. Rhett, through the *Mercury*, quelled that idea. Admitting that the recent Kansas controversy made him feel that he could be useful in the Senate, he had no desire at his age actually to make a contested run for a place in the House, which would be "extremely distasteful to his feelings, while derogatory to his dignity."

Apparently, having served in the Senate, he regarded any lesser office as beneath him. Besides, in an utterly disingenuous protest of disinterest, he averred that "any mere ambition he may once have had, has been extinguished by the events of time in his somewhat stormy and unsatisfactory career as a public man."[71] Having been three times a candidate for the Senate and once nearly for the governorship during the past three years did not exactly sound like extinct ambition.

For now, undoubtedly disappointed far more by this defeat than by his previous foiled attempts to return to office, Rhett went to his Darien plantation for the winter to put behind him the scene of his misfortunes. He told his cousin Barnwell that he intended to devote his attention to his planting for a change, something he had said before and would say again but never really do. It delighted Barnwell to hear it, though, for he had always wanted to see his volatile cousin out of the maelstrom of political life. "There are few modes of living which afford more happiness than that of a Planter if he lives on his Plantation," he told Rhett in January 1859, "& few which produce more disquietude if he lives away from his negroes." Even in Georgia, however, Rhett could not escape the hands of debt, for Barnwell pleaded to be paid long-overdue interest and principal on a loan. Rhett had no choice but to put another thirty-one of his slaves up for sale and with them one of his remaining Lowcountry plantations. This prompted a neighbor girl that January to remark on "what a dreadful confusion [his] mind must be in, the plantation for sale 13 children to feed some with long coats. . . . Two others with lace & spangles, crying, fretting." She declared, "Alas and Alas for the poor man." Of course, had he but given up the *Mercury* and paid attention to his plantations instead of sinking everything into the paper, he would not have been in such a deep predicament, but always politics came first—sometimes, as now, even before his family. Somehow he did hire a teacher for his smaller children at the plantation. However, in the spring when they all returned to the Oaks on the Ashepoo, the children seemed ravenously hungry to visitors when a neighborhood picnic was held beneath one of the giant oaks from which the place took its name. Rhett could hardly know on that April evening, while watching his boys and girls gobbling up the confections "like starved hounds" and listening to a neighbor girl sing sweetly in the moonlight, that his days in Coventry were about to come to a dramatic end.[72]

EIGHTEEN

The Tea Has Been Thrown Overboard
1859–1860

NOT SURPRISINGLY HIS RESURRECTION BEGAN with a speech. Protesting that "many of your predictions are daily being verified," citizens organizing the 1859 Fourth of July celebration at Grahamville, in his old district, invited Rhett in April to address them one more time and share his views.[1] The continuing debate over slavery in the territories was only getting hotter after the Lecompton failure in the Kansas referendum. It may have prevented Kansas from becoming a free state in the immediate future, but by giving settlers the option Congress had implicitly accepted Douglas's hated popular sovereignty policy while at the same time establishing a precedent that Congress did have some authority over slavery. Both policies were anathema in the South, further alienating the region from Douglas and at the same time critically dividing the Democratic Party just when it most needed unity in the face of a strong Republican challenge in 1860. Worse, the fall elections of 1858 showed dramatic gains by the Republicans in congressional seats.

It was significant, then, that the people of the old Beaufort-Colleton district were sufficiently concerned, even alarmed, that they once more turned to their old leader. No one had asked Rhett to give a public address in South Carolina for seven years, as the state retreated from him and his brand of extremism. Always ahead of the people, as he said repeatedly, he could hardly lead when they were too far behind to see him. Gradually they were catching up, although not because of his continuing agitation, for that had been much toned down and, in any case, repeatedly rebuffed. Events of the past five years, and not Rhett, had propelled the people back to where he stood waiting. When he studied classics at Beaufort College nearly half a century before, he surely heard stressed the principles of the ancient Greek rhetoricians. In the fifth century before Christ, just after the invention of popular democracy, they argued the importance of saying the right thing to the right audience, and at the right time. If the occasion were propitious, they said, even a feeble speech would succeed, while brilliance was wasted if ill-timed. The result was to give even the commonest of men untutored in oratory a chance to best the most able professional. Rhett was not a common man, nor was he unskilled in public debate, but for him and his cause now at last the man, the hour, and the audience at Grahamville were right.

He told them nothing new. The only real difference was that they were receptive to his message. Always fond of the image of his own martyrdom, he implied comparison of his former political career to the ministry of John the Baptist, in that he, an outcast in his own state, was crying South Carolina's rights in a congressional wilderness where no one listened. He implied, too, that he was the last of the once-long list of great Carolinian champions of state rights. He proudly pointed out that even if their condition now were pitiable, still this, his old district, and they, his old constituents, had been ready to make the issue in 1832 and 1844 and again in 1850, only to be let down by the rest of the state. Their mettle had always been true, like his. They were the only people in the United States ever to have elected to Congress a representative, Rhett, who advocated an independent Southern nation.

National affairs were at the crisis, he said. The foolish Buchanan, for whom Rhett confessed high personal regard, had seen his administration ruined by slavery agitation. The compromise bill putting statehood and slavery to referendum in Kansas had failed to protect slavery or Southern rights; the Union was thoroughly sectionalized between North and South over the issue; and the so-called Compromise of 1850 was proven a humbug. The South should have seceded in 1820 rather than submit to the Missouri Compromise, but instead it had yielded, and it had yielded ever since so that the growing majority in the North now looked on them with contempt. It was folly ever to suppose that they could expect in the future anything but more aggression and more subjugation. There must inevitably come a full consolidation of all power in Washington, dominated by Yankee interests and reducing the South to vassalage. In effect, according to Rhett, the North had already abolished the Constitution by its repeated violations.

Even if the North were to repudiate all its transgressions, however, and halt all oppression, still he would reject it now. "To be a free government to us," he declared, "we must be able to control it." It must be *their* government, not that of others no matter how charitable they might be. There, and there only, lay security from oppression, especially considering the unique feature of the South, its slave population. Without naming a single example, he asserted that there were many nations and peoples who maintained the perfect equality of all races, who thought that all men were equally fit to govern themselves whether individually or politically, and it was the duty of the South to demonstrate the error of such propositions. White and black could only be happy together in society with the latter enslaved to the former, and the South could only demonstrate this conclusively if independent. Moreover, the nations of the world would support them, not out of love necessarily but out of fear and intimidation thanks to "the hostages for peace which our productions take from them." There was "King Cotton" again, and Rhett's old instinctive resort to threat as a means of statecraft.

He did not stop there. He elaborated considerably on a theme he had first addressed several years before in declaring that the Southern people required expansion and that their special combination of white ownership and black labor was the only way to cultivate the rich territory in their latitudes. Boldly he declared that "expansion shall be the law of the South, as of the North," and proclaimed, "we are of the dominant Caucasian race, and will perform our part in civilizing the world." Everything for thirty degrees of latitude above and below the equator on their continent ought by rights to be theirs by "civil conquest," and it would be; nor did they have to ask anyone to grant them title to what by rights they were entitled to take. All of Mexico and Central America, and three-fourths of South America should make up their empire, the greatest the world had ever seen, and the current colonial owners in England, France, Spain, and Portugal presumably would not risk the loss of cotton by resisting their advance. If not mere rhetorical hyperbole, the idea held at least a hint of megalomania, and yet the audience cheered the prospect.

Independence, slavery, and empire—those were his promises to them and the stakes they had to lose by remaining in the Union. "We must act," he demanded. "We must resist." Even if all the other wrongs they still faced in unjust taxation and tariff were not enough to move them to action, the denial of this their destiny surely should be. "Delay is the canker of great enterprises," he admonished them, as he had so many times before. They had been patient for thirty years bought only by degradation and shame. The abolitionists, not content with stealing the territories, would soon move for the abolition of slavery where it already existed. Inevitably they would use their majority in Congress and the probability of a Republican president in the near future to spread their control to the last defense of rights, the Supreme Court, which was already embattled after the Dred Scott decision. "The mutterings of the political tempest, which the next presidential election must produce, already break upon the ear," he told them. "To submit to the encroachments of this vulgar crew of plunderers and fanatics, is a degradation no other free people than the people of the South ever endured," he charged, "but to submit to their *rule* will be the desperation of a weak and conquered race—conquered without a fight."

That is what was likely to happen in 1860. They must demand their full rights and a candidate to fully represent them. He did not have to say that Douglas was not the man. He saw good signs that at last the South was aroused enough to unite more than ever before on such a course, but they must make certain that they allow no lesser questions to arise to divide them, a reminder of the cost of the slave trade debate. Then if they won the return of their rights in 1860, the future looked bright for them within the Union. If they failed, however— as he fully expected and wanted, without so saying—"let this election be the last contest between the North and the South; and the long, weary night of our dishonor and humiliation be dispersed at last, by the glorious day-spring of a Southern confederacy." He declared that the only epitaph he wanted on his grave when he died was the statement that after twenty years of trying to save the Constitution and the South, he "did all I could to dissolve her connection with the North, and to establish for her a Southern Confederacy."[2]

The speech was remarkable and showed that while he had lost none of his radicalism, still he had either matured or else managed to restrain his excesses in order to meet the ancients' admonitions to suit the message to the audience. Not once did he utter the actual words *secession* or *disunion,* though throughout their presence was implicit. Absent, or greatly restrained, was the usual distortion and misrepresentation of his enemies, and there was no mention whatever of dissenting opinion within South Carolina. His defense of slavery came in perfect keeping with Southern opinion, and his statements on liberty and free government he so couched as to sound inescapably logical. Indeed, almost everything in the speech seemed transparently sensible, yet he interwove throughout a constant thread of Southern independence as the only true means of salvation. His appeal to a virtual hemispheric imperialism on a scale never before advanced by him, and by few others, dangled before Southerners the prospect of fantastic wealth and security as a result of independence, for he did not have to say that if they remained in the Union, a North that would not allow them to spread slavery westward would hardly let them take it south.

Grahamville represented the presentation of a new Rhett, or at least the appearance of one, in a renewed bid for leadership—not in office, for a change, but directed toward the single immediate goal of the 1860 election as a step on the road to his perpetual objective of secession. Widely republished, the speech played well, even outside the state in Georgia, where one reader applauded his consistency for Southern rights and prayed that disunion was not far off. "I for one hope to have the pleasure of casting my vote for you as *President* of a *Southern Confederacy,*" he declared. "May God give you life to see this 'glorious' Union dissolved & to see the establishment of a Southern Confederacy & you the president of it."³ It was the first time that someone seems to have suggested Rhett's likely role in a new slave nation, but the role was surely something Rhett had considered long before this.

Some saw it as more than coincidence that just four days after Grahamville, Yancey came to Columbia and in a speech suggested that Southern rights people should participate in the coming 1860 convention—which through delicious irony would meet in Charleston—and present unnegotiable demands for their rights in the territories for the platform. If rebuffed, they should walk out of the convention and hold their own to select a suitable candidate. Then if the Republicans won the election—which dividing the Democratic Party was all but certain to guarantee—the governors of the slave states ought to call state conventions while Buchanan was still in office and secede.⁴ Yancey seemed to be taking Rhett's proposal for convention participation—which in itself was uncharacteristic—and giving fuller practical voice to its logical finale, leading some to conclude that Rhett and Yancey were working out some mutually hatched course of action.⁵ It was possible, though Rhett and Yancey in fact were never close personally and did not know each other well, even if Yancey did regard Rhett as a model for his own policy.⁶ Still the perception of collusion upset the cooperationists. "We must be guarded & warned of the impracticable, radical, visionary & provincial partisanship of such schemers and ambitious demagogues as Rhett, Yancey & co," a friend from Alabama warned Hammond, "or the country will drift into either ruin or disgrace or both."⁷

Certainly the two fire-eaters did begin to cooperate later that summer, when Yancey wrote to Rhett and suggested that he draft an outline for Southern policy and publish it in the *Mercury*. Rhett's "Measures for Southern Resistance to Northern Rule" appeared on October 19 and showed a more sophisticated program than he had ever proposed theretofore. While dodging the matter of whether the South ought even to attend the Charleston convention, he laid out a series of six well-crafted resolutions that ostensibly presented two distinct alternatives, though in fact all aimed toward a single end. The state legislature should issue a declaration of Southern rights and refuse to support any candidate who did not subscribe to them, particularly the Dred Scott decision that Congress had no authority over slavery in the territories. If the platform at Charleston endorsed those rights, then Southern Democrats ought to support the nominee. Should that candidate be defeated by the Republican in the general election, then the legislature ought to withdraw its congressional delegation as soon as possible and ask fellow slave states to do the same and consult on their common course. On the other hand, if the Charleston convention failed to affirm the statement of rights, then slave-state delegates should walk out at once and hold their own convention, producing their own nominee. If their candidate were elected, they should take no further action, but their candidate's defeat would call once more for withdrawing representatives in Congress and consulting with the other slave states on "means for their common safety" in a Southern convention.[8]

While seeming to offer a policy either for abiding by the 1860 election and remaining in the Union or rejecting it and presumably seceding—though again the word was not used—Rhett in fact constructed a plan aimed solely at disunion, for he, like everyone else, knew full well that Douglas men would likely dominate at Charleston and that they would be unwilling to accept what amounted to a repudiation of popular sovereignty in return for Southern support. Equally, Rhett had to know and expect that no separate Southern candidate would have a chance of victory in a three-way race for the presidency except by the remotest contingency should the election be thrown into the House of Representatives. Thus, without explicitly saying so, his measures were little more than a prescription for secession. Meanwhile the *Mercury* also continued the policy of encouraging Southern unity by counseling against any further agitation of the lingering slave-trade issue. It was not something on which Southerners could unite for breaking the Union, so it was better abandoned so that concentration could focus on the coming election.[9]

The struggle for that unity came hard, especially when so many saw clearly enough that Rhett's true goal was to disrupt the Charleston convention and thus guarantee Republican victory, creating a crisis in which finally the South would have seemingly no choice but to secede. It was madness, thought Hammond. "This is what our Rhetts . . . are working for," he told Simms, but he believed that the fire-eaters were "infatuated and besotted." Even the election of a Republican would not propel the slave states to disunion; they would acquiesce, thought Hammond.[10] There were simply too many conflicting loyalties and factions, especially in South Carolina, including those who supported Douglas in spite of popular sovereignty. Only an explosion could bring them all together.

It came just as Rhett's six points appeared in the *Mercury.* Two days earlier the abolition fanatic John Brown had forcibly taken over the United States Arsenal at Harpers Ferry, Virginia, intending to use its arms to equip a spontaneous slave uprising in the South. It was a madman's plan that was quickly and easily foiled, with Brown and his raiders captured or killed on October 18. But it electrified the South, for here was a plot to create a servile insurrection greater than anything planned by Vesey or Nat Turner, with all the horrors of rape, murder, and destruction that seemed likely to ensue. Brown's financial and spiritual support from prominent New England abolitionists was soon well known, confirming Rhett's declarations of Yankee hatred and plans for subjugation and even racial amalgamation in the South. Harpers Ferry, he declared, was "fact coming to the aid of logic."[11]

Suddenly partisans of every hue in South Carolina were homogenized by the fear of servile insurrection and Yankee conspiracy. Regardless of whether they were slave traders or submissionists, secession men or cooperationists, they all felt the same horror and fear. John Brown did more to unite them, in fact, than all the Rhetts' equivocating or Hammond's conciliations, but because of the radical nature of the perceived threat, it naturally tended to strengthen Rhett's radical solution to the Southern dilemma. Suddenly secession seemed possibly a safer risk than the alternative of waiting within the Union for the abolitionists and their black minions to murder Carolinians in their beds. Stories quickly circulated of abolition spies in their midst trying to foment rebellion among their slaves, and suddenly vigilance committees sprang up throughout the state. Rhett felt uneasy with the committees, for he was always a believer in regularly constituted authorities, and the idea of extralegal squads of frightened men arresting and expelling or even perhaps executing the innocent on mere suspicion disturbed him. "In our indignation at the aggression of the North we are in danger of dealing with men as if they were guilty without proof," the *Mercury* warned. Even when he slowly came around to support such groups, he still spoke for the need for cool heads and full justice for the accused, and a regular system of organization rather than ersatz bands of vigilantes.[12]

Carolina congressmen such as Miles started walking the streets of Washington armed, in the expectation of an outbreak of violence in the House of Representatives, and someone in the South Carolina delegation proposed to Gov. William Gist that they should be prepared to use force if necessary to prevent the election of a Republican as Speaker of the House. Gist declared that he was willing "to wade in blood rather than submit" but protested that such action would start a revolution. Nevertheless, he told Miles that if the Southern delegates in Congress decided to use force to keep the Speakership from the enemy, he would send a regiment of militia to the Capitol or some nearby spot to be ready. "I do not wish to be understood as not desiring the war to begin at Washington," he told Miles, "but I would prefer it should begin in sudden heat & with good provocation, rather than a deliberate determination to perform an act of violence which might prejudice us in the eyes of the world."[13] At Cahaba, Alabama, the newspaper *Slaveholder* suddenly and unexpectedly raised Rhett's name to its masthead as its candidate for the presidency in 1860. Though of course he could not be a serious candidate, still the act demonstrated once more that some were willing to look to him as leader not just of the moment in South Carolina but in the South, and to support the action the 1857 biography by

Wallace was reprinted as a pamphlet, this time with the Grahamville speech appended.[14]

Faced with all this momentum, Rhett capitalized on the hysteria by declaring these fears the natural outcome of trying to remain in a government with the North, hoping that when the legislature met that fall the Harpers Ferry outrage might in itself precipitate some definitive action even in advance of the coming election. Immediately he abandoned his previous call for participation in the Charleston convention, which he never sincerely wanted in the first place, believing it would only be dominated by cooperationists and that by participating South Carolina would be honor bound to go along with the majority. Meeting with the Northern Democrats would only result in a patchwork of "hollow truces," the *Mercury* bellowed. Indeed, it was impossible to meet with them now because their principles were so antagonistic. And for the Southern delegations to withdraw from the convention if disappointed on the platform actually suggested bad faith in their attending in the first place. "To go into the Convention with a determination to act with it only on the terms of a minority, is by no means a very honorable policy," an editorial proclaimed. "You put yourself in the position of being faithless to your party, or faithless to the South. Both are wrong." Indeed, now he could reveal that for two years or more he had known that the Charleston convention was doomed to failure because the Democrats would be too fragmented to achieve consensus.[15] Instead in the *Mercury* he and his son published a call to arm the state to put down any insurrection, to refuse to participate in the Charleston convention, and to pledge the state to oppose any Democratic candidate who did not come out against Douglas and squatter sovereignty. This was a sharp shift from Rhett's earlier proposals and showed how he felt he could use Harpers Ferry to abandon his caution and ratchet up his position and demands.[16]

He overestimated, however, for the unity of fear did not produce any corresponding unanimity on course of action. His brother Edmund tried to make progress on a convention boycott in the senate but failed, and all that came in the end were puny resolutions calling for cooperation among the slave states, appropriating one hundred thousand dollars for strengthening the militia, and reaffirming the old declaration of the right to secede but with no threat to do so. Once again Rhett misread, not public sentiment, but the ability of the state's leaders to commit themselves to action. Worse, the legislature's paltry resolutions rendered nugatory all of his editorials of the past summer and fall calling for action, for the legislature would not meet again until the fall of 1860, allowing another year to pass and more time for passions to cool. Hammond thought that the legislature's action finished his old antagonist for good. The

Rhetts, he said, were "dead and ought to be dead as a political clique in South Carolina."[17]

Hard on that disappointment came the crushing blow of the death of three-year-old Ann Elizabeth on New Year's Day.[18] And yet Rhett could not withdraw himself entirely from the crisis to grieve. The call for a Southern convention was almost a joke. Memminger, whom Rhett never liked and who recently earned his disdain even more by authoring the watery resolutions, undertook early in January a mission to Richmond in the hope of promoting the convention, but to no good purpose, and South Carolina's legislature did not even bother to appoint delegates. The meeting would never take place, nor could it have accomplished anything, as Rhett would have been happy to tell them all along. Nor would the South take any action so long as its leading men continued trying to remain within the national organization of the Democratic Party.[19]

Indeed, Rhett now predicted that the state rights men would not be strong enough to get what they wanted at Charleston and that Alabama and Mississippi would probably walk out over failure to sustain the Dred Scott decision and reject squatter sovereignty. That would lead to organization of a Southern States Rights Democratic Party that would form its own platform and select its own presidential candidate, thus ensuring the defeat of Douglas and the Northern Democrats and giving them an organization in place to face the almost certainly victorious Republicans. In that event their delegations should immediately leave Congress, and they would dissolve the Union. Barnwell Rhett Jr. declared that the War of 1812 was started by a "mere handful of fearless and patriotic Southern men, regardless of consequences," and that the people were only being restrained now by the cowardice and venality of their statesmen too anxious for office and power to stand for resistance. Hunter and Wise had both been trimming in Virginia, apparently with an eye on the presidential nomination, but the only effect Rhett could see from their actions was that Wise had ruined himself politically and Hunter was in danger of betraying the South on squatter sovereignty. The state rights men, Rhett's son Barnwell feared, would have to turn their backs on the Old Dominion entirely for support in the struggle. "Men having both nerve and self-sacrificing patriotism must head the movement and shape its course controlling and compelling their inferior contemporaries," he averred. There was no question, of course, as to the person the younger Rhett thought fit that requirement.[20]

The elder Rhett expressed himself unhappy with men such as Miles representing the state in Washington, fearing that they were too satisfied with office and not sufficiently aware of what was needed from them. After two months there still was not a Speaker in the House, as ballot after ballot came and went in the deadlock. There was also a rumor that Rhett wanted somehow to displace Miles in Congress. Rhett went to Washington in April for the first time in eight years but only to encourage Miles to be more active, for in fact the two were cooperating, Miles passing a steady stream of news back to Rhett. Still, when after forty-four ballots a Whig about to turn Republican was finally chosen Speaker in February, Rhett somehow thought that Miles had not done enough. He felt the same dismay when he saw that the men elected to the state Democratic convention in Columbia to choose delegates to Charleston were weaklings from the Orr faction, who refused to repudiate either Douglas or popular sovereignty the way Alabama and Mississippi had done with resolutions in their legislatures. He hoped to see a meeting in Charleston take place perhaps concurrent with the convention that would pressure South Carolina's delegation to sustain her sister states. "He is not a person, you are aware," Simms said of Rhett, "to be easily pleased with any party who does not recognize himself as the guide." Nevertheless, Hammond and others opposed the idea. "I will not be drawn into any movement of the Rhetts, whom I like but don't trust," he protested.[21]

Finally came the Democratic convention in Charleston, and it looked unrelentingly bleak for Rhett's hopes. Rhett was not a delegate and had not even been a candidate, nor would he have allowed himself to be one, given his repudiation of any participation in what he expected to be a Douglas and Orr affair from the outset. But he was there in Charleston all the same, watching carefully. On April 22, the day before the first gavel, the South Carolina delegation, almost entirely men from Orr's camp, met in caucus. Everyone already knew that Alabama was pledged to walk out if the platform did not stand on Dred Scott and the repudiation of popular sovereignty, and one state rights delegate offered a resolution that they should do the same after Alabama. Perry sat in the delegation and opposed the proposal, which was rejected. Then they decided not even to attend a general caucus of Southern delegates. "They had no more idea of going out than flying," complained the *Mercury*'s editor contemptuously. Rhett was "an active lobby member," as he called himself, and the head of one of the delegations, perhaps even South Carolina's, asked him as a contingency to draft a manifesto to be used in case the state found it necessary to join a walkout after all.[22]

When the convention opened, it was clear that the Douglas forces were in control, with sufficient majority to decide the platform but not the two thirds they needed to make a nomination. As he entered Institute Hall where the meeting was being held, Rhett met Douglas's convention manager William Richardson of Illinois, whom he had known in Congress years before. Immediately he issued terms for Southern support that, not being a delegate, he had no authority but his own to offer. "Give us an endorsement of the decision of the

Supreme Court of the United States in the Dred Scott case," Rhett said, "and
we will give you the whole South for Mr. Douglas; but fail to do this, and the
South leaves you—the Democratic Party will be divided—and Mr. Douglas
defeated." There must be affirmation of Dred Scott or a repudiation of squatter
sovereignty. In response Richardson only smiled, confident so Rhett thought,
that in the end the South would split and that enough cooperationists would side
with Douglas to give him the nomination without any bargains on the platform.[23]

When the platform fight came, a majority of the platform committee favored
affirmation of Dred Scott and a specific statement of the rights of slaveowners
in the territories, but the Douglas majority on the floor wanted to go no farther
than a statement of willingness to leave the whole issue to the Supreme Court.
That evasion was transparent, and men such as Rhett could no longer even trust
in the Supreme Court, since the Republicans could well pack it in the future to
produce any decisions they wished. The states themselves must be able to overrule the court as what Rhett now called the "final arbiter" or there was no security for the South at all.[24] Day after day the debate went on, and by April 26 one
of Rhett's old Bluffton Boys Daniel H. Hamilton, counting noses from the
wings, believed that Alabama, Mississippi, and three other states would walk out
over the platform, but South Carolina disgracefully showed no inclination to act.[25]

Finally the convention majority rejected the platform on April 28, and two
days later Yancey ostentatiously walked out of Institute Hall. His delegation followed him, and so did most of the delegates from seven other states. Amazingly
enough, South Carolina went with them, only Perry and one other remaining.
The pressure on the Carolinians to maintain solidarity with Alabama and Mississippi mounted on them from the moment they arrived, the Rhetts attribut-
ing it to the pervading public sentiment in Charleston and the fear that if they
did not go out with the other bolters, the South Carolina delegation risked meeting violence at the hands of the people outside.[26] Peer pressure, rather than decisive conviction or any influence from Rhett, sent them out. Nevertheless, that
evening a crowd gathered outside the *Mercury* office to serenade the father and
son whom many saw as the true spirits behind what happened that day.[27]

That same evening the bolters met informally and determined to convene
again the following day, May 1, to propose holding a new convention in Richmond, representing Southern interests and affirming the platform rejected by
the Douglas men in the Institute Hall convention. Sitting in the Charleston
Theatre, they referred to their recent action as "retiring" rather than seceding
from the regular convention. They determined to wait and see who the other
convention nominated, if anyone, and then their new convention in Richmond
should either endorse that candidate or nominate one of its own. On May 3 the

Institute Hall meeting broke up, with Douglas too powerful for anyone else to get a nomination but not powerful enough to get it for himself with the bolters withdrawn. They would meet again in Baltimore in June, hoping that the seced-ers would return or their states would appoint new delegates in their place. For their part, the men at the theater simply resolved on a call for the states to send delegates to their own June meeting in Richmond. Yancey denied any motive for disunion, but one delegate made it clear that they were there to save not the Union but the Constitution. Rhett, of course, took no official part, but he was there watching their deliberations all the same. The *Mercury* congratulated them on withdrawing from the "ignoble struggle" of the Douglas convention, and he and his editor son immediately began fighting any movement to persuade the state's delegates among the seceders from returning to the Douglas convention when it met in Baltimore, threatening to publish the names of any who did so.[28]

Immediately after the breakup the Democratic state convention was called to convene again at the end of the month in Columbia to choose delegates to the Richmond meeting. Men were shifting now as the heat around them grew. Lawrence Keitt and William Porcher Miles had opposed withdrawing from the Institute Hall convention, but now Miles came over into the disunion camp and began providing information to Rhett of what his recent associates among the moderates were planning, which would be helpful since it was feared that Orr and his faction would try to dominate the Columbia meeting and its chosen delegates to Richmond. There were suggestions that the new delegation should reflect all opinion in the state, but that was not enough for Rhett. He could not forget that, without the pressure around them, most or all of the state's delegates who walked out of Institute Hall might not have done so but would have stayed and likely gone along with a Douglas nomination on the hated squatter sover-eignty platform. Rhett wanted the Democrats in Columbia to select an entirely new delegation, and aided by Miles and others, he worked steadily to ensure that only men of his own leaning would be sent to Richmond so there would be no danger of the delegation simply voting to rejoin the rest of the party at Baltimore, as the Orr faction would certainly do. Soon the *Mercury* denounced the old delegation, even though it had walked out, and called for a new one. Promising not to seek a seat among them or to attempt to direct the delegates' course, Rhett even agreed to stay quiet and conciliatory, endorsing the notion that the future delegation should represent all shades of opinion. Privately, of course, he had no such intention.[29]

Just before the state convention met, a blow came from Southern members of Congress attempting to quell the rising passion by recommending to their states that they send their old delegations to the convention in Baltimore. This undermined hopes for defeating Douglas and his platform, and the Rhetts reacted bitterly, condemning the suggestion.[30] Meanwhile his old Democratic constituents in Colleton elected Rhett to lead their representatives at Columbia, Charleston chose his editor son as a delegate, and brother Edmund Rhett was to represent Beaufort.[31] Now Rhett would have a platform from which to reassert himself in state politics, and a crisis made to order for his skills.

The Democrats met in Columbia on May 30, and quickly all unity broke down in a hard battle for control. Almost from the first Rhett and his forces held the upper hand, which may have been helped by the fact that the *Mercury* had withheld its barbs on Orr recently, thus persuading some undecided Democrats that Rhett had become more moderate and could be trusted. The vacuum of leadership became painfully apparent. When Calhoun lived, his personal authority commanded obedience. "We did this implicitly and kept up the appearance of a solid column," Alfred Huger told Miles. But no one now filled Calhoun's place, least of all Rhett, and Carolinians who had acquired the habit of following seemingly had "lost the habit of thinking."[32] Thus when the convention voted for the first delegate at large to head their Richmond delegation, the two candidates were Rhett and Isaac Hayne, the Orr man, and Rhett won handily. The moderate Orr people were stunned, regarding Rhett as a lifelong enemy of the Democratic Party. As a result they virtually boycotted their own convention, refusing to nominate any more delegates, which left the field entirely to Rhett and his people.[33] "Madness ruled the hour," said Hayne.[34] The moderates looked on Rhett and his following as undisguised secessionists, bent not on party harmony in the coming election but on a sinister agendum of their own.

Ironically, now it was Rhett making conciliatory speeches to try to keep the Orr forces in the convention at least for a show of unity. He could not have been unaware of the unusual nature of his selection. Through a peculiarity of the state convention system that gave undue weight to the Lowcountry parishes, his 84 winning votes represented 112,713 white Carolinians, while Hayne's losing total of 67 came from delegates representing 148,309. Thus delegates representing a substantial majority of the people had rejected him. It was only the Lowcountry that gave him the post, and the rapid growth of Upcountry population was steadily reducing the power of the Lowcountry voters who elected him.[35] The message was clear that if this trend continued, any disunity and delay hereafter only made any future action all the more unlikely. At the same time he could hardly hope to influence other states to follow any South Carolina move if the state itself stood publicly divided. Ruffin of Virginia was in Columbia at the time and told Rhett that his state would never act first for secession, though it might follow others. If South Carolina could not be united itself, it could hardly lead.[36]

Now Rhett declared himself all but opposed to any disruptive action at Richmond. In fact, though he did not say so, the debacle at Columbia, combined with the damaging call from the Southern congressmen, had taken most of the spirit out of the Richmond movement. They would be lucky to achieve anything, and only a refusal by Douglas forces at Baltimore to accede to Southern platform demands would likely achieve the true party disruption that his critics feared was his object. Rhett tried to calm fears, unconvincingly pleading that he was never a disunionist by choice but had been forced to it by events, and that he was still willing to see them remain in the Union if it could be reformed. Even if secession should come, he promised that it would take no more than two years to reform the Union with guarantees acceptable to the South. He deliberately misrepresented his own beliefs and desires, and the futility of his dissembling now was evidenced by the fact that almost no one believed him.[37] Rhett put to the lie all his trimming statements now when he admitted a few years later that he accepted the delegate at large election, "believing that a revolution had begun."[38]

"I knew Rhett had no popularity out of So Ca," Hammond declared after the meeting, "but I had no idea he was utterly *odious*." Even friends in Washington, and fire-eaters among them, wrote to him almost tearfully when they learned that Rhett was to head the delegation. Henry W. Ravenel, a distinguished Lowcountry planter, felt fearful of dire results. "Mr. Rhett I hold to be the most untrustworthy politician in the state," he wrote on hearing the news from Columbia. "He is truly devoted to his state & to the South, but he wants judgment, & can never be relied on for statesmanship as a leader." In Ruffin's Virginia, Gov. John Letcher felt despair at the news. Now the Richmond convention had no hope of harmony, he told Hunter. "I do not think it possible, that any party can survive the leadership, of two such politicians, as Rhett and Yancey," he lamented. "Their purpose is the disorganization and overthrow of the Democratic party." Hayne bitterly spat out "Rhett!" to Hammond. Such men, he said, "would ruin any cause."[39]

The delegates to Richmond assembled on June 11, though Rhett arrived two days earlier to meet with Ruffin and others. David F. Jamison had already urged him to press the state delegation not to accept a Douglas nomination, while others only prayed that Rhett would take no active part in the meeting rather than being the divisive force that most expected.[40] In the event, almost no one did anything active. The convention sat a mere two days. The delegates from the other states were far more moderate than Rhett and his people, and as a result he was all but ignored, receiving no committee appointments and taking no part in the discussions. When they decided to adjourn and apply for readmission to the regular Democratic convention in Baltimore, South Carolina opposed

adjournment but stood alone, and only Florida joined her in repudiating returning to the Baltimore meeting.[41] It was a repudiation of everything Rhett and his
delegation had come for, and Perry, who was there, believed that Rhett was the
reason, being personally so disliked by the other delegates that they refused to
associate themselves with him.[42]

While all the others went on to Baltimore, Rhett and his delegation and a
smattering of others remained in Richmond to maintain a pointless show of continuing their convention, with no one there to convene with them. He watched
what happened in Baltimore when the regular Democratic convention reconvened on June 18 and saw soon enough that there would be no accommodation,
for this time Douglas forces controlled with an iron hand. Rhett was denounced
on the floor as one who would rather dissolve the Union than keep it together.
Then the convention refused to readmit the delegations from states that had
bolted at Charleston, guaranteeing Douglas's nomination. The Southern delegations from Richmond met in their own caucus and nominated their own candidate, John C. Breckinridge, the sitting vice president and a moderate from
Kentucky. On June 26 those delegations returned to Richmond and met again
with the Carolinians in a ratification of their nomination.[43] There it was at last.
The Democratic Party was fatally split, virtually guaranteeing the election of the
Republican candidate in the fall, and the previous May that party had nominated Abraham Lincoln of Illinois on a platform opposing any further spread of
slavery in the territories. A Republican victory on such a platform could be, at
last, the act that would push the South to secession, the program that Yancey had
advocated for some time and which Rhett had foreseen. Yet through all of these
climactic events Rhett had been a mere bystander rather than a dynamic participant, his very unpopularity robbing him of influence in the South, in the
Democratic Party, and even in South Carolina.

Rhett returned to Charleston to find a family tragedy in the sudden death of
his son Barnwell's wife Josephine from typhoid on June 30. Barnwell Rhett Jr.
felt at first so distraught that he thought for a time of giving up editorship of the
Mercury, but soon he rallied and, like his father before him, took solace from grief
by burying himself in the work of the season.[44] Immediately upon Rhett's return
from Richmond he addressed a meeting in Charleston ratifying the Breckinridge nomination. He reminded his audience of all the warnings he had given
them over the years, and of how they had lost California, thus accentuating the
danger to their interests in all the remaining and future territories posed by Lincoln. Congress for a decade now had been "the grand 'propaganda' of incendi-
arism and abolitionism," he told them. "Sectional hatred, rages throughout the
Union." Indeed, so far as sympathy or affection were concerned, the Union had

been dissolved for some time now, and Southern men like he who spoke of resistance to aggression were called traitors. The government had become a sectional despotism.

Rhett told his audience that in these dark times the true conservative man would stand first by the Constitution and accept disunion rather than see the existing government perverted into one of arbitrary power. "To preserve the Union of the Constitution and the liberty it guarantees, I have striven for thirty years," he declared, which somehow sounded strange placed beside his proclamation less than a year before at Grahamville that for twenty years he had done all he could to dissolve that Union permanently. Thrice had he asked South Carolina to interpose its sovereignty to save that Union, to no avail. She would not act without other states, and now it appeared that the restoration of the old Union of their fathers was hopeless. Now the Republicans, a sectional party with a sectional candidate committed to opposition to slavery, had nominated Lincoln of Kentucky, "a renegade Southerner" traitorous to his birth. Equally bad, his running mate Hannibal Hamlin of Maine bore black blood, an unfounded assertion that Rhett made with no basis other than an unconfirmed statement in an obscure Southern newspaper, but to his mind a rumor that was useful instantly became fact. "To reward a traitor to the South, and to insult the South, by placing over the Southern States, in the Senate, a man of negro origin, is the policy of this sectional party," he charged. "Hatred and malignity, as well as sectional ambition, has dictated the choice of their candidates." If they succeeded, the South would become little more than a subject colony of the North.

The course the state must pursue should be obvious, but the North now held them in such contempt that Southern threats, which in the past the Yankees repeatedly declined to back by action, would be meaningless. "They hate, without respecting us," he warned. Nevertheless, his people could still prevail if resolved. Lincoln could be beaten, he told them, though certainly he never for a moment believed it himself. Defeat the Republicans, and the South might be safe within the Union. But if Lincoln won, then the Constitution was lost and the old Union they had known and loved was overthrown. He did not tell them what then they ought to do but counseled them to "ponder well on your condition under such a state of things, and be prepared to meet it. It may be the turning point in the destinies of you and yours forever."[45]

Significantly, Rhett did not call for secession or even mention the word. Sensing that his prestige had been wounded by the Richmond fiasco, and by the uproar over his election as a delegate, he took a circumspect tone in the summer following the nominations. Even Miles complimented the temperate nature of Rhett's speech. Hammond mused on the ancient myth of Cassandra: she was given the power of prediction in return for her love, but when she reneged on the contract, Apollo ensured that no one would heed her warnings of calamity. Rhett seemed to have been born under her star. "How unfortunate that Cassandra came to preside over his birth & make him say the wisest things, so out of time & place, that they are accounted by those who rule, mere foolishness," Hammond said of him now. "What a pity that such fine talents should be thrown away on such a perverse temper." No one listened to Rhett in 1828, or in 1833, or in 1844, and now it appeared at last that it was not because of the message, but the medium.[46]

The *Mercury* suffered as well in public opinion after its past course, yet now when its counsel was most needed men seemed reluctant to heed its advice. To regain its position of trust, now it proclaimed its goal of placing matters squarely before its public "without bias or exaggeration." However, the father and son Rhetts simply could not control their instinct for hyperbole and defamation. They refrained from attacking South Carolinians and Southerners in general, as before, but no Northerner and certainly no Republican was safe from vilification without regard to fact. The paper gave its readers the impression that the only points of view in the North were those of the abolition extremists such as Owen Lovejoy, William Lloyd Garrison, Charles Sumner, and more, ignoring entirely the broad base of moderates, including Lincoln and even Seward, or else distorting their views.[47]

The Hamlin slur was but one example. There was not a word of truth in the suggestion that he was a mulatto or quadroon. Although the younger Rhett had tried to investigate the rumor inconclusively, Rhett stated it as fact from the podium and his son in the *Mercury,* with much of the Southern press quickly echoing the charge. It was an entirely new usage of the race issue, inaccurate and irresponsible, and designed solely to raise the level of racial outrage to a new height in which the Republicans posed not just a threat to slaveowners but to all whites for whom the subordinate place of blacks in their society was a necessity, and for whom the prospect of having a man of Negro blood just a step away from the presidency raised threats that went beyond economics to strike at the very heart of their culture and society.[48] Such outrage, however, could be useful for the Rhetts' own ends now. "Success is no criterion of duty," the *Mercury* proclaimed early in July, but much of its editorial policy this season suggested that success did at least justify any means used to achieve it.[49] Soon those who sincerely backed the Breckinridge candidacy let it be known that they preferred that the Rhetts and the *Mercury* not come out actively for their candidate, fearing that support from such a quarter promised more harm than good. In fact, Hammond told Simms, "so rampant have Rhett, Yancey & Co. made *Unionism,*" that the Breckinridge men "would *pay* largely I believe if the Mercury would *attack* them."[50]

Some saw other motives behind Rhett's apparent change of tone, and Miles for one showed that though he thought Rhett sounded temperate for a change, still he was not taken in entirely by the fire-eater's new pose of moderation and general silence as the campaign proceeded. Agreeing that Rhett's recent Charleston speech had been correct in all its positions, still Miles remarked that "it is undoubtedly the fact that nothing coming from him carried any weight or accomplished any good." Certainly he, like others, did not believe Rhett's assertion that his efforts had ever been to save the Union. "The truth is," Miles told Hammond, "Rhett finding that his ultra course has not given him control of the state is now bidding for the suffrages or at least the approbation of the more moderate of the states Rights men."[51]

Miles, Keitt, and several others thought they saw the reason too, which was that Rhett hoped to displace Hammond that fall when the legislature met to fill the Senate seat he currently held. Hayne had suspected as much since April.[52] A few years earlier they would have been right, but for once they were probably mistaken in their judgment of Rhett's ambitions. His real goal was secession, as it had been for some time, and if that happened, any seat in the Senate would be meaningless. He did have his eyes on an election, though this one the fall contest for seats in the legislature. If Lincoln were elected, it would be up to the legislature to issue a call for a state convention to meet the issue, and Rhett wanted to have the right votes in place to accomplish the object. Despite the denials of some, it soon became apparent that Rhett and the *Mercury* were working toward promoting candidates friendly to their cause. Rumors of a "Mercury ticket" circulated, attached to hints that the paper's support for candidates would hinge on their support of Rhett, though he disavowed any desire for men to commit themselves to him for any office. As a first step, in mid-September, Barnwell Rhett Jr. was nominated for a legislative seat from Charleston.[53]

Yet Rhett trod a tortuous path this season, for it was evident that many, even in secessionist ranks, still rejected any idea of leadership by him. Indeed, should Hammond retire from the Senate, they were prepared to back Gov. William Gist for the Senate rather than Rhett, and Keitt told Hammond that he need have no worry of a serious challenge. Even secessionist editors such as John Cunningham of the *Charleston News* repudiated Rhett's leadership, and a friend of Hammond assured him that "you can beat any spavined old horse like Rhett."[54] The problem was the confused state of South Carolina. The state had come close to secession before, then backed away. The new crisis now was the greatest yet faced, but the long years of acquiescence might have fatally weakened any resolve to resist. As a result Rhett seemed to waver from constituency to constituency, trying to overcome his own reputation and at the same time build some consensus. Maintaining that resistance would preserve rather than break the Union, he was even rumored to have declared again for the Union in September, despite the fact that other moderates, including even Orr, were now coming out for secession in the event of a Lincoln victory. Others, such as Chesnut, dodged the issue, while Hammond opposed any separate state action.[55]

Most of the discord centered on the matter of South Carolina acting on its own, for no one could forget that when she tried it before in 1832 she found no other states coming to her side. In August, Keitt and Boyce declared that the state should secede alone after a Lincoln election, but Rhett trimmed, saying in the *Mercury* that separate action could not be considered "until events shall make up the issue." Rhett now said he favored unified action by all Southern states. Failing that, then the Deep South cotton states should act together. "If this fails, then we should strive to get the co-action of four, three, or two of the Cotton States" and only then consider separate action. That stance found many adherents, even among those not used to agreeing with Rhett, who felt that discussion of separate state action now was premature. It was their way of avoiding facing a difficult decision, one that Rhett would have welcomed, but if it helped to build a constituency by binding the cooperationists more closely with the outright secessionists, then Rhett could continue to trim his sails for the time being. The *Mercury* continued to make it clear, however, that even just one state alone had the right to break up the Union and even to "produce a Southern Confederacy," though Simms urged Rhett that any talk of a new Southern nation now risked losing the moderates and the fearful. "The fruit is not ripe," he told him, but it would be soon enough.[56]

Rhett never expected that South Carolina would be alone for long if she went out separately. Once the Union was broken, the other slave states would have to rally to her to resist abolition rule. The debate hinged on the proper response to a Lincoln victory. Buchanan would be a lame duck for four months thereafter, which would give them time to act if they chose.[57] Some people favored calling a Southern convention, while others took the view that united action with only two or three other states would be sufficient for secession, which the *Mercury* had echoed. Gist sent letters to the governors of all the other slave states asking if they would secede after a Republican victory, and not one replied that his state would unless South Carolina or some others went out first. When questions were put to candidates for the legislature on what course they favored, almost to a man they hedged, espousing resistance but declining to explain what that should entail. Only a few, including Keitt and Gist, forthrightly called for unilateral secession. "I think we will have to secede first," Rhett told his cousin Robert Barnwell in October. "I have aimed at nothing but a Southern Confederacy," which would come if they took the lead.[58]

In such a sea of opinion Rhett could hardly see the true course to steer. All he could do was continue to speak out for resistance but, like the legislative candidates, avoid committing himself or the *Mercury* on a specific policy. Behind the scenes, however, the Rhetts laid plans and even began to prepare the public to deal with the possibility of an outbreak of violence in the wake of the election. Discussing the hypothetical possibility of secession followed by a new Southern nation, the *Mercury* declared in September that "for the *speedy* formation of a Confederacy of *all* the Southern States, the best instrument, we believe, will be the sword."[59] By early October there were rumors in Charleston that Francis Pickens, former governor James H. Adams, and the younger Rhett had helped organize a group called the Minute Men for the Defense of Southern Rights, which formed itself October 7 in Columbia. They reputedly held meetings to hear inflammatory speeches, wore blue cockades in their hats as symbols of resistance, and required each member to have a rifle or pistol ready to use in a march on Washington to prevent a Lincoln inauguration. Columbia had three hundred members, and another four hundred joined in Edgefield, with the Charleston membership unknown. The organization was genuine enough, though its aims were shrouded. The charge of intended interference with the inauguration may have been nothing but rumor, but it was pervasive enough to reach Northern ears and have officials worried, and certainly the *Mercury* gave the Minute Men some editorial backing.[60]

At the same time the Rhetts tried to dilute any fears their people might have about their prospective enemies should it all come to blows. Secession would be quiet and easy. The Yankees were a grasping and cowardly people fitted by nature for manufacturing but not for war. "That a people, like the people of the North, prone to civil pursuits and money-making, should get up and carry out the military enterprise of conquering eight millions of the only people on the continent, who from education and habits, are a military people," said the *Mercury*, "is one of those absurdities which none but a professed panic-maker could be capable of announcing."[61] In what was only the first of a number of hyperbolic banquet boasts, James Chesnut came off the fence to declare that he would drink all the blood shed as a result of secession, and the elder Rhett reportedly remarked in Charleston that he would join the feast by eating the bodies of all those slain, so great was his confidence that there would be no war as a result of secession.[62]

Both Rhetts meanwhile played a role growing out of the formation in Charleston in September of the 1860 Association. Concerned about the prospect of a Lincoln victory, they organized committees of correspondence and printed 166,000 copies of pamphlets urging the necessity of resistance and preparation for defense, showing special concern for Georgia, where the elder Rhett had often in the past placed hopes for independent action or an alliance with South Carolina in secession. They did not bother with the border states. "They must be made to choose between the North & South," he told Ruffin, "and then they will redeem themselves but not before." Hoping to give Alabama, Mississippi, or Georgia the opportunity to take the lead, they initiated a correspondence with the leading men in those states, including Jefferson Davis, trying to elicit from them their views on what their states would do in the wake of a Republican victory and seeking in an interchange of ideas and views the preparation of the Southern people for the crisis to come. The responses were not encouraging for any independent action, and by late October the Rhetts doubted that any of the three would act. Already the younger Rhett began to plan on publishing a scheme to effect a Southern confederacy once the election was so close that he could not be accused of influencing the outcome with his plan. "I believe we are going to break up the Union if Lincoln is elected," he told Ruffin, and a few days later he assured his brother Robert Woodward Rhett, "we expect to secede."[63]

Of Lincoln's victory in November there had never been any real doubt, though earlier in the campaign some had hoped that Douglas and Breckinridge, and another entrant, John Bell of Tennessee, might take enough states to deny the Republicans an electoral victory, thus throwing the election into the House of Representatives. That possibility looked increasingly remote by the fall, however. Partly for the reason that efforts to defeat Lincoln were futile, as well as because a Lincoln victory served his ends, Rhett contributed little active leadership during the campaign. It was to his purpose not to be seen as a leader just now, for fear of frightening the moderates away from the growing secession mood, for if he had learned anything in politics, it was that the personal animosity he could generate often worked against his policy. Besides, during the weeks leading up to the election Rhett fell ill again and simply could not be active beyond letter writing and contributing editorial columns to the *Mercury*, and holding no public office, he had no legitimate forum for asserting leadership had he been so inclined.[64]

By early November, Rhett felt well enough to plan on going to Columbia for the opening of the legislature, and it was vitally important to him that he be there. Neither Alabama nor Georgia, the only states other than South Carolina that might take the lead in secession, would have its legislature convene until after the election. That meant that South Carolina would be the only one in session when the results of the balloting came in, and thus, like it or not, she would be forced into the position of facing the decision first. He thought the legislature looked good for action, for the election on October 8 packed the statehouse with men committed to secession, their only differences being the question of when and whether to act alone.[65] William Trescot wrote him from Washington that Howell Cobb of Georgia, now Buchanan's Treasury secretary, advised delay on secession until after the inauguration, which would allow more time to build Southern unity and also allow the harvest of the current cotton crop and produce the cash necessary to fund a new government, for he agreed with Rhett that their goal must be a new Southern confederation.[66] Rhett, however, would never sanction delay. Now in Columbia he might well exert the necessary influence to bring the legislature to action, though some feared that he came to pull wires and seek election to the governorship, which terrified the more moderate.[67]

On November 5 the legislators convened, their only duty being to cast the state's votes for electors in the Electoral College, and not unexpectedly they chose electors pledged to Breckinridge. Gist asked them to remain, however, until the result of the general election should be known so that they would be in place to receive his request for calling a special convention. That same evening, before leaving Charleston for Columbia, Rhett spoke at a mass meeting in Charleston where he joined others in calling for separate state secession, and they received an enthusiastic reception from the crowd.[68] He arrived in Columbia to find that his adherents had already given up their attempt to elect a speaker from among their number, which some saw as a repudiation of any move for separate action. Now the Rhett forces instead spoke of trying to enact secession by legislative act rather than waiting for a convention, for if a convention went against them it would likely end the question of secession forever. Along with several others he made a public speech that evening advocating calling a convention for immediate and unilateral secession, and he let it be known that he was daily in communication with men in Georgia, Alabama, and Florida who said that their states would follow South Carolina if she took action.[69] More than that, he told the audience outside the Congaree House Hotel that secession was their only remedy to Yankee tyranny. The Yankees, a nation of cobblers fit for nothing better than carving wooden nutmegs, were too cowardly ever to risk fighting for their Union, Rhett told them. Out in the crowd Congressman Milledge L. Bonham did not think much of Rhett's bluster. "Mr. Rhett is mistaken in charging the Yankees with cowardice," he told a bystander. "I have seen them fight in Mexico." He would not be surprised to see them fight again.[70]

Then they got the news. On November 7 the returns from the polls made it evident that Lincoln, despite receiving just under 40 percent of the popular vote, had carried enough states to win in the electoral count. At once secession sentiment in Columbia seemed unanimous, and crowds gathered to call for speeches from Rhett, Chesnut, and others. Ruffin was there, as he always appeared when secession was in the air, and Rhett turned at once from the immediate success to the next step, wanting to know what Virginia would do now. Back in Charleston the *Mercury* hung a flag with a palmetto and a lone star out its upper-floor window and published an exultant declaration. "The tea has been thrown overboard," the editorial stated. "The revolution of 1860 has been initiated."[71]

NINETEEN

The Fist of South Carolina
1860–1861

RHETT'S HOUR HAD COME AT LAST. Yet it was the moment of greatest peril for his objectives, for he had seen too often before how fear and hesitation could set in immediately after South Carolina took a bold step. They were almost all secessionists in the legislature, but faced now with making the move that would bring it about, the old pockets of conservatism quickly reemerged, fueled by talk of waiting for other states to act with them or even to see what Lincoln did in office. As Rhett told his son, the prime rule in revolutions was not to wait and give the people time to cool. In hearty agreement, Barnwell Rhett Jr. introduced in the house a resolution calling for an election for delegates to a state convention on November 22 and for the convention itself to meet on December 17, and Edmund Rhett did the same in the senate, but neither passed.

Instead the timid fought for time. By November 9 it became evident to the cooperationists that they did not command the strength to prevent separate action by the majority, but at least they could find enough support among the more fearful to delay the convention call, and that might accomplish their ends by another means. That same day the senate passed almost unanimously a bill calling for the election on January 8 and the opening gavel of the convention a week later. That was more than two months away. It needed only house action to become law. Rhett felt almost inexpressibly frustrated. "Why do we pause in so vital a cause when all are, or ought to be ready to resent our injuries & daily insults," he grumbled to his son. The North would soon be threatening their domestic peace and even sending infiltrators to foment uprising and unrest among the slaves; of that he was certain. "Will not delay cool the ardor of our people, who incensed now would resist promptly?" Rhett asked.[1]

Rhett had already taken steps to apply the needed pressure to shut off delay. From the outset he saw the hesitation in the legislature and found it especially strong among the members from Charleston who, with the most to lose in any economic upheaval, seemed inclined to align themselves with the Upcountry moderates. Rhett knew that he dare not interfere directly himself. "He is deemed the head of the extreme secession party," observed Ruffin, who was with him in Columbia, "& his views, though adopted by all now, have previously rendered him very unpopular with all who were more 'conservative,' and more patient."[2] Now he asked friends in Columbia to telegraph an old Bluffton Boy, William Colcock, currently port collector at Charleston, and others in the city's 1860 Association advising them of what their delegates were doing and suggesting an immediate public meeting of outrage. Colcock did his part. It helped that as soon as word of Lincoln's election came, several prominent Carolinians in federal office had resigned, exciting the citizens considerably. When Colcock and the others called their meeting at Institute Hall on the evening of November 9, the people were ready to stay excited. Several Georgia leaders were there promising their state's support in secession, and at that very moment arrived a false rumor that Sen. Robert Toombs of Georgia had resigned and that the governor of his state was calling for a convention. The result was a wildly enthusiastic groundswell for immediate action, and soon three men from Charleston were on a train for Columbia, propelled by the citizens of the city on a mission to stiffen their wavering representatives in the legislature.[3]

Rhett's last-minute intervention worked perfectly. When the Charleston men arrived at noon on November 10, they quickly changed the minds of the wavering delegates, and within hours the convention bill was altered to call for an election on December 6 and the convention itself on December 17, the very day originally proposed by Barnwell Rhett Jr. It passed both houses unanimously. That evening there were celebrations in Columbia and innumerable speeches, and Rhett spoke out in bellicose terms of the "fright already spreading over the Abolition communities of the North" and warned of "the merited retribution and ruin sure to follow" in the wake of Southern independence.[4]

Rhett returned to Charleston at once to keep the popular passion high and resolve strong. He arrived to find people already starting to decorate the city with talismans of resistance, banners and flags, liberty poles. Calhoun's portrait appeared everywhere, which no doubt struck Rhett as an irony, since the old man had always stood in the way of secession. More satisfying, however, was the Charleston Restaurant's window with its life-sized transparency of Rhett fully illuminated every night. Indeed, Rhett found himself the man of the hour, a satisfying moment indeed for one so often rejected in the past. Newly formed militia paraded under the name of the Rhett Guard, and people walked down sidewalks past expressions from his speeches emblazoned on banners. He could hardly help being immensely satisfied with all these expressions of the fact that he had been right all along and that at last South Carolina had caught up to him.[5]

No sooner did he arrive than the people arranged for him to address them at a ratification meeting for the convention call at Institute Hall on November 12, and now with the movement under way, he could afford to relax his recent moderation and come out once more in his true color. "We are in the midst of a revolution," he declared in opening. Rhett informed them that they were a different people from those in the North and that they must think carefully as they faced the question of separation or possible reunion with guarantees. As of old, he gave them a long history lesson on their sectional grievances, reminded them that New England had once flirted with secession at the Hartford Convention, and did not fail to point out that he had stood for resistance as far back as 1828. He touched their memories of the state's volunteers killed in the war with Mexico, the further to outrage them that they were denied the fruits of their blood sacrifice by being excluded from California. Now had come the last insult, the election of Lincoln, "a Southern renegade—spewed out of the bosom of Kentucky into Illinois—and a Northern whitewashed or octoroon mulatto, to be President and Vice-President." The people were to be the victims of a despotism "as hating as it is hated—with all the fury of fanaticism, and all the lust of avarice and ambition, to direct its power."

For twenty years Southern generosity and honesty and faith had been met by Yankee villainy and greed and betrayal, Rhett charged. Northerners were not fit to live with any other people, for they had no concept of free government. "Their idea of such a government is, that a majority shall rule a minority," he said contemptuously, and the South had given in to them so often in the past that they looked upon Southerners with contempt now. How could the South ever hope to live peacefully under their domination? "Swollen with insolence, and steeped in ignorance, selfishness and fanaticism, they will never understand their dependence upon the South, until the Union is dissolved, and they are left naked to their own resources," he declared. He predicted economic and social calamity in the North in the wake of secession—failing banks, stilled factories, stock and real estate collapse, and bread lines in the streets. It would lead to the overthrow of the abolition fanatics, and a new Union party would reemerge, seeking reunion with the South upon its own terms and singing all the old tunes of brotherly love. But he warned them to "make your hearts adamant, to resist such affectionate appeals." Despite his opening remarks about their having a choice before them, he made it clear that their one and only alternative was complete and eternal separation. Indeed, he begged the North to pass a force bill to coerce South Carolina, for that would bring Virginia and all the border states to her side, and a strong Southern confederacy would be inevitable.

In fact, forming that new nation would only be the beginning, not the ending, of their challenges, for they would have to prevent free states from seceding to join them; of that he was certain. Theirs must be exclusively a slaveholding confederacy, however, like ancient Greece and Rome, whose glories of intellect he attributed to slavery. They must also avoid the pitfalls of universal white suffrage with the whole population controlling the government. The only safe form of government in a country where population grew faster than capital, and where the majority owned no property, was an oligarchy such as South Carolina's, for otherwise those who had not would soon use their votes to take from those who had. Further to that end, they must reform taxation in their new nation and engage in free trade with other nations, with tariffs for revenue only, no internal improvements, and no monopolies allowed or encouraged by government. Every man must have the same chance to rise or fall strictly on his own merits. And finally, even if a new confederation should be formed, South Carolina must maintain full control over the forts in Charleston harbor and never again allow any other power, even a new Southern government, to control them. Already he voiced the hint of distrust of any sort of nationalism or strong central authority in their future alliances.

Impelled by these ideas, the South could form a new constitution and a new confederacy that would last the ages and make them powerful as well as great. The nations of the world would bow to them and their produce. And that was not all. "We will expand, as our growth and civilization shall demand—over Mexico—over the isles of the sea—over the far-off Southern tropics—until we shall establish a great Confederation of Republics—the greatest, freest and most useful the world has ever seen." It was the same expansionist promise he had made ten years before at Walterborough. The South would be the new Rome, extending its brand of localism, conservatism, and slavery across half a hemisphere.

"The Union is dissolved," he told them in closing. It had been spiritually for years, and now that separation was about to become statute fact. "By the fist of South Carolina, it will be amongst the wrecks of past things." He said it over and over again. "Would that I could speak, not in the voice of the earthquake, but could whisper to the startled ear of the oppressor and fanatic, in the still small voice of conscience—the Union is dissolved!" To the North they left all the empire won in three wars by Southern generals and Southern blood, and civilized by generations of Southern statesmen. "The long weary night of our humiliation, oppression and danger is passing away," he told them, "and the glorious dawn of a Southern Confederacy breaks on our view." God blessed them, and they would soon be happy, prosperous, and free—a great people once more.[6]

The old Rhett was back—arrogant, threatening, and dictating not just to the North but to the world. Within a few days prominent men in the North took note especially of his declarations of future empire, arousing fears that slavery would be spread to Mexico and the tropics.[7] More immediately frightening to some in South Carolina was the repudiation of the wait-and-see policy. Chesnut had already resigned his United States Senate seat when he heard the Toombs rumor, and now Hammond resigned his own. But there were still great dangers from that quarter. Rhett's nephew Charles Haskell Rhett worked in the Interior Department at Washington and heard advice from Secretary of the Interior Jacob Thompson of Mississippi that South Carolina should not move so rapidly as to separate herself from the rest of the South, implying that they must act together. Jefferson Davis wrote to Barnwell Rhett Jr. on the very day the convention bill passed, bringing the unsatisfactory news that he doubted that the Mississippi legislature would call a state secession convention or send delegates to any Southern convention at this time. Even if South Carolina seceded first, he doubted that Mississippi would do so, for she sat isolated to the west. Only if contiguous states such as Alabama or Louisiana went out would Mississippi likely take real action. Worse, Davis actually counseled against South Carolina seceding unless certain that Georgia would go with her, for without the security of Georgia, neighboring Alabama might not go and thus neither would Mississippi. It was a case of dominoes in reverse. Rather than each state felling the next in line, each needed the next to stand, and it appeared that the only probable successful progression would be South Carolina followed in turn by Georgia, then Alabama, then Mississippi. Only the use of force by Washington to coerce South Carolina would likely bring all the slave states out in support, thought Davis. Meanwhile he counseled waiting until cooperation could be achieved.[8]

But Rhett was not about to stand idle now. Filing Davis's lackluster response with the other small list of grievances against the Mississippian, Rhett decided to risk leaving the state to aid the cause of secession in Georgia. It had cost him dearly when he tried it in 1850, but now the atmosphere was more favorable, and he needed to learn firsthand how affairs stood in Milledgeville, the capital. Not for nothing had he and the 1860 Association peppered Georgians with their pamphlets, believing they had been read to good effect. He went there on November 20 in company with Ruffin and the next day spoke first with three of the delegates to the legislature then just convened. They all assured him that though Georgia would not secede first, she would follow South Carolina. Then they took him to see Gov. Joseph Brown for a long and frank discussion, which revealed considerable support for secession but also a healthy opposition. That evening Rhett met with several others over dinner where the conversation turned exclusively on secession, and champagne came out for toasts to disunion. Rhett dined with Brown the next day and learned that the senate and house had both passed resolutions granting him seats on their floors as a mark of esteem.[9]

Rhett did not stay to take the proffered seats, but seeing that Georgia was on the right path with good secession managers, he quickly returned to Charleston on November 23 and turned his eye northward. Just as he had shown two faces toward Van Buren and Polk—one publicly flattering and even fawning, while the other harshly condemned them—so he also felt toward Buchanan. There had been repeated expressions of friendship and respect over the years, but they could not hide Rhett's disdain for him as a weakling and coward. Now Rhett sought to maintain his momentum by persuading and even bullying the president. In the guise of advising Buchanan of what was happening in South Carolina, and after expressions of warm personal friendship and sympathy, he told him that South Carolina's secession was a certainty and warned that if Buchanan sent any more troops to the forts in Charleston harbor as a result, there would be open bloodshed. "I trust you will not suppose that I intend to direct your judgment as to your course of duty, but simply to inform it," he added disingenuously. Then he turned even more subtle. If Buchanan had any hope of reconstructing the Union after secession, he said, a move to coerce South Carolina now would put such hope to ruin forever.[10]

By so saying, Rhett implied that reconstruction was indeed possible, even though he had rejected it entirely in his Institute Hall speech just twelve days earlier. Now he held out to Buchanan what he avowedly regarded as a future impossibility, as a carrot to circumvent immediate peril to what he believed to be a certainty. It was a sound tactic and showed a good appraisal of the gelatinous spine of the president. Yet it was an exercise in deceit all the same, a resort to one of those low tricks that separated the mere politician from the lofty statesman that Rhett pretended to be, an act he would have condemned contemptuously in someone else.

Rhett meanwhile found the campaign for delegates to the convention well under way and tickets listing several candidates for the different parishes in Charleston about to be put before the people. The tickets were prepared while he was in Georgia, and he denied having any role in their composition or even knowing who actually selected the nominees.[11] Nevertheless, his name headed most of them, and on November 26 the *Mercury* raised his name in nomination, but then in its hubris the paper almost went too far by attempting to dictate to the public those who should be acceptable as delegates. Almost without exception nominees were to run unopposed, for virtually all agreed on secession now, but still there was fear of those who favored it later rather than sooner.

Returning, like Rhett, to its old ways, the *Mercury* abandoned the pretense of moderation and now tried to influence the coming election by demanding that Charleston send a solid bloc of twenty-two delegates pledged to secession. There was an immediate outcry at the paper's effrontery, and quickly the Rhetts backed away. Instead the paper now called on all candidates to declare their positions on secession in advance of the election. Would they vote for secession as soon as an ordinance was presented to the convention, and would they thereafter oppose being reunited with any free state or states? After the candidates sent in their responses, the *Mercury* began publishing a daily list of them along with its own appraisal of whether they were "explicit" for secession or "non-explicit."

No candidates were pitted directly against one another for specific seats, but rather there were more nominees than seats in the coming convention, and only those receiving the greatest number of votes would be elected. Thus the Rhetts hoped to influence the voters to back only those explicitly committed to secession. It elicited anger in some quarters as a clear attempt to rig the convention in advance, and even some of Rhett's political friends declared the *Mercury*'s conduct "outrageous." Yet it was all parcel of Rhett's long-held notion of leadership in which the bold few dictated to the timid many and leaders were the makers and not the servants of public opinion.[12]

In the midst of the campaign another chimera arose to trouble the Rhetts, for a rumor spread just days before the election that the legislature was going to elect Rhett governor when it chose Gist's successor in a few days. Rhett seems to have made no overt efforts to advance himself for the office, though being governor of an independent South Carolina after secession would make him virtually a president and that much more powerful in dictating the conditions of association in a Southern confederacy. Gist thought the post more likely to go to David Jamison, with Rhett and his old antagonist Pickens each probably able to command no more than about 15 percent of the votes on a first ballot.[13]

Still that was enough to frighten many. Simms must have had Rhett in mind when he said that some of the candidates were "able enough, but odiously selfish," while one man who hoped for a position on the future governor's staff declared that he would withdraw his application should Rhett be that governor.[14] "For Gods sake and the sake of our beloved state don't let Rhett be elected Governor," one Carolinian begged of a member of the legislature. "It will be disastrous to us." Citing Rhett's "rashness, impracticability, arrogance, selfishness & unpopularity," he predicted that making him governor would frighten at least ten thousand Georgia voters into turning against secession in their own state and perhaps doom the entire movement. "I expect no good result under his leadership," he said. "I would look for blunders, defeat—possibly disgrace." Given the recent news that Toombs—who had not resigned—was counseling South Carolina to postpone secession until the following February and that he, Thompson, Davis, and Howell Cobb were forming a movement to induce the state to delay until then, a Rhett governorship promised only more division rather than the unity they needed now.[15]

Fortunately the fear of a Rhett governorship disappeared almost as quickly as it arose, and apparently without doing any real damage. The *Mercury* was doing enough on its own, however. Hard on publishing the candidate ratings, it presented a draft of a secession ordinance from W. F. Hutson that was so long and involved that if it were taken up by the convention, the debate would inevitably delay the actual moment of secession at a time when any delay worked against the ultimate result. The convention should simply frame a secession ordinance but leave all subsequent matters of detail to be handled later, said the Rhetts.[16]

The reaction to its high-handed attitude led the less radical men in the city to hold public meetings and advance tickets of their own in some parishes headed by more moderate men such as Memminger, and excluding Rhett's name entirely. The cooperationists, who had been at first frightened away from seeking to participate in the convention by the *Mercury*'s posture, now began to reassert themselves, and Rhett found himself attacked and indeed almost the only real issue of debate in Charleston. Only the efforts of friends, including those who supported him in spite of a personal dislike for the man, kept his name on some of the tickets in the city. There was talk of votes being purchased and even an attempt by someone using Rhett's name to get Miles, who was committed to immediate secession, to withdraw his own candidacy.[17]

Had the election campaign lasted another few days or weeks, Rhett might not have been elected at all. As it was, when the votes on the various tickets were counted for Charleston, he came in seventh overall, chosen to represent the parishes of St. Michael's and St. Philip's, with William Porcher Miles, Andrew G. Magrath, and others well ahead of him and his old opponent the moderate Memminger immediately behind. There was no concealing that it represented a repudiation of both his own leadership and that of his *Mercury.* Even one of his supporters complained after the election that Rhett was "so damned impracticable, that I am afraid he will kick up hell in the Convention." Rhett confessed his mortification at this most public display of disapproval and dislike.[18] The election of Pickens a few days later as governor, with Rhett's name never seriously in the running, only added to the embarrassment.

But nothing was going to deter Rhett from his relentless pursuit of his ultimate goal. Though the success of a few cooperationists in the convention election, and the selection of Pickens and the high ballot for Memminger, revealed a resurgence of moderate feeling, he charged ahead, even allowing the *Mercury* to attack Virginia and Maryland as weak and deluded "fleshpots" for remaining in the Union. South Carolina, Alabama, Florida, Georgia, and Mississippi would be more than enough to form a new confederation, and confident of them at least, he took it upon himself to determine the foreign policy of the new nation even before its presumed components had faced secession itself.[19]

On December 15, Rhett paid a call on Robert Bunch, the British consul at Charleston. Whatever his chagrin over his recent humiliations, Rhett appeared to Bunch to be quite full of himself with pride that his long-held doctrine was about to come to pass. Indeed, despite recent evidence that his support in the state was marginal at best, he succeeded in persuading the consul that he wielded considerable influence, and from that position he proceeded to dictate to Her Majesty's representative the nature of the proper future relations between Great Britain and South Carolina. Secession was a certainty, and Buchanan would not interfere, he said. Indeed, Buchanan would soon give up the forts and other federal installations and offices in the state, he averred, ignoring the president's annual message to Congress twelve days earlier in which he said nothing of the sort but rather stated that the garrison in the forts would defend against any attempt to expel them.

Now Rhett wanted to settle the terms on which South Carolina and the future confederacy would trade with England, for he predicted that there would be enough states seceded to form a new nation by February 15 if not sooner. They would want an alliance with Britain and would prefer to trade with her above all other nations. The South would demand free trade with nominal rates only for necessary revenue, perhaps 15 percent import duties to start but rapidly falling to 5 percent, and eliminating duties altogether with nations that made treaties on the South's terms and overlooked any objections to slavery. Boldly telling Bunch that his nation was dependent on Southern cotton while the South needed British manufactures, Rhett explained that theirs should be a relationship of mutual dependency.

Rhett dismissed English opposition to slavery as incidental and ignored Bunch's reference to Britain's moral antipathy toward slavery and the hope that his nation might be an example to the South. According to Bunch, the British government at least would probably want a repudiation of any intention to reopen the slave trade before entering an association with the new confederacy, but Rhett bristled at that. It was not negotiable, he declared. "To prohibit the Slave trade was, virtually, to admit that the Institution of Slavery was an evil and a wrong," he protested, "instead of, as the South believed it, a blessing to the African Race and a system of labour appointed by God." If Britain insisted on this point, there could be no relations between them, and the South would grant most-favored-nation status to France or Germany instead, both of which would gladly overlook the slave trade to get the trading terms the South offered. The threat was implicit that Britain would be left behind other nations, and Rhett counted especially on the ancient antipathy toward France to influence English opinion. But Bunch was not to be bullied and reminded Rhett that he was a bit hasty in counting on France and others. All European nations were signatory to a treaty outlawing the slave trade and binding them to suppress it, and they would hardly tolerate in one nation what they condemned in others. Rhett immediately backed off and then disingenuously suggested that he did not himself favor bringing any new slaves into the country but expected that states farther west that needed more fresh labor would insist on a revival. He offering the opinion that the South might agree to limiting a reopening to just a few years and then cease.[20]

Good diplomat that he was, Bunch listened without committing his government to anything, but he quickly formed the conviction that Rhett was a man unduly impressed with himself. He suspected that the Carolinian might harbor hopes of being the new confederacy's ambassador to England but had no doubts that he "indulges in an abundance of utterly absurd invective against all who differ from him."[21] Two weeks later, seemingly quite satisfied with his call on Bunch, Rhett told Ellison Capers that England and France would grant diplomatic recognition to the new nation by April 1861, and that if Washington tried to impose a blockade on Southern ports, those nations would break it and leave the North "like a chicken, with his head cut off." Rhett communicated his cocksure certainty to his brother Edmund, too, who soon told a British visitor, "you must recognize us, sir."[22] Once more Rhett was at his old habit of assuming authority he did not have, speaking for constituencies he did not represent, and expecting eventualities to occur simply because he so willed them.

For Rhett's plans to take shape, first South Carolina had to secede. On December 17 he joined the other delegates, two-thirds of them planters and almost all slaveowners, as they gathered in the First Baptist Church in Columbia. When the call went out for nominations for president of the convention, his name was put forward along with others, but on the first ballot he received a mere 5 votes out of 169 present and thereafter disappeared from the voting entirely—yet another facial slap to any ideas he had of exerting real leadership. Instead they selected the old Blufftonite David F. Jamison as president of the convention, which showed that it was Rhett himself and not his ideas that they rejected. Undeterred, Rhett entered the brief debate that day to suggest that they should not only decide on an ordinance of secession but also consider the nature of their relations to the other states and perhaps consider amendments to the state constitution made necessary by their revolutionary action.[23]

Those issues and a unanimous resolution that they should secede were as much as they accomplished, for an outbreak of smallpox had Columbia in a panic, and the members deemed it unwise to remain any longer. They adjourned to meet again the next day at Institute Hall in Charleston, away from the epidemic, and at 4:00 A.M. the next morning Rhett joined the hundreds of others at the South Carolina Railroad depot in the scramble to escape the pestilential capital. It was well into the afternoon when they reached Charleston and hurried to Meeting Street and Institute Hall, which sat between the Circular Church and the Teetotal Restaurant that served soda water instead of spirits. They found the hall decorated with a banner showing an arch composed of fifteen blocks of stone, each named for a slave state, with South Carolina the keystone, and a Roman-garbed Calhoun perched atop. "Built from the Ruins," proclaimed the banner, and there was also a banner with fifteen stars and the words "Southern Republic" emblazoned across it, flying from a palmetto next to the arch. At the foot of the arch—which perhaps significantly rested on foundation stones named for Texas and Virginia—lay the crumbling remains of blocks identified as Massachusetts, New York, and the rest.[24]

The delegates met for barely an hour before adjourning at 5:00 P.M. Jamison named several committees, including one to draft a secession ordinance, and appointed Chesnut, Orr, Gregg, Benjamin F. Dunkin, W. F. Hutson, and Rhett, with John A. Inglis as chairman. Rhett proposed another to prepare an address to the Southern people explaining their action, and Inglis put Rhett at its head.[25] The committees met during the balance of the day, and the next morning when the convention reassembled, some debate commenced on the floor over the functions and purview of the committees. Even at this eleventh hour there was the possibility that moderates and extremists in the body might prejudice their efforts either by trying for delay or pushing too hard, and Miles and others tried to cut debate off. When some raised fears that Buchanan might reinforce the forts in retaliation for secession, Miles declared that he had himself warned the president that any such attempt would result in Carolinians storming and taking the forts themselves. On the other hand, to the hotheads who wanted the forts seized unilaterally now—and he may have been addressing Rhett here—Miles wisely pointed out that a garrison of scarcely less than one hundred men hardly posed a threat to anyone and could be taken at will at any time without risking fomenting armed conflict. Bide their time, attend to secession, and Buchanan would have to yield them peaceably, he reassured them.

Immediately afterward arose the issue of what to do when other states followed them out of the Union. One delegate suggested appointing deputies to meet with invited representatives of other future seceded states in a general convention. Another proposed that a provisional government for the seceded states be inaugurated, taking the old Constitution with any needed changes for its charter until a new document could be framed. Rhett rose to urge caution and careful thought. A lot could happen between their secession and the framing of a permanent Southern government, yet with the timing of the conventions being called for most of the other slave states, he pointed out that Alabama, Florida, Mississippi, and Georgia could all be out by the end of January, meaning that a convention to form a permanent government could commence as early as the first of February 1861. What need was there, he asked, for a provisional ruling body with so short an intervening period? And the old Constitution clearly had failed, or else why were they there? It would be folly to burden themselves with it again. Even if it should be a year before a new Southern constitution could be framed, he would never agree to live again under the old document.

"Why do you seem to be in such haste to run away from independence?" he asked. South Carolina was the ruling state in the South, and the South could dictate to the world. They had perfect freedom before them if they were wise and deliberate now, so why tie themselves even temporarily to a charter that had been the means of their ruin in the old Union? Indeed, he warned that once they formed their new nation under its own constitution, it was possible that South Carolinians might have to reject the document, for it might reflect interests of other states that were incompatible with their own. The idea of allowing others to form a constitution for him made him indignant. "I send a Commissioner to make a Constitution for me!" he shouted. "I give a batch of men the right to make a Constitution for me!" Not for a day or even an hour would he submit to such an outrage. Let South Carolina remain independent as she was about to be until other states had joined her in secession, and then they would continue to follow her lead. He did not say so overtly, but it was implicit in his remarks that he believed South Carolina should dictate the terms of any new constitution and that the rest of the South would follow. Just as implicit was the suggestion that he expected to be the guiding hand in that constitution.[26]

That ended the discussion of an immediate provisional government, and the convention soon adjourned. But it was to be a busy day for Rhett, for the Inglis committee resumed their deliberations immediately afterward. At least one of the committee, Hutson, came armed with a proposed draft of a secession ordinance, the same that he had sent for publication in the *Mercury* three weeks before. Rhett likely had a draft of his own too, since he always seemed to have appropriate documents prepared in advance for any occasion, and others may have as well. Hutson's was the most comprehensive but also the lengthiest. Orr probably introduced it on his behalf, but they all quickly realized that its length would only afford opportunity for extended debate, when they needed a quick vote with as little deliberation in the convention as possible. Rhett undertook cutting the draft down dramatically, until its effective provision merely declared that South Carolina's 1788 ratification of the Constitution and all subsequent ratifications of its amendments were thereby repealed, "and that the union now subsisting between South Carolina and other States, under the name of 'The United States of America,' is hereby dissolved." By that evening the committee members were agreed on the text and ready to report it to the general convention in the morning, and Rhett was proud that he had, as he put it, "shaped" the ordinance.[27]

Just before 1:00 P.M. on December 20 the committee reported the ordinance to the convention, which had assembled in St. Andrew's Hall, and Inglis read it to the delegates. There was no discussion, for there was nothing in the brief statement to arouse debate. They simply voted in a roll call, alphabetically and unanimously. It took just eight minutes to accomplish what Rhett had striven more than thirty years to bring about. South Carolina was going to resist. It was moved that they have the ordinance engrossed on linen parchment and then reassemble again at Institute Hall that evening with the public in attendance for the formal ceremony of signing. Meanwhile they spent the next couple of hours in general debate.

Even now, after the vote for the ordinance, some spoke out for caution, wishing to postpone promulgating their act until they saw what reaction Washington might have in the way of concessions. Others wanted to pass resolutions dealing with immediate trade measures and the retention or expulsion of current federal postmasters and customs collectors and other such officers, and including the continuation of all federal laws currently in existence until they could enact their own statutes and even allowing federal collectors to continue receiving customs duties. Rhett had wanted to keep them from bogging down in immediate detail. "I think we ought to endeavor to let this revolution go on with as little injury as possible to the interests of the country," he declared. But he could not consent to be ruled for an hour by federal laws or agents. South Carolina could collect taxes by her own authority and her own laws now, and only for this would he assent. They could simply transfer all federal employees into state employ and levy duties themselves to cover the expenses. Their independence must be not only at once but complete.[28] Rhett also managed to kill any talk of an immediate provisional government based on the Constitution, but he did introduce a resolution calling for invitations to be sent to the other slave states asking them to meet with South Carolina in convention to form a new confederacy.[29]

.

At 6:30 P.M. they gathered at St. Andrew's once more and marched in parade to Institute Hall, arriving in fifteen minutes to find members of the legislature awaiting them at the foot of the stairs and an exuberant crowd of three thousand within. The applause began to roar as they entered, and it continued until they had all taken their places. After an opening prayer Jamison read the ordinance, and as the cheering commenced anew, the signing began. Two hours later it was done. The thunderous applause echoed in the booming of the cannon of the East Bay Artillery on the Battery, the tolling of church bells throughout the city, burning bonfires and rockets sent into the night sky, and the continual blaring of brass bands. Amid the din the local militia paraded past the Mills House on Meeting Street where the new governor was staying, while newsboys distributed throughout the city a special extra of the *Mercury* that the younger Rhett had printed earlier that day in anticipation. It said, simply, "The Union is Dissolved."[30]

Much work still remained, and even as the sound of the parades and the salutes continued in the days ahead, Rhett went to work with his own committee to draft a statement to the Southern states. Cheves and others served on the committee, but Rhett wrote the *Address to the Slave-holding States* himself in only a few hours.[31] He had the old list of grievances memorized by now and traced them back to the beginning. The Constitution had failed to be able to unite two distinct peoples under one government, he said. The election of Lincoln was only the most recent and most outrageous in a long litany of injustices and insults to the slave states. Southerners made up a great nation and deserved to be one in their own right.[32] Circumstances beyond South Carolina's control had put her in the lead of a great movement, he asserted. She would have preferred that some other state act first, but having done so now—and in direct contradiction of his statements in the convention a day or two earlier—she had no desire to lead or dictate to her sister states. Providence bound them together, and South Carolina asked for their "sympathy and confederation." Fate and Yankee hate drove them together. Let the North go its own way, he said, with labor and capital in perpetual combat, with starvation in the laboring classes controlling population, with men and children worked to death, and with civil order maintained only by the sword and the bayonet. No one could ever accuse him of recoiling from hyperbole. They preferred their own system, with labor and capital the same, population doubling every generation, and abundance and plenty for all in a land where civil order, not steel, kept the peace. "All we demand of other peoples is, to be let alone, to work out our own high destinies," he declared. "We ask you to join us, in forming a Confederacy of Slaveholding States." United, the slave states must be the greatest nation on earth, the fruit of their soil sufficient to conquer peace with all. To do anything less in this crisis risked losing everything—their freedom, their society, and their slaves.[33]

The convention adopted Rhett's *Address* and also another statement drafted by a committee headed by Memminger, a *Declaration of the Immediate Causes* leading to secession, which largely repeated points made by Rhett, though with less fire and eloquence and ignoring entirely his broader philosophical position on the innate right of the South to be free. Never really close, Rhett and Memminger had grown far apart in recent years thanks to the latter's reluctance on secession, and the cautious phrasing of the *Declaration* now would do nothing to bring him back into Rhett's favor.[34] Rhett's *Address* left no room for looking back or returning to the Union under any circumstances; Memminger's *Declaration* seemed less decisive, and certainly less joyous at independence. The convention heard some objection to Memminger's centering his objections on slavery, wanting to soften their stance before the world, but Rhett felt no such problem in his *Address,* for slavery, though not the root cause of secession in his mind, was certainly the occasion that brought it about.[35] As for Rhett's document, seeing in it echoes of the arrogant posture Rhett displayed in his office just a week before, Consul Bunch frankly thought that the Carolinian had forced on the convention "a most weakly reasoned and, in some respects, offensive Manifesto."[36]

The very day after adopting the ordinance, Rhett's sixtieth birthday, the convention created a commission composed of Barnwell, Orr, and Adams to go to Washington and attempt to negotiate for the peaceful turnover of the forts and arsenals, and to address the state's just debts due to the national government. Then they turned to the forts themselves. Fort Sumter sat out in the harbor more than a mile from the waterfront, with Castle Pinckney on a small island much closer to the city and Fort Moultrie on Sullivan's Island six miles distant. Scarcely a dozen soldiers were at the dilapidated Pinckney, which offered no threat. Sumter at the moment was unfinished and ungarrisoned, while Maj. Robert Anderson commanded the 127 men and officers at Moultrie. There they posed no danger to the city, but if Anderson should move his men to Fort Sumter, its cannon would command not only the city but also the main shipping channels.

Rhett favored taking all of the forts by force if necessary, an easy task given that militia units flocked to Charleston and batteries of artillery were already going up all around the harbor. By the right of eminent domain, he argued, the sovereign state was entitled to the property, regardless of the fort sites having been ceded to the federal government years before and Fort Sumter itself being constructed on an island created by national authorities. Besides, the Barnwell commission would negotiate in good faith to compensate Washington for its lost property. Their sitting out in Charleston's harbor was an affront to the state's dignity, he would argue. What he did not say was that taking them forcibly would accomplish the same goal he had hoped to achieve almost ten years before when he suggested the same act to Governor Means. An outbreak of violence was sure to propel the rest of the slave states into secession, even the wavering such as Virginia and Kentucky, which would only accomplish the objective of a strong and self-sustaining new confederacy that much sooner, guaranteeing that the North could not and would not attempt coercion.

No one else shared his views sufficiently to launch such a movement, but he was still concerned lest Anderson's garrison be reinforced and urged that the Barnwell commission be advised to state to Buchanan that any attempt at reinforcement would be regarded as an act of war.[37] Indeed, Rhett felt some chagrin at the reluctance of his fellow delegates to risk confrontation and feared that while they delayed, the Yankees would take the initiative. His son the editor called on Pickens the day before Christmas to suggest that a steamer then in the harbor ought to be manned with five hundred volunteers with rifles and cannon, and anchored in the harbor between Forts Moultrie and Sumter, where it could prevent any attempt by Anderson to move. Pickens dismissed the suggestion, stating that he already had a spy on Sullivan's Island to warn him of any Yankee movement and a vessel in the harbor patrolling every night. There seemed to be no danger of Anderson occupying Sumter.[38]

Christmas Day was a happy one in Charleston and certainly at Rhett's home on the corner of Vanderhorst and Thomas Streets, a property he had somehow purchased a few years before from James Legaré. The substantial three-story Greek Revival house sat well back from the streets in a beautiful and spacious yard shaded by cape jasmines, japonica, and oleander trees up to twenty feet high.[39] Still harassed by debt, he could scarcely afford so ostentatious a house, but with half a dozen children at home he could hardly live anywhere smaller. The Oaks and Drainfield, his remaining plantations, harvested 202,500 pounds of rice that year, an excellent yield that relieved the burden somewhat.[40] Better yet, the crisis had done wonders for the *Mercury.* Circulation grew rapidly as Carolinians all over the state sought the news from Charleston, and they found the Rhetts' editorial stance—if not the Rhetts themselves—increasingly palatable. The paper was actually making a profit and soon would have to invest in newer equipment with a capacity for meeting the demand. Rhett would never be rich, but he was more comfortably set than he had been in years, and it behooved a man of his status in the newly sovereign state to live in a befitting style.

The joy of the season lasted scarcely a day. On December 26 came first a personal loss. Rhett's elder brother Thomas, for whom he still felt great affection despite the sometime estrangement over his plantation management, unexpectedly died. Scarcely did Rhett have time to come to grips with his grief when he heard two cannon shots in the harbor that evening after dark. He did not know their meaning, though some suggested that perhaps Pickens had taken Fort Moultrie after all. Only the next morning did he discover with the rest of Charleston that they had been a signal from Anderson that he had embarked the last of his command for Fort Sumter, spiked the guns of Moultrie, and set fire to what he could not remove. Under their very noses the Yankees had done what Rhett so long feared by establishing themselves in Sumter astride the main channel and putting the city under their guns.[41]

Rhett was livid. Pickens's precautions had come to nothing, and Rhett charged him privately with "lamentable incompetency" and railed at the humiliation to South Carolina. They should have seized the forts the moment they seceded; he had told them so, and they had not listened. Here was the result. "With the most conclusive means of success in our hands," he railed, "we were completely outwitted." Their whole policy toward the United States over the forts had been ill-conceived because they had not listened to him. Now the Barnwell mission had to be recalled, and Rhett accused Buchanan of being duplicitous in dealing with them without revealing his intention. In fact the decision had been Anderson's alone, but Rhett could not have known that then.[42]

His low opinion of Pickens confirmed, Rhett grudgingly went along with the convention in an emergency measure that same day conferring on Pickens presidential powers to make treaties and to appoint and receive ambassadors, and ordering him to appoint an executive council both to assist him and in the hope that it could make up for his presumed laxity.[43] A week later Pickens appointed Magrath as secretary of state, Memminger as treasury secretary, and Jamison as secretary of war. They became in effect a cabinet, though as Rhett sarcastically noted, they were only "a feeble immitation" of the real thing, devoid of power.

The weakness of Pickens only confirmed for Rhett the need for better men to be in control of state and Southern affairs. Possibly at the urging of his son Barnwell, he renewed his call for the formation of a permanent government and proposed that the suggested convention of seceding states be held in Montgomery, Alabama, as an honor to the city's great son Yancey, but also because of its central location in the anticipated lower tier of seceding states between South Carolina and Louisiana. Now in the interest of time he wanted the convention held prior to his earlier suggested time in mid-February.[44] In opposition there arose once more the suggestion of a provisional government founded on the Constitution as an interim measure, and several days of debate followed. The delegates raised such issues as the assertion of state sovereignty in dealing with their fellow slave states, the nature of representation in the planned Southern convention and whether it should be by population or by state, the taxing power, foreign trade, resistance to protectionism, strict control of governmental expense to defeat any return to internal improvements, and more. Some matters, especially what Cheves called "shirking the name of Slavery" in justifying their course, promised to be points of disagreement with some of the more moderate states.[45]

Responding to the evident pressure for some provisional form of immediate government, Rhett drafted a plan suggesting that each seceding state ought to cast ballots for a president and vice president for the provisional government prior to an unspecified date in February 1861. Each state would then cast as many votes for the victors as that state had been entitled to cast in the electoral college of the United States, and the persons receiving the majority in all of the seceded states aggregately would then be declared elected. This was a cumbersome process at best, for each state could theoretically select a favorite son as president, and thus there might well be a candidate with a plurality but no one with a clear majority. At the same time the states should choose two senators each and twice the number of representatives as they recently had in the House of Representatives. They should all then assemble in February in an unspecified city and organize themselves into a provisional congress "with the constitution adopted for said Provisional Government," by which he did not specify the United States Constitution, and install their president and vice president. If no candidates came with a majority of the electoral votes, then the new house of representatives would select candidates according to the process of the old Constitution, the only reference Rhett made in his plan to the charter of the Union. Above all, this new provisional regime was to rule for no more than one year, and less if a permanent constitution and government could be formed sooner.[46]

Rhett could not carry his plan before the convention, and soon another proposal gained favor on the floor. According to this proposal, appointed commissioners would be sent to the several slave states to enlist cooperation and could determine the precise time and place of the convention, with February 12 suggested as a date for selecting a new president and vice president on a poll of electors chosen by the several states; the new government would be inaugurated on February 22, George Washington's birthday. Then they would proceed to frame a permanent government, and whenever three-fourths of the participating seceded states ratified the new constitution, the old provisional government would be abolished.[47]

In the end, on December 31 the convention combined the several propositions. The commissioners were to propose to the other states formation of a new confederacy by adopting the old Constitution for a provisional government, thus

rejecting Rhett's earlier arguments. It terrified Rhett with the prospect of reconstruction, but the best he and his friends could do was alter the mandate to
require that the new confederation be organized before March 4 and that as soon
as the provisional government was formed, the Southern convention would
immediately turn to framing a permanent constitution of its own, with no more
than two years to accomplish the task before the provisional government must
expire. They suggested that each seceding state should send representatives to
the Southern convention equal to the number in their current congressional delegations, but that in all deliberations of the new body the states should vote as
blocs, with one state, one vote. Thus little Florida, with only three prospective
delegates, would speak just as loudly as Georgia with ten. Rhett could heartily
accord with this, at least. There would be no tyranny by a numerical majority,
but each sovereign state would be the equal of the others.

The convention chose the commissioners on January 2, and the next day
they met before leaving on their missions and agreed to adopt Rhett's proposition of Montgomery as the meeting place and setting February 4 as the date.
Barnwell Rhett Jr. proudly wrote to Yancey that his father had "used his persuasion" with the convention to select Montgomery and that it was done to
honor Yancey's leadership in the movement, but it was only another case of
claiming undue credit and authority.[48] Nothing from his own provisional plan
made the final vote except a February meeting date, for there was no stipulation
at all placed on how officials should be elected, or a congress formed, or even
that there should be a congress, for nothing in the resolution made it binding
that the coming convention adopt the old Constitution. Rhett may have suggested the Alabama capital earlier, but the choice was made by the commissioners, not the convention, and apparently without consultation with Rhett,
thanks no doubt to the logic of holding the meeting in the center of the anticipated seceded states. Nevertheless, in the end Rhett had gotten some of it his
own way, with the call for a February convening at Montgomery. Already, however, he began to make plans not to let that convention get out of hand if he
could help it.[49]

In the interim Rhett and the convention debated daily on a host of other
issues. Old Judge Thomas Withers raised the impossibility of dealing with their
late companions of the North on the basis of free trade. As neighbors they were
bound to quarrel. They must have at least a revenue tariff. Withers feared there
would be no need for judges such as he, and then in an unrelated series of positions he argued for a constitution founded on Christianity and predicted that
South Carolina could not stand alone long, especially if Charleston were blockaded. Rhett's old friend Gregg demanded perfect equality among the states of

any new confederacy, with the states, and not their new national government, controlling forts and levying tariffs. Rhett had to fight strenuously against a proposal that the state's delegates to Montgomery should withhold from any future confederacy the power of levying taxes and import duties. He made a lengthy speech outlining his whole program as he had proposed it to Bunch, arguing how essential it was to obtaining diplomatic recognition, as well as to their future relations with the United States. Given the power to levy tariffs, the new nation could virtually exclude the old Union from any commercial intercourse with it if it so chose. Once the confederacy achieved independence, then member states could revert to perfect free trade, but for now favorable duties were their best lure to England and France. Old animosities came out when Keitt launched a rather personal attack on Rhett during the debate for his inconsistency in now seeming to abandon free trade, and he reproached him for opposing their proposed restriction on their delegates. However, the soundness of Rhett's policy in this issue carried the day. The debate sometimes became so diverted from the main issues that Alexander Mazyck actually discussed his fear that a new government might apply taxes to carriages.[50]

The convention's last act before adjourning on January 5 was to elect the eight delegates who would represent South Carolina in the coming convention. The opposition to Rhett was still strong enough that one ticket was prepared that omitted his name entirely from the list of potential candidates, although the attempt, probably mounted by Keitt, failed.[51] To his delight Rhett found that he finished at the head of the list, the first time in many a year that he had received such a demonstration of approbation. Of the rest, Keitt was the only true fire-eater, and perhaps Miles, while Withers, William W. Boyce, and Chesnut had been on the fence for years, and Barnwell and Memminger were cooperationists right to the end, thus revealing the continuing division of opinion in the convention. The nature of the rest of the new delegation suggested strongly that the vote for Rhett was less an expression of confidence than simply a compliment to his undeniable surpassing efforts for secession and a new Southern nation. Nevertheless, his ranking at the top of the list made him de facto head of the delegation and might carry with it considerable power if he would use it, and if the others would let him.[52]

Soon Rhett learned that this same day in Washington a caucus of senators and representatives from Mississippi, Texas, Louisiana, Georgia, Florida, Arkansas, and Alabama agreed on recommendations to their states to secede and joined South Carolina's call for a convention in Montgomery to form a new nation. Years later in bitterness, Rhett would persuade himself that they went beyond this, conspiring among themselves to choose the direction of that new nation and even to select its leader.[53] He would be mistaken, but for now the news gave cause for rejoicing. Meanwhile state militia and citizens in Alabama and Georgia seized Federal arsenals and armories in their states, and two days later on January 7, Floridians did the same. That same day a telegram came to Rhett's son from New York informing him that Washington was sending a ship, the *Star of the West,* to provision Fort Sumter. That could only be good news, for when Charleston's guns inevitably opened fire when the ship arrived, it could be the outbreak Rhett had prayed for to galvanize all of the South.[54]

At the same time there was evidence of growing influence for the Rhetts in the city, or perhaps fear of them. The wives of Anderson's officers did not go into Sumter with them but attempted to find temporary room and board in local hotels before leaving for the North. Since the innkeepers depended on local business, they felt unwilling to risk the ire of their neighbors by taking in the Yankees, and some demanded that the women get the sanction of the Rhetts before they would feed or house them. Should the *Mercury* come out against a hotel or boardinghouse for disloyalty in the current temper of the city, it could be disastrous for business.[55]

The momentum accelerated on the morning of January 9 when the *Star of the West* appeared off the harbor and tried to reach Fort Sumter. While Rhett and a crowd of thousands watched from the Battery, Carolinian artillery opened fire and easily persuaded the ship to turn around. Though the vessel had not returned fire, Charlestonians regarded the little incident as a victory. Scarcely was the vessel out of sight before the wires brought news that Mississippi had seceded, and at last South Carolina was not alone. Rhett immediately made plans to go to Georgia to assist if he could in bringing her out, for in her January 2 election for convention delegates the popular vote revealed a state evenly divided between secession and remaining in the Union awhile longer. Even before he left, Florida went out on January 10.

By the following evening, when he arrived in Savannah to meet Ruffin and others, he heard that now Alabama, too, had left the Union. Rhett had been in correspondence with members of Georgia's state convention for some time now, and on his arrival he found the debate still heavily divided but tending toward secession and the momentum from the other states exerting a powerful influence. All they needed now was Georgia to have a solid band of seceded slave states from the Atlantic to the Mississippi. In addition to meeting with prominent men, he found time to give Ruffin his own account of the *Star of the West* and then to detail to him other affairs in Charleston, all of them boding well but bound to carry, he feared, a heavy expense due to the inevitable disruption of business and trade in the crisis. Rhett also revealed that, like almost everyone else in Charleston, he thought himself an amateur military strategist. Others had been sending him plans for taking Fort Sumter, and he sketched for Ruffin his own ideas on how to storm the fort.[56]

Meanwhile the *Mercury* carried on its policy of unfettered partisanship, vilifying the North and any Southern politicians in Washington such as those from the border states that sought some accommodation or compromise. Barnwell Rhett was anxious to find and publish actual proof of Hamlin being an octoroon, meanwhile picking up some of his father's suspicious nature and coming to believe that Yankees were interfering with or stopping his editorial correspondence from the North, which he now had sent to a front address. He also turned his attention, as a member of the legislature, to choosing a new flag for the independent "nation" of South Carolina, despite the fact that this independence was not likely to last long. He came up with a blue field with a white palmetto and a blue union in the corner, and upon that a white crescent, which the legislature adopted late in the month. To any such as Keitt, whom he called "would be fireeaters," who differed from his father's policy, he advised his correspondents to criticize them, "and don't be squeamish about using names." He also began adding his own views to letters from his correspondents, to make it appear as if they came from people outside Charleston rather than being his own editorial opinions. Like his father, young Barnwell Rhett had long since abandoned anything more than the pretense of objectivity.[57]

On January 19, by a satisfyingly large majority, Georgia finally voted to secede, and the elder Rhett could return his attention to Carolinian affairs in the few days before he would have to leave for Montgomery, for each of the seceded states had agreed to send delegates to the proposed convention, and on the terms proposed by the South Carolina convention. He opposed all efforts at conciliating the men from Virginia and Kentucky who were wavering, for he did not trust them not to attempt to reconstruct the Union if they gained any influence in the new confederation to come. They must come, if they came at all, on no terms but full acceptance of the perpetuity of secession.[58]

On his return from Georgia the nagging problem of Fort Sumter remained. Pickens had been allowing fresh meat and vegetables to be sent to the garrison from the city's markets and then on January 21 actually agreed to let the Federals buy for themselves in the town. Rhett and his friends immediately raised an uproar over this trading with an enemy, and according to local gossip an outraged Rhett stormed into Pickens's temporary office on Meeting Street to demand that the fort should be taken at once and without further delay. "Certainly, Mr. Rhett; I have no objection!" the governor replied, obviously enjoying the moment. "I will furnish you with some men, and you can storm the work yourself." That took Rhett aback. "But, sir, I am not a military man!" he protested. "Nor I either," shot back Pickens, "and therefore I take the advice of those that are!" The two had been making points against each other for fully a generation, and this was one more the governor could chalk to his credit in a personal feud that would only become increasingly petty as the years progressed.[59] In the interest of a public facade of harmony, Rhett decided not to attack Pickens in the *Mercury* over delay in taking Sumter. "He is trifling with the honor of the state and the cause of a Southern Confederacy, under the pretext of unpreparedness to take it," his son complained to a *Mercury* correspondent. The danger was that sooner or later a reinforcement might get through, and then they would have five hundred instead of one hundred to deal with. They would hold off awhile yet, but not indefinitely.[60]

With the convention in Montgomery due to meet on February 4, Rhett found the closing days of January as busy as any he had known. He was refining his ideas for future foreign policy for the new nation, intending to meet head-on the British prejudice against slavery by the offer of an irresistible trade package that included a twenty-year treaty with a fixed tariff of not more than 20 percent. The recently concluded fiscal year ending in June 1859 saw the South export more than $188 million in produce, chiefly to England and carried mostly in British vessels. No nation would risk that level of trade in vitally needed raw materials just because of some moral scruple over dealing with a slave state, especially with preferential duties on its own manufactured exports in the offing.[61] Not surprisingly, too, Rhett had for some time been at work on his own proposal for a constitution for the new confederacy, which he took to calling the "Federal Republic of America" in his notes. As so often in the past, he planned to come fully prepared to present the convention with a document that, reflecting his own opinions, ought by right to secure their agreement as well.[62]

Barnwell came to Charleston on Thursday, January 31, and stopped at the Mills House on Meeting Street, intent on joining his cousin and others of the delegation for the trip to Montgomery. Rhett was elated, yet worried too. Scarlet fever had settled in the house on Vanderhorst and Thomas Streets, and his daughters eleven-year-old Ann Barnwell, or "Nannie," and little Katherine Ethelind, just turned three, were both ill. Yet on the shoulders of his great triumph and that of South Carolina, his concern was tempered by his excitement for what lay ahead, as well as some apprehension of the pitfalls in his path. His son Barnwell took him to the studio of the local photographer George Cook to have his portrait taken.[63] He looked tired, his hair wind-blown and unkempt, and there was a hint of the little sticking plaster that now perpetually adorned the side of his nose. He was sixty. The career that he had thought a failure seemed about to be vindicated, perhaps even crowned with anticipated laurels in the new nation to be. When he boarded the train with Barnwell the next morning, February 1, 1861, the long and painful past promised only to be a prologue now of what lay ahead at the end of the track.[64]

TWENTY

We Will Have Run Round a Circle

1861

THE ROUTE TO MONTGOMERY took Rhett by four different railroads through Augusta and Atlanta before he and Barnwell and a few other delegates stepped off at the Montgomery & West Point station in the Alabama capital at noon on February 2. Unpaved streets filled with mud from recent heavy rains greeted them, and as their carriage struggled through the morass toward their hotel, they saw men and animals spattered with grime to their necks. Rhett watched as a dog nearly choked in mud as it tried to cross a street to bedevil a pedestrian and then futilely attempted to wipe its eyes on its foreleg. It made him think of the newly sovereign slave states trying to wipe the filth of abolition from their eyes, and he wondered to himself how the delegates would ever get through the swamp a half-mile from the hotel up Market Street to the capitol building, where the senate chamber had been set aside for them.[1]

The proprietor of the Exchange Hotel on Court Square at the foot of Market gave Rhett room number six when he arrived, and on entering he found that Gov. Andrew Moore had had his and the other delegates' rooms furnished with an abundance of stationery and other things they might need in the days ahead, as well as some tasty sweetmeats.[2] Later that afternoon Rhett joined other arrivals in the hotel parlor, which had already become what he would describe as a "conversational parliament." While occasionally looking out the window as the relentless rain continued to fall, he took note of the others there and those continuing to arrive through the evening.[3] Most of the Alabamians were already in town and came down to the hotel to meet the new arrivals. A commission of North Carolinians had come with Rhett on the train, though their state was nowhere near secession yet, and now some of the Mississippians were there too. The evening train brought the first of the Georgians and more of his own delegation, all but Chesnut and Withers, and those Carolinians present decided to spend an extra five dollars a day to rent a private parlor just for their delegation.[4] The next morning's train brought the last two Carolinians and also the real giants from Georgia, Toombs and Alexander H. Stephens.[5]

Already that parlor parliament in the Exchange seethed with ambitions, con-flicting purposes, and disturbing rumors. Rhett did not like the North Carolina people being there, nor the fact that commissioners from Tennessee and Vir-ginia had also been invited by Alabama to attend. Distrustful as ever of the border states, he feared they might try to delay their proceedings to allow time for some compromise to wreak reunion.[6] To the extent that he was a Southern nationalist at all, his vision encompassed really only the most solidly slavery-based states in the Deep South, the cotton, rice, and sugar states that could be trusted to see their interests wholly wrapped up in maintaining their institutions free of the taint of lingering Union pangs.

There was rampant speculation on who might be their new president. Cer-tainly Rhett thought he deserved the spot, not only as reward for this culmina-tion of his life's efforts but also because he would have the best vision of the shape their new nation should take. Nevertheless, in a show of wisdom and restraint, he and his delegation had already agreed that South Carolina would not seek to dominate the convention, at least overtly, for fear of creating a back-lash among the more skittish states such as Georgia, some of whose delegates, such as Stephens, had to be dragged to secession, and Alabama, which was so torn that Yancey failed to be chosen as a delegate. Consequently they were agreed that they would not put forward any of themselves as candidates for office. Of course, should other states wish to nominate and vote for one of them, that would be altogether different. Rhett did not know, however, that Chesnut had told Stephens during their train journey that the South Carolina delegation looked to Georgia for the president, meaning either Toombs or himself.[7]

It did not bode well for Rhett that members of his own delegation were apparently making policy without consulting him, but it was only the first of what would be an unbroken string of demonstrations that none of them really looked on him as their leader, regardless of his official position, and that none of them would make an effort to advance his hopes for high office. He was cer-tainly self-deluded enough to believe that he could be an effective leader for the new nation, but however much many of the fire-eaters back at home wanted Rhett to be the new president—and many did—that sentiment did not make the journey to Montgomery.[8] In other parts of the South the opposition was more outspoken. Referring to this convention as "the provisional abortion at Montgomery," a New Orleans paper declared that it was just the place for "the Yanceys, the Toombses, the Rhetts, the Jeff Davises and the mighty swarm of equally brilliant aspirants for fame and high office at the head of such a govern-ment."[9] Stephens felt fearful of the influence of personal ambition on their pro-ceedings, doubting that anything good would come of the convention, in which he feared "the want of high integrity, loyalty to principle, and pure, disinterested patriotism in the men at the head of the movement." He did not speak of Rhett by name but surely had him in mind along with others whom he found "selfish, ambitious, and unscrupulous."[10] Passed by and all but forgotten back in South Carolina, Hammond undoubtedly thought bitterly of Rhett when he told Simms that "*big-man-me-ism* reigns supreme & every one thinks every other a jealous fool, or an aspiring knave."[11]

Though the convention was not to assemble until Monday, February 4, the crowd of delegates at the Exchange spent all day Sunday discussing what should be done, and Rhett's sense of alarm grew rapidly as he discovered that delegates from the other states had come with very different ideas of what should be done from those of South Carolina. He and others of his delegation had planned only on meeting to frame a provisional government and then have the delegations return with the proposal to their separate state conventions and legislatures for acceptance or rejection. But now as he talked with Stephens and other Georgians in the parlor, he found that they had a different plan.[12] The "Georgia project," as he called it, proposed that this convention should assume legislative power for the new Confederacy, choose a president, create executive departments and offices, raise revenues, frame a provisional constitution, and then proceed to work on a permanent constitution, submitting only the latter to the state legislatures for ratification.[13] Toombs and Stephens argued that conditions in Georgia were so precarious at the moment that if the South Carolina plan were carried out and a proposal for a provisional government submitted to its voters before being put in operation, it would likely be defeated in their state, with disastrous consequences for the movement overall. Alabamians argued that their state offered the same peril, and they seconded the Georgia scheme, but Rhett regarded the whole thing as a "usurpation."[14]

At the same time Rhett talked to the Mississippi delegation, only to find that they had their own "project," which simply was to adopt the United States Constitution as it was, elect a president, and then go home, leaving it to the states to choose representatives for the new congress, or else do as Mississippi already had and designate the same senators and congressmen who so recently sat in Washington to serve them in the new congress. Moreover, Rhett saw immediately that their further intent was to see their own Jefferson Davis chosen to head the new government, though Davis was not a delegate.[15]

Rhett felt outraged. Mississippi had not even sent her most distinguished men there to represent her, and now they wanted to dictate policy. Moreover, this convention had no vested authority from the states to elect a president, for that must be done by the states themselves in their conventions. And the Mississippi plan made no comprehensive provision for the manner of choosing representatives to the new congress, which meant that at the moment they would be electing a president and vice president who would be what Rhett called "powerless puppets" with no congress to work with, to confirm cabinet appointments, to raise revenue, or to wage war if necessary. To his mind, the adoption of the old Constitution was tantamount to cooperationism, a sop to the border states, which would be allowed to join the new confederation and—barring the reforms needed in a new constitution—be able to bring their protective tariff and internal improvements with them. Worse, such a policy would actually allow free states to join them in the future under the existing Constitution. Clearly it was nothing but disguised reconstruction with the old charter and even the old representatives. "After all, we will have run round a circle, and end where we started," Rhett grumbled. "We will only have changed masters."[16]

Despite having their own caucus room, Rhett did not attempt to call a meeting of his delegation that evening to discuss the emergency before them. This was probably because he found that half of them seemed in fact to favor the Georgia project, including even his cousin Barnwell, who said that since the state of things facing them in Montgomery was so different from what they had expected, it was necessary for them to assume legislative power immediately or risk destruction by the moderates and Unionists in Georgia, Alabama, and indeed all across the slave states.[17] Instead, that evening Rhett sent a gloomy dispatch to his son outlining the two plans for the *Mercury.* "The enclosed will show you the danger here," he groaned. Though he had only spoken with Stephens, apparently he believed that Toombs and Howell Cobb also favored the Georgia project. As for the other program, "Jefferson Davis and Mississippi have acted very meanly," he said. "Instead of being here to give all the weight possible to the proceedings of the Convention, they cook up offices for themselves, and send tools here, to carry out their selfish policy." It was almost too much, and he feared that this unexpected state of affairs would leave his own delegation with little to do. "The Poor South!" he moaned. "If I had no trust in God, I would despair, utterly."[18]

Certainly the chief presidential talk seemed to be for Davis at the moment, though that could change.[19] That evening, before they convened the next morning, he tried to counter the Georgia and Mississippi schemes by suggesting that instead of making itself a congress and electing president and vice president, the convention should just modify the existing Constitution in those areas of concern to Southern rights, telegraph the changes to their state conventions, and wait for their ratification, which he felt could be achieved speedily. At the same time those conventions could also cast their electoral votes for president and vice president and select senators and representatives. Unrealistically Rhett thought all that could be accomplished in a week, with the new congress meeting by February 20–25 to count the electoral ballots and declare the president and put the new government in operation, and all with no "usurpation" of power. In just the time element alone it was almost hopelessly impractical, and his proposal also ignored entirely the warnings from Georgia and Alabama about the divisiveness within their conventions, which almost certainly would have led to fatal delays in their action. A three-state confederacy of Mississippi, South Carolina, and Florida, with a huge gap between them, would have been ridiculous and pointless. Desperate to prevent what he saw about to happen, it was the best proposal Rhett could make at the last moment.[20]

Rhett must already have accepted defeat by the next morning when he joined the exodus for the walk up Market Street to the statehouse, for by then the Georgia project had taken firm root, with only some of the South Carolina delegation in opposition. Rhett confessed that the plan was practical and consistent, that as popularly elected delegates they would be closer to the will of the people as congressmen than any others appointed by their conventions, and that at least it did not have within it the seeds of reconstruction contained in the Mississippi proposal. All he could hope to do now was to resist any further usurpations or concessions. Even as they walked, the delegates were already referring to themselves as "the Congress."[21]

With the temperature barely above freezing, the delegates filed into the senate chamber just before noon. Rhett saw many familiar faces there, for he had served in the U.S. Congress in Washington with several of them and knew others from the commercial conventions of past years. After they had presented their credentials, and by an agreement made the day before at the Exchange, he opened the business of the convention by calling for the election of a president of the "congress" to preside over their deliberations. The act was a compliment to him for his role in bringing them there, and in recognition of Georgia's being the largest delegation, he proposed that Howell Cobb be selected by acclamation, which carried.[22]

Other than appointing a committee to devise rules for their conduct, they did nothing more that day, which was just as well, for Rhett felt ill, his unease in mind over the future matched by the return of one of his recurring maladies. In the inevitable discussion back in the Exchange lobby that evening he continued to object to the Georgia plan, raising what Tom Cobb thought "petty technicalities" over power and privileges, but of course he had always been a master of technicalities.[23] They were of no avail to him now, and worse, he was too ill to take his seat the next day and missed Memminger introducing a resolution calling for a committee to prepare a plan for a provisional government based on the United States Constitution, and Thomas Cobb's amendment—the Georgia plan—calling for them to choose a president and vice president and constitute themselves a congress. He was not there to speak in dissent, and no one else from his delegation chose to do so, so Memminger's resolution carried. Cobb withdrew his, which was in any case redundant, since even before the vote on Memminger's resolution they adopted another to refer to themselves then and thereafter as a congress. The "Georgia project" had succeeded, and to cap it all, by being ill Rhett was not there to assert his right for a place on the new framing committee. Instead, the spot he assumed would have been his went to Barnwell, and the other from South Carolina went to Memminger. Despite his love for his cousin, he knew not to expect a proper charter from their likes, for both had been unreliable on secession almost to the last.[24]

Rhett's dislike of Memminger had grown steadily and did not lessen that evening when it became known that Memminger had come to Montgomery with his own plan for a provisional government that called for taking the old Constitution, having all the states carry over their congressional delegations from Washington to Montgomery, and allowing the new congress to elect not only the president but also a general-in-chief for the army they knew they would have to raise, and quickly.[25] Then Boyce came up with his own plan proposing that the convention elect not only president and vice president but also senators and representatives for all the states. "Such a proposition is a monstrous commentary upon representation in Government," Rhett railed, for it would allow Georgia, Alabama, and Louisiana to have a hand in choosing representatives for South Carolina. "Why are all these expedients brought forward?" he complained that evening, writing petulantly back to the *Mercury* that "it is very doubtful whether you have not committed a great error in proposing any Provisional Government at all!"[26] Denied the chance to push his own plan for organization in the committee, Rhett bristled that Memminger would be able to do so instead. Declaring that "a portion of our Delegation behaved abominably," he promised to expose the offenders when the convention adjourned. He could not do so now since they operated under a self-imposed vow of secrecy on their deliberation, but when he returned to his seat in the state convention to report their actions, he would speak out.[27] Indeed, the cloak of secrecy was something else that he condemned, for the people had a right to be informed, and certainly he wanted Carolinians to know what he said and did in their behalf as well as to know that which he opposed.[28] Yet there was nothing for it in any event, for with support precarious in several of the states, they could not risk presenting anything other than a united front, and publishing their debates or holding them before the public would only reveal the deep divisions within the new congress.

There was nothing for the congress to do the next day as the framing committee did its work, and again Rhett did not attend. Instead he wrote yet again to the *Mercury* to complain that "words are certainly very shadowy in their meaning," for South Carolina intended one thing by inviting the seceding states to a convention, while others in accepting read something entirely different into the invitation, and now here they were forming an unlawful government with no authority from their states to do so. Louisiana had seceded, and her delegates were with them now and seemed to join with Georgia and Alabama in the drive for usurpation.[29] If he could not stop it here, at least he could complain in the pages of the *Mercury* to the extent that he could speak in generalities without breaking his oath of silence. His complaints, sometimes several letters to the editor in a single issue, began appearing February 5, and thereafter they occupied the editorial columns day after day. Within two days some in South Carolina began to see that something was amiss. A concerned Trescot wrote to Miles in Montgomery to complain of the "very injudicious" correspondence, revealing as it did division and disagreement in the delegation and the congress, and a confusion over their purpose. "This is all 'bosh,'" Trescot complained, suspecting that such opinions reflected prejudices taken to Montgomery by their author rather than being formed by circumstances on the spot. "They do harm to us and must prejudice us out of the state," he warned Miles, especially the nonsense that Davis might go for reconstruction.[30]

Others found the *Mercury* accounts equally disquieting, and though none knew with certainty who authored them, everyone shared the same suspicion. Chesnut described Rhett as "a very bold & frank man," one who "avowed opinions and acted upon them with energy," and that was the Rhett whom others clearly recognized in the *Mercury* letters.[31] Memminger had no doubt of authorship. "We are annoyed by the chief of our Delegation being the correspondent of the Mercury, and undertaking through that paper to lecture the rest and the Congress," he complained.[32] Soon the South Carolinians in Montgomery began to receive entreaties to put a stop to the damaging leaks from their own delegation. Yet those who knew who was doing the leaking also knew how impossible it would be to stop its flow.

Rhett was back in the chamber again on February 7, the fourth day of the session, and he was now determined to assert control. Without knowing what would be in the provisional constitution being drafted by the committee, he could well suspect that it would be unacceptable, dangerous even, containing the potential for their destruction. Though determined to fight any offending passages when it was reported to the congress, he sought to strike preemptively in the next and more important fight. Others on his delegation had suggested to him that he introduce a resolution to appoint a committee to frame a permanent constitution. Now he did so, and none too quickly, for the next delegate to stand was Memminger, ready to report the proposed provisional charter.[33]

It was no better than he expected, being a hastily assembled collection of six articles in nineteen sections borrowed almost verbatim from the U.S. Constitution with a few specific changes to meet their exigency. Certainly he did not see it as any improvement. Though it prohibited internal improvements, it left the powers of taxation vague and did nothing about the tariff or free trade. On the other hand, it continued the prohibition of the African slave trade that he regarded as a "positive condemnation of the Institution of Slavery." The congress set aside all of the next day for debate, but Rhett had so little interest in the document that he scarcely spoke out except to propose unsuccessfully that they soften the slave trade clause to state merely that the congress had the power to prohibit, without expressly doing so. It was midnight before they finished and took their vote. The provisional constitution passed unanimously, each state voting as a bloc with one vote as per their rules, though a voice vote would likely have found Rhett still going along with the majority, knowing that this was a small skirmish lost in a much greater campaign. He moved their adjournment until the next morning, when they would elect their president and vice president, and within hours wrote to his son at the *Mercury*. He could at least report that the congress now seemed bent on making a new nation with lessening threat of reconstruction, and in that at least he felt highly pleased. Some states were still too solicitous of gaining the border states to their cause, and he believed that the new constitution was no better than it was in order to lure them to secession. All the same he wanted Barnwell Rhett Jr. to denounce the document because of its failure to address the tariff and its slur on slavery. They could only accept it as a temporary expedient while awaiting the permanent document that he would frame properly. The son did as he was told, publishing regrets that "any Provisional Government was formed at all."[34]

Even before the congress addressed the provisional constitution, the anticipation of the choice of president had many of them in considerable excitement. Mississippi had made its desire for Davis clear from the outset, offensively so to Rhett, who accused them of working on a fixed mandate to "get Davis elected President." Yet there were other contenders. Some spoke of Yancey, and at least a few such as Duncan Kenner of Louisiana heard Rhett's name proposed, while others expected South Carolina to get the vice presidency. Moderates, with their eye cocked toward the skittish border states, believed that it would be foolhardy to choose a radical such as Yancey or Rhett, and they suggested Toombs or Stephens, to which Rhett made his opposition well known.[35]

Throughout the previous days members of the South Carolina delegation had remained fixed in their determination not to push any candidate of their own, and they actually won the praise of others for their forbearance. Rhett even complimented them on February 6 in a letter to the *Mercury,* saying, "your delegation seem to be wisely pushing forward others rather than themselves, I presume, that the great cause they are engaged in may not be injured by any personal aspirations of theirs." Rhett did not call the delegation together to discuss whom to support or for any other cause, and he made no effort to influence them individually either. Most looked to Barnwell or Miles for leadership, while Governor Pickens ignored him entirely and dealt chiefly with Miles. There was frank and free interchange between them on every subject, but each man was left to form his own opinion. This was very much unlike the old Rhett, and Chesnut and Miles agreed afterward that Rhett had exerted no control over them. Keitt openly detested him as well as his brother Edmund and the *Mercury* in the bargain, and Rhett regarded Memminger as an open enemy now too. Ironically, while Toombs at least thought that Rhett had his delegation firmly under his control and favoring Toombs himself, Rhett in fact risked being openly rebuffed if he tried to dictate a meeting to them, let alone attempt to guide their choice of candidates. In any event his ill health no doubt sapped him of the physical strength to face such an ordeal even if he had been willing to try.[36]

Of course Rhett was the only one of them with high aspirations, and one of the little Florida delegation fed them by telling him that their state would vote alongside South Carolina and that they expected the Carolinians to nominate Rhett. Unfortunately there was nothing he could do to build on that tiny base. Even if he thought he could successfully call a caucus of his delegation, it would hardly become him as their head to propose to them that they should put his name forward, and plainly none of them would do so otherwise. "I stood rather isolated in the Delegation," he later complained, and never did he feel it more than now.[37] In fact, there was nothing that he could do.

As early as the opening day of the congress Rhett warned his son that Davis would be elected, if for no other reason than he was a military hero of the war with Mexico and the possibility that a confrontation over Federally occupied forts on Southern soil might lead to an armed conflict.[38] Rhett maintained that he had no personal acquaintance of Davis whatever, despite having served in the House and Senate with him and occasionally even exchanging remarks in debate. Indeed, he could not, that he recalled, remember even hearing Davis in a conversation outside the old Capitol, but he knew that he did not trust him.

Rhett did not forget Davis's support of Zachary Taylor nor Davis's occasional remarks against disunionists in the 1850s, especially his 1858 speech "at sea" in which he referred to "trifling politicians" trying to break up the Union. Rhett did not like Davis's onetime advocacy of a transcontinental railroad, yet another internal improvement, nor his equivocal reply to his son Barnwell's inquiry about Mississippi and secession the previous fall, and he especially did not like the spectacle of Davis in tears when he resigned his seat in the United States Senate barely a month earlier. He suspected Davis of being behind the press of the Mississippians to get him elected and to push their reconstructionist "Mississippi project," and now he even began to suspect that during that meeting of Southern representatives in Washington in January, before their resignation, a plan had been put in place to bring about his election now.[39] Naturally he would resent Davis supplanting him as Calhoun's successor. Davis might be a man of some intellect and ability, but Rhett did not trust him, even though he did not know him. The rumor among others that Davis was at heart a reconstructionist hardly disquieted him.[40]

Meanwhile Rhett's cousin Barnwell had been active in the cause of Davis, whom he thought the right man for the time and place even though he, too, had some doubts about his record and knew him to be of a prickly temper.[41] Sometime before the adoption of the provisional constitution, Barnwell called on Rhett and asked him who he favored for the presidency. Whether sincerely or not, Rhett replied that he thought Thomas Cobb the best man for the job, "a man, pious, honest, earnest, able and brave—altogether, I thought the best man in the Congress," he claimed. It was a strange reply, since Rhett had probably never met Cobb before the previous Sunday. The Georgian was conceited, smug, arrogant, often utterly impractical, detested even by most of his own delegation, and to date notable only as a distinguished local jurist and outspoken secessionist. In short, he was almost the mirror image of Rhett himself, and perhaps therein lay the attraction. But Rhett also knew that the Georgia delegation would never support this Cobb, erroneously believing it more likely that they would nominate his brother Howell instead, whereas in fact Howell had as little support as his brother. The only Georgian likely to have been put forward by a majority of that delegation was Toombs, who had unfortunately made an embarrassment of himself at a party the evening before they adopted the constitution and thereby spoiled his chances.[42]

Now Rhett told Barnwell that he felt no enthusiasm for either Davis or Cobb, and there the matter rested. But Barnwell called again a day or so later, and this time Rhett gave him all his reasons for not favoring Davis, thinking him inconsistent on Southern principles and rights, and too much a Unionist. Rhett doubted his capacity for high office. Barnwell responded that, unlike Rhett, he knew Davis personally and well, and knew him to be honest, reliable, and trustworthy. Admitting that he was not the most able man, still Barnwell said he had sufficient ability to recognize merit in others, and that was the great necessity in a president who must bring the best talent into his administration. If Davis's previous statements and positions did not entirely meet Rhett's approval, he needed to remember that conditions had been different before 1861 and had little bearing on the moment at hand. Besides, if Rhett were to hold out for a candidate who matched precisely his own opinions in all matters, there was not a man in the congress fit to be president. Rhett had to admit the truth of that and finally decided that as he had faith in Barnwell's judgment, and if Barnwell had faith in Davis, then he could support him if given no alternative. It did not require greatness to be a president, he reflected, for Monroe, Tyler, Polk, and even Washington had not been men of great mind, but they had integrity, and that was enough. If the choice came to Cobb or Davis, Rhett would support the man from Mississippi.[43]

While Barnwell made the same approach to others in the delegation, Rhett heard from Louis T. Wigfall of Texas and Clement Clay of Alabama, both men whom he regarded highly, and they too urged Davis as the right man.[44] Though still distrustful in some measure, Rhett bowed to what seemed the inevitable, especially since there was no movement for himself and Howell Cobb was certainly less palatable than Davis. Moreover, Barnwell soon told him that a majority of the other Carolina delegates had come over to Davis, thus making Rhett's vote in opposition to Davis pointless, or so he believed. In fact, it appeared that Barnwell said the same thing to the others and thereby built a majority where none would have existed otherwise, but Rhett was not to discover that until too late.[45]

The next morning, February 9, Rhett arose convinced that either Davis or Cobb would be elected, and more likely Davis, so he wrote to Barnwell Rhett before leaving for the capitol and the election.[46] In a solemn scene hardly reminiscent of the cheering throng that witnessed the signing of the secession ordinance in Charleston, Rhett and his delegation walked forward to Howell Cobb's stand when called and there took their oath to the new provisional government.[47] That done, the congress appointed some standing committees and then turned to the election. Those delegations that had not caucused beforehand, such as South Carolina, polled their members now. Three or four Carolinians had declared for Davis by the time it became Chesnut's turn. Not entirely easy with his choice, he turned around to Rhett at the desk behind him and declared, "Uncle! I suppose I must vote for him." Chesnut's vote may have decided South

Carolina for Davis, though Rhett believed that it was his own vote that made the majority. If so, it was a fateful casting, for had South Carolina gone for Cobb or anyone else, then according to Rhett's reckoning Florida would have as well. With the states voting as blocs, that was two out of six against Davis, and given that Georgia first cast its vote as a favorite son tribute to Howell Cobb, the tally would have stood with Mississippi, Louisiana, and Alabama for Davis and three opposed, which by their rules constituted a defeat. Either another candidate would have been found or else some hard bargaining would have ensued. In any event, Rhett would always believe that it was his own vote that made Jefferson Davis president of what they now styled the Confederate States of America.[48]

As head of his delegation Rhett had to announce South Carolina's vote for Davis, a bitter moment to be sure.[49] The delegations gave the vice presidency to Stephens, mainly as compensation to Georgia for having lost the presidency. Outside a cannon boomed at the news, and Rhett joined Toombs and another as a committee to telegraph Davis officially with news of his election—yet another twist of the knife.[50] He could not know that at that very moment readers in the North were seeing that day's issue of *Frank Leslie's Illustrated Newspaper,* one of the most influential sheets in the region, which featured a portrait of Rhett and a substantial biographical sketch clearly influenced by some who knew him personally and well. If only affairs had gone differently, there might have been much more to say about him in that profile. "Life is nothing but a continual series of disappointments," he lamented to his daughter Elise two days later.[51]

Rhett might still have been hopeful for his own place in history, however, for the same day he began his campaign to get the deliberations of this congress known outside the walls of the senate chamber by moving that they remove the veil of secrecy so far as to allow the members to explain their actions at home before their state conventions, and to this the body assented. Before they adjourned that day Cobb announced his appointments to Rhett's constitution committee, the first to be so appointed, and they included Toombs, Thomas Cobb, and Chesnut among others.[52] In the next few days the congress went about the business of further organizing itself under the provisional constitution, and Rhett gained the chairmanship of the foreign affairs committee in addition to his own, which well suited him, for he already had Confederate foreign policy settled, in his own mind at least. If he could dominate the permanent constitution and dictate the terms of their relations with other nations, he might actually be more powerful than the president-elect and exert an impact lasting far longer than the elective term of Davis or anyone else.

Typically, he was not willing to wait for the new president to set his own foreign policy. Rhett had already enunciated his own expectations to Consul

Bunch and publicly to many others in recent weeks. On February 13, with Davis still en route for Montgomery, Rhett attempted a preemptive move by asking that they go into secret session and then proposing, as head of his committee, that the congress appoint commissioners to go immediately to England and France under instructions of this body until Davis took office.[53] His intent was transparent. If they could appoint and dispatch commissioners immediately, they would be on their way days in advance of Davis taking office and in Europe acting under the instructions of Rhett's committee well before Davis could get orders recalling them or changing their mandate. If British or French ministers took the bait of Rhett's policy immediately, then Davis would be presented with a foreign policy fait accompli that he dare not reverse without looking foolish and drawing to himself unbearable condemnation in the face of success. The congress passed Rhett's resolution after some debate and efforts at amendment but insisted that they wait for Davis to appoint the commissioners, which largely defeated Rhett's purpose. But by now Rhett had an alternative approach, and even more power in mind, for during the week, while they awaited Davis's arrival for his inauguration, he did not hide his desire that he be offered the portfolio as secretary of state. South Carolina, as leader in secession, was logically entitled to the premier spot in the cabinet. Not forgetting that in the old Union the state office had been considered a prelude to the presidency, he felt that with such an office he would have stature almost matching that of the president.[54]

Davis reached Montgomery on February 16, but if Rhett saw him at all prior to the inauguration it was only a courtesy call with his delegation. Two days later Rhett stood at the foot of the statehouse steps at the end of Market, dressed in the appropriate statesman's black, and watched as the inaugural procession slowly moved up the half-mile toward him from the Exchange.[55] Already that morning he and the rest had signed the engrossed copy of their provisional constitution. In a last galling irony, he had been appointed to the arrangements committee to prepare for this occasion, and now it was his part to greet Davis as he alit from his open carriage and escort him, arm-in-arm, into the chamber to take his oath. By now he knew of Barnwell's deception, which only made it more painful. Rhett's face was almost always red now thanks to that peculiar skin irritation, and the ever-present plaster no doubt paled as the occasion raised his color even more while they passed through cheering crowds that should have been cheering for him instead of the Mississippian reconstructionist. Once inside, much as the words must have stuck in his throat, Rhett presented Davis to the congress and expressed his confidence in the new president and in the wisdom of the body in selecting him.[56]

Now the rumors renewed with added vigor as speculation seethed over Davis's cabinet appointments, for he had said nothing about them prior to his arrival. Despite letting it be known generally that he wanted the state position, Rhett knew well before then that he could not expect anyone on his own delegation to do anything to advance his cause. "There is no little jealousy of me by a part of them," he thought, preferring to interpret their personal dislike as envy, though he hardly had any influence or position to arouse such feelings in them. "They will never agree to recommend me for any position at all under the Confederacy," he added, while confessing that of course he could not suggest his ambitions to any of them. A week before the inauguration he believed that he had but one friend among the Carolinians, and that was Barnwell, who wanted no office for himself and, Rhett expected, would act on that same principle when it came to his cousin. "I have never been wise in pushing myself forward to office or power, and I suppose never will," he said on February 11. "I will do my duty as the occasion requires, and leave office to be intrigued for by others." He could not change even if he wished, and so he warned his son to "prepare for disappointment." Clearly in his own mind, anyone who might achieve office in his place would do so only by chicanery.[57]

At least Rhett read his own associates well. Still there were others who might act for him, and in Montgomery generally there was speculation that he would get the state portfolio or the treasury. When Yancey called on Davis, the new president apparently offered him any cabinet post of his choosing, though he declined and instead accepted a diplomatic mission to Europe. Still the offer apparently showed that Davis harbored no prejudice against the old-time fire-eaters, unlike some in the South who had hailed Davis's election as evidence that "the Yancey-Rhetts—God be praised,—are few indeed, and *we trust and believe,* (that, like dogs) 'they have had their day.'"[58]

Yet Davis made no call on Rhett and almost certainly never even considered him. Davis was wise enough to know to steer clear of the extremists and to sense that in a revolution the greatest security lay toward the center. Moreover, Davis was a man every bit as jealous of his prerogatives as Rhett was, and if he had learned of the Carolinian's attempt of the previous week to preempt his foreign policy direction, it would have killed Rhett's chances of any appointment on the spot, especially to head the state department. The South Carolina delegation made no suggestions to Davis, and apparently neither did any of the others officially, though Magrath had asked the delegates to put him forward for attorney general.[59] Instead, on February 19, Davis spontaneously summoned Barnwell and offered the state department position to him. When Barnwell declined and suggested instead that Davis ought to appoint Howell Cobb or Toombs and might honor South Carolina by making Memminger secretary of the treasury, the president agreed. After the interview Barnwell told Rhett what he had done, apparently blithely unaware of how the news would affect him, and he added that Rhett's name had not come up in any connection during the interview. "I was too sick of heart to ask any information beyond what he thought proper to impart," Rhett told his son.[60] The state portfolio went to Toombs.

"He waited, as always, for the office to seek the man," his son wrote in the *Mercury* a week later, "and nobody suggested him." Even the paper admitted that all of the delegation were old cooperationist opponents except for Keitt, whose animosity was purely personal.[61] The Rhetts laid the disappointment at the feet of petty hatreds and old political resentments, neither grasping nor willing to grasp that when it came to any form of advancement depending on the good-will of others, his own actions and personality were his most decisive foes. "He has already brought himself into evil odor with some of the Delegations as well as our own," Memminger told a friend a week after they convened.[62] Rhett's red face was not seen at many of the parties and social gatherings held by Montgomery's social leaders for the delegates, and he would have looked with some disdain on the number of saloons, billiard halls, and bordellos in the city, hardly choosing to socialize with the other delegates patronizing all. During the successive nights of celebration after the announcement of Davis's election, crowds gathered outside the Exchange and other hotels, calling out Toombs, Stephens, Chesnut, and both Cobbs. On one occasion they begged just for "somebody!" to come out and make speeches to them, but there were no such calls for Rhett.[63]

A *Mercury* correspondent in the North noted that same week that Rhett was known to have few intimate friends and lacked the gifts of conciliation and flattery needed for public popularity. "He has never been wise in the arts of pushing himself for office," he said, "nor has he had personal friends sufficiently interested to do it for him."[64] Chesnut actually took to using Rhett's name as an uncomplimentary sobriquet for others who were querulous or arrogant, including his own wife on one occasion, and Thomas Cobb, while admitting Rhett's undeniably generous nature, still found that this kind heart came burdened "with a vast quantity of cranks and a small proportion of common sense." A quarter-century later Barnwell Rhett Jr. would make a statement that applied more to his father's inability to get along with people than to his own. "Devoted personal friendships are essential to success in politics, as in other things, *with men,*" he wrote. "I, like my father, have not sought them and hence am neglected."[65]

In a letter to the *Mercury* that he probably wrote himself, Rhett declared that he, "the prime mover of secession," had been "over-slaughed" for high office by others who he did not have to say were unworthy, and the paper denounced

Davis for failing to see that Rhett was the best man for the state office.[66] In Charleston some of his fire-eater friends regarded it as a "savage slight" to their leader, and others did not fail to note that their extremist friends in Montgomery had been ignored entirely in Davis's appointments.[67] Worse, a rumor soon went out that the whole delegation had recommended Memminger, and Rhett angrily tried to put a stop to that with open denials in the *Mercury.* It was bad enough to be passed over, but he was not about to have it put about that his old opponent had gotten office with his recommendation or that of his delegation.[68] "The course of things appear to consign me to retirement, after I shall have accounted to the Convention of South Carolina for my course here," he sadly told Barnwell Rhett Jr. In the face of his disappointments, the prospect of leaving public life looked attractive at the moment, though he had said that before more than once. Still, once again he was close to financial ruin and needed the employment. He would leave it all up to his god. "I can say with St Paul, at least in my public course—'I have fought the good fight, I have kept the faith, I have finished my course' but I cannot like him say, that I have a 'crown of righteousness laid up for me,'" he concluded. It was not the first time he likened himself to a martyr to his rectitude and his principles, nor would it be the last. Indeed, it was the only alternative to the much less palatable admission that his failures lay not in his fates but in himself.[69]

Disheartening news came from Charleston as well. Rhett had not abandoned his conviction that Pickens ought to attack and take Fort Sumter at once without awaiting the outcome of the convention in Montgomery. Probably at Rhett's behest, Hayne renewed the suggestion to the governor a few days after they convened, but on February 8, while the congress debated the provisional constitution, two telegrams arrived from Charleston. One, from Hayne, announced that Pickens rejected the suggestion. The other, from Pickens, addressed Memminger and not Rhett and told him to get the delegation to push on quickly in completing organization of the new government so that he could turn the matter of the fort over to the new authority. Keitt suggested that they submit Pickens's telegram to the congress as evidence that they must hurry, but Rhett and Barnwell opposed the idea, thinking it would make South Carolina look weak and vacillating. Their opposition alone, thought Rhett, prevented their being disgraced in front of their colleagues. Rhett thought that Pickens was a vain imbecile and that his cowardly submission to the presence of Yankee soldiers in the harbor weakened, if not ruined, the delegation's effectiveness in the congress, and he referred to him the next day in outrage as "that miserable Poltroon Pickens." How could they argue a strong policy for the new government with a weakling governor undermining their stance?[70]

With all the rest of the delegation except Barnwell favoring a delay on taking Fort Sumter until the new president could take office and power, Rhett urged his son on the scene to do something to bring it to a head first. "For heavens sake, cannot a fight be got up in Charleston Bay?" he wrote on February 9. If nothing else, they should burn Pickens in effigy and serenade him in his office with the Rogue's March. "Let the People drive him out of office or into the Bay," Rhett pleaded. "Can no way be found to extricate ourselves from the position of shame and dishonor in which we are?" Meanwhile he argued with Toombs against the introduction of a resolution in the congress, inspired by Miles and Memminger he suspected, requesting Charleston to do nothing to start hostilities, and Toombs gave in. Meanwhile Hayne telegraphed again to cry that if the fort were not taken soon, the state would be disgraced. "We the State are disgraced already," Rhett fumed. "No reasoning on Earth can satisfy the people of the South that in these two months a whole State could not take a fort defended by but 70 men. The effort is absurd. We must be despised." And all this was because of "the miserable imbeciles in Charleston."[71]

That Pickens ignored protocol and addressed Memminger rather than him only added to Rhett's fury. Rhett quickly accused Memminger of going into a panic over the telegram, though in fact Memminger seemed quite calm and was even then discussing with Charlestonians some mode of keeping the peace there until Davis could take office.[72] The younger Rhett could not precipitate an outbreak of violence, but he could turn up the heat on Pickens in the *Mercury*, and in the days to follow he took an increasingly antagonistic line, especially after the governor started allowing the Sumter garrison to buy food again.[73] It only produced a backlash. "Is there no way of controlling the Charleston Mercury," a worried Wigfall wrote to Davis on inauguration day. "It is doing us immense harm."[74] When Rhett told an Alabamian shortly after Davis's election that there would be no war with the North, the other fellow remarked that there seemed to be fighting enough going on in the *Mercury*.[75]

Wigfall wrote to Robert W. Barnwell giving Rhett a terrible chastising for his behavior and asked Barnwell to read the letter to Rhett to bring him to his senses. They were attacking not only Pickens but also the border states, fearful that compromise measures from Kentucky and Virginia then being considered in Congress in Washington might still lead to pressure for reconstruction. Keitt condemned the brothers Edmund and Barnwell Rhett Jr. for using their editorials and paper for "abusing every body & calling them submissionists *but* his father." Some began to speak only half in jest of South Carolina seceding yet again, this time from the new Confederacy. Rhett believed that people would have understood him better if only their important debates were not taking place in secret session. "I have spoken a great deal," he wrote his son in Charleston on February 11, but with the secrecy imposed, the public could not form a correct idea of his position, or the clear rectitude of his arguments, or the urgency that called for his criticism. "What a pity," Chesnut's wife observed at the time. "These men have brought old hatreds & grudges & spites from the old Union." She began to suspect that the Rhetts would knowingly damage the cause itself in their quest to have their own way, and perhaps to injure Davis in the offing for having gotten the chair that should have gone to Rhett. When Barnwell read the letter from Wigfall, his cousin was unmoved. His defense of his course, he said, was simply that he was right.[76] As far away as Arkansas readers saw what was being said and divined the Carolinian's determination to dictate to those around him. One of them derisively referred to Rhett the day before the inauguration as "King Barnwell the first."[77]

There yet remained the permanent constitution, and if Rhett could have his way there, then he could still hope to give some personal direction to the new Confederacy. He declared that his intention would be to rise above party and faction, make no compromises, and produce a document closed to "constructive usurpations." It must be a charter impervious to "doubt, dissatisfaction or revision here, in order to please others," he said, meaning the border states. If those states seceded, they were going to have to take a pure Southern rights document or none at all. "A failure now," he warned, "will probably be a failure forever."[78]

The committee met immediately after its initial appointment, and at first Rhett hoped they would be able to report a permanent constitution to the congress by February 16. He anticipated that some would attempt a delay to wait for the border states to secede and have their influence on the document, but he was having none of that. He was also determined, if possible, to see that when he delivered the document it would not be debated behind closed doors. "What took place on the provisional government satisfies me that we must have the Constitution considered in open session," he told his son Barnwell, and he urged him to get a reporter there quickly to record and report the debates back to the Mercury's columns.[79]

In the first meeting of the committee Rhett proposed that under such a constraint of time it made sense to take the old United States Constitution as a template, with only the most necessary changes being made. After all, in the main the South had not quarreled with the old Constitution itself so much as with the way it was interpreted and abused by the Yankees. If they could eliminate all possibility of such usurpations from their document, then they would produce what he called "a matter of restoration, than of innovation." Fortunately, he had it all ready in advance and produced for them a bound copybook into which he had already laid out his proposed changes in the old Constitution, and now they would use it as the starting place for their deliberations. He could not have forgotten his own assertion that the original document was fathered not by James Madison but by Charles Pinckney of South Carolina, and now here he was, another Carolinian, doing the same for another new nation. Between the two of them this permanent constitution would be pure South Carolina if he had his way, and the rest of the South would have to fall in line.[80]

The changes he proposed echoed his thirty years and more of fighting against consolidationism. There would be no preamble with its unfounded talk of "the People of the United States" implying a primary national allegiance. They were a confederation of sovereign states, and he stated explicitly that each one retained "its sovereignty freedom and independence and every power jurisdiction and right" except those explicitly delegated therein. Congress would be constituted and elected just as before, except that in apportioning representatives each inhabitant, excluding Indians, was to be counted in full, and not as before where slaves were numbered at three-fifths of their white counterparts. That way states with a high percentage of slaves, such as South Carolina, would have representation commensurate with their stake in and commitment to a slave nation. Rhett would make it harder to overturn a presidential veto by requiring a two-thirds vote of all members of the House, rather than just two-thirds of those present.

He struck hard for reform in the taxing power by specifying that the congress could only collect taxes and duties for revenue to carry on the government, specifically adding that "no tax duty impost or excise shall be laid to foster or promote one branch of industry rather than another; nor shall any tax or duty be laid on importations from foreign Nations, higher than fifteen per cent on their value." Congress could, however, lay lower duties on imports from foreign nations of choice "to enduce friendly political relations," his old most-favored-nation proposal to Bunch. He also toyed with laying a poll tax on slaves as on whites for raising revenue but abandoned that almost at once. The Confederacy, too, should have the right to accept from a state or states a district for the capital city, but he emphatically provided that the congress would have no power to interfere with slavery in that district. There would be no petitions from any Southern "Old Man Eloquents" here. And whereas the old Constitution granted complete authority over any state property purchased by the national government for forts, arsenals, and other such installations, in his Confederacy the states would have the prerogative to retain possession of such places. If they chose to surrender them to the national government for defense in time of war, possession must be restored to the states upon demand, a policy that could potentially cripple a new nation's ability to defend itself if state and national authorities fell out. If Pickens would not assert South Carolina's right to Fort Sumter, Rhett would do it for him in the new constitution. That done, Rhett inserted again his failed proposal for the provisional charter that congress could prohibit the slave trade, but there would be no exclusion of it in his document. Ever devoted to his quixotic goal of a direct tax, he removed the prohibition against it from the old Constitution.

When it came to the presidency Rhett had equally definite reforms in mind. His president should serve for six years rather than four and be limited to a single term, though he would be eligible again after someone else served an intervening term. He had tried for the single-term limit in Washington as far back as 1838. He wanted no two-term dictators like Jackson now. There would be no abuse of executive patronage or abuse of power in the quest for reelection. He retained the old prohibition against the president receiving any other emolument than his salary but amended the oath of office to add an avowal to "preserve protect and defend the Sovereignty of the States" as well as the constitution. His president would retain the power of appointment as before, but if the Senate rejected one, he would not be able to get around that by reappointing that same person again during the Senate's recess. This was a blow against patronage abuse.

When it came to the fugitive slave provisions he took no chances of misunderstanding or interpretation. The governors of the states would be bound by law to deliver up any runaways from other states, and when slaves were abducted or otherwise rescued from slavery, the state in which it happened must pay the owner the full value of the slave. He also dealt with another grievance over the issue of territories. The old document referred to territories belonging to the national government, but he specified that they belonged to "all the states and the peoples thereof" and that they all had equal and full rights to the enjoyment of all "property" recognized as lawful in the states to which they belonged. It was his old common property doctrine, and there would be no "squatter sovereignty" raising its head in this Confederacy. And finally, to make certain that no state would ever have to suffer challenges to its dignity or sovereignty from sister states or the national government, he added that "any State whenever it deems it expedient may exercise its sovereign right of withdrawing peaceably from the Confederacy."[81]

Aside from a few minor housekeeping changes, that was it—enough to guarantee some debate, no doubt, but every change mandated by the injustices and abuses they had suffered in the old Union. But Rhett soon found that he could not impose his will on his committee and that, in fact, some of them had definite ideas of their own. More than once the tyranny of the majority that so offended his autocratic nature overruled him. The result was much more discussion that he had expected. After only a few days, by February 14, he saw his hopes in shambles in the committee and wrote bitterly for the *Mercury* that fear for the future and a want of statesmanship were about to paralyze all hopes for reform from his committee, though he did not name it specifically as the culprit. "Let your people prepare their minds for a failure in the future Permanent Southern Constitution," he warned, "for South Carolina is about to be saddled with almost every grievance except Abolition." By then he had already lost on eliminating the prohibition of the slave trade and the three-fifths clause so important to his state's power in the congress, since she had the greatest proportion of blacks to whites. There was no telling what else he would lose in the days ahead. "The fruit of the labors of thirty odd long years, in strife and bitterness, is about to slip through our fingers," he continued in the *Mercury.* Those were *his* thirty years, and so had been most of the strife and bitterness.[82] February 16 came and went, and the speedy reporting of his version that he had anticipated disappeared in long evening meetings and revisions.

When they were done, the committee members had rejected almost all of his changes and made several of their own. They reinserted a preamble with the dangerous words "the people of the Confederate States," though it went on emphatically to assert state sovereignty. Gone was his enumeration of slaves at full value, and instead the three-fifths clause remained. Especially irritating, the committee demanded retaining the prohibition of the African slave trade. Gone, too, was his change in the veto override procedure. The new version allowed cabinet heads to hold seats on the floor of the congress when invited; rebuffed Rhett's reforms on taxing power, tariffs, and internal improvements; likewise eliminated his stipulations on possession of forts and arsenal property; ignored the provisions on slavery in any capital district; and eliminated the special inducements to foreign powers for amity and friendship. His only significant changes to pass the committee were the guarantee of slavery in the territories (though the committee only provided this during the territorial stage and thus left the door open to possible free states being formed) and the six-year presidential term, and even there they rejected the one-term limit. They also accepted his prohibition against the reappointment of rejected presidential appointees, a minor point at best.[83]

It was yet one more stunning blow to his battered ego. He was being rejected at every turn, it seemed, and then during the losing battle with his committee it suddenly appeared as if his god had deserted him too. Indeed, much of his failure to carry a large share of his program probably lay in the effects of a telegram that came from Charleston just a day or two after the inauguration. Little Nannie had died of scarlet fever. "My poor bleeding heart," he moaned to Barnwell Rhett Jr. "Nannies departure has broken one more link which bound me to life." The anguish threw him into a melancholy despair unlike anything before except the death of his first wife. He felt as if his own life were meaningless now except insofar as he could continue to support those of his family who remained, and yet even there he appeared doomed to failure. "My life," he said, "appears to me to be worthless to any body."[84] Katherine took the train to Montgomery to console her husband, even though it meant leaving their youngest daughter, Katherine, still ill herself. By February 25, the day Rhett somehow tore himself from his mourning to announce that he would be ready to report the constitution the next day, she was with him.[85]

Perhaps she should have remained in Charleston. Rhett reported his committee's results on February 26 and lost one more battle when a majority on his committee declared that they wanted the constitution considered behind closed doors. There was too much in it likely to produce serious debate and deep division for them to risk letting the outside world see the cracks in their unity. With the debate set to begin on February 28, all Rhett could do the day before was to move that stenographers be employed to take down word for word the debates to come so that one day the people would know what he had fought for.[86] Even there he lost, and then came another telegram that made it all pale for the moment. Just past her third birthday, little Katherine had died that same day.[87]

The news so stunned him that he could hardly speak of the double loss outside his family. To a man of such tender sensibilities and such affectionate, not to say doting, devotion to his children, it was a blow that would mark him for the rest of his life. The death of Elizabeth nine years before was still with him, and always would be, and it was not yet fourteen months since the loss of three-year-old Ann Constance. Now two more beloved children gone in scarcely more than a week was shattering. Having his wife with him must have helped, but even his faith could hardly lift from him the anger and frustration at losses so senseless. As of old, Rhett could only hope to lose himself in activity. The constitutional debate was just the battle he needed. It was a field on which perhaps he could win back some of the ground lost in committee, and if he needed a foe on which to focus the rage that must have seethed within, he had already had one in his sights for some weeks now—Jefferson Davis. "South Carolina—Bluffton Rhetts, &c," said Mary Chesnut, had "heated themselves into a fever that only bloodletting could ever cure—it was the inevitable remedy."[88] She was speaking of a state full of fire-eaters in South Carolina, but her words applied as well to this one man. Robert Barnwell Rhett needed a battle now more than ever. For him, too, it was "the inevitable remedy."

TWENTY-ONE

A Pompous, Hard, Ambitious Man
1861

HE HARDLY LOOKED LIKE A WARRIOR. An Alabama newspaperman thought that "Rhett, that awful fire-eater, is a mild looking man, with gold spectacles, and a patch on his nose." To date the only thing people in Montgomery had seen him attack were the meals at the Exchange dining room. "How much fire he can eat I do not know," said one observer, "but if Watt, of the Exchange, makes much out of him at $2.50 *per diem,* I am greatly deceived. The way he lays in on the boiled turkey and oyster stuffing is a caution to tavern keepers."[1] He had always had a formidable appetite, but in the wake of his family tragedy and the near-collapse of his long dreams for a new Southern political utopia, his only hunger now seemed to be to strike out to relieve his frustration. The new president of the Confederacy became his target barely three days after taking office.

The provisional constitution provided a salary for the president but prohibited him from being paid any further fees or "emoluments," as in the old Constitution. Davis had taken rooms at his own expense at the Exchange, but with Washington and the White House as the model, some in the congress thought it befitting their new executive that he should have a mansion too. On February 22 an Alabama delegate introduced a resolution that the appropriate committee should lease "a furnished mansion" to be the presidential residence. Rhett immediately spoke up to point out that the measure was unconstitutional, since providing a residence constituted an emolument beyond Davis's salary. Others in his delegation agreed, and so did most of the Louisiana members, but when a vote was taken the resolution passed with four states in favor against their two. That was bad enough, for the change in their constitution had been made specifically, thought Rhett, to avoid the way the United States president had seemingly no limit on what he could receive. But then Davis, who Rhett thought should have seen the unconstitutional nature of the measure and vetoed it, instead signed it into effect. To Rhett nothing but a "spirit of indecent avarice" could have actuated Davis in doing so, though he confessed that it was a paltry matter. Still the principle was what mattered, and even if not already envious and distrustful of Davis, Rhett now started to conclude that he had made a terrible mistake in voting for Davis, one that he would one day claim to be the greatest of his life.[2]

Even while he wrote to the *Mercury* by his non de plume "Reviewer" of the outrage and the "enormous rent" of five thousand dollars to be paid for the house, Rhett was already exercised over another presidential failure.[3] It had been apparent to Rhett from the beginning that the success of their movement might depend on the friendship or intervention of England and France. He already had foreign policy mapped out for his committee, and it was virtually what he had proposed to Bunch two months earlier. To effect his combination of minimal tonnage duties on foreign imports sufficient only for harbor maintenance, punitive tonnage duties on those nations failing to recognize Confederate independence, free navigation of Confederate ports to allies, the lure of most-favored-nation status with 15 or 20 percent import duties for twenty years in return for alliances, and if necessary a twenty-year agreement with Britain to help her protect her Canadian territory from Northern aggression, he wanted Confederate diplomats to be invested with considerable authority to make treaties.[4] He had already asserted this position to the South Carolina convention as well, especially championing the right to use importation taxes and preferential rates to lure other nations toward recognition. As for the twenty-year periods involved, he believed that in that span of time the Confederacy would grow so large and powerful that it would have need of no alliances with anyone afterward to maintain itself.[5]

Rebuffed in his earlier attempt to start his own foreign policy, Rhett had to wait until Davis selected his three commissioners, and as head of his committee he brought the nominations to the floor for confirmation on February 26. Yancey was to lead the mission, assisted by Pierre Rost of Louisiana and Ambrose Dudley Mann, the only career diplomat of the three. Distracted by the death of his second child a day later, Rhett did not actually speak to Yancey in the matter for a few days after confirmation of the appointments, but in the meantime he encountered Secretary of State Toombs on the stairs of the Exchange. When he asked what Yancey's instructions were for his mission and whether they included Rhett's expectations, Toombs told him that Davis had not taken account of them. At once Rhett called on Yancey, who seemed to confirm that the president had not given him unilateral authority to conclude commercial treaties.

"What, then, can be your instructions?" asked a puzzled Carolinian. Yancey replied that he was to plead the justice of their cause, give assurances of their peaceful intent and of their power to establish and maintain themselves, and point out the advantage to Europe of the consequent weakening of the United States as a commercial and political competitor. That, of course, was all pointless diplomatic jargon, as Rhett well knew. Where was the real persuasion, where were the concrete benefits they had to offer if they were recognized, and where—being Rhett—were the threats if they did not? "I suppose on our cotton," was all Yancey could reply. Davis had emphasized the importance to Europe of Southern cotton and was counting on the foreign manufacturers' hunger for the fiber to prod their governments. "He says that 'cotton is king.'"

Rhett was shocked. When he told Yancey what he thought the mission's powers ought to be, Yancey agreed fully but did not know what he could do. "If you will take the counsel of a friend, do not accept the appointment," Rhett responded. "You will meet nothing but failure and mortification." He should return to Davis and demand the necessary power to make his efforts a success, or else stay at home. "You have no business in Europe. You carry no argument which Europe wishes to hear," he went on. He had to have something to offer nations in compensation for the risk they would take in recognizing the Confederacy. "Without powers, you cannot approach a single Minister or ruler of a Foreign nation," he charged. "You will have nothing to propose; and nothing therefore, to treat about."[6]

In fact, Rhett's policy may have offered the brightest prospect of success in obtaining recognition, since it appealed to the self-interest that inevitably motivated nations as well as men, but Jefferson Davis was not about to have policy dictated to him.[7] In the final instructions to the commission before their departure Toombs—presumably with authority from Davis—did order them to propose treaties of friendship, commerce, and navigation, giving them full powers for that purpose.[8] Thus perhaps Rhett's urging did prompt Yancey to exact greater authority for his mission, but by then Rhett was already attempting to influence affairs even more. He met with Mann by chance in the street early in March just before the commission was to leave for Europe, and after no doubt pressing again his views on what they should demand from and offer to Great Britain, he advised Mann that if they met with any reluctance from the British on recognition, they should cross immediately to France, where he expected they would be warmly received.[9] Rhett did not learn what the commission's final authority was before they left, though as chairman of the foreign affairs committee he certainly could have asked, but by that time he seems already to have adopted a policy of having nothing to do with Davis whatever.[10] Instead, he planned his next approach to be to the congress itself, where he would try to make foreign policy on the floor and force it on Davis. However, that would have to wait awhile, for there were other failures of the president's to address first.

Rhett soon came to the conclusion that Davis was going to support protective tariffs. "It is impossible to obtain a simple Revenue Tariff from this Congress,"

Rhett grumbled on February 25, and no one showed any disposition to take his ideas into account. "My uncompromising Southernism and anti-Tariffism, I suppose, renders me unfit for the councils of the Provisional Government," he said.[11] Two weeks earlier Keitt had told Hammond there would be no free trade coming out of Montgomery, no resort to Rhett's direct taxation ideas, for no man would willingly give ten dollars out of his pocket once he had it, in preference to paying that sum as part of the price of purchase of dutied goods.[12] They had to have a revenue tariff, though to Rhett anything more than 15 to 20 percent for covering expenses constituted protectionism.[13] But they could not wait on the tariff to finance their new government. They had to have much more money, and quickly. The states were going to make loans and outright gifts to the government to get it going, South Carolina having a million dollars or more available.[14] But there was something even better immediately at hand, and that was their cotton.

Some of the previous crop was still unsold—though not as much as Rhett believed—and soon another two hundred thousand bales would come ready from the new crop.[15] To Rhett, of course, that cotton was the carrot to lure foreign recognition. He did not believe that an embargo on cotton would alone bring about recognition, but certainly it would apply such pressure that their other diplomatic inducements—if his were in fact applied—must soon bring England to their door. Instead he found that Davis and Memminger were not only allowing the continued shipment of bales by Southern merchants but actually encouraging it, as when Memminger overruled an executive council embargo imposed in South Carolina. It was all part of the same corrupt scheme. Instead of a simple direct tax that would raise money quickly and equitably all across the Confederacy, they were going to rely on high tariffs while at the same time bowing to pressure from the rich planters not to interfere with their own profits on which they had no fear of having to pay taxes. Moreover, if war came or if the North blockaded Confederate ports, customs duty would be drastically reduced if not eliminated. Only foreign recognition could end the blockade, but Davis had prejudiced any chances of that at the outset. Meanwhile, with planters willing to offer hundreds of thousands of bales of cotton to the government at large discounts out of patriotism, Montgomery could have sold the bales and realized millions almost immediately. But Davis argued that such would be unconstitutional, meanwhile allowing all of that cotton to continue going out of the country to the profit of the planters themselves. Rhett thought the government ought at least to buy the cotton at the fair rate of eight cents a pound, ship it abroad for sale, and keep the money in the Bank of England to meet drafts for purchase of munitions and supplies. The only other alternative was direct taxation.[16] The failure to adopt any of Rhett's ideas was just another black mark against Davis, more evidence that he had never had the stomach for the real revolution around them and that he remained, as before, the weak tool of protectionists.

Worse than all that was the president's utter failure to prepare properly for war. Rhett said repeatedly that there would be no conflict. He had been saying for a generation that the Yankees were too mean and cowardly to try to stand up to the South. That was one of the reasons he so blithely tried to commence hostilities in Charleston harbor, for he did not expect the Union to fight back. Yet he admitted the possibility that there might be an attempt at coercion that would lead to warfare, and thus even before they finished their permanent constitution he urged speedy and strong military readiness. "We should prepare for war as if war was inevitable," he would say.[17] If there had to be a war, they should be ready to make it short, sharp, and decisive, for he instinctively understood that with its disadvantages, any protracted conflict inevitably worked against the Confederacy. They must act while their spirit and patriotism were at an absolute high. It was his old argument that delay meant defeat, and it was never more sound than now.[18]

On February 28 the congress authorized the president to receive into the national service all state forces then under arms and followed that with more acts calling out state militia, creating a regular corps or professional army to one day replace the volunteers. In addition the president was authorized to call for up to one hundred thousand more men to serve for a year. Of course the management of all this was up to the president, as commander-in-chief, and Rhett would sarcastically comment of Davis that "his military pretensions and tastes, he did not permit to be unknown." Indeed, during debate over the February 28 act Rhett complained to several fellow delegates that the bill gave Davis too much control over the army, but no one took his grumbling seriously. Yet from the first Davis seemed reluctant to take full advantage of what was available. He buried himself with the chairman of the military affairs committee day after day and did not ask the congress for the money to finance an ambitious and aggressive military and naval buildup when the enthusiasm and wherewithal seemed to Rhett to be most available. Moreover, thanks to the reforming provision in the provisional—and later the permanent—constitution that all appropriations had to originate from the president or one of the executive departments, thus eliminating pork barrel legislation, the congress itself could not initiate money. Otherwise Rhett would have taken it upon himself to start appropriations and thereby try to force Davis, by veto overrides if necessary, to prepare for war in a manner that suited Rhett's expectations.[19]

Late in February, thinking himself firmly in the president's bad books after the objection to the leasing of the mansion, Rhett decided not to approach Davis with his concern about creating a navy. Instead, as on so many occasions before when he knew his own personality might work against his aims, he persuaded another member of the congress to ask Davis to request a substantial appropriation of several million dollars to buy cotton and ship it to England to pay for a fleet of new ironclad warships. Davis rebuffed the suggestion as impractical, or so Rhett thought, possibly in terms suggesting that he did not like others telling him his business, which would have been just like the president. All Rhett could do was turn the matter over to his son to get the *Mercury* to add the pressure for a navy to its columns of complaint.[20] Rhett even got his editor son to send to Montgomery a series of expensive imported color lithographs showing uniforms of European armies for Davis to use in designing Confederate uniforms, and which in the main Davis did himself. The president never returned the pictures, adding yet one more grievance to the list.[21]

In his military and naval preparations Jefferson Davis, of course, answered to a host of circumstances and dictates of which Rhett was unaware, or to which he simply would not have given cognizance in any case since they ran counter to his own preconceived notions of how affairs must unfold if done his way. The supply of arms was limited, and Davis, expecting a long war if there were one since he doubted even now that foreign powers would come to their aid, preferred to use them to equip volunteer regiments that he would enlist for three years' service, rather than put them in the hands of the current wave of twelve-month enlistees. Before long he would be turning down the offer of new twelve-month men, holding out for the longer enlistments. Rhett, wanting a short and decisive war, believed they should arm everyone now regardless of term of enlistment, as he was counting on quick European recognition and intervention thanks to the allurements of his generous foreign policy.

Both Davis and Rhett envisioned well-integrated plans, but the president's was the more sound. Never expecting foreign support, he based his hopes on a long-range military policy; should recognition come anyhow, it was only so much the better. If either of Rhett's two lines of offensive failed, however, the other could not stand alone. If they counted on recognition and intervention to be decisive in a short war, and it did not come, then the twelve-month regiments could hardly win a quick victory on their own; on the other hand, if those volunteers failed in the field during their term of service, foreign recognition would never come. Even if they had attempted to compare their views dispassionately, it would have availed nothing. Davis was not a man to explain himself to anyone, and Rhett was not one to listen to opinions counter to his own. In time, in a grotesque exaggeration, Rhett would accuse Davis of turning down whole armies—hundreds of thousands of volunteers—because of lack of arms. In fact, Davis did reject a few thousand for inability to arm them, but they were the twelve-month troops that his own policy wisely looked beyond.

The one great strength in Rhett's overall concept was the sale of cotton overseas by the government. Had Davis been willing to do so, then he might well have been able to buy enough arms to accept and equip every regiment regardless of enlistment period. Yet as events would demonstrate, even raising an army three times the size of what the Confederacy would field in its first year would not have changed their course, for being resolved to stand on the defensive and to present themselves to the world in that attitude, they needed only enough strength to protect their borders, and that they would do for the next year.

Rhett's rapidly growing distaste for Davis fed as well on the handling of affairs in Charleston. He took special interest in the local regiments being raised, trying to ensure that the February 28 bill allowed for acceptance into the Confederate service of an artillery company in which his son Alfred had enlisted as a lieutenant; Rhett was seeking in the manner of all politician fathers to advance the career of his son.[22] There at least he got satisfaction, but the continuing delay in taking Fort Sumter made him livid. As early as February 11, Rhett predicted that Davis would not attack and take Fort Sumter or the other spot of contention, Fort Pickens outside Pensacola, Florida. Rhett believed that instead the president would try to negotiate, or else delay any attack until Lincoln's inauguration in March.[23] Hayne sent a panicky telegram on Davis's inauguration day that if they did not take Sumter immediately, he feared a Yankee fleet would occupy the harbor, though there was no such fleet in sight or even preparation. The next day he complained that South Carolina was not ready to attack the fort but said that Davis should order it anyhow.[24]

Rhett and Barnwell did not believe that Pickens did not have force enough to take the fort and wired back to ask him when he could. He responded that within a week, perhaps, he would be ready, then asked for more experienced officers to be sent to Charleston for the effort when it came.[25] Davis sent an inspector who reported back that Pickens had sufficient strength, and by the end of the month the governor was begging that Sumter be taken at once, though now the order had to come from Montgomery. While still holding no intention of taking overt action, Davis turned the command of Charleston over to a new general, P. G. T. Beauregard of Louisiana, who met with Rhett and the other Carolinians before going to his command. But there was no order to attack.[26] Pickens's dithering and indecision was costing them time, and Davis seemed no more disposed to action, one more evidence that the president did not have his heart in the cause.

In the main, Rhett could only fight back through the *Mercury*. By the end of the month he was calling the provisional government "useless" and preparing readers to find the permanent constitution less than satisfactory in all respects, suggesting that the convention would have to demand amendments to remedy its shortcomings on his prime issues. "Affairs here are not conducted in a way always agreeable to the policy and wishes of South Carolina," he said, and he advised his audience to use "a very long mental telescope" to see any positive results in the future.[27] His cousin Barnwell, who could say almost anything to Rhett without offending but who could never influence him to change, saw clear enough the origin of the *Mercury*'s increasing malice toward the government, and Davis in particular. In fact, he told Chesnut's wife that the Rhetts had started attacking Davis even before he had a chance to do anything wrong. "They were offended—not with him so much as with the man who was put in what they considered Barnwell Rhett's place," he said, and she agreed. "The latter had howled nullification, secession, &c so long," she believed, that "when he found his ideas taken up by all the Confederate world, he felt he had a vested right to the leadership."[28]

Hers was an astute observation, matched by others. A Mobile editor declared that the *Mercury*, "always discontented and grumbling, arrogant in tone, flippant in judgment, intolerant of any opinion but its own," did not speak for South Carolina but only for its owner and editor.[29] And almost everyone understood that it was that owner who was speaking, whether he signed himself as "Reviewer" or not at all. "I say nothing about the Mercury," Trescot wrote from Charleston to Miles in Montgomery in mid-February, "because if report speaks the truth, you are much nearer its source of inspiration than I am."[30] The rumors and public condemnation became so prevalent that the younger Rhett resorted to falsehood and denied them repeatedly in his columns, at the very same time that his father was sending him even more critical articles and advising him on what anti-Davis material to publish and when.[31] Outrageous or not, it was good for circulation, which had quadrupled by now since the Rhetts took over. They would soon be buying another new press to meet the demand.[32]

While his contempt for Davis steadily grew, and even after the debate on the permanent constitution commenced, Rhett was active in the daily affairs in the congress. Concerned always with fiscal thrift, he tried unsuccessfully to amend a funding bill calling for accepting loans from the several states, by limiting the amount that could be borrowed unless there was war with the Union. To forestall such a war he initiated a commission that would be sent to Washington seeking to negotiate the outstanding differences between the two nations, and even to secure friendly relations. He also authored legislation to create commercial agents and foreign consuls, one more step in his program of securing European interest and amity.

In the debates themselves his votes remained unwaveringly true to his staunch conservatism. He unsuccessfully opposed an act making violation of the slave trade prohibition a felony, seeking to reduce it to a misdemeanor instead, and he then voted in the minority to override a veto when Davis rejected the bill because it provided that illegally imported slaves would be kept in the Confederacy and sold to benefit the government. If Rhett could not keep slave trading from being a crime, at least he could try to keep the slaves once in the country. He opposed an export duty on specific raw materials shipped out of the Confederacy but stood with the majority in favor of an overall export duty on all goods, thus remaining true to his position against favoring any one industry or product. Rhett even tried to prevent the carriage and delivery of mail on Sundays by their new Post Office Department.[33] Occasionally some of his old fire flared up, especially in debate with Charles Conrad of Louisiana, who seemed to lie in wait for the Carolinian, pouncing on him over some point whenever he spoke.[34] The two were what Mary Chesnut called "everlasting speakers and wranglers."[35] The clerk of the congress even composed a bit of doggerel about the debates on February 21 when no chaplain appeared to open the day with prayers:

> The place left vacant by the priest
> Just call on Rhett to fill,
> And if the Lord don't answer him,
> Conrad of Louisiana will.[36]

Barnwell and Miles and others took great glee in circulating copies of the verse to their friends, though if Rhett ever read the poem, he failed to comment on whether or not he thought it amusing.

By the time the debates on the permanent constitution were to commence, few failed to note Rhett's contentiousness, or that of his fellow Carolinians. A reporter rated the different delegations by their characteristics—Georgia most boisterous, Mississippi most braggartish, and so on—and concluded that South Carolina was "the most bellicose."[37] Indeed, the fact that they did not get along among themselves escaped few. "The South Carolina delegation are all Ishmaelites amongst themselves," Alexander Stephens commented early in March. "No two of them agree." Each seemed jealous of the others, and though they were respectful in debate, out of the statehouse they talked incessantly against one another. Stephens saw clearly Rhett's compulsion to be their chief, but "none of them will acknowledge his leadership." Only Barnwell got along with him, but he, too, would not be led by him.[38] Despite their seeming friendship, Withers did not except Rhett when he said that month that Barnwell was the only honest man in the delegation, and Rhett would have words of his own.[39] After Withers told Keitt that Rhett had lost all his influence by speaking too much on the floor and asked, "why will he make such a fool of himself?" Keitt could only laugh a short time later when Withers held the floor and Rhett commented to him, "just listen to that old fool."[40]

That exchange came during the debate on the permanent constitution, which was always destined to strain tempers and patience. The congress made it a special order of business every day from the commencement of the debate on February 28. Rhett had tried to postpone the debate until March 4, but all of the other states voted against him and South Carolina stood evenly divided. Clearly he wanted to wait until they knew the content of Lincoln's inaugural, hoping no doubt that it would be sufficiently threatening or insulting that inflamed passions in the congress would work to his advantage in amending his committee's version to return the charter to his original design.[41]

At first they started work on the constitution at noon every day, but within a few days the task became so heavy that they expanded their hours, starting at 10:00 A.M. and working until 3:30 or 4:00 and then again in the evening from 7:00 to 11:00 or later.[42] They began with the preamble, and though Rhett would have been pleased to see it eliminated altogether, in the end they settled for "We the people" followed by an explicit statement that each state was acting in its independent and sovereign capacity. After that, much of the first lengthy article of the constitution was passed without substantial debate over the powers delegated to the congress. But then they stuck on definitions of citizenship and eligibility for office, and Rhett and virtually all the rest rejected an attempt to place a term of residence and citizenship requirement on officeholders. The moment any Southerner became a Confederate, Rhett believed, he was entitled to hold office.[43]

The larger issues appeared soon thereafter, beginning with Rhett's attempt once again to have the slave trade exclusion eliminated or softened. Broadening his definition to include any form of bonded service, involuntary or otherwise, he proposed that they merely assent that the congress could if it wished in the future exercise the power to exclude not only foreign slaves but also Chinese coolies and any other variety of indentured servant. Every state but South Carolina went against him. The slave trade exclusion would stay, to his eternal chagrin.

Undaunted, he tried again and again to make the new document more emphatically the basis of a slave nation, sometimes without regard to the logic of where such provisions should go. When they debated the clause prohibiting states from entering treaties and alliances, he tried unsuccessfully to insert an amendment providing that no state could remain in the Confederacy if it abolished slavery. He then tried later to insert the same clause, and when that failed, he supported a doomed substitute prohibiting any state from abolishing slavery without the unanimous assent of the other states. It was an explicit denial of absolute state control over this one domestic institution, and a direct contradiction of his whole argument for years past. In short, having maintained all along that only the states individually had the right to decide on the issue of slavery for themselves, once having embraced the institution, he maintained that a state did not have the right to exclude it again without the approval of outside sovereignties. Whether that outside agency were a state or a federal government, the violation of his long-proclaimed principle was the same. In short, for Rhett slavery was a power superior even to state sovereignty.

He also supported an amendment that would ban the admission of free states, addressing his old fear that Northern and western states would want to leave the old Union and align themselves with the new one, just leading to the same problems they had left behind. That failed, and Rhett helped pass a version by Miles that would not admit any state that denied the right to hold slave property or to protect fully such property to the owner, but that, too, failed to survive. He also tried unsuccessfully to get passed his original fugitive slave law clause forcing the executive of any state to surrender a fugitive or provide reimbursement to the owner. Throughout, on every issue touching slavery, Rhett remained rigidly consistent to his long-held belief in the legal and ethical sanctity of the institution and the necessity for making an assertive statement of such part of the fundamental law.[44]

He remained equally consistent on other issues that had been part of his political creed for the past three decades. Toombs had introduced and then withdrew an amendment banning internal improvement expenditures to aid commerce, but Rhett then proposed a similar one of his own, got it past an attempt to table, and then supported it to passage with help from a Louisiana delegate and a minor amendment from Thomas Cobb allowing for appropriations for navigational aids. When a motion came up to eliminate the provision prohibiting the congress from initiating any appropriations except for its own expenses, requiring them to originate from the executive departments, Rhett stood with the majority that defeated the motion. He defended state prerogatives rigidly, joining a majority to deny their national judiciary any jurisdiction over disputes between citizens of different states and unsuccessfully trying to deny the anticipated Supreme Court jurisdiction over any case already settled by a state court. He did not want to risk a high court's interpretation of state rights and laws, and even opposed a clause permitting the congress to allow appeals from state courts to go to the higher bench. Boyce's attempt to reinsert an outright statement of the right of a state to secede found South Carolina standing alone in favor, and it was tabled for good.[45]

Rhett tried to reinstate his original clause preventing a president from succeeding himself without an intervening term, and that failed, but South Carolina supported a successful amendment by Boyce simply limiting any chief executive to one term, which largely accomplished his object. Rhett's effort to make eligible for the presidency any natural-born citizen of any state, even a United States citizen, at the time of this constitution's adoption seemed at first puzzling. No doubt he had in mind men such as Hunter of Virginia and Breckinridge of Kentucky who might join them yet whose states had not seceded as yet, and might never. They were far more able than many in the Confederacy, and no doubt he had Davis in mind especially. Congress tabled his amendment but then with his help passed a version that achieved the same results.

As to the manner of electing the president, the congress adopted the committee report, which merely copied the United States Electoral College. Rhett had not proposed any changes in his original draft submitted to the committee, thinking that any faults that existed were not in the system itself but in the way it had been put in practice in the Union, and of course he distrusted the only logical alternative of a simple popular election in which the dreaded majority will risked cutting off the oligarchy from rule.[46] South Carolina preferred having electors selected by the legislature, which still kept control in the hands of an elite, but not one other state would go along with her. This issue became especially contentious in the debate and so seemingly insoluble that the members simply decided to leave it to be reformed later. Rhett objected to cutting off debate with passage, however, wanting to keep fighting it out then until they found some better solution. In congressional apportionment he understandably tried yet failed to get more representatives for South Carolina, having lost the elimination of the three-fifths clause that would have accomplished the same end. And he supported another failed amendment by Thomas Cobb that would prohibit the congress from requiring any citizen to work on a Sunday except in time of emergency.[47]

Rhett enjoyed other successes. His proposal for a six-year presidential term came through intact, and so did his provision that the congress could only levy taxes and duties to raise revenue for carrying on the government but could not grant bounties to favor trade or levy duties to foster industry. He did have to do some behind-the-scenes work speaking personally with the wavering Alabama delegation to get one of them to work on his colleagues before that state cast the deciding favorable vote, however. In a blow to reform patronage, he successfully inserted a clause allowing the president to remove from office his cabinet and foreign diplomats at pleasure. But as for all other civil officers, they could be dismissed, but such removals along with justifications would have to be reported to the senate. There should be no rampant spoils system as under Andrew Jackson. He also proposed Article V of the new constitution, providing that conventions of any three states could issue a call for a convention of all the Confederate States for the purpose of amending this constitution, and that any amendments passed by that convention should require ratification by two-thirds of the state conventions or legislatures to become law, instead of the three-fourths demanded under the old Constitution. Thus he took the power to initiate amendments out of the hands of the congress entirely but made it much easier than in the old Union for the states to initiate change and as well made it easier for such amendments to become law.[48]

The debate seemed endless at times, and after a few days Rhett began once more to despair. He wrote to the *Mercury* that South Carolina's members were fighting hard for a constitution of which their state could approve but that success looked doubtful.[49] Still he never quit, and he often took critical members aside to argue for support or opposition on a provision or change.[50] Late one evening as Rhett held the floor during the constitutional debate, Keitt said to Stephens in jest that he would love to find a deaf man, but the little Georgian went him one better by saying that at the moment he could almost fall in love with a mute. "Just look at Rhett now," he said, "speaking and no body listening."[51] Still Stephens had to admit that most of the really substantive improvements in the final document came from Rhett, and J. L. M. Curry of Alabama credited the Carolinian as one of the ones who accomplished the most in promoting the changes in the committee report.[52]

Certainly Rhett felt proud of what he had accomplished. He struck a seemingly decisive blow at internal improvements with an explicit prohibition that still allowed state ports and harbors to levy duties sufficient for maintenance but that required any surplus revenue, beyond what was needed to sustain navigational aids on the rivers and coastline, to be paid over to the Confederate treasury, thus discouraging state abuse of the taxing power. He incorporated the free trade provision that prohibited bounties or special duties to encourage industry. Of course his six-year executive term passed, and so did his provision to provide for independent tenure of office, one of the first civil service reforms in American history. And in making amendment of this constitution easier he eliminated, he believed, the onerous will of the majority, for no matter how large this Confederacy should become, only three states could require a constitutional convention, and then the majority would have to meet with them and address issues. In contrast, the Northern majority for generations had refused to entertain constitutional amendments to settle the South's complaints.

Unsaid, but implicit in his revision of the amendment process, was that it would be easier in the immediate future to insert changes that the congress had rejected in debate. Time after time in the slave trade prohibition, free state admission, and other vital issues three states had stood with Rhett only to see the other four—Texas had now seceded too—go against or else stand undecided, in either case producing defeat. If those same three states—usually South Carolina, Florida, and Texas or Mississippi—stood together in the future, they could force reconsideration at a time when there would be no distraction from framing the constitution as a whole, and after the people and their state conventions had been sufficiently aroused. Rhett was nothing if not a political strategist.

Looking at all this, Rhett concluded that he authored "perhaps the most important part" of the new charter, his goal throughout being to remove the ambiguities in the old Constitution that had been the source of all their grievances.[53] He accomplished more revision on the old United States Constitution than any other delegate and succeeded with at least six substantial reforms. It is a fact that he failed to achieve his fully integrated program of making the Confederacy a congruous or uniform slave society, but to expect any one delegate or even state to so thoroughly dominate such a proceeding would have been unrealistic. In the context of what could be done, the divisions within the congress, and those facing them in the Confederacy as a whole, Rhett deserved credit for substantial success. In politics "half a loaf" is almost always a victory, and Rhett cut several of the best slices.[54] He also accomplished at least a part of his goal not to relax correct principles in order to appeal to the border states. In fact, his free trade success and his proposals to eliminate the three-fifths clause and reopen the slave trade left many in Virginia and Kentucky shocked, fearful that South Carolina extremists were going to dominate the new government.[55]

Yet clearly they were not, for in spite of all he had gotten into the document, Rhett was not satisfied, and a couple of days before the debate closed he advised Barnwell Rhett Jr. that though it was the best constitution ever devised by men, still he was not happy with it, especially over the lingering stigma on slavery of the slave trade prohibition.[56] On March 11 the debate ended, the congress voted unanimously to adopt the permanent constitution, and almost immediately Rhett moved on his long-held determination to get the debates made public. That would show who had been loyal to Southern rights and who had wavered. Moreover, it would be the first battle in the war to arouse sufficient public opinion, especially in the state conventions, to demand further amendment before they agreed to ratify. He was still determined to have his way on the slave trade, making slavery a precondition for admission to statehood, eliminating the three-fifths provision that denied South Carolina her just representation, a specific limit of 15 percent on their tariff, and some revision of the manner of electing the president.[57]

The whole issue of secrecy had rankled him from the beginning, which is not surprising for one whose whole political career had shown such a keen perception of the value and malleability of public opinion. Both the provisional and now the permanent charter made provision for keeping a journal of congressional proceedings, and indeed the congress did so both for open and closed sessions. The constitutions further required that those journals be published from time to time, excepting portions deemed to require continued confidentiality. They were too new as yet for a program of publishing their daily debates to get under way, though he was anxious for that to start, and now he proposed that they relax the injunction of secrecy and release the debates on the permanent constitution for publication. It might have served his ends in South Carolina, but the majority from the other states easily saw that doing so would only reveal their internal divisions and encourage the wavering and reluctant, as well as the strong seam of Unionists in states such as Georgia and Alabama, and perhaps discourage the border states from taking the risk of joining a new nation revealed to be anything but unified in its sense of itself and its future goals. Wisely they rejected Rhett's appeal, going only so far as to allow their members to reveal confidentially to their several state conventions what had taken place in their deliberations.[58]

This was the best Rhett was going to get, though all along he had counted on being able to bring his disagreements before the state convention with this new charter; and just two days after the passage came a summons from David Jamison calling the Carolinians to a meeting in Charleston on March 26.[59] On March 16, its business done until the required five states should ratify the new charter, the congress adjourned after Rhett proposed a vote of thanks to Howell Cobb for his deportment and moved that as soon as they signed the permanent constitution, it should be lithographed and copies sent to each state. He had three days earlier joined the majority in voting for an adjournment until June 16, and that done, they went home.[60]

Rhett felt deeply disturbed as he and Katherine took the train back to Charleston. Despite the improvements in the new constitution, it still left the door to reconstruction far too open. The failure to exclude free states from joining or to expel any slave state that enacted abolition was the most dangerous of all, in his mind. If he had been able to bring about a reopening of the slave trade or pass his stringent fugitive slave law, then those provisions alone would have been enough to discourage any free state from wanting to be admitted, thus still accomplishing his purpose. The fear of reconstruction plagued him as it did most of the radicals, and the gossip that Davis or Stephens, or this delegate or that, were at heart in favor of rebuilding the old Union under their new constitution only fueled his discontent. Thirty years in public life had already convinced him that the people of the North and the West were so fundamentally different from Southerners that they could not live in amity under the same roof. Worse, their loss on the three-fifths clause worked against the states with the greatest number of slaves, while if border slave states and free states were admitted, with their large and predominantly or exclusively free populations, soon the cotton states would be reduced to a minority within their own nation. At the same time the prohibition on reopening the slave trade would naturally limit Southern expansion and the creation of the vast slave empire that he foresaw, further making them a minority.

Somehow the gorgon of reconstruction and his growing distaste for Davis became increasingly joined in Rhett's mind, despite the fact that Davis had nothing whatever to do with framing the permanent constitution and that this was, of course, fueled by the persisting rumors that the president himself earnestly desired reconstruction. Certainly, Davis had emphatically enough stated his wish to have the border slave states with them, though in his inaugural he all but ruled out any complete reconstruction with the rest of the old Union. Still on one occasion he did actually say that he would not be surprised if the good conservative state of New Hampshire might want to go Confederate, and that was enough to raise horror in Rhett's imagination. Rhett increasingly suspected that the perceived reconstructionists in the congress were acting with Davis's support, if not his active encouragement, and before long he would imagine as well that the refusal to publish their debates was somehow part of a plot by Davis and his friends to protect him from public scrutiny and to hide their ultimate aim. Already convinced that they had elected the wrong man, Rhett saw in this the beginnings of a division in the government. They had entertained the idealistic notion that there would be no political parties in their new Confederacy and that they could leave all the partisanship, acrimony, and demagoguery attendant to such a system behind them. However, the first few weeks of the convention put an end to that happy dream, for it simply failed to take into account the basic nature of politicians and of democratic government. Certainly it failed to allow for the nature of Robert Barnwell Rhett.

Years later his editor son, surely echoing his father's expressions, claimed that within six weeks of Davis's election the realization of their having chosen the wrong man led some to fear that they were about to split into administration and antiadministration parties centered not so much on policies as on Davis the man.[61] When he got home to Charleston, Rhett called on his first wife's brother Andrew Burnet and his son Barnwell Burnet at their house on South Bay and inevitably began discussing events in Montgomery. He told the story of how he was misled into voting for Davis and how deeply he felt his mistake, concluding by averring that Davis's actions thus far "so impresses me with fear for our cause Andrew that I wish it placed on my tomb stone that the worst and most to be regreted act in life was my voting for Mr Davis."[62] He did not say what so many others could see, which was that the chief source of his regret was that Davis held the office he thought he deserved, nor did Rhett reveal that he was already the very center and foundation stone for the slowly growing second "party" in Montgomery. Even at the far remove of Vicksburg, Mississippi, an editor even now foresaw that "the first attempt at a party formation in the Confederate States, will be by those who have selfish ends to promote." They did not need parties, he argued, and "the formation of parties is always fraught with mischief."[63] They were going to have them nevertheless.

Now the place to continue the fight was before the state convention, for if Rhett could persuade those attending not to ratify the constitution without the amendments he wanted, then South Carolina would simply stand free of the new Confederacy. Then, if just two other states also withheld ratification—and he could hope at least for Florida—then the constitution could not by its own provision go into effect. They would have to start over, or the congress would have to accept amendments to win South Carolina's assent. That plan collapsed before the Charleston debates began, for Alabama had ratified the constitution the day after it passed the congress, and Georgia did so the very day that congress adjourned. Louisiana and Texas followed within days, and then Mississippi made it five on March 29. Thus when Rhett began his arguments on April 1 the adoption of the new constitution was an accomplished fact. The convention only handed Rhett additional disappointment. From the opening gavel there was a general disposition to take the constitution as it was. The old moderate spirit of South Carolina at large reasserted itself as the reality of secession and the possibility of war set in. Once again, as before, Rhett saw how even the passage of a little time could dilute the state's radicalism.[64]

The convention rejected every one of the amendments Rhett wanted it to require, and he found his fellow delegate Chesnut on the floor more than once speaking in opposition to him. His plea for a demand to reopen the slave trade was ignored, and he decided simply not to bring it up again, though the *Mercury* would never stop condemning the prohibition as weak and short-sighted.

He found himself on the defensive and having to deny false reports that in Montgomery he had said that only slaveowners should have the vote, when his real demand had been that only slave states should be admitted. But now his repeated attacks on the failure to restrict future admissions to slave states was rebuffed. He railed against the three-fifths clause and the selection of presidential electors by popular vote and the failure to secure absolute free trade, but no one paid heed.[65]

The debate, despite his consistent setbacks, raised alarm in Georgia and elsewhere that South Carolina might actually secede from the Confederacy, and in Montgomery the new government watched with some apprehension.[66] Davis knew there would be some opposition to the constitution, but no one supposed that the fight in Charleston would be easily won. Yet on April 3 the convention ratified by an overwhelming vote of 114 to 16, and Rhett was beaten. Only Florida had yet to be heard from, and she, too, ratified three weeks later.[67] The best he could do was move several resolutions—one that they add a proviso to their ratification stating that in ratifying, South Carolina did not recognize itself as bound to remain in the Confederacy if it should admit free states; and another calling for a state convention in the event that any free state were ever admitted.[68] Rhett's enemies were elated. "The Constitution has been adopted by an overwhelming majority against Rhett & Co, Slave traders, Free traders, fire eaters and extremists," gloated Hammond, "and I suppose this is an end of them." He thought that, certainly, Rhett and his kind brought about secession, and he was delighted to see him repeatedly repudiated. They were instruments in the hands of God, just as Judas had been, he believed. "Restless, reckless, ambitious, selfish and fanatical as they were, I do not think they would have been bribed by the 30 or 30 thousand pieces of silver, and therefore they are not bound to hang themselves as Judas did."[69]

Certainly, Rhett had no intention of hanging himself, despondent though he may have been that, after all, they had achieved none of the truly vital reforms he sought. As he plodded on with the other less interesting business of the convention, including chairing a subcommittee appointed to audit the records of Pickens's treasury and finance managers, he continued to look with apprehension on affairs beyond Charleston. He had hopes that midterm elections in the North would sweep the Republicans from power in the fall of 1862, meaning that the Confederacy might only have to last until then before a change in Yankee public opinion would make their independence a fact without resort to war, which now he did not anticipate. Yet it could happen now if only Davis in Montgomery and Pickens in Charleston were not so passive. He was convinced that the president and most of the congress favored admitting the border slave states, then the northwestern states, and eventually all but New England, and that it would happen unless something occurred first to galvanize Southern public opinion into opposing reconstruction. War would do that, and they needed it right away.[70]

Just ten days after his son Barnwell echoed those sentiments to one of his correspondents, Rhett got his war. Convinced that Lincoln would soon give up Fort Sumter without a fight when the garrison ran out of food, Rhett was taken somewhat by surprise when news of a Union intent to resupply the fort reached Charleston and Davis sent Beauregard instructions to take it by bombardment first. Rhett probably knew some hours beforehand, as did many others in the city, that Confederate batteries would open fire in the predawn half-light of April 12, and during the ensuing thirty-six hours he spent some time with his friend John Williams watching the bombardment from the Battery or a rooftop.[71] Two of his sons were out there now, Robert Woodward Rhett as a lieutenant in the First South Carolina Infantry, which would not be involved, and Alfred commanding a battery at Fort Moultrie whose barrage set fire to the Sumter barracks. Indeed, it was that fire that eventually forced the garrison to agree to surrender on April 13, and the next day Major Anderson and his command gave up the fort.[72]

Thousands flocked to Charleston in the next few days, many of them making an excursion to see the battered fort, and most likely Rhett made an inspection to see the damage and exult in the victory.[73] A few days later he was in the *Mercury* office when visiting British newspaper correspondent William H. Russell paid a call, and none of the Rhetts could conceal their hubris at so easily whipping the Yankees, oblivious of the fact that there had never been a question of a one-hundred-man garrison holding out against several thousand Confederates surrounding them with cannons. Russell found Rhett to be "a pompous, hard, ambitious man," yet seemingly one of ability who could not resist trying to impress the visitor with his own English ancestry and his personal fondness for Britain. Russell had already heard that the Rhetts were "not over-well pleased with Jefferson Davis for neglecting their claims to office," and perhaps to impress upon him his qualifications, Rhett actually gave him a copy of the Daniel Wallace biography of himself. Nor, with the subject of reconstruction still paramount in his mind, did he neglect to denounce New England and any association with those states. If the whole effect of the visit were to leave Russell impressed with a lack of modesty, it was only enhanced when he met a few days later with brother Edmund Rhett, who told Russell, as if there were no room for question in the matter, that England "must recognize us, sir, before the end of October."[74]

From Rhett's point of view, the attack on Sumter did not start the war. That came a few days later when Lincoln issued a call for seventy-five thousand volunteers to put down "the rebellion." In fact, he traced a whole chain of events that led to conflict, including Van Buren and Douglas destroying the Democratic Party for their separate ambitions, "so far as the ruin of that party could influence the war." Lincoln's election also caused the war, Rhett felt, and he believed that the Republican had it in mind from the first to bring about a conflict. He reasoning that Lincoln's entering Washington in disguise before his inauguration somehow revealed a self-consciousness of his malign purpose, although in fact Lincoln was simply reacting to rumors of an assassination plot. Rhett felt that the rejection of a proposed border-state compromise the past winter also brought on the war, even though Rhett himself had condemned the attempted compromise measures launched by Kentucky's John J. Crittenden because they would lead to reconstruction. The failure of those same border states of Virginia, North Carolina, and Tennessee to secede when the other states did produced the war, by weakening the phalanx arrayed against the Union and emboldening it to attempt coercion. Anderson's midnight move from Fort Moultrie to Fort Sumter produced the war too, for somehow Rhett reasoned that if he had remained in the former place, Confederates would not have attacked him. The failure of Pickens to heed Barnwell Rhett Jr.'s suggestion of putting a steamer between the two forts to prevent Anderson's act produced the war, and so did Lincoln's sending the relief fleet; and indeed, the fact that during the bombardment that fleet stayed out to sea instead of coming in to assist Anderson proved to Rhett's mind that the only purpose of the fleet in the first place was to precipitate a conflict and make the Confederates fire the first shot. Of course he had to admit that the actual firing on Sumter also helped start the war, but he argued that since every man in the country knew the Confederates would attack if an attempt were made to reinforce, therefore the responsibility lay with Lincoln for forcing them to do so. And Lincoln's unconstitutional call for volunteers, made when his Congress was not in session to stop him, showed his premeditated design and started the war.[75]

Rhett did not see Southerners as rebels. Southerners were citizens of their states, not of the United States, and their only allegiance was due to that one sovereignty. They could only be rebels if they rebelled against their own states. In 1860–61 they faced the alternative of free government and liberty or despotism, and that was why they seceded. The North that now intended to make war upon them was seeking to abolish that freedom. "What language can fitly describe the foul and barbarous attrocity of making war upon them and murdering them for their fidelity?" he asked, and of course there was no answer.[76] The greedy money power consolidationists of the North had been working toward this end for generations. "They wanted war; for war would produce the grand end of all their

Party-policy, co-eval with the existence of the Government. It would spread law-less force over the land,—extinguish the Constitution,—bring creditors to the support of their Party, and boundless taxation, with vast enrichment to monop-olists, manufacturers, and Paper-money jobbers."[77] It was all part of a grand con-spiracy, and now the South must battle for freedom and its life.

In all his lengthy enumeration of the causes and contributors to bringing the sections to this pass, there was one whom he left out. James Chesnut's father, who had known him for years, could think of one other. "For fifty years Bluff-ton has been spoiling for a fight," he complained. "That is the center spot of the fire-eaters. Barnwell Rhetts and all that," he grumbled. "And now I think he has got it."[78]

TWENTY-TWO

Litterally Eaten Up with Envy

1861

IMMEDIATELY AFTER THE TAKING of Fort Sumter and Lincoln's call for volunteers, President Davis issued a summons for a special session of the congress to address the crisis. Along with Barnwell and the rest Rhett rushed to Montgomery, this time bringing Katherine with him, and on April 29 he met once more with his colleagues in the Alabama statehouse before galleries packed with expectant spectators. His first act was to move that all members who had not to date signed the constitution ought now to do so. While the members went about the usual organizational business, Davis sent a special message to them along with a copy of Lincoln's proclamation, and it immediately went to Rhett's foreign affairs committee.[1]

"It was plain that it might be no easy task, to make European nations understand the true nature of the contest," Rhett forthrightly admitted. "The rights of the Southern people under the terms of the Constitution, were unfortunately implicated with African slavery; and it might appear to European nations, that not the principles of Free Government, but the perpetuation of African slavery, was the real issue in the contest." Indeed it would so appear to anyone who noticed his attempt in the constitutional debate to deny states the right to exclude slavery, but for the present the secrecy of the debates that he so derided actually protected his inconsistency from exposure. Meanwhile Rhett felt it necessary to erase any such confusion right away, and consequently even while his committee drafted the brief and expected declaration of a state of war, he applied himself to an accompanying report to set forth the nature of the conflict before them and its causes, not for the congress but for the world.

The issue was "the great principle of self-government," he declared, and whether a majority in one section should have the power and right to rule a minority in another or should they by right govern themselves? He likened the Northern tyranny to that of Britain over its colonies in 1776, perhaps not the most apposite comparison in a document intended to win English favor. From the first the North had sought to circumvent the limits of the old Constitution upon centralized majority rule, and finally they had gone too far. One people simply could not rule harmoniously over another with different institutions, industries, and social habits, and it hardly mattered to be represented in a legislature when such a majority stood firmly in control, for resistance was futile. "Between a representation incompetent to protect, and no representation, there is no difference where there are conflicting interests in a common legislative body," he argued. And what point was there in voting for a president, when even if every single man in the minority section should vote against the majority section's candidate "they cannot prevent his election?" With their old Constitution subverted and Washington in the hands of the Yankees, not just liberty but self-preservation required the secession of the South. Their permanent sovereignty was all they needed to accomplish that, and he asserted that "there is not a fact in all history more indisputable" than that those states did not renounce their sovereignty when they ratified the Constitution.

Rhett had to address slavery, of course, but only briefly and only to dismiss it as a cause of the conflict. Affirming that Lincoln had stated he had no intention or motive of interfering with slavery where it then existed, Rhett went on to say that "the laws of party progress, are sometimes as inexorable as the laws of nature." The Republicans might have no design on slavery until now for no reason other than that to do so would have risked disunion before it actually came. Rhett also dismissed any sense of humanity as a Republican motive in opposing the institution. It was simply political policy, linking Republican fortunes with the majority free states to guarantee power, and he pointed to the struggle in the territories as one motivated not by concern for slaves, but as a quest for power—the South needing more for protection, the North for dominance. The Southern claim to territory had been constitutional, however, by right of common property. The victory of the Northern position, in spite of the Constitution, signified a virtual overthrow of that charter, and that alone justified secession. "Abolish the Constitution," he said, "and the Union is destroyed." Adroitly, in denying that there was any humanitarian aspect to Northern opposition to slavery, Rhett avoided the logical necessity of presenting the Southern moral defense of the institution that would have alienated so many abroad.

The South had submitted for two generations to Northern aggression, to protectionism, unlawful use of the national treasury, exclusion from the territories, and more. Yet all the while those states paid more than their fair share and came forth in inequitably large numbers when called to war, even in the War of 1812 when the issue, he said, was British wrongs to Northern seamen and commerce. "No narrow sectionalism—no ignoble jealousies, limited the broad views of their great statesmanship," he declared, ignoring as always the fact that

Southern enthusiasm for that war had a great deal more to do with the expectation that it would destroy the predominantly Northern Federalist Party and leave the Southern Jeffersonians in sway, as indeed it did.

Now it was time to leave the Union, and they sought to take nothing with them, he claimed, ignoring the forcible seizure of millions in federal property at forts, arsenals, and customhouses, since it had been their intent to negotiate some compensation to Washington, even though negotiation at gunpoint after seizure hardly seemed to constitute fair or good-faith bargaining. The South left the North to its own concept of freedom, simply removing itself from further association and control. In return the Union offered Southerners "violence and war." Rhett did not mention the fact that it was the Confederacy that first used "violence and war" at Fort Sumter, nor that he had been trying to get those shots fired for fully a decade. As always, whether in debate or in the *Mercury*, to Rhett inconvenient or contrary facts were the same as irrelevant.

Future historians would be amazed at how long the South stood the indignities heaped upon it, he said, but Rhett reminded them that traditional attachment to the Union had been strong, a passion handed down through generations. Washington was a Southerner. Southerners were chiefly responsible for the Constitution and all of the presidents but five—six in fact; Rhett could be cavalier even with unimportant facts—had been from the South. In the cabinet and on the battlefield "the genius of the South for command" displayed itself. Not surprisingly the people of the region came to separation slowly, but come to it they had, and they faced the judgment of the world without fear. If they must fight for their liberty, they accepted the trial before them.[2]

Characteristically, Rhett may well have had his statement in preparation before he arrived in Montgomery, though if not, it certainly required little thought, for it repeated all of his old grievances and justifications, and even some of his exact wording on former occasions. For the purpose it was to serve, it was one of his better efforts—concise, well organized, not as repetitious as many of his productions, and incisively framed for European ears, both in the way it dodged slavery as a cause of the war and also for the underdog appeal it could have to a host of nations just recently emerged from a series of wars of social unification and revolution against arbitrary authority. Equally significant, it revealed no intent or suggestion that the Confederate States should pursue an aggressive war. They wanted only to be left alone, which meant that the rampant talk of the moment of marching on Washington or invading the North was to be discouraged. On May 1, Rhett reported the declaration of war from his committee and presented his report, and three days later the congress passed the declaration without a dissenting vote, one of the first unanimous ballots achieved in that body outside the final vote on the constitution.[3] It only affirmed Rhett's long-held conviction that precipitating a crisis could weld the disparate elements in the South into unity far faster and more effectively than endless deliberation and negotiation. If only they could have fired those shots years earlier, even just four months ago, he lamented. Had Pickens taken Sumter in December when Rhett wanted him to, he told friends now, they would not have a war on their hands. Unwittingly his report almost led to shots being fired at his own family, for when the *Charleston Courier* ran a disparaging editorial on Rhett's report, his high-tempered son Edmund threatened the editor with a duel until an apology was forthcoming.[4]

But now there was a war and no time to waste. In fact, the day before introducing the declaration he went to the state department offices in a converted building on Commerce Street now called Government House, and there met Toombs on the stairs. He later claimed that when he asked if the Yancey mission had been empowered to make treaties of commerce and navigation, Toombs replied that they had not, which is all but impossible since his instructions to them explicitly ordered them to propose such agreements. However, Toombs did not give Yancey exact guidelines or unilateral authority to negotiate specific rates of duty, only promising that duties in the Confederacy would be so low as almost to constitute free trade, and that may have been the actual cause of Rhett's exclamation to him: "I am astonished that you have sent them at all. They will fail!"[5]

Rhett missed no opportunity to make his case for European and especially British recognition of the Confederacy. A week after the special session opened, Russell appeared in Montgomery to report its activity for his paper the *Times of London.* On May 6 he walked into their chamber and someone presented him to the house, but when they went into secret session he stood to leave with the other spectators as they were ushered out. Rhett jovially called to him that he ought to keep his seat and said, "If the *Times* will support the South, we'll accept you as a delegate." Russell, already disposed not to care overmuch for Rhett, responded icily that he could not consent to be a delegate to "a Congress of Slave States."[6]

If Rhett felt the cut, he said nothing of it but only renewed refinement of his rationalization that slavery, in fact, should be no obstacle to foreign recognition. He pointed out that the Yankees averred in their Congress that they were not going to wage war to abolish slavery and that in his inaugural Lincoln did the same. Indeed, the Union then maintained the posture that if the Southern states would put down their arms and return to the fold, their slave property would be protected as before. "These acts clearly removed Slavery out of the sphere of diplomacy, between the Confederate States and Foreign nations," Rhett would argue, because whether the Confederacy won or lost, Northern declaration made it evident that slavery would persist. Thus the continuation of slavery afforded no legitimate ground for European reluctance to deal with the South, since they all dealt with the Union, which, by Rhett's absurd logic, was just as committed to the continuation of the institution as the South.[7]

The real impediment to recognition was Davis's ineptitude, according to Rhett. Feeling that nothing would happen if he did not bring it about himself, Rhett went to work preparing a resolution to introduce in the congress calling on Davis to empower the Yancey mission to propose commercial treaties with a maximum of 20 percent duty for a period of twenty years on all imports, and he intended to follow that with a similar resolution to propose free navigation of Confederate ports and harbors. He showed it to Toombs first, who approved, and then brought the secretary of state before his foreign affairs committee to express his approbation. That done, the committee backed Rhett's introducing the resolution in Congress, which he did on May 13, and the congress referred it back to his committee for consideration. Rhett addressed the committee briefly in advocacy of his measure, and no one dissented, but John Perkins of Louisiana did propose that instead of twenty years they should grant the preferential rates for only six years. Rhett argued that the war just started might not be over in six years, and that even if it were it would take much longer for the Confederacy to establish smoothly the channels of international trade such treaties would open. To offer other nations only six years would be laughable to them, he said, and if the committee backed the Perkins motion he would consider it the same as a rejection. On May 20 when Rhett reported the resolution back from committee, there was no specification of time limits of commercial treaties, but then his friend Thomas Cobb echoed Perkins by successfully attaching a five-year limit. Giving up on it entirely, Rhett moved that his committee's resolution be tabled, his only reward being to have Withers come to his desk, extend his hand, and compliment him for his principled statesmanship.[8]

His disappointment with Davis's military preparations were no less severe, especially the failure to accept every volunteer who came forward without regard to terms of enlistment. It did not help when Davis rebuffed Rhett's own relatives. Despite his protestations about patronage reform and his soon-burgeoning complaints about the president's favoritism in making appointments, Rhett was no different from any other politician in wanting special favors and places for his friends and relations. Jehu Marshall of Charleston came to offer a one-thousand-man cavalry regiment raised and equipped, ready for service, yet Davis turned him down because they were only enlisted for one year. With no evidence but his own prejudice against Davis, Rhett blamed this act on patronage. At the same time Rhett's cousin William Cutting Heyward came to Montgomery seeking authorization to raise a regiment but waited for days without getting an interview with the president. He went home, where he later raised the Ninth South Carolina Infantry anyhow. Unmoved by the enormous demands on the president's time and the scores if not hundreds of callers on the same sort of mission, Rhett could not forgive Davis for ignoring his cousin.[9]

On a larger scale, he still waited for Davis to use fully the authority of the February 28 military bill to call out one hundred thousand twelve-month volunteers, which Davis would never do. Rhett quibbled that Davis dragged his feet in the appointment of officers for the mandated Regular Army, oblivious of the fact that this small corps of only eleven thousand was created for the long-term military establishment of the Confederacy and played almost no role in the war immediately at hand, putting it rightly low on the president's list of priorities. On May 8, Rhett joined the majority in passing a new military bill authorizing Davis to call out volunteer regiments enlisted for the term of the war, which the president had wanted from the first. Three days later Davis was authorized to accept into service units already raised before he made his call, settling their periods of enlistment himself. Whatever his carping about Davis's presumed sloth, no one could accuse Rhett of not supporting the speedy buildup of military force for the war ahead. Moreover, in a striking example of practicality overcoming principle, he also supported the policy of directing that general officers in the national Confederate service should supercede in command any state militia officers of equal rank whenever their forces should act in conjunction. However much that might seem to violate states' rights, even one as doctrinaire as Rhett could see that otherwise they would suffer from divided counsels and command chaos. Yet even here Rhett quibbled, for the legislation produced by Davis and the military affairs committee called for officers of no higher rank than that of brigadier general. Unfazed by his own lack of a single second of military training or experience—and he was soon to produce other opinions that would make calling his military judgment sophomoric, extravagant praise—Rhett would later conclude that this was completely inadequate for management of large armies. Even at the time he seems to have complained to fellow members of Congress, who told him to let Davis have his way since he had been a military man himself.[10]

Once more Rhett complained the day before the new military bill passed that if only they had taken Sumter months before, they would not face these problems, nor would they be hostage to the president's dilatory and inadequate management.[11] Taking it upon himself to try to force sense into their foreign and military policy, he felt obliged also to seek some management of their financial affairs. He managed passage of a bill to raise revenue from imported commodities and tried to support a bill by Memminger to authorize up to $15 million in direct taxes on property, only to see it fail in debate over what sorts of property to exclude from taxation. He still favored his cotton-buying scheme, as did Stephens and others, but it got nowhere. To save expenditure he even opposed for the moment the reimbursement to congressmen of mileage expenses for their travel to and from Montgomery.[12]

The best news of the session was the secession of Virginia, followed by Arkansas. Rhett welcomed the Old Dominion's first representatives into the congress on May 7 and then a week later introduced the resolution to ratify a convention with Tennessee, then just seceded. Oddly enough, given his near obsession with the secret sessions, the *Mercury* now actually gave them some support, since otherwise everything would find its way into the press and be read north as well as south of the Potomac. Yet Rhett did want the veil of secrecy removed from all acts signed by Davis, in part for the public information but also just as likely so that he could show the people what the president had not done. He had friends from the press there, including E. G. Dill of the *Mercury,* of course, but also his old associate John Heart, and thus he had every opportunity to feed the press if he could secure anything to serve his ends.[13]

Watching Rhett's machinations against Davis from her own perch in Montgomery, and occasionally receiving a call from Rhett personally, Mary Chesnut had to confess that "he is clever, if erratic." Still there was little in the way of socializing for Rhett, especially with the sorrow of his children's deaths still wreathing his every hour. Katherine in her black mourning was often his only companion as they sat with their sorrows at the dining table at the Exchange. "My heart bleeds for them," confessed Thomas Cobb as he looked on. By the second week of May, expecting the congress to finish its emergency bills and appropriations and adjourn within ten days, Rhett sent Katherine to the Darien plantation where she could be near her family awhile before he came for her.[14]

But first there was one more outrage to begrudge the president. On May 18 when an appropriation bill from the committee for public buildings came before the congress, it contained a provision for $987.50 for furniture Davis had requested for the executive mansion, for which they had already allowed $5,000 to lease. Withers immediately seized upon it to rant at some length about unconstitutionality. He even produced a dictionary and read from it the definition of the word *emolument* to show that all such appropriations constituted additions to the president's compensation, though the fact that the furniture in question would be owned by the government, and not Davis personally, argued against that. Had they just left the usurpation of the North only to start the same corruption and profligacy in their own nation? he asked. Turning to Rhett, he said: "If my colleague will support me in the motion, I will call for the Ayes and Nays on the Resolution." Rhett responded, "If you do not call for them, I will call for them myself." With no debate they took the vote, with only Rhett, Withers, Barnwell, and one other member supporting the motion to strike the appropriation. The next morning when Rhett went to the capitol to write some letters at his desk before the gavel, Withers came to his desk and damned the appropriation for house and furniture. "The fact is, Davis is venal and corrupt, and the Confederate Congress is no better; and I will not continue a member of such a body," he declared. "I will resign my seat as soon as it adjourns." Despite Rhett's entreaties that he needed Withers there to help him fight just such abuses, the old judge resigned as soon as he got home. Rhett regarded it as a great loss; the rest of the congress, including even Withers's niece Mary Chesnut, thought it good riddance.[15] It was only the first evidence that henceforward Rhett would allow a man's hostility to Davis to overrule a host of shortcomings as he made alliances and chose those in whom to place his trust.

As early as May 10 a motion came to the floor to move the Confederate capital to Richmond when they next convened. It had been a part of the bargain worked out when Virginia seceded, and it made every sense militarily and politically; and yet there were good-faith reasons to oppose the move as well. Rhett thought it would arouse more bellicosity in the North thanks to Richmond being threateningly close to Washington, which was sound enough. In the Confederacy he saw it drawing strength from the center of the nation to what was nearly its frontier, which was certainly true, but he overlooked the undeniable fact that if the Yankees invaded in the East, they would do it through Virginia, which contained much of the South's vital industrial, financial, and transportation facilities. Virginia had to be protected, and it would be hard to manage that defense from a capital almost seven hundred miles away. Rhett opposed the motion by trying to postpone consideration but failed; he then unsuccessfully voted against the resolution itself. When Davis vetoed it a few days later as being unconstitutional, Rhett tried first to postpone an attempt to override the veto, which was consistent with his own position, but when that lost he then surprisingly voted with the unsuccessful minority to override. There seems no logical explanation other than that his antipathy toward Davis was already at the point that he would rather spite the president than have his own way and keep the capital at Montgomery.

The measure came up again on May 21, the final day of the session, and despite changes to win Davis's approval, the bill still seemed destined for defeat by 2 P.M. when they adjourned until later that afternoon. Since all that seemed to remain were some signing formalities on bills already passed, Rhett and a number of others boarded afternoon trains for home. When the congress reassembled, the removal resolution was reintroduced and quickly passed with most of its opposition gone, and Davis signed it that same day. Rhett was not yet home the next morning when he got word of the passage. It reeked of the sort of close dealing and corruption that had tainted Washington, and he suspected without real foundation that it had been planned thus all along in order to get past opponents like himself. Worse, he saw in the move to Richmond the shadow of the ever-dreaded reconstruction. Most of the Virginia delegates to the congress had been cooperationists in the old days, and now he even suspected his onetime associate Hunter of favoring reconstruction. The move to Richmond put the government on the soil and seemingly in the clutches of people Rhett firmly believed did not wish to see a permanently independent Confederacy. He saw the same design in the passive waiting policy of the administration too. They should be aggressively taking the war to the enemy, he thought. "Fighting exasperates, and exasperation is the probable defeat of reconstruction."[16]

Rhett went to Darien first to look at his crops and collect Katherine, and then on to Charleston. Once home he and his son Barnwell immediately planned an offensive on the administration. Though they would largely refrain from attacking Davis by name for the time being, they decided to exercise little or no restraint in questioning the administration itself. Indeed, they actively sought critical articles from their correspondents. "I want facts and criticism, to affect public opinion," the younger Rhett instructed a new stringer in Richmond. "Criticize with perfect fearlessness," he went on, wanting assaults on Davis's policy. Moreover, he edited the material he received "to suit the precise requirements of this locality," by which he may have meant Charleston but was just as likely thinking of the more immediate locality of his editorial chair and his father's parlor.[17]

The effect became immediately apparent. Within no more than a week Simms lamented that the *Mercury*, "I am sorry to see, is beginning that sort of pic[k]ing upon the Confederate Govt in the management of the army, which it kept up, on our own, before the taking of Sumter." He knew many Carolinians felt indignant at what they read. "It is wild, mischievous & idle." So it was. "What an exasperating Paper," Mary Chesnut exclaimed in June after reading an article that implicitly, if not explicitly, complained that Rhett had not been given a post in the government.[18] Throughout the early summer the Rhetts hammered on every perceived shortcoming. Through timidity they had lost the slave state Maryland to the Union. In May the Yankees had invaded and occupied a few miles of northern Virginia. Missouri was up in the air, while Kentucky had declared itself a neutral, showing how unreliable the border states were on Southern principles. Admitting that they did not know with what powers the Yancey mission was cloaked, they declared it a failure. Frustrated by his powerless position, Toombs had announced his intent to resign as secretary of state. It was time to dismiss all foreign consuls from their ports, withhold cotton from all nations that failed to recognize the Confederacy, recall Yancey and his associates at once, and wait for England and France to come on bended knee to the South, which in nine months time they must do or see every loom in Europe go idle. With typical smugness, they declared that "the people and Governments of Europe are evidently a little in the dark—a little dull of perception—a little mystified" when it came to the power the South had over them. "They require instruction as to their own best interests." Now that negotiation had failed, and proclaiming that "Cotton is Peace," the *Mercury* predicted that an embargo would cause immense distress in six months and social revolution in nine, and that eventually through unemployment and starvation it would kill fifty times more than would fall in the war in America. "Let President Davis and King Cotton form an alliance, and all the powers of the earth cannot overthrow them," the paper asserted.[19]

Davis said that he thought the war could last up to five years or more, but the Rhetts questioned in the *Mercury*'s pages whether the Confederacy could sustain itself that long on its own, and the reason was the failure to organize speedily and efficiently. The current funding plan of having planters subscribe a portion of their crops to the government in return for interest-bearing bonds was bound to fail. The government had to sell the cotton overseas to fund itself and repay the bonds, but Lincoln had imposed a blockade of their ports after Fort Sumter that, if not fully effective, was still bound to greatly retard foreign trade. If only they had followed the Rhett plan of stockpiling cotton overseas before hostilities, they would have abundant funding available to them, while any shortage of further shipments by the blockade would only drive up the price they could realize on their bales in Europe.

Cataloging the "blunders about the organization of the army," they took Davis to task for all the things he had not done in calling out every available man. "Congress has exhausted its wisdom in supplying the Executive with every kind of power to carry on successfully the war in which we are engaged," they said. If their army now were insufficient, "Congress is not to blame"; it was all up to Davis. Gone now was Rhett's policy of early May of acting on the defensive. The war would be over already if Davis had launched an offensive, he said in a neat and unexplained reversal of attitude, and the congress had given him power to do everything needful. "His energy makes the war long or short," and at the moment he was needlessly prolonging it through vacillation and a defensive policy. The country must "look with a watchful and jealous eye on all our officials," they said, moving judiciously and reluctantly to condemn, but they must determine the cause of their successes and their failures, for soon they would be tested on the battlefield and must be ready or perish.[20]

That first battlefield test came sooner than expected. Rhett and Barnwell took the train together to Richmond for the opening of the next session of the congress on July 20, and on the way Rhett's cousin upbraided him for the editorial policy of the *Mercury,* which of course was not about to change.[21] Scarcely had they arrived when, on July 21, the first real battle of the war was fought ninety miles north of Richmond near Manassas, ending in a startling Confederate victory for the combined armies of Generals Beauregard and Joseph E. Johnston. Four of Rhett's sons were in uniform now. Alfred was in the artillery at Charleston; Edmund was a captain in a sharpshooters battalion; Burnet was a captain in the Second South Carolina Infantry; and Robert Woodward Rhett held a commission in the First South Carolina. Both Burnet and Robert had been in the battle at Manassas, while Rhett's nephew Thomas was an aide at Beauregard's headquarters, and so he had excellent inside sources of army information. The most immediate concern was a report that Burnet had been killed in action, which happily proved to be false, but soon Rhett spoke with leading Carolinian officers to get information on other survivors to send to families back home, and of course he collected information for the *Mercury.* "The victory is most marvellous," he declared, more so even than Fort Sumter.[22]

Yet it had not been enough. With the demoralized Union army running in a panic from the field, the Confederates had failed to pursue them vigorously back to the Potomac, even into Washington, which many thought could have ended the war at a stroke. The fact was that the Southern army was just as exhausted and disorganized as its foe, and when Davis, who arrived on the field as the rout began, urged Johnston and Beauregard to follow up the victory, they plainly said that their army could not do it and that he could not get them to try. Just four days later Rhett declared that their forces should have been annihilated, presuming them—falsely—to have been heavily outnumbered, "but God, not our Government, has saved them."[23] When his old friend Benjamin Perry visited him a few days after the battle, Rhett gave him a good description of the action and then complained that like Hannibal's great victory at Cannae, the failure to follow it up had cost them dearly. "The Confederate army ought to have gone on and taken the Federal city," he grumbled. It was a line that came straight from Beauregard's headquarters; if he had had more men, he would have taken Washington.[24]

On July 25 the *Mercury* began to blame the administration. The full fruit of victory had slipped away, it accused, "not from want of generalship, but *for the want of troops.*" Had Davis not been dilatory in taking every volunteer offered, there would have been double their numbers at Manassas and no question that they would have marched into Washington. "Our Government has blundered in this particular from the very beginning," said an editorial aping the elder Rhett's familiar complaint. "This war should have been conducted on the soil of the enemy." Instead there they were on the defensive thanks to Davis's "suicidal system" of rejecting twelve-month volunteers. The emergency was such that the people and the press had to speak out. They must take every twelve-month volunteer they could get, and the congress must give Davis every facility to do so and make certain that he did. Rumors circulated in Richmond that Davis had actually commanded on the field during the battle and even that he ordered the army not to pursue the enemy—both false—and though he said nothing to encourage the former and denied the latter, the *Mercury* wanted to ask questions.[25]

Rhett wanted to ask them in congress too but found soon after it convened that there was little disposition to take any decisive action. He would make up for that with his own activity. He introduced a resolution demanding from the president his instructions to the Yancey mission and copies of all correspondence with the European commissioners, and he then followed up his renewed attempt to dictate foreign policy by offering a resolution to ask his foreign relations committee to investigate the expediency of offering special trade advantages to the first nations granting formal recognition, which failed. Striking another blow against the specter of reconstruction, he proposed laying a 15 percent duty on top of the tariff already established when any goods were introduced from the United States and prohibiting the introduction of any foreign goods into the Confederacy through the North. That would total 30 percent duty, hardly the free trade he said he championed, but of course a punitive tariff against the North was an allowable exception to a general principle in his view. Even if political reunion did not take place, which seemed less likely the longer the Confederacy lived, there were alarming signs that some in the South might go halfway with a commercial reunification. And there were notions that after their beating at Manassas, the Yankees might offer peace if they could get back the preferential benefits they once enjoyed with Southern trade in the former Union. Rhett's tariff was designed to shortcut any such reunion by making it economically unattractive.

Resorting to his old trick of getting others to introduce measures for him when he feared that his own authorship, if known, would prejudice their chances, he engineered resolutions introduced by Wigfall on July 26. These called for

Rhett's foreign affairs committee to present opinions tending toward legislation to expel from their ports foreign consuls originally sent prior to secession, and at the same to recall the failed Yancey mission and to recommend an embargo. In committee Rhett presented evidence that cotton and tobacco were being exported privately. He drafted a bill for an embargo but once more stepped into the background by getting James Mason of the committee to introduce a resolution calling on the committee for a report and recommendations in the matter on August 21. The next day Mason introduced the actual embargo bill, but for the rest of the life of the provisional congress neither he nor Rhett could get it called onto the floor for debate and a vote. Memminger steadily opposed consideration of the bill from his seat on the floor, just as he opposed the policy as secretary of the treasury, leaving Rhett to regard administration opposition as making further effort futile. Rhett's only success on the diplomatic front, in fact, was to move the appointment of new foreign diplomats to other nations and propose that the Confederacy accept and operate under the maritime law decreed by the congress of Paris in 1856, the accepted law of nations.[26]

Rhett also moved on the economic front. He supported selling unwanted government property to boost the treasury and opposed any immediate settlement of claims against the central government by the several states, believing that should wait until after the war when money was more plentiful. After being appointed to the new committee on commercial and financial independence, he supported the issue of treasury notes to have a medium of exchange in circulation while the government swallowed most of the specie available, just as he had for Van Buren a quarter-century before. He also ardently supported a war tax of fifty cents of every one hundred dollars' worth of real property to back and redeem them. It was almost his old direct tax, falling on those who could pay and in proportion to their wealth. With it came a provision for "tax in kind" payments by which planters pledged crops or livestock to the government in lieu of their tax and the government could then realize the sale and proceeds from the commodities. The debate on the bill was heavy and heated, reflecting Keitt's old warning about men being unwilling to part with money already in their pockets. Finally on August 16 one opponent stood and changed his position and, for the good of the country, called on the rest of the opposition to do the same. In a moving scene, former President John Tyler, now a congressman from Virginia and never well regarded by Rhett, then took the floor and made an eloquent appeal before changing his vote as well. Rhett called for the yeas and nays, and one by one the opposition came over, unanimously passing the tax bill and realizing the beginning of Rhett's lifelong dream of tax reform, though it had taken war and emergency to get it.[27]

He might not be in uniform like his four sons, but he could also strike at the enemy. In response to the Yankee seizure of property in the North owned by Confederates, he supported a retaliatory sequestration act and fought repeatedly to keep it alive. He also demanded that the secretary of state's office take and retain testimony from owners of slaves abducted or harbored by the enemy, or of any other seized property, so there would be a complete record should a day of reckoning come. More immediately, hearing that two South Carolina soldiers had been hanged by the Yankees just prior to Manassas and that other "cruelties" had been practiced by the invader, Rhett demanded an investigation and that Davis cooperate, quite probably with some sort of retaliation in mind. More to the point, it served his purpose of depicting Yankees as so vicious that no sane Confederate would contemplate reconstruction with them.[28]

All the while the stridence of the *Mercury* continued attracting attention and criticism, impressing many in and out of government that Rhett had a personal agenda. The administration had crippled the Yancey mission, it said, and then the diplomats failed to act assertively on their own—the first and only time Rhett ever criticized his fellow fire-eater. Congress must eject foreign consuls, stop dithering and declare an embargo on cotton and tobacco, establish direct foreign trade in the South's own hulls, and more. The paper questioned why they did not have a real navy as yet. "We seem to have sat down in a kind of torpor," it argued, warning Carolinians that they might have to defend themselves and their coastline on their own if the administration did not wake up. "The same system," it cried, "of timid, shrinking, injudicious diplomacy, which has hitherto characterized our counsels and conduct in regard to our foreign relations, is likely to mar our prospects." To those who complained of the *Mercury*'s continual carping, the sheet responded that they did not yet live in a Lincoln dictatorship, though hinting that Davis's acts suggested that he might be tending in that direction. A private citizen still had the right to speak his mind, and proudly the *Mercury*—now certainly speaking for the senior Rhett—pointed out that it had "*something* to do with the construction of this new Government" and therefore had a vested interest in its success and knew better than most how it was formed and by whom. "We are not ready to be led blindly, like an ass by a halter."[29]

If anything, to some it looked as if the *Mercury* were intent on leading itself, and what it sought to lead was what they had all hoped to avoid, a new anti-Davis party. "The opposition begins before he has time to offend," complained Mary Chesnut in August, seeing Keitt, Boyce, Hammond, and especially "the Rhetts & *Mercury* influence" in operation as the leading elements.[30] Even a prospective reporter for the paper frankly told Miles that the course of the editors had been such as not "to elicit very favorable consideration" either with the government in Richmond or the army at Manassas. "Mr R. has not made himself altogether *convenable* to those in authority," he said, and he hoped that by writing only facts of public interest and eschewing partisan editorializing he might promote harmony between the administration and the *Mercury*.[31]

But he reckoned without the Rhetts. Commenting early in August on rumors that a minority in the congress wanted to establish a standing opposition party, the paper placed no blame on the malcontents but rather said it was only the natural outcome of the poor condition of the army—of whose medical and supply departments Rhett was even then trying to launch an investigation in the congress—and the public outrage at Davis for neglect. Beauregard, more politician than general, brought to the South Carolina delegation his complaints that he could not go on the offensive for want of supplies, and Rhett would make much of them. What some called factionalism the *Mercury* called "the exposure of incompetency." Sounding much like the elder Rhett speaking, the paper charged that far from trying to hinder the president with an antiadministration party, members of the congress "have covered up his errors and deficiencies with the veil of secrecy." Still, by the end of August the criticism forced the Rhetts to an even more explicit denial. "The Mercury is not—never has been—never will be,—whilst in the hands of the present proprietors—*a party organ,*" they declared. It had its own opinions and its own policy, "and asks for no party lead, or man-god to worship." Pointing to the fact that they found fault with the administration from the very formation of the government, they could hardly be accused now of coming in train behind some new party. They stated, "We desired a purely Slave Confederacy," yet their constitution would allow free states to join them. They wanted free trade, but the framers took too much latitude on the tariff. They expected future troubles on both those points, and the continuing secrecy in the congress only increased the opportunity for abuse and excess.[32] It was their duty to speak out. If others agreed, it did not mean that the *Mercury* was following them into some new faction, but rather that others saw the wisdom of the paper's positions. It was pure Rhett, going all the way back to his earliest flirtations with the Democrats under Van Buren. He did not shape his views to conform with a party; he expected a party to conform to him, and so too now with his *Mercury*. The fact that some men now did so only proved that he was right. Yet still there might have been a motive in trying to build an antiadministration constituency at home in Carolina, one that would reveal itself in the fall when the first regular elections for the congress to take over under the permanent constitution came.

In the scant time remaining in the short session, Rhett fought against waiting for current soldiers to be fully armed before accepting more into the service, which was consistent with his policy from the first of raising as large an army as possible regardless of enlistment terms or availability of weapons. To encourage foreign-born men to enlist he also voted for a naturalization law that would provide citizenship to all Confederate soldiers. There was a second motive to the latter, in that such men, having served under arms and now made potential voters, would be likely to oppose any move toward a reconstruction that would render their sacrifices wasted.[33] There was little more to do, or that he could do, before the session adjourned on August 31.

Almost immediately, however, he found another example of the chicanery and autocratic instincts of the president. At the adjournment one substantial piece of unfinished business was a bill to continue in office a number of military and naval officers appointed by Davis but not yet confirmed by the congress. The body had passed it, but somehow it did not get to Davis before the adjournment, and under their rules, any bill not returned within ten days either signed or vetoed automatically died. Though most of the delegates left for home on September 1, Davis issued a call for those remaining in the capital to assemble in special session two days later to address this matter. Rhett had already left and did not learn of it until afterward. Indeed, only Miles of South Carolina was still there, and six other states only had one delegate each still in Richmond. Still, by their rules one delegate could constitute a quorum, so a mere eighteen men met for barely an hour on September 3 and passed a bill continuing the appointees in office until they could be confirmed or rejected at the next regular session, and Davis signed it right away.[34]

It was a perfectly sensible solution to an immediate problem, but Rhett saw in it a design to get around the congress by keeping in office for several months men who might theoretically otherwise have been denied confirmation. This was the easy road to despotism, for with each state voting as a unit, it revealed that all Davis had to do to make legislation at any time was to call a sudden session when no one was in town and bring in just one congressman from any six of the eleven states, and he would have the majority to do as he pleased.[35] The particular instance also signified to Rhett that Davis was attempting to pursue a policy of favoritism in his appointments, rewarding old friends and family and West Point graduates, while ignoring the friends or relatives of those who did not fawn on him. This was first suggested to Rhett by the case of his own nephew Maj. Thomas Rhett of Beauregard's staff, who that August complained of being held back from promotion, while an old friend of Davis who had been out of uniform for more than twenty years was made a colonel. It was one more sign of the meanness of character in the president that Rhett would feel bound to monitor and expose when the time came.[36]

No wonder that when he got home, the *Mercury* began to launch several attacks on the growth of presidential power and began to propose that they must strengthen the powers of the congress as a counter. The Rhetts also renewed the charges against Davis for Manassas. "He, and only he, we have reason to believe, prevented an advance on Washington," the paper charged, which was a falsehood that even the denial of Johnston and Beauregard could not persuade the Rhetts to abandon. Now due to poor supply, health problems, and inadequate organization there had been weeks of inactivity by that army following the victory. It was not the fault of the generals, of that Rhett was convinced. Beauregard had asked permission to lead an advance, but Davis denied him, true enough thanks to the utterly fantastical nature of Beauregard's plans, but now Rhett condemned Davis virtually for not wanting to win the war. While he may not yet have formed any close personal alliance with Johnston or Beauregard, Rhett instinctively sensed allies as he watched their own growing disaffection from Davis, and thereafter the *Mercury* would be their unquestioning defender.

The purpose in stopping a pursuit and preventing any subsequent advance could only be more evidence of an intention to seek reconstruction. As for the mooted idea of commercial reunion on the basis of peace and independence in return for making the Union a most favored nation, it was little but treason to the South, for inevitably they should become commercial vassals of the Yankees once more. The Confederates ought to invade the North, take Washington, and force a treaty on the enemy with not a single trade concession or favor. The great danger facing them now was not from enemy armies but from their own statesmen for financial and commercial reunion. "We know what we say and we say it deliberately," they declared.[37]

Lashing out beyond Davis, the Rhetts took on those in South Carolina who had gainsaid their paper's positions since the days before the Montgomery convention, indulging in a sweeping "I told you so." The current position of the Confederacy, which was engaged in a war that was not necessary, victorious on one battlefield yet unable to win on any other front diplomatic or economic, and faced with a strong current for reconstruction, was all the result of failing to listen to the Rhetts. They had said to take Sumter in December 1860 when the North could not, and under Buchanan would not, have attempted coercion. They had argued for quick and decisively advantageous commercial treaties with Europe that would have produced instant recognition. They had been for ignoring the border states, waiting until the Confederacy had established its independence and could then make them come in on its own terms without risking the introduction of unhealthy political viruses. Instead the Confederacy was in a war, ignored by Europe, and in danger of reconstruction—all because of "the inefficient policy, the shuffling, sideway, timid conduct of our affairs, domestic and foreign, by the authorities of the Confederate States." It was all a repudiation of those who opposed reopening the slave trade, who said there would be no war, and who said the war when it came should be defensive.[38] Some thought this latest barrage "frantic" and merely saw it as more evidence that Rhett was laying down the boundaries to contain a new party for himself.[39]

The war on the administration continued into October, even though shortages forced the *Mercury* to go to a reduced sheet early in the month. The failure of the army's capability of advancing, the paper charged, was because Davis did not want it to do so, and the Rhetts accused him of being unwilling to advance into the North because it would ruin chances of reconstruction, the same reason that the Congress refused to legislate commercial independence for the Confederacy. The navy office sat inactive, suggesting that their warfare on the seas would be defensive too, whereas the Rhetts advocated from the first building a strong fleet and employing a host of privateers to prey on Yankee shipping.[40]

The Rhetts turned much more sharply on the subject of an embargo now. Disingenuously the paper's editorials stated that they assumed the subject had been raised and rejected in congress but that the secrecy cloak left them in the dark. Of course it had been discussed repeatedly in two sessions and rejected, but this was Rhett's way of saying so in the guise of a speculation and thus not actually breaking his vow of silence. He suggested that it would probably come up again in the session due to open in November, meaning that he would likely introduce it himself, and he declared that it was the only true policy for bringing the war to a speedy end by forcing other nations to take the side of the Confederacy. The *Mercury* harped on the embargo for several weeks, as planters voluntarily began to withhold their bales from shipment, but it was imperative that the congress and the president take strong action to make it effective and universal. On the other hand, if they failed to enact an embargo, then everyone would know where the responsibility lay. At the same time Rhett dropped all pretense of keeping congressional secrets when he described the rest of the diplomatic policy that he had tried to get through and failed, the free trade policy he had proposed, and more. He printed all this in the *Mercury* under the pretext of answering public clamor at inactivity, thanks to the proceedings in the congress being closed to the public, but most of that clamor was being raised by the *Mercury* itself.[41]

They also attacked the policy of the government purchasing cotton and paying in treasury notes so that the planters had currency for paying taxes and supporting themselves during an embargo, which they saw as not constitutional under the taxing authority, since it was not a tax, nor under the fund-raising power of the military acts for supporting armies. Worst of all, it did not work, because when the taxes were paid, the treasury just got back its own worthless notes. The problem was not in the government buying but in what it used to pay. If paid in specie or banknotes, then the treasury would have something of real value, while by purchasing cotton with those notes it also acquired a commodity that it could not sell thanks to the embargo. Rhett preferred having the state legislature authorize the state to purchase the cotton using its credit with its own banks to produce the real money for the exchange. Then the planters would have something real with which to keep themselves and their four million slaves provided for during the time that the embargo forcibly put an end to their profitable employ, and they would also have money for paying their taxes to support the government.[42]

In October, Rhett got his first direct inklings that his policy of embargo and favored-nation promises would not have any effect even if attempted. Ambrose Dudley Mann wrote to him from England that Britain was stubbornly resisting granting recognition and that it was not trade or cotton concerns that might move them, but the military outcome of the war. The open hostilities made the British quite reluctant to risk getting involved, and soon afterward word came from Yancey that there was simply no interest in dealing diplomatically with the Confederates. Indeed, Yancey's commission could scarcely get an audience with anyone of importance and found their time largely wasted, while no one was talking of panic in the streets if there were a cotton shortage. Nor, with their markets girdling the world in the Empire, did they feel much stimulated by the prospect of favorable tariff rates from the Confederacy. Like so many others, Rhett had grossly misjudged the authority of King Cotton and the importance of Southern trade to Europe. It was a blow, yet faced with information from the men on the scene, he all but gave up henceforward his attempts on the trade treaty front and greatly scaled down the once-arrogant pronouncements of the omnipotence of Southern cotton. If they were to get recognition henceforth, he said now, it would have to be on the basis that Mann advised, as belligerents.[43] Ironically, years later, in spite of the abundant evidence to the contrary, Rhett would come around again to his now-abandoned assertion that early and advantageous treaty proffers would have won recognition. He could do so not because of any demonstrable evidence, but rather because the lack of any experience to the contrary allowed him, from the vantage point of failure, to look back and proclaim without fear of contradiction that since the foreign policy that was adopted failed, therefore his idea that was not adopted would have worked if attempted early enough. It was another example of that species of dialectic that allowed him, in his own mind, to remain undoubting of his own rectitude, certain that he had never lost an argument.[44]

The realization that cotton and trade were not going to bring recognition came hard, and as late as the first of November, King Cotton advocates still pleaded that the Confederacy need only hold out until the winter for the imaginary cotton shortage to force Europe to act.[45] This only made Rhett and the *Mercury* turn even more strident on military inactivity. By the end of September they were declaring that the whole nation, soldiers and civilians alike, opposed Davis's defensive posture. The lie that Davis halted in the pursuit after Manassas came up again and again. "We know President Davis on the battle field, ordered the pursuit to be arrested," they charged at the end of October. Then after Beauregard explicitly went on record again saying that such was not the case, Rhett simply extended the same argument from Davis opposing offensive action immediately at the end of the battle to his opposing it indefinitely as a matter of policy. "President Davis, and no one else, was responsible for the war—or, rather, anti-war policy of our army on the Potomac," said the *Mercury,* for the first time attacking Davis directly by name instead of merely referring to "the Executive."[46]

Then the *Mercury* escalated the campaign against Davis, virtually ensuring that there would never be a healing of the breach and at the same time playing a small role in widening the gap in relations between the president and Beauregard. It took the general some time to write his report of the battle at Manassas, and when he did it proved to be bombastic and vain to suit its author. He sent it to the war department on October 14, but through some misadventure the secretary of war, now Judah P. Benjamin of Louisiana, failed to pass it along to Davis. The first the president knew of its contents was a misleading synopsis that appeared in the Richmond press on October 23 which suggested that Davis had disapproved a campaign plan by Beauregard to march on Washington prior to the fight at Manassas, and that Davis had also opposed the junction of the two armies of Beauregard and Johnston that achieved the victory.

Unaware that the report had only been in the government's hands for less than two weeks, the *Mercury* correspondent in Richmond concluded on the basis of the damaging synopsis that Davis was intentionally withholding the full text from the public, for every time he asked to see it he was told that Benjamin had not yet had a chance to give it a reading. When an anonymous but well-informed defense of Davis appeared a few days after the synopsis pointing out the errors, the correspondent believed Benjamin himself the author, but he then learned from a government clerk that Benjamin was known to have read the report and thus could not deny in print what he knew must eventually become public. The problem, of course, was that the charges in the synopsis were not true. Both were false, and neither claim was contained in Beauregard's actual report, but the unauthorized synopsis from an anonymous source did untold damage at a time when Davis was already under attack by the Rhetts and a few others. Acting on their correspondent's speculation, the Rhetts repeated the synopsis in the *Mercury* and immediately began speculating on what could be so awful in the report that Davis withheld it from public scrutiny. In the controversy that mushroomed out of the affair Davis and Beauregard suffered a permanent break in relations; the alliance between Beauregard and the Rhetts was further strengthened, especially because the general's mention of an attack on Washington conveniently matched the offensive posture they had now adopted; and the *Mercury* took hold of another arrow to sling at the president and kept on using it long after the synopsis was discredited. Soon they declared that the executive could be dangerous to public liberty because it controlled the military, accusing Davis of seeking "to curb the expression of opinions and muzzle the press" by withholding Beauregard's report, not to mention the secret proceedings of congress over which Davis had no control—although they claimed this did not matter to them.[47]

The provisional government was going to expire and cease existence in February 1862, and legislation provided for an election in November 1861 to choose the members of the house and senate, as well as the president, under the permanent constitution. It had been assumed by most that Davis would automatically be reelected without opposition, but the furor with Beauregard that summer and fall, combined with the growing frustration over military inactivity and the discontent assiduously cultivated by Rhett and others in the still-nascent opposition, had led to talk of running Beauregard against Davis. But for one thing the *Mercury* likely would have raised his name on its banner. What stopped them was that the *Mercury* itself was under fire as never before since secession.

Reading the pages of the newspaper that October as the attacks and the controversy unfolded, Mary Chesnut concluded as did others that if only Rhett had been chosen president, or if Davis had made him secretary of state as he expected, there would have been no war on the administration in the *Mercury* now, a conclusion that was half right but which missed Rhett's essentially controversial nature. If chosen for the state department, he would still have fought with any president placed over him, especially Davis; as president, Rhett would inevitably have gone to war with this moderate and unsteady congress, and in either circumstance the *Mercury* would have marched to combat with him. She saw even more signs of the paper seeking overtly or covertly to coalesce an opposition party around its owner, and though it was doubted that it would be strong enough to do anything, still it could cause trouble. "The *Mercury* was more than usually *atrocious,*" Chesnut found late in October. "He ought to be burned, this *traitor*—who published such."[48]

Even Robert W. Barnwell declared that "the rancor, malice & folly of our Newspapers have heretofore been almost innocuous" compared to the *Mercury* by the end of October on the eve of the election. Rhett's old foe Samuel McGowan saw the cause much as did Mrs. Chesnut. "This world is litterally eaten up with envy," he said, while Ellison Capers, soon to be a South Carolina general like McGowan, agreed that the editorial course of the paper was due chiefly to pique over Rhett's not getting the presidency or other high office.[49]

Rhett could not see that his own attitude and his paper's was doing irreparable harm. Simms found the *Mercury* regarded as odious throughout much of the state by election day, thanks to its attacks on Davis and the administration. "The Rhetts cannot bear prosperity," he told Hammond, "and they have kicked over the milk tub of theirs."[50] The backlash began to manifest itself among the literate civilians such as Chesnut and Simms first, then the officers such as McGowan and Capers, and finally the soldiers. His own son Burnet had communicated to the paper his Second South Carolina Infantry's disillusionment at its inactivity after Manassas and a determination not to reenlist when its twelve months were out in the coming spring. But when the *Mercury* published the report, the regiment recoiled in anger and denounced it as a lie and furthermore affirmed their faith in the president. Though Burnet Rhett no doubt did not go along in the vote of his comrades repudiating his father and brother, still the act stung in the *Mercury* office, and the editors reacted predictably with an even more strident attack on Davis for keeping the army idle out of a desire for commercial reconstruction at least and political reunion at worst.[51]

The senior Rhett realized too late the effect his course was having on his own standing. For some time his friends mooted putting him before the legislature in December for one of the state's senate seats in Richmond, and by mid-October it was generally believed that he would be nominated, though some also felt just as certain that he would be defeated.[52] By the end of the month Rhett knew that his chances were almost nil. He was in Charleston running the paper while the younger Barnwell Rhett went away for a week, but he already regarded his prospects as "desperate." Barnwell, Pickens, and Orr seemed the most likely candidates, along with Boyce and Chesnut, who now regarded Rhett as nothing but "bluster." His absent son confessed that "his chance is exceedingly slim." Worse, the war and its own editorial policy were doing what Simms had observed, for people were now beginning to turn away from the *Mercury* again, starting once more the slide into ever deeper debt. Rhett was broke, the banks would give him no more credit, and he faced suddenly the possibility that he would have to sell the paper and declare bankruptcy. There is even a hint that Burnet Rhett may have shared his regiment's rejection of the *Mercury's* negativism. "On the whole," said Barnwell Rhett, "the condition of the family is desperate."[53]

Too late did the Rhetts finally see that they ought to change their tone before they destroyed themselves. By late November, a week after the elder Rhett returned to Richmond for the long winter session, his son concluded that it was more important now to sustain the will and courage of the people than to carp. "Criticism, unless plainly and palpably beneficial, does more harm than good," he advised a reporter rather late in the day. The state of the Confederacy seemed to be such that it would take little more to demoralize everyone, and as a result he began heavily editing and even discarding critical reports from the capital. "The Mercury has been clearly right but it is now necessary to let Davis alone and put the best face on matters," he said. "People cannot always stand too much truth." The great majority of the people were too weak to stomach absolute truth of the sort that only the Rhetts could supply, and so for the present their editorial policy would soften to offer "the truth, but not all the truth."[54] He did not say, because neither he nor his father likely would admit, that for the Rhetts "truth" was always malleable for expedience.

Earlier that month, condemning the idea of commercial reconstruction, the Rhetts reiterated their call for a Northern invasion and dismissed the idea of such an act engendering hatred between the sections. For their ends, such hatred would only be a further barrier to any form of reconstruction, and that was positively beneficial. Hatred, they said, "is the sole compensating utility of the war."[55] Yet by now they had lost track of the hatred launched in their pages and actions. Some barbs went true to aim and struck the Yankees, but more had fallen short of the North, to land in Richmond instead. Most perilous of all for them, however, was the mounting hatred they bred when so much of their vituperation only called down animosity upon themselves, and from the very people they sought to lead. Men might live on hate, but men's hopes could not.

TWENTY-THREE

There Is Something Wrong Somewhere
1861–1862

RHETT REACHED RICHMOND IN SOMETHING of a state, for the Yankees had finally moved and the war suddenly struck close. Just days before he left home Jefferson Davis was elected president of the permanent government without opposition. That was bad enough, but the next day, November 7, a Union fleet attacked Confederates protecting Port Royal Sound, and that same day enemy soldiers occupied Beaufort, where his brother Edmund still lived in the home that had hosted many secession discussions over the years. Rhett's birthplace and boyhood home were now to be occupied by the Yankees. Worse, the Confederate defender Gen. Thomas Drayton was a local man who had been a West Point crony of Jefferson Davis, and Rhett charged him with incompetence, thus chalking another personal grievance against the president. In a further disappointment, the local planters placed such confidence in Drayton that they did not destroy their cotton beforehand to keep it out of Yankee hands. Now their confiscated crop would be clothing Union soldiers or going overseas to profit the enemy and lessen the hoped-for cotton shortage in Europe. When the overall commander in South Carolina, Gen. Robert E. Lee, suggested that the coastal forts should be garrisoned with naval men, Rhett objected, wanting military force, and a lot of it, to protect the rest of his state and, it was to be hoped, reclaim Beaufort. He would stay excited and apprehensive about the military situation in the Lowcountry for some time to come, and with good cause. Meanwhile, he sent Katherine and the younger children off to Aiken, South Carolina, to keep them safely out of the way of the war.[1]

Trouble was to come in threes, for the day after the fall of Port Royal Sound, the new commissioners to replace the failed Yancey mission, James Mason and John Slidell, were forcibly taken by Yankee authorities from the British ship taking them to England. Though he had little time for Slidell, Rhett had been a friend of Mason for much of his public career, and two of his nephews married Mason's nieces, giving them a distant family connection. But more than any concern for his friend's safety, Rhett saw immediately the diplomatic potential attendant to the seizure of accredited ministers from a neutral vessel. He could hope that Britain would regard it as an act of war and that it might propel White-hall toward recognition or even intervention, accomplishing at a stroke what cot-ton and trade lures had not. Hunter and Memminger wrote an inflammatory article for the Richmond press about the matter, leaving it unsigned, and at once people thought it must be by Rhett since he chaired the foreign affairs commit-tee, although it was not. Still he sent it on to his son for republication in the *Mer-cury,* which at first speculated that England would do nothing in protest since the Yankees had acted within international law in the capture. Rhett wanted to encourage the British government that the seizure constituted an act of war, and soon the *Mercury* changed voice and sounded the call for outrage and retribu-tion from abroad.[2] Nothing came of it, chiefly because of excellent diplomacy from Washington and London. Davis had condemned the action in his message to the congress on November 18, but thereafter he took a strangely passive atti-tude toward the possibilities of the situation. Ten days later Rhett moved that that portion of the message be referred to his committee for action, perhaps hop-ing that he could make some capital from it, but the whole problem ended on January 1, 1862 when the Union released Mason and Slidell and sent them on to England.[3] The missed opportunity only further served to convince Rhett that the president was the wrong man in the wrong job.

On reaching Richmond, Rhett at first lodged at the Spottswood Hotel, bring-ing the pretty and talented Elise with him to charm the other guests, but then they moved to a boardinghouse on Eighth Street for the balance of the session, enjoying a small but convivial society there. Rhett only had eyes for renewed attacks on the president. Memminger told him definitively that Davis did not halt a pursuit after Manassas but that his generals had told him it could not be done. Rhett did not trust Memminger now and would later accuse him of being willing to write or say any lie that Davis wanted. For now he abated his charges about the pursuit but happily found another to replace it, for rumors had also circulated that Davis actually commanded on the field in the battle and that the laurels for the victory were rightfully his. It was untrue of course, an accidental confusion that quickly died away in Richmond and a claim that Davis never made. Unfortunately, he did not repudiate the story emphatically enough to suit Rhett, and thereafter the Carolinian would charge that the venal and vain pres-ident was trying to steal the credit due to others.[4]

Rhett launched his campaign on the military front now, with two assaults. One was a continuation of the imbroglio over Beauregard's Manassas report, still not published, and he introduced a resolution in the congress on November 26 calling on the president to furnish copies of all battle reports received from commanders in the field, though of course the only one he was interested in was Beauregard's.[5] When finally the congress saw it, however, any gain Rhett hoped to realize evaporated as they saw that, in fact, there was nothing in the document for Davis to try to hide.

By then Rhett had his teeth in a much juicier morsel, Davis's usurpation of power and favoritism in military appointments. Early in the month, before Rhett went to Richmond, the *Mercury* had already commenced criticism of the president for elevating a number of officers from brigadier to major generals. The congress had only created two grades of high rank, brigadier and full general, and had not authorized any such office as major general, the paper argued. Thus Davis had no right in law to make such appointments.[6] Rhett was correct, but the armies had grown to such proportions that the original enabling legislation for high command was quickly outmoded. A brigadier should command a brigade, and a full general an entire army, but as the armies now might encompass twenty or thirty brigades in a single field command, some intermediate refinement into divisions and even corps was clearly necessary for efficiency, and intermediate ranks of major and even lieutenant general were called for. Rhett freely confessed the need for the new ranks and would even in time add the failure to anticipate this to his growing list of Davis's failures, but the law now was the law, and when Davis submitted a list of his recent promotions to major general to the congress on November 21 for confirmation, Rhett pounced, introducing a resolution calling for an inquiry to determine under what authority such promotions were made.

Four days later the military affairs committee reported that legislation was, indeed, needed to authorize such promotions, and Rhett moved to refer the matter to the judiciary committee to prepare the proper legislation. But then the report and Rhett's motion were tabled, not to rise again until December 2 when Rhett moved that they lay aside a communication from the president with a long list of military appointments and first consider his new resolution for the judiciary committee to inquire into Davis's promotions. It was a clear attempt to embarrass the president by holding up new appointments until the earlier issue—which most in the congress seemed to wish to ignore—had been fully explored, and no doubt publicized. Rhett's resolution passed. Then Miles produced a report from the military committee moving that they proceed to approve the promotions, but the majority, including Rhett, tabled the report. Rhett was not about to let Davis off that easily. For two more weeks the matter hung fire, and on December 13, Rhett introduced another resolution in the matter. Only an appearance and personal appeal from Benjamin, newly installed as secretary of war, finally got confirmation of Davis's earlier promotions, and meanwhile the congress passed the legislation to create the new ranks needed.[7]

Even while holding Davis's feet to the coals over the promotions, Rhett found another instance of executive usurpation that enraged him even more. Just the day after his call for the battle reports Rhett voted with the majority to ratify a convention with a rump secession legislature in Missouri, adding one more star to the flag.[8] On December 2 two delegates from the new state called on Rhett to describe a meeting they had just had with Davis.[9] Command of the secessionist forces in Missouri was in chaos between supporters of the popular Gen. Sterling Price and others, and Davis had let it be known that he intended to solve the problem by placing his own man, Henry Heth, in command out there, making him a major general for the job. In the course of their courtesy call the Missourians began to sing the praises of Price, obviously urging Davis to leave him in unequivocal command, but Davis met them with firm, perhaps impatient resistance, reminding them as he would many others that he would not be influenced or dictated to in his appointments.

Later that day Rhett mentioned the Missourians' complaint to William C. Rives, delegate from Virginia, who said that a delegation from his own state had encountered precisely the same imperious attitude when they laid a proposition before the president. In fact, Davis would soon be so noted for such demeanor that congressmen other than his close supporters rarely approached him. Naturally the Missourians were in an uproar at having one of their own, Price, superseded. Heth called on them to tell them he had been appointed and would be leaving soon but did not wish to leave before meeting with them to hear their views. He was told that they intended to oppose his confirmation when Davis submitted his promotion to the congress. Soon several other people called on Davis asking him to change his mind, but he only replied anew that he would not be dictated to when it came to the prerogatives of his office. Gradually word of an impending battle got out, and Davis decided to change his mind for the sake of political expedience rather than risk alienating a new state and its soldiers. On December 9 he said he had no intention of superseding Price and that indeed he could not because of a technicality with the troops to be commanded, an obvious device to make it appear that he was not in fact backing down.

For Rhett, this only confirmed Davis's meanness and inadequate character. "Jefferson Davis is not only a dishonest man, but a liar," Rhett fumed to his son at the *Mercury.* "What is to become of us under this man for six years," he wondered. "He is a mean-born swine, utterly unworthy and unfit for his great office." As usual, Rhett believed that he had been well in advance of others in spotting Davis's shortcomings and said, "No wonder he instinctively hates me." But for his prescience he found himself accused instead of disloyalty or disappointed ambition. He sent his son all the details he could get so that the paper should expose the president's duplicity, but Barnwell Rhett, still briefly committed to backing off criticism of the administration, would not publish it. Nor did the *Mercury* cover the story until the following March, when the elder Rhett was back in Charleston and no doubt overruled his son.[10]

There were other influences acting on Rhett's already-deplorable opinion of the president. The *Mercury* correspondent in Richmond, George Bagby, described the Davises as "the Imperial family," passing along stories of their rude Mississippi behavior and dictatorial manner with friends and other people's servants. Davis did not visit the sick and wounded in hospitals, nor did he donate to soldier charities, and Varina Davis, his wife, did little more. Bagby even repeated rumors that Mrs. Davis was behind the Heth-Price affair for Heth's wife had supposedly persuaded her to influence her husband in his favor. Davis was an "unhappy and diseased hypocrite," bent on becoming dictator.[11] It could hardly be surprising that with such influences adding new rumor and venom to his own prejudices, Rhett's antipathy for the president grew dramatically toward the point of obsession.

It hardly helped that Davis had just been reelected, whereas the legislature in Columbia, meeting to select its first two senators for the new congress, scarcely gave Rhett a thought. Instead they chose Barnwell and Orr. Rhett did not put himself before the people of Charleston for reelection to a house seat, probably since having been a United States Senator before secession, to accept any lesser position now would be a comedown. Also it was quite evident that there would be a real contest for the seat, with Jamison and Lewis M. Ayer both anxious and on the hustings. Ayer was finally triumphant. By the time Rhett realized how little chance he had for the senate seat, it was too late to get into the house race, and in any case his temperament simply did not allow him to engage in adversarial stump politics. Whether that came from squeamishness toward the sometimes rough-and-tumble business of seeking office or a belief that after long experience of the oligarchs receiving office by right of birth it was beneath him to vie for it, he never said. But it all meant in the end that when the provisional congress expired in February, he would be out of a job and thrown back on his newspaper and his plantations, neither of which was flourishing. Adding further gall to the mix, after the senatorial elections the Columbia legislature went on to pass a resolution of support and confidence for Davis and calling on all Carolinians to back him as their patriotic duty.

With much before them Rhett opposed a long three-week Christmas recess and, like the rest, remained at his post, almost his only social recreation being visits to an artist's studio on Twelfth Street to have his bust sculpted. The sculptor found him of such a generous nature that he went out of his way to accommodate Rhett's limited means.[12] In fact, where once Rhett had opposed paying travel mileage to members, his personal finances were now so precarious that he changed position on this too, most likely because he needed the money himself.[13] Despite opposing the recess, after it was defeated Rhett went home at Christmas for a brief session of the state convention. There he took little part other than a surprising opposition to calling on Richmond for more troops to protect the state, but only because he knew how endangered other fronts were about to be.[14]

Rhett returned to Richmond just after the new year, and then John Tyler died. The Virginia delegation asked Rhett to take part in the tributes paid to the old patriot in the city, which he happily did, though Tyler had never been among his favorites in earlier days. There were also some happily uncontroversial affairs to handle, as when he voted to admit Kentucky as a state after a rump convention there opted for secession. Rhett introduced the resolution on December 10, referring the bill for Kentucky's admission to the judiciary committee, an ironic act to say the least, considering his long suspicion and even opposition to the border states. Continuing his new policy with the northern slave states, he raised a motion to make it a provision of any future peace treaty with the United States that it must provide for Maryland to have the opportunity of joining the Confederacy, adding an amendment that the congress should issue a resolution of sympathy and support for her current trials under Yankee domination. A few weeks later, as a rump Unionist convention in western Virginia declared that part of the state independent from the Old Dominion and made overtures to be received into the Union as a new state, Rhett offered a resolution of hearty support and a pledge of assistance to Virginia in resisting dismemberment. With the war seeming to go nowhere, and with so many of the other avenues of strength and advantage he envisioned cut off, he had no choice but to reverse himself and start cultivating the border states for the support they could provide.[15]

During that winter session he continued true as ever to his basic convictions of policy. Seeing the need for national economy as well as in his own finances, he opposed a salary increase for soldiers while also coming out against a proposed pay decrease for officers, though he stood in favor of noncommissioned officers receiving an increase. He continued to oppose using treasury notes to pay advances to growers for cotton and tobacco subscribed to the government as tax in kind, and he still supported the by-now-deceased notion of an embargo. In December he learned that three shipments of tobacco had recently gone out of Virginia's James River bound for Europe, which he brought to the attention of his foreign affairs committee. The committee prepared another embargo bill that was introduced on December 11, but as usual it died on the floor.[16] He continued his support of sequestration of enemy property in the Confederacy too, though calling for it not to apply to persons born in the Confederate states. And in a rare break from his opposition to any interference between a master and his property in slaves, he voted against excluding slaves from being subject to confiscation when they were the property of enemies of the state.[17]

Rhett seemed truer to form on slave property when in mid-December he favored exempting slaves owned by railroads from being assessed as part of the value of their stock for tax purposes, but perhaps that was only because he was fighting a much bigger battle on a much larger issue. In his message to the congress on November 19, Davis had called for an appropriation to construct a connection between the Danville, Virginia, terminus of the Richmond & Danville and the Greensboro terminus of the North Carolina Railroad. It was vital to the efficient and speedy movement of troops and supplies, and made perfect sense as a military necessity. But it constituted a first step toward that great tyranny that had first inspired Rhett in his entry into politics some thirty-three years earlier—internal improvements. He saw it as clearly unconstitutional. An appropriation bill containing a provision for the rail connection appeared on December 9, and when it came up for consideration he moved to strike the provision. When that failed, he voted against the whole bill. On February 6 it arose again, and he tried to kill it by voting against a postponement of regular business to take it up, but that failed. Then when a delegate called for the question on the measure, Rhett voted against that too and failed again. A day later he voted with a minority trying to postpone consideration of the bill indefinitely. Finally on February 10 when a vote to reconsider passage of the bill failed, he joined with Toombs and other opponents in registering a lengthy protest into the record, the first and only time such occurred during the life of the provisional congress.

The act gave Davis too much power, they complained, for he could contract with whomever he chose to build the rail link regardless of the wishes of the two states involved, in effect overriding their sovereignty. Worse, as a military necessity the president would be able to impose military protection on the line, superceding the civil authority in those states. The congress did not have the power under the constitution to give the president this authority. Moreover, they said, it was unnecessary, since men and material were currently transported by other means in the main and always would be, or so they predicted without much foresight. Most of all—and this was probably Rhett talking now—they feared the rise of the excuse of "military necessity," for it could in future cloak all manner of usurpations. Such excesses under that same guise were even then outraging the old Union, and was this not, after all, one of the evils from which they all seceded in the first place? In registering their protest Rhett and the others called on the people at large to look into the danger this move posed, since those opposed in the congress could not defeat it. Four days later Rhett voted against similar appropriations for two other rail connections in other states, but both passed.[18]

"Congress today passed the first Internal Improvement Bill recommended by the President," Rhett grumbled in an unsigned editorial sent to his son for the *Mercury.* "It was supported on the ground of a military necessity," he explained, and he warned that it only laid the foundation for untold aggressions on the constitution and public liberty in the future. There was other evidence too. The previous August the congress had authorized the president to sell a steamer partially owned by alien enemies, but it died along with five other measures when an ailing Davis was unable to prepare veto messages on them before the ten day time limit expired, though he sent Benjamin, then attorney general, to explain his action. In the steamer case his objection was that the decision belonged to the courts and not to the congress, and that the vessel was also partly owned by loyal Confederate citizens. But a few months later Davis ordered the same vessel seized by the government for public use in violation of the rights of the loyal owners. Furthermore, at the same time that the railroad bill passed, the government had also started seizing niter, a necessary component of gunpowder, from private sources that were in the habit of charging exorbitant prices. While condemning profiteering, Rhett railed against the confiscation, calling it "simply a military usurpation" and pointing out that the president had done nothing about establishing the Confederacy's own sources of niter and other needed resources, despite congressional encouragement, which made the resort to confiscation all the more objectionable. Davis and his administration were bathing themselves in illegality.[19]

The evidences to support Rhett's contention that Davis was an arbitrary tyrant mounted rapidly. Even while fighting the losing battle over the railroad bill, Rhett took up the cause of Gen. Milledge Bonham, with whom he had never been on close terms until antipathy toward Davis allied them. Bonham commanded a brigade at Manassas, but immediately afterward one of his regiments was transferred, reducing his command to less than a full brigade, and Davis took the position that this terminated his commission as a brigadier. Bonham protested, enlisting congressional aid, and in October, Davis reappointed him but without backdating his seniority, which thus made Bonham junior to other brigadiers appointed since Manassas.

Rhett always took an interest in high commissions for Carolinians and now got fully involved in the Bonham controversy. He warned Bonham that during the recess before the winter term Davis might have decided not to submit his reappointment for confirmation, and Rhett concluded to bring the whole matter to the floor.[20] On January 22 he introduced a resolution for the military affairs committee to investigate the nature of the tenure of brigadiers, and two weeks later he followed with another calling on the committee to report on whether a brigadier's commission expired when his command was dispersed or reduced to less than a regulation brigade, including by the action of the expiration of terms of service. By this time Bonham was no longer involved, since he had gotten his commission after all but resigned in January preparatory to taking a seat in the new congress the following month. But that did not stop Rhett, for there was a principle of power and prerogative here, and another barb with which to prick Davis. In February the *Mercury* took up the battle, publishing a series of articles exposing the whole affair and charging Davis with eliminating Bonham in order to make a place for one of his favorites.[21]

Indeed the nepotism accusation in appointments came more and more frequently from the Rhetts now, and not without some foundation, for Davis gave brigadier's commissions to relations such as Richard Taylor and David Jones, while others not among his favorites sometimes seemed to languish. In January the *Mercury* charged that government could not be free when "there is nothing radical but corruption," and the paper accused Memminger of firing a whole bureau of officeholders in spite of the presumed civil service reform that Rhett had worked into the constitution. "Incompetency weighs heavily on the efficiency of the public service," charged an editorial, "while nepotism and partizanship reign supreme."

No concerns about favoritism seem to have inhibited Rhett from using his position to advance the careers of his own sons, however. Young Burnet Rhett complained to him that his superiors would not furlough twelve-month men, who had enlisted in a new artillery company he was trying to raise to be commanded by him when their previous enlistments expired so that he could properly organize the command for acceptance into the army. The elder Rhett called on the secretary of war and got complete satisfaction, but in spite of that he would never have a good word to say about Benjamin, nor would he stop condemning perceived favoritism in Davis.[22] Perhaps this was in part because the *Richmond Enquirer,* in an article believed to have been written by Benjamin, responded to the *Mercury* and the Rhetts' attacks on the Bonham case by charging that "there are a class of persons, small, and, happily powerless, who, adopting the opposite extreme of the monarchical theory that 'the King can do no wrong,' put themselves to great trouble to prove that the President can do no right."[23]

In at least one area Rhett unfailingly supported the administration, and that was in the raising of more volunteers. He voted for every military enlargement bill that went through the congress, fought to get them passed quickly, supported the expansion of the staff and support services to eliminate the problems that had plagued the army after Manassas, and likewise supported any effort to build the infant navy.[24] The problem was that Davis would not ask for enough, so even here Rhett remained an opponent. He never countenanced Davis's policy of offering furloughs and bonuses to twelve-month men as an inducement for them to reenlist in the new three-year regiments, and he repeatedly voted against bills to accomplish that purpose, assisted in opposition by Thomas Cobb and Toombs. Rhett tried unsuccessfully to frame a military bill himself, aided by Cobb, who urged him on in the work. When Davis vetoed one act for raising troops in Missouri, Rhett tried to override unsuccessfully and was dismayed to find Cobb changing sides to support the veto. When he took the Georgian to task, Cobb replied that he was about to lead his own command in the coming spring campaign and feared that if he offended Davis now, it would cost him when he needed the president's support in the field. Rhett generously granted that standing with him could only prejudice Cobb's fortunes as a soldier, and he released him from any obligation to help further.[25]

Toombs took up Cobb's cudgel, however, and Rhett's last effort to increase the army in spite of Davis came on February 5 when Toombs introduced a bill for a vigorous levy to raise 50,000 or more by calling on the several states to bring out their militias, using compulsory conscription if necessary. Rhett ultimately envisioned the legislation leading to 250,000. The situation seemed all the more urgent because their new commander in the Mississippi Valley, Gen. Albert Sidney Johnston, had been under the impression that he would have 50,000 or more, only to find on his arrival that his forces were substantially fewer with which to face a probable Union invasion. Worse, the lawful legislature of Kentucky's abandonment of neutrality and alignment with the Union meant that enemy forces were now free to move across the state to invade Tennessee and parts farther south. Rhett maintained that the bill was introduced more to state the policy of Davis's opponents than out of any expectation of passage, for a scant two weeks of the session remained before the provisional congress went out of existence, and they could hardly expect to push through such a controversial measure in that short time. What Rhett was really doing with Toombs was setting up yet another issue with which to drub the president, an illustration that his dilatory policy had driven the congress to such an extremity, while if it had actually passed and inevitably been vetoed by Davis, then he would have the veto as a weapon. Either way Rhett gained a point to use in his war with the administration.[26]

The bill went to the military committee, but its response on February 13 was that the country had sufficient legislation in place already, having already called for four hundred thousand three-year men. What Rhett regarded as "an angry and excited debate" ensued on the floor over the bill, Rhett and Toombs hot in support, and it continued sporadically over several days. The chairman of the military committee, Stephen Hale of Alabama, led the fight against the bill, at one point ridiculing Rhett that men who knew nothing of the military pretended to know more about what was good for the army than its commander-in-chief. Toombs replied hotly in what would be his last speech on the floor, since he, too, had taken a military commission. Having done his duty by proposing this legislation and affirming what he and Rhett thought ought to be the proper policy of the government, he withdrew the bill in what Rhett called "disgust, perhaps indignation." Rhett wanted to force a voice vote on the bill so that men would have to go on record, rather than being able to hide behind the unit votes of their states, but Toombs advised against wasting the time, and thus it died.[27]

The timing of the bill had been prophetic, for as it failed, Federal forces in Tennessee captured Fort Donelson on the Cumberland River, a victory that followed the fall of Fort Henry on the nearby Tennessee. Combined, the two gains opened the whole center of the Confederate heartland to invasion by army and naval forces. It was a disaster, perhaps unavoidable but made the worse because Albert Sidney Johnston's army was too small and too spread out to resist. In the wake of the victories the Confederates had to abandon their foothold in Kentucky and virtually all of middle Tennessee, including Nashville. Two months later, when reenlistments proved disappointing and Virginia was being invaded as well, the administration passed its first conscription bill, and Rhett could at least indulge in some grim satisfaction. However, even here he would castigate Davis for making conscription a national act, rather than asking the states to conscript their own men, which lay exclusively within their sovereignty.[28]

As the close of the session approached, the *Mercury,* never able to stay restrained for long, turned the heat up again on Davis, perhaps reflecting Rhett's frustration that he was about to be cast into civil life. The paper still preached against the tendency to reconstruction that it saw in every act, championing now propositions to replace the old naturalization law adopted from the United States and imposing in its place a new one that would prevent Yankees from flooding the South after the war, taking citizenship, and gaining access to the ballot box where they would weaken the solid majority of sound conservative men.[29] Though remaining optimistic for the future, it decried the inactivity of the past six months. "Audacity—*audacity*—AUDACITY!" it cried. Citing Sterling Price, whom Rhett was coming to regard as one of the great generals of the war, the newspaper proclaimed his taking of Lexington, Missouri, the previous fall as an example of what daring could do, ignoring the fact that he gave it up two weeks later. The editorials railed on about the secret sessions, hinting that there were liars in government who needed to be exposed and raising the prospect that someone in Richmond sought to be a "political Bounaparte," while leaving it to the readers to guess who. After the fall of Forts Henry and Donelson, the *Mercury* began to suggest that the states should raise regiments and acquire arms on their own. They were not wholly dependent on the central government and could themselves act unilaterally without awaiting authorization. Then they could present legions of regiments, even gunboats for the navy, and Richmond would have no choice but to accept them.[30]

Rhett undoubtedly wrote several of the unsigned letters and editorials appearing now, and once more his authorship was an open secret in Richmond. When the *Richmond Enquirer* accused him of doing so, the *Mercury* blustered and hedged but never forthrightly denied the charge.[31] Rhett protested especially against the secret sessions. "Conscience and the Constitution, duty and policy," he argued, dictated that the people should be informed. He was unable or unwilling to understand that the full disclosure that he believed would force Davis to conform to Rhett's idea of government, would also reveal their weakness to the enemy and provide much-needed encouragement. He pointed especially to the provisional constitution's call for the periodic publication of congressional proceedings and asked why it had not been done.[32] Meanwhile he had become so reckless in disclosing the spirit, if not the actual content, of closed proceedings, that complaints had been on the f.oor since July, and an actual inquiry initiated at the end of the summer session was too late to accomplish anything.

Rhett and the *Mercury* were never specifically named, but it seemed generally understood that they were the prime objects. On January 25 his old antagonist Charles Conrad reported the result of a fresh inquiry into the matter of secret proceedings being made public, and he recommended ejecting everyone but members and officers from the building half an hour before they went into secret session. That would eliminate any question as to the leaks coming from anyone other than the members themselves, and since most appeared first in Rhett's *Mercury*, it would not tax logic overmuch to expose the source.[33] Rhett's repeated efforts to get their journals published would have given him away if nothing else, and as late as January 30 he was still trying unsuccessfully to get at least the journals of the convention that adopted the provisional and permanent constitutions released.[34] When a bill came forth early in February, further in response to the leaks, making it treason to publish in the press anything that revealed military information, the *Mercury* immediately railed that it was a new Sedition Act and a violation of the basic freedom of the press. The people must awaken, the paper said. "It is time for them to know what their Government is doing."[35]

Rhett especially wanted them to know of the autocratic way he saw Davis trying to rule by veto. Back in December he introduced a resolution asking the judiciary committee to investigate the series of bills that died at the end of the last session when Davis was too ill to prepare veto messages.[36] To his mind, Davis had been trying to kill legislation without having to run the risk of having a veto overridden, thus overturning the constitutional checks and balances, and Rhett accused him of merely hiding behind his illness. Worse, by sending Benjamin to deliver the message and to answer on behalf of the president any questions about his objections to the bills, Rhett saw Davis making a studied insult to the congress. Moreover, he thought Davis violated a tradition—which Rhett invented for this argument—that past presidents in the United States had only used the veto to stop legislation that they thought to be unconstitutional. On February 5, Rhett delivered a lengthy address on the floor charging that Davis was seeking to usurp the legislative authority by using the veto to stop bills. The veto power, which he supported when properly used, could not be applied in all legislation but only against that which violated the constitution. He declared—erroneously—that not a single veto had ever been imposed in the Union on any basis other than constitutionality. He then charged that Davis had already vetoed more bills than all the presidents from Washington to Jackson combined—another example of Rhett's cavalier attitude toward facts when they conflicted with his aims. The first seven presidents issued a total of eighteen vetoes, whereas Davis had issued only ten. Years later he would exaggerate those ten vetoes into being greater than the combined total of all presidents from Washington to Buchanan, in fact some forty-five.[37]

A week before the close of the session Rhett was again voting unsuccessfully to override Davis's most recent vetoes, and he was soon complaining in the *Mercury* that the president "did little or nothing, that we can perceive, except to appoint individuals to office, keep the army in check, and control the Congress by vetoing their bills and shaping their legislation." Derisively correspondent Bagby, writing as "Hermes," began calling Davis "the Great Almoner" and "the Great dispenser."[38] The complaints against Davis became more frequent and more pointed. "There is something wrong somewhere," his pages alleged; "somebody is either *traitorous* or *utterly incompetent*." On the day they heard of the attack on Fort Donelson, the *Mercury* proclaimed Davis's military approach "a monstrous absurdity," one that had squandered their early advantages on "a petty, piddling policy." The people were disregarding wise counsel and warnings, and even condemning those such as Rhett who sought to make the public aware of the true nature of their president and the perils before them. "In war, as we support imbecility, and faithlessness and folly," the pages railed, "we must take the natural results of confusion, failure and suffering."[39]

Mary Chesnut believed now that Rhett acted as if he believed Davis had been specifically invented by the Yankees to torment the Confederacy, and even old Edmund Ruffin, every bit as radical as Rhett and now a close associate, still saw that the opposition to the president had gone beyond policy to become personal obsession. "He [Rhett], & many others of the earliest & staunchest movers of secession, & defenders of southern rights & interests, now that the great measure has been brought about, have to experience that the conduct of affairs, & the honors & rewards of office, are withheld from the men of their class, service & merit," Ruffin commented on February 6. He did not doubt that there were good grounds for some of Rhett's criticism of Davis, "but their sharpness is added to by Rhett's feelings of neglect & disappointed ambition."[40]

In the last days of the provisional congress Rhett could do little more than he had accomplished in the earlier sessions. Still clinging to the goal of free trade and economic independence, he hoped right to the end of the session to get through a downward revision of customs duties, supporting even a temporary bill allowing all imported goods to enter the Confederacy duty free. To prevent any goods from coming to the country via the United States, he introduced bills requiring all imports to come directly from their countries of manufacture and a navigation act to establish direct trade requiring goods to be shipped either in Confederate vessels or those of the exporting nation. After peace and independence he did not want Yankee merchants profiting by controlling the carrying trade to the South as before. He still clung to King Cotton and the embargo, arguing that it was working, only slowly, and that soon five million Britons would realize that the Confederacy controlled their livelihood. Not one of his measures passed, and he even lost when he tried to settle the patterns for the great seal and emblems of the Confederacy before the adjournment. Rhett did not stay until the adjournment on February 17. In poor health, he left two days earlier immediately after casting his last vote, fittingly in a failed attempt to override Davis's veto of a furlough bill. As he left Richmond he met Yancey, who was just arriving back from Europe and was now to sit in the new senate. Rhett later claimed that Yancey told him, "You were right, sir. I went on a fool's errand." It was a sadly appropriate way to end his service in the congress. He had failed to impose his vision of the shape of the Confederacy when they first met a year before, just as now he could not even influence the design of its flag. All he could do was strike out one last time at the man who was ruining all his hopes, while at least Yancey told him he had been right all along. In a final irony, when Rhett and Elise left their boardinghouse to go home, the ex-congressman's room was immediately rented to young Burton Harrison, private secretary to Jefferson Davis.[41]

"We do not cast able men aside at the caprices of a mob, or in obedience to some low party intrigue," his son Edmund had haughtily declared shortly after

Fort Sumter, "and hence we are sure of the best men."[42] Yet now his father was cast aside; the mob had had something to do with it, and certainly his enemy had been the intrigues for power of the low party that fawned on Jefferson Davis. At least Robert Barnwell Rhett could say that he had stood his ground for state and individual rights; for the perpetual independence of the Confederacy militarily, economically, and diplomatically; and for the perpetuation of slavery as a social and moral benefit. No one could point to any inconsistency in his stands, no points compromised for expedience. He had been the unyielding champion of the federation of sovereign slave states. What he could not do, what he could never do, was overcome his own personality and temperament and thereby persuade others to follow his lead, for he offered a pathway strewn with spite and bitterness, a blinkered vision of his own infallibility, and the arrogant assumption that none but he saw the true way or held the true faith. He saw his failure and rejection as the same old story. Rhett went to Montgomery not to find a Southern consensus for independence and a future nation, but to allow others to fall in line behind his vision. He was ahead of his people, and thus they did not accept his bidding. If the Confederacy lived long enough, still it might catch up to him, as South Carolina and the South had finally caught up to him on secession—that is, if the malicious plotters and traitors who ruled the country but sought its ruin in reconstruction did not achieve their ends first.[43]

Rhett thought that at least being out of the congress left him free to speak out forthrightly at last—as if he had not been doing so all along—taking the view that the expiration of the provisional congress meant as well the end of any binding oath to keep its secrets. "I wish the people I have represented to know, that it has not been with my assent, that they are kept ignorant of my course," he declared soon after reaching South Carolina. "I did all I could, to bring to their knowledge all I said or did as their Representative." When he felt better he would give them a full account of his service.[44] Meanwhile he could help his son with fresh ammunition for the *Mercury,* and the attacks took on even more intensity. As soon as he read Davis's message to the new congress that convened on February 18, he attacked. In an editorial saying only that their information came "from a good source," Rhett gave details of Davis's vetoes, of treasury problems, and of congressional calls for increased arms that went unanswered and urges to build the navy that Davis seemingly ignored. As for the cabinet, Rhett declared that none of them were statesmen but rather were little more than clever neighborhood politicians. Arguing that Davis expected a war yet made no preparation for it, Rhett revealed that he had himself supported every bill for fielding a strong army, as indeed he did. Somehow Rhett read into Davis's message a criticism that lack of cooperation from the provisional congress hindered the creation of a navy—although no such statement appeared in the document—and using this manufactured argument against the president, he proceeded to rehearse the efforts to force a navy on Davis. "That fellow is certainly a great rascal," Rhett told his son in providing the information for the editorial and much of its literal substance. Rhett told him how to introduce his own contribution and what points to stress, and he included opinions on forthcoming actions in the congress, a fair example of how he personally shaped and guided the editorial commentary of the *Mercury,* for which he and his son so assiduously denied his authorship.[45]

By March the Rhetts' campaign grew even more aggressive, charging the president for false policy and "his incompetency in carrying out even that." He could have been forced on track by public pressure, a free press, and a strong congress, but until now everyone had chosen instead to cover his bumbling. "When the Provisional Congress elected Mr. Davis," said a March 22 editorial, "it is clear that they knew nothing about him—most probably he did not know himself." Now the congress should rectify that error. If he could be controlled, then control him; if not, then discharge him. The constitution allowed them means and a procedure. The *Mercury* had decided early to oppose Davis, it declared, and was attacked as a result because others did not know what the paper knew, thanks to information it was not at liberty to disclose; this was a clear—and perhaps unwitting—admission that the senior Rhett had been the inside source of its news all along. Now the evils they had predicted were realized. If Davis would change his ways, the paper would still support him, but it held out little hope. He had too many fawning supporters, "pimps and parasites" the *Mercury* called them as the level of its invective stooped ever lower.

Soon Rhett revealed that Davis's election had not been unanimous, and he then went on to accuse him of twenty vetoes by the late spring, when in fact there had been but thirteen. He said that now Davis was attempting to suppress the press even more by banishing reporters from the armies—another untruth—and likened Davis's aim to that of despots. The new congress in February gave him the power to suspend the privilege of the writ of habeas corpus as well, which could only lead to tyranny, and which Rhett had predicted six months earlier Davis would use to muzzle the press. This sorry tale of inadequacy and vanity and incompetence would continue, he predicted, unless the people could learn the truth of what was happening in the congress and the tented field, or until "the people, through their professed representatives, coerce justice and efficiency in the Administration." The president must be chastened and put in his place by "the strong men of the South," of whom Rhett presumed himself to be one. To those who assailed the *Mercury* for its accusations, especially the administration organ, the *Enquirer,* which met the Rhetts' exaggerated charges with some embarrassing contradictions with real facts, the Rhetts weakly replied that "President Davis and the Richmond *Enquirer* are so fallible in their assertion of facts, as to deprive them of all authority or credibility in their assertions with regard to us." It had come to this, said the Rhetts, because "the men who had been mainly instrumental in bringing about the Southern Confederacy, were not placed in power to complete its independence." The *Mercury* would not let people forget who at least one of those men was.[46]

The younger Rhett felt inclined to back away. Editorial invective had risen to the point that George Cuthbert, commander of a South Carolina regiment, threatened to challenge the editor to a duel for his remarks about Davis and those such as his regiment who supported the president. As the criticism of the *Mercury* rose and sales declined, he advised his correspondent in Richmond to curb his criticism of Davis. Rhett Jr. began editing excessive remarks out of Bagby's letters and told him to avoid all personal comment on the president and limit himself solely to political matters. "People will not tolerate the expression of mere opinions derogatory to this great little head of a great country," he warned. As long as secret sessions and executive patronage protected the president, "Davis cannot be broken down," and any victories, such as the success seemingly just achieved at the Battle of Shiloh a few days earlier, only made him stronger with his followers. It was time to "give the dear weekly public as much as possible of the bright side of things," he advised, noting that the rival *Courier* was thriving economically on flattering everyone and everything.[47]

But his father was having none of it, and in what may have been a bit of a struggle between the two for the editorial voice of the paper, Rhett Sr. kept up his attacks, especially after April saw Shiloh turn to a defeat, with Johnston killed on the field, and soon thereafter came the fall of New Orleans and loss of control of the Mississippi. "To this point the military policy and administration of Mr. Jefferson Davis has reduced the fortunes of the Confederate States," he complained; "disaster, peril and suffering at the hands of one man—incompetent, perverse." With the exception of Price and Thomas J. "Stonewall" Jackson, Davis had appointed no great generals, and he seemed to frown even on them. Soon Rhett had his son back on course and even challenging Robert W. Barnwell when he asserted that his own confidence in Davis remained unshaken and that the charges being leveled against him were false.[48] Edmund Rhett, acting the younger sibling by trying to outdo the rash proclamations of his older brothers, declared publicly now that Davis was "conceited, wrongheaded, wranglesome, obstinate, a traitor," an opinion that could only have come from his father.[49]

It helped, perhaps, that now there was a genuine movement to remove some power from Davis when the congress sought to impose a general-in-chief on him. And after Davis vetoed that bill there was even talk of impeachment or calling a general convention of the states to depose him. Davis did in fact respond to the former when he withdrew Lee from Charleston to act as an advisory general-in-chief in March, but he only further aroused Carolinians by replacing him with the Northern-born John C. Pemberton, another old crony. Then in May the Federals began a drive to take Charleston that put the city in a panic and under martial law briefly. Rhett and the *Mercury* had been the first to call for such things publicly, but now Rhett, like Davis's foes still in congress, knew that removal of Davis would only make Stephens president, and they suspected him even more of being a reconstructionist.

As a result, even though they did not want to do so, the Rhetts started trying to dampen the impeachment talk. "That President Davis is an incubus on our cause, we do not doubt," said an editorial certainly written by the elder Rhett. The editorial stated that the president would be speedily deposed if the constitution permitted such, but its impeachment provision only allowed for removal for "high crimes and misdemeanors," not incompetence. Then in May and June, Lee took field command in Virginia and began to achieve stunning victories, driving the invading army back, and the Federals were repulsed outside Charleston. Such success made Davis untouchable, so Rhett reemphasized his position that they need not depose the president, but rather only exert the will of the congress and the people to change his course, especially the disastrous defensive military policy that had cost them so much territory and that recently seemed destined to lose Charleston as well. In that struggle the press must be heard.[50]

The Rhetts were usually sensitive to public backlash against their paper's declarations, but almost always not soon enough. By the summer, with Lee victorious on every field in Virginia and the Federals stymied on the Mississippi at Vicksburg and in central Tennessee, their carping was even more out of touch with the public mood, and it cost them. "The Mercury," complained Capers, now commanding a regiment of South Carolinians, "pushes its recusant spirit with so much energy & power, as at times to endanger the public confidence in the government, & to gain a point against him, this paper has divulged matters of the state & army." He dismissed, as did most, the plea that the Rhetts did so for patriotism, cause and country, and instead found their actions rooted in selfishness and vanity. "The *real* secret of it all is, that Mr Rhett's personal ambition has been greatly mortified, & the Mercury is *his* paper."[51]

The reaction told where Rhett would feel it the most, financially. Where the paper's circulation stood at ten thousand when the war began, by June 1862 it fell to eighty-eight hundred for the triweekly edition and down to forty-eight hundred for the daily. Moreover they found themselves forced to reduce it in size yet again from four pages to two thanks to economy and paper shortage and then had to buy a new press to handle the smaller size.[52] Nor were Rhett's other financial affairs any more flourishing. Determined to manage his own plantations personally now, since he could not afford managers or overseers, he remained only a few days in Charleston at the close of the congress and then went to Darien to inspect his crops, only to find them looking anything but promising for the harvest. When he returned to Charleston in March he found his two rice plantations in poor repair and his slaveholdings reduced to 197 by the earlier sales to meet debts. His indebtedness left him no choice but to sell the grand house on Vanderhorst and rent a place in Walterborough, close to his Ashepoo plantations, but then the sale fell through when the buyer could not raise the money. He could not afford enough salt to supply his slaves and was reduced to selling rice in quantities as small as three hundred bushels to raise immediate money for food. By the summer he was trying to renew an unpaid note on the state bank, but Barnwell balked at signing as surety yet again, since his own property was greatly reduced in value by the war and many of his slaves had been confiscated by the Yankees. Rhett rented the Charleston house now while seeking a buyer and was even forced to rent one of his slaves to meet a payment due on another note. The levy by Pemberton of slaves from planters around Walterborough to work on the defenses around Charleston only further reduced what Rhett could produce from his fields, for unlike some other local planters he cheerfully contributed his slaves to the cause.[53]

There was much worse to come. The Rhetts took an interest in collecting casualty lists for the information of their readers, and the elder must always have feared that with four sons in the military it was inevitable that one day one of his own boys would appear in the notices.[54] The news he dreaded came late in June. In the Battle of Gaines's Mill, one of the series of bold offensives by which Lee was pushing the Union army that threatened Richmond away from the capital, his nephew Lt. Grimké Rhett was shot through the head and killed instantly. His son Lt. Robert Woodward Rhett fell with a desperate wound and the next evening died at nearby Beulah Church. The exigencies of the campaign and Rhett's own poor health made it impossible to retrieve his son's body immediately, and so the boy was buried near Richmond, while his shattered father went to Florida for a few weeks to mourn and try to recover his health.[55]

The death of the one son would only have made Rhett more concerned for his others in uniform. Burnet remained in Virginia with Lee, while Edmund received a commission in July as captain of the First South Carolina Battalion of Sharpshooters.[56] Most promising of all was Alfred, now major of the First South Carolina Artillery and second in command at Fort Sumter. But he had inherited his father's intemperate mouth, as had all the boys, and his impetuous and hot-headed nature as well. Moreover, Alfred, like Robert Barnwell Rhett Jr. and Edmund, could be arrogant and touchy on points of honor, ever ready to let an argument escalate to a degree that their father would not. On August 7, Alfred and Edmund sat with Arnoldus Vanderhorst drinking in the Charleston Club when a discussion about the relative merits of West Point–trained officers as against volunteers grew heated. Vanderhorst said that Fort Sumter's commander, Col. W. Ransom Calhoun, a nephew of John C. Calhoun, was an excellent West Pointer. But Alfred and Calhoun had a long-standing animosity between them going back to Fort Sumter and exacerbated when Calhoun had been promoted ahead of Alfred Rhett thanks to his education. Alfred, like his father, resented someone else getting a place he rightfully felt was his and said that Calhoun was nothing but a "puppy," which taken figuratively meant only callow and inexperienced but literally, of course, meant "son of a bitch." When Vanderhorst found that offensive, Alfred told him, "you may take it as you please." W. R. Calhoun heard of it and threatened to horsewhip Rhett after the war, but the next day Vanderhorst published a notice demanding an apology or satisfaction. He and Alfred Rhett met on August 9, and both fired and missed. When Rhett still refused to apologize, they reloaded, but then Vanderhorst fired and missed, and Rhett discharged his pistol over his head, ending the meeting. Then Col. W. Ransom Calhoun challenged Rhett on August 31. They met on September 5 at the Charleston Oaks Club with smoothbore dueling pistols at ten paces. In the first exchange of shots Calhoun fell, and he died within an hour.[57]

The *Mercury* said not a word about the affair, despite its protestations of the right of the people to know what was happening in their armies and its desire to cover local news of interest. But everyone else talked of it, and the act was roundly condemned. In Richmond the secretary of war gave instructions that the articles of war covering such matters be observed and proceedings against Major Rhett initiated, with a court-martial soon to sit. For Robert Barnwell Rhett it was only another full measure to the bitter cup that summer brought. Despite his own unwillingness to engage in violence, even when it touched on his honor, he had condoned and even encouraged it in his sons when it came to theirs. Now his teachings had come around to curse him and show him the cost of what was, in its way, his own hypocrisy. For years before secession he proclaimed his willingness to give his life in defense of his holy cause. Now, instead, he watched helplessly as the gore of one son made a payment for Southern freedom, while another son shed hallowed Calhoun blood as the price for being a Rhett.

TWENTY-FOUR

Cast Out of Public Life

1862–1864

THANKFULLY RHETT HAD ONE REMAINING public duty to distract his mind from the tragedies of the summer. The South Carolina state convention had adjourned the year before after installing an executive council to help Pickens run the state in the wake of the fall of Port Royal, only to find that the body assumed to itself increasingly greater power. This led some to raise cries of dictatorship for, among other things, requiring an accounting of all privately held precious metals in case they had to be seized by the state. Whereas the convention represented the people acting in their sovereign capacity, the council, being appointive, had no such sovereignty or accountability. In ordinary times Rhett would have been in the midst of the battle against this dictatorship in his own field, but his preoccupation with Davis for the past year completely distracted both him and the *Mercury*.[1]

The outcry against the council became the focus for every sort of discontent in the state, not just because of the Yankee invasion and war hardships, but because it opened again all the old regional and political divides that dated back for generations. There was a demand for another session of the convention to address the council and also to be a forum for the tide of discontent sweeping the state, and in September the delegates reconvened. Rhett still held his seat at the convention and attended from the first, though as usual with his own agenda. He scarcely addressed the imbroglio over the council but instead relaunched his attack on the administration and his campaign to force reform in the permanent constitution.

Rhett opened on September 12 when another delegate introduced resolutions calling on the state to take upon itself the raising of troops without asking for authorization from Richmond. This was much the same policy countenanced in Rhett and Toombs's recent bill, and a proposal that may in fact have been influenced by Rhett since it came from a man representing the same parishes that had sent Rhett to the convention. Rhett revealed that he had proposed much the same thing in congress, but since the congress had passed a national conscription act in April, the perils of the moment were so great that he could not support a competing state plan, even though national as opposed to state conscription was probably unconstitutional. For a change he argued that the times were too perilous to split hairs now.[2]

Then he went on to attack Davis for "imbecility and want of forecast" in the aftermath of Manassas, saying that the government was justly chargeable for shortsightedness and vacillation. He railed against an ineffective system of raising men and supplies and now declared that the late Johnston found only fifteen thousand men in his western army when he took command rather than the fifty thousand Davis supposedly misled him to believe. Rhett probably never learned that in fact Johnston had almost forty-eight thousand when he took command, nor would he have wished to know. His information on this, as on much else, was coming to him from his ally Beauregard, and he would not want his arguments diluted by inconvenient truth. He charged Davis with the loss of Fort Donelson and with keeping the Manassas army idle for six months unnecessarily. He was unaware that even when supplied and reorganized, Joseph E. Johnston was too timid to lead it forward in spite of Davis's entreaties, and Beauregard's plans were too fantastical to be risked. Barnwell rose immediately to defend the administration, though admitting it had made mistakes, and blamed the military inactivity after Manassas on illness in the army.[3]

Undaunted, Rhett went on to his main task the next day when he presented three resolutions. One warned of the danger of admitting any free state into the Confederacy; another condemned making any favorable trade concessions to the United States not made to other nations; and the third asserted that internal improvements of any sort were unlawful under their constitution, making Davis's recent railroad bills "usurpations of power." He defended all three with the same arguments as before, though he produced a new rationalization for the opposition to slavery. Implying that its appearance during the past two centuries when civilization had made its greatest advances was evidence that slavery constituted one of those advances, he remarked that where slavery had been practiced primarily in colonies, opposition to it arose chiefly in the home countries. Thus an inequality existed in the issue from the first, for the colonies and their institutions could not stand on the same footing as the parent nations. Revolutionary France, with its declaration that there was no God, abolished slavery in its colonies, and thus he associated atheism with abolitionism.

"Slavery makes the free man a privileged being," he argued. "To rule, is his habit from infancy." Having no slaves, the Yankees were themselves ruled instead as laborers, which only made them jealous of the South. "The Southerner values his honor more than his life," he said, risking reminding them of

Albert's recent affair, while "the Northerner does not understand the meaning of the term." It was but one evidence of how the peoples of the two sections could never live in harmony, and the conduct of the war presented another, for the Yankees were bent on a grand money grab, speculating among themselves while at the same time clamoring for reunion so they could plunder the South. Their seizure of slaves in the Port Royal area was but one example. The South, of course, was fighting only for liberty. Without citing any examples, he charged the Yankees with inhumane barbarities, while Confederates had been, if anything, too forbearing.

Rhett asserted that the majority of those who framed their constitution in Montgomery wanted to allow for the admission of free states in the future, but he claimed that if they let one in, soon they would have them all, and then "the vast Northern hive" would "hang over our destinies like a portentous cloud." Their majority would force the same crisis all over again, and once more slave-holders would face the impossibility of living peacefully with free-state men under the same government. "They combine all the vices of the savage, with the intelligence and enterprise of the civilized man," he charged, and he said that experience had shown them faithless. He said, "They are a nation of criminals— the greatest criminals of the present century—not against us only, but against mankind in all ages to come," for they had forfeited not only their own freedom but that of their posterity to the usurper Lincoln and the consolidationist policy he represented. They had set back free government for centuries, guaranteeing that future generations would have to spill oceans of blood to regain it again. "Shall we take such a people into our embrace?" he asked. He cited an *Enquirer* editorial demanding that, as a condition of any peace treaty with the Union, all states should have the option to choose in which government they chose to reside, Union or Confederacy. Rhett charged that this was clear admission that the administration favored reconstruction. He even suggested that Richmond would use the alternative of continued war to force the Confederacy into accepting reconstruction. The administration did not represent the people, he averred. The people fought and bled and won the battles, but then their rulers cheated them of the fruits of victory.

His attack on any commercial ties to the North after the war was in similar vein, denouncing any idea of ever being able to carry on free trade with the Yankees as merely a reward to them for invading the South and denying its rights. As for internal improvements, he showed that he had been turning his fertile mind to yet newer arguments and more ingenious rationalizations. Davis wanted the railroad connections because of "military necessity," he had said. Dispensing quickly with the problem that there was no such authority as "military necessity" recognized in their constitution, Rhett went on to argue that thanks to the blockade and their own lack of industrial capability, the railroad links could not in any event be completed during the duration of the war. That meant that they would not be finished until peace came, and thus "military necessity" would have disappeared. "They are appropriations to be carried out in peace," he charged, "and, therefore, are appropriations to carry out a general system of internal improvements." In short, Jefferson Davis was using the war as merely an excuse to continue the attack on their liberties begun by Henry Clay forty years before. If nothing else, Rhett certainly demonstrated that years of disappointment, failure, and recently tragedy had not dimmed his skill at twisting an argument to its logical absurdity.[4]

Barnwell rose again, calling Rhett's resolutions "mischievous," and then continued his defense of the administration. Rhett was back on the floor again on September 14 to reply. He revealed more details of the Toombs state conscription plan, rehearsed again the military failings of the administration, and then returned once more to the failure to pursue the beaten Yankees after Manassas or to launch an offensive during the balance of the summer and fall of 1861. Sickness did not cause that, he said, but Richmond's failure to provide adequate food and transportation did. At that Chesnut arose to challenge Rhett, and he made good points, since he had been on Beauregard's staff and testified firsthand that the health of the army in fact put it in no condition to pursue after Manassas, even though in saying so he made an enemy of Beauregard. By a deliberate misreading of Beauregard's much later claim that he was prevented from advancing "after" the battle by want of rations and wagons, Rhett tried to dismiss Chesnut's correction as well as the by-now-widespread knowledge that even Johnston and Beauregard had denied that Davis called off an immediate pursuit. Where the general meant several weeks or even months after the battle, Rhett chose to interpret "after" as meaning immediately, thus construing Beauregard to contradict his own denial of the charge against Davis and allowing Rhett to renew one of his own. "I think that the commanding general is a rather better authority for the state of things in his army than either or both of these gentlemen," he said to Chesnut and Barnwell.[5]

Then Rhett went back to his resolutions and raised even more explicitly the specter of Davis coercing the Confederacy into accepting a peace treaty allowing free states to join them or else he would impose more war upon them. It was utterly ridiculous, manifesting nothing other than Rhett's inability by now even to think rationally where it concerned Davis. The same tendency toward obsession to the exclusion of rationality, logic, or even incontrovertible conflicting evidence that had seized him years before, when he became a doctrinaire extremist on the secession question, focused itself now on this new fixation with Davis. It was given additional fuel perhaps by the recent death of his son, for Rhett could well reason to himself that had Davis conducted the war as Rhett would have him do, it would have been over before that awful day in June and Robert Woodward would still be alive. In his mind Rhett could easily see the president as directly responsible for the bullet that killed his son.

Reconstruction was dead as an idea among the people; of that he was certain, for the war and invasion had hardened the population against any reunion with the Yankees. It dwelled as a goal only among some of the politicians in Richmond now, chiefly in Davis himself, and they must fight his policy and his ability to usurp enough authority to impose that policy on the country. Admitting that this might well be the last time he ever spoke in a deliberative body, he wanted his final words to be those calling for independence and liberty, and eternal freedom from their former brethren of the North.[6]

The convention tabled Rhett's resolutions on internal improvements and free trade with the Union after the war, and amended his free state resolution to note that it only reiterated that body's previously stated objections and therefore required no further action. Still seeing the chimera of reconstruction on the horizon, especially after hearing of moves in the congress that looked toward luring the northwestern states, Rhett was not content to wait for the convention to publicize its proceedings. Returning to Walterborough, he oversaw his son's publication of his speeches in the *Mercury* and at the same time instructed him to approve the final ordinance of the convention that continued the despised council and the convention itself until the legislature could elect a successor to the failed Pickens that December. As soon as his speeches appeared in print, Rhett found himself attacked anew by the *Enquirer,* and there ensued a hairsplitting debate in print between the two papers that did credit to neither.[7]

The debate came in time for the fall elections for the legislature, and both his son Barnwell and his brother Edmund were candidates representing the old secessionist faction, as was as his uncle Nathaniel Heyward. Rhett took no personal part in the campaign but did leave Walterborough for Charleston in late September, no doubt in order to free his son from the *Mercury* office for a few days as the race came to a close. Yet his voice was always in the background through the *Mercury,* and the attack on Davis and his cabinet was incessant. Benjamin having taken over the state department, Rhett turned on him as he had on Stephen Mallory, the beleaguered head of the naval office. "Our Secretary of State is a far greater nonentity than the Secretary of Navy," he declared in October just as Carolinians were going to their polls. "The diplomacy of the Administration has been very remarkable. It has consisted in doing nothing."[8]

And yet at that very moment a Confederate army was in Kentucky. It had briefly taken the capital and installed a governor, and though now in retreat, it had still tactically won a battle at Perryville and shown that the South had the strength to drive to the Ohio River even if it could not stay there. Meanwhile in the East, Lee not only pushed the Federals decisively away from Richmond in the summer, but then went on to deliver two serious defeats to them in northern Virginia and then to drive into Maryland. Though his invasion was stopped in September at Antietam, he won a tactical victory there too, and the Yankees were so cowed that they had made no attempt to invade Virginia for two months. After a seemingly desperate spring the battlefronts looked good everywhere, and the Federals had even been repulsed at Vicksburg, keeping at least a part of the Mississippi in Confederate hands. In such a climate the croaking and fault-finding of the *Mercury* and the Rhetts seemed more out of touch than ever, and the voters rejected them almost unanimously. Heyward was defeated, Barnwell Rhett lost his seat, and only Edmund Rhett managed to hold his place in the state senate, though his brother had dejectedly expected him, too, to be beaten. Robert Barnwell Rhett looked on it all as a rejection not of them but of himself, and in sour mood he told his son, "I believe it is I who have killed you all."[9]

It was to be a winter of loss. Scarcely did Edmund take his seat in Columbia than he died after a brief illness in February. He had remained Rhett's law partner and ran the Charleston practice, especially after Beaufort fell and his own handsome house became headquarters for Union tax commissioners who were rapidly transferring his and others' property to Northern hands by confiscation laws.[10] Then a month later Rhett's old mentor and old friend Petigru died. His editor son had never thought much of Petigru, disdaining him as a self-made man "of Irish or no antecedents," the son of an Irish drunkard, and gifted with nothing but "a thoroughly Irish dish face and Irish mother-wit." With nothing like the editor's Gaelophobia, Rhett truly lamented his friend's passing. He appeared with others of the Charleston bar on March 25 to honor Petigru as "my tutor in boyhood, my friend in early manhood, my better friend in advanced life, whom neither time nor fortune, private duties nor troubles, nor the angry public contests and differences of more than thirty years, ever induced to say to me an unkind word or to do an unkind deed." It was one of the peculiarities of the basically gentle and generous nature so often avalanched by his political passions and temper that Rhett's closest friends came from those with whom he differed the most radically.[11]

Edmund's death only added to Rhett's daily burden, since he had to administer his brother's estate while trying to manage his own two plantations. His advice to others was not to plant cotton but to sow corn and thus be able to feed their soldiers while starving European looms, and he turned some of his own land to corn now. For the rest he continued planting rice. He made one good crop to help retire some of his debt, and on a continuing basis he sold rice straw and hay for fodder to the local military, realizing a few hundred dollars of inflated Confederate money every few months to sustain the family. Soldiers from a regiment posted in his neighborhood frequently came to one of his plantations and bought produce as well, or Rhett went to their camps.[12] Still, the burden of what he owed to Barnwell and others remained so heavy that in the fall of 1863 he finally succeeded in selling the Thomas Street house to George Trenholm for thirty-three thousand dollars, substantially more than he had paid for it. He reimbursed Barnwell, but the other large debt was that still remaining to his sister Claudia Stuart from his purchase of her late husband's share of the *Mercury*, and her executor, his brother Benjamin Rhett, refused to accept payment then because of the depreciated value of the currency. Instead he preferred to continue holding a mortgage on the slaves Rhett had pledged for the debt, for their real value would not deflate.[13]

In fact, perhaps the only personal success Rhett achieved was to save his son Alfred from serious consequences for the death of Colonel Calhoun. In September 1862 when Beauregard returned to command in South Carolina, the *Mercury* lavished high praise on him. No doubt most of it was sincere, for Rhett thought the Louisianian a great general. More important, Beauregard was his companion—and sometime source of information—in the war with President Davis. For the immediate moment Beauregard would be Alfred Rhett's commanding officer and could have considerable influence in quashing any proceedings against him. In December, Rhett prepared a small pamphlet setting out the circumstances of the duel and sent copies to the war department in Richmond, hoping to mitigate any sentence. He called on Beauregard several times to enlist his sympathy and support. He at first won the promise that Alfred would not be tried after all, but would have to be transferred away from his regiment and Fort Sumter. Accustomed to having his own way, Alfred wanted to stay, seeing nothing reprehensible in his action.

A court did meet and inevitably found Alfred Rhett guilty of a breach of the applicable articles of war, but then Rhett appealed to Beauregard again. The bond between them was already growing closer thanks to the fact that Col. A. B. Roman, Beauregard's most trusted staff officer, had started courting Rhett's daughter Sallie. Moreover, the general was canny enough to know that the *Mercury* could be a powerful ally in his own war with Davis and in the future promotion of his career. As a result he disapproved the findings of the court and allowed Alfred Rhett to remain with his command. It greatly pleased the Rhett family, though it outraged others who were privy to the proceeding. "Beauregard, though a genius, is too ambitious & too vain to be a pure general," complained one of his officers, Colonel Capers. "He is swerved from the path of *duty* by political men." Capers thought Beauregard's catering to Rhett dishonorable.[14] It would not have occurred to Rhett to see anything inconsistent in his use of influence to aid his own while he castigated Davis for his favoritism. Indeed, he and his family only continued to hold it against Davis that Benjamin's son, his nephew Thomas Rhett, could not seem to rise above the rank of major, which Benjamin Rhett regarded as "a tyranny that seeks in the nephew a victim for the hatred borne the Uncle."[15] Meanwhile, for the other son who was beyond his help, Rhett sent a man to Richmond to disinter and return with Robert Woodward's body. By the summer of 1863 he had him at home once more, reflecting in sadness mixed with pride of "his gentle and affectionate, but brave and noble nature."[16]

Following the defeat in the legislative elections; the trend against reconstruction and the continuing rise in Confederate fortunes with a crushing victory at Fredericksburg, Virginia, in December 1862; and a near miss at reclaiming middle Tennessee, Rhett took less part in the *Mercury's* columns. He was too busy with his plantations, and the repudiation of his position and his personal misfortunes must have robbed him of some of the spirit to keep up the fight. His son Barnwell frankly asked him in October to stop writing articles assailing the administration, which may have led to some temporary friction between them, since the *Mercury* continued running critical pieces by others. After January 1863 the younger Rhett wrote almost all of the editorial columns for some time, and there were fewer of them as economy forced them once again to reduce the size of the paper.[17]

In fact, by March 1863 *Mercury* writers confessed seeing little point in continuing their lonely battle against the administration, since the paper's positions were virtually ignored by the state authorities, while the public seemed to have no interest in opinions on the conduct of the war. Even they had to confess that prospects looked bright after the new year, with a near-victory in Tennessee and the enemy pressing them nowhere at the moment except in the Southwest. It was "hardly worth troubling ourselves to write," they announced with some petulance. Nevertheless still it did, though without the old vehemence. When Lincoln issued the Emancipation Proclamation effective January 1, 1863, the Rhetts chided Davis for having said that the Yankees would never try such a measure and reminded the diminishing number of readers that their paper had predicted it all along. They argued that conscription be pressed seriously, saying, "we want crushing victories, and have all along had men enough in the South to achieve them." Hearing that when Pemberton was in command in South Carolina he had recommended abandoning the forts around Charleston to the enemy—and two were given up as he concentrated his forces—Rhett expressed fears for Vicksburg, where Pemberton commanded now. Signing himself as "Fort Moultrie," Rhett wanted Richmond to investigate. Being born a Yankee and a crony of Davis as well, Pemberton might just give up without a fight again.[18]

Depending on his son to keep him informed of what was happening while he lived in some isolation at Walterborough or out at the Oaks, Rhett freely confessed that spring, "I do as little as I can." Occasionally he visited the nearby camps of Confederate soldiers, whom he found well behaved, or went to the post office at Ashepoo Ferry to receive the latest *Mercury*. But then he became seriously aroused at the end of February 1863 when a bill was introduced that would renew the February 1862 grant to Davis of the power to suspend the privilege of the writ of habeas corpus. "If the effort is successful, he will be a Despot," Rhett told his son, and immediately he put his pen to work. "To suspend this act, is to authorize the President to seize whom he pleases, without process of law," Rhett complained in print. "It converts the President into a despot, and the people into his subjects and slaves of his will and pleasure." He dismissed as cant the arguments that such a move was necessary for security. "Never, since the first struggle for political liberty, have any people been more orderly among themselves, or more unanimous in supporting the great cause for which they are contending, than the people of the Confederate States," he proclaimed. Among such a people there was no need to worry about treason.

The evidence of disaffection, Unionism, and willful resistance to Confederate authority throughout the Upcountry and the mountainous and more remote parts of the South was plain to everyone and was the cause of the congress's action. This was the same constituency, in fact, in which the reconstructionism he once saw as rampant most dwelled, but now when he had a different point to make, he chose to ignore it all. Indeed, the people of the Confederacy had supported the government better than it had supported itself, he said, and now, as ever, the congress was only being subservient to the president. A month later, while the congressional debate continued, he came out even stronger, declaring that "we want no despotism in the person of President Davis." At the same time, having found an issue that reawakened his old fire, he corresponded with Ayer in the congress, who had asked him for his views in the matter. "Don't let our Washington! Put our liberties under his feet," challenged Rhett. Ayer must call for the ayes and nays when it came to vote, so that every delegate should be on record. "Let the world see then who are for surrendering the liberties of our Confederate States," he urged, referring to Davis as "such a poor apology for greatness."[19]

Thus aroused, Rhett came somewhat out of his lethargy and began to write more, though his son edited his father's productions so that the criticism of the administration remained restrained, at least by their standards. Rhett reopened his old complaints about financing the war and turned especially antagonistic in May when a bill came up to impose a tax on land and slaves, even though it represented substantially his old direct tax cause. The problem was that the apportionment of such taxes to the states, like that of representation in the congress, must constitutionally be based upon a census, but no census had been or ever would be conducted in the Confederacy. It was only more evidence to him that "ultimately there has been no plan, no scheme, and all is confusion & inconsistency."[20]

Even while renewing his old fight from afar, Rhett saw the war firsthand on April 7 when a Union fleet steamed into the harbor and attacked Fort Sumter. In a gallant defense the garrison, commanded by his son, now Col. Alfred Rhett, repulsed the Yankees with considerable damage, aided by the ring of batteries encircling the harbor. Immediately afterward Barnwell Rhett Jr. went to Richmond to meet with Secretary of War James Seddon to press for his brother's promotion, and he came away believing that the victory had at least neutralized any remaining prejudice against Alfred as a result of the duel. No doubt urged to do so by the Rhetts, the South Carolina delegation to the congress recommended Alfred's promotion to brigadier general as a reward, and Beauregard and the immediate area commander both seconded the recommendation. A few months later his father asked Seddon if the duel were still a hindrance to his son's advancement and was given the good news that it was not. There was no bar against further promotion if it were merited, though Rhett himself could think of one, for all generals had to be nominated by Jefferson Davis. Even though Davis had nominated Alfred for promotion to colonel, and thus seemingly held no brief against the son for the actions of his father, no nomination for the next promotion would ever be forthcoming. The fact that Alfred never got his brigadier's star would be just another in the catalog of grievances against the president.[21]

The summer swept Rhett back onto the full offensive against the administration when the lull of good fortune on the battlefield came to an abrupt end. Even when Lee won his most crushing victory of the war at Chancellorsville in May, the *Mercury* was niggardly with its praise. The paper said that the triumph owed as much to the slain Stonewall Jackson and to the magnificent army built by Johnston and Beauregard as to Lee's management, and it argued that the latter two commanders deserved a share of the praise. But then Lee invaded

Pennsylvania in June. Ignoring his own previous calls for a northward move out of Virginia and his condemnation of Davis for not doing so, Rhett now raised doubts about the wisdom of Lee's campaign and even suggested that he could not have undertaken it of his own volition. "He may not have the control of his own army in conducting the war," Rhett wrote, a veiled hint that Davis had forced this campaign on the general. When initial reports indicated success, the *Mercury* was jubilant. "Let Yankee cities burn and their fields be laid waste," it crowed, hoping that Washington and Baltimore would be captured and their public buildings destroyed, with Philadelphia and New York to follow.

Then came news of disaster. On July 4, after seven weeks of siege, Vicksburg fell. "It is the greatest disaster which has befallen the arms of the Confederate States," Rhett declared, and he immediately started casting blame. It was all the result of inefficiency, he said. Still thinking that the Pennsylvania campaign was going well, Barnwell Rhett Jr. echoed an idea his father would ever after champion, which was that Lee should have stayed in Virginia and sent part of his army to reinforce Pemberton instead. Then in mid-July came definitive word that Lee, too, had been repulsed—not only beaten in a bloody fight at Gettysburg on July 1–3 but forced to retire, leaving no burned cities or wasteland in his wake. If Vicksburg could have held out until the winter frost, it would have been safe, the paper declared. Lee could have spared thirty thousand to do the job and held the Yankees at bay in Virginia, or he could equally well have sent the same thirty thousand to the army in Tennessee under Gen. Braxton Bragg, who could have cleared the state of the enemy and moved into Kentucky once more and decisively, forcing the enemy to give up the siege of Vicksburg.

Instead, Davis "sends the whole army on a chivalric raid into Pennsylvania." Having withheld the army in Virginia from offensive operations through most of 1861 and 1862, when finally Davis did get aggressive—and now the assumption was plain that Davis ordered Lee to go north—he did it in the wrong place. Significantly, this was not entirely the Rhetts talking but also Beauregard speaking through them. These were the complaints that he would make for the rest of his life, and his connection with the family now was such that they had ready access to his views, and he to the editorial columns of the *Mercury*. What Robert Barnwell Rhett added to the story was his conviction that Lee would never have invaded Pennsylvania if not forced to do so. Despite its being completely fallacious and repeatedly gainsaid by Lee himself and everyone else conversant with the planning of the campaign, father and son Rhett would spend the rest of their lives arguing otherwise.[22]

Scarcely was news of the disaster at Gettysburg absorbed before a more personal blow came with word that the ailing Yancey had died. Though he and

Rhett were never close personally, still there had been a spiritual bond between them, made the stronger by their mutual disgust with the administration and enhanced by Yancey's acknowledgment of Rhett as his political mentor. The *Mercury* paid high tribute to its dead ally in an obituary that Rhett would have wanted written for himself. "Of an ardent temper, and intrepid will, frank and self-confident, perhaps to haughtiness, political enemies swarmed around his path; but they never impeded his tread onward to the goal where duty and honor called," it read. He had his enemies, but that was natural, for "those we fear, we usually hate." Yancey, like Rhett—like Christ—had espoused the true faith and been despised by lesser men in reward. With unwonted humility, Rhett concluded that "he probably did more than any other man to instruct and nerve" the South for the contest before them.[23]

The war came to Rhett's hearth yet again in August when the Federals, now in position on Morris Island below Charleston, began to bombard the city. Some shells landed within two hundred yards of the Vanderhorst house not long before he sold it to Trenholm. Everything had seemed so bright a few weeks before, the *Mercury* lamented, but now the Mississippi was gone, Lee was beaten, and the Yankees stood almost at the gates of Charleston. "We should search out and expose the true causes of our disasters," he preached, "in order that they may not be repeated." Calling on the men of the country to enlist in greater numbers and on the people to support the government, he then went on to condemn Davis for his poor appointments, inattention, caution, and more.[24]

There was more to this than just Rhett's usual renascent antagonism. He felt that the only way to save the country was to curb or control Jefferson Davis, which only the congress could do, and which it would do if enough of the right sort of men replaced the toadies and weaklings who composed the current house. Their terms expired in February 1864, and the race to fill their seats would be run that fall. In August an anonymous communication appeared in the Charleston press nominating Rhett for the seat currently held by Ayer. A few days later Rhett called on Gen. Roswell Ripley, then in immediate command in Charleston, and while there he met his old antagonist Keitt, now colonel of a regiment in the defenses. To his considerable surprise Rhett learned that Keitt had written the nomination. He was fed up with Davis's ineptitude. In the course of a long discussion Keitt revealed his belief now that most of the South Carolina delegates at Montgomery had opposed Davis's election as president but that because they never caucused and spoke so little to one another, they did not know each other's sentiments. Therefore the efforts of Barnwell and the general trend otherwise toward Davis had swayed them. Had they but known their own collective minds, they might have voted against him. Then with Florida following their lead and Georgia going for Cobb, Davis might have been stopped. Keitt felt that now they must stop him in the congress. If Rhett agreed to run, he would easily win, since it was assumed that Ayer would step aside in his favor.

It took Rhett little time to agree to seek the office, even though it represented a step down from his previous more-exalted position in the old Senate. Some friends asked him not to run, no doubt fearing the effect of the inevitable wrangling and controversy in Richmond on his frequently frail health. But Rhett sensed a mission, a final opportunity to turn the tide both for himself and for the Confederacy. Convinced that the congress was the only hope, and that it either must control Davis or remove him from office, he could hardly refuse an office that might give him personally the opportunity to save the nation. He did not forget that he first attracted attention to himself in politics some thirty-five years before with his action in using constitutional measures for impeachment. Could he not do so again? Did he not have a duty, as he put it, "to impeach the President before Congress, for incompetency, and remove him or compel his resignation"? Indeed, he feared that he could not prevent his own election, so confident was he of his old constituents' regard. The old arrogance returned quickly, if indeed it ever left, for he was soon convinced that he could remove Davis almost single-handedly.[25]

No sooner was Rhett's active candidacy announced than he met the first setback. Ayer refused to stand aside. Though the two had been on friendly terms, Ayer regarded Rhett's attitude toward Davis and the administration as so unreasoningly hostile that he thought Rhett only entered the race to embarrass the president. Ayer declared that electing Rhett would be tantamount to declaring war on the Confederacy.[26] Instead of simply sitting back, perhaps writing a public letter or two for the press and waiting to be swept into office, Rhett suddenly found that he had to campaign actively, something he had not done since the race with Grayson almost thirty years earlier. He scheduled a series of public meetings in the old districts of Beaufort, Colleton, Orangeburg, and Barnwell and meanwhile allowed his son to turn the *Mercury* to the wheel—not in attacks on Ayer, but rather in renewed assaults on the administration. They raised again Davis's sloth in raising troops and revealed more of Rhett's role in trying to remedy that in the Toombs bill. They echoed all of the other old arguments, only slanting them now to show that the present emergency represented Davis's failure in every instance.

When Bragg won a spectacular victory in September at Chickamauga, the *Mercury* gave it high praise, especially since it was done in part by sending a corps from Lee's army in Virginia to Tennessee. But the paper then went on to remind readers that if this had been done before Gettysburg, they might still

have Vicksburg and the Mississippi. Rhett wrote to the secretary of war expressing his delight, yet added there, too, the proviso that he hoped this had been
truly decisive, instead of the "mere repulses" that constituted most Confederate victories in his mind. Still there were the inevitable missteps, as when the
Rhetts declared that Davis had lost the confidence of the army and the people.
Immediately came a remonstrance from a South Carolina brigade with Lee, which
included Burnet Rhett's regiment, declaring that *they* still had confidence in the
president. At once his father and brother backed away, claiming that they really
meant only the armies outside Virginia.[27]

When Rhett went out to meet with the voters, he found that the impertinent Ayer was there to meet him, and for the first time in his political life he
had to engage in old-fashioned stump debate. Moreover, though nervous at first,
Ayer soon gained confidence in dealing with the old warrior, though one listener
described his speaking as "miserable, like some clumsy schoolboy." Still he
quickly succeeded in making the attitude of the Rhetts toward Davis the only
real issue, for on the war itself or other policies there was no basic disagreement
between them. As a result Rhett spent much of the campaign on the defensive.
He denied that he was a factionalist trying to establish an antiadministration
party and instead attacked Davis for his vetoes as an example of his dictatorial
rule. Rhett opposed Davis not on personal grounds, he assured them, but for
the good of the country. That said, he declared that he would never be guided
by such a one as Davis, and that he was his own man and too old to change. He
would be the tool of no man, and if they elected him they would have to take
him as he was.

More than once Rhett and Ayer got into verbal exchanges, and with his years
of experience behind him, the elder seemed to get the better. "Rhett is decidedly
the man of the two," concluded a soldier in whose camp the candidates met on
October 9 near McPhersonville. "Ayr follows him about wherever he goes to
speak in order to speak also and thus nullify the effects of Rhett's speeches, but
he ruins his prospects by that very act as he cannot compare with Mr Rhett
either in his carriage as a gentleman or as a speaker." When Rhett finished, there
was always applause, as befit a seasoned public speaker, while Ayer sometimes
finished to silence. Most of all Rhett showed that he had lost none of the inspiration or zeal of youth, nor his conviction that he was, as usual, ahead of everyone else. He could see what the people could not see, he told them, and that was
why he opposed the administration. It was the same old story. He had to lead
because he knew better; it was their duty to follow him. Sometimes he even used
an illustration from the life of Napoleon. Prior to launching the campaign into
Russia the emperor argued with his uncle Cardinal Joseph Fesch, who could not

grasp the purpose of the campaign or what it would benefit France. Napoleon took Fesch to a balcony and pointed into the night sky, asking if his uncle could see a certain star. "No, Sire," said the cardinal. "But I do," replied Napoleon, and he dismissed him. Rhett could see it too.[28]

Despite his handicaps from lesser experience, Ayer fought back well in substance when he argued that even though he, too, differed with the administration on some issues, it was their overriding duty in the crisis to stand behind Davis. To elect Rhett was to endorse the reprehensible and unpatriotic course of the *Mercury,* and that was an argument that made sense to many who had seemingly spent all their lives reading injudicious Rhett-motivated attacks on people in the *Mercury.* The repudiation of the brigade of soldiers in Virginia did not help either, suggesting that the men who really had their lives on the line, the sons of these voters, did not approve of the Rhetts' course. In addition the *Charleston Courier,* always opposed to Rhett as a disunionist, had come to the support of the administration, and thus backed Ayer.[29]

The election was destined to be unlike any before. For a start, many of the citizens in his old stronghold in the town of Beaufort and in portions of the Beaufort and Colleton Districts were now behind enemy lines and would not be able to vote. Moreover, hundreds of potential voters served in the military, many of them with that brigade in Virginia, and their voice, too, could not be heard. As a result, when the day came, the turnout in Beaufort and Colleton was small, though Rhett took both districts with a majority of 88. However, in the interior districts, where he had never had great strength, especially in Barnwell, the Ayer majority was a commanding 592. Overall that gave Ayer the election by 504, a decisive defeat even despite the conditions of the election. Twenty years earlier, out of 3,000 votes cast in this congressional district, Rhett won by 1,000. Since then population had not grown markedly in his two strongest districts, which were always less populace than Barnwell and Orangeburg, while the resolutions of the brigade with Lee suggest that most of those in uniform would not have voted with him had they been at home. In short, even without the war drain of voters and the inability of some behind enemy lines to cast ballots, Rhett would have lost. His was a message they did not care to hear, and indeed that they had been hearing for far too long in the *Mercury.* His was a star they did not believe was there or care to see.[30]

Predictably, the *Mercury* chose to all but ignore this final rejection by the people Rhett hoped to save. Rhett in later years would look back and conclude that he lost because the public could not get beyond his opposition to the administration and because he could not overcome "folly and false confidence," what he regarded as "the popular ignorance of the causes of our downward

progress to ruin."[31] His son would be less restrained. "Government is a most difficult affair, and Free Government, next to an impossibility to establish or perpetuate," he editorialized. "The vast majority of men are man-followers." The
weak and timid were easily led by those in power and resented those who upset
their peace by challenging authority. Thus "the vindicator of the truth, who
would inform, arouse, warn, benefit, and may be, save the people," was vilified.
"The Saviour of the world was rejected of men" too, the younger Rhett reminded
his readers. In the course of a few weeks his father had transformed from
Napoleon to Christ.[32]

The defeat left Rhett resolved never to seek public office again, and he would
not.[33] The only good news during the campaign was his daughter Sallie's marriage to Colonel Roman on September 14, which further cemented his close
relations with Beauregard and his circle. It took some persuading on the father's
part to overcome her fears that it would be inappropriate to wed during the war.
"The times are very unpropitious for marrying," he confessed, but he saw no
reasonable objection. Roman being a Catholic, Rhett even encouraged her to convert and seek confirmation as soon as possible.[34] Happily Rhett did not have to
share Beauregard's irritation on November 2 when President Davis came to make
a public visit and protocol required the general to greet him at the railroad depot.
Col. Alfred Rhett, as commander of Fort Sumter and Beauregard's subordinate,
had no choice but to be present, but Rhett could at least avoid that indignity.
The Mercury only made passing mention of the event on the back page, especially
after Davis made a public address in which, without stating names, he condemned those who could only carp and complain. The greater indignity came
a few days later when the legislature renewed its previous expressions of confidence in the president. On all sides Rhett found himself repudiated, rebuffed,
and publicly humiliated by being ignored.[35] It hardly helped that some others
were slowly coming around. Hunter told Miles, who communicated it to Barnwell Rhett Jr. in December, that he had resigned as secretary of state in March
1862 because "no gentleman can stay in the cabinet with Mr. Davis," and even
Senator Orr complained now that the Confederacy was without direction.[36]
There was little satisfaction in being right without recognition.

Rhett apparently became so despondent after the loss, or else his debts pressed
so heavily on him in spite of selling his house, that in December he raised the
idea of selling the Mercury. He wanted two hundred thousand dollars, but in
real terms it was much less thanks to the heavy inflation in Confederate currency. Keitt, still no admirer of Rhett despite their recent policy rapprochement,
initiated a movement in which he enlisted Andrew G. Magrath and a few others,
and sought to sign on Hammond as well, to raise the money. "The paper can be

made of great power," he thought. He wanted to make Boyce the editor, which meant little real change in attitude toward Davis and his policy, though Boyce did not generate the antipathy of the Rhetts and had been, and would be again, amenable to calling a convention of all the states North and South to try to resolve their differences. In the end, however, they could not raise the money or Rhett changed his mind, for the *Mercury* soldiered on under its rightful alter ego.[37]

"Our coasts are desolated—our people are driven from their homes, and their houses laid in ashes," the *Mercury* lamented. From now on it preached determination, sacrifice, and commitment to the cause as their only salvation, and for the next several months Rhett confined himself to his plantations and his own immediate salvation.[38] Keeping his eye ever on the proximity of the Yankees at Beaufort and along the coast, he presumed on his connection to Beauregard to pass along suggestions for the defense of the area in which he had "so much pecuniarily at stake," and the general accepted his advice cheerfully.[39] He cultivated good relations with Gen. Beverly Robertson when he assumed immediate command in the Charleston area, under Beauregard's overall department command, and took an interest in finding lighter duty for invalid soldiers unable to stand the rigors of regular campaigning. In a profound irony, he saw the largest single customer for the *Mercury* turn out to be the very government he had been fighting, for the paper took in hundreds of dollars in government advertising and thousands for subscriptions furnished to the local military hospitals' inmates.[40]

As for his two rice plantations and the 170 slaves still on them, they at least produced one more good crop worth thirteen thousand dollars, but in that economy it still was not enough to eliminate his debt. The quarterly sales of fodder and rice straw to the military became all the more important for daily living expenses, though they never amounted to more than a few hundred dollars at a time.[41] One consolation, at least, was that after three years of war, and with the Federal lines within relatively easy reach, not one of his slaves attempted to run away. However much Rhett could not get along with the powers in place trying to keep them in bondage, his relations with the slaves themselves seemingly never wavered from the indulgent and patriarchal model set by his father, James Smith, and encouraged by his promise to Stapleton. Despite the social upheaval around them, the blacks seemingly preferred—for the moment—the life they had known with an easy master to the uncertainty the future promised.[42]

Rhett's best hope for financial stability now lay with his Darien plantation. His cotton crop there proved good in the spring of 1864, and by April he and other local planters had twenty-two thousand bales worth an estimated $8 million in Confederate currency collected on the coast nearby at the mouth of the Altamaha. All they had to do was get it through the blockade to Europe. Seeing the voluntary embargo a failure and Richmond indisposed ever to make it government policy, and having finally given up on his old notion that they could starve British textile manufacturers into forcing recognition and intervention, Rhett was finally ready to join those whom he had so long opposed. Indeed, in years to come he would continue to condemn the planters who profited by selling cotton through the blockade for their personal benefit, but now necessity seemingly overrode principle. Ironically, it came just at a time when the administration was finally putting a ban on exports except those handled by the government itself, and the *Mercury* complained that it had come too late. Predictably Rhett complained of the way in which it was done. Memminger simply issued an edict, which to Rhett meant that the treasury secretary was by "insolent interference" violating the sovereign authority of South Carolina in the absence of a congressional act. Now he and the other planters enlisted Memminger's assistance in arranging to get it through the blockade, since the treasury was to take a one-third share of all cotton exports. Hammond was financing the building of an ersatz steam ram at Savannah in the hope that it could sally out and decoy the enemy fleet long enough for blockade runners to race in and load the cotton, intending to land near Rhett's plantation, and then convoy the bales to Cuba or the Bahamas. Unfortunately the plan never came to fruition, or Rhett's concerns about debt would surely have been eliminated entirely.[43]

Rhett now alternated between the Oaks and Charleston, and he was in the city in March 1864 when he received a letter from Wigfall that frankly asked his advice about the propriety of attempting to depose Davis. "I had great fears from the incompetency of the Confederate Government, that our cause might fail," Rhett told his sister Claudia, and back in January the *Mercury* warned yet again against the dangers of a military despotism. Soldiers were bound by the articles of war not to speak out against the government, and now with an enormous proportion of the male population in uniform, that dramatically reduced those who could lawfully protest. Fearing that Davis would soon legislate against a free press, and with most of congressional sessions still secret, the Davis despotism looked nearer to completion than ever before.[44]

Wigfall suggested the solution of the congress calling a convention to enact a constitutional amendment that would take the power of controlling the military away from Davis, vesting it instead in an appointed commander-in-chief subject to the advice and consent of the congress. Wigfall sent substantially the same inquiry to Hammond and a number of others, seeking some consensus. Rhett could not resist responding by pointing out that in 1861, with Wigfall's urging, he had voted for Davis against his better judgment, and events had, as usual, proven him right. "You were all deceived," Rhett claimed. He had tried to stop Davis in the congress and failed, and he had since been "cast out of public life," while the president continued on an unchecked career of "mischief, more ruinous than even I apprehended." But he did not agree that a constitutional convention was the remedy. It would be impractical to try to do so during the war, since most of the voters were in the army. They could hardly get a fair hearing of their case before the people in any case. The soldiers, used by discipline to following orders, would never defy their superiors, while the officers of the army, all beholden to Davis for their appointments, would likely stand by Davis, especially those ambitious for further advancement. Such men would hardly support amending the constitution to take power from him, for they could expect him to have a long memory when their promotions came across his desk. Even in the congress the delegates all needed favors from the president from time to time, and those could only be obtained, Rhett believed, by being subservient.

"I can see no other course now, to arrest the future calamities, he may yet bring upon us, but the one I tried to get Congress to pursue," Rhett told Wigfall. The congress must insert its own power. The senate must stop approving his appointments of incompetent friends and relatives and sycophants. The congress as a whole must ensure that he respect the constitution. They must end secret sessions and publish their debates quickly, and then they would "reestablish a responsibility to the country." There would be time enough to amend the constitution appropriately after the war, when the army was disbanded and the soldiers and officers were out from under the control of the president. As civilians once more, they would quickly regain the feelings and jealous protection of their liberties as citizens that the military necessarily discouraged. "We will then I hope be able to repair the shattered walls of the constitution," he said. "We will win our liberties and independence," Rhett closed with confidence, "but it will be in spite of the most terrible incompetency and perversity in our Executive, which have ever afflicted a noble people."[45]

That spring and summer the *Mercury* renewed the assault on Davis, as if to back the advice Rhett gave to Wigfall and mirroring a rising discontent throughout the Confederacy as war weariness and the inexorable advance of Yankee armies evaporated any remaining enthusiasm from the heady days of 1861–62. "It is useless to attempt to deceive ourselves," said the paper. "Our military disasters have been our folly." Davis had violated every rule of common sense and all the established rules of war, they said. Unless the congress forced him to change, "we will go on blundering in blood, and can win success only in spite of the disasters they must produce." To the rumors—unfounded—that Lee was about to invade Pennsylvania again, the Rhetts responded with disbelief. Had not Davis learned his lesson at Gettysburg? Their brightest hopes now lay in

Beauregard and Joseph E. Johnston, they said. Johnston was just then beginning his toothless defense against William T. Sherman's advance toward Atlanta in May, and despite the fact that Johnston had done nothing notable since Manassas, the *Mercury* proclaimed that in defending north Georgia, "he is the man to do it." His real qualification, of course, was that he was at war with Jefferson Davis even more than Beauregard was. As if further evidence of woeful military judgment were needed, Rhett also still expected great things from old Sterling Price, who had done nothing successful for two years now.[46]

They kept up the pressure on the government as well, calling for the resignations of Memminger, Mallory, and Benjamin. Confederate foreign policy was such an obvious failure after three years that even Davis should see the need for a change, if it were not too late. In February a new tax act passed charging an ad valorem tax on slaves and land. It was virtually the direct tax that Rhett had preached for a generation, but still it was unconstitutional because no census had been taken. Ignoring that objection, Rhett pointed out that in the straightened state of the country now, the act would only force many planters to sell some of their land and blacks in order to have money to pay the tax on the rest. Once again, when slavery mixed in a matter, it overrode even a policy such as direct taxation that Rhett had championed, often alone, for decades. "The Secretaries do not represent the country," the *Mercury* complained; "they only tax it." When Memminger finally resigned in July, the Rhetts were delighted, especially since his replacement was George Trenholm, now living in Rhett's old house.[47]

Rhett found it more cheering at least that in June the senate finally called for stenographers to take down the debates for publication, putting part of his advice into practice. But it would take more than that to save them, especially as the months rolled on into the fall. Johnston never seriously tried to stop Sherman, and Davis quite properly relieved him when he was on the verge of giving up Atlanta without a fight in July. Gen. John B. Hood replaced him and made a bold if foolish attempt to drive the Yankees back; he then was forced to give up the city in September. The month earlier a Union fleet took Mobile Bay, while in Virginia, after a brilliant effort to stop his advancing foe in the field, Lee and his army were finally forced into trenches around Richmond and nearby Petersburg to endure a siege. To the objective, the only remaining hope of independence for the Confederacy lay in Lincoln failing in his bid for reelection in November, and in the wake of all these victories that seemed most unlikely.

Rhett believed that much of what was happening was Davis's fault. Davis had never supported Johnston, Rhett believed, because he was jealous of his capability and popularity, and his malignant hatred of Beauregard prevented him from putting him in his place instead of the unfortunate Hood. If Mallory and

Davis had ever tried to build a navy, they could have held Mobile, and as for Lee, while Rhett regarded him as the central general of the South now, as did everyone else, still he suspected that his being tied down to a siege must also in some way be traceable to the president. The fall of central Georgia was especially worrying, for it was plainly evident from the map that it made South Carolina vulnerable. With enemy forces at Port Royal and just below Charleston, and Sherman likely to advance from the interior, they could be cut off and carved into pieces.

Then Richmond made it even worse. Within the span of only a few days the greatest evils imaginable arose to threaten not only their political existence but the very foundation of their civilization and their nation. Reconstruction had not died after all but only slumbered, and now with cruel irony the prince who kissed it into life was a South Carolinian. Far worse than that, however, and unthinkable even from Davis, there was suddenly a plan for Confederate emancipation.

TWENTY-FIVE

Let Us Go On Striving
1864–1867

ILL HEALTH DID NOT PUT Rhett in any better mood for what was to come. The pesky lump beside his nose had not been a pimple at all but a skin cancer, which started to grow alarmingly during the war. In September 1862 he submitted himself to a physician who treated it by simply burning away the diseased tissue, and successive treatments over the next two years left an ugly hole in and beside his nose, but still the growth advanced. He spent some of the summer of 1864 at a resort near Flat Rock, North Carolina, seeking respite from the discomfort, but from now on a pain in his face would be a constant companion, and with it an increasing reluctance to go out in public with his disfigurement.[1] Sadder still to him was the news that his son Edmund, while serving in the army, had contracted tuberculosis. Rhett had seen its ravages on Clay and Calhoun, and the frustration of knowing that he could do nothing for his son only added to his anguish. It was a slow death, but by July 1864 it was generally known that Edmund had no more than a few years to live.[2]

Now it appeared to Rhett that the cause was dying as well, or would, and not from the Yankee armies but from traitors and reconstructionists within, as he had always feared. In fact, exhaustion, widespread social dislocation, horrific losses in the field armies, rabid inflation and attendant hardship all added to war weariness by the summer of 1864 to persuade hundreds of thousands of Confederate citizens that they could not go on. Desertion from their armies sapped the generals' strength when they could fight, and people at home increasingly urged their men to desert. The South had neither the will nor the wherewithal to resist much longer. The result was a rapid growth in talk of peace short of independence. When Sherman took Atlanta in September and a few weeks later Union forces started to rout the Confederates out of the Shenandoah Valley in Virginia, the talk only increased. Already there were rumors that Gov. Joseph Brown of Georgia had put out feelers to Sherman for making an independent peace for his state, while the prospects for Lincoln being defeated in November dwindled rapidly.

In such an atmosphere the *Mercury* reacted strongly in August when the *Richmond Enquirer* suggested that when both sides really wanted peace, the war would end. Since this was the presumed administration organ, the Rhetts asked if this were administration policy now, the hint being that here at last was the realization of all their fears of reconstruction, and that Davis had never been a committed Confederate. There could be no peace commission, said the Carolinians, for the Confederate government did not have the authority to discuss peace. That lay only with the states in their sovereign capacity. When rumors suggested that the Democratic Party in the North would propose a peace convention as a plank in their platform for the fall election, the *Mercury* called for the people of the South to repudiate the suggestion, and should Richmond try to answer any such overtures, the states must intervene.[3]

Then at the end of September, Boyce issued a public letter to Jefferson Davis in the press, warning that they were rapidly approaching a military despotism and asking for an armistice followed by a convention of all the states North and South to negotiate a settlement. Boyce believed that it would make the Democrats even more potent in their battle with Lincoln in November. The Rhetts reacted immediately. It was ridiculous to seek protection from Jefferson Davis by going to the Yankees, they argued. Boyce was a reconstructionist and ought to resign. The *Mercury* even attacked Vice President Stephens, known to be sympathetic to Boyce's proposal. When it was further suggested that the constitutional problem of Richmond not having the power to treat for peace was to be gotten around by an amendment prepared by Boyce, Rhett declared that any such amendment would be a violation of the Constitution by granting to the central government a sovereignty that the states could not surrender. Most foolish of all, of course, was the idea that the Union would honor the result of any such convention if it actually did meet. "The original Yankee—the New Englander—is notorious for his propensity to deception," said the *Mercury.* The Confederacy did not need to talk of reconstruction but only keep heart and courage.[4]

Lincoln's election in November ended any hope of conventions and reconstruction, for his terms for ending the war—an end to the Confederacy, full reunion, and an end of slavery—were well known, and there was no room for compromise or negotiation there. Indeed, to Rhett the triumph of Lincoln was almost welcome, for it meant that the South had to give up the unrealistic dreams of Boyce and others and fight on for complete independence or complete defeat. He might even have hoped that Barnwell Rhett Jr.'s election to the legislature in October signified some return of resistance spirit. But then came perhaps the greatest shock of all, something that he would not have imagined even Davis could conceive. The president wanted to arm slaves to fight and to offer them freedom as an incentive.

The idea of using slaves in the armies dated back to the formation of the Confederacy, but Davis turned away all such proposals in the early years of the war and continued to do so even when a petition came to him from some of his more influential western generals in the fall of 1863. A year later the situation had altered so dramatically that he was forced to reconsider. In October 1864 several state governors met in Georgia and concluded that since advancing Yankee armies were already appropriating their slaves and putting them in uniform to fight, perhaps the Confederates should do the same. They already used slaves as cooks and teamsters and in other noncombatant roles, but now slaves should be soldiers. Owners should freely contribute them, but if they did not, then the congress ought to allow the government to conscript them, with emancipation for those who served faithfully. Rhett thought the idea monstrous and also unconstitutional, since South Carolina for one had laws that prohibited owners from emancipating slaves unless the blacks were expelled from the state immediately afterward. No free blacks could return to the state, nor could free blacks from other states enter. How, then, could they deal with such freed slaves after their terms as soldiers were done? "The freemen of the Confederate States, must work out their own redemption, or they must be the slaves of their own slaves," the Rhetts argued. "Assert the right in the Confederate Government to emancipate slaves, and it is stone dead." The only reason they had a manpower problem in their armies, the Rhetts stated, was that the patronage-mad Davis had provided exemptions from military service for hundreds of thousands of able-bodied males—one of whom just happened to be Robert Barnwell Rhett Jr., by the way —and that hundreds of thousands of others were allowed to be absent without leave.[5]

Davis actually proposed a limited program of purchase of slaves from their masters and using them as laborers, with the promise of emancipation after service, in his message sent to the congress on November 7. He made it clear that he did not suggest using them as soldiers, but the wording of the message made it clear that such would be an acceptable eventuality if the Confederacy were forced to the alternative of defeat. Rhett was livid. From the first he made it clear that the reason for Southern independence, for fighting the war, was to preserve the constitutional liberties that guaranteed to slaveowners their right to their slaves. How could the government then suggest that it had the right to conscript them for purchase or to emancipate them?

Rhett took his case to former governor William Aiken, not because Aiken had any political power but because it could then appear as a nonpolitical personal letter when Rhett published it in the *Mercury,* which was his original purpose. Both being out of office, he suggested in a logical non sequitur, he and

Aiken were better able to judge of policy than were those in power. "Nothing since this war commenced, has struck me with such alarm and despondency, as the late message of the President of the Confederate States, claiming for the Confederate Government the power to emancipate our slaves," Rhett began. Davis may only have asked for an appropriation to buy slaves to be laborers, he confessed, but he added that this was all Davis recommended at the moment. His declaration that slaves should be put in the army in preference to defeat revealed his ultimate purpose.

Rhett reminded Aiken that when South Carolina seceded she put forth in justification—in the document that he wrote himself—the interference with slavery as their "proximate or *immediate cause.*" The North had been refusing them the right to take slavery into the territories, had imposed abolition in the District of Columbia, and had interfered with the fugitive slave law. Yet they never asserted that their congress had the right to emancipate a slave in the slave states themselves. Still the South chose to withdraw for such outrages, and it would be ridiculous to suppose that anyone in the secession conventions or the framing congress at Montgomery ever supposed that their new government should have the power to do that for which they abandoned the old one. Davis seemed to find support from the constitutional clause authorizing the congress to raise and support armies, yet Rhett charged that with being only an inference, a "construction," the very sort of thing that destroyed the Constitution of the Union.

In a series of examples Rhett showed how the Confederates' constitution nowhere left open the door for interpretation, and moreover that if the congress had unlimited power to raise armies through conscription of all classes of people, free and slave, then it ultimately could obliterate all state government by conscripting all state officers. It was a reminder that such officers now held their positions thanks to being exempted, and many sought office in order to evade the military in fact. If Davis could take their slaves, then sooner or later he could take them too. Slavery was a recognized element in the constitution, and slaves were part of the enumeration for apportionment. Conscript them and the government removed from the states one of the sources of their representation, and since the constitution did not recognize free blacks at all for census purposes, the emancipation of blacks afterward made the disruption in apportionment perpetual. Just as slavery had been the paramount element in defining power in the Congress in Washington, so it could be in Richmond too. Neither was there any provision in the document that would authorize the treasury to appropriate money for such a purpose. Throughout the whole constitution, said Rhett, its meaning was clearly that this was to be a Confederacy of free white men. Nowhere did the charter state that, no doubt because it had been taken for granted by the framers, but now, ironically, Rhett resorted to an "interpretation" of his own, even though he had spent a career denouncing those who interpreted the old Constitution. "They propose emancipation—faithlessness—wrong," he declared. South Carolina, for one, he hoped would never surrender her sovereign right to determine exclusively the subject of emancipation within her borders, nor would she ever abandon slavery so long as she had life.

"Few of us, I fear, realized the difficulty of maintaining a free Government in war," he concluded. Executive usurpation invariably led to the deaths of those free governments that had failed in the past, and in time of war, such amalgamation of power was especially to be feared. In the great contest they fought, it was especially vital that the great principles of state rights and slavery for which they began their existence should be rigidly defended. "For this, we have fought; for this, our people have died." If they needed any power beyond that of the central government to carry on their war, that power resided in the states, to whom the appeal should be made. But Davis thought otherwise. "To ignore the States, and to usurp any power deemed expedient to carry on the war, has been the policy pursued," he charged. It was a policy that had wasted their manpower and dampened the ardor of true lovers of freedom. "The Confederate Government threatens to put upon us all the evils we threw off the dominion of our Yankee enemies to avoid." It encouraged reconstructionism and so demoralized their soldiers that whole armies of absentees shirked their duty.

Their soldiers would not fight beside slaves, Rhett promised. Moreover, once commenced, emancipation must spread until it freed all. "Who would live in such a country as ours without slaves to cultivate it," he asked, "and who but slaves will live in any country with four millions of emancipated slaves?" Their slaves had behaved well during the war, and their labor had benefited the war effort. "They are in their normal condition as slaves, by the decree of God himself." True, the Yankees made soldiers of them, but only by compelling them into uniform, for to soldier was not within the preordained compass of the black, and regardless of the wisdom or morality of what Davis proposed to do, Rhett declared emphatically that the president had not the power to do so. There was still time for Davis to change his course, to honor the constitution and stop fighting it, to honor the rights of the states and seek their cooperation. "With our affairs thus administered," Rhett finished, "I have not a doubt of our success."[6]

The timing of Rhett's letter, just before the session of the new legislature, was not accidental, especially now that his son was once more a delegate, for it was designed to prepare and encourage that body to take some definitive action. While the *Mercury* kept up its criticism of the administration's proposed policy, Barnwell Rhett Jr. went to Columbia at the end of the month and, in perhaps the greatest irony of the war, enacted virtually a repetition of his father's entry on the national scene of politics thirty-six years before. In resolutions that well may have been authored by the senior Rhett, he declared that the Confederacy must only consider peace on the basis of independence, condemned censorship, renewed condemnation of the direct tax, and now demanded the exemption of state officials from conscription. Above all, he asserted the principle that slavery was and must ever remain inviolate. When the Richmond government acted in violation of any of these stated purposes, it should be the duty of South Carolina to refuse to submit. It was to be nullification in the Confederacy.[7]

The Rhetts' entire program did not get through the legislature, though on December 23 an act was passed repealing all previous bills covering furnishing slave labor to the military and placing the subject under the exclusive jurisdiction and management of the governor and state authorities. Its effect was to interpose the state between Richmond and any conscription of a slave by a government that might later put him in uniform or emancipate him. At the same time the legislature enacted a bill authorizing the new governor, Magrath, to claim the exemption of all members of the legislature, state militia officers, and almost all state and local civil officials down to the level of clerks, bank tellers, and of course newspapermen. Indeed, about the only class not covered by the exemption was that of simple farmers, and even they could be included whenever the governor felt that local citizens were required to maintain order on the plantations among the slaves.[8]

It was almost a declaration of independence. South Carolina had never resisted conscription before, but faced now with the waste of her troops in an inefficiently run military organization and their perhaps being forced to fight alongside blacks, she chose to keep every man possible at home to defend the state, a pressing concern now that Sherman's victorious army was even then in Savannah, poised to march north into South Carolina any day. Gen. John S. Preston, charged with overseeing slave impressment, declared that "this legislation is an explicit declaration that this State does not intend to contribute another soldier or slave to the public defense, except on such terms as may be dictated by her authorities." In disgust as a Carolinian himself, he lamented that "the first treason to the Confederate States in form of law has been perpetrated," believing it the work of "designing knaves."[9] South Carolina had interposed her state sovereignty to halt governmental usurpation, and by now even Robert Barnwell did not speak up to scold the Rhetts or defend the president. Jefferson Davis, he said, had no policy but merely drifted from crisis to crisis. No wonder several of the states were starting to look out for themselves, and no reason South Carolina should be an exception.[10]

The new year saw the *Mercury* looking sorrier than ever, a single sheet now with badly worn type, dwindling advertising, and no good news to print. It had reported Sherman's inexorable march from Atlanta to Savannah and now covered the beginnings of his sweep northward into South Carolina, with no force sufficient to stop him. That was Davis's fault too, of course, and the Rhetts blasted him for withdrawing local forces to other theaters. Condemning the submission meetings being held in other states, the *Mercury* preached defiance to the end and argued that Beauregard could save them now, but he remained out of favor with the president, so there again Davis was dooming their cause. Sherman was succeeding because he and his army had nerve, whereas Davis was "impracticably obstinate and lamentably weak." The Rhetts even gave Lincoln credit for being an effective leader and statesman with a bold policy. "Blackguard and buffoon as he is, he has pursued his end with an energy as untiring as an Indian, and a singleness of purpose that might almost be called patriotic."[11]

By mid-January 1865 the editorials almost ranted in their abject loathing of "King Davis," suggesting that the editors had lost the last remaining vestiges of reason where it came to the president. A Northern officer and newspaperman, Charles Halpine, looked on "the Rhett faction," as he called them, as "never at home save when in the attitude of contradiction; men whose lives were expended in the negative." The president kept his opinion of them to himself, but two years later, when Halpine compared Rhett to a man who, with no one else with whom to quarrel, threw open his window and argued with a night watchman calling "two o'clock—all well," Davis responded tersely that he was "not even as fair as that."[12]

No man who could not obey the congress and the laws could be a leader. Indeed, the Rhetts questioned whether Davis might have secretly decided to surrender some time ago, explaining his mismanagement now and the ineptitude of those he chose to surround him. "In friends, in counsellors, in the Cabinet, in Congress, no men of force, or energy, of will, of wisdom or knowledge or experience are sought for," the *Mercury* complained, "but tools and sycophants, and men subservient to Mr. Davis' will and whims and dictations." There was more than a hint of pique that Alfred had never gotten his star when the Rhetts grumbled that "political tools are made brigadiers," but beyond that they declared that the time was at hand when brave men had to face the president and tell him, "do as we command, or vacate your position." The only alternative was defeat.[13]

Inevitably the logic of Rhett's words turned him more and more to deposing the president. He had discouraged Wigfall in the spring of 1864, and as late as November the *Mercury* declared that "we utterly eschew all irregularity—all violence—all revolution—any—the least departure from the plain mandates of the Constitution and law." They did not want a dagger in the night or a palace coup, but the president was not omnipotent—an open urge to impeachment. As the weeks went on the Rhetts' position gradually shifted. "Can Congress find no remedy for the incompetency and mismanagement which is riding us down to ruin?" they asked early in January, excoriating "the incorrigible intermeddling, mischievous dictations, malignant prejudices and petty partizanship" of the president. "It is these things which are destroying us, and which must be eradicated by the action of Congress." They must put "the knife to the seat of the disease."[14]

Rhett's rantings found a sympathetic ear with several people, among them Toombs, who had concluded that Davis must be deposed or killed, or else their cause was lost. The Speaker of the house in Columbia, A. P. Aldrich, came to the conclusion that Davis must be hobbled, and he consulted Rhett on January 9. With Atlanta gone and Sherman in Savannah, the only way to save Georgia—not to mention South Carolina—was to "take control of military affairs out of the hands of the President." Meetings in Georgia spoke again of calling a state convention to make a separate peace. If that happened, the backbone of the Confederacy would be gone and with it any remaining hope. He proposed that the congress should make Lee "the military head of the Government," leaving the conduct of all armies entirely up to him. He did not suggest deposing Davis but only removing the commander-in-chief function from his authority, much the same as Wigfall's earlier suggestion.[15]

That was not enough for Rhett. Now he wrote to the vice president and suggested to Stephens that Davis must be removed entirely or the Confederacy would fall. He urged that the congress should remove Davis immediately and place General Lee at the head of the government. So great was the country's confidence in the general that the people would willingly allow congress to pass whatever emergency legislation needed to be undertaken to get around the constitutional obstacles to an immediate removal, and without the prolonged process of impeachment and trial. Of course, removing Davis should have made Stephens president in his place, which was one of Rhett's earlier objections to talk of impeachment, but in the emergency he assumed that Stephens would be willing to step aside and that legislation to encompass such an unconstitutional action could be framed. Rhett asked Stephens to circulate his letter among members of congress to sound their interest, and meanwhile he began to trumpet in the *Mercury:* "Is there no high toned gentleman in the land, like General Lee, or General Joseph E. Johnston who could be raised by Congress to the position now held by this incompetent man?" He wondered if the congress had "forgotten the power of the people to impeach."[16]

The objection of most to Rhett's plan was that Lee was too good a soldier and too loyal a citizen ever to go against the president, his constituted immediate superior. Rhett reasoned, however, that if the congress deposed Davis first, thus removing Lee's constitutional superior, and then waited on him in a body and asked him to take over, he would be too much the patriot to decline. In a crowning irony, Rhett said that the congress had the power to do this "on the revolutionary ground of military necessity," the same justification for which he had spent four years damning Davis.[17] Stephens may simply have pocketed Rhett's letter, for by now he knew they were beaten and just wanted the war over, and he already had another mandate before him in the abortive Hampton Roads peace conference with Lincoln on February 3. It never had a chance, for Lincoln's terms were reunion and emancipation, while Stephens could negotiate on neither point. Predictably the *Mercury* condemned it as fruitless but said that instead the time had come for the cotton states to deliberate together on their immediate destiny. The paper did not state for what purpose, but it could only have been for the states to overrule the congress by directly deposing Davis, for the president had committed yet another outrage by proposing to England that in return for recognition and intervention the Confederacy would emancipate its slaves.[18]

Rhett never lost his conviction that England *ought* to have recognized the Confederacy, nor the belief that it would have but for Davis's limp foreign policy. Throughout the war he even continued to hope that somehow Britain could be persuaded to see the obvious benefits to an alliance with the Confederacy. In these last months of the war he spent idle hours drafting a fictional conversation between a Confederate and an Englishman, designed to present the Confederate case and meet all the objections and misconceptions that he felt stood in the way of recognition. The Confederates were not rebels, as they were called, but an independent people, made so by the states to whom they owed their only paramount loyalty. Slavery did not cause the war, for the Yankees had been willing to leave it alone by their own declaration, saying that they only wanted the Union whole again. "It was the occasion, but not the cause of the war," said Rhett's Confederate. The real cause was in the agitations of the Yankees to use the government against slavery and the election of a sectional president on a platform pledged to unconstitutional assaults upon slave rights.

He addressed the problems with majority rule, no doubt thinking this would appeal in Britain especially, since the landed elite still controlled government. He revealed the abuses of freedom in the Union now, including the unlawful seizures of dissidents and newspaper editors, which was justified by the tyrant's plea of "military necessity." "Admit the plea to be honest," his Confederate said, and it amounted to the silly paradox that to save the Constitution, it had to be violated. "All scoundrels, from the autocrat to the modern Caesar, have used the same paradox to abolish Free Government, and to authorize their despotisms." Presumably it did not constitute despotism when Rhett offered the same plea to eliminate Davis. And to all of the Confederate's arguments the Englishman replied by saying, much as Rhett had said and thought after so many of his political pronouncements over his career, that "such facts, it appears to me do not admit of argument." Having spent a lifetime convincing himself that his arguments were unassailably right, it was only natural that his fictional Englishman should agree.[19]

One thing Rhett did not address in his imaginary conversation was emancipation as a lure for recognition. In January the congress had finally created anew the position of general-in-chief and pressured Davis into appointing Lee, and hard on that came Davis's call to enlist blacks into Confederate arms in return for emancipation, as Rhett had expected would happen. Despite his high regard for Lee, Rhett was convinced that it was an idea the general had instilled in the president, for he thought Lee was at heart an old-time Federalist as his father had been. He opposed slavery and needed more men, and that led him to author "this nigger soldier idea." Lee was a better general than a politician, concluded the *Mercury*, and should stay in his proper sphere. The idea of putting the black into the gray would find no sympathy in the Rhetts' pages. "The mad remedy of driving our quiet negro producers into the war, and forcing them to fight" was ludicrous on its face. Given the choice of fighting for the South for his own emancipation or fighting for the Union for the freedom of his family and his entire people, which choice would a slave make? Arm them, and they would just desert to the enemy where conditions were better.

It was just emancipation by another means and more evidence, if any were needed, that Davis had long believed abolition was inevitable and free labor to be desired. Remove slavery and they destroyed republican government, replacing liberty with mobocracy. Ignoring the fact that free blacks were certainly willing to fight for emancipation, the *Mercury* argued that such people—"ignorant, idle vagrants"—would not work of their own accord without slavery compelling them, and that the loss of their labor would reduce the planters to penury. Worse would be the social result, especially for the poor white. "He is reduced to the level of a nigger, and a nigger is raised to his level," said the *Mercury*. "Cheek by jowl they must labor together as equals. His wife and his daughter are to be hustled on the street by black wenches, their equals. Swaggering buck niggers are to ogle them, and to elbow them." Was this what their brave white soldiers had been fighting for, "to reduce themselves to the level and companionship of niggers?" Raising the inevitable specter of interbreeding, the Rhetts warned of "mongrels" and miscegenation. These would be the results of putting slaves in the army and emancipating them for their efforts, "mobocracy on the one hand— nigger equality and gradual miscegenation [on] the other." Nor would the slave fight for anything less than freedom. "There are some simple things that he is able to understand," said the paper. "He is not altogether a monkey."[20]

"Slavery and independence must stand together, or they must fall together," the *Mercury* decreed early in February. Kill the former, and the latter died with it. "Sink or swim, live or die, we want all, or we want none." And that applied as well to the proposal to emancipate in return for recognition, a proffer made too late and that offered something that was never a serious obstacle to recognition in the first place. To talk of abolishing "the institution which lies at the base of our whole Government, and our whole system of civilization" was treasonous. Comparing the idea to the belief that Lincoln at Hampton Roads might offer a twenty-year continuation of slavery in return for reunion, the *Mercury* declared that "both are ruin."[21]

Nothing came of the overture to England, and only a handful of blacks were raised to start training as soldiers before events overtook the Confederacy. The *Mercury* ranted against Davis right to the end, on February 7 calling him "Jeff, 1st, Autocrat of the Confederate States." What were the people of the Confederacy, it asked, "white negroes, or serfs, or what?" And "what is this little man Jeff. Davis?" Who could fathom what his monomania was leading them to, and what was the congress doing, or the clerks who composed his cabinet? What had happened to their world, and why had God let it happen to them in the guise of Jefferson Davis? "Is the millenium coming, or the day of judgment?" it implored. "What is the matter?" Four days later, still complaining, they published the last issue of the *Mercury.* Sherman was at their gates.[22]

Rhett later claimed that he gave up the cause as lost when Davis removed Johnston from command of his army outside Atlanta in July 1864, but that was hindsight, of which Rhett always had a considerable quotient. It is evident that he made few preparations for the coming of the Yankees, while Barnwell Rhett Jr. only shut down the *Mercury* and started packing his papers and his father's, and the press and type on February 11. Meanwhile out at the Oaks the elder Rhett did nothing about packing his personal papers or effects there, but he did take some steps to have his slaves and movable livestock ready to get out of Sherman's path if he came through. By late January word that Sherman would soon begin crossing the Savannah River into South Carolina reached Charleston and the outlying areas, and on January 26 some of his advance units skirmished briefly at Pocotaligo, just twenty miles southwest of the Oaks.[23]

That night a sharp knock at their door at the Oaks awoke Katherine Rhett, who roused her husband and sent him down. It was a soldier sent by his captain to tell them that the enemy gunboat *Pawnee* had passed the obstructions at the mouth of the Ashepoo earlier that day and seemed threatening to continue coming up the narrow river.[24] Rhett calmly thanked the man and set about getting ready to leave. He had planned for some time that when and if they had to evacuate, he would take the family west across Georgia to Eufaula, Alabama, where he had rented some property. He had done that recently after selling the Darien plantation for seventy thousand dollars, which finally got him out of debt except for what he still owed his sister Claudia.[25] If the Yankee gunboat got to the one bridge over the Ashepoo before they did, however, they would be cut off and might be trapped, with Sherman's advancing columns between them and the Georgia line.

It was a frantic time, with neither Rhett nor Katherine knowing what the other was doing in preparation. She lit candles and ran to the back door, ringing the plantation bell furiously to summon her maid to help her dress and to awaken the slaves. As he dressed, Rhett yelled for a servant to go find their slave driver and have him get their two buggies and every plantation wagon harnessed and ready to leave. "The yankees are coming up the river," he yelled, "and we must try and cross the bridge before they arrive." He ordered that all the slave children be put in the wagons, which meant that there would be no room for baggage, and the adult blacks would have to walk. Six men were to stay behind to protect the house from looters and would rejoin them later. Katherine meanwhile gathered some silver and a few sentimental belongings, but Rhett had no time to pack any of his books and papers from a lifetime of public activity. He and Katherine's sister got in one of two buggies and immediately drove off, leaving Katherine and her maid to follow in a second.

Mrs. Rhett tarried a few moments for a last look at the home she loved. Years later she recalled "how beautiful yet mournful the scene appeared as I looked around, a waning moon cast its melancholy light upon the silent fields, the river was hidden in a silver line of mist, the distant woods were dark and sombre, the garden flowers threw out a stronger and most refreshing fragrance, and the perfume of the magnolia blossoms was almost overpowering." When she came out of her brief reverie she looked down the road to see Rhett's buggy almost out of sight. She had left slowly, having sent a servant back for yet another keepsake, and finally after the slave caught up, Katherine turned into a wooded lane and almost crashed into her husband. Suddenly realizing that she was not behind him, he had stopped in a fright to wait for her. He shouted a scolding at her for her tardiness, but she only yelled at him to get going again. As they drove on, her maid Betsy comforted Katherine: "Massa call you fool but no mind him, he donno what he do say."

The lane led them in time to a Confederate outpost that halted them until Rhett gave their names, and he left word that his slaves would be coming along behind them. It was a tense time now, and the soldiers warned them that there were more outposts ahead and that most would fire at anything. Thereafter as the Rhett buggies neared a Confederate picket line they started shouting their names as they approached and then raced by, and so they kept on through the night. At dawn they came at last to the bridge, and once he had Katherine safely across, he left her to proceed at a slower pace while he drove back to rush on the other wagons.[26]

Over the next two weeks Rhett and the slave wagons, along with some small livestock driven along by the adults, caught up with Katherine, and slowly they made their way. Unfortunately, whereas they thought originally that Sherman's objective was Charleston—which is what he wanted Confederates to think—in fact he was pushing north toward Columbia. This meant that the Rhetts could not move due west to get into Georgia but had to keep going north in hopes of getting around the enemy's advancing columns. They probably passed through Orangeburg and then moved along the north bank of the Edisto River by about February 11, just before the Yankee army took it the next day. They may even have reached Columbia before they headed west toward Augusta, some fifty-five miles away, where Beauregard had a small command that could give them some protection. By February 17 they stopped to make camp on the Little River, twenty miles west of Columbia. The caravan made quite a sight. While they ate a mid-day meal another refugee came upon them and remarked on "the Rhetts with an immense train of wagons, his man-servant and his maid servant, his ox and his ass and everything that was his, including a drove of about 40 hogs and a flock of at least 50 turkeys, fleeing with all his family and substance from before the face of Sherman."[27]

It was a clear, dry afternoon in the camp, and they remained that evening when a high wind came up out of the east, and soon it began to smell of smoke. It was their first hint that Sherman had taken the capital, and Columbia was in flames. What Rhett would not know until later was that much more than a city was burning. His son Barnwell Rhett had shipped the *Mercury* press and type as well as his own and some of his father's personal papers off to Columbia in a special train car, wanting it forwarded on to Charlotte, North Carolina, where he expected to continue operations. Once in Columbia, however, the car sat on a siding during the panic of the evacuation before Sherman, and Rhett's agents with the car simply left it there. Now, like the rest of the city, it burned, and part of what the elder Rhett could smell on the wind on the Little River was the scent of his past being consumed. He could not know that this very same day Confederate forces including his sons Alfred and Burnet were evacuating Charleston. Within hours plundering Union soldiers would be looting both the small house he rented in the city and the Oaks, taking his furniture, shipping his books north as souvenirs, and scattering his papers to the winds. One Yankee found the door wide open to the Charleston house and walked in to see floors strewn with books and magazines and several slave children playing among them. Rhett had kept his papers in an old Chinese chinoiserie desk there, but now the soldier found his letters scattered all about by looters. He picked up a few of the letters and was unable to read Rhett's handwriting, which he called "a dose of hieroglyphics." But he intended to send them to a newspaperman in New York in the hope that he might be able to read them and from them discern some of the secret history of the rebellion. One of them was the letter that began, "Jefferson Davis is not only a dishonest man, but a liar."[28]

By February 21, Rhett reached Eufaula and there finally stopped traveling. He found the house he had rented awaiting him, but it had no furniture and he could find none locally, so his family had to make do with the little that they had brought with them. His hired plantation twenty miles out of town had no cabins for his slaves. "Such are the troubles of a fugitive," he wrote back to his eldest son. Desperate for money to buy seed corn, he asked Barny to secure payment from the Confederate authorities for several thousand bushels of rice they had commissioned, but when he got it on May 3 it amounted to a mere $107.56 in near-worthless Confederate money, barely enough to plant seed on his new plantation. No doubt to suit the surroundings to his mood Rhett called the place Castle Dismal, ironically borrowing the name from one of William Gilmore Simms's literary productions. Nothing in the ensuing months promised any relief from the constant budget of bad news. Sherman had it all his own way in South Carolina and then marched north into North Carolina, where on March 16 at Averasborough he met and defeated troops including those who had evacuated Charleston. Though Burnet came through unscathed, Alfred Rhett, commanding the rear guard of the Confederate force, was captured by Yankee cavalry and sent north to prison. By now Rhett would have known the fate of the *Mercury* press and his personal things. Three weeks later came word that Lee had been forced to surrender at Appomattox, and a few weeks after that the only remaining Southern army in the East capitulated to Sherman. Despite some forces still being under arms out to the west and on the run from the foe, the day of the Confederacy was done. The same day that Rhett got his rice money, Jefferson Davis and his fleeing cabinet reached Washington, Georgia, with just one week of freedom to go before his capture.[29]

There were some who thought ill of Rhett for leaving South Carolina, remembering all his vows over the years to stand by his state and share her fate. When the time came his only remaining fortune was invested in his slaves, and he took them with him rather than risk losing that investment. "Old Barnwell Rhett & his whole family moved to Eufaula, *Ala.*—out of danger!" Mary Chesnut commented indignantly when she heard. Rhett later confessed that he fled because he knew the cause was lost, though in admitting that to himself he also knew that in a short time his slaves would be emancipated no matter where he took them. Most likely his real fear was for his family, with a ten-year-old son, a teenaged daughter, and one or two of his adult daughters living with him. After all he had suffered and lost, perhaps he was entitled to put his own first before his now-pointless pledges to a Lost Cause. Certainly he did not fear for his own safety, though his son Burnet did. A few weeks after the last surrender, Burnet told Edward Barnwell that he worried that his father, "the greatest of seceders," might be the object of Union vengeance. "You need not be," Barnwell assured him. "The Yanks are too grateful to the *Mercury.* The *Mercury* did them yeoman service during the war—disintegrating the Confederacy. They will never allow a hair of the head of anybody connected with the Charleston *Mercury* to be singed."[30]

Indeed they would not, though Rhett could regard his current circumstances as punishment enough. All of his furniture and books being lost at the Oaks, he had nothing to fill the rented house at Castle Dismal but his family. They were in time to get in a planting, but only to discover they had come for a growing season of unparalleled heat and drought, and month after month Rhett simply watched as his crop burnt up in the fields. Illness among the slaves cost him money he did not have, and his vacant Carolina plantations had been occupied by the Freedmen's Bureau, an agency established to care for former slaves and help with their transition to freedom. On top of all that, for a long period that fall he suffered from a recurring fever that sapped his already frail strength. He watched from afar as the dying echoes of the war and the Confederacy faded away. In June his old friend Edmund Ruffin, unwilling to live under Yankee rule, committed suicide, and Rhett lamented that if only Ruffin had had faith, he would have been able to face whatever this life presented, knowing that there would be a better one. He felt outraged when Henry Wirz, commandant of Camp Sumter prison compound at Andersonville, Georgia, was tried and hanged as a war criminal. Rhett argued that the man had only been obeying his orders and that if his prisoners went hungry, it was because the inefficient supply system of Davis's military cronies failed to provide enough.[31]

Like many other Southern leaders, Rhett had hoped that Lincoln's Emancipation Proclamation, being a war measure, would cease effect with the end of the war and that the Union would continue to recognize slave property in the existing slave states as it had stated it was willing to do in 1861. But time and war had changed everything, and a new amendment to the Constitution, the thirteenth, was even then being ratified by states in the old Union and soon would be a condition of readmission by the former Confederate states. As the time approached for the election of delegates to a state convention in Alabama, some of Rhett's neighbors called on him to ask what he thought their convention ought to do. If the convention were merely to reinstate the old Union in conformity with resolutions of the Congress to that effect, then they should cooperate heartily, he told them. However, if the real expectation from the convention was that it would ratify the Thirteenth Amendment, as he suspected, then they ought to do nothing. The Union could force compliance, but it could not force them to act as agents of their own social destruction. "They should rule us directly by the sword," he said, rather than "that we should attempt to rule ourselves *under their authority*," for that would be merely to sanction their despotism. "Obey and suffer, and bide our time" was his counsel.

Indeed, he almost feared that the Union would be too lenient and forbearing with them, for it would only lure the South once again into the impossible notion that the two sections could live together. He hoped that the Yankees would harass them sufficiently that it would create a reaction among Southerners so great as to achieve "the union of the White Race of the South" to a degree they had not been united during the war, defeat forever the evil delusion of reconstruction, and set them on the course to revolution and independence once more "under the great principles of the Confederate States' Constitution." Rhett's South would rise again, and quickly he hoped. He even reduced his arguments to resolutions for publication in the local press, but when the Alabama convention met, the sympathy for reunion was so strong that no one even introduced his resolutions, and on December 2, Alabama ratified the Thirteenth Amendment.[32] It ended slavery forever. Expecting its coming, Rhett had already been forced to hire his former slaves as employees that summer. This was yet another expense he could scarcely meet, though not one of them left him.

Severely reduced by his fever, his crop a ruin, and recoiling from associating with the strangers around him thanks to the deformation of his face from the cancer, Rhett quickly resolved that summer to get back to South Carolina if he could. He got his son Robert Jr. to approach Union authorities overseeing the confiscated plantation property along the coast, making the case that the Oaks and Drainfield were not abandoned, that they were never inhabited in the summer anyhow thanks to weather and isolation, and that thus he should be allowed to return and resume occupancy. To facilitate this goal, hard though it was for any

Rhett to stomach, Robert Jr. even signed an oath of allegiance to the United States. Late in the year, after Rhett Sr. salvaged what little he could of his Alabama crop, he received word that the Freedmen's Bureau would yield his property to him and he could go home. He had already gone to Aiken for his health, and in January 1866 his son Alfred, now released from prison, joined him to help work the land. By spring, however, Rhett had decided to return home. Barny found a house to rent in Charleston where all of them could live while the blacks worked the Ashepoo plantations, but money was so tight that, faced with the choice of going to South Carolina or sending Alfred to Europe to study medicine, Rhett at first preferred to spend it on his boy, since he could keep living in Aiken rent-free thanks to friends. In the end they left at the end of May, and in a gratifying gesture every one of his former slaves except the house servants engaged to make the return trip and go to work for him at their old home.[33]

Once more in South Carolina, Rhett confessed, "My blackest fears, have been realized." He lamented to his sister Claudia, "I am worth nothing." Friends had saved the carpets and curtains from his Charleston house at the end of the war, and there still remained some parlor furniture and bedding at his Altamaha plantation. He had buried the family china before the end of the war and hoped to dig it up again. By combining all the bits and pieces of their prewar homes he hoped to be able to furnish a townhouse with enough bedrooms for all of them, but he admonished that "we *must accommodate ourselves to our means.*"[34] He did not intend to give way to despair in his bankruptcy, however. He still had good land and the house at the Oaks, and all the slave cabins remained in good repair. His former slaves seemed loyal and willing to work for him. He could still pull himself out of this deep hole. When South Carolina ratified the Thirteenth Amendment—and he was still convinced that only the state could do so, not Washington—he felt that the state should have compensated slaveowners for the property it thus took from them, but of course that did not happen. With no other money available, Rhett was forced to pledge the family silver, all they had saved in the evacuation, in order to raise money to keep going and start a new rice crop. Alfred felt confident that he could bring in a good crop if he could keep the black workers fed, no doubt promising them a share of the proceeds when the rice sold.

Barnwell Rhett Jr. meanwhile, on his father's advice, went north early in 1866 to try to raise capital to restart the *Mercury.* Rhett felt that he ought to reopen his law practice "even though it is profitless." At least he could earn enough for the office rent, and he contemplated writing for hire as a last resort for raising the money to keep them going. Indeed, he took it for granted that he would be earning money writing for the resurrected *Mercury.* And if Barny did not succeed in finding financing to start the press again, then his father would go to Charleston and hire out his pen to whomever would pay for what he had to say. "I am not content to do nothing," he told Barny, "or not to strive to do something to support my family." He could not prevent some sad reflection on the past. "What a tumult has been my latter years!" he said in January 1866. "A strange life it has been! For more than thirty years, amidst oblique suspicion, abuse and hate, I have strived to save my country from the ruin I saw coming over her. I have failed. My country is ruined, and me and mine left stripped of the means of living." His cause may have been beaten, but he was not ready to give up. "I have five years yet, before the three score years & ten," he declared, "and with Gods blessing I will use all the faculties with which he has endowed me."[35]

Most of the old planters of the area had to scrape, sell, or rent their property to get going again after the war, so at least Rhett was not alone. He lamented that he could not afford both a cook and a house servant, and the family had to get along with two male servants and a maid. Aged sixty-five, with his health too unsteady to allow him to manage the plantations actively himself, he leased them to Alfred, and in March 1866 he mortgaged both Drainfield and the Oaks to two sisters in New York in return for ten thousand dollars to plant cotton, rice, and corn. The first half of the note was due in two years, and Alfred was to share one-third of the proceeds of his crops as well as paying interest. Since the former slaves came under the aegis of the Freedmen's Bureau, the Rhetts also had to meet its regulations for the hire and care of their onetime property. That done, the planting began, Rhett looked for some legal business, and they tried to renew life where it had left off a year before. All things considered, he told Barny, "I think we have done wonders."[36]

It was a difficult year. Alfred's first crop that summer failed, and Rhett's older brother Benjamin was murdered on July 6 on his plantation by an angry man to whom he had refused permission to hunt on his land. Yet there were lighter moments. Shortly after he returned to South Carolina, the First South Carolina Association, composed of veterans of Alfred's old regiment to care for the invalids from the war and preserve their history, elected him an honorary member. Mostly Rhett stayed at the Oaks, venturing out only infrequently, listening to his daughters Elise and Claudia playing the piano that had been too heavy for the Yankees to carry away, and sitting up late into the nights singing. There were two little dogs to amuse him, a yellow one called Ginger and a black one whom they named Nigger. He could even take some delight in the little domestic upheavals on occasion, as when one morning he got up at sunrise, as was his custom, and called for a cup of tea, only to see the servants go into some confusion over fetching the tea and his gold-rimmed cup and then trying to find the most precious commodity of all, the sugar. They discovered that Katherine had to be awakened, for she kept the tea in a caddy under lock and the sweetener in a closet similarly protected. At the same time other servants ran into each other trying to get a fire started with wood chips to brew the water, and the two dogs so bedeviled one black woman that she accidentally fell into the well. It was a scene, thought Rhett, "exemplifying Southern house-keeping."[37]

Meanwhile he did what he could to help his son get the *Mercury* going again. In August, Barnwell Rhett went to New York to seek capital, and his father borrowed another eight thousand dollars from the sisters, probably to help launch the paper. With the money in hand his son hired the noted Richmond journalist Francis Warrington Dawson to come to Charleston as assistant editor and then engaged his old Richmond correspondent George Bagby—"Hermes"—to cover Washington news for him. "I have not a dime to throw away," the younger Rhett warned Bagby, so Bagby must be economical in using the telegraph for especially timely news. "Our people are so poor it will take several months to reinstate the Mercury, and in the meantime it will be hard scratching." On November 19, 1866 the *Mercury* reappeared, and four days later young Rhett was already attacking the constitutionality of the Thirteenth and Fourteenth Amendments to the Constitution, arguing that there were no representatives in Congress during the war when they were passed, thus making them unlawful. The old *Mercury* was back.[38]

In the months that followed, the son echoed the advice his father had given the Alabamians. The elder Rhett played a lesser role in the paper editorially now, though he still wrote for it occasionally and found his son rather careless in his editing. However, Rhett's ideas dominated the commentary on national affairs. There was another amendment before them now, the Fourteenth, a civil rights bill that granted former slaves the right to vote while at the same time taking the vote away from Confederate leaders who had previously sworn an oath to uphold the Constitution. The *Mercury* argued that Southern representatives, now back in the Congress under Reconstruction, ought to resist. In the wake of the previous amendment's ratification by most of the former Confederate states and their acceptance of the yoke of Union rule once more, he said nothing more now about another Southern rebellion. Instead Rhett advocated something much like the old nonintercourse policy of Hammond after the Compromise of 1850, a move that would preserve their personal integrity until the rest of the Union came to its senses and restored the proper balance between state and federal sovereignty. He saw the new president, Andrew Johnson, as the helpless tool of the radical elements in his Congress, with a paralyzed judiciary and even the Senate no longer independent. Rhett was quick to spot the basic contradiction in Washington policy. Having argued all through the war that the South never left the Union, because secession was unlawful, the victorious Republicans now treated the South like a conquered province, denying it the rights previously granted to it in the Constitution. For the first time addressing former South Carolina slaves as free men, the *Mercury* urged those who could vote to stand beside white voters in resisting further attacks upon the Constitution. By the spring of 1867 the Rhetts saw themselves and the South as "standing amidst the ruins—the miseries—the sorrows which *violations of the constitution* have produced."[39]

Robert Barnwell Rhett faced some immediate ruins of his own. After one failed crop in 1866 Albert confronted the prospect of another in the spring of the next year, and Rhett had to borrow twenty-six hundred dollars to keep his son going on the plantations. Meanwhile his namesake son found receipts from the *Mercury* coming so slowly that one check to Bagby bounced, and the younger Rhett had to borrow four hundred dollars in May just to keep going because his advertisers were not paying their bills. By the fall his infrequent salary payments to Dawson led to a breach, and the assistant editor left and joined another to take over the *Charleston News,* making it into a dynamic and successful competitor and creating no small amount of bad blood between him and the Rhetts. "Our failures are often our greatest blessings; and the greatest success the greatest failure," the elder Rhett reminded his son amid the turmoil. He pointed out, as he had so often, that Jesus, too, was spurned, suggesting yet again that Christ and the Rhetts had a lot in common.[40]

Amid his misfortunes Rhett turned his imagination to new ways to get his family by, and inevitably his focus fixed on writing. Already some of the war's participants were rushing into print with memoirs and apologia. Stephens was known to be at work on an autobiography; Lee was collecting materials in hope of producing an account of his campaigns; and a diary by a former clerk in the Confederate war department was published in the North to a fair sale. With the conflict over, it seemed that a large audience yearned to learn more of it from the pens of those in the front rank, and so why not from Rhett, the man who, in his own estimation, founded the Confederacy? Of course a memoir was always in Rhett's nature. Here was an opportunity for him to have the last word and to place the best gloss on his failures and make them those of others, while taking full credit for his successes. Most of all, in his undying bitterness toward Jefferson Davis, he could use a memoir to tell the whole story of the founding and foundering of the Confederacy. Captured in May 1865, Davis was imprisoned for more than a year, which won him immense sympathy as a Southern martyr. To Rhett that had to seem an unbearable injustice, since in his view the South had really been the martyr and Davis the executioner. There were rumors that Davis, too, intended penning a memoir after his release in May 1867 pending a trial (which never came). Who knew what lies and villainies he would tell in such a book? "When despotism, (which is by its nature false) endeavors to establish its power," Rhett believed, "it seldom regards history or truth." The answer to Davis was for Rhett to combine history and truth in a memoir of his own. "The Confederate States, after a struggle of four years, yielded, more from the weakness of their own Government, than from the strength of that of the North," he maintained. This would be his chance to prove his case.[41]

The idea had been with him, in fact, at least since the spring of 1866 if not earlier, and he had actually started writing while living in Aiken, although he soon had to stop for lack of reference books. Once in Charleston he would be able to find what he needed, he hoped, and renew the work. Meanwhile, when he read a new book purporting to be a physician's account of Davis's life in prison, Rhett found some of the statements attributed to Davis to be outrageous. In fact, Charles Halpine ghostwrote the book, and much of it was pure fiction. Although Rhett knew or soon would know of Halpine's authorship, he found it easy to believe that Davis would have said some of the things attributed to him. Not surprisingly, Rhett wanted most immediately to establish how Davis became president in Montgomery and how his cabinet members were chosen, and he began corresponding with some of the fellow delegates who met with Rhett there.[42] Seized by the old enthusiasm that always accompanied his writing, he began collecting what could be found of his own papers once in Charleston and acquired a few reference books. In April 1867 he wrote an affectionate letter to his old friend Buchanan and in passing commented, "I will certainly never enter the triumphant North." Yet three weeks later he was on his way to New York and Washington. What survived of the Confederate archives had been taken to the capital, and Rhett hoped to gain access to them for further material in constructing his case against Davis while at the same time calling on prominent men to seek further support for the *Mercury.* A dual mission such as this, to preserve the truth of the past while ensuring that his son could keep the truth before the eyes of the present, was a fit quest for an old warrior such as Rhett. "I have determined to get to work in earnest as soon as possible, to perform the great task I propose to accomplish before I die," he wrote Katherine the day after he arrived in New York. "If I fail, it will be like all else I have attempted as regards this world; yet it may please God to give me the strength and means to accomplish it." He would need her help, and in either event, succeed or fail, he admonished her in words that echoed his old motto about persistence, which had become almost a synonym for his life itself: "Let us go on striving."[43]

TWENTY-SIX

To Humble My Pride

1867–1876

IT WAS A DISAPPOINTING TRIP, which perhaps Rhett should have expected from any foray of his into Yankee land. The steamer passage proved rough, and he suffered from seasickness and cold, during which he fell into a long reflection on his future prospects and began to plan the shape of his memoir. But when he reached New York he discovered he had forgotten his overcoat and toothbrush, and then he was shocked when he found he would have to pay thirty-five dollars a week at the New York Hotel. Rhett soon moved to a more modest room east of Broadway, where he could look out his window and see the local women sitting on their window ledges or doorsteps, and he concluded that "it is clear that they are open to intrigue." He called on prominent Democrats, including future presidential hopeful Samuel J. Tilden, seeking their aid in strengthening the *Mercury* as an organ of opposition to the Republicans in the South, but nothing seems to have come of the effort. After nearly a month in the city he had had enough.[1]

"I am disgusted beyond expression at the wretched business I have been engaged in," he complained. Everyone seemed to regard the South as a primitive bog that would swallow any capital investment without trace, and there was no credit to be found. "To think of the men before whom I have appeared—so mean—so ungracious—so heartless—is most humiliating," he wrote Katherine in June. "I have done all that my wit and energy could suggest to stave off the ruin which presses on us." Yet his every effort failed. "Perhaps for this reason, God sent me here, to humble my pride," he thought in a rare moment of clear introspection brought on by his dejection. "Yet I will try on." At the end of his stay, with nothing to show for it, he returned by rail, stopping in Washington to see his onetime friend Secretary of State William Seward and to pay a social call on Andrew Johnson, who he then thought an honest, if inept and weak, president. Any hopes of getting into the Confederate archives were defeated, however, for the War Department was not yet ready to allow former Confederates to delve into records.[2]

Matters did not improve when he returned home. His son sent an agent north to canvass for advertising, without success, and to keep the paper going Rhett borrowed another twenty-six hundred dollars, pledging the Oaks and Drainfield as surety. Meanwhile an old eight-hundred-dollar judgment for debt against the plantations reappeared from 1860. They were getting themselves deeper and deeper into debt. Albert had suffered two failed crops in a row, and the *Mercury* simply was not paying its way, in large part because the younger Rhett persisted in trying to make it what it had been when it was failing in the 1850s, an advocacy journal. While other papers in the South, including Dawson's *News,* flourished giving the public what it wanted, the *Mercury* insisted on publishing what he thought they ought to have, a distinction Barnwell Rhett Jr. was never willing to make.[3]

It was a bleak spring. For months they had no meat, coffee, rice, or potatoes. One day in January their dinner was nothing but a pint of gruel and some corn pone that was originally intended for Herbert's pet pigeons. Without that, said Rhett, "we would have gone supperless to bed, having litterally nothing to eat." Mostly they subsisted on last year's rice and dried corn. The lack of nourishment told on Katherine, while Rhett, all of his life accustomed to meat twice a day, sometimes had to go without for weeks at a time. Thanks to Alfred's fair corn crop, that summer things improved to the point that they could put a small dish of meat on the table and afford enough fresh vegetables to keep themselves healthy at least. Hardship and sad reflection on his lifetime of failure made Rhett draw within himself, apologizing to his wife for "what a solitary creature I am." When an outbreak of yellow fever threatened Charleston shortly before his trip to New York, he had sent her away to the country for a time, and he missed her during her absence. Barny, too, had gone away for his health, leaving the running of the debt-ridden *Mercury* to his father. Rhett could take almost no exercise, finding anything an effort. Moreover, he recoiled from going into town, especially Charleston. "It adds to my sadness to meet those I know," he told his sister Claudia. Seeing their own poverty depressed him, while he feared the look of pity he found in their eyes as they saw him. Then there were other looks. "I know that I am thoroughly hated and feared," he wrote his wife, and he resolved to try to ignore the inevitable slights. He said, "I labour at all times under a sense of deep depression," which was enhanced by his inability to be active. "Every day, I am more sensible of my sad imperfections." The death of his brother Benjamin and his sister Mariana the year before, and then in February 1867 of his sister Emma only added to his mood. He was tired of outliving his siblings and his children, and of the former now only he and Claudia, always the closest to him, were left. "How little would we have anticipated, that we would have survived so many of our Brothers and sisters," he mused to her, "yet here we are, by Gods will, old and struggling with the most tremendous difficulties, which ever bent the People of a ruined country." As usual he blamed his difficulties on unforeseen events. "No man could have anticipated them," he complained. "They are of God. My wisdom, my strength, is turned to nought, by his sovereign will, and dispensation." He often went to bed as early as possible, just to bring an end to the day, wondering how he had offended his god and saying to himself as did David in the Old Testament, "why art thou disquieted with me?" When he thought of joining Katherine and Herbert in the country during their absence, he was so dejected that he believed he would not be welcome.[4]

Almost his only pleasure now was his son Herbert. Unable to afford Beaufort College, of course, Rhett tutored the boy himself, arising at dawn to give him his Latin lessons before breakfast and then continuing with grammar after the meal. He boasted proudly of the boy, as well as of his other grown children and now the grandchildren that a few had produced. "I am like a small shop-man, who opens his shop to the sun," he said, "and hangs out his brightest goods to allure the admiration of customers." That done, he sat down to write an editorial for the *Mercury* perhaps, until Kate brought him a meager lunch of bread and tea. He might go back to the editorial after eating, working on it until time for dinner, and then perhaps spend a little while reading. Compared to the activity of earlier years, most of it seemed almost pointless. "Anything more than duty I cannot do," he complained, but he took pride in the *Mercury* all the same. Even though it was failing he thought it among the most vigorously and thoughtfully edited papers in the nation.[5]

By early 1868 the *Mercury* was speaking in its old voice despite all advice that some restraint might produce more readers and advertisers. When Washington began to impose military reconstruction, the Rhetts, surely father and son both, responded in its columns. "They deliberately trample on four years of lies, running through huge volumes of laws," and had now installed "an unscrupulous and bloody despotism," they accused the Yankees. Of course the dividing of the former Confederacy into four military districts and putting them under the command of generals and occupation forces was unconstitutional, and merely an attempt to intimidate the Southern states into going along with the continued mutilation of the Constitution with the Fourteenth and Fifteenth Amendments. Shifting from passive nonparticipation, they declared now that Southerners must resist. When Alabama voted down a new state constitution proscribing former Confederates from holding office and swaying power to the newly enfranchised blacks and their white Republican allies, the *Mercury* crowed and at the same time repeatedly condemned a similar "negro convention" meeting in Charleston, even though their own family warned that it would do no good. White boycotts of the delegate elections virtually handed the convention to their foes, and despite the considerable reforms contained in the constitution they produced, the old oligarchy such as the Rhetts could see in it only disintegration and tyranny of the mob. Their attacks took on such a tone that Rhett's nephew A. R. Stuart warned that the editors' personalities would likely get them "a drubbing at the hands of one of the black members," and one *Mercury* reporter was assaulted at the convention amid angry threats to storm the newspaper's office.[6]

No mob needed to destroy the *Mercury,* for the Rhetts could not make the paper pay its way. By the spring of 1868 the *Mercury's* position had become critical, and the younger Rhett went to New York for one more attempt to find capital. "If he fails, the Paper stops," Rhett told his old friend Burt. Barnwell Rhett Jr. tried every avenue, but when potential financiers looked to the credit analyst R. G. Dun, the word on the Rhetts and the *Mercury* put them off. They had no means of their own; the paper was doing marginal business, but only because the elder Rhett bore and always had borne the brunt of its indebtedness, and now his own plantations were no longer his without encumbrance. Such a report could only close doors, and Barnwell Rhett Jr. came home empty-handed.[7]

The strain told on all the family. Somehow Dawson of the *News* fell afoul of Alfred Rhett and found himself challenged to a duel. However, he responded, with an irony that should not have been lost on the Rhetts, that he could not accept it because "being a member of the Catholic Church, I cannot, under any circumstances, engage in a duel." It was, of course, the same explanation given by Rhett himself years before.[8] Then came another crop failure, which only added to the problem. For some time now the Rhetts had been missing the payments due to the New York sisters and their other creditors, and Rhett had to admit to his sister Claudia now that there was no prospect of him ever paying the debt he owed her unless he could make something from his memoir. Even that, however, moved with agonizing slowness. It all proved so debilitating that Rhett sank further into despondence. "I feel so dead to the external world," he told his sister, "that it is with difficulty I can force myself out of the house."[9]

Then his precarious health took a turn for the worse. In March and April he suffered three attacks of erysipelas on his face, right beside his afflicted nose. Iodine seemed to arrest the problem, but a doctor warned him that if the fever and inflammation spread to his eyes or into his nose, they could do nothing for it, and now he was treating the problem with muriatic acid. He suspected his poor diet to be the cause, especially the lack of meat.[10] The cumulative effect of all his financial and health troubles was to make Rhett so nervous, irritable, and despondent that he believed he had become "a weight, instead of a help, a source of anxiety, instead of a source of comfort," to Katherine. She became irritable and impatient with him. Despite his sixty-seven years, his ill health, and the emotional burdens of failure and near penury, the powerful sex drive that fathered fifteen children and helped to kill his first wife remained strong, but now she turned away from him in their bedroom. He decided that the best thing for him to do was pay a long visit to one of the health resorts in the North Carolina mountains, remembering the time he spent at Flat Rock in 1864. He desperately needed to get away from the sources of his frustrations and all the reminders of the past.[11]

Rhett left early in July, convinced that his departure was a relief to Katherine as well. He first went to a resort in South Carolina, intending only to remain for a couple of weeks before returning to Charleston to face the inevitable problem of continuing the *Mercury* and also the need to rent a house in the city.[12] His nose seemed to improve on the brief hiatus, but after only a few days in Charleston it took a turn for the worse once more, and he left almost immediately for Greenville, where his old friend Benjamin Perry had told him of a local physician who might be able to help. Rhett went to see the doctor and submitted to a minor operation, but afterward he visited with Perry and actually laughed at the surgeon's rude practice, finding him ignorant, illiterate, and suspecting he was not a real doctor at all. Still the clumsy operation seemed to help for a time, and certainly the laughter with an old friend made even better medicine.[13]

Rhett decided to go on to Flat Rock to stay at least a month to enjoy the healthy air, try to regain his strength by walking on the hillsides, and perhaps work on his memoir. He made a brief stop in Columbia but avoided old political colleagues, and he then rode on to Flat Rock, accompanied for the journey by George A. Trenholm and his first wife's brother William DeSaussure. Told that he looked "much wilted" by those who had not seen him since the war, he could hardly disagree. "My own ill condition is a sad mortification to me," he told Katherine. "We are all of us very tired." Unfortunately the trip to Flat Rock proved exhausting and hot, and during much of it he was exposed to the sun, which only inflamed his face anew and made it worse than before. Still he slept a lot and was able to start taking brief walks twice a day, and soon he felt somewhat better, though it would be some time before his spirits lifted. "The load upon my breast is stern," he complained. "Will it ever be lifted again, but by the hand of death?"[14]

The month at Flat Rock brought back much of his old spirit, though in fact his physical health got worse for a time as he suffered from an attack of rheumatism, and at the end of his stay he was so unwell that he had to remain longer until he was well enough to travel. Yet the mornings sitting at his window watching the mist rising over the Blue Ridge Mountains were spiritually rejuvenating, and the absence from Katherine made him reflect on his love for her. "You have been the companion of my days of adversity; and cheerfully and bravely have you done your duty," he wrote to her. "You have stood by me with unflinching fidelity." In expressing from afar his gratitude for the years she had given him, he could even tease her as he had in their courting days many years before when she complained that he did not express his feelings for her often enough. "You can make the *nicest* little allusions, and they seem to mean nothing," he bantered in his letters. "Your gentle fancy, *toys* with its object; and makes it *aspire* to your love. How many times must I *repeat* Oh Dear! To *satisfy* you?" He could even tease about her denying him in bed, asking what she thought of a woman who "hushes off her husband" in the night, having "passed beyond the hey-day of joyous amenities" and preferring to melt "her reciprocities of love, into the enjoyment of tending chickens and sound sleep." Protesting pleasantly an end to such "foolish language," he teasingly threatened that "I may not write to you any more."[15]

He was able, too, to take renewed interest in national politics. His editor son was chosen at the state Democratic convention in the spring as a delegate to the national convention in New York, though a brief confusion led to a rumor that it was to be the father who was coming instead, raising anew the old fears of agitation and disruption until the *Mercury* published a correction. What Rhett thought of the presidential nominee, Horatio Seymour, he kept to himself, though Rhett would not likely have approved of a New Yorker who had been much favored in 1860 by the cooperationist and reconstructionist factions. Still he hoped for a victory in the fall. If the Republicans won, he expected nothing but rule "by negro courts and juries," and that was important to him just then for it looked increasingly as though the default on the New York loans could lead him into a foreclosure court on his plantations. Not surprisingly, he and the *Mercury* railed against "carpet-baggers and negroites" ruling the South, and they warned that if they tried to use their military force to impose domination, they risked awakening once more the slumbering Southern spirit of resistance. The United States was intended to be a white man's government, he declared, deploring those who favored providing education and property to black men to qualify them to vote, for he accused them of doing it only to conciliate the Radical Republicans. Some in the South believed that they could manipulate qualified black suffrage in the South to cast off the Reconstruction yoke, but Rhett argued that the Radicals would reject that and wanted only complete black suffrage that they could themselves manipulate to perpetuate their own power. A remainder of his old bravado even emerged during the campaign when someone published the old story that in 1861 he had boasted about drinking all the blood spilled in the war and now he had to deny it, though admitting that his friend Burt had made such an injudicious boast.[16]

Finally late in October, unable to pay for printing or paper, let alone to meet past debts, the Rhetts stopped the *Mercury*, intending it only as a temporary measure while they once again sought financing. Barny still hoped to keep it going and once again went looking for financing. His father had had enough, however, and decided to leave Charleston for the Ashepoo. "My labours for the paper cease with my going into the country," he told his son before leaving for Flat Rock. "Indeed I do not intend to read a paper," he said, wanting to cut himself off entirely from the bad news of the world. But he was also removing himself from the growing discord between Barny and Edmund, for he could never bear to see his sons quarrel. Edmund had begun working as an editor on the *Mercury* again but soon bristled at the idea that his older brother might have editorial veto over what he wrote. It was all right so far as public and political questions were concerned. "I don't care enough about any public question to make it a matter of difference between us," Edmund complained to his father. However, once the *Mercury*'s line of policy was laid out, he insisted that he be allowed to publish what he pleased without being edited by his older brother. "I cannot conform my taste to his," he declared. "He is a religious man, and not a man of the world." Edmund went on, "I write for men, by and large, as I see them and know them—not troubled over much with either religion or propriety." In short, he said that Barny did not know enough to edit his work. The older brother objected that Edmund's writing was too sensational, which all Charleston should have known after the Taber episode, but the message did not register with Edmund Rhett. "I object to his taking up my articles, for which I alone am responsible, and striking out this, as irreligious, that, blasphemous, a third, as harsh, a fourth, as improper &c," he insisted. Robert Jr. was too "proper" to run a successful newspaper, he argued, for to pay its way a sheet had to be "sharp, aggressive, and pungent." Edmund wanted the paper to be profitable, and he said, "it is impossible to publish the views of the Charleston Mercury without giving ground for offense to somebody."[17]

In the end there was no money to be found, and the next month Rhett told his son Robert, "I fear you have failed entirely." The true men in the South wanted the paper to continue, he argued; they wanted "the truth spoken," meaning the Rhetts' truth. But the Rhetts could no longer deny the sheet's financial collapse. They published a special broadside as "A Farewell to the Subscribers of the Charleston Mercury." Though the son signed the statement, in fact his father wrote it for him, and it echoed all of the elder Rhett's ideas and spirit.[18]

The South lived now under a despotism of consolidation, the states and their sovereignty absorbed by Washington. With universal male suffrage it would only get worse. "Swelling the multitudes of voters" would not make liberty but be its downfall, while the military Reconstruction now in place attempting "to put the half savage negro over the civilized Caucassian, may not be forgotten or forgiven." History would remember it as an act of abject hatred and bigotry. The South, a more tolerant and congenial region, did not like change and revered the past, while the North, "fond of novelties, misnamed progress," was the slave of its own dogmatism. The South had lost thanks to the ineptitude of her political leaders—he did not have to charge Davis by name—and now the foolish North thought that by freeing and enfranchising almost two million black males they could keep the South subservient. Forgetting that his own revered ancestor William Rhett briefly dealt in the importation of slaves, Rhett repeated the happy myth that Yankee avarice was responsible for foisting slaves on the South in the first place.

"There is no ground for forgetfulness—no possibility of forgiveness, with these black, moving memorials of our wrongs, polluting our sight, crossing us in all the walks of life, and vaunting their consequence as the tools of our tyrants," the newspaper's "Farewell" concluded as it condemned "a despotism of vagrant white men, and ignorant, filthy negroes." Even Kentucky now was feeling the heel of Reconstruction, her sympathy with the other Southern states greater than ever before, and a spirit of resistance was growing throughout the old Confederacy, refueling "the hatred and regional unity that will one day regain Southern freedom and power in national counsels." The Union was destined to fall apart from its own corruption one day, and then "the people of the Southern States will yet be a great and free people." Only now the *Mercury* would not be there to see that ultimate triumph when it came. In a cruel final irony, the Rhetts had to have their "Farewell" printed on the press of their old rival the *Courier*.[19]

Scarcely did they lay the *Mercury* to rest, with all the memories that entailed, when Rhett's nose disease flared again even worse than before. He believed that malnutrition as a result of his poverty contributed to the flare-up and had been treating it himself by applying poultices made of a stinking weed. By January 1869 the disease on his face was such that he expected that, unchecked, it would make him unfit to be seen within the year. Worse, the pain and effect on his eyesight would make it impossible for him to do anything productive for his support. "I am under the impression that as soon as I can do nothing I will die," he told Barny. "Indeed I hope to die." But his daughter Sallie Roman, living in Louisiana with her husband Colonel Roman, suggested that her father see a specialist in New Orleans, and propitiously his son Barnwell had seventy dollars that he could spare at the same time that Rhett received another seventy dollars for an article he wrote for a monthly publication. Thus funded, he went to New Orleans early in 1869 for the treatment, which once again consisted of simply burning out the apparently cancerous growth. There was talk of fitting what Rhett called "an ornamental addition" to his nose, but a decision was made to wait a year and have him return to see if the cancer was arrested. Until then, Rhett wrote Katherine, "you can enjoy my deformity." Meanwhile his son-in-law made a fruitless attempt to find a backer in New Orleans to support the writing of Rhett's memoir.[20]

If Roman had gotten him any money, it would have been sucked away by his debt, for when Rhett returned to South Carolina he found yet another crop failed on the plantations and the creditors out of patience. Alfred was at his wit's end, clearly a failure as a planter, and his father had neither the strength nor the temperament to try to manage the Oaks and Drainfield himself. Indeed, Rhett had finally to admit to himself that his debts were so great that he could no longer hold on to the plantations. "My father is insolvent to a dollar," his son Edmund admitted. "Even his table silver is held by parties who have loaned him money to live on." In July, after some discussion involving sparing Albert's feelings at being shunted aside, Edmund came up with a scheme—perhaps influenced by his father since he was living with him at the Oaks—whereby Edmund wanted the creditors to foreclose immediately, and then he would buy the plantations himself. That way he could keep the two plantations together, and also he and his father wanted to continue to employ their former slaves who had "grown up with us." His father was amenable, and the creditors agreed.[21]

But then other ghosts of past financial infelicity returned to thwart the plan. Just a few days after Edmund worked out his arrangement, another creditor filed suit for recovery of some $3,800 that Rhett owed. It came as a shock, the more so because he was not even informed in the customary manner. Worse, though the amount was relatively small, he had used the plantations as security, which meant that this debt could force foreclosure before Edmund's scheme could be consummated, thus leaving the creditors in New York unsatisfied and Rhett still heavily in debt to them. Now Rhett desperately wanted the New Yorkers to foreclose first, and they filed their suit soon thereafter, leaving Rhett facing combined debts of $22,707.78. By December it looked as if Edmund's idea would work out after all, for the New York creditors got their claim in first, and on December 31, 1869 it was ordered that the Oaks and Drainfield be sold at public auction. On January 25, 1870, they went on the block and passed into the hands of Hamilton Shields, acting for his sisters in New York. Thanks to the arrangement with Edmund, however, the Rhett family was allowed to remain at the Oaks and continue planting while Edmund and Shields worked out the details of their transaction. It was close, and humiliating to be beholden to a Yankee, but at least Rhett's family still had a home.[22]

By the time of the foreclosure Rhett was back in New Orleans with the Romans, having his nose examined again and submitting to another operation to remove even more tissue. At first he opposed the proposal of taking healthy flesh from his forehead and applying it to his nose. "I have no intention of being further tortured for the sake of looks," he told Katherine, but the operation also promised at least partial relief from the almost constant pain in his face that now was so bad he could not concentrate to work on his memoir. Thus he underwent the burning and the knife yet again, for if things continued as they had been for another six months, he doubted that he would ever be able to support his family at all. In mingled pride and dejection he declared, "I will die first before I will be a burden on others." There had been talk of Katherine and Herbert coming to Louisiana to be with him, but since he could find no employment to afford to hire a house, she had to remain in South Carolina. He warned her cheerlessly that if the doctor's efforts failed, "I will return to you, to linger a wretched burden on your charity." He took a rented room instead and struggled by writing little articles and reviews to make enough to keep himself and send something back to the Oaks. It was frustrating work, not least because generally he valued the worth of his writing much higher than did editors, whom he regarded as "generally rascals, flourishing on the brains of poor men." He had entirely forgotten how little he and his son paid the *Mercury*'s contributors. "I am a student, and shut out every-body," he warned Robert Jr., even Katherine when later she came for a visit. Even then he was uncertain if he could even meet his rent for more than a few months, yet somehow he managed to keep her and Elise with him for a time and even to send a little money to his son Herbert, enjoining the boy to use it to have some fun. Before long Elise would become his closest companion, a reminder of the first wife who was always his first love, and an important helpmate in the work on his writing. She copied all of his hieroglyphic scrawl into fair copies of his articles, while he enlisted his son Barny to submit his work to publishers.[23]

As before, the operation seemed to bring some relief, and by the summer of 1871 Rhett could return to Katherine. Now he was trying to treat himself as well, having found a cancer "cure" in a newspaper that involved applying zinc chloride to burn out the tissue covering the cancer, which then supposedly allowed the tumor simply to fall out. It was a quack remedy, to be sure, but in desperation he was ready to try anything and even used carbolic acid.[24] Whatever he tried, at least it gave him enough relief to get about the house and to do some writing. His son Herbert was away at an inexpensive boarding school, and Rhett now corresponded with him regularly on the course of his studies. "You can say nothing to me so interesting as what you *achieve* in the way of performing your duty and acquiring knowledge," Rhett told him. He regularly corrected spelling errors in his son's letters and tried to get books to send him. "Whatever you learn, try to learn *thoroughly*," he implored. Rhett had hopes of sending Herbert to the Virginia Military Institute, the school where the great Stonewall Jackson had taught before the war. It was a fine school trying to rebuild itself after 1865 and a fitting place for a new generation of Rhetts to start rebuilding the family fortunes. Meanwhile the doting father cared for his son's pet pigeons and chickens, even feeding one old cock by hand because he was too slow to compete with the others. "The Old Fellow reminds me of myself," he told Herbert, "both of us much battered by the wear of life, and rather helpless."[25]

They ate a little better than before, especially that summer when Alfred killed a fat bear and Katherine traded some of the meat for fresh vegetables. Better fed, Rhett was more productive in his writing. He submitted articles on politics and "Free Government," as he called it, to *Blackwood's Magazine* and to the *Southern Quarterly Review,* intending them to be chapters in his later book. His daughter Elise was still unmarried and at home, and she took his abominable scrawl and copied it neatly for submission. When he sold something, he anxiously sent money to Herbert for him to have some of the fun that boys ought to have, despite complaints from Katherine that the boy was already "too prompt in spending money." For Rhett, no money was so well spent as that which pleased his children.[26]

And there was no greater shock than losing one of them. Already he had outlived five: his son Robert Woodward, the infant Caroline, Ann Barnwell, Ann Elizabeth, and Katherine. On July 29, 1871, the consumption that had been slowly killing Edmund finally completed the job. His father watched his decline for days, helpless, and now it was a double tragedy, for Edmund had been unable to complete his scheme of buying the two plantations before his death. On February 11, Shields sued again for foreclosure, though he continued to allow the Rhetts to live at the Oaks. However, in turn Shields could not meet the taxes for 1870 and 1871, and as a result, in June 1872 the plantations went to sheriff's sale again. This time the new buyer took over the property, evicting the Rhetts from their home of decades and in the process finally severing them forever from the blacks who had remained so loyal over the years. For all of the financial commitments he was never able to honor, at least Rhett had kept that ancient promise to Colonel Stapleton to treat them, at least those he had not had to sell, with charity and humanity, and to all outward appearances they returned his love— albeit condescending—with an affection of their own.[27]

"The Southern people were badly broken by the results of the sectional war and its gross mismanagement by the man put at the head," Barnwell Rhett Jr. would explain to his daughter in years to come. "Few families were worse used up than my father's." In the fall of 1871, with the suits for debt threatening, Rhett transferred to Katherine ownership of "all that remained to me, from the war," including all their parlor and bedroom furniture, tables and chairs, bookcases and even his books, china, cutlery, the little remaining silver, carpets, and even bed and table linens. It was all in redemption of some two thousand out of sixteen thousand dollars that he owed her, probably from an inheritance of her own that she had loaned him for the plantations or the *Mercury*, but of course the real reason for the transfer of ownership was to protect their remaining possessions from seizure for his debts, for which she was not liable.[28]

For the first time in his life as one of the most noted South Carolinians of his time, and after two and one-half centuries of his family's intimate involvement in its affairs, Robert Barnwell Rhett owned nothing at all in the state he loved. Then came worse. On June 30, 1872 he lost a seventh child, as his daughter Mary Burnet died at aged thirty-six. She had been a concern to him for several years, ever since he discovered in January 1868—in spite of her brothers' efforts to hide it from him—that she had become an alcoholic since the death of her husband John Vanderhorst during the war. He had ordered her brought to live with him, vowing that "she shall live or die temperate," and apparently with her father's help she had recovered and married John Lewis in August 1869, only to succumb now. Rhett loathed her father-in-law John W. Lewis Sr., who repeatedly snubbed him publicly and had beaten Edmund to a favorable plantation lease shortly before, but he entertained the kindliest feelings for the younger Lewis. Mary's husband carried her to church on her last day so she could take communion before her death.[29] The final blow came on August 8. Rhett and Katherine had just moved to a large rented house, with only two black serving girls left, Herbert away at school, and their remaining daughters Elise and Claudia grown adults on their own. Heavy rains all the previous night softened the ground under a defective foundation, and around 10 A.M. that morning the house simply collapsed on the Rhetts and the servants. Though covered by the ruins, they emerged uninjured, despite the fact that the accident was powerful enough to be heard more than a mile away.[30]

If they needed any remaining calamity to convince them that it was time to leave, surely here it was. It was all finally more than Rhett could bear. There had been too much death in South Carolina, too much debt and disappointment, too many great dreams blasted, and a whole way of life gone with the war. His eyes were failing him, and rheumatism kept him from taking even light exercise.

There was nothing to remain for now. His son Barnwell Rhett had taken a job with the *New Orleans Picayune,* and of course the Romans lived on a plantation in St. James Parish, not far from the city. There was the one place where his children were doing well, and the only recourse for himself and Katherine now. Though it may have galled his old Francophobia a bit to have to depend on the French-speaking Roman and to live in the midst of the still predominantly French culture of south Louisiana, he had no choice, and that fall Barnwell Rhett left South Carolina, destined to return only once more.[31]

Being away from South Carolina, no longer having to worry about the *Mercury,* and being now close to his son Barnwell again and to Roman, who was helping Beauregard collect material for a memoir, Rhett was able to devote more time to his own autobiography and to call on the two of them for assistance with sources. Over the years he had gathered a few things, mostly copies of some of his more memorable speeches. He had a copy of Halpine's ghostwritten account of Davis in prison, and he could use that to charge Davis with saying demonstrable falsehoods, even though Halpine had told the younger Rhett several years before that it was not at all a genuine memoir, which the father must have known, and therefore was not to be relied on for Davis's sentiments. Since Davis had not come out publicly and discountenanced what the book had him saying, then as far as Rhett was concerned that meant that Davis stood by it, just as the president's failure to proclaim loudly that he had not led the forces in battle at Manassas meant to Rhett that Davis really wanted to take credit for doing so.[32] He also had access to his son's run of the *Mercury* for the war years. Other memoirs were appearing now, including Alexander Stephens's in 1870, with more coming all the time, and of course he had direct access to Beauregard. He corresponded with William Porcher Miles back in Charleston, asking him to get the published laws of the Confederacy, and copies of other books that Rhett lost when the Yankees looted the Oaks in 1865. Joseph E. Johnston let him have a look at the manuscript of his own forthcoming narrative, and Rhett returned the favor by sharing some of his recollections and papers with the general. Early in January 1869 he put his son Barny to work gathering a number of works: Horace Greeley's *American Conflict,* the Richmond editor E. A. Pollard's anti-Davis *Lost Cause,* Stephens's *Constitutional View of the War between the States,* and even several works by Northerners on the war. He also tried to find published statements made by Lincoln back in the 1840s supporting the right of revolution, in order to convict the late president of hypocrisy out of his own mouth for denying the South the right to seek its independence.[33]

But it all went so slowly. On April 18, 1870 he began writing on one of the issues that divided North and South before the war and came upon an immediate roadblock. "I find myself stumped at the very threshold of the investigation," he complained to his oldest son. Not surprisingly, he already knew the conclusion he would come to in the matter but actually confessed, "I cannot move a step in treating the matter without a knowledge of the facts accompanying it." In short, as so often before, his conclusion predated his investigation. He pleaded with his son to send him more books. "How am I, in this wilderness, to obtain a knowledge of the facts, this question requires to be completely exposed?" he complained. He had to have at least the published statutes and reports of Davis's administration. "How can the details and conduct of the Confederate Government be described and considered with not one of these sources of information in my possession?" he grumbled. Barny did at least get him the statutes at large enacted in Montgomery and Richmond, but that was not enough.

"I am writing something," Rhett complained, "but it must be uncertain and unsatisfactory without authority before me." The fact that he hit such an abrupt stumbling block so early disheartened him temporarily. "In despondency and disgust I throw down my pen," he declared. It would be impossible "to write a history, which will be worth any thing." Edward Gibbon took twenty years to write his history of the decline of the Roman Empire, and he had a great library near at hand. "With no library, and no money to buy one, how can any man write a history worth reading?" he pleaded. Then the old determination reasserted itself, and he added a postscript urging Barny to send him everything on the subject he could find, and as well to a.k friends for contributions of a few hundred dollars to buy the books necessary. He had a great work, a great duty, to perform; of that he was certain. "As matters have gone on, and are going on with me, when I am gone, the niggards and fools will wake up to a sense of the loss they have encountered, by not supplying the cheap means ($200 would give them) in the way of Books, by which their country and themselves might be vindicated to their posterity," he declared in disgust. "Instead of Free men upholding the greatest cause the last five centuries has produced, they may go down to future ages, as mean & paltry Rebels, against the meanest and most depraved People on Earth."

In short, only Barnwell Rhett could properly tell the Confederate story, and former Confederates owed it to him and themselves to fund his efforts. Having conceived the "History" as a means of staving off penury, he now saw it as a sacred calling. "As to myself, I have done my part, with all my might and means; and what future generations may think of me, if indeed I am worthy of any thought, is to me of not the slightest consideration," he self-righteously mused. "I was not regarded in life, when I tried to save them; and in death, let them if they please, forget or slander me," he went on. "I will be where neither malignity nor folly can reach me." The South failed to listen to him in 1861 and after and the Confederacy failed, which to Rhett was a simple proof of cause and effect. He could still save them in history, however, if the world would listen now. He was not giving up yet.[34]

Rhett was hampered by his health and the need to write other things when he could in order to bring in a little money. He did a few editorials for his son at the *Picayune* and produced a few longer essays and reviews. When Martin Van Buren's posthumous *Inquiry into the Origin and Course of the Political Parties in the United States* appeared, Rhett spent some time on a lengthy review that took the former president to task for all his failings, making no mention of how ardently Rhett at least professed to support him during his incumbency. Now Rhett charged that Van Buren had been ignorant, unable to see what was happening in the Union around him, and that he had helped set in motion the destruction of the Democratic Party that, in turn, led to the Republican victory in 1860, the Civil War, and now the despotism of the Fourteenth and Fifteenth Amendments. Van Buren had helped put the country in the hands of the dreaded "money power" of the North, and only the overthrow of it and its foul corruption would ever bring the return of free government. Universal suffrage and representation, instead of checking the evil, contributed to it by allowing absolute majority rule. He never stopped arguing the old Calhoun thesis of concurrent majorities.[35]

As he watched the swirl of political and social events in the North, Rhett also found inspiration to pen an essay on "Northern Civilization in the United States," this time attacking the atheism and immorality he saw as integral parts of Yankee society. He saw them especially fueled by the 1872 sexual scandal involving the Reverend Henry Ward Beecher, which only further reinforced his belief that the peoples of the two sections were fundamentally different and that their old foes were by nature debauched and immoral, in large part caused by the immigrant population from the poor and ignorant countries of Europe, the corrupting influence of greed and avarice that he saw everywhere in the North, and again universal suffrage.[36] That this all came out in an election year, 1872, was no surprise to him, for Yankee politics was itself corrupt and immoral. He wrote a number of editorials on the Democratic presidential candidate, the New York editor Horace Greeley. Though certainly Rhett favored him over the Republican Ulysses Grant seeking a second term, Rhett held out little hope for the Democratic Party, even though Northern Democrats such as Greeley and Tilden were now protesting Reconstruction too. It was too late. Being Yankees, they were weak and easily led, and duplicitous by nature. "The Northern People are so corrupt, so ignorant, and so indifferent to political liberty, that no appeals to lift from themselves or from us the burden and degradation of such a Government, can be effectual," he declared.

Grant won the election, of course, which convinced Rhett more than ever that "the blessings of Free Government can only be obtained by the Southern People ruling themselves." All of the governmental offices in the South were filled with corrupt Republican partisans, he believed, and he even suspected that his own mail was tampered with by dishonest Yankee postal employees. He wanted to see in the region a Southern party condemning the old Constitution, with its now perverting amendments proscribing former Confederates from holding office and giving the vote to the blacks, and instead organizing Southern power for a day of deliverance. They should stop submitting voluntarily to Reconstruction laws. He wanted them to eschew all party affiliations with Yankees, but then he changed his mind to suggest the more practical approach of cooperating with the "least hostile," meaning the conservative Democrats, rather as Irish members who sat in the British Parliament, while pursuing Irish independence, still voted with the Whigs because they were friendlier. "The Southern States must seek *now,* and seek *forever,* a separate Federal Independence." The Southern people would not be inactive, he hoped. "Whether sitting around their hearths; or worshipping in the Temples of God; or standing over the graves of our Confederate dead—they will ever remember that they died for them; and spurn from them, as an imputation of the foulest dishonour, the mere suggestion that they can ever abandon their great cause—the cause of Free Government for which their glorious dead suffered and died." The South would rise again, not just to achieve its own independence but to save free government and political liberty for the world. They had but to will it to see it accomplished. For this reason among others he would never be one of the thousands taking an oath of allegiance and seeking the return of his full civil liberties.[37]

Rhett went first to Louisiana, and Katherine followed him a few months later in February 1873. They initially lived with his son in New Orleans so that Rhett could be close to the physicians who continued to labor over his face.[38] "I have become a hideous old man, with my nose gone and my mouth twisted," he lamented to his granddaughter Josephine, who was back in South Carolina. "I am really not fit to see anyone." In May 1873 the doctor held out some hope of recovery, and the Rhetts moved out to Roman's plantation, Cabanocey, but in July he had to submit to another operation. "The Doctor had to burn down in my head," he told Josephine; "my nose is all gone excepting a little piece of the left nostril." The pain of the operations and recovery was so acute that it left his nervous system all but shattered. He could do nothing, concentrate on little, and scarcely even carry on a correspondence, much less finish the memoir.

His eyesight was failing him too, and as he sadly confessed, "withall, there is the inertia of 73 years weighing on a diseased body."

The greatest sadness to such an affectionate man was that he was so far from his grandchildren, and yet he told them, "you ought not to desire to see me." He doubted now that they would recognize him if they met by accident in the street. "My face is so marred that I cannot even seek the innocent enjoyment of my Grand children here," he complained. He no longer had the energy to play with them as of old, and it hurt him to see the way they recoiled at his face. "They are shy of such deformity," he confessed sadly. "You must not imagine me to be so ugly, as to be afraid of me," he begged Josephine. "Think of me always, as when I loved you most, and was most loved by you."

There was little company for him in the parish, and just as well, since he kept to himself much of the time. "I am a poor companion to any one," he confessed after the ruin of his nerves. Katherine was with him and still loving and attentive, but as he could bear little company, she spent most of her time reading poetry or novels, or she simply slept. They heard occasionally from Herbert, still away at school, and his father happily believed that the teenaged boy had come down with a disease that he teased was worse than smallpox; "*he is in love.*" There was a little dog they named Paps to play with, and this, sporadic work on the memoir, and dreams of better days when all his family were alive and around him passed the time, but it was not living for a man of his temperament. "Your Old Grandfather, must sit silent and sad, hoping that God will not allow him to be long a burden, and a source of anxiety to the kind hearts around him," he told his granddaughter. He was ready to die.[39]

But not just yet, for despite the cancer devouring his face and the condition of his nerves, his vital organs remained strong for his age, and so did his own case of that particular disease afflicting Herbert. In April 1874, on their twentieth anniversary, he composed a sonnet for Katherine in thanks for all she had suffered for him:

> This day, for twenty years, we have been one;
> And faithful to thy vows, thou'st been to me,
> In sickness, sorrow, death—thy love has grown,
> And proudly faced the storm, which others flee.
> With heart still bleeding on thy children gone,
> And friends and country crushed in blood and war,
> Closer and firmer still, to me thou'st shown
> Thy priceless wealth of love, no time can mar.
> Oh! How the poor heart vainly strives to tell,
> In voiceless praise, for all thou'st done for me.

Deep, where the tenderest love and memory dwell,
Responsive beats, its very pulse for thee.
Dear God! Thy loving wings spread oer her head
And make us meet in thee, when life is fled.[40]

There was the side of Rhett that only his family and a few friends ever saw, the hidden nature that would have shocked the millions who knew him only as the fire-eater, the center of storm, the preacher of sectional hatred and revolution. Yet to those whom he loved, there was a man entirely at odds with that public persona. "Depend upon it, happiness is not in the things without us," he wrote his granddaughter a few months after writing that sonnet. "It is from within—*the heart!*" Perhaps this was the tender side that even as a child he felt constrained to cloak in public, the side nurtured in loneliness and self-imposed isolation, helping to form that original "Madam Modesty" that hid so many inner fires.

In his closing years Rhett showed that despite his lifelong conservatism, he was not resistant to all change, especially when it came to the spread of education. However much he railed against the state conventions after the war—none in fact dominated by blacks, as he accused—one thing he never objected to in the new state constitutions they produced was universal education. He tutored his daughter Sallie Roman's children himself and pressed always for his son Herbert and his grandsons to gain comprehensive learning, for they "carry the name and future fortunes of the family." He grew especially interested in education for women. "The time is short, for women to acquire and improve in mental culture," he wrote in 1874, "unless they seek steadily, and obtain the habit of reading." He did not mean novels of the sort his wife read, "for they are worse than useless." Rather, he wanted young women to read "the great realities, and lofty aspirations, of the highest virtue, and the noblest features of humanity." A young woman should be constantly doing something to acquire knowledge and mental stimulation. "This habit of reading is worth more than money," he said, for it would "imbue us with thoughts sentiments and principles, which remain with us for life." He believed that the greatest ruin to the South from the war was not the destruction of property and fortunes, nor even the loss of slavery, "but it is the ignorance which poverty breeds and poisons, and thereby paralyzes and degrades. Knowledge is power, not only for those who have it, but *over those who have it not.*"[41]

But of course that power depended upon knowing the truth, and despite his infirmities, Rhett never stopped trying to promulgate *his* truth. Someone years before had called him a one-idea politician, and if that was rather hyperbolic, still it struck at the essential fact that Rhett had only ever had a few basic political tenets, and he stated and restated them over and over again for half a century, just as he did in the summer of 1875 when he wrote his final essay, a review of Charles Ingersoll's *Fears for Democracy.* Indeed, Rhett largely used the review, for the *Southern Magazine,* as a vehicle to carry an essay he had already written on that old adversary the "Money Power" of the North. It was all there—the discussion of power, state sovereignty, Northern perfidy, congressional usurpation, protectionism, and more. There never had been and never would be a "people of the United States," but rather two distinct peoples, Northern and Southern. Democracy existed only in the states themselves and not in the national government. The Union had no sovereignty, republican free government was dead in America, and despotism reigned. He railed as of old against the convention system of choosing presidential candidates and even more so at making electors chosen by popular ballot rather than appointed by the legislatures. Majority tyranny held full sway, and now with talk of Grant seeking a third term in 1876, he saw the inauguration of imperialism. There were no new ideas and no shifting at all from the positions of that first speech in Colleton nearly fifty years earlier. Now, ruled as they were by a common despotism, the people of North and South had lost all constitutional liberty. If their freedoms were not regained, then the future of the United States would be "the peace of the bayonet, with the scabbard thrown away." Would that be their ultimate end? he asked. His answer, as always, was "no!"[42]

As he could, Rhett worked at the memoir, but his failing strength, the pain, and his poor eyesight made it increasingly difficult. Moreover, he seemed never entirely to settle on the format or even the intent of the book, whether it was to be a straightforward memoir or more a collection of his essays and extracts from speeches illustrating his views on government and economy. With the example of Calhoun to emulate, he had dreamed of producing penetrating insights into the nature of the state, yet for the most part he could only repeat what he had said in dozens of speeches and papers decades before, while his inability to countenance any views or facts to the contrary inevitably reduced his conclusions to mere expressions of personal opinion. Then, too, his weakness forced him to take advantage of as much of his previous writings as possible, rather than write it all anew, and the fact that his opinions remained unchanged over the decades meant that nothing had gone out of date.

He intended first to title it "The Last Decade, seen in the extinction of Free Government in the United States, and the Downfall of the Southern Confederacy, in connexion with the Political Life and Services of the Honorable Robert Barnwell Rhett." That was a lot of title, and later he shortened it to "Political Life and Services of the Honorable Robert Barnwell Rhett." To save going over the same ground, he determined to begin it with a verbatim inclusion of much of the old Daniel Wallace biography from 1857, unchanged. This was further evidence, if any were needed, that Rhett served as Wallace's principle source, if he did not, in fact, author the sketch himself. Rhett edited a copy of Wallace's text, and with that as base he then went on to extend the narrative through the Grahamville speech in 1859, the tumult of 1860, and the conventions, secession, and his role in the provisional congress of the Confederacy, with some limited commentary following. To it, as illustrating his positions and thinking, he also intended to append his defense of secession for the convention in 1860, his report accompanying the declaration of war in May 1861, an 1867 letter written to a nephew in which he set out his role in framing the permanent constitution, three essays on free government, his review essay on party politics in response to the Van Buren book, and his essay on Northern civilization. By 1875 he also envisioned a concluding chapter that he would call "Chivalrous Southrons," though he never got it written.[43]

Aside from the actual documents to be included, his essays were all of a piece and, like so much up to and including the recent review of the Ingersoll book, covered the same old ground over and over again. Repetition never bothered Rhett but rather seemed to form a part of his political personality, as if his great truths had to be repeated without end in order to embed them in the minds of his people. The real meat of what he wrote was to be his actual recollections of his part in forming the Confederacy and his experiences during its first year, and here he revealed that the passage of years had done nothing to dim the old bitterness and resentment. If anything, they had only fermented into an even more powerful hatred of Jefferson Davis, for throughout, his Confederate memoir was a scarcely disguised diatribe against the president, leveling all the old charges and presenting—and inventing—some new ones.

Rhett's obsession with Davis was such that in three separate places he told and then retold the story of Davis's election, making over and again the points that he had been misled as to Davis's character and that it was only his own vote that turned South Carolina, and thereby Florida, for the Mississippian. He hinted that, but for that misapprehension, he might have stopped Davis and perhaps even been elected himself. Any hearsay that reflected badly on Davis he included unquestioningly; any enemy of Davis, from the bumbling Sterling Price to the egomaniacal Thomas Cobb to the crackpot Thomas Withers, he magnified to be paragons of their age; any useful known fiction, such as the Halpine prison account or the falsehood that Hannibal Hamlin was a mulatto, he used anyhow. He resorted repeatedly to speculative arguments on what would have happened had Davis followed Rhett's naive military policy rather than his own and, thanks to his association with Beauregard, incorporated many of that general's fanciful ideas of grand concentrations and lightning invasions into the North to produce one great Napoleonic battle that would have settled Southern independence at a stroke. Rhett also incorporated arguments given him by Joseph E. Johnston, including Johnston's intentionally falsified figures of troop strengths, to show that he had been so outnumbered in the Atlanta campaign that he had no choice but to fall back before Sherman, and yet asserting that Davis removed him from command just at the moment that he had Sherman where he wanted him and was ready to deliver a decisive counterstroke. It was all self-serving fable, but it struck at Davis and so Rhett chose to believe it.[44]

Everywhere, Davis was the usurper, from the trivial matter of the rented house and furniture to the number of his vetoes, which Rhett consistently exaggerated. Any refusal by Davis to entertain an idea or to promote an officer was transformed into a studied insult or an example of blatant favoritism. The actions Davis took to build the army and navy were ignored, and instead Rhett harped on his own proposals that the president had not adopted. Rhett's memoir would be the first work to include an entirely new charge, furnished to him by Beauregard, that in 1861 Davis had been offered a fleet of modern warships belonging to the old East India Company but turned them down, a charge unknown until 1874—and of which not one person involved in the government in 1861 had any recollection or record. On cotton policy and the treasury and foreign affairs Rhett hammered Davis just as hard, and often just as recklessly, and all with the perfect hindsight that allowed for the logical syllogism that since Davis's policies had not produced victory and independence, it followed therefore that Rhett's would have. There was not a man in the Confederacy who could have led it to defeat except Davis, Rhett finally concluded in his hatred. "He was created for this work," he said, "as Judas Iscariot was for his."

Throughout his memoir Rhett consciously or subconsciously sought to sanitize the record as well, reducing or even eliminating slavery's role in bringing about secession despite his own former declarations to the contrary, ignoring his own brief attempt to participate in the cotton trade that he condemned, disclaiming any personal ambition in the government even as his epithets toward Davis reeked of envy and disappointed hopes. And when he came to treat of Reconstruction, his pen wrote with no less venom than in his attacks on Davis. The South was ruled by "gangs of robbers and thieves" who had erased all liberty or justice with their amendments to the Constitution. The states had become mere counties of the central government, with no power over their own affairs and no security from federal interference. When the South fell, so did that free government that he always capitalized, and again and again he emphasized that not superiority of numbers or generalship led to Confederate downfall, but rather Jefferson Davis, whom he now felt more certain than ever had been the almighty's "special creation for a special purpose."

Rhett concluded with a measure of hope. Three decades' passage would see the people of the South their own masters again. Until then they must bear their injustices with patience while they "cherish the hot antagonism, which seethes and boils over in our hearts, still beating with the blood of our children—fathers—brothers—friends—fallen in battle in defense of their Country." Their persecutions now might be a blessing, reinforcing the impossibility of living with the Yankees and making them covet liberty more than ever. With a territory greater than that of Europe, with a climate and soil superior to all others, and with a population of heroes, the Southern people would rise again. Not content to stop at that, he even added an appendix that proved to his satisfaction that the North, and not the South, actually started the war. "My task is done," he concluded at the end.

> The laboring heart is still;
> No longer burning with the sacred fire
> To tell how fell my country; how her will
> Baffled and prone, may yet rise the higher,
> Her cause the altar, not the Funeral pyre.
> Where nations yet may kneel, and tyrants pale,
> When Freedoms trumpet tones again inspire,
> Calling from mountain top to answering vale,
> "Stand forth! in life or death & my cause shall never fail."[45]

Rhett dedicated the work to his sons Robert Woodward and Edmund, the one killed in the war and the other a victim of it by having contracted tuberculosis in camp. Both of them, in their father's words, were "martyrs in defense of the Confederate States, and the liberties of their country." Having worked at the memoir off and on for several years, it is not to be wondered he was so repetitious, nor that it came out very wordy, since his speeches had always been over-long as a rule, taking much longer to make a point than was necessary. Rhett wrote the first draft himself, finishing it as early as 1870, but as writing became more difficult for him, Katherine made a fair copy and he did his subsequent editing and revision on that, and on a later draft made around 1872 that he continued to edit occasionally. He occasionally read portions of the memoir aloud to friends and family to get their opinions, and lent copies of portions to Johnston and others for use in their own memoirs.

Yet another operation on his ravaged face came in early 1875, which likely forced him to set aside the work. By January 1876 he was intermittently at it again, though now he could not write at all and dictated everything to Katherine.[46] Despite his condition, he was after his son Barnwell to get him copies of more of his past speeches and old issues of the *Mercury,* and his son responded with all the help he could, as well as suggestions on expanding the memoir to include more of Rhett's prewar life, his relations with Calhoun and Polk, and even the story of the near-duel with Huger. The younger Rhett would have been happy to produce the final text himself but for the press of business, but he urged his father to run it through one more draft, dictating to Katherine and including more personal anecdotes to lighten the narrative.[47]

But Rhett no longer had the strength for another revision, nor would the memoir have been finished even if he had, for unlike his opinions and attitudes that remained fixed and complete at birth, he could not stop tinkering and revising. To his credit, some of this included toning down his invective except where it applied to Davis. By now many people knew what he was at, and some had high hopes. "I am sure it will be a valuable contribution to the literature of the State," his old friend Benjamin Perry remarked.[48] Yet by the summer of 1876, as the United States observed its centennial and he saw his seventy-sixth birthday approaching, Rhett was not so certain. In fact, he felt considerable concern, knowing that Davis was working on his own memoir. Rhett did not like the idea of his book appearing first so that Davis would have an opportunity to rebut his criticisms at a time when Rhett might be no longer living to retort. As a result, intending to find and use even more evidence in building an irrefutable case against Davis, Rhett expressed the wish that if he died before the memoir was completed, it should be destroyed, thus denying Davis a target. If Rhett could not have the last word, even from beyond the grave, then he preferred not to publish at all.[49]

It was a difficult summer for Rhett. His son Barnwell, back in Charleston now editing the *Journal of Commerce,* had not long before narrowly averted one duel and in August tried to precipitate another in a slanderous attack on Dawson at the merged *News and Courier.* While the disagreement may have gone back to Dawson's argument with Alfred Rhett in 1868, or more likely to Dawson's unhappy departure from the *Mercury,* it unquestionably now had much to do with the fact that Rhett was editing the *Journal of Commerce* no more successfully than he had the *Mercury,* while the *News and Courier* repeatedly showed itself to be better edited and consequently thrived. Rhett and friends even paraded the streets of the city well armed, hoping to incite an incident, but Dawson refused to take the bait. In an editorial Rhett viciously castigated Dawson for hiding behind his religion to avoid a duel, claiming that Dawson preferred "to play the part of an insolent coward" by slinking "in safety behind what is, with him, but the shield of a base hypocrite."[50] The adjective "hypocrite" would seem to have been misapplied, since Barnwell Rhett Jr. always defended his father for making precisely the same plea of religion to avoid a duel.

The summer was difficult, too, because by then Reconstruction was all but over in the former Confederate states except for Louisiana, Florida, and South Carolina, and whichever way the coming presidential contest in the fall should go, it was confidently expected that the last military occupying forces would be withdrawn. Rhett would never have thanked Washington for pulling out its soldiers, but he would have rejoiced to see them go, weary of waiting for Southern soil to be free from the invader's heel. Indeed, waiting is what he had been doing for years now, ever since the end of the war—waiting for the misery of penury to end, for the pain in his face to leave him, waiting for death to relieve him of an existence that had become burdensome to others and an intermittent misery to him. He was denied even the comfort of knowing that when he died he could be buried where he most desired to be, which was beside his father, James Smith, in the family vault at St. Philip's in Charleston. There had been so many deaths, so much disturbance of the caskets and bones over the years, that no one any longer knew which were his father's or where they were. Finally it ceased to matter. The cancer and the disappointment and the years did their work, and on September 14, 1876 at Cabanocey, Rhett's long wait was ended.[51]

When the family got around to going through his papers after his death, they found among the essays and the drafts of the memoir, and all the other reminders of a turbulent life, a simple poem that he had written, no one knew when:

Waiting—waiting—waiting
Waiting at the door.
Weak and weary, day is breaking;
Winds are chill and sore
Beyond is rest forever more,
Forever more.[52]

TWENTY-SEVEN

Do You See Yonder Star?

1876–1939

IN 1865, AS SHERMAN'S VICTORIOUS ARMY marched through South Carolina, one of his officers noted the empty houses of the Rhetts and others who had fled. "When first these men became traitors they lost honor," he said in a memoir published that same year. "To-day they have no local habitations; in the glorious future of this country they will have no name."[1] Indeed, when word of Rhett's death reached the press, many had not heard the name in so long that they thought him already gone. "The name of Mr. Rhett will seem like a ghost evoked from the dead past," read one obituary. "The great mass of people will doubtless be surprised that he lived so long."[2]

Katherine's first desire was to take him home, back to Charleston where he belonged, but there was not the money. She returned herself, perhaps to live for a time with her stepson Barnwell. Many years before he had purchased a plot in Magnolia Cemetery on the outskirts of the city overlooking the Cooper River, and there his mother, Elizabeth, already lay, and his first wife, Josephine. Now others were scattered about the plot, some of those who had died since the war with no headstones because the family could not afford them.[3] They selected a spot for his father, and Katherine and her stepdaughter Elise took it as a sacred duty to find the money to bring her husband to join two of her own children by him already there interred. Sometimes she visited the cemetery just to view the spot where he would rest, and finally they were able to bring him back, to lay him nearly in the center of the plot. All she could do was have neat turf placed over the grave; they could afford no stone. Often thereafter she went to Magnolia. Once after meeting a man who had gathered some leaves from the Charleston grave of Calhoun as keepsakes, she wondered to Herbert "if any one would ever do as much for your Father." Elise dressed the spot frequently with flowers, but they were the only memorial her father would ever have. Years later, in better times, the family placed a single monument in the center of the plot, not to mark any grave specifically but to remember all there buried, though it would have been perhaps the most appropriate for the one grave that wore Elise's garlands.

It bore only the single word "Rhett." Two generations of South Carolinians and millions of Americans who lived in the turmoil of his times knew that could mean only one man.[4]

Rhett himself had said at Grahamville in 1859 that his declaration for secession there should be his epitaph, and none of the few obituaries that appeared after his death could separate the man from the moment in 1860 when his life reached its zenith. His old foe the *News and Courier* called him "the father of secession," and his son writing in the *Journal of Commerce* made much the same claim.[5] Old friends could not divorce him from his politics either. "Mr. Rhett was always a disunionist as well as a nullifier and secessionist and despised the Union from the bottom of his heart till the day of his death," said Benjamin Perry, while William Grayson charged him as one of those "eager to sever the Union because they saw nothing more in the act than their own personal advantage." Another regarded him as perhaps the most persistent and consistent of all the secessionists, saying, "He paid for his sincerity & his one idea by the entire loss of his estate."[6]

It might have been added that Rhett also paid the price of being largely ignored by posterity, just as he had been so often in life. In his later years, when at last he occasionally reflected upon himself and his weaknesses of character, he gave some thought to one of the charges most often leveled at him, his arrogance:

> There is nothing that men dislike more than conceit. Our estimate of ourselves amongst men, is generally comparative. Conceit therefore, is not merely a false assumption for ourselves, but a depreciation of others. Yet this weakness (which if not a delusion, would be a combination of selfishness and falsehood) is a striking manifestation of the goodness of God. The world at large consists of inferior people. The superior are few. If the inferior realized to themselves their inferiority, they would lose the strongest motives to effort— the esteem of others, and the hope to rise in the world, and shine in its favour. But buoyed up by conceit, and the flattering opinion of themselves, it excites, they fight their small battle of life with comparative energy and cheerfulness, and fulfil, in spite of its disadvantages, their narrow round of duties. In a strong man, Conceit is weakness;—in a weak man, strength.[7]

There is no doubt that Rhett saw himself as one of those "superior" people, and as one of the strong, though whether he ever admitted that his own conceit weakened him—as surely it did—he did not say. Proud as he was of his editor son, still it would have hurt his vanity to know that future generations would not even differentiate between him and Barnwell Rhett Jr., treating the two as interchangeable and often confusing the words of one for the other.[8] Most likely

Rhett would have been outraged, had he lived another five years, to see that in a final insult his hated enemy Jefferson Davis did not mention him even once in a massive two-volume memoir. Davis simply wrote Rhett out of Confederate history, as he did most of those who feuded with him. Yet Rhett had been a part of that history, in the first few weeks an influential part and a constant presence throughout, just as he had been a loud voice on the public stage for fully a generation before secession and the war.[9]

Rhett's was a life haunted by his ancestors, by the Revolution, and by the shadow of Calhoun, a life steeped in the past that he maintained made him a prophet of the future. Just as he looked back on men such as William Rhett and John Barnwell who threw off the yoke of the old proprietors of the South Carolina colony, or looked to the Smiths and Barnwells who fought the British, so he saw himself in their mold as he tried to propel South Carolina and the South toward their own independence. "History," he said, "is an anticipation almost prophetic, of the future."[10] So thoroughly grounded was he in history, that he convinced himself that it put him in advance of the rest of his people in anticipating what lay before them and what they must do to protect themselves. In much of his augury, it has to be said, events proved him right. It was his tragedy, and that of the South, that he overlooked the greatest lesson of all from history and tried to resist its inexorable march toward change.

He grew up a product of his time and place, to become a mixture of the conservative, the libertarian, and the populist—three sometimes warring, but all essentially conservative, approaches to the world that can be quite compatible when sieved through the right personality. Like most other conservatives of his time, he was heir to attitudes that began to emerge two centuries before him when the rise of capitalism coincided with the decline of absolute monarchy, creating a middle class and an inexorable erosion of the political and social rule of the elite. Anti-majoritarian as long as he lived, Rhett would have felt very much at home in the England of James I but, like his ancestors, far less so under James II. His brand of conservatism attempted to maintain control of society and culture and the state against the pressures of an increasingly restive mass. Two years before Rhett's death, the eminent jurist Sir James Fitzjames Stephen neatly summarized Rhett's attitude when he declared, "I think that wise and good men ought to rule those who are foolish and bad." It was classic conservatism for his time.[11]

The problem for Rhett arose in the questions that the American Revolution left unsettled. However much it reformed the political institutions of the new nation, it left untouched and unresolved the old social order, especially in South Carolina. This meant that Rhett had to face a population with an ever greater impetus toward more diversely spread capitalism and fuller democracy, while he tried to represent and be a part of an oligarchy unchanged for nearly two hundred years, the very social institution that the rise of capital was bringing down everywhere else. Like conservatives on the defensive elsewhere, he could only defend the old order by the fact of its longevity and by the assumption of a natural aristocracy, of the superiority and inferiority of men and races, and of divine ordination. They were powerful forces for preserving a status quo but were impotent in the face of the relentless pressure of democracy. He would maintain his world where it was or, better yet, take it back to a better time when he and his were not under threat. It is no accident that Rhett remained all his life so familiar with the classics, for the ancient Greek model of the state and society would be for him ever the best, as it was run by an aristocracy and was founded on slavery. Since that was unattainable, Rhett fought instead a futile rear-guard action to prevent the American Revolution from marching beyond 1787. Like many who either lived through or grew up amid the repercussions of that turbulent era, he craved stability and predictability, and the more he experienced of the upheavals of his own century, the more he wanted what had been.

The great danger for him was that dreaded Enlightenment idea that a popular majority might contain within itself an inherent tendency to choose that which was best for the majority. Such an idea spelled doom for the elite in the South, and Rhett had to try to find some persuasive justifications as to why people should continue to be led by a social and political aristocracy that ran the state for their own ends. State sovereignty was mandatory, of course, for difficult as it was becoming by the 1850s to maintain control over the growing pressure of the masses within South Carolina, it would have been disastrous if any of that power shifted to an even more uncontrollable body politic outside the state. Indeed, every act in Washington in the first half of the century, from the abolition of the slave trade, to internal improvements, to the protective tariff and then the Compromise of 1850, showed how the wealth, the slaves, and the power of the oligarchy were increasingly eroded by centralization and the tyranny of the majority. In such an atmosphere it was only natural that he should venerate the past even more, a past when the right of the few dominated the reason of the masses.

And yet while Rhett the oligarch always tried to dictate to South Carolina, he often otherwise reflected the better side of what conservatism had become, for desiring that the South be left to choose its own way of life and institutions, he never sought to impose those choices upon the North. Never did he argue that slavery ought to spread to the North, nor that Yankees should not raise high duties on imports to protect their industry or spend that money to promote transportation or manufacturing in their section. He argued only that they should not so tax Southerners, or spend their money outside their section, or threaten their property rights. Consistently he was happy to leave the North to its beliefs and practices, whether he liked them or not. He did not have to respect them or their institutions but felt it his duty to tolerate them, as he wished them to tolerate his. Yet that did not keep him from asserting that a slave section and a free section could not remain under the same government indefinitely, for the labor of each inevitably aspired to what the other had—Southern slaves to Northern freedom, and Northern laboring masses to the employment that could be available in the South. Both must tend eventually to destroy slavery.

In his conceit and arrogance, that of all ruling elites, he knew that his way was the best and spent half a century trying to show Carolinians and Confederates that the ideal state he would construct for them on slavery, free trade, and state sovereignty offered them the stability and order and prosperity that they all wanted. Any proposition that eroded his way, to the extent of the erosion had to be resisted, to the point of violence if necessary, for once the rot began, it could hardly be stopped. The one thing he could not accommodate was contingency. Having ordained what his version of American democracy should be, how it would operate, and the benefits to be derived, he could not countenance variation or accident or the caprice of men and time. To do so would have been to admit that he could be wrong and that it was not possible for his perfect political and social system to function indefinitely and immutably.

This led naturally to the streak of libertarianism that ran through Rhett's life, though it was never fully developed. He admitted that some degree of government was necessary as a practical matter, but in almost all areas except divorce he denied that government, state or nation, had any right to reform men, whether by prohibition of alcohol or emancipation of slaves, whether voluntarily or by mandate. Left to themselves, men would look after themselves, and though he was more charitable toward lawbreakers than most libertarians might have been, he still supported punishment for infraction, whether removal from office for malfeasance or execution for desertion. The example to control behavior should come not from law imposed by interfering government, but rather from the standard set by the natural aristocracy that he defended, thus blending conservatism and libertarianism in what, to him, seemed a quite compatible combination.

But there was a problem faced by Rhett and all the others who wanted to maintain the South and the nation as they were. Despite history and all their pretensions, the spread of property from the elite down through the middle class ever deeper into the working people meant that appeals to natural right and expectations of blind obedience could no longer work with a growing electorate, especially in the explosion of popular democratic spirit that arose during the Jacksonian era. The rise of the so-called "Common Man" created a force that could vote as it chose, stand up to an aristocrat, and demand to be persuaded rather than taken for granted. Given the cynical attitude that Rhett and all of the oligarchy shared about the stupidity, ignorance, irrationality, and malleability of those "inferior" people, he inevitably turned to the sort of approach that worked best with them, and which just happened to accord perfectly with his own personality. He became a populist.

Rhett's talk was always a monologue, not a conversation, with the voters, he the teacher and they the students. No other politician of his time was more didactic. God and the superiority of his own station and intellect had given him a perfect vision of the proper order of things, one not to be questioned, and when gainsaid it had to be by men of malign purpose or inferior mind. If another sought to control or manipulate him as he did the voters, he would have cried "tyranny." When he did it to them, it was leadership. Always his was a bold vision, but unlike most political ideals, it was not his direction that made it so, for to step backward is rarely as daring as to go forward. Rather his audacity lay in his presentation and in his alternative, secession.

"One of the hallmarks of the populist down the ages is the yelp," a later observer remarked. "He is the yelp made flesh." Always there was someone bigger who posed a threat, external forces seeking to undermine Rhett, and his opponents were dishonest, corrupt, venal. "The populist litany becomes the sustained whine punctuated by the snarl and—when enough of them gather—outbreaks of hysterical barking in the night," the observer said, and they thrive on umbrage. "His are the politics of complaint. His mode is inherently oppositional. When the populist actually wins, he is quickly insecure and his platform falls apart. Political generosity is beyond him. Courtesy escapes him. It spoils his world view to conciliate, even where that would be in his interest. . . . all dissent must be foul play. Their own past foul play was 'principled,' concerned something 'too important' for mere unity to trump. They do not, however, extend to rival creeds the courtesy of allowing that these, too, might hold their beliefs to be important. Even as he conspires, your populist mutters about the overarching conspiracies of others. These define him and his world, to himself."[12]

Written twelve decades after his death, the description might have been an epitaph for Rhett. Yet for an unsophisticated audience this very approach, which seemed to come instinctively to Rhett, was easily the best designed to achieve his ends. Disdaining the intellect of the people at large, he could use his appeal to emotions—to fear, resentment, envy—to stir the baser passions of his listeners.

Even as he distrusted the common man, Rhett understood instinctively that his best weapon for overcoming the evils of democracy was to mold this new electorate into a body of opinion that would actually help him retain a social and political order bent on containing the spread of their rights and prerogatives. It helped, too, that Rhett was born with all the instincts of the classic ideological agitator—the grasp of the uses of propaganda and the power of the press, the willingness to bend or break the truth and ignore inconvenient facts in shaping public opinion, the zealot's conviction that the end justified the means and that violence is always an acceptable, if lamentable, last resort. This helped explain his constant injunctions to excite the people dramatically, even by fomenting confrontation if need be; his relentless urgings to take action while passions were high; and his ever-present threat of bloodshed. Aristocrat, conservative, populist, revolutionary—he would have been a familiar figure in Paris in 1789, or Petrograd in October 1917, or most especially perhaps in Germany in 1933, not because he was evil or bloodthirsty—which certainly he was not—but because he had a genius for stirring the passions and the prejudices that could propel millions to uprising. He was a man familiar in all times and all nations, the perfect revolutionary.

Without a doubt he could be effective. Certainly no Southerner except Calhoun was so influential in giving the state rights cast to the Democratic Party that it began to take in the 1840s, and as an inside manipulator Rhett was probably more effective than Calhoun, who always had to assume the pose of being above political wire-pulling. It should be noted, however, that Rhett was only truly successful and influential when Calhoun was behind him, even if in the background; after Calhoun's death Rhett was almost impotent in Washington or the Democratic Party. But for Rhett, the wires were the greatest challenge and probably the greatest fun of politics. He had the instincts of the grassroots organizer, the party functionary, the sort who makes the everyday affairs of a political organization happen while the figureheads carry the banner. He could show brilliance as a publicist when he restrained his extremism and intolerance for opposition within party ranks, and his unquestionable instinct for manipulating and capitalizing on the popular mood were repeatedly manifest.

Unfortunately, the obverse of the coin was that, knowing the moment to push public sentiment, he never knew when to stop pushing and so time after time overreached his audience and the patience of those who backed him. No one who knew him ever denied that his worst enemy was his own public personality; he was arrogant, didactic, condescending, and intolerant of dissent whether from foe or friend. Indeed, it is peculiar that of the few men who knew him who left kindly portraits of Rhett, most were political opponents such as

Petigru or Perry. Since they were open and avowed foes by party and policy, whom he could have no expectation of winning to his side, he seemed able to accept their differences and look beyond them to form warm and affectionate friendships. But with men in his own political camp he seemed to regard any deviation from his own revealed word as apostasy. His greatest personal enemies were often those who should have been among his close political friends.

Then there was his ambition. Rhett always denied it, as was expected of every politician of his time. Yet friend and foe alike saw ambition as a thick seam running through all his public career, from his first maneuverings to supplant Pickens and Hammond in Calhoun's favor, down to his bitter disappointment at being ignored in Montgomery in February 1861. He would not have been human if he did not crave approval, and in his incessant protest at the failure to publish the debates in the Confederate congress can be seen more than just a struggle for the public's right to know. It was irritation that the public did not more specifically know what *he* had done. Rhett was never a follower. His long association with Calhoun was more of an alliance in his eyes than a relationship of leader and led. When Calhoun's views did not accord with his own, Rhett balked, and he did it again and again, compelled to be independent despite the cost to himself or his cause, and compelled even more by ambition to lead rather than follow. Robert Barnwell Rhett was never entirely a member of any team or party. Eyes fixed on that star that he often believed only he could see, he simply could not turn away to gaze toward any lesser light.

And of course his star was secession and Southern independence. Despite his no doubt sincere protestations that in his earlier years he invoked secession only as a threat to awaken the North and bring about a return to the Union that his brand of conservatism required, there can be no reasonable doubt that he early on contemplated the eventuality that the North would not give way and that secession would go from threat to fact. By the time of Bluffton in 1844, and in fact probably rather earlier, as early even as 1833, he became a secessionist not only at heart but in commitment. And yet when secession finally came to South Carolina in 1860, there is every reason to conclude that it happened not because of Rhett but in spite of him.

Repeatedly, in 1832, again in 1844, then in 1852, secession fever began to sweep the state, and Rhett ably spread the virus as quickly as he could before the natural antibodies of reason, reflection, and calm drove it out. Though he was certainly from the first the most able, ardent, and inflammatory of all advocates of separation, he could never overcome the basic moderation and conservatism of the mass of Carolinians. In the greatest battle on the national stage over the Compromise of 1850 he played no more than a supporting role, the debates with Foote and Clemens providing some heat but no fire. If anything, his extremism sent many recoiling into the ranks of the cooperationists and a few cooperationists into the Unionist camp. Conversely, not a single piece of testimony survives by which a Carolinian declared that Rhett made him a secessionist. Rather, the record of the years makes it abundantly clear that Carolinians advanced toward secession in a series of fits and starts and steps backward as well as forward, not propelled by the invective of leaders but motivated by events. When Rhett retired in a funk from the Senate in 1852, secession was as dead as it had ever been in South Carolina, so dead that even with his confidence in his ability to command men and events, he gave up and went into his "profound retirement." When the crisis renewed, it was Kansas and Lecompton, and John Brown at Harpers Ferry, and the election of Lincoln that did the job. All of the threats to South Carolina's peace of mind in the Union before had come singly and at substantial intervals, but here within four years was a quick succession of shocks, each more threatening than the one before.

Rhett had no role whatever in making them happen. He, like the rest of Carolinians, simply reacted to them, and in his case that meant capitalizing on them in the *Mercury* and later on the stump. The fact that public sentiment and reaction to these events was much the same in other slave states such as Louisiana, Florida, and Mississippi that had no outspoken or ardent fire-eaters molding public opinion in 1860 suggests more strongly than anything else that in South Carolina, too, it was the inevitability of events, and not this one fire-eater, that swayed the decision. Rhett had kept secession talk before the eyes and ears of his public for thirty years. To that extent he had sustained it as an open topic, and perhaps by making it familiar he made it seem somehow less frightful, though time after time his people recoiled from it as well as from him when presented the option. By November 1860, however, it seemed the only option left, though it is significant that when it came, Rhett was out of office and out of any real influence other than the *Mercury,* and the lead was taken and sustained by other men. Yancey, not Rhett, precipitated the breakup of the Charleston convention and the Democratic collapse that inaugurated the final crisis. Nor did Rhett in any way dominate the secession convention in December, for the delegates were virtually all of like mind by then. When he walked down the aisle at Institute Hall to sign the ordinance, he came as one who had almost been left out of the convention. The cheers and applause were not for a man who had made that day happen, but for an aged warrior who was now the grand old man of secession, given recognition for his efforts years ago in a movement that he no longer led. Indeed, secession in 1860 resurrected Rhett from the obscurity in which the repeated rejection of the people had cast him. His son could not have been more mistaken in that obituary. This was not the father of secession; rather, secession in 1860 had fathered the rebirth of Robert Barnwell Rhett.[13]

And yet his revolution failed, and he and almost all of his kind with it. The true fire-eaters of importance were few in number—a dozen, perhaps more.[14] Stephens thought them unified by their being "more or less blinded by passions, prejudices, or zeal," and that they all lacked the cool wisdom of the true states-man, which certainly described Rhett.[15] Though they all shared some basic attrib-utes, they were a diverse lot, each subject to the peculiar influences and demands of his state, his background, and even his age. No two were alike, and they defy any uniform portrait.[16] But one thing that does characterize almost all of them is that, once their goal of secession was achieved, whatever real power they had up until that time diminished thereafter. It is in the nature of revolutions that once the crisis comes and a bold step is taken, all parties almost instinctively race toward the center, for there lies the greatest security. The Dantons and Robes-pierres and Michael Collinses rarely outlast the opening years or even months of the insurrections they help incite, and neither did the Rhetts and the Yanceys.

The founding fathers of the Confederacy never for a moment seriously con-sidered a fire-eater for the presidency or vice presidency, and not one of them was considered for a cabinet post either. Those first top leaders were cooperationists to a man, and some such as Stephens reluctant even in that pose. Yancey's post at the head of the first diplomatic mission to Europe was practically a sinecure with little authority and no influence, a pointless exercise by his own admission and, according to some, merely a device for getting him away from Montgomery. Of all the fire-eaters only Yancey, Wigfall, and Miles held seats in the Confed-erate congress under the permanent constitution, while Keitt gave up his seat and Rhett was rejected by the voters. Yancey never succeeded in being more than an irritant to Davis in the senate, nor did he author or guide significant legisla-tion that influenced Confederate affairs, while Wigfall chiefly differed with the president on executive authority. Both senators stunted their potential by giving way to resentment and vanity over disappointed ambitions, and what Wigfall did that was successful was almost all in the way of furthering Davis's military policy. Only Miles actually served through the entire life of the Confederacy. Granted he become perhaps the most powerful member of the congress, but only after he came almost entirely over to President Davis's policy. By the clas-sical definition of influence as the potential or kinetic ability to control or pro-duce effects, Rhett and the other fire-eaters were all but powerless after secession. They affected none of Davis's policies, nor did they materially direct or alter the policies of any of the states. They complained and criticized, but they changed nothing, decided nothing, and failed even to persuade enough Confederates to their way of thinking to form a significant following. At best they were an annoyance and an irritant. To the small extent that any of these men achieved active influence in the Confederacy, it came in inverse proportion to their abandonment of their hallmark stances as fire-eaters. Otherwise they were impotence incarnate.[17]

The Confederacy simply could not afford to give power to a man like Rhett, nor is there any indication that he would have used it wisely or productively. For a start, his personality was just as difficult as Davis's. Like the president, Rhett could not get along with men he could not dominate. Like Davis, he did not understand how to compromise or deal with dissent. Like the Mississippian, he was a poor judge of men, if his expressions of admiration for the likes of Price and Cobb and Withers were genuine. Despite his complaints of Davis's trampling over the congress, there is nothing in Rhett's life to suggest that, had he as president met with opposition from that body, he would not have done much the same, while the ability at fomenting dissent and animosity that he demonstrated abundantly in his life would hardly help him in forging unity and cohesion among the disparate factions composing the Confederacy. A proud South Carolinian who fully believed that Southerners were a superior race apart from the Yankees, Rhett did not—and never would—become a true Southern nationalist, nor even a slave state nationalist, but rather opposed all manifestations of nationalism.

Only an approximate judgment of the value of the actual policies he later *claimed* that he would have imposed can be made, but the lens of hindsight casts no roseate tint. Only in domestic policy would he appear to have had the better of Davis, but here as elsewhere any judgment is based only on what Rhett said he *would* do. That the congress would have let him might have been a far different matter. Certainly his cotton embargo would not have put the Confederacy in a better financial position than otherwise, for to starve Britain of cotton meant to starve the South of money. His state conscription might have raised more troops, however, and sooner. His call to accept all volunteers regardless of terms of service might have created a larger army in 1861, though given the time that history revealed it took for generals on both sides to learn to handle large forces, there is no reason to suppose that the timid and ineffectual Joseph E. Johnston—who was senior to Beauregard—would have done anything more than he did anyhow. Rhett's concern for building or acquiring a larger navy could have helped, although with the goal being to break the blockade and thereby help attract foreign recognition and intervention, he would have run into the impenetrable wall of European neutrality no matter how large his fleet.

Indeed, his all-or-nothing foreign policy certainly would have failed, as evidenced by his own eventual admission that King Cotton had lost its power. Four years of British indifference to Confederate diplomatic feelers displayed the undeniable fact that the South simply never had anything to offer to Britain worth the risk of going to war with the Union and jeopardizing its transatlantic trade with the North, or its merchant hegemony on the globe. As ever in the way of nations looking out for their own interests first, Europe was never going to help the Confederacy until it could demonstrate that it needed no help. Rhett's military policy is kindly described as sophomoric. Most of his later pronounce-ments came to him after the fact, borrowed entirely from Beauregard and John-ston. His sole contemporary policy seems to have been to attack immediately with whatever could be assembled, to invade the North, capture Washington, and thereby presumably achieve a quick and decisive victory. It was a policy based on his contempt for the patriotism and staying power of the people of the North, an underestimation that characterized all his attitudes toward enemies.

It also ignored practical military realities that an experienced man such as Davis recognized but which a tyro such as Rhett never thought to consider—for example, the impossibility of even getting across the Potomac to reach Washing-ton and the North unless obliging Yankees left the few bridges open and intact. And given the posture that Rhett espoused that the Confederacy only wanted to be left alone and that it wanted nothing from the Yankees, an invasion and battle on Northern soil and the capture of Washington would have been a diplo-matic catastrophe for the Confederacy, casting it instead in the role of an aggres-sive invader. Meanwhile, if Rhett's great invasion happened to lead to a defeat instead of the victory that he took for granted, his army could have disintegrated under his nose. With no tradition of victory to sustain them through setbacks, such as the one the Confederates weathered in 1863 after two years of battle-field success, the soldiers and the people at home simply might not have had the staying power to sustain the cause, and there is no telling what encouragement a humiliation in its first great battle might have given to the still-widespread sen-timent for reconstruction in 1861. That was the problem with all-or-nothing strategies like Rhett's.

In short, the Confederacy under a President Rhett faced the probability of a significantly shorter life span than even its four short years under Davis, and a regime even more turbulent and divisive, for Rhett's personality alienated so many leading men in the decades before the war that it certainly must have prej-udiced their willingness to work with him in the crisis. Yet Rhett would never have countenanced such a thought. Rather, the Confederacy had been his by right since he gave it birth. Among the proudest achievements of his life were the genuine reforms he inserted into the permanent constitution, and even if they did not significantly alter the framework of government or achieve all his aims, still in his eyes they were his most lasting monument to the struggle for free government. Indeed, disappointed as he was with the finished constitution in 1861, it grew more and more perfect in his recollection in after years.

Among the poems and other notes intended for his memoir, but never actually incorporated, he wrote a brief statement titled "The wreck of the Confederacy": "Mine was a singular fate, in the affairs of the Southern Confederacy. I built the ship; and with my own hands, put into it, its best ribs and soundest planks—and then was turned out of it to be navigated by others, some of whom shed tears at its construction. Well!—wise men did not do this; and wise men did not wreck the Ship."[18]

Rhett had always lived in something of a dream world, not the dream of the megalomaniac or the insane, but a vision of a South that could be strong and secure and prosperous with state sovereignty as its cornerstone, great among the nations, and expanding its empire to the Pacific and beyond on the backs of cotton and slavery. To his credit, he was one of the few to admit—declare, in fact—that slavery brought about secession, though after the war, like the others, he would attempt to gloss over that. Slavery, to Rhett, was an institution that was right in the natural order of the world and worth fighting for, though of course slavery had merely been the catalyst for the outbreak founded on a much older and more fundamental constitutional malady.

He did not and would never accept or understand that in a century witnessing the growth and unification of nation-states throughout the western world, his brand of localism was becoming as archaic as the city-states of Renaissance Italy, which was itself struggling to unify under a central rule at that very moment. In an age of steam-powered industry, increasing social mobility, an ever-rising middle class, and growing popular participation in politics, a return to the halcyon days of Greece was impossible. Rhett never did address or explain away the fundamental dilemma posed by his hatred of majority rule. If the minority could not prevent the election of a president, he had complained, then there was no point in voting at all, and the Constitution and the Union had failed. But if a minority should have the right to do so, then how was democracy to continue? Like all the rest of his compatriots, he never considered that the South might not be the only minority. In fact, the 39 percent of Americans who elected Lincoln were certainly a minority and yet they won, which disproved Rhett's argument right before his eyes though he would not see or admit it. The West was a minority, and New England was a minority, yet later each would determine elections against a presumed majority candidate. The plain fact was that for all of Rhett's talk of minority rights as a constitutional issue, it really came down only to Southern rights, and even that more than once succumbed to his ultimate

dedication to slaveholders' rights. His pretense of high principles of free government worth fighting for, were reduced in the end in practical terms to parochial concerns for his own section, and even more so his own class. Rhett always
believed that he did not succeed because he was too far ahead of his people. In
the end more likely he failed because they had left him too far behind. Arcadia
had become anachronism.[19]

It was left to Rhett's family to try to make a berth for him aboard the posterity of that ship he thought he had built. Katherine preserved the several drafts
of the unfinished memoir along with such other private papers as she could
gather, "mournful relics only valuable as he once possessed them," she called
them.[20] But Robert Barnwell Rhett Jr. would have a better use for them than as
relics, for with his father's death he undertook to carry on Rhett's attack on Davis,
and vindication of himself. Davis's memoir, *Rise and Fall of the Confederate States
Government,* appeared in 1881 and stimulated Barnwell Rhett to begin anew collecting sources to refute the onetime president. He gleaned quotations from Orr
and Toombs and Barnwell, among others, all testifying to Davis's shortcomings
as a leader, and he declared that Davis had been allowed to play the role of
Southern martyr for seventeen years since Appomattox and that now it was time
to expose him since he had put his story on record.

Rhett's first avenue of attack was to furnish everything he had to Beauregard,
who was really writing most of his memoir despite Roman's putative authorship.
The editor tried to guide Beauregard and Roman in their handling of Memminger's and Trenholm's financial failures, as well as the cotton embargo, and other
matters that interested his father especially. In fact, Rhett wrote the concluding
chapter of Beauregard's second volume, which was little more than a restatement
of all of his father's old complaints about diplomatic failures, the semimythical
East India fleet, and more. He believed that the book, finished in January 1883
but not published until the following year, would be sensational, and he continued sending material even after its completion so that the authors would have
"some fixed ammunition, reserved for use when Davis and his friends assault
your work."[21]

Not long afterward Rhett contributed under his own name an article to the
popular *Century Magazine* series Battles and Leaders of the Civil War covering
the formation of the Confederate government at Montgomery; he drew his
material almost entirely from his father's memoir and a few letters he had collected for Beauregard and Roman. Beauregard expected it to be a strong blast at
Davis, and Rhett said that he was writing the piece to "prevent the suppression
of important facts in history, and injustice to eminent men, now dead, who have
been much misunderstood," meaning his father, of course.[22] Yet there was nothing

new in the article not already revealed during the war in the *Mercury* years before or in what was furnished for Beauregard's memoir.

Rhett did not intend to stop there. Several years later in 1889 he was still collecting material to use against Davis, who by this time had joined Rhett in death. When defenders stood up for Davis and Roman decided to write more himself, Rhett could only say "the more the merrier." He began work on an article on the management of the Confederate government, intending it to be his final word, though he never saw it published. Then when he heard that Varina Davis intended to publish her own memoir of her husband and the Confederate years, Rhett collected more material with renewed vigor, declaring, "I have the material to answer all." As every new Confederate memoir came off the press, he judged it on how much it did or did not augment his case against Davis. Like his father before him, he could not let go of the determination to discredit the former president.[23]

Rhett was liberal in loaning copies of his father's memoir to other writers, including Beauregard and Roman, of course, and particularly John Witherspoon DuBose, who was then writing his biography of William L. Yancey. Much of the senior Rhett's pertinent material found its way into the final work, especially the by-now seemingly ubiquitous charge about the East India fleet, which even Stephens took up in a volume subsequent to his memoir.[24] Indeed, in a wonderful irony, the memoir that Rhett never finished proved to have considerably more influence on the writing of the history of the Lost Cause than Rhett himself ever had on the course of the Confederacy.

By the turn of the century there were fewer and fewer of the family he so loved left to perpetuate his message. Burnet died three years almost to the day after his father, and Katherine outlived her husband by less than six years. His quarrelsome son Alfred died in 1889. Herbert, whose pets he doted over, never married and died unmarried in 1892 despite the early afflictions of love. Claudia, too, died unwed, while Sallie Rhett Roman lived until 1921 and became a minor writer in her own right. Robert Barnwell Rhett Jr. continued his quest to vindicate his father. By 1900 he contemplated writing a biography of the elder Rhett and was still collecting material, but he never finished. The editor of the *American Historical Review* even approached him about publication of the now dog-eared Rhett memoir, but Barny Rhett's death in 1901 prevented any further action.[25] Elizabeth Rhett, the Elise with whom her father shared so much during his later years in Charleston, outlived them all, married her sister Mary's widower, and kept the flowers on Rhett's grave for years. In her later years she happily cooperated with a biographer who finally put her father's eventful and ultimately tragic life into print.[26]

Yet it would be left to others to ensure in a roundabout way that Rhett was not entirely forgotten. Almost exactly sixty years after he died, a book far more influential than anything he ever could have written appeared to reawaken that dream vision he had of the South. *Gone With the Wind* not only fixed its romantic —but inaccurate—image of the Old South and the Confederacy in the minds of millions then and later, but it also unintentionally made the long-forgotten Rhett a household name in American popular culture. Margaret Mitchell's fictional hero had nothing in common with the so-called father of secession other than coming from Charleston, but in seeking to give him a name she could think of nothing more archetypal of South Carolina than Rhett. The fictional Rhett was no fire-eating secession hothead, however, but rather a voice of reason. Forthrightly he criticized the real secessionists around him for their "arrogance." In perhaps the ultimate irony of a life spent largely in condemning others, Robert Barnwell Rhett would only be remembered in popular posterity because of a namesake who condemned everything he had stood for.[27]

All his life Barnwell Rhett had seen a "yonder star" that others would not see, and his dream had died. Yet to the end he expected that those who followed him would one day see his vision anew and take up his cause to make it a reality. The South would rise again, and it would be free and independent and dedicated to principles that would vindicate him and his struggle. Of course it did not happen, nor could it have happened, for his were visions of what was gone and buried, much of it dead long before his birth. For an America about to emerge as a leader in the world community, making Rhett's past a part of its future would have been no dream at all, but a nightmare.

Notes

Abbreviations Used in the Footnotes

CM   Charleston Museum, Charleston, South Carolina
Crosby   Robert Barnwell Rhett Jr. Papers, in possession of Leslie Crosby,
          Huntsville, Ala.
JHRSC   Journal of the House of Representatives of the Legislature of the State of
          South Carolina
LC   Library of Congress, Washington, D.C.
PRO   Public Record Office, London
SCDAH   South Carolina Department of Archives and History, Columbia
SCHS   South Carolina Historical Society, Charleston
SCL   South Caroliniana Library, University of South Carolina, Columbia
SHC   Southern Historical Collection, University of North Carolina, Chapel Hill

The Signing

1. Charles H. Lesser, *Relic of the Lost Cause: The Story of South Carolina's Ordinance of Secession* (Columbia, S.C., 1996), 1, 9–10; *New York Evening Post,* December 13, 21, 1860; *Frank Leslie's Illustrated Newspaper,* February 9, 1861; Claudine Rhett, Reminiscences of Secession, Aiken Rhett Collection, Charleston Museum (hereafter cited as CM), Charleston, S.C.; George S. Bernard Scrapbook, 195, Duke University, Durham, N.C.; Francis William Guess, *South Carolina: Annals of Pride and Protest* (New York, 1960), 223.

Chapter One

1. William Howard Russell, *My Diary North and South* (New York, 1954), 69.
2. Lawrence S. Rowland, Alexander Moore, and George C. Rogers Jr., *The History of Beaufort County, South Carolina: Volume 1, 1514–1861* (Columbia, S.C., 1996), 58–61.
3. G. H. Ladson, Genealogy of the Smith Line, Rhett Genealogy Notes, South Carolina Historical Society (hereafter cited as SCHS), Charleston, S.C. Accounts of the early Smith genealogy are confused and contradictory, most of them being family accounts based on oral tradition that tend inadvertently to eliminate a couple of generations in the early 1700s, and they are further confused by there being no fewer

than seven Thomas Smiths in successive generations. The basic outline of the Smith line here and hereafter is based on A. S. Salley, "The Family of the First Landgrave Thomas Smith," *South Carolina Historical and Genealogical Magazine* 28 (July 1927), 169–75; and A. S. Salley, "More on Landgrave Smith's Family," *South Carolina Historical and Genealogical Magazine* 30 (October 1929), 255–58. This fills in the gaps in the family accounts and also eliminates some family legend, such as the belief that the immigrant Thomas was the son of Sir George Smith where in actuality his parents were Thomas and Joan Smith. There is also a common legend that the wife of the immigrant Thomas Smith was the widow of a Dutch baron (though it is improbable that Atkins was a Dutch surname). The confusion probably arose because the twelve-thousand-acre grant that apparently came to her was of a size often called a barony. See "The Lower Country of South Carolina," *The Land We Love* 1 (October 1866), 385.

4. *Charleston Sunday News,* August 1, 1897.
5. Rowland, Moore, and Rogers, *History of Beaufort County,* 85–86.
6. "James Smith, A Genealogy," September 10, 1802, Rhett Genealogy Notes, SCHS. Elizabeth A. Poyas to Robert Barnwell Rhett Jr., June 18, 1864, in Elizabeth A. Poyas, "The Olden Time in Carolina," SCHS, says that Thomas Smith brought the rice seed over with him on the *William and Ralph* when he immigrated in 1670–71, which is almost certainly incorrect.
7. Converse D. Clowse, *Economic Beginnings in Colonial South Carolina, 1670–1730* (Columbia, S.C., 1971), 81–82, 125–26, 130–32; Bernard C. Steiner, ed., "The South Atlantic States in 1833, As Seen by a New Englander," *Maryland Historical Magazine* 13 (December 1918), 361.
8. *Charleston Sunday News,* August 1, 1897.
9. D. E. H. Smith Papers on the Rhett Family, Rhett Genealogy Notes, SCHS; Elizabeth A. Poyas to Rhett, August 4, 1864, "The Olden Time in Carolina," SCHS.
10. Letter of Attorney, February 2, 1699, deed book for 1694–1704, Court of Probate, Charleston County, Charleston, S.C.
11. Elizabeth A. Poyas to Rhett, August 4, 1864, "The Olden Time in Carolina," SCHS; William Rhett to the Commissioners of the Customs, December 31, 1717, Records Relating to South Carolina, 7:104–6, Public Record Office, London.
12. Rhett to the Board of Trade, October 21, 1718, Records Relating to South Carolina, 7:205, Public Record Office, London.
13. Clowse, *Economic Beginnings,* 192–94.
14. Rhett to the Board of Trade, December 21, 1719, Records Relating to South Carolina, 1A:28, Public Record Office, London.
15. *Boston News-Letter,* February 7, 14, 1723. The genealogical sources on Rhett agree that he died on January 12 (one mistakenly says June 12) 1722, as does his tombstone, which may not be immediately contemporary, however. The Boston newspaper would seem to establish beyond question that 1723 was correct, however, and that date has been accepted here, though it must be considered as possible that the date was a misprint.

16. "James Smith, A Genealogy," September 10, 1802, Rhett Genealogy Notes, SCHS.

17. *Charleston Sunday News,* August 1, 1897; G. H. Ladson, Genealogy of the Smith Line, Rhett Genealogy Notes, SCHS; "James Smith, A Genealogy," September 10, 1802, Rhett Genealogy Notes, SCHS. Thomas Smith the younger's wife, Anna Cornelia Van Myddagh, is probably the origin of the family tradition of a nameless Dutch wife, except it attributes her to the father rather than the son.

18. Several of the early Rhett genealogies state that when Landgrave Thomas Smith arrived in the Carolina colony, a brother James or Paul came with him but later settled in Massachusetts. If that is true, then the first Thomas Smith of Boston may have been the son of such a brother. On the other hand, the coincidence of names when Sabina married Thomas may simply have led to a later family tradition of a relationship between the Massachusetts and South Carolina families.

19. "James Smith, A Genealogy," September 10, 1802, Rhett Genealogy Notes, SCHS; Barnwell Rhett Heyward, "James Smith," Smith-Rhett Genealogy, Barnwell Rhett Heyward Papers, SCHS.

20. John Adams to Abigail Adams, May 17, 1776, in L. H. Butterfield, Marc Friedlaender, and Mary-Jo Kline, eds., *The Book of Abigail and John: Selected Letters of the Adams Family, 1762–1784* (Cambridge, 1975), 130.

21. Barnwell Rhett Heyward, "James Smith," Smith-Rhett Genealogy, Barnwell Rhett Heyward Papers, SCHS; "James Smith, A Genealogy," September 2, 1810, Rhett Genealogy Notes, SCHS.

22. Stephen B. Barnwell, *The Story of an American Family* (Marquette, Mich., 1969), 11, 28, 30–31, 51; Robert Barnwell Rhett, sketch of James Smith, n.d., Robert Barnwell Rhett Jr. Papers, in possession of Leslie Crosby, Huntsville, Ala. (hereafter cited as Crosby).

23. Robert Barnwell Rhett, sketch of James Smith, n.d., Crosby; Joseph W. Barnwell and Mabel L. Webber, comps., "St. Helena's Parish Register," *South Carolina Historical and Genealogical Magazine* 23 (October 1922), 188; Robert Barnwell Rhett Sr. autobiographical fragment, n.d., and Robert Barnwell Rhett, "My letter opposing the Tariff of 1842," n.d., Robert Barnwell Rhett Sr. Papers, SCHS. In the autobiographical fragment cited above, Rhett appears to date his birth as December 24 rather than 21, but this is most likely simply his terrible handwriting at work. As with much of the Smith-Rhett genealogy, there is some confusion as to the number of James Smith's children. Laura A. White, *Robert Barnwell Rhett: Father of Secession* (Washington, D.C., 1931), 5, states that there were fifteen siblings. Stephen B. Barnwell, *American Family,* 164, lists only ten but presumably omits stillbirths or those who died in infancy. James Smith himself, in an undated "Genealogy of the Rhett Family" in the Rhett Genealogy Notes, SCHS, states that he had fourteen, but he may well have been writing prior to the birth of his last daughter, Elizabeth, in 1815, and it should also be noted that the fact of the document being headed with the name Rhett rather than Smith means that it cannot be in the hand of James Smith himself, who died before the 1837 name change, but is a later copy made afterward. Thus it is possible that an error or a change in the number was made by whoever prepared the extant copy.

Hereafter, in order to differentiate him from his son Robert Barnwell Rhett Jr., citations will refer to the son by his full name and his father simply as Rhett.

24. Joseph W. Barnwell and Webber, "St. Helena's Parish Register," 188; James Smith, "Genealogy of the Rhett Family," n.d., Rhett Genealogy Notes, SCHS.

25. Stephen B. Barnwell, *American Family,* 51.

26. "The Low Country of South Carolina," *The Land We Love* 2 (November 1866), 8. Though this article carries no identity as to its author, the attitudes and expressions in it are somewhat resonant of those of Rhett himself.

27. Stephen B. Barnwell, *American Family,* 62–63.

28. Ibid., 39–43.

29. *Charleston Mercury,* March 11, 1863; Robert Barnwell to Rhett, December 30, 1842, in John Barnwell, "Hamlet to Hotspur: Letters of Robert Woodward Barnwell to Robert Barnwell Rhett," *South Carolina Historical Magazine* 75 (October 1976), 247–48.

30. Rhett to Robert Barnwell Rhett Jr., June 10, 1847, Crosby.

31. Rowland, Moore, and Rogers, *History of Beaufort County,* 285.

32. Robert Barnwell Rhett Jr. to Josephine Bacot, February 9, 1896, Bacot-Huger Collection, SCHS.

33. Ibid.; William J. Grayson, *James Louis Petigru: A Biographical Sketch* (New York, 1866), 48, 64–66.

34. *Memorial of the Late James L. Petigru. Proceedings of the Bar of Charleston, S.C., March 25, 1863* (New York, 1866), 23.

35. Robert D. Bass, "The Autobiography of William J. Grayson," Ph.D. diss., University of South Carolina, 1933, 117–18.

36. Barnwell Rhett Heyward, "Robert Barnwell Rhett the Elder," Smith-Rhett Genealogy, Barnwell Rhett Heyward Papers, SCHS. It should be noted that, with the exception of occasional personal additions such as this comment about Smith's school days, the Heyward sketch up through 1859 is taken verbatim from Daniel Wallace, *The Political Life and Services of the Hon. R. Barnwell Rhett, of South Carolina. By "A Contemporary"* (Cahaba, Ala., 1859).

37. Rowland, Moore, and Rogers, *History of Beaufort County,* 285–87.

38. Stephen B. Barnwell, *American Family,* 62–63; Rhett to Robert Barnwell Rhett Jr., July 30, 1845, July 29, 1847, Crosby. Some of the readings listed for Smith are based on his later demonstrated familiarity with those works.

39. Rhett, Autobiographical fragment, n.d., Rhett Papers, SCHS.

40. James Smith notes, n.d., "Genealogy of the Rhett Family" Rhett Genealogy Notes, SCHS; Heyward, "James Smith," Smith-Rhett Genealogy, Rhett Genealogy Notes, Barnwell Rhett Heyward Papers, SCHS.

41. Rhett to Claudia Stuart, October 21, 1867, Stuart Family Papers, SCHS.

42. Stephen B. Barnwell, *American Family,* 51, 165, 285; Heyward, "James Smith," Smith-Rhett Genealogy, Rhett Genealogy Notes, Barnwell Rhett Heyward Papers, SCHS.

43. Steiner, "South Atlantic States," 359; Rhett, Sketch of James Smith, Rhett to Robert Barnwell Rhett Jr., July 27, 1865, Crosby.

44. Rhett, Autobiographical fragment, Rhett Papers, SCHS; Rhett, Sketch of James Smith, Crosby; Heyward, Rhett, "Rhett the Elder," Smith-Rhett Genealogy, Barnwell Rhett Heyward Papers, SCHS; *Frank Leslie's Illustrated Newspaper,* February 9, 1861.

45. Rhett, My letter opposing the Tariff of 1842, Rhett Papers, SCHS.

46. Rowland, Moore, and Rogers, *History of Beaufort County,* 333, 335; Stephen B. Barnwell, *American Family,* 68.

47. *Congressional Globe,* 29th Cong., 1st sess., 1846, 143; 31st Cong., 2d sess., 1851, appendix, 320; Robert Barnwell Rhett Sr., "Political Parties in the United States," Aiken Rhett Collection, CM.

48. Ibid.

49. Robert Barnwell Rhett Sr., "Essay on Money Power in United States," n.d. [1866–76], Rhett Papers, SCHS.

50. Rhett, "Political Parties," Aiken Rhett Collection, CM.

51. Ibid.

52. Rowland, Moore, and Rogers, *History of Beaufort County,* 333–35.

53. *Memorial of . . . Petigru,* 25.

54. Robert Barnwell Rhett, "Tract on Government," *Southern Quarterly Review* 18 (April 1854), 502.

55. Ibid., 513–14.

56. Henry H. Perritt, "Robert Barnwell Rhett: South Carolina Secession Spokesman," Ph.D. diss., University of Florida, 1954, 362.

Chapter Two

1. Rowland, Moore, and Rogers, *History of Beaufort County,* 290–91.

2. *Charleston Mercury,* October 27, 1834.

3. Rhett, Autobiographical fragment, Rhett Papers, Heyward, Rhett, The Elder, Smith-Rhett Genealogy, Barnwell Rhett Heyward Papers, SCHS; Stephen B. Barnwell, *American Family,* 157; *Frank Leslie's Illustrated Newspaper,* February 9, 1861.

4. Heyward, Rhett, The Elder, Smith-Rhett Genealogy, Barnwell Rhett Heyward Papers, SCHS.

5. Autobiographical Sketch, 1858, Robert Barnwell Rhett Sr. Papers, South Caroliniana Library, University of South Carolina, Columbia (hereafter abbreviated SCL). In his Autobiographical fragment in the Rhett Papers, SCHS, Rhett says that he formed the partnership with Barnwell in Coosawhatchie in 1824, and together they moved to Walterborough in 1824. Stephen B. Barnwell, *American Family,* 109, says, too, that the partnership was formed at Coosawhatchie. However, the majority of other statements by Rhett maintain that the partnership commenced in Walterborough in 1824.

6. White, *Rhett,* 6; *Charleston Mercury,* March 16, 1824; Stephen B. Barnwell, *American Family,* 136.

7. *McLean* vs. McLellan, n.d., Rhett Papers, SCHS; Robert Barnwell Rhett Jr. to J. Franklin Jameson, May 19, 1899, J. Franklin Jameson Papers, Library of Congress (LC).

8. Elise Rhett Lewis, "A Few Personal Notes About the Hon. Robert Barnwell Rhett," n.d., Lucy Marmier to Rhett, n.d. [1859], claret receipt, n.d., Rhett Papers, SCHS; Robert Barnwell Rhett Jr. to Josephine Bacot, March 10, 1903, Bacot-Huger Collection, SCHS; *Charleston Journal of Commerce,* September 16, 1876; Rhett to Robert Barnwell Rhett Jr., June 9, 1847, November 13, 1848, Rhett to Alfred Rhett, August 3, 1847, January 7, 1848, Crosby.

9. Rhett, "Tract on Government," 492; *The Death and Funeral Ceremonies of John Caldwell Calhoun* (Columbia, 1850), 120.

10. Stephen B. Barnwell, *American Family,* 68; Rhett, "Political Parties," Aiken Rhett Collection, CM.

11. Rowland, Moore, and Rogers, *History of Beaufort County,* 336.

12. Robert W. Barnwell to Rhett, November 1, 1844, in John Barnwell, "Hamlet to Hotspur: Letters of Robert Woodward Barnwell to Robert Barnwell Rhett," *South Carolina Historical Magazine* 77 (October 1976), 253; Mary Delaney McConaghy, "Ordinary White Folk in a Lowcountry Community: The Structure and Dynamics of St. Bartholomew's Parish, South Carolina, 1850–1870," Ph.D. diss., University of Pennsylvania, 1996, 335.

13. Rhett, Autobiographical fragment, Rhett Papers, SCHS; Rhett, Synopsis of life, n.d. [1858], Rhett Papers, SCL.

14. Rhett, Autobiographical fragment, n.d., Rhett Papers, SCHS.

15. Journal of the House of Representatives of the Legislature of the State of South Carolina (hereafter JHRSC), 27th General Assembly, 1st sess., 1826, 2, 6, 12, 15, 19, 32, 67–68, 151, South Carolina Department of Archives and History, Columbia, S.C. (hereafter SCDAH),

16. Ibid., 56, 78, 87–88, 154, 185.

17. *Congressional Globe,* 30th Cong., 2d sess., 1849, 418.

18. Journal of the House of Representatives, 27th General Assembly, 1st sess., 1826, 56, 78, 79, 88, 90, 81, 93, 114–15, 118, 185, 192, SCDAH.

19. Ibid., 90, 188, 193.

20. Benjamin Franklin Perry, *Reminiscences of Public Men, with Speeches and Addresses* (Greenville, S.C., 1889), 129.

21. Journal of the House of Representatives, 27th General Assembly, 1st sess., 1826, 32, 77, 90, SCDAH; Rhett, Autobiographical fragment, Rhett Papers, SCHS; Heyward, Rhett, Smith-Rhett Genealogy, Barnwell Rhett Heyward Papers, SCHS; Robert Barnwell Rhett Jr. to Josephine Rhett, July 11, 1885, Bacot-Huger Collection, SCHS; White, *Rhett,* n 7.

22. Perry, *Reminiscences,* 129.

23. Ibid., 131; Emily B. Rhett genealogical notes, April 21, 1879, Rhett Family Papers, SCHS.

24. *Memorial to the Citizens of Colleton District, June 23, 1827,* Crosby. That Smith chaired the memorial committee is implicit in all the names of the members being listed alphabetically except his, which appeared first on the list. White, *Rhett,* 13, states that Smith's name did not "appear in connection with the popular or legisla-

tive discussion of the tariff during 1827," so somehow she missed this document in her research.

25. Thomas Grimké, *An Oration, on the Practicability and Expediency of Reducing the Whole Body of the Law to the Simplicity and Order of a Code* (Charleston, S.C., 1827), n.p.

26. Journal of the House of Representatives, 27th General Assembly, 2d sess., 1827, 1, 10–11, SCDAH.

27. Rhett, Autobiographical fragment, Rhett Papers, SCHS.

28. Stephanie McCurry, *Masters of Small Worlds: Yeoman Households, Gender Relations, & the Political Culture of the Antebellum South Carolina Low Country* (New York, 1995), 249.

29. McConaghy, "Ordinary White Folk," 320.

30. Journal of the House of Representatives, 27th General Assembly, 2d sess., 29–30, SCDAH.

31. Rhett, Autobiographical fragment, Rhett Papers, SCHS.

32. Journal of the House of Representatives, 27th General Assembly, 2d sess., 1827, 29–30, 35, 53, 68–70, 138–39, SCDAH.

33. Ibid., 186–87, 194, 199, 227–35, 245; Rhett, Autobiographical fragment, Rhett Papers, SCHS.

34. Journal of the House of Representatives, 27th General Assembly, 2d sess., 1827, 186–87, 219–23, SCDAH.

35. Ibid., 399; Rhett, Autobiographical fragment, Rhett Papers, SCHS; *Charleston Mercury,* February 1, 4, 1828.

36. See, for instance, John B. O'Neall, *Biographical Sketches of the Bench and Bar of South Carolina* (Charleston, S.C., 1859), 1:236–40.

37. Emily B. Rhett genealogical notes, Rhett Family Papers, SCHS.

38. Rhett, "Political Parties," Aiken Rhett Collection, CM.

39. Stephen B. Barnwell, *American Family,* 136; H. Hardy Perritt, "Robert Barnwell Rhett: Prophet of Resistance, 1828–1834," *Southern Speech Journal* 21 (Winter 1955), 103; Rowland, Moore, and Rogers, *History of Beaufort County,* 335.

40. Rowland, Moore, and Rogers, *History of Beaufort County,* 333.

41. Rhett, Autobiographical fragment, Rhett Papers, SCHS.

42. *Charleston Mercury,* June 18, 1828.

43. Rhett, Autobiographical Sketch, 1858, Rhett Papers, SCL.

44. McCurry, *Masters,* 257–60.

45. Perry, *Reminiscences,* 131.

46. Rhett, Autobiographical fragment, Rhett Papers, SCHS.

47. Perritt, "Prophet," 105. White, *Rhett,* 15, calls his language in the address "sophomoric," as indeed it was.

48. Rowland, Moore, and Rogers, *History of Beaufort County,* 317.

49. *Charleston Mercury,* July 9, 1828. Arnold Whitridge, *No Compromise! The Story of the Fanatics Who Paved the Way to the Civil War* (New York, 1960), 25, argues that in fact Rhett had been "a flamboyant nationalist" before the 1828 tariff made him a sectionalist, but Whitridge offers no evidence to support what is a clearly erroneous contention.

50. Perritt, "Prophet," 106; Rowland, Moore, and Rogers, *History of Beaufort County,* 337; Rhett, Autobiographical fragment, Rhett Papers, SCHS.

51. *Charleston Mercury,* July 9, 1828. White, *Rhett,* 16, says that this statement, signed only "Colleton," is probably by Smith, and certainly it bears all the hallmarks of his later position and is the first public statement of such a policy from anyone, which argues strongly in favor of his authorship.

52. Perritt, "Prophet," 106; Rhett, Autobiographical fragment, Rhett Papers, SCHS. Some of Smith's opinions stated here are not contained in the source cited but reflect his later comments on his beliefs and motives at the time.

53. Elizabeth Rhett to Alfred Rhett, March 12, 184–, Robert Barnwell Rhett Papers, Southern Historical Collection, University of North Carolina, Chapel Hill (SHC).

Chapter Three

1. "Nullification Resolutions of 1828," *Publications of the Southern History Association* 3 (Washington, D.C., 1899), 212, 219–20.

2. *Charleston Mercury,* August 6, 1829.

3. Journal of the House of Representatives of the Legislature of the State of South Carolina, 29th General Assembly, 1st sess., 1828, 9, 12, 57, 76, 85, 127–29, SCDAH; Rhett, Autobiographical fragment, Rhett Papers, SCHS.

4. Rhett, Autobiographical fragment, Rhett Papers, SCHS, acknowledges Calhoun's authorship of the *Exposition,* but says Legaré wrote the *Protest.* Perritt, "Prophet," 107, agrees. Having served on the committee, Smith should have known who wrote the document, but at the time Calhoun wanted his authorship kept quiet, so perhaps Legaré simply allowed the other members to believe that he had written it, and Smith never learned otherwise.

5. Rhett to Richard Crallé, October 25, 1854, in "Robert Barnwell Rhett on the Biography of Calhoun," *American Historical Review* 13 (January 1908), 33.

6. Journal of the House of Representatives, 28th General Assembly, 1st sess., 1827, 169, 178, 203–5, SCDAH.

7. Ibid., 118–21, 135.

8. *Charleston Mercury,* July 29, 1829.

9. Ibid., August 4, 1829.

10. Journal of the House of Representatives, 28th General Assembly, 2d sess., 1828, 6, 16, 93, 140, 171–72, SCDAH.

11. Rhett, Autobiographical fragment, Rhett Papers, SCHS; Heyward, Rhett, The Elder, Smith-Rhett Genealogy, Barnwell Rhett Heyward Papers, SCHS.

12. Journal of the House of Representatives, 28th General Assembly, 2d sess., 1828, 42, 48, 50, 65, 138, 194–95, SCDAH; *Charleston Mercury,* December 7, 1829. The *Mercury* article says the resolution passed 92 to 26, but the house journal should be the more accurate.

13. Journal of the House of Representatives, 28th General Assembly, 2d sess., 1828, 21, 146–48, SCDAH.

14. White, *Rhett,* 19.

15. Francis W. Pickens to James Henry Hammond, March 13, 1830, James Henry Hammond Papers, LC.

16. *Charleston Mercury,* July 12, 1830.

17. Ibid., October 19, 1830.

18. Perritt, "Prophet," 108.

19. *Charleston Mercury,* November 30, 1830.

20. Ibid., November 27, 1830; Robert Barnwell Rhett Jr. to J. Franklin Jameson, May 19, 1899, J. Franklin Jameson Papers, LC.

21. Journal of the House of Representatives of the Legislature of the State of South Carolina, 29th General Assembly, 1st sess., 1830, 1, 5, 10, 32, SCDAH; *Charleston Mercury,* November 26, 28, December 9, 1830.

22. *Charleston Mercury,* November 30, 1830.

23. Robert Barnwell Rhett Jr. to Josephine Bacot, September 14, 1890, Bacot-Huger Collection, SCHS.

24. N. Louise Bailey et al., eds., *Biographical Directory of the South Carolina Senate 1776–1985* (Columbia, S.C., 1986), 2:771–72.

25. Journal of the House of Representatives, 29th General Assembly, 1st sess., 1830, 200–202, SCDAH.

26. *Charleston Mercury,* December 10, 14, 1830.

27. Journal of the House of Representatives, 29th General Assembly, 1st sess., 1830, 200–202, SCDAH; *Charleston Mercury,* December 16, 1830; Perry, *Reminiscences,* 129.

28. Robert Barnwell Rhett Jr. to Josephine Bacot, September 14, 1890, Bacot-Huger Collection, SCHS.

29. *Charleston Mercury,* December 20, 1830.

30. Perry, *Reminiscences,* 129–30.

31. James L. Petigru to Hugh Legaré, January 9, 1831, James L. Petigru Papers, SCL. This letter is a bit confusing and actually appears to be dated 1839, but the only occasion of a "fracas at Columbia," as Petigru calls it, between Smith and Huger was in December 1830. There is also the fact that Petigru refers to Smith as Rhett, which would argue for 1839 being the correct year, but neither Rhett nor Huger was serving in Columbia at that time.

32. Robert Barnwell Rhett Jr. to Josephine Rhett, July 11, 1885, September 14, 1890, Bacot-Huger Collection, SCHS.

33. *Charleston Mercury,* December 21, 1830.

34. Robert Barnwell Rhett Jr. to Josephine Rhett, July 11, 1885, September 14, 1890, Bacot-Huger Collection, SCHS.

35. *Charleston Mercury,* 22 December 22, 1830; Journal of the House of Representatives, 29th General Assembly, 1st sess., 1830, 200–206, SCDAH.

36. *Proceedings of the Celebration of the 4ᵗʰ July, 1831, at Charleston, S.C. by the State Rights and Free Trade Party: Containing the Speeches & Toasts, Delivered on the Occasion* (Charleston, S.C., 1831), 3–36 *passim.*

37. *Charleston Mercury,* July 14, October 17, November 1, 9, 1831.

38. Ibid., August 4, 1831.

39. Ibid., December 2, 1831; Robert Barnwell Rhett Jr. to J. Franklin Jameson, May 19, 1899, J. Franklin Jameson Papers, LC.

40. *Charleston Mercury,* December 10, 1831.

41. Journal of the House of Representatives, 29th General Assembly, 2d sess., 1831, 64–65, SCDAH; *Charleston Mercury,* December 5, 9, 1831.

42. Journal of the House of Representatives, 29th General Assembly, 2d sess., 1831, 107, SCDAH; *Charleston Mercury,* December 17, 1831; White, *Rhett,* 23.

43. Robert Barnwell Smith (Since all of Rhett's correspondence prior to his name change in 1837 was signed Smith, citations here us that name for precision, hereafter cited as Smith.) to Charles Glover, June 12, July 10, 1832, Joseph Glover Papers, SCHS.

44. Smith to Waddy Thompson, February 10, 1832, Rhett Papers, SCL.

45. Stephen B. Barnwell, *American Family,* 165, 167; James L. Petigru to Jane Petigru, June 13, 1832, James L. Petigru Papers, LC.

46. *Charleston Mercury,* July 11, 14, 1832.

47. Perritt, "Prophet," 109. Perritt argues that in this speech Smith revealed that he was already beyond nullification, aiming toward, if not actually espousing, disunion.

48. *Charleston Mercury,* July 17, 1832.

49. Ibid., August 25, September 14, 1832.

50. Perritt, "Prophet," 110.

51. Henry D. Capers, *The Life and Times of C. G. Memminger* (Richmond, 1893), 107, 569ff.

Chapter Four

1. Rhett, "Political Parties," Aiken Rhett Collection, CM.

2. McConaghy, "Ordinary White Folks," 276; McCurry, *Masters,* 150ff.

3. James Smith to William H. Barnwell, March 1833, Barnwell Family Papers, SCHS.

4. Rhett to Burnet Rhett, n.d. [1872], Rhett Papers, SCHS; *Memorial of . . . Petigru,* 25.

5. Rhett, "Tract on Government," 494.

6. McCurry, *Masters,* 150–53.

7. Heyward, Rhett, The Elder, Smith-Rhett Genealogy, Barnwell Rhett Heyward Papers, SCHS.

8. Smith to William H. Barnwell, March 1833, Barnwell Family Papers, SCHS.

9. James L. Petigru to Hugh Legaré, October 29, December 21, 1832, James L. Petigru Papers, SCL.

10. Perritt, "Prophet," 110.

11. Journal of the House of Representatives of the Legislature of the State of South Carolina, 30th General Assembly, Special sess., 1832, 1–17, SCDAH.

12. *Charleston Mercury,* November 22, 1832.

13. *Journal of the Convention of the People of South Carolina: Assembled at Columbia on the 19th November, 1832, and again, on the 11th March, 1833* (Columbia, 1833), 53.

14. Journal of the House of Representatives, 30th General Assembly, 1st sess., 1832, 43, 80, 92, 99, 101–2, 107, 120–21, 142–43, 147–48, SCDAH.
15. Ibid., 151, 157, 171, 181–82.
16. Perry, *Reminiscences,* 133; Rhett, Autobiographical Sketch, 1858, Rhett Papers, SCL.
17. Smith to William H. Barnwell, March 1833, Barnwell Family Papers, SCHS.
18. Smith to William H. Barnwell, February 23, 1833, Barnwell Family Papers, SCHS.
19. Stephen B. Barnwell, *American Family,* 118.
20. *Charleston Mercury,* February 21, 1863.
21. Rhett, "Political Parties," Aiken Rhett Collection, CM.
22. Ibid.; Robert Barnwell Rhett Sr., Conversation concerning the late war in the United States, Robert Barnwell Rhett Sr. Papers, Southern Historical Collection, University of North Carolina, Chapel Hill (SHC).
23. James L. Petigru to Hugh Legaré, February 6, 1833, James L. Petigru Papers, SCL.
24. Perritt, "Prophet," 111.
25. In the Rhett Papers, SCHS, is an abstract of one of Clay's speeches on tariff modification, in Smith's handwriting.
26. Rhett, "Political Parties," Aiken Rhett Collection, MC.
27. Steiner, "South Atlantic States," 365.
28. *Journal of the Convention,* 93.
29. *Charleston Mercury,* March 18, 1833.
30. Ibid., March 20, 1833.
31. Smith's speech is found in two variants, first the immediate reporter's version in the *Mercury* for March 20, 1833 and then a fuller one furnished in writing by Smith in the March 26 issue. It has to be assumed that this later version has been corrected and probably considerably expanded by Smith for publication, as it contains much that is not in the first reporting. It was also printed in *Speeches Delivered in the Convention,* 21–27.
32. Perry, *Reminiscences,* 133.
33. *Charleston Mercury,* March 18, 22, 1833.
34. Ibid., 18, March 22, 1833; *Speeches Delivered in the Convention,* 6–11; Perritt, "Prophet," 114–15.
35. *Charleston Mercury,* March 26, 1833.
36. McCurry, *Masters,* 209.
37. Steiner, "South Atlantic States," 361–65.
38. *Charleston Mercury,* June 20, 1833.
39. John S. Coussons, "Thirty Years with Calhoun, Rhett, and the Charleston Mercury: A Chapter in South Carolina Politics," Ph.D. diss., Louisiana State University, 1971, 65; Robert Barnwell Rhett Jr. to J. Franklin Jameson, May 19, 1899, J. Franklin Jameson Papers, LC.
40. *Charleston Mercury,* November 19, 1833; James L. Petigru to Hugh Legaré, November 20, 1833, James L. Petigru Papers, SCL.
41. Thomas Cooper, *Hints, Suggestions, and Contributions toward the Labours of a Convention* (Columbia, 1832).

42. "Letters of Dr. Thomas Cooper," *American Historical Review* 6 (July 1901), 725–26.
43. *Charleston Mercury,* December 9, 1831.
44. Ibid., November 19, 20, 28, 1833; James L. Petigru to Hugh Legaré, November 20, 1833, James L. Petigru Papers, SCL.
45. James L. Petigru to Hugh Legaré, November 20, 1833, James L. Petigru Papers, SCL.
46. *Charleston Mercury,* November 19, 1833.
47. McConaghy, "Ordinary White Folks," 282–83.
48. *Charleston Mercury,* August 7, 1833, April 2, 1844; Stephen B. Barnwell, *American Family,* 118.
49. "Genealogy of the Rhett Family," n.d., Rhett Genealogy Notes, SCHS.
50. Lacy K. Ford, *Origins of Southern Radicalism: The South Carolina Upcountry, 1800–1860* (New York, 1988), 149.
51. *The Book of Allegiance; or, A Report of the Arguments of Counsel, Opinions of the Court of Appeals of South Carolina on the Oath of Allegiance* (Columbia, 1834), 3–4.
52. Ibid., 14ff.
53. *Charleston Mercury,* April 3, 1834.
54. *Argument of R. Barnwell Smith, Esq. Delivered in the Court of Appeals of the State of South Carolina, Before the Hon. David Johnson & William Harper; on the Third April, 1834; in the Case of the State, Ex Relatione Edward M'Crady, Against Col. B. F. Hunt; on the Constitutionality of the Oath in the Act for the Military Organization of This State, Passed 19th December, 1833* (Charleston, 1834), 3–10.
55. *Book of Allegiance,* 114, 123.
56. Perritt, "Prophet," 118; Perritt, "Rhett," 106–7, 222ff.
57. *Charleston Mercury,* July 7, 1834.
58. Perritt, "Rhett," 108–9; *Charleston Mercury,* December 11, 1834.
59. Steiner, "South Atlantic States," 361; Albert M. Smith to Smith, n.d., Rhett Papers, SCHS; Stephen B. Barnwell, *American Family,* 174; *Charleston Mercury,* December 11, 1834.

Chapter Five

1. Bond, January 28, 1835, Rhett Papers, SHC; "Genealogy of the Rhett Family," Rhett Genealogy Notes, SCHS.
2. *Charleston Mercury,* October 27, 1834.
3. Heyward, James Smith, Smith-Rhett Genealogy, Barnwell Rhett Heyward Papers; Robert Barnwell Rhett Jr. to Josephine Bacot, April 21, 1898, Bacot-Huger Collection, SCHS.
4. Rhett, Sketch of James Smith, Crosby.
5. Heyward, Smith-Rhett Genealogy, Barnwell Rhett Heyward Papers, SCHS.
6. Elise (Elizabeth) Rhett Lewis to Laura White, n.d., in Perritt, "Rhett," n 369; *Congressional Globe,* 32d Cong., 1st sess., appendix, 62. The original of the Lewis letter, like several other Rhett items, did not find its way to the Rhett Papers at

SCHS along with the rest of what Elise Lewis had when she helped White with her research in the 1920s. The papers were still in family hands when Perritt did his research.

7. Rowland, Moore, and Rogers, *History of Beaufort County,* 343.
8. The dating of this visit to England is conjectural. Higham & Fife to John Stapleton, February 17, 1836, John Stapleton Papers, SCL, says clearly that "when in England" Smith had been asked by Stapleton to assist Grimké in a case he was to handle for Stapleton. This definitely dates Smith's visit to before February 1836 and certainly before Grimké's death in October 1834.
9. Higham & Fife to John Stapleton, February 17, 1836, John Stapleton Papers, SCL.
10. Ibid.
11. James L. Petigru to Hugh Legaré, February 17, 1836, James L. Petigru Papers, SCL.
12. Suzanne Cameron Linder, *Historical Atlas of the Rice Plantations of the ACE River Basin—1860* (Columbia, 1995), 178, 311.
13. Heyward, Rhett, Smith-Rhett Genealogy, Barnwell Rhett Heyward Papers, SCHS; John Stapleton to Smith, July 28, 1836, Rhett Papers, SHC.
14. John Stapleton to Smith, July 28, 1836, Rhett Papers, SHC.
15. *Death and Funeral Ceremonies of John Caldwell Calhoun,* 151.
16. Rhett to Armistead L. Burt, June 24, 1845, Armistead L. Burt Papers, Duke University, Durham, North Carolina.
17. Smith to John Stapleton, n.d. [1836–37], Rhett Papers, SHC.
18. There is no explicit statement by him that he believed the story, but the fact that his father repeated it in his September 10, 1802 Genealogy, Rhett Genealogy Notes, SCHS, and that Robert's brother Edmund told the story in 1833 suggest that all of the sons would have gotten and accepted it from James Smith, as well as from local lore. See Steiner, "South Atlantic States," 361.
19. Heyward, Rhett, Smith-Rhett Genealogy, Barnwell Rhett Heyward Papers, SCHS.
20. Steiner, "South Atlantic States," 364.
21. Christopher G. Memminger to Rhett, November 27, 1844, Rhett Papers, SHC.
22. Coussons, "Thirty Years," 87–91.
23. Smith to Henry L. Pinckney, n.d. [February–March 1836], Rhett Papers, SCHS. This was written apparently as an open letter for the press, probably the *Mercury,* though it has not been found in print.
24. Ibid.
25. James L. Petigru to Hugh Legaré, February 17, 1836, James L. Petigru Papers, SCL.
26. *Charleston Mercury,* September 30, 1836.
27. Rowland, Moore, and Rogers, *History of Beaufort County,* 343.
28. James L. Petigru to Hugh Legaré, May 25, 1828, James L. Petigru Papers, SCL; *Charleston Mercury,* October 17, 1834.
29. Smith to the editor, August 18, 1836, *Charleston Mercury,* August 23, 1836, William Grayson to the editor, September 8, 1836, *Charleston Mercury,* 19 September 1836.
30. Bass, "Grayson," 163. Grayson in his memoirs does not mention Smith in his discussion of the leaders of nullification.

31. The extended correspondence by Smith, Thomas Smith, Grayson, and others, explaining this and the ensuing controversy, will be found in the *Charleston Mercury,* August 23, September 19, 21, 28, 30, October 7, 1836.

32. *Charleston Mercury,* September 28, December 29, 1835, January 22, 1836.

33. Ibid., September 4, 1836.

34. Ibid., October 7, 1836.

35. Ibid., September 29, October 6, 1836.

36. Ibid., October 14, 15, 16, 18, 24, 26, 1836.

37. Ibid., March 15, 1837. As probable evidence that Grayson retained some animosity toward Smith, in his memoirs written years later he never once mentions Smith/Rhett by name, even in discussing his retirement from office. See Bass, "Grayson."

38. Perry, *Reminiscences,* 130–32.

39. Rhett to John Stapleton, n.d. [fall 1837], Rhett Papers, SHC.

40. Perry, *Reminiscences,* 132; *Memorial of the Late James L. Petigru,* 20.

41. Deed, June 29, 1837, Rhett Papers, SCHS.

42. *Memorial of the Late James L. Petigru,* 20.

43. Rhett to John Stapleton, two letters, n.d. [summer–fall 1837], Rhett Papers, SHC.

44. *Charleston Mercury,* July 13, 1837.

45. George C. Rogers Jr., "South Carolina Federalists and the Origins of the Nullification Movement," *South Carolina Historical Magazine* 71 (January 1970), 30.

46. *Frank Leslie's Illustrated Newspaper,* February 9, 1861; Robert Barnwell Rhett Jr., Rhett Genealogy Notes, Rhett Genealogy, Rhett Family Papers, SCHS.

47. Perry, *Reminiscences,* 129.

48. "Historical Notes: The Date of the Changing of the Name Smith to Rhett," *South Carolina Historical and Genealogical Magazine* 30 (October 1929), 257–58.

49. *Frank Leslie's Illustrated Newspaper,* February 9, 1861. This sketch of Rhett's life up to 1861 is unusually well informed, especially in some areas for which other sources are silent, leading to the conclusion that it was based either upon information directly from Rhett himself or someone close to him in a position to know. Perritt, "Rhett," 114, offers no explanation of the name change, and White, *Rhett,* 34, gives it but a sentence, citing only this newspaper account.

50. Robert Barnwell Rhett Jr., Rhett Genealogy Notes, Rhett Genealogy, Rhett Family Papers, SCHS.

51. Rhett, "Political Parties," Aiken Rhett Collection, CM; Rhett, Essay on Money Power in United States, n.d., Rhett Papers, SCHS. White, *Rhett,* 34, states without citing a source that Rhett "enrolled as a Whig." In fact, no source has come to light that reveals Rhett ever in his own words stating that he was a Whig at that or any other time.

52. *Congressional Globe,* 25th Cong., 1st sess., 2.

53. James L. Petigru to Jane P. North, September 17, 1837, James L. Petigru to Thomas Petigru, September 18, 1837, in James Petigru Carson, ed., *Life, Letters and Speeches of James Louis Petigru* (Washington, D.C., 1920), 191.

54. White, *Rhett,* 33, maintains that between 1835 and 1837 Rhett "achieved a profound readjustment in his political outlook. Calhoun supplanted Turnbull and Hamilton

as his guide, philosopher, and, later, his friend. Turning from the thought and the vocabulary of revolution, he now mastered Calhoun's political theories, accepted them implicitly and prepared himself to support with all his abundant energy Calhoun's purpose and desire to preserve the Union as well as protect the South." There is little in Rhett's record, starting with his September 29, 1837, speech on the issue of treasury notes, to support such a contention.

55. *Congressional Globe,* 25th Cong., 1st sess., appendix, 152.

56. Coussons, "Thirty Years," n. 102, says that Rhett was a sudden convert to the sub-treasury idea, probably at Calhoun's direction, but again this is unconvincing, his support being entirely consistent with some of his actions when in the state legislature ten years earlier.

57. *Congressional Globe,* 25th Cong., 1st sess., 41.

58. Charles Francis Adams, ed., *Memoirs of John Quincy Adams* (Philadelphia, 1874–77), 9:386.

59. *Congressional Globe,* 25th Cong., 1st sess., appendix, 151–53.

60. Ernest M. Lander Jr., "The Calhoun-Preston Feud, 1836–1842," *South Carolina Historical Magazine* 59 (January 1958), 26.

Chapter Six

1. Adams, *Memoirs,* 9:396.

2. *Congressional Globe,* 25th Cong., 1st sess., 70, 72, 93, 105; Adams, *Memoirs,* 9:396, 398.

3. Rhett, "Political Parties," Aiken Rhett Collection, CM; Heyward, Rhett, Smith-Rhett Genealogy, Barnwell Rhett Heyward Papers, SCHS; *Charleston Mercury,* February 13, 1843.

4. Heyward, James Smith, Smith-Rhett Genealogy, Barnwell Rhett Heyward Papers, SCHS.

5. Capers, *Memminger,* 126.

6. Lander, "Calhoun-Preston Feud," 28–30; John Niven, *John C. Calhoun and the Price of Union* (Baton Rouge, 1988), 231–32.

7. Adams, *Memoirs,* 9:451.

8. *Congressional Globe,* 25th Cong., 2d sess., 21–22; *Charleston Mercury,* December 21, 1837. This 14 December 1837 letter is not signed by Rhett but merely attributed to a member of Congress, but it so clearly mirrors his attitudes that he was almost certainly the author. White, *Rhett,* 38, concurs in Rhett's authorship.

9. *Congressional Globe,* 25th Cong., 2d sess., 41; Henry Wilson, *History of the Rise and Fall of the Slave Power Conspiracy in America* (Boston, 1872), 1:352. Henry Wilson was not in Congress in 1838, and so was not an eyewitness to this scene, but his description is so vivid as to suggest that he had it from someone who was there.

10. Henry Wilson, *Slave Power Conspiracy,* 1:352.

11. John B. Edmunds Jr., *Francis W. Pickens and the Politics of Destruction* (Chapel Hill, N.C., 1986), 45.

12. John McCardell, *The Idea of a Southern Nation: Southern Nationalists and Southern Nationalism, 1830–1860* (New York, 1979), 64.

13. Heyward, Rhett, Smith-Rhett Genealogy, Barnwell Rhett Heyward Papers, SCHS; *Charleston Mercury,* December 27, 1837.

14. *Address to the People of Beaufort and Colleton Districts, upon the Subject of Abolition, by Robert Barnwell Rhett. January 15, 1838* (N.p., 1838), 3. Jesse T. Carpenter, *The South as a Conscious Minority 1789–1861* (New York, 1930), 185, apparently basing it on an earlier source, implies that Rhett only introduced the secession motion, ignoring the previous resolution, and the fact that secession was an alternative and not an end in itself.

15. *Charleston Mercury,* January 6, 1838.

16. *Address to the People of Beaufort and Colleton,* 3–13.

17. McCurry, *Masters,* 232, 234.

18. *Charleston Mercury,* February 9, 1838; Rowland, Moore, and Rogers, *History of Beaufort County,* 342–43.

19. James L. Petigru to Hugh Legaré, February 14, 1838, James L. Petigru Papers, SCL.

20. *Charleston Mercury,* February 20, 1838.

21. Adams, *Memoirs,* 9:468; *Congressional Globe,* 25th Cong., 2d sess., 83.

22. Rhett to Jesse Hoyt, February 20, 1838, Rhett Papers, Duke University, Durham, N.C.

23. Adams, *Memoirs,* 9:485; *Congressional Globe,* 25th Cong., 2d sess., 152, 157, Appendix, 93–94.

24. *Congressional Globe,* 25th Cong., 2d sess., 317, 319; *Charleston Mercury,* May 16, 1838.

25. *Congressional Globe,* 25th Cong., 2d sess., 21–22, 189, 288.

26. Ibid., 189, 489, 496.

27. Adams, *Memoirs,* 9:529.

28. *Congressional Globe,* 25th Cong., 2d sess., 369–70.

29. Ibid., Appendix, 94, 331–34.

30. Francis W. Pickens to Patrick Noble, May 23, 1838, in Alice Noble Waring, "Five Letters from Francis W. Pickens to Patrick Noble, 1835–1836," *South Carolina Historical Magazine* 54 (April 1953), 80.

31. *Charleston Mercury,* June 25, July 6, 1838.

32. Ibid., June 14, 1838; James L. Petigru to Hugh Legaré, May 7, 1838, James L. Petigru Papers, SCL.

33. *Charleston Mercury,* June 28, 1838.

34. *Congressional Globe,* 25th Cong., 2d sess., appendix, 503–9.

35. Rhett, "Political Parties," Aiken Rhett Collection, CM; Heyward, Rhett, Smith-Rhett Genealogy, Barnwell Rhett Heyward Papers, SCHS.

Chapter Seven

1. "Genealogy of the Rhett Family," Rhett Genealogy Notes, SCHS.

2. *Charleston Mercury,* September 10, 1838.

3. Ibid., August 22, 27, 29, September 6, 1838.
4. Ibid., September 10, 1838.
5. John C. Calhoun to George Elliott et al., August 19, 1838, *The Papers of John C. Calhoun,* Clyde N. Wilson, ed. (Columbia, 1981), 14:402–3.
6. Edmunds, *Pickens,* 53; Chauncey Samuel Boucher, "The Annexation of Texas and the Bluffton Movement in South Carolina," *Mississippi Valley Historical Review* 6 (June 1919), 17.
7. Rowland, Moore, and Rogers, *History of Beaufort County,* 342–43.
8. Coussons, "Thirty Years," 157.
9. John C. Calhoun to Rhett, September 13, 1838, Wilson, ed., *Papers of John C. Calhoun,* 14:425–26.
10. Coussons, "Thirty Years," 124.
11. Wallace, *Political Life,* 16.
12. *Charleston Mercury,* December 14, 15, 1838.
13. Heyward, Rhett, Smith-Rhett Genealogy, Barnwell Rhett Heyward Papers, SCHS.
14. Ibid.; Wallace, *Political Life,* 16; Adams, *Memoirs,* 10:60, 114.
15. *Congressional Globe,* 25th Cong., 3d sess., appendix, 132–34.
16. Ibid., 317.
17. The Salt Ketcher is now known as the Salkehatchie River.
18. *Speech of Robert Barnwell Rhett, to His Constituents on the Salt Ketcher River, at a Dinner Given on 4th day of July, 1839* (Charleston, S. C., 1839), 3–19. Rhett's speech also appeared in the *Mercury* on July 31, 1839.
19. Rhett to James K. Polk, August 21, 1839, in Wayne Cutler, ed., *Correspondence of James K. Polk, V 1839–1841* (Nashville, 1979), 201–2. Variations in portions of this letter quoted in the text from the published version cited are due to errors in editorial transcription of Rhett's difficult handwriting.
20. Franklin H. Elmore to Jesse Hoyt, April 30, 1839, Franklin H. Elmore Papers, SCL.
21. James L. Petigru to Hugh Legaré, October 5, 1839, James L. Petigru Papers, SCL.
22. James L. Petigru to Hugh Legaré, n.d. [1838–39], James L. Petigru Papers, SCL.
23. Francis W. Pickens to James H. Hammond, January 12, 1840, James Henry Hammond Papers, LC.
24. James H. Hammond to Francis W. Pickens, December 24, 1839, James Henry Hammond Papers, LC.
25. This comment appears in the margin of James L. Petigru to Hugh Legaré, October 5, 1839, James L. Petigru Papers, SCL, and is almost certainly a comment written after Petigru's death by someone of his family, perhaps his grandson James Petigru Carson, who edited his papers for publication in 1920.
26. Harold S. Schultz, *Nationalism and Sectionalism in South Carolina, 1852–1860: A Study of the Movement for Southern Independence* (Durham, N.C., 1950), 12–13.
27. Francis W. Pickens to James H. Hammond, December 1, 1839, Francis W. Pickens to Franklin H. Elmore, January 18, 1840, James Henry Hammond Papers; C. E. Haynes to Franklin H. Elmore, January 6, 1840, Franklin H. Elmore Papers, LC.

28. Francis W. Pickens to James H. Hammond, December 1, 1839, Francis W. Pickens to Franklin H. Elmore, January 18, 1840, James Henry Hammond Papers, LC; Adams, *Memoirs,* 10:144.

29. John C. Calhoun to Patrick Calhoun, December 4, 1839, Wilson, ed., *Papers of John C. Calhoun,* 15:6, John C. Calhoun to Anna Clemson, December 18, 1839, 20.

30. Adams, *Memoirs,* 10:144; *Congressional Globe,* 26th Cong., 1st sess., 20, 30th Cong., 1st sess., 528; Heyward, James Smith; Heyward, Rhett, Smith-Rhett Genealogy, Barnwell Rhett Heyward Papers, SCHS.

31. Adams, *Memoirs,* 10:144, 148–49, 151, 158, 160, 171; *Congressional Globe,* 26th Cong., 1st sess., 20.

32. Adams, *Memoirs,* 10:171; *Congressional Globe,* 26th Cong., 1st sess., 67–68; Heyward, Rhett, Smith-Rhett Genealogy, Barnwell Rhett Heyward Papers, SCHS.

33. Francis W. Pickens to James H. Hammond, January 12, 1840, James Henry Hammond Papers, LC.

34. James P. Carroll to Francis W. Pickens, March 8, 1840, Francis W. Pickens Papers, Duke University, Durham, N.C.

35. Francis Mallory to Robert M. T. Hunter, January 12, 1840, in Charles Henry Ambler, ed., *Correspondence of Robert M. T. Hunter, 1826–1876. Annual Report of the American Historical Association for the Year 1916* (Washington, D.C., 1918), 2:32.

36. Coussons, "Thirty Years," 124, and John Barnwell, *Love of Order: South Carolina's First Secession Crisis* (Chapel Hill, N.C., 1982), 37, both conclude that Rhett was acting on Calhoun's instructions with the Richardson nomination. Hammond, on the other hand, believed that Calhoun knew nothing about it, or even that Rhett did it in defiance of Calhoun (James H. Hammond to Francis W. Pickens, January 18, 1840, Francis W. Pickens Papers, Duke University, Durham, N.C.). Drew Gilpin Faust, *James Henry Hammond and the Old South* (Baton Rouge, La., 1982), 215, suggests that the degree of Calhoun's involvement or foreknowledge, if any, is unclear though adding that he said nothing for or against the move after the fact. The general impression at least among Hammond's friends is that Rhett acted on his own, but being loyal followers of Calhoun they would prefer that view to the idea of Calhoun betraying one of his favorites.

37. Butler to James H. Hammond, January 17, February 5, 1840, James Henry Hammond Papers, LC.

38. James H. Hammond to Francis W. Pickens, January 18, 1840, Francis W. Pickens Papers, Duke University, Durham, N.C.

39. James P. Carroll to Francis W. Pickens, March 8, 1840, Francis W. Pickens Papers, Duke University, Durham, N.C.

40. L. M. Butler to James H. Hammond, January 17, February 5, 1840, James Henry Hammond Papers, LC.

41. John C. Calhoun to James H. Hammond, February 23, 1840, James Henry Hammond Papers, LC.

42. Coussons, "Thirty Years," 124ff.

43. Franklin H. Elmore to Francis W. Pickens, January 3, February 24, 1840, Francis W. Pickens to Franklin H. Elmore, March 6, 1840, Franklin H. Elmore Papers; Thomas T. Player to James H. Hammond, February 9, 1840, James Henry Hammond Papers, LC.

44. John Stapleton to Rhett, June 21, 1840, Rhett Papers, SHC.

45. Adams, *Memoirs,* 10:283; *Congressional Globe,* 26th Cong., 1st sess., 287, 382–84, 386, 397, 475–76, Appendix, 95–98.

46. Adams, *Memoirs,* 10:315.

47. Higham & Fife to John Stapleton, April 20, 1838, John Stapleton to Higham & Fife, July 17, 1838, John Stapleton Papers, SCL; John Stapleton to Rhett, October 30, 1839, June 21, September 12, 1840, Rhett Papers, SHC.

48. J. Robinson to Rhett, October 21, 1840, April 2, 1841, Planters & Mechanics Bank of South Carolina Letter Book, Duke University, Durham, N.C.; T. Street to John C. Calhoun, August 19, 1840, Wilson, ed., *Papers of John C. Calhoun,* 15:334.

49. Rhett to unnamed son, March 24, April 1, 1840, Elizabeth Rhett to Edmund and Alfred Rhett, May 5, 1840, Rhett Papers, SHC.

50. John Stapleton to Rhett, June 21, 1840, Rhett Papers, SHC.

51. John C. Calhoun to James H. Hammond, April 29, 1840, Wilson, ed., *Papers of John C. Calhoun,* 15:190.

52. Faust, *Hammond,* 217–19; *Charleston Mercury,* June 17, 1840; *Edgefield (S.C.) Advertiser,* July 16, 1840.

53. James H. Hammond to Catherine Hammond, August 25, 1840, James Henry Hammond Papers, LC.

54. White, *Rhett,* 46.

55. "Genealogy of the Rhett Family," Rhett Genealogy Notes, SCHS.

Chapter Eight

1. *Congressional Globe,* 26th Cong., 2d sess., 118, 132; Adams, *Memoirs,* 10:402–3.

2. Barnwell to Rhett, January 23, 1841, in John Barnwell, "Hamlet to Hotspur," 241; ibid. May 15, 1841, 243. (All citations employing last name "Barnwell" alone are to Robert W. Barnwell).

3. Ibid., May 15, 1841, 237–39; Thomas Rhett to Robert Barnwell Rhett Jr., n.d., Rhett Papers, SHC.

4. Heyward, Rhett, Smith-Rhett Genealogy, Barnwell Rhett Heyward Papers, SCHS.

5. Elizabeth Rhett to Alfred Rhett, March 12, 1841, Rhett Papers, SHC.

6. Barnwell to Rhett, January 23, May 15, 1841, in John Barnwell, "Hamlet to Hotspur," 238–39, 243–44.

7. Rhett to John Stapleton, January 16, 1841, John Stapleton to Rhett, October 30, 1839, July 31, 1841, Rhett Papers, SHC.

8. Rhett to Richard Crallé, October 25, 1854, in "Robert Barnwell Rhett on the Biography of Calhoun," 311; Robert Barnwell Rhett Jr. to J. Franklin Jameson, May 19, 1899, J. Franklin Jameson Papers, LC.

9. Edmunds, *Pickens,* 56; Barnwell to Rhett, January 23, 1841, Rhett Papers, SHC; Carol Bleser, ed., *Secret and Sacred: The Diaries of James Henry Hammond, Southern Slaveholder* (New York, 1988), 58, 60.

10. Rhett to the Editor, January 20, 1843, *Charleston Mercury,* January 24, 1843.

11. Barnwell to Rhett, May 15, 1841, in John Barnwell, "Hamlet to Hotspur," 242.

12. James L. Petigru to Rhett, September 17, 1841, Barnwell to Rhett, May 15, 1841, Rhett Papers, SHC.

13. Notes headed "What might be done after 1842," Rhett Papers, SCHS.

14. *Charleston Mercury,* January 25, 1841; George McFarlane to Rhett, June 6, 1841, Rhett Papers, SHC.

15. *Congressional Globe,* 27th Cong., 1st sess., 57, 100–101, 155–56; Adams, *Memoirs,* 10:497.

16. *Congressional Globe,* 27th Cong., 1st sess., 166–67; Adams, *Memoirs,* 10:499.

17. *Congressional Globe,* 27th Cong., 1st sess., 207, 212.

18. Ibid., 244–45, 254; Adams, *Memoirs,* 10:509. Rhett's copies of the Rhode Island and Massachusetts tariff resolutions are in the Rhett Papers, SCHS.

19. *Congressional Globe,* 27th Cong., 1st sess., 367–68.

20. *Charleston Mercury,* July 22, 1841.

21. *The Right of Debate, Considered in Three Letters, Addressed to the Editors of the National Intelligencer, by the Hon. R. Barnwell Rhett* (Washington, D.C., 1841), 3–19.

22. *Charleston Mercury,* August 31, September 23, 1841.

23. John Bassett Moore, ed., *The Works of James Buchanan* (Philadelphia, 1908–11), 5:69.

24. Coussons, "Thirty Years," 142–43.

25. John Stuart to John C. Calhoun, November 19, 1841, Wilson, ed., *Papers of John C. Calhoun,* 15:819–20; Edmunds, *Pickens,* 57–58.

26. *An Address from the Hon. R. Barnwell Rhett to the People of Beaufort and Colleton Districts* (Washington, D.C., 1841), 3–7.

27. Stuart to John C. Calhoun, November 19, 1841, Wilson, ed., *Papers of John C. Calhoun,* 15:819–20; M. E. Carn to James H. Hammond, November 18, 1841, James Henry Hammond Papers, LC.

28. A. P. Butler to Rhett, December 9, 1841, Rhett Papers, SHC; Charles R. Carroll to James H. Hammond, August 23, 1841, James Henry Hammond Papers.

29. Report of Edmund Rhett, December 1841, Rhett Papers, SHC; "Genealogy of the Rhett Family," Rhett Genealogy Notes, SCHS.

30. Adams, *Memoirs,* 11:50.

31. *Congressional Globe,* 27th Cong., 2d sess., 25, 50–51, Appendix, 39–42.

32. Adams, *Memoirs,* 1:141.

33. *Congressional Globe,* 182, 211; Adams, *Memoirs,* 11:56.

34. Receipt, 30 May 1842, H. M. Fuller to Rhett, January 21, 1842, Higham & Fife to Rhett, April 7, 1842, Rhett Papers, SHC; Charles R. Carroll to James H. Hammond, August 23, 1841, James Henry Hammond Papers, LC. Carroll's letter actually says that Rhett owed seven hundred thousand dollars, but this must certainly be a simple error of adding one too many zeros.

35. A. Campbell to Rhett, September 17, 1842, Clement Cox to Rhett, 2 September 1842, Rhett Papers, SHC.

36. Rhett to Claudia Stuart, April 1, 1842, Stuart Family Papers, SCHS.

37. Robert Barnwell Rhett, To the Steeple of Christ Church in Georgetown, August 23, 1842, Rhett Papers, SCHS.

38. Albert Rhett to Rhett, June 18, 1842, Rhett Papers, SHC.

39. Rhett, "Tract on Government," 492.

40. John C. Calhoun to Franklin H. Elmore, May 30, 1842, Wilson, ed., *Papers of John C. Calhoun*, 16:264; John P. Richardson to Rhett, January 21, 1842, Rhett Papers, SHC.

41. Thomas Rayson to Rhett, January 7, 1842, Rhett Papers, SHC; Rhett to John C. Calhoun, January 17, 1842, Wilson, ed., *Papers of John C. Calhoun*, 16:49.

42. *Congressional Globe*, 7th Cong., 2d sess., 708–9, Appendix, 605–8.

43. Claudia Stuart to Elizabeth Rhett, July 8, 1842, Rhett Papers, SHC; Heyward, Rhett, Smith-Rhett Genealogy, Barnwell Rhett Heyward Papers, SCHS.

44. *Congressional Globe*, 27th Cong., 2d sess., 749.

45. Niven, *Calhoun*, 254.

46. Robert Barnwell Rhett Jr. to Josephine Bacot, February 23, 1896, Bacot-Huger Collection, SCHS.

47. Barnwell to Rhett, October 1, 1842, Rhett Papers, SHC. Carpenter, *Conscious Minority*, 81, suggests that in 1842 Rhett was an "aggressive advocate of Southern co-operation." This rather misses the point. In 1842 Rhett was advocating cooperation within South Carolina and *national* cooperation between state rights men and Democrats. There was nothing regional in his scheme or Calhoun's, other than the message to the Democrats that they could not win in 1844 without the South.

48. Franklin H. Elmore to Andrew P. Butler, August 11, 1842, Rhett Papers, SHC; E. G. B. Hart to Robert M. T. Hunter, October 5, 1842, in Ambler, *Hunter*, 50; Joseph A. Scoville to Robert M. T. Hunter, November 21, 1842, 52, Rhett to John C. Calhoun, October 3, 1842, Wilson, ed., *Papers of John C. Calhoun*, 16:485–86; ibid., October 13, 1842, 493.

49. Rhett to John C. Calhoun, October 13, 1842, Wilson, ed., *Papers of John C. Calhoun*, 16:493–96.

50. Albert Rhett to Rhett, June 18, 1842, Rhett Papers, SHC.

51. Thomas T. Player to James H. Hammond, February 9, 1840, James Henry Hammond Papers, LC.

52. Albert Rhett to Rhett, August 13, October 22, 1842, Rhett Papers, SHC.

53. Bleser, *Secret and Sacred*, 115.

54. Francis W. Pickens to John C. Calhoun, Wilson, ed., *Papers of John C. Calhoun*, 16:535.

55. Niven, *Calhoun*, 259.

56. John C. Calhoun to Robert M. T. Hunter, October 26, 1842, Wilson, ed., *Papers of John C. Calhoun*, 16:516; John P. Richardson to Rhett, May 17, 1842, Stuart to Rhett, January 9, 1843, Rhett Papers, SHC.

57. William C. Preston to Waddy Thompson, December 17, 1842, William Campbell Preston Papers, SCL.

58. Barnwell to Rhett, December 30, 1842, Rhett Papers, SHC.

59. Edmunds, *Pickens,* 57–58.

60. Stuart to Rhett, January 9, 1843, Rhett Papers, SHC.

61. Bleser, *Secret and Sacred,* 116, 212.

62. William C. Preston to Waddy Thompson, December 17, 1842, William Campbell Preston Papers, SCL.

63. Rhett to James Buchanan, October 20, 1845, James Buchanan Papers, Historical Society of Pennsylvania, Philadelphia.

64. *Charleston Mercury,* February 13, 1843.

65. Edmund Rhett to Rhett, December 1842, Rhett Papers, SHC.

66. James L. Petigru to Hugh Legaré, March 2, 1843, James L. Petigru Papers, SCL.

67. Barnwell to Rhett, December 30, 1842, Rhett Papers, SHC.

68. Franklin H. Elmore to Rhett, January 4, 1843, Rhett Papers, SHC.

69. John C. Calhoun to James H. Hammond, January 23, 1843, Wilson, ed., *Papers of John C. Calhoun,* 16:628.

70. Franklin H. Elmore to Rhett, January 4, 1843, Rhett Papers, SHC.

71. *Charleston Mercury,* January 24, 28, 1843.

72. Ibid., February 9, 10, 14, 17, 24, March 3, 1843.

73. James L. Petigru to ?, February 24, 1843, in Carson, *Petigru,* 213.

Chapter Nine

1. Robert B. Rhett, "An Appeal to the Democratic Party," January 1843, Wilson, ed., *Papers of John C. Calhoun,* 16:584; *Charleston Mercury,* January 25, 1843.

2. [Robert Barnwell Rhett], *The Compromises of the Constitution Considered in the Organization of a National Convention* (Washington, D.C., 1843), 1–13; Peter Manning to Rhett, January 26, 1843, Rhett Papers, SHC.

3. Robert M. T. Hunter to My dear Sir, February 20, 1843, Virginia Historical Society, Richmond.

4. E. G. B. Hart to Robert M. T. Hunter, October 5, 1842, in Ambler, *Hunter,* 50.

5. Stuart to Rhett, January 9, 1843, Rhett Papers, SHC; Robert Barnwell Rhett Jr. to J. Franklin Jameson, May 19, 1899, J. Franklin Jameson Papers, LC.

6. Robert M. T. Hunter to My dear Sir, February 20, 1843, Virginia Historical Society, Richmond; Rhett to Richard Crallé, October 25, 1854, in "Rhett on the Biography of Calhoun," 311. The fullest examination of this episode, establishing Hunter's role, is James L. Anderson and W. Edwin Hemphill, "The 1843 Biography of John C. Calhoun: Was R. M. T. Hunter Its Author?," *Journal of Southern History* 38 (August 1972), 469–74. The conflict with Rhett's 1855 account to Crallé, which claimed that the book was almost entirely autobiographical and that Hunter contributed only a page and a half, is best explained by Rhett's not being present when Hunter undertook the writing task and then not being told by Hunter of his authorship when they read it together. Unlikely as this seems, Hunter told his wife that he did not want his role in the work to be known

outside their family. Thus, seeing only the page and a half that Hunter actually wrote in front of him, Rhett could believe that this was all that Hunter contributed.

7. *Charleston Mercury,* February 10, April 7, 1843; Wilson, ed., *Papers of John C. Calhoun,* 17:153n.

8. Coussons, "Thirty Years," 146–48, 150; Rhett to Robert M. T. Hunter, May 12, 1843, R. M. T. Hunter Papers, University of Virginia, Charlottesville.

9. Rhett to Orestes Brownson, May 19, 1843, Rhett Papers, SCL.

10. James L. Petigru to Hugh Legaré, May 13,1843, James L. Petigru Papers, SCL; William C. Preston to Waddy Thompson, May 27, 1843, William Campbell Preston Papers, SCL.

11. James L. Petigru to Hugh Legaré, June 3, 1843, James L. Petigru Papers, SCL.

12. Edmunds, *Pickens,* 73.

13. Rhett to Robert Barnwell Rhett Jr., December 28, 1849, Crosby.

14. Albert Rhett to John C. Calhoun, July 17, 1843, Wilson, ed., *Papers of John C. Calhoun,* 17:309, August 3, 1843, 332–33, August 17, 1843, 361, Virgil Maxcy to John C. Calhoun, August 6, 1843, 338, Rhett to John C. Calhoun, July 22, 1843, 312–13, August 25, 1843, 376; *Charleston Mercury,* July 19, 1843.

15. Niven, *Calhoun,* 257ff.

16. Rhett to John C. Calhoun, August 26, 1843, Wilson, ed., *Papers of John C. Calhoun,* 17:379–80.

17. Rhett to John C. Calhoun, August 25, 1843, Wilson, ed., *Papers of John C. Calhoun,* 17:76–77; Robert M. T. Hunter to My dear Sir, February 20, 1843, Virginia Historical Society, Richmond.

18. Franklin H. Elmore to Robert M. T. Hunter, August 18, 1843, Hunter Family Papers, Virginia Historical Society, Richmond; Rhett to John C. Calhoun, August 26, 1843, Wilson, ed., *Papers of John C. Calhoun,* 17:379–80, Franklin H. Elmore to John C. Calhoun, September 4, 1843, 398–400, note, n.d., 534.

19. Franklin H. Elmore to John C. Calhoun, September 4, 1843, Wilson, ed., *Papers of John C. Calhoun,* 17:398–400, Maxcy to John C. Calhoun, September 20, 1843, 458, October 13, 1843, 507, Rhett to John C. Calhoun, September 21, 1843, 460, October 7, 1843, 491.

20. Rhett to John C. Calhoun, September 21, 1843, Wilson, ed., *Papers of John C. Calhoun,* 17:460, October 7, 1843, 491, Robert M. T. Hunter to John C. Calhoun, September 19, 1843, 455, Albert Rhett to John C. Calhoun, September 12, 1843, 434, September 15, 1843, 447.

21. Rhett to James Buchanan, September 15, 1843, James Buchanan Papers, Historical Society of Pennsylvania, Philadelphia; Rhett to John C. Calhoun, October 8, 1843, Wilson, ed., *Papers of John C. Calhoun,* 17:493.

22. Robert M. T. Hunter to John C. Calhoun, September 19, 1843, Wilson, ed., *Papers of John C. Calhoun,* 17:455.

23. Joseph Scoville to John C. Calhoun, October 25, 1842, Wilson, ed., *Papers of John C. Calhoun,* 16:508, Rhett to John C. Calhoun, August 25, 1843, 17:376–77.

NOTES TO PAGES 178-183

24. Rhett to James Buchanan, September 15, 1843, James Buchanan Papers, Historical Society of Pennsylvania, Philadelphia; William Smith to John C. Calhoun, September 24, 1843, Wilson, ed., *Papers of John C. Calhoun,* 17:465, Rhett to John C. Calhoun, September 21, 1843, 459–60.

25. Haym Solomon to John C. Calhoun, October 1, 1843, Wilson, ed., *Papers of John C. Calhoun,* 17:479, Robert M. T. Hunter to John C. Calhoun, October 10, 1843, 495, Rhett to John C. Calhoun, October 7, 1843, 491–92, October 8, 1843, 493.

26. Rhett to John C. Calhoun, October 16, 1843, Wilson, ed., *Papers of John C. Calhoun,* 17:509–10.

27. Rhett to James Buchanan, September 15, 1843, James Buchanan to Rhett, September 25, 1843, James Buchanan Papers, Historical Society of Pennsylvania, Philadelphia.

28. Rhett to John C. Calhoun, October 16, 1843, Wilson, ed., *Papers of John C. Calhoun,* 17:510–11.

29. Rhett to John C. Calhoun, October 7, 1843, Wilson, ed., *Papers of John C. Calhoun,* 17:492.

30. Ibid., October 16, 1843, 509–10.

31. Francis W. Pickens to John C. Calhoun, October 22, 1843, Wilson, ed., *Papers of John C. Calhoun,* 17:520.

32. A Statement of the last sickness and death of Alb. Rhett, by Robert B. Rhett, n.d. [early November 1843], Rhett Papers, SCHS.

33. Rhett to John C. Calhoun, December 8, 1843, Wilson, ed., *Papers of John C. Calhoun,* 17:597.

34. Rhett to Robert Barnwell Rhett Jr., December 14, 1843, Crosby.

35. Rhett to John C. Calhoun, November 1843, Wilson, ed., *Papers of John C. Calhoun,* 17:529, December 2, 1843, 582–83, December 8, 1843, 595–96, Maxcy to John C. Calhoun, December 10, 1843, 599–600; Rhett to Robert M. T. Hunter, December 27, 1843, R. M. T. Hunter Papers, University of Virginia.

36. Alexander Jones to John C. Calhoun, December 7, 1843, Wilson, ed., *Papers of John C. Calhoun,* 17:592–93.

37. Boucher, "Annexation," 7.

38. Rhett to John C. Calhoun, December 8, 1843, Wilson, ed., *Papers of John C. Calhoun,* 17:596.

39. Maxcy to John C. Calhoun, December 10, 1843, Wilson, ed., *Papers of John C. Calhoun,* 17:600; Boucher, "Annexation," 8–10.

40. Rhett to Robert M. T. Hunter, December 27, 1843, R. M. T. Hunter Papers, University of Virginia.

41. Rhett to John C. Calhoun, December 9–10, 1843, Wilson, ed., *Papers of John C. Calhoun,* 17:603; *Charleston Mercury,* December 15, 1843.

42. Coussons, "Thirty Years," 150.

43. Rhett to Robert M. T. Hunter, December 27, 1843, R. M. T. Hunter Papers, University of Virginia.

44. Ibid.

45. Boucher, "Annexation," 9–10.

46. Coussons, "Thirty Years," 150–51; Boucher, "Annexation," 10; Robert M. T. Hunter to Rhett, February 1844, Rhett Papers, SHC; Franklin H. Elmore to John C. Calhoun, January 13, 1844, Wilson, ed., *Papers of John C. Calhoun*, 17:696; *Charleston Mercury*, February 2, 1844.

47. "Genealogy of the Rhett Family," Rhett Genealogy Notes, SCHS.

48. Boucher, "Annexation," 11; Coussons, "Thirty Years," 151.

49. Rhett to John C. Calhoun, February 21, 1844, Wilson, ed., *Papers of John C. Calhoun*, 17:797–98.

50. Rhett to Martin Van Buren, February 21, 1844, Martin Van Buren Papers, LC.

51. Rhett to John C. Calhoun, February 21, 1844, Wilson, ed., *Papers of John C. Calhoun*, 17:797–98.

52. Wright to Martin Van Buren, March 1, 1844, Martin Van Buren Papers, LC.

53. Martin Van Buren to Rhett, March 10, 1844, Martin Van Buren Papers, LC.

54. Rhett to John C. Calhoun, March 5, 1844, Wilson, ed., *Papers of John C. Calhoun*, 17:816.

55. Rhett to John C. Calhoun, March 7, 1844, Wilson, ed., *Papers of John C. Calhoun*, 17:837.

56. Francis W. Pickens to James Edward Colhoun, February 7, 1844, Wilson, ed., *Papers of John C. Calhoun*, 17:n 774.

57. Edmunds, *Pickens*, 75.

58. Francis W. Pickens to John C. Calhoun, March 3, 1844, cited in White, *Rhett*, 66.

59. James Wishart to John C. Calhoun, March 28, 1844, Wilson, ed., *Papers of John C. Calhoun*, 17:900.

60. George McDuffie to John C. Calhoun, March 10, 1844, Wilson, ed., *Papers of John C. Calhoun*, 17:855–56. The unsigned article apparently by Rhett is "The Issue at Stake," *United States Magazine and Democratic Review* 13 (November 1843), 542–47. Its positions are largely in agreement with Rhett's, and he is known to have written something for this journal about this time.

61. Coussons, "Thirty Years," n 159, 159.

62. *Congressional Globe*, 28th Cong., 1st sess., 44, 98.

63. Barnwell to Rhett, May 5, 1844 in John Barnwell, "Hamlet to Hotspur," 251; Adams, *Memoirs*, 12:11; *Charleston Mercury*, April 22, 1844.

64. *Congressional Globe*, 28th Cong., 1st sess., 528, 582; Rhett to Robert Barnwell Rhett Jr., December 12, 1848, Crosby.

65. Ibid., 81, 325, 520; Adams, *Memoirs*, 11:464.

66. *Congressional Globe*, 28th Cong., 1st sess., 134; *Remarks of Messrs. Rhett, Belser, and A. V. Brown, on the Constitutional Power of Congress to Receive or Reject Petitions; and in favor of the retention of the 25th Rule, prohibiting the reception of Abolition Petitions* (N.p., 1844), 1–2; Adams, *Memoirs*, 11:483. The *Remarks* pamphlet contains portions of Rhett's speech left out of the *Congressional Globe* and probably reflects those parts indistinctly heard by House reporters and provided subsequently by Rhett for distribution in the pamphlet.

67. Quoted in White, *Rhett,* 66.

68. Notes on John C. Calhoun, n.d., Rhett Papers, SCL.

69. Ibid.; Robert Barnwell Rhett Jr. to J. Franklin Jameson, May 19, 1899, J. Franklin Jameson Papers, LC.

70. *Charleston Mercury,* May 22, 1844.

Chapter Ten

1. *Congressional Globe,* 28th Cong., 1st sess., appendix, 656ff; *Charleston Mercury,* May 20, 1844.

2. White, *Rhett,* 71.

3. Ibid., 69.

4. *Charleston Mercury,* 4 August 1851; Niven, *Calhoun,* 280; Daniel Huger to Rhett, April 9, 1844, Rhett Papers, SHC; Wilson, ed., *Papers of John C. Calhoun,* 19:121; Bleser, *Secret and Sacred,* 122.

5. Barnwell to Rhett, May 5, 1844, Rhett Papers, SHC.

6. Rhett to My Dear Sir, n.d. [May–June 1844], Ed Fishburne to A. Campbell, June 23, 1844, Barnwell to Rhett, May 5, 1844, Rhett Papers, SHC.

7. *Congressional Globe,* 32d Cong., 1st sess., appendix, 62; Rhett to Orestes Brownson, July 1, 1844, in possession of Shinaan Krakowsky, Encina, Calif.; Rhett to My Dear Sir, n.d. [May–June 1844], Rhett Papers, SHC. The identity of the addressee cannot be pinpointed, unfortunately. It is possible, in fact, that its survival in Rhett's own papers as a "My Dear Sir" letter could mean that it is really the prototype of a "To Whom It May Concern" letter that he sent to several potential sources of loans.

8. *Address of Hon. R. Barnwell Rhett, to His Constituents, the Citizens of Beaufort, Colleton, Orangeburgh and Barnwell Districts* (N.p., 1844), 3–11.

9. Bleser, *Secret and Sacred,* 122; *Charleston Mercury,* July 20, 1844.

10. Isaac E. Holmes to James H. Hammond, July 23, 1844, James Henry Hammond Papers, LC.

11. Bleser, *Secret and Sacred,* 120.

12. Coussons, "Thirty Years," 182.

13. Niven, *Calhoun,* 280–81.

14. Rhett to Armistead L. Burt, September 9, 1844, Armistead L. Burt Papers, Duke University, Durham, N.C.; Rhett to Orestes Brownson, July 1, 1844, in possession of Shinaan Krakowsky, Encina, Calif.; *Charleston Mercury,* July 26, 1844.

15. Rowland, Moore, and Rogers, *History of Beaufort County,* 384, 420; *Charleston Mercury,* August 8, 1844; Heyward, Smith-Rhett Genealogy, Barnwell Rhett Heyward Papers, SCHS.

16. *Charleston Mercury,* August 8, 1844; Regular Toasts, n.d. [July 31, 1844], Pope Family Papers, SCHS.

17. *Charleston Mercury,* August 8, 1844.

18. Ibid., August 7, 24, 1844.

19. Ibid., August 12–28, 1844; White, *Rhett,* 75.

20. R. W. Singleton to George Frederick Holmes, August 6, 1844, George Frederick Holmes Letterbook, Duke University, Durham, N.C.

21. *Charleston Mercury,* August 20, 1844; Virginia Louise Glenn, "James Hamilton Jr., of South Carolina: A Biography," Ph.D. diss., University of North Carolina, 1964, 362; James Hamilton to John C. Calhoun, September 12, 1844, Wilson, ed., *Papers of John C. Calhoun,* 19:760.

22. Henry L. Conner to John C. Calhoun, August 8, 1844, Wilson, ed., *Papers of John C. Calhoun,* 19:545, William D. Porter to John C. Calhoun, August 8, 1844, 545, Francis Wharton to John C. Calhoun, August 21, 1844, 625–26; James A. Seddon to Robert M. T. Hunter, August 22, 1844, Ambler, *Hunter,* 69; George Frederick Holmes to Joseph D. Pope, August 20, 1844, George Frederick Holmes Letterbook, Duke University, Durham, N.C.; *Charleston Mercury,* September 3, 19, December 2, 1844.

23. Wharton to John C. Calhoun, August 21, 1844, Wilson, ed., *Papers of John C. Calhoun,* 19:625–26, Francis W. Pickens to John C. Calhoun, August 10, 1844, 552; Edmunds, *Pickens,* 85.

24. Francis W. Pickens to James Edward Colhoun, September 14, 1844, Wilson, ed., *Papers of John C. Calhoun,* 19:785.

25. Rhett to Armistead L. Burt, September 9, 1844, Armistead L. Burt Papers, Duke University, Durham, N.C.

26. *Charleston Mercury,* August 16, 21, 22, 31, September 4, 1844.

27. William J. Grayson to Rhett, August 27, 1844, Rhett Papers, SHC.

28. Franklin H. Elmore to John C. Calhoun, August 26, 1844, Wilson, ed., *Papers of John C. Calhoun,* 19:661–62.

29. Rhett to Armistead L. Burt, September 9, 1844, Armistead L. Burt Papers, Duke University, Durham, N.C.; Christopher G. Memminger to Rhett, November 24, 1844, Rhett Papers, SHC.

30. Glenn, "Hamilton," 382; *Charleston Mercury,* August 21, 1844.

31. Coussons, "Thirty Years," 172–73; Rowland, Moore, and Rogers, *History of Beaufort County,* 420–21.

32. James A. Seddon to Robert M. T. Hunter, August 22, 1844, Ambler, *Hunter,* 69.

33. Rhett to Armistead L. Burt, September 9, 1844, Armistead L. Burt Papers, Duke University, Durham, N.C.

34. *Charleston Mercury,* September 3, 1844.

35. Ibid., August 30, September 4, 1844.

36. Ibid., September 14, 1844.

37. Coussons, "Thirty Years," n. 191.

38. Rhett to Robert M. T. Hunter, August 30, 1844, Ambler, *Hunter,* 70–71.

39. *Charleston Mercury,* September 5, 12, 1844.

40. Rhett to Armistead L. Burt, September 9, 1844, Armistead L. Burt Papers, Duke University, Durham, N.C. Andrew Jackson to Joel R. Poinsett, 12 November 1844, as quoted in Robert Remini, *Andrew Jackson and the Course of American Democracy, 1833-1845, III* (New York: Harper and Row, 1984), 3:44.

41. White, *Rhett,* n 76.

42. The terms *secessionist* and *disunionist* are often used interchangeably in discussing Rhett, but the difference in meaning is vital to understanding what he was thinking in 1844. White, *Rhett,* 76–78, discusses Rhett's motivation and confuses the two expressions, concluding that he was not a disunionist or a secessionist, meaning one wishing for a permanent breakup of the Union. She is clearly mistaken, for Rhett is undeniably advocating the actual act of secession, which by definition made him a secessionist. However, his statements, public and private, including those to Burt, with whom he was much more open than with Hunter and others, portrayed him as viewing secession as temporary and that once its aim had been achieved, South Carolina would return to the Union. Of course, given Rhett's record with the truth, he could have been dissembling in this. Certainly White is wrong when she argues that all Rhett really wanted was resistance and that the manner of it did not matter (*Rhett,* n 77), for his letter to Burt makes it perfectly clear that he no longer regarded nullification as a useful means of resistance. That left only secession, which he also clearly indicated as his method of choice. Coussons, "Thirty Years," n 191, suggests that Rhett's statements of loyalty to a constitutional union were insincere and implies that he was a disunionist at this stage, and this may be right.

43. Rhett to Armistead L. Burt, September 9, 1844, Armistead L. Burt Papers, Duke University, Durham, N.C.

44. *Charleston Mercury,* September 11, 1844.

45. Ibid., September 20, 1844.

46. Rhett to Armistead L. Burt, September 18, 1844, Armistead L. Burt Papers, Duke University, Durham, N.C.

47. Boucher, "Annexation," 25.

48. Rhett to Armistead L. Burt, September 18, 1844, Armistead L. Burt Papers, Duke University, Durham, N.C.

49. Langdo Cheves to Rhett, October 16, 1844, Rhett Papers, SHC.

50. Coussons, "Thirty Years," 173.

51. Rhett to Armistead L. Burt, September 18, 1844, Armistead L. Burt Papers, Duke University, Durham, N.C.; Adams, *Memoirs,* 12:91.

52. Boucher, "Annexation," 25; Francis W. Pickens to John C. Calhoun, December 28, 1844, Wilson, ed., *Papers of John C. Calhoun,* 20:657.

53. Coussons, "Thirty Years," 173; Stephen B. Barnwell, *American Family,* 168–69. McCardell, *Southern Nation,* 65, makes the trenchant suggestion that Rhett's intellect and capacity for leadership were inferior to Hammond's, and that as a result Calhoun regarded him as less of a threat to his own dominance.

54. Stuart to Rhett, November 11, 1844, Rhett Papers, SHC.

55. Christopher G. Memminger to Rhett, November 27, 1844, Rhett Papers, SHC.

56. Barnwell to Rhett, November 1, 1844, Rhett Papers, SHC.

57. Stuart to Rhett, November 11, 1844, Rhett Papers, SHC.

58. Franklin H. Elmore to Rhett, November 18, 1844, Rhett Papers, SHC.

59. Christopher G. Memminger to Rhett, November 27, 1844, Rhett Papers, SHC.

Chapter Eleven

1. Stuart to Rhett, November 11, 1844, Rhett Papers, SHC.

2. *Congressional Globe,* 28th Cong., 2d sess., 28.

3. Rhett to James H. Hammond, November 3, 1844, James Henry Hammond Papers, LC; Bleser, *Secret and Sacred,* 127; Boyce to John C. Calhoun, November 28, 1844, Wilson, ed., *Papers of John C. Calhoun,* 20:383; William Gilmore Simms to Armistead L. Burt, January 1, 1845, Mary C. Simms Oliphant, Alfred Taylor Odell, and T. C. Duncan Eaves, eds., *The Letters of William Gilmore Simms* (Columbia, S.C., 1956), 2:7.

4. McCardell, *Southern Nation,* 64; Bleser, *Secret and Sacred,* 130–31, 141; Coussons, "Thirty Years," 184, 188–89; *Charleston Mercury,* January 3, 1845; Rhett to James Buchanan, October 20, 1845, James Buchanan Papers, Historical Society of Pennsylvania, Philadelphia; Boucher, "Annexation," 20.

5. Rhett to Armistead L. Burt, September 18, 1844, Armistead L. Burt Papers, Duke University, Durham, N.C.

6. *Charleston Mercury,* December 3, 1844; References to Debates for the Suppression of the African Slave Trade, etc., Rhett Papers, SCHS.

7. Boucher, "Annexation," 30–31.

8. Adams, *Memoirs,* 12:156, 233; John Witherspoon DuBose, *The Life and Times of William Lowndes Yancey* (Birmingham, Ala., 1892), 1:141; Rhett notes in his copy of Wallace, *Political Life,* 19, Crosby.

9. Niven, *Calhoun,* 270; Robert Dale Owen to Rhett, July 1, 1844, Rhett Papers, SHC.

10. Robert W. Johannsen, *Stephen A. Douglas* (New York, 1973), 154–55.

11. Ibid.; Adams, *Memoirs,* 12:139; *Charleston Mercury,* January 9, 1845.

12. *Congressional Globe,* 28th Cong., 2d sess., 166–67 and appendix, 143–46.

13. *Charleston Mercury,* February 5, 1845.

14. The claim of Rhett's suggestion to Brown appears in Heyward, Rhett, Smith-Rhett Genealogy, Barnwell Rhett Heyward Papers, SCHS, though Heyward confuses Milton Brown for Aaron V. Brown. Rhett's authorized "biography," Wallace, *Political Life,* 20, to which Rhett undoubtedly contributed, was more restrained, saying only that "Mr. Rhett took part" in the Brown resolution. The more specific claim by Heyward, like other variations from Wallace in his pre-1857 account, apparently came from Rhett himself or family close to him.

15. Francis W. Pickens to John C. Calhoun, December 18, 1844, Wilson, ed., *Papers of John C. Calhoun,* 20:584.

16. Wallace, *Political Life,* 19–20; Coussons, "Thirty Years," 195; Heyward, Rhett, Smith-Rhett Genealogy, Barnwell Rhett Heyward Papers, SCHS; Robert Barnwell Rhett Jr. to J. Franklin Jameson, May 19, 1899, J. Franklin Jameson Papers, LC.

17. Barnwell to Rhett, February 19, 1845, John Barnwell, "Hamlet to Hotspur," 256.

18. Dixon Lewis to John C. Calhoun, May 9, 1845, Wilson, ed., *Papers of John C. Calhoun,* 21:544.

19. Rhett to Armistead L. Burt, June 24, 1845, Armistead L. Burt Papers, Duke University, Durham, N.C.

20. *Charleston Mercury,* August 7, 1845.

21. Niven, *Calhoun,* 292–93.

22. Milo M. Quaife, ed., *The Diary of James K. Polk* (Chicago, 1910), 1:21–22; Matthew Forster to Rhett, December 29, 1845, Charles Simpson to Matthew Forster, October 15, 1846, Rhett Papers, SCHS; Rhett to James Buchanan, September 18, 1845, James Buchanan Papers, Historical Society of Pennsylvania, Philadelphia.

23. Rhett to John C. Calhoun, September 18, 1845, Wilson, ed., *Papers of John C. Calhoun,* 22:149.

24. White, *Rhett,* 86.

25. Quaife, *Polk,* 1:17; Rhett to John C. Calhoun, September 18, 1845, Wilson, ed., *Papers of John C. Calhoun,* 22:148–49; Coussons, "Thirty Years," 199.

26. Richard Crallé to John C. Calhoun, September 23, 1845, Wilson, ed., *Papers of John C. Calhoun,* 22:163; Coussons, "Thirty Years," 199.

27. James M. Walker to James H. Hammond, October 6, 1845, James Henry Hammond Papers, LC; Rhett to James Buchanan, October 20, 1845, James Buchanan Papers, Historical Society of Pennsylvania, Philadelphia.

28. Franklin H. Elmore to John C. Calhoun, December 5, 1845, Wilson, ed., *Papers of John C. Calhoun,* 22:318; ibid., December 16, 1845, 345; ibid., James Edward Colhoun to John C. Calhoun, January 7, 1846, 420; ibid., John C. Calhoun to Andrew P. Calhoun, 7 December 1845, 327.

29. Franklin H. Elmore to John C. Calhoun, December 5, 1845, Wilson, ed., *Papers of John C. Calhoun* 22:318; ibid., December 16, 1845, 345.

30. Rhett to James Buchanan, October 20, 1845, James Buchanan Papers, Historical Society of Pennsylvania, Philadelphia.

31. Adams, *Memoirs,* 12:230–32.

32. Heyward, Rhett, Smith-Rhett Genealogy, Barnwell Rhett Heyward Papers, SCHS.

33. *Congressional Globe,* 29th Cong., 1st sess., 142–43.

34. Ibid., 147, 156–58, 318.

35. Wallace, *Political Life,* 20–22; Heyward, Rhett, Smith-Rhett Genealogy, Barnwell Rhett Heyward Papers, SCHS; *Frank Leslie's Illustrated Newspaper,* February 9, 1861. The Wallace account, of course, had at least some influence from Rhett himself, as did the Heyward sketch. It also appears that the *Leslie's* sketch may have in some degree reflected input from Rhett; thus the sources cumulatively suggest that Rhett at least *believed* that he influenced the Oregon debate.

36. *Congressional Globe,* 29th Cong., 1st sess., 437–38, 529.

37. Ibid., 793–95, 808, 1187.

38. Robert Barnwell Rhett Jr. to J. Franklin Jameson, May 19, 1899, J. Franklin Jameson Papers, LC.

39. Franklin H. Elmore to Rhett, August 22, 1846, Franklin H. Elmore Papers, LC.

40. [Robert Barnwell Rhett], "The Memphis Convention," *Southern Quarterly Review* 10 (October 1846), 377–417 *passim.*

41. Coussons, "Thirty Years," 204–5.

42. Rhett to Franklin H. Elmore, September 6, 1846, Franklin H. Elmore Papers, LC.

43. Rhett to Armistead L. Burt, September 3, 1846, Armistead L. Burt Papers, Duke University, Durham, N.C.

44. Robert M. T. Hunter to Rhett, September 8, 1846, General Holdings, Henry E. Huntington Library and Art Gallery, San Marino, Calif.

45. Rhett to Armistead L. Burt, September 3, 1846, Armistead L. Burt Papers, Duke University, Durham, N.C.

46. Franklin H. Elmore to Rhett, August 22, 1846, Franklin H. Elmore Papers, LC; Robert M. T. Hunter to Rhett, September 8, 1846, General Holdings, Henry E. Huntington Library and Art Gallery, San Marino, Calif.

47. Barnwell to John C. Calhoun, June 21, 1846, Wilson, ed., *Papers of John C. Calhoun,* 23:187.

48. White, *Rhett,* 89.

49. Heyward, Rhett, Smith-Rhett Genealogy, Barnwell Rhett Heyward Papers, SCHS; Rhett to Richard Crallé, October 25, 1854, "Rhett on the Biography of Calhoun," 312.

50. Bleser, *Secret and Sacred,* 155.

51. Rhett to James H. Hammond, September 11, 1847, James Henry Hammond Papers, LC.

52. *Congressional Globe,* 29th Cong., 1st sess., 93.

53. Robert Barnwell Rhett Jr. to J. Franklin Jameson, May 19, 1899, J. Franklin Jameson Papers, LC.

54. Emily B. Rhett genealogical notes, April 21, 1879, Rhett Family Papers, SCHS; Rhett to Robert Barnwell Rhett Jr., n.d. [1846–47], Crosby.

55. Barnwell to Rhett, February 19, 1845, Rhett Papers, SHC.

56. Rhett to James Buchanan, March 3, 1846, James Buchanan Papers, Historical Society of Pennsylvania, Philadelphia; James Buchanan to Louis McLane, July 13, 1846, Moore, *Works,* 7:27.

57. Louis McLane to Charles Barry, May 5, 1846, Matthew Forster to Rhett, June 18, September 18, 1846, Charles Simpson to Matthew Forster, October 15, 1846, Rhett Papers, SCHS; Rhett to Franklin H. Elmore, November 11, 1846, Franklin H. Elmore Papers, LC.

58. W. B. Fickling to James H. Hammond, June 6, 1846, James Henry Hammond Papers, LC.

59. Bleser, *Secret and Sacred,* 161.

60. Simms to James H. Hammond, December 11, 1846, Oliphant et al., *Letters,* 2:236, December 25, 1846, 246; James H. Hammond to Simms, November 10, 1846, James Henry Hammond Papers, LC.

61. Simms to James H. Hammond, November 17, 1846, Oliphant et al., *Letters,* 2:207; Rhett to Franklin H. Elmore, November 19, 1846, Rhett Papers, Duke University, Durham, N.C.

62. Coussons, "Thirty Years," 342; Rhett to John C. Calhoun, November 12, 1846, Wilson, ed., *Papers of John C. Calhoun,* 23:536.

Chapter Twelve

1. *Congressional Globe,* 29th Cong., 2d sess., 15–16.

2. Ibid., Appendix, 244–47.

3. Robert R. Russel, *Critical Studies in Antebellum Sectionalism* (Westport, Conn., 1972), n 12.

4. Rhett to John C. Calhoun, May 22, 1847, Wilson, ed., *Papers of John C. Calhoun,* 24:376–77.

5. [Robert Barnwell Rhett], "The Wilmot Proviso: Proceedings of the Twenty-Ninth Congress," *Southern Quarterly Review* 11 (April 1847), 377–406 *passim.*

6. Rhett to Robert Barnwell Rhett Jr., May 31, 1847, Crosby; Rhett to John C. Calhoun, May 22, 1847, Wilson, ed., *Papers of John C. Calhoun,* 24:376–77.

7. Coussons, "Thirty Years," 223, 229; *Charleston Mercury,* February 1, April 2, 5, 1847; Rhett to Claudia Stuart, April 25, 1868, Stuart Family Papers, SCHS.

8. Joseph Allen to Rhett, February 13, 1847, *Charleston Mercury,* March 1, 1847.

9. Simms to James H. Hammond, March 2, 1847, Oliphant et al., *Letters,* 2:280.

10. *Charleston Mercury,* May 13, 1847.

11. Simms to James H. Hammond, June 4, 1847, Oliphant et al., *Letters,* 2:322.

12. Conner to John C. Calhoun, May 7, 1847, Wilson, ed., *Papers of John C. Calhoun,* 24:348–50.

13. Rhett to John C. Calhoun, May 20, 1847, Wilson, ed., *Papers of John C. Calhoun,* 24:371.

14. Ibid., Rhett to John C. Calhoun, May 20, 1847, 371, May 22, 1847, 322, September 8, 1847, 541–42; Coussons, "Thirty Years," 253.

15. Rhett to John C. Calhoun, May 20, 1847, Wilson, ed., *Papers of John C. Calhoun,* 24:371–72, May 22, 1847, 376, June 21, 1847, 412; ibid., September 8, 1847, 542.

16. Rhett to John C. Calhoun, May 20, 1847, Wilson, ed., *Papers of John C. Calhoun,* 24:371–72; Rhett to John C. Calhoun, May 16, 1847, Chauncey S. Boucher and Robert P. Brooks, eds., "Correspondence Addressed to John C. Calhoun 1837–1849," in *Annual Report of the American Historical Association for the Year 1929* (Washington, D.C., 1930), 376.

17. *Congressional Globe,* 29th Cong., 1st sess., 318.

18. Rhett to John C. Calhoun, June 21, 1847, Wilson, ed., *Papers of John C. Calhoun,* 24:412–13; ibid., September 8, 1847, 541.

19. Coussons, "Thirty Years," 283–88.

20. Rhett to James H. Hammond, September 11, 1847, James Henry Hammond Papers, LC.

21. James Buchanan to R. B. Campbell, October 20, 1847, Moore, *Works,* 7:438; Rhett to unknown, February 7, 1847, Rhett to James Mason, February 25, 1847, April 1, 1848, Rhett Papers, SCL; Richard Simpson to John Y. Mason, March 3, 1848, Richard Simpson Papers, SCL.

22. Rhett to Franklin H. Elmore, November 3, 1847, Appointment, November 3, 1847, Statement of deliveries, 1847, Franklin H. Elmore Papers, SCL; Rhett to

James H. Hammond, September 11, 1847, James Henry Hammond Papers, LC; Simms to James H. Hammond, October 20, 1847, Oliphant et al., *Letters,* 2:353; Robert Barnwell Rhett Jr. to J. Franklin Jameson, May 19, 1899, J. Franklin Jameson Papers, LC.

23. Rhett to Charles Simpson, October 17, 1847, Bradhurst Hill to Rhett, October 19, 1847, Rhett Papers, SHC; Duff Green to John C. Calhoun, October 27, 1847, Wilson, ed., *Papers of John C. Calhoun,* 24:631.

24. Rhett to Franklin H. Elmore, November 3, 1847, December 8, 1847, Franklin H. Elmore Papers, SCL.

25. Wallace, *Political Life,* 23; Heyward, Rhett, Smith-Rhett Genealogy, Barnwell Rhett Heyward Papers, SCHS; Rhett to Franklin H. Elmore, December 8, 1847, Franklin H. Elmore Papers, SCL.

26. Quaife, *Polk,* 3:236.

27. *Congressional Globe,* 30th Cong., 1st sess., 27–28.

28. White, *Rhett,* 94–95.

29. *Congressional Globe,* 30th Cong., 1st sess., 286–86 and appendix, 239–42.

30. Quaife, *Polk,* 3:458.

31. Armistead L. Burt to Henry L. Conner, March 29, 30, 1848, Henry L. Conner Papers, Charleston Library Society, Charleston, S.C.

32. Quaife, *Polk,* 3:458.

33. Ibid.; Rhett to Franklin H. Elmore, May 12, 1848, Franklin H. Elmore Papers, SCL.

34. Rhett, "Political Parties," Aiken Rhett Collection, CM.

35. *Charleston Mercury,* June 6, 1848; Coussons, "Thirty Years," 289; David S. Heidler, *Pulling the Temple Down: The Fire-Eaters and the Destruction of the Union* (Harrisburg, Pa., 1994), 16–17.

36. Coussons, "Thirty Years," 295; *Congressional Globe,* 32d Cong., 1st sess., appendix, 64; Rhett to Robert Barnwell Rhett Jr., May 31, 1848, Crosby.

37. *Congressional Globe,* 30th Cong., 1st sess., appendix, 655–59.

38. Rhett to Robert Barnwell Rhett Jr., June 7, 1848, Crosby.

39. Rhett, "Political Parties," Aiken Rhett Collection, CM; Coussons, "Thirty Years," 295.

40. Armistead L. Burt to Conner, July 4, 1848, Armistead L. Burt Papers, Duke University, Durham, N.C.; *Congressional Globe,* 32d Cong., 1st sess., appendix, 64; Rhett notation in Rhett's copy of Wallace, *Political Life,* 23, in possession of Leslie Crosby, Huntsville, Ala.

41. Henry D. Gilpin to Martin Van Buren, July 28, 1848, Martin Van Buren Papers, LC; *Charleston Mercury,* August 18, 1848.

42. Simms to James H. Hammond, July 20, 1848, James Henry Hammond Papers, LC; Coussons, "Thirty Years," 298.

43. Coussons, "Thirty Years," 295.

44. Rhett to Franklin H. Elmore, May 12, 18, 23, 1848, Franklin H. Elmore Papers, SCL; Rhett to Robert Barnwell Rhett Jr., September 8, 1848, Crosby.

45. Rhett to Robert Barnwell Rhett Jr., September 5, 1848, Crosby; John Barnwell, *Love of Order,* 75.

46. Simms to James H. Hammond, August 29, 1848, Oliphant et al., *Letters,* 2:440.

47. *Charleston Mercury,* September 21, 23, 29, 1848.

48. James H. Hammond to Simms, September 7, 1848, James Henry Hammond Papers, LC.

49. Simms to James H. Hammond, August 29, 1848, Oliphant et al., *Letters,* 2:440.

50. Rhett to Robert Barnwell Rhett Jr., May 13, 1847, Crosby; Rhett to Robert Barnwell Rhett Jr., September 10, 1848, Autograph Letters and Portraits of the Signers of the Constitution of the Confederate States, Charles Colcock Jones Papers, Duke University, Durham, N.C.

51. Rhett [though not in Rhett's hand] to E. B. Foote, n.d., Rhett Papers, SCHS.

52. Rhett to Robert Barnwell Rhett Jr., March 20, 1848, Crosby.

53. Rhett to Alfred Rhett, March 11, December 8, 1848, Rhett to Robert Barnwell Rhett Jr., September 11, 1847, n.d. [1848], Crosby.

54. Rhett to Robert Barnwell Rhett Jr., n.d. [November–December 1845], August, 21, September 1, December 24, 1847, March 20, May 12, 30, 31, July 20, December 5, 1848, Crosby.

55. Rhett to Robert Barnwell Rhett Jr., June 10, August 17, 19, September 1, December 24, 1847, January 8, March 12, April 22, May 17, 30, 31, July 5, 9, 15, 20, November 13, 1848, Rhett to Alfred Rhett, March 11, May 17, December 4, 8, 1848, Crosby.

56. Rhett to Alfred Rhett, June 5, July 15, August 29, December 8, 1848, Rhett to Robert Barnwell Rhett Jr., May 22, June 9, n.d. [July], July 29, November 9, 1847, n.d. [1848], December 5, 15, 1848, June 18, 1849, Edward Everett to Rhett, January 29, 1849, Crosby. Rhett to Robert Barnwell Rhett Jr., n.d. [1845–46], July 22, 1848, Crosby.

57. Conner to John C. Calhoun, November 2, 1848, J. Franklin Jameson, ed., *Correspondence of John C. Calhoun* (Washington, D.C., 1900), 1184–85.

58. John Barnwell, *Love of Order,* 75–76.

59. Simms to James H. Hammond, November 24, 1858, James Henry Hammond Papers, LC; Coussons, "Thirty Years," 307; *Charleston Mercury,* May 26, 1848.

60. Rhett, "Political Parties," Aiken Rhett Collection, CM.

61. Simms to James H. Hammond, November 24, 1848, James Henry Hammond Papers, LC.

62. Nathaniel Beverly Tucker to James H. Hammond, December 6, 1848, James Henry Hammond Papers, LC.

Chapter Thirteen

1. Rhett to Robert Barnwell Rhett Jr., December 12, 18, 1848, Crosby.

2. J. F. Thomas, ed., *The Carolina Tribute to Calhoun* (Columbia, S.C., 1857), 369. This account comes from Rhett's later oration over Calhoun and thus may well have been embellished or even invented to serve the purposes of the event and the speaker.

3. *Charleston Mercury,* January 22, 23, 27, 1849; Quaife, *Polk,* 4:309.

4. *Charleston Mercury,* January 31, 1849.

5. Coussons, "Thirty Years," 307, 339–41, 345, 350.

6. *Congressional Globe,* 30th Cong., 2d sess., 418.

7. Thomas Rhett to Rhett, September 12, November 5, 1849, various sureties, bonds, and notes, Henry Eubank to Rhett, August 3, 1849, Rhett Papers, SHC.

8. Robert Barnwell Rhett Jr. to Josephine Bacot, February 9, 1896, Bacot-Huger Collection, SCHS.

9. Rhett to Robert Barnwell Rhett Jr., fragment n.d. [January 1849], January 31, June 12, 1849, February 5, 1851, Crosby.

10. Rhett to Alfred Rhett, May 17, June 11, 1849, Rhett to Robert Barnwell Rhett Jr., November 13, 1848, May 2, 23, June 12, 1849, Crosby.

11. McConaghy, "Ordinary White Folk," 345.

12. Rhett, "Political Parties," Aiken Rhett Collection, CM; Rhett to John C. Calhoun, July 19, 1849, Boucher and Brooks, "Correspondence," 517–18.

13. Coussons, "Thirty Years," 342.

14. Robert Barnwell Rhett Jr. to J. Franklin Jameson, May 19, 1899, J. Franklin Jameson Papers, LC.

15. Amos Lawrence to Rhett, December 12, 1849, William Lawrence, ed., *Extracts from the Diary and Correspondence of the Late Amos Lawrence* (Boston, 1855), 274–76.

16. Edmunds, *Pickens,* 114; Bleser, *Secret and Sacred,* 195.

17. Emily B. Rhett Genealogical Notes, April 21, 1879, Rhett Family Papers, SCHS; Margaretta Childs and Isabella G. Leland, comps., "South Carolina Episcopal Church Records," *South Carolina Historical Magazine* 84 (October 1983), 258; McConaghy, "Ordinary White Folk," 7, 314–15, 345. McConaghy is contradictory on the number of Rhett's slaves, citing 375 in one place and 396 in another and citing 1850 slave schedules for St. Bartholomew Parish as authority for both. The schedules actually suggest that he had either 306 or 380, so the figures remain indefinite.

18. Rhett to William Elliott, March 11, 1850, Elliott and Gonzales Family Papers, SHC.

19. McCurry, *Masters,* 15.

20. *Charleston Mercury,* February 14, 20, 1850.

21. Niven, *Calhoun,* 343.

22. Coussons, "Thirty Years," 383; Margaret L. Coit, *John C. Calhoun, American Patriot* (Boston, 1950), 489–90. For the Davis-Calhoun relationship, see William C. Davis, *Jefferson Davis, the Man and His Hour* (New York, 1991), 185–86, 193–94, 198, 205–6.

23. Rhett to Richard Crallé, October 25, 1854, "Rhett on the Biography of Calhoun," 312.

24. Coussons, "Thirty Years," 394.

25. *Charleston Mercury,* April 12, 1850; Bleser, *Secret and Sacred,* 199.

26. Bleser, *Secret and Sacred,* 199; *Charleston Mercury,* April 12, 1850.

27. Carl R. Osthaus, *Partisans of the Southern Press: Editorial Spokesmen of the Nineteenth Century* (Lexington, Ky., 1994), 78; Rhett to anonymous, n.d., Rhett Papers, SCHS.

28. *Charleston Mercury,* May 10, June 1, 13, 1850; Telegram, May 29, 1850, Franklin H. Elmore Papers, SCL.

29. Edmunds, *Pickens,* 117; Bleser, *Secret and Sacred,* 203.

30. St. George L. Sioussat, "Tennessee, the Compromise of 1850, and the Nashville Convention," *Mississippi Valley Historical Review* 2 (December 1915), 331.

31. Perry, *Reminiscences,* 134.

32. Sioussat, "Tennessee," 339.

33. *Charleston Mercury,* June 20, 1850.

34. James H. Hammond to Simms, June 27, 1850, James Henry Hammond Papers, LC.

35. James H. Hammond to Simms, June 16, 1850, James Henry Hammond Papers, LC; Edmunds, *Pickens,* 117; Sioussat, "Tennessee," 337.

36. *Charleston Mercury,* July 2, 1850.

37. Rhett to Henry Benning, July 20, 1850, Rhett Papers, SCL; *Charleston Mercury,* July 20, 1850.

38. *Charleston Mercury,* July 20, 1850.

39. James H. Hammond to Simms, June 27, 1850, James Henry Hammond Papers, LC; Bleser, *Secret and Sacred,* 203.

40. Rhett to Benning, July 20, 1850, Rhett Papers, SCL.

41. "The Southern Convention," *Southern Quarterly Review* 18 (September 1850), 230–31.

42. John Barnwell, *Love of Order,* 108; *Charleston Mercury,* August 16, 1850; Theodore Rosengarten, *Tombee, Portrait of a Cotton Planter* (New York, 1986), 502, Journal of Thomas B. Chaplin, July 19–24, 1850.

43. Richard H. Shryock, *Georgia and the Union in 1850* (Durham, N.C., 1926), 275; Rhett to Benning, July 20, 1850, Rhett Papers, SCL.

44. Daniel Wallace to Whitemarsh B. Seabrook, June 8, October 20, 1850, Whitemarsh B. Seabrook Papers, LC.

45. Yancey wrote a letter to this effect to Rhett at an unknown date, and though the letter is lost, Robert Barnwell Rhett Jr. made a note about it in the margin of the July 31, 1863 issue of the *Mercury,* now in the Charleston Library Society.

46. Shryock, *Georgia,* 284–86.

47. What appears to be a manuscript draft of a portion of this speech is in the Rhett Papers, SHC.

48. *Charleston Mercury,* September 25, 1850.

49. Ibid.; Heidler, *Pulling the Temple Down,* 72.

50. James A. Meriwether to Howell Cobb, August 24, 1850, Ulrich B. Phillips, ed., *The Correspondence of Robert Toombs, Alexander H. Stephens, and Howell Cobb. Annual Report of the American Historical Association for the Year 1911* (Washington, D.C., 1913), 2:210.

51. Heidler, *Pulling the Temple Down,* 57–58.

52. Shryock, *Georgia,* 286–87.

53. Ibid., 319; Eric H. Walther, *The Fire-Eaters* (Baton Rouge, La., 1992), 2.

54. *Charleston Mercury,* September 12, 13, 1850.

55. Sumter District broadside, October 1851, SCL; James H. Hammond to Simms, September 30, 1850, James Henry Hammond Papers, LC.

56. McConaghy, "Ordinary White Folk," 345; H. Hardy Perritt, "Robert Barnwell Rhett: Disunionist Heir of Calhoun, 1850–1852," *Southern Speech Journal* 24 (fall 1958), 40.

57. *Charleston Mercury,* November 8, 1850.

58. Elizabeth Rhett to Rhett, November 7, 1850, Rhett Papers, SCHS.

59. Ibid.

60. John A. Quitman to Rhett, November 30, 1850, Whitemarsh B. Seabrook Papers, LC.

61. Sioussat, "Tennessee," 344; Simms to Marcus C. H. Hammond, December 14, 1850, Oliphant et al., *Letters,* 3:83; Bleser, *Secret and Sacred,* 205.

62. Glenn, "Hamilton," 403–4; Stephen B. Barnwell, *American Family,* 70.

63. Perritt, "Disunionist," 40; Chauncey S. Boucher, "The Secession and Co-operation Movements in South Carolina, 1848 to 1852," *Washington University Studies* 5 (April 1918), 106.

64. Perritt, "Disunionist," 40–41; *Death and Funeral Ceremonies of John Caldwell Calhoun,* 119–68 *passim.* Perritt, a speech specialist, maintains that this oration was the finest of Rhett's career.

65. L. M. Ayer to James H. Hammond, December 18, 1850, James Henry Hammond Papers, LC.

66. Perritt, "Disunionist," 42–43.

67. Bleser, *Secret and Sacred,* 211, 216.

68. Butler to Samuel McGowan, December 5, 1850, Samuel McGowan Papers, SCL.

69. James L. Petigru to Jane Petigru North, December 19, 1850, Carson, *Petigru,* 286.

70. Ibid., 207.

71. Bleser, *Secret and Sacred,* 218–19, 223.

Chapter Fourteen

1. James H. Hammond to Simms, December 23, 1850, James Henry Hammond Papers, LC.

2. Simms to James H. Hammond, January 30, 1851, Oliphant et al., *Letters,* 3:88.

3. Bleser, *Secret and Sacred,* 219–20.

4. Elizabeth Rhett to Rhett, January 7, 10–11, 16, 31, 1851, Rhett Papers, SCHS.

5. Ibid., January 10–11, 1850; Rhett to Alfred Rhett, January 13, 1851, Rhett Papers, SCL.

6. *Congressional Globe,* 31st Cong., 2d sess., 178.

7. Drayton Nance to Rhett, January 28, 1851, Rhett Papers, SCHS.

8. Elizabeth Rhett to Rhett, January 31, 1851, Rhett Papers, SCHS.

9. Drayton Nance to Rhett, January 28, 1851, Rhett Papers, SCHS.

10. Rhett to Alfred Rhett, January 15, 1851, Rhett Papers, SCHS.

11. John A. Quitman to Rhett, January 24, 1851, Rhett to John A. Quitman, February 22, 1851, J. F. H. Claiborne Papers, Mississippi Department of Archives and History,

Jackson; Rhett to N. Foster, February 1, 1851, Rhett Papers, SCHS; Robert E. May, *John A. Quitman, Old South Crusader* (Baton Rouge, La., 1985), 248–49, 260, n 426.

12. *Congressional Globe,* 31st Cong., 2d sess., 148, 344, 460–63, 477 and appendix, 405; Dunbar Rowland, comp., *Jefferson Davis, Constitutionalist: His Letters, Papers and Speeches* (Jackson, Miss., 1923), 2:25; C. Vann Woodward, ed., *Mary Chesnut's Civil War* (New Haven, Conn., 1981), 289.

13. Rhett to Matthew Forster, February 1, 1851, Rhett Papers, SCHS.

14. Elizabeth Rhett to Rhett, February 5, 1851, Rhett Papers, SCHS.

15. James H. Hammond to Simms, February 14, 1851, James Henry Hammond Papers, LC.

16. Ibid.; Rhett to Robert Barnwell Rhett Jr. February 10, 1851, Crosby; Bleser, *Secret and Sacred,* 230.

17. Elizabeth Rhett to Rhett, January 7, 10–11, February 5, 1851, Rhett Papers, SCHS.

18. Rhett to Robert Barnwell Rhett Jr., January 9, 1850, Crosby; Stephen Meats and Edwin T. Arnold, eds., *The Writings of Benjamin F. Perry* (Spartanburg, S.C., 1980), 2:80–81.

19. Stanley W. Campbell, *The Slave Catchers: Enforcement of the Fugitive Slave Law, 1850–1860* (Chapel Hill, N.C., 1970), 29; *Congressional Globe,* 31st Cong., 2d sess., 579.

20. *Congressional Globe,* 31st Cong., 2d sess., appendix, 317–21.

21. Ibid., 414, 418.

22. Elizabeth Rhett to Rhett, February 13, 15, 1851, Rhett Papers, SCHS.

23. Rhett to Alfred Rhett, February 2, 1851, Rhett Papers, SCL; Rhett to Robert Barnwell Rhett Jr., March 27, 1850, Crosby; Rhett to Matthew Forster, February 1, 1851, Elizabeth Rhett to Rhett, February 13, 23, 1851, Mary Rhett to Rhett, February 13, 1851, Rhett Papers, SCHS.

24. *Charleston Mercury,* March 4, April 29, 1851; Simms to Nathaniel Beverly Tucker, March 2, 1851, Oliphant et al., *Letters,* 3:94, March 12, 1851, 99–100.

25. *Charleston Mercury,* April 29, 1851; Perritt, "Disunionist," 47–48.

26. Rhett to Alfred Rhett, April 13, 1851, Rhett Papers, SCL.

27. *Charleston Mercury,* April 8, May 6–9, 1851; Philip M. Hamer, *The Secession Movement in South Carolina 1847–1852* (Allentown, Pa., 1918), 94–95.

28. Rowland, Moore, and Rogers, *History of Beaufort County,* 432; Heidler, *Pulling the Temple Down,* 91.

29. Hamer, *Secession Movement,* 99–100; *Charleston Courier,* May 5, 1851; James F. Cooper to Howell Cobb, May 5, 1851, Phillips, *Correspondence,* 233.

30. James H. Hammond to Simms, May 29, 1851, James Henry Hammond Papers, LC.

31. James H. Hammond to Simms, May 24, 1851, James Henry Hammond Papers, LC.

32. Rhett to ?, n.d. [summer 1851], Crosby.

33. John Barnwell, *Love of Order,* 170; John B. Lamar to Cobb, July 3, 1851, Phillips, *Correspondence,* 242; *Charleston Mercury,* July 2, 1851; *Congressional Globe,* 32d Cong., 1st sess., appendix, 60.

34. May, *Quitman,* 260. Rhett's actual reference to Quitman has not been found.

35. Rhett to John A. Quitman, July 22, 1851, J. F. H. Claiborne Papers, Mississippi Department of Archives and History, Jackson.
36. *Charleston Mercury,* June 4, July 15, 1851; John Barnwell, *Love of Order,* 169.
37. *Charleston Courier,* July 30, 1851; *Charleston Mercury,* 1 August 1851.
38. John Means to Rhett, July 30, 1851, Rhett Papers, SHC. Rhett's actual letter to Means has not surfaced, but its content can be surmised from Means's response.
39. *Charleston Mercury,* August 1, 2, 4, 14, 16, 1851.
40. Hamer, *Secession Movement,* 110–12; *Charleston Mercury,* August 4, 7, 25, 1851.
41. *Charleston Mercury,* September 8, 20, 25, 1851; Perry, *Reminiscences,* 132–33.
42. *Vicksburg* (Miss.) *Sentinel,* September 18, 1851; May, *Quitman,* pp. 260, 426n, 428-29n.
43. John Barnwell, *Love of Order,* 180; Simms to Nathaniel Beverly Tucker, July 14, 1851, Oliphant et al., *Letters,* 3:138; Bleser, *Secret and Sacred,* 235; William C. Preston to William C. Campbell, August 22, 1851, Campbell Family Papers, Duke University, Durham, N.C.; William Elliott to his wife, September 1, 1851, Elliott and Gonzales Family Papers, SHC.
44. Paul H. Hayne to Minnie Hayne, September 18, 1851, Paul H. Hayne Papers, Duke University, Durham, N.C.; Rhett, Autobiographical fragment, Rhett Papers, SCHS; *Charleston Mercury,* September 25, 27, October 11, 1851.
45. Don Higginbotham, "Fomenters of Revolution: Massachusetts and South Carolina," *Journal of the Early Republic* 14 (spring 1994), 28; Woodward, *Mary Chesnut,* 366.
46. *Charleston Mercury,* October 11, 1851.
47. Bleser, *Secret and Sacred,* 238; Maxcy Gregg Journal, September 2, 29, 1851, Maxcy Gregg Papers, SCL.
48. Rhett to Alfred Rhett, April 13, 1851, Rhett Papers, SCL; Rhett to Matthew Forster, February 1, 1851, Rhett Papers, SCHS; White, *Rhett,* n 123.
49. *Charleston Mercury,* October 10, December 2, 1851; Hamer, *Secession Movement,* 88–101 *passim;* Rowland, Moore, and Rogers, *History of Beaufort County,* 432; Stephen B. Barnwell, *American Family,* 70.
50. McCardell, *Southern Nation,* 306; Hamer, *Secession Movement,* 125; William Elliott to his wife, October 17, 1851, Elliott and Gonzales Family Papers, SHC; Perritt, "Disunionist," 48.
51. Elizabeth Rhett to Rhett, October 17, 1851, Rhett Papers, SCHS.
52. Rhett, Autobiographical fragment, Rhett Papers, SCHS.
53. Bleser, *Secret and Sacred,* 239–40.
54. Alfred P. Aldrich to James H. Hammond, November 10, 11, 1851, John Cunningham to James H. Hammond, November 10, 1851, Maxcy Gregg to James H. Hammond, November 14, 1851, James Henry Hammond Papers, LC.
55. F. W. Byrdsall to Rhett, December 27, 1851, Abbott Laurence to Rhett, November 14, 1851, Simpson to Rhett, November 27, 1851, Rhett Papers, SCHS; Bleser, *Secret and Sacred,* 243; Lewis M. Ayer to James H. Hammond, December 1, 1851, James Henry Hammond Papers, LC; James H. Hammond to Edmund Ruffin, November 21, 1851, Edmund Ruffin Papers, SHC; Rhett notes on Hammond plan, n.d., Crosby.

56. Bleser, *Secret and Sacred*, 243; James H. Hammond to Edmund Ruffin, November 21, 1851, Edmund Ruffin Papers, SHC.

57. G. W. Gayle to Rhett, December 23, 1851, Rhett Papers, SCHS.

58. F. W. Byrdsall to Rhett, December 27, 1851, Rhett Papers, SCHS.

59. Rhett, "Political Parties," Aiken Rhett Collection, CM.

Chapter Fifteen

1. *Congressional Globe,* 32d Cong., 1st sess., appendix, 62.

2. Ibid., 32d Cong., 1st sess., 32, 40, 49.

3. Ibid., 96.

4. The notes for Rhett's December 15 speech are in the Rhett Papers, SCHS.

5. *Congressional Globe,* 32d Cong., 1st sess., appendix, 42–49.

6. Ibid., 49–64.

7. John Bradley to Rhett, January 6, 1852, J. Galluchat to Rhett, January 23, 1852, Joseph B. Kershaw to Rhett, December 22, 1851, Benjamin F. Porter to Rhett, January 12, 1852, W. S. Snethen to Rhett, February 2, 1852, various requests for copies of speeches and autographs, Rhett Papers, SCHS.

8. Bleser, *Secret and Sacred,* 247–48.

9. John Slidell to Cobb, January 28, 1852, Phillips, *Correspondence,* 276.

10. Rhett to Thomas Laurence, January 7, 1852, Rhett Papers, SCHS.

11. Rhett to Robert Barnwell Rhett Jr., January 20, 11, 24, February 25, 1852, Crosby.

12. Rhett to Alfred Rhett, February 20, 1852, Crosby.

13. Rhett to Henry Gourdin, January 11, 1852, Rhett Papers, SCHS; Rhett to Andrew Burnet Rhett, January 18, 1852, Rhett Papers, SCL.

14. Mary Rhett to Rhett, December 20, 1851, Rhett Papers, SCHS; Maxcy Gregg to James H. Hammond, March 9, 1852, James Henry Hammond Papers, LC; Bleser, *Secret and Sacred,* 239–40.

15. Rhett to Alfred Rhett, January 7, 1848, Rhett to Robert Barnwell Rhett Jr., n.d. [1847], April 15, 1847, May 13, 1847, December 18, 1848, Crosby.

16. Rhett to James Reeves, January 22, 1852, Rhett Papers, Duke University, Durham, N.C.; *Charleston Mercury,* January 26, 1852; Rhett to Mary Rhett, February 22, 1852, Crosby.

17. Rhett to Andrew Burnet Rhett, January 18, 1852, Rhett Papers, SCL.

18. W. R. Nicholls to Robert M. T. Hunter, January 18, 1852, Ambler, *Hunter,* 133, indicates that Rhett may have been expected at Hunter's on his way to Washington.

19. *Congressional Globe,* 32d Cong., 1st sess., 640, 641.

20. Wallace, *Political Life,* 25–26.

21. Rhett to Robert Barnwell Rhett Jr., February 9, 12, 18, 25, 26, 1852, Crosby; *Congressional Globe,* 32d Cong., 1st sess., 602, 604, 637, 640.

22. *Congressional Globe,* 32d Cong., 1st sess., 654; Rhett to Andrew Burnet Rhett, February 27, 1852, Rhett Papers, SCL; Rhett to Robert Barnwell Rhett Jr., February 27, 1852, Crosby.

23. Perry, *Reminiscences,* 133; Heidler, *Pulling the Temple Down,* 139; Waldo W. Braden, *Oratory in the Old South 1828–1860* (Baton Rouge, La., 1970), 71, 244, 252, 255. White, *Rhett,* seems to have originated the oft-borrowed description of Rhett's oratory as "sophomoric," an apt if not always accurate representation. Hardy Perritt in an essay in Braden, *Oratory,* 244, says that Rhett's speeches appealed to reason, whereas South Carolinians wanted emotion. In fact, a reading of Rhett's addresses reveals if anything that they contained too much emotion.

24. Rhett to Robert Barnwell Rhett Jr., March 3, 1852, Crosby.

25. *Congressional Globe,* 32d Cong., 1st sess., 640–56 *passim.*

26. Rhett to Robert Barnwell Rhett Jr., February 29, March 3, 1852, Crosby.

27. Ibid., March 3, 8, 1852; Rhett to Andrew Burnet Rhett, February 29, 1852, Rhett Papers, SCL.

28. *Charleston Mercury,* March 3, 6, 12, 13, 1852.

29. Lorenzo Sabine, *Notes on Duels and Duelling* (Boston, 1855), 326–29.

30. John Barnwell, *Love of Order,* 185; Paul H. Hayne to Minnie Hayne, March 2, 1852, Paul H. Hayne Papers, Duke University, Durham, N.C.

31. *Charleston Mercury,* March 8, 1852.

32. Bleser, *Secret and Sacred,* 247–48, 251.

33. Rhett to Robert Barnwell Rhett Jr., March 8, 1852, Crosby.

34. *Congressional Globe,* 32d Cong., 1st sess., 729, 762–63, 769, 787, 908, 922, 942, 985, 992–93.

35. Rowland, Moore, and Rogers, *History of Beaufort County,* 432–33; Bleser, *Secret and Sacred,* 251; Rhett to Robert Barnwell Rhett Jr., February 25, March 3, 8, 1852, Crosby; John Barnwell, *Love of Order,* 185.

36. White, *Rhett,* 130.

37. Meats and Arnold, *Writings,* 1:128–29.

38. Alfred P. Aldrich to James H. Hammond, May 3, 1852, James Henry Hammond Papers, LC.

39. Rhett, Proceedings of Convention, n.d., Rhett Papers, SCHS. Rhett says that the 26 April caucus took place on a Saturday, which is an error, suggesting that he wrote this account of the proceedings sometime afterward and with faulty memory of some details. Other content suggests that he wrote after the Civil War, and perhaps as a part of his intended memoir.

40. Meats and Arnold, *Writings,* 1:128.

41. Ibid., 130.

42. *Charleston Mercury,* April 30, May 4, 1851. Though unsigned, this letter so clearly represents Rhett's known views, and even some of his expressions, and at the same time shows such inside knowledge of caucus proceedings, that it could only have been written by a member present, all of which points to Rhett himself.

43. Rhett, Proceedings of Convention, n.d., Rhett Papers, SCHS.

44. Ibid.

45. Ibid.; *Charleston Mercury,* May 3, 5, 1852.

46. Perry, *Reminiscences,* 134; Meats and Arnold, *Writings,* 1:132.

47. Meats and Arnold, *Writings,* 1:132.

48. *Mercury,* May 4, 5, 1852. White's account of the convention in *Rhett,* 130–32, is badly garbled in chronology.

49. Rhett, Proceedings of Convention, Rhett Papers, SCHS; Columbia, *Daily South Carolinian,* May 10, 1852.

Chapter Sixteen

1. Meats and Arnold, *Writings,* 1:134–35; Stephen B. Barnwell, *American Family,* 169–70.

2. Bleser, *Secret and Sacred,* 249–50, 253.

3. *Charleston Courier,* January 7, 1856; Bleser, *Secret and Sacred,* 253; Simms to James H. Hammond, January 28, 1858, Oliphant et al., *Letters,* 4:31.

4. *Charleston Mercury,* May 5, 10, 15, 17, 1852.

5. *Columbia Daily South Carolinian,* May 10, 1852.

6. "I could not in the correspondence assign all the reasons which induced my resignation," Rhett, Proceedings of Convention, Rhett Papers, SCHS.

7. Kenneth S. Greenberg, *Masters and Statesmen: The Political Culture of American Slavery* (Baltimore, 1985), 18, sees in the resignations of Quitman, Yancey, and Rhett a pattern of "turning away from conflict" on the part of the fire-eaters. It seems a strained point at best. Quitman resigned to avoid personal scandal, and Yancey left office in disgust with Congress's avoidance of conflict, and neither Yancey nor Rhett eschewed conflict after their resignations.

8. Perritt, "Disunionist," 55.

9. McConaghy, "Ordinary White Folk," 366ff.

10. Rhett to Andrew Burnet Rhett, February 11, March 27, 1852, Rhett Papers, SCL; Rhett to James H. Thornwell, July 10, 1852, James H. Thornwell Papers, SCL.

11. Rhett to Robert Barnwell Rhett Jr., December 15, 1848, May 23, 1849, January 9, 1850, January 18, July 21, 1851, January 28, February 10, 11, 26, 27, March 12, 15, 16, 19, 1852, Rhett to Thomas Rhett, n.d. [1852], Crosby.

12. Stephen B. Barnwell, *American Family,* 136.

13. Rhett to Daniel Webster, March 1, 1849, Rhett Papers, SCL; *Charleston Mercury,* November 1, 3, 1852.

14. Rhett to Asbury Dinkins, November 22, 1852, Rhett Papers, SCL; Heyward, Rhett, Smith-Rhett Genealogy, Barnwell Rhett Heyward Papers, SCHS; Wallace, *Political Life,* 26.

15. Bleser, *Secret and Sacred,* 258.

16. "Genealogy of the Rhett Family," Rhett Genealogy Notes, SCHS; Robert Barnwell Rhett Jr. to Josephine Bacot, April 21, 1898, Bacot-Huger Collection, SCHS.

17. Rhett to Elise Rhett, 1864, quoted in White, *Rhett,* 134.

18. Rhett to Claudia Stuart, January 9, 1866, Stuart Family Papers, SCHS.

19. Rhett, Autobiographical Sketch, 1858, Rhett Papers, SCHS.

20. Linder, *Atlas,* 175, 178, 302, 311; *Alfred M. Rhett* vs. *Nathaniel Heyward,* 1858, Rhett Papers, SCHS.

21. Linder, *Atlas,* 175–76; C. M. Furman to Rhett, January 21, 1845, Rhett Papers, SHC; Rhett to Andrew Burnet Rhett, August 15, 1855, *Alfred M. Rhett* vs. *Nathaniel Heyward,* 1858, Rhett Papers; Rhett to Langdon Cheves, March 11, 1858, Langdon Cheves Papers, SCHS; McConaghy, "Ordinary White Folk," 100. McConaghy gets some of the chronology of property transfer and management incorrectly here.

22. Robert Barnwell Rhett Jr. to Bacot, June 5, 1887, Bacot-Huger Collection, SCHS.

23. Rhett to Robert Barnwell Rhett Jr., February 12, 1852, October 30, 1869, Crosby; Rhett to Asbury Dinkins, June 11, 1851, Rhett Papers, SCL; *Alfred M. Rhett* vs. *Nathaniel Heyward,* 1858, Rhett Papers, SCHS; Heyward, Rhett, Smith-Rhett Genealogy, Barnwell Rhett Heyward Papers, SCHS; Plantation Account Book, 1853–1857, Rhett Papers, Duke University, Durham, N.C.

24. Plantation Account Book, 1853–57, Rhett Papers, Duke University, Durham, N.C.

25. Edward Dent to Rhett, n.d., three letters circa 1853–54, Rhett Papers, SCHS.

26. Rhett to Claudia Stuart, October 21, 1869, Stuart Family Papers, SCHS; Rhett to Elise Rhett, April 10, 1859, quoted in White, *Rhett,* n 182.

27. Rhett to Katherine Dent [Rhett], n.d., Rhett Papers, SCHS.

28. Rhett-Dent Family marriage notes, n.d., Rhett Papers, SCHS; Heyward, Rhett, Smith-Rhett Genealogy, Barnwell Rhett Heyward Papers, SCHS.

29. Rhett to Richard Crallé, October 25, 1854, "Rhett on the Biography of Calhoun," 312; Stephen B. Barnwell, *American Family,* 171; Perry, *Reminiscences,* 134.

30. Rhett to Andrew Burnet Rhett, August 15, 1855, Rhett Papers, SCHS.

31. Rhett to James Morse, June 25, 1853, Rhett Papers, SCL; Rhett to Jefferson Davis, November 10, 1855, Lynda Laswell Crist and Mary Seaton Dix, eds., *The Papers of Jefferson Davis* (Baton Rouge, La., 1985), 5:465.

32. Richard McCardle to Rhett, October 13, 1854, Rhett Papers, SCHS; Rhett to Richard Crallé, October 25, 1854, "Rhett on the Biography of Calhoun," 311–12.

33. Rhett, "Tract on Government," 486–520. Rhett to Daniel H. London, March 18, 185[4–5], Daniel H. London Papers, Virginia Historical Society, Richmond, establishes Rhett's authorship of the essay.

34. James Murdock Walker, "What Is Our Government?," *Southern Quarterly Review* 18 (July 1854), 128.

35. John McQueen to Rhett, February 3, 1854, Rhett Papers, SCHS.

36. Rhett, "Political Parties," Aiken Rhett Collection, CM.

37. Rhett to Jefferson Davis, October 17, 1854, Crist and Dix, *Papers of Jefferson Davis,* 5:381; Richard Crallé to Rhett, October 13, 1854, Rhett Papers, SCHS.

38. Rhett to Armistead L. Burt, December 22, 1855, January 17, February 19, August 24, 1856, Armistead L. Burt Papers, Duke University, Durham, N.C.

39. *Charleston Mercury,* February 24, 1855, January 17, 1856, January 14, 1857.

40. Rhett to Andrew Burnet Rhett, August 15, 1855, Rhett Papers, SCHS.

41. Rhett to Armistead L. Burt, August 24, 1856, Armistead L. Burt Papers, Duke University, Durham, N.C.; Linder, *Atlas,* 176, 178, 306; *Alfred M. Rhett* vs. *Nathaniel Heyward,* 1858, Rhett Papers, SCHS.

42. Heyward, Rhett, Smith-Rhett Genealogy, Barnwell Rhett Heyward Papers, SCHS.

43. Plantation Account Book, 1853–57, Rhett Papers, Duke University, Durham, N.C.

44. Rhett to Armistead L. Burt, 24 June 1845, Armistead L. Burt Papers, Duke University, Durham, N.C.

45. Rhett to Andrew Burnet Rhett, August 15, 1855, Rhett Papers, SCHS; Plantation Account Book, 1853–57, Rhett Papers, Duke University, Durham, N.C.

46. Stephen B. Barnwell, *American Family,* 67.

47. Virginia Clay-Clopton, *A Belle of the Fifties* (New York, 1905), n 219.

48. Charles F. Deems, ed., *Annals of Southern Methodism for 1856* (Nashville, 1857), 259.

49. Heyward, Rhett, Smith-Rhett Genealogy, Barnwell Rhett Heyward Papers, SCHS.

50. Elise Rhett Lewis to Laura White, n.d. [1920s], Rhett Papers, SCHS.

51. Robert Woodward Rhett to Rhett, June 14, 1856, Rhett Papers, SCHS; Edmund Rhett to Rhett, December 8, 1855, Rhett Papers, SHC.

52. Perry, *Reminiscences,* 133.

53. Isaac E. Holmes to Andrew P. Butler, March 17, 1856; Ambler, *Hunter,* 182.

54. Rhett, "Political Parties," Aiken Rhett Collection, CM.

55. Robert Barnwell Rhett Jr. to William Porcher Miles, April 17, 1856, William Porcher Miles Papers, SHC.

56. Rhett to Armistead L. Burt, August 24, 1856, Armistead L. Burt Papers, Duke University, Durham, N.C.

57. *Charleston Mercury,* 29 August, September 1–15, 1856.

58. Osthaus, *Partisans,* 80.

59. Burke Davis, *Sherman's March* (New York, 1980), 229.

60. Rhett to Robert Barnwell Rhett Jr., December 15, 1850, Crosby; Woodward, *Mary Chesnut,* 318, 619, 622, 626.

61. James L. Petigru to Susan King, November 28, 1856, Carson, *Petigru,* 318–19; Rhett to Henry Wise, November 7, 1856, Simon Gratz Autograph Collection, Historical Society of Pennsylvania, Philadelphia.

62. Rhett, "Tract on Government," 513–14.

63. *Charleston Mercury,* 7 November 1856.

64. James L. Petigru to Susan Petigru King, November 28, 1856, Carson, *Petigru,* 318.

Chapter Seventeen

1. Rhett to Armistead L. Burt, February 4, 1857, Armistead L. Burt Papers, Duke University, Durham, N.C. The year of this letter is in some doubt, thanks to Rhett's poor handwriting, and it is even possible that it is 1868, but the content suggests 1857 as the more likely.

2. Rhett-Dent marriage notes, n.d., Rhett Papers, SCHS.

3. *Charleston Mercury,* February 5, 1857.

4. Rhett to Armistead L. Burt, February 4, 1857, Armistead L. Burt Papers, Duke University, Durham, N.C.

5. Osthaus, *Partisans,* 80–81. Osthaus says trenchantly that "the Rhetts disdained openness in journalism as a sign of a lack of principles and a species of moral cowardice."

6. Anonymous to Rhett, November 13, 1857, Rhett Papers, SCHS.

7. Rhett to Edmund Rhett, October 22, 1857, Rhett Papers, SHC.

8. *Charleston Mercury,* July 2, 3, 1857.

9. William K. Scarborough, ed., *The Diary of Edmund Ruffin* (Baton Rouge, La., 1972), 1:66, May 13, 1857.

10. Simms to James H. Hammond, January 28, 1858, Oliphant et al., *Letters,* 4:31.

11. Ibid.

12. Ronald T. Takaki, *A Pro-Slavery Crusade. The Agitation to Reopen the African Slave Trade* (New York, 1971), 1–2, 188–89.

13. *Charleston Mercury,* June 25, 1857.

14. Wallace, *Political Life,* 5–28 *passim.*

15. *Charleston Mercury,* August 10, 17, 1857.

16. Ibid., August 17, 1857; *Spartanburg* (S.C.) *Spartan,* August 13, 1857.

17. *Charleston Mercury,* November 27, 1857.

18. Paul H. Hayne to James H. Hammond, December 18, 1857, James Henry Hammond Papers, LC.

19. Charleston, *Mercury,* November 27, December 1, 1857; Bleser, *Secret and Sacred,* 270–71.

20. Rhett-Dent Family marriage notes, n.d., Rhett Papers, SCHS.

21. Robert Woodward Rhett to Rhett, July 1, 1858, Elise Rhett to Rhett, March 11, 1858, Rhett Papers, SCHS.

22. Plantation Account Book, Rhett Papers, Duke University, Durham, N.C.; Rhett to Langdon Cheves, February 19, 1858, Langdon Cheves Papers, SCHS.

23. List of a Gang of 38 Negroes, February 1858, Louis DeSaussure to Langdon Cheves, telegram February 1858, February 4, 12, 15, 19, 23, April 6, 1858, Rhett to Langdon Cheves, February 8, 19, 22, March 11, 1858, J. A. Wragg to Langdon Cheves, February 19, 1858, Langdon Cheves Papers, SCHS.

24. Osthaus, *Partisans,* 77, 81; Simms to James H. Hammond, March 27, 1858, Oliphant et al., *Letters,* 4:43; Robert Barnwell Rhett Jr. to George W. Bagby, January 27, 1858, Bagby Family Papers, Virginia Historical Society, Richmond.

25. Robert Barnwell Rhett Jr. to James H. Hammond, January 6, 1858, James Henry Hammond Papers, LC.

26. Paul H. Hayne to James H. Hammond, March 25, 1858, James Henry Hammond Papers, LC; James H. Hammond to Simms, February 7, 1858, Oliphant et al., *Letters,* 4:n 42.

27. Simms to James H. Hammond, April 12, 1858, Oliphant et al., *Letters,* 4:49; *Charleston Mercury,* November 14, 25, 28, 1857.

28. Alfred P. Aldrich to James H. Hammond, April 22, 1858, Simms to James H. Hammond, March 27, 1858, James Henry Hammond Papers, LC.

29. Simms to James H. Hammond, March 27, 1858, Oliphant et al., *Letters,* 4:43, April 12, 1858, 49, Simms to William Porcher Miles, March 27, 1858, 47, James H. Hammond to Simms, April 3, 1858, n 44.

30. Simms to James H. Hammond, April 12, 1858, Oliphant et al., *Letters,* 4:48–49.

31. Paul H. Hayne to James H. Hammond, 17 April 1858, James Henry Hammond Papers, LC; S. G. Tripper to William Porcher Miles, April 19, 1858, William Porcher Miles Papers, SHC.

32. Tripper to William Porcher Miles, April 19, 1858, Paul H. Hayne to James H. Hammond, April 21, 1858, William Porcher Miles Papers, SHC.

33. James H. Hammond to Simms, March 24, 1858, Oliphant et al., *Letters,* 4:n 43.

34. White, *Rhett,* 141–44.

35. William H. Trescot to William Porcher Miles, May 30, 1858, William Porcher Miles Papers, SHC; *Charleston Mercury,* June 7, 8, 1858.

36. *Charleston Mercury,* July 5, 15, 1858.

37. Robert Barnwell Rhett Jr. to William Porcher Miles, September 15, 1858, William Porcher Miles Papers, SHC; George A. Gordon to Dear Knilla, July 3, 20, 1858, George A. Gordon Papers, Duke University, Durham, N.C.

38. Rhett to Daniel H. London, March 18, 1854, Daniel H. London Papers, Virginia Historical Society, Richmond.

39. Takaki, *Pro-Slavery Crusade,* 150–51.

40. *Charleston Mercury,* May 14, 1858; Scarborough, *Diary of Edmund Ruffin,* 1:184, 186.

41. *Charleston Mercury,* May 11–19, 1858; John A. Campbell to Daniel Chandler, November 12, 1860, "Papers of Hon. John A. Campbell—1861–1865," *Southern Historical Society Papers* 62 (September 1917), 18–19; Heidler, *Pulling the Temple Down,* 130–32.

42. Rhett notes in his copy of Wallace, *Political Life,* 28, Crosby.

43. Robert Barnwell Rhett Jr. to James H. Hammond, August 2, 1858, James Henry Hammond Papers, LC.

44. *Charleston Mercury,* June 9, 1858.

45. William C. Davis, *Davis,* 264–65.

46. *Charleston Mercury,* July 17, 30, August 10, 25, 1858.

47. William H. Trescot to James H. Hammond, December 5, 1858, James Henry Hammond Papers, LC.

48. Robert Barnwell Rhett Jr. to James H. Hammond, July 25, August 2, November 5, 1858, James Henry Hammond Papers, LC.

49. Maxcy Gregg to Rhett, September 14, 1858, Rhett Papers, SCHS; *Charleston Mercury,* August 2, 1858; Robert Barnwell Rhett Jr. to James H. Hammond, August 2, 1858, James Henry Hammond Papers, LC.

50. Osthaus, *Partisans,* 80, 84; Rhett, "Political Parties," Aiken Rhett Collection, CM; Rhett to Edmund Ruffin, April 5, 1860, Edmund Ruffin Papers, Virginia Historical Society, Richmond.

51. N. D. Banks to William Porcher Miles, September 7, 1858, William Porcher Miles Papers, SHC.

52. George A. Gordon to Knilla, July 27, September 4, 1858, George A. Gordon Papers, Duke University, Durham, N.C.

53. Osthaus, *Partisans,* 84.

54. Robert Barnwell Rhett Jr. to James H. Hammond, November 5, 1858, James Henry Hammond Papers, LC.

55. Osthaus, *Partisans,* xii, 83.

56. *Charleston Mercury,* November 5, 19, 1858; Osthaus, *Partisans,* 206–7.

57. Rose Miller Betts, "William Henry Trescot," Master's thesis, University of South Carolina, 1929, 39–40.

58. George A. Gordon to Knilla, August 30, 1858, George A. Gordon Papers, Duke University, Durham, N.C.

59. *Charleston Mercury,* July 28, November 12, 1858.

60. Ibid., August 2, 1858.

61. Ibid., September 13, 1858.

62. Takaki, *Pro-Slavery Crusade,* 212–14.

63. James Buchanan to Rhett, September 3, 1858, Rhett Papers, SCHS; *Charleston Mercury,* September 13, 1858.

64. Chauncey S. Boucher, "South Carolina and the South on the Eve of Secession, 1852 to 1860," *Washington University Studies* 6 (April 1919), n 93. Boucher agrees that Rhett sought to get involved in the *Echo* case in order to use the courtroom as a forum for arguing the unconstitutionality of the abolition of the slave trade.

65. George A. Gordon to Knilla, September 30, October 4, 5, 1858, George A. Gordon Papers, Duke University, Durham, N.C.; Rhett to Josephine Rhett, October 5, 1858, Bacot-Huger Collection, SCHS.

66. William Branch to Robert Barnwell Rhett Jr., August 26, 1858, Rhett Papers, Duke University, Durham, N.C.; Rowland, Moore, and Rogers, *History of Beaufort County,* 435.

67. *Charleston Mercury,* December 10, 1858.

68. White, *Rhett,* n 152.

69. William Branch to Robert Barnwell Rhett Jr., August 26, 1858, Rhett Papers, Duke University, Durham, N.C.

70. Peyton Bowman to James H. Hammond, January 24, 1859, James Henry Hammond Papers, LC.

71. *Charleston Mercury,* January 3, 1859.

72. Barnwell to Rhett, January 31, 1859, Rhett Papers, SCL; Ann M. Vanderhorst Diary, January 25, 1859, Vanderhorst Collection, SCHS; Lucy Marmier to Rhett, n.d. [1858–59], Rhett Papers, SCHS.

Chapter Eighteen

1. *Charleston Mercury,* April 25, 1859.

2. Ibid., July 7, 1859.

3. George B. Miller to Rhett, July 25, 1859, Rhett Papers, SCHS.

4. *Charleston Mercury,* July 14, 1859.

5. White, *Rhett,* 154–55, first suggests that the two were working together in this instance, and Henry H. Perritt, "Robert Barnwell Rhett: South Carolina Secession

Spokesman," Ph.D. diss., University of Florida, 1954, 293–94, repeats this, while admitting that there is no evidence of any contact between the two for a year prior to Grahamville. Of course collusion cannot be ruled out, for almost all of Yancey's correspondence is lost, as is much of Rhett's, yet there is no need to speculate on overt cooperation between them at this time, for each was really just reiterating and expanding on ideas already in place for more than a year.

6. *Charleston Mercury,* July 31, 1863. In the margin of the obituary of Yancey in this issue of the *Mercury* in the Charleston Library Society, and also in the microfilm edition, Robert Barnwell Rhett Jr. wrote a comment about a letter Yancey wrote his father in which he acknowledged his being "a follower" of the Carolinian.

7. J. J. Seibels to James H. Hammond, August 15, 1859, James Henry Hammond Papers, LC.

8. *Charleston Mercury,* October 13, 18, 1859; DuBose, *Yancey,* 2:440.

9. Takaki, *Pro-Slavery Crusade,* 228–29.

10. James H. Hammond to Simms, April 22, 1859, James Henry Hammond Papers, LC.

11. *Charleston Mercury,* October 31, 1859.

12. Ibid., November 23, December 5, 1859.

13. Hamilton to William Porcher Miles, December 9, 1859, Alfred Huger to William Porcher Miles, December 12, 1859, William Gist to William Porcher Miles, December 20, 1859, William Porcher Miles Papers, SHC.

14. Wallace, *Political Life,* 2.

15. *Charleston Mercury,* November 29, December 1, 5, 7, 1859.

16. Ibid., November 29, December 5, 1859.

17. James H. Hammond to Simms, April 3, 1860, James Henry Hammond Papers, LC.

18. Rhett-Dent Family marriage notes, n.d., Rhett Papers, SCHS.

19. Christopher G. Memminger to William Porcher Miles, December 27, 1859, January 3, 1860, Robert Barnwell Rhett Jr. to William Porcher Miles, January 29, 1860, William Porcher Miles Papers, SHC.

20. Robert Barnwell Rhett Jr. to William Porcher Miles, January 20, 29, 1860, William Porcher Miles Papers, SHC; Robert Barnwell Rhett Jr. to Edmund Ruffin, April 5, 1860, Edmund Ruffin Papers, Virginia Historical Society, Richmond.

21. Robert Barnwell Rhett Jr. to William Porcher Miles, March 28, 1860, Simms to William Porcher Miles, February 5, 1860, William Porcher Miles Papers, SHC; James H. Hammond to Simms, April 3, 4, 1860, James Henry Hammond Papers, LC; Simms to William Porcher Miles, April 9, 1860, Oliphant et al., *Letters,* 4:210.

22. Benjamin F. Perry to Benson J. Lossing, September 2, 1866, Benjamin Franklin Perry Papers, SCL; Robert Barnwell Rhett Jr. to William Porcher Miles, May 12, 1860, William Porcher Miles Papers, SHC; Robert Barnwell Rhett, Memoir, Aiken Rhett Collection, CM.

23. Rhett, Memoir, Aiken Rhett Collection, CM.

24. Rhett, "Political Parties," Aiken Rhett Collection, CM.

25. Daniel H. Hamilton to William Porcher Miles, April 26, 1860, William Porcher Miles Papers, SHC.

26. Robert Barnwell Rhett Jr. to William Porcher Miles, May 12, 1860, William Porcher Miles Papers, SHC.

27. *Charleston Mercury,* May 1, 1860.

28. Robert Barnwell Rhett Jr. to William Porcher Miles, May 10, 1860, William Porcher Miles Papers, SHC; *Charleston Mercury,* May 2, 1860.

29. Robert Nicholas Olsberg, "William Henry Trescot: The Crisis of 1860," Master's thesis, University of South Carolina, 1967, 33, 38–40, 42–43; *Charleston Mercury,* May 6, 1860.

30. Robert Barnwell Rhett Jr. to William Porcher Miles, May 10, 1860, William Porcher Miles Papers, SHC; *Charleston Mercury,* May 12, 14, 17, 1860.

31. Rowland, Moore, and Rogers, *History of Beaufort County,* 435–36.

32. Alfred Huger to William Porcher Miles, June 1, 1860, William Porcher Miles Papers, SHC.

33. Olsberg, "Trescot," 42; Schultz, *Nationalism and Sectionalism,* 218; Channing, *Crisis of Fear,* 214–24.

34. Isaac Hayne to James H. Hammond, June 3, 1860, James Henry Hammond Papers, LC.

35. White, *Rhett,* n 167, 167.

36. Scarborough, *Diary of Edmund Ruffin,* 1:423–24, 434.

37. *Charleston Courier,* June 6, 1860.

38. Rhett, Memoir, Aiken Rhett Collection, CM.

39. James H. Hammond to Simms, July 10, 1860, Paul H. Hayne to James H. Hammond, June 3, 1860, James Henry Hammond Papers, LC; Arney Robinson Childs, ed., *The Private Journal of Henry William Ravenel, 1859–1887* (Columbia, S.C., 1947), 20; John Letcher to Robert M. T. Hunter, June 6, 1860, Ambler, *Hunter,* 332.

40. Scarborough, *Diary of Edmund Ruffin,* 1:427; Simms to William Porcher Miles, July 15, 1860, Oliphant et al., *Letters,* 4:232, 234.

41. Schultz, *Nationalism and Sectionalism,* 219; William B. Hesseltine, ed., *Three Against Lincoln: Murat Halstead Reports the Caucuses of 1860* (Baton Rouge, La., 1960), 180–83.

42. Perry, *Reminiscences,* 320–21.

43. Hesseltine, *Three Against Lincoln,* 203–4; Channing, *Crisis of Fear,* 225–26.

44. Fannie Colcock to her mother, June 28, 1860, Walter Horton to Robert Barnwell Rhett Jr., July 15, 1860, Bacot-Huger Collection, SCHS; Sarah Woolfolk Wiggins, ed., *The Journals of Josiah Gorgas, 1857–1878* (Tuscaloosa, Ala., 1995), 35.

45. Rhett, Memoir, Aiken Rhett Collection, CM.

46. William Porcher Miles to James H. Hammond, July 10, 1860, James Henry Hammond Papers, LC; James H. Hammond to William Porcher Miles, July 10, 16, 1860, William Porcher Miles Papers, SHC.

47. Olsberg, "Trescot," 48; Osthaus, *Partisans,* 89–90.

48. Abner Doubleday, *Reminiscences of Forts Sumter and Moultrie in 1860–61* (New York, 1876), 16; Donald E. Reynolds, *Editors Make War: Southern Newspapers in the Secession Crisis* (Nashville, 1970), 58.

49. *Charleston Mercury,* July 9, 1860.

50. James H. Hammond to Simms, July 10, 1860, James Henry Hammond Papers, LC.

51. William Porcher Miles to James H. Hammond, August 5, 1860, James Henry Hammond Papers, LC.

52. Lawrence Keitt to James H. Hammond, August 4, 1860, Paul H. Hayne to James H. Hammond, September 19, 1860, James Henry Hammond Papers, LC.

53. William H. Trescot to William Porcher Miles, August 10, 1860, William Porcher Miles Papers, SHC; *Charleston Mercury,* August 24, September 15, 1860.

54. Paul H. Hayne to James H. Hammond, September 19, 1860, Keitt to James H. Hammond, August 4, 1860, John Cunningham to James H. Hammond, July 30, 1860, Alfred P. Aldrich to James H. Hammond, October 4, 1860, James Henry Hammond Papers, LC.

55. James H. Hammond to Paul H. Hayne, September 19, 1860, James Henry Hammond Papers, LC.

56. *Charleston Mercury,* August 10, September 21, 1860; J. D. Ashmore to James H. Hammond, August 30, 1860, James Henry Hammond Papers, LC; White, *Rhett,* 168.

57. Rhett to Barnwell, October 16, 1860, Rhett Papers, SCHS; *Charleston Mercury,* September 24, 1860.

58. Rhett to Barnwell, October 16, 1860, Rhett Papers, SCHS.

59. *Charleston Mercury* September 24, 1860.

60. G. D. Tillman to James H. Hammond, October 9, 1860, James Henry Hammond Papers, LC; Channing, *Crisis of Fear,* 269–70; Lucius E. Chittenden, *Recollections of President Lincoln and His Administration* (New York, 1891), 39, 46; *Charleston Mercury,* October 4, 15, 19, 1860.

61. Osthaus, *Partisans,* 88; *Charleston Mercury,* October 5, 1860.

62. *Charleston Daily Courier,* October 27, 1863. The *Daily Courier*'s claim that Rhett boasted of eating bodies may be an exaggeration, since the paper had been opposed to him for years, but unlike the *Mercury* it was not in the habit of outright fabrication, and thus this probably reports an actual event.

63. Robert N. Gourdin to Langdon Cheves, November 19, 1860, Langdon Cheves Papers, SCHS; Rhett to Edmund Ruffin, October 20, 1860, Edmund Ruffin Papers, SHC; Robert Barnwell Rhett Jr. to Edmund Ruffin, October 20, 1860, Edmund Ruffin Papers, Virginia Historical Society, Richmond.

64. Fannie Colcock to Robert Barnwell Rhett Jr., October 6, 1860, Bacot-Huger Collection, SCHS.

65. Robert Barnwell Rhett Jr. to Edmund Ruffin, October 20, 1860, Edmund Ruffin Papers, Virginia Historical Society, Richmond.

66. William H. Trescot to Rhett, November 1, 1860, William H. Trescot Papers, LC.

67. A. M. McGowan to Samuel McGowan, November 3, 1860, Samuel McGowan Papers, SCL.

68. Dwight Lowell Dumond, *The Secession Movement 1860–1861* (New York, 1931), 138.

69. R. C. Griffin to D. L. Dalton, November 6, 1860, Milledge L. Bonham Papers, SCL; Heyward, Rhett, Smith-Rhett Genealogy, Barnwell Rhett Heyward Papers, SCHS.

70. McCarter Journal, 1860–1866, LC.
71. Scarborough, *Diary of Edmund Ruffin,* 1:483–84; *Charleston Mercury,* November 8, 1860.

Chapter Nineteen

1. Rhett to Robert Barnwell Rhett Jr., November 10, 1860, Rhett Papers, SHC.
2. Scarborough, *Diary of Edmund Ruffin,* 1:489–90.
3. Rhett, Memoir, Aiken Rhett Collection, CM; Channing, *Crisis of Fear,* 249–50.
4. *Charleston Mercury,* November 12, 1860.
5. Lesser, *Relic of the Lost Cause,* 1; White, *Rhett,* 181.
6. *Charleston Mercury,* November 21, 1860.
7. Francis P. Blair Sr. to Francis P. Blair Jr., November 22, 1860, Blair Family Papers, LC.
8. Jacob Thompson to Charles H. Rhett, November 15, 1860, Jacob Thompson Letterbook, Entry 467, War Department Collection of Confederate Records, Record Group 109, National Archives, Washington, D.C.; Jefferson Davis to Robert Barnwell Rhett Jr., November 10, 1860, Crist and Dix, *Papers of Jefferson Davis,* 6:368–70.
9. Robert N. Gourdin to Langdon Cheves, November 19, 1860, Langdon Cheves Papers, SCHS; Rhett, Memoir, Aiken Rhett Collection, CM; Scarborough, *Diary of Edmund Ruffin,* 1:500–502; Charles G. Campbell to Rhett, November 22, 1860, Rhett Papers, SCHS.
10. Rhett to James Buchanan, November 24, 1860, James Buchanan Papers, Historical Society of Pennsylvania, Philadelphia.
11. Rhett to William Porcher Miles, November 8 [December] 1860, William Porcher Miles Papers, SHC. In his Memoir, Rhett states that he returned from Georgia "just after the election" to discover himself selected as a delegate. This is entirely in error, for his November 24 letter to Buchanan was dated in his own hand at Charleston, and the election did not take place until December 6, some twelve days later. Rhett's memory may simply have been faulty on this point, or he may have wished in later years to imply that he had no role in the delegate campaign and that his election came as a surprise to him. Certainly he says nothing about the fact that he was nearly not elected.
12. White, *Rhett,* 183; John R. Horsey to William Porcher Miles, December 10, 1860, William Porcher Miles Papers, SHC. Osthaus, *Partisans,* 87, is particularly good on the Rhetts' attitude in this election.
13. William Gist to Milledge L. Bonham, December 6, 1860, Milledge L. Bonham Papers, SCL.
14. Simms to William Porcher Miles, n.d. [December 1860], William Porcher Miles Papers, SHC; G. Allen Wardlaw to Samuel McGowan, December 2, 1860, Samuel McGowan Papers, SCL.
15. J. J. Wardlaw to Samuel McGowan, December 3, 1860, D. Wardlaw to Samuel McGowan, December 2, 1860, Samuel McGowan Papers; Milledge L. Bonham to William Gist, December 3, 1860, Milledge L. Bonham Papers, SCL.

16. Lesser, *Relic of the Lost Cause,* 4.

17. Rhett to William Porcher Miles, December 8, 1860, John R. Horsey to William Porcher Miles, December 10, 1860, William Porcher Miles Papers, SHC.

18. *Charleston Mercury,* December 6, 8, 1860; John R. Horsey to William Porcher Miles, December 10, 1860, William Porcher Miles Papers, SHC; White, *Rhett,* 184.

19. *Charleston Mercury,* December 12, 1860.

20. Robert Bunch to John Russell, December 15, 1860, "Despatch from the British Consul at Charleston to Lord John Russell, 1860," *American Historical Review* 18 (July 1913), 783–87.

21. Ibid., 783; Robert Bunch to John Russell, January 8, 1861, quoted in White, *Rhett,* n 190.

22. Ellison Capers to his wife, January 1, 1861, Ellison Capers Papers, Duke University, Durham, N.C.; Russell, *My Diary,* 79.

23. *Charleston Mercury,* December 19, 1860.

24. Lesser, *Relic of the Lost Cause,* 2. This banner is now on display at the SCHS.

25. Unaccountably, in his Memoir, Rhett claims that he was chairman of the committee to draft the secession ordinance, which he had to know was manifestly untrue, as the *List of the Committees of the South Carolina Convention, December 17th, 1860* (Charleston, S.C., 1860), 3, and several other contemporary sources make perfectly evident. He was chair of the committee to draft the address to the Southern people, however, and perhaps careless writing, failing memory, and his perpetual penchant to exaggerate his own importance left him confusing the two.

26. *Charleston Mercury,* December 20, 1860.

27. Lesser, *Relic of the Lost Cause,* 6–7, provides the finest discussion of the authorship of the ordinance, which was at one time attributed entirely to Rhett and then to others. In his Memoir, Rhett states that he "shaped the ordinance of Secession," and Heyward, Rhett, Smith-Rhett Genealogy, Barnwell Rhett Heyward Papers, SCHS, asserts that he was "the person who gave its final shape to that document." Rhett later denied authorship and told his son Barnwell Rhett Jr. that he only edited a version submitted by Orr, which Lesser concludes was the Hutson draft. This derives from a statement by the younger Rhett in the *Charleston Sunday News,* July 12, 1896.

28. *Charleston Mercury,* December 21, 1860.

29. Armand J. Gerson, "The Inception of the Montgomery Convention," in *American Historical Association Annual Report* (Washington, D.C., 1910), 183.

30. Lesser, *Relic of the Lost Cause,* 6–10.

31. Heyward, Rhett, Smith-Rhett Genealogy, Barnwell Rhett Heyward Papers, SCHS; Rhett, Memoir, Aiken Rhett Papers, CM.

32. Eric H. Walther, "Fire-Eaters and the Riddle of Southern Nationalism," *Southern Studies* n.s. 3 (spring 1992), 69, appears to argue that Rhett was not truly a Southern nationalist, or that he did not regard Southerners as a nation in the social and cultural sense. Rhett's declarations in the *Address* and elsewhere, as well as his repeated declarations of the different—though fallacious—social and economic origins of Northerners and Southerners, would seem to argue otherwise.

33. Rhett, Memoir, Aiken Rhett Collection, CM.

34. [Christopher G. Memminger,] *Declaration of the Immediate Causes Which Induce and Justify the Secession of South Carolina from the Federal Union; and the Ordinance of Secession* (Charleston, S.C., 1860), 3ff; Capers, *Memminger,* 227, 569ff.

35. Lesser, *Relic of the Lost Cause,* 11; Conversation concerning the late war in the United States, n.d., Rhett Papers, SHC. Internal evidence shows that this document was originally drafted by Rhett during the war as a discussion between a Confederate and an Englishman, and was edited after the close of the war.

36. Robert Bunch to John Russell, January 8, 1861, quoted in White, *Rhett,* n 190.

37. Heyward, Rhett, Smith-Rhett Genealogy, Barnwell Rhett Heyward Papers, SCHS.

38. Rhett, Memoir, Aiken Rhett Collection, CM. The *Mercury* made references more than once during the war to the younger Rhett's suggestion of an armed steamer on guard, so much did it annoy him to be disregarded.

39. Jane Wilkes to Charles Wilkes, November 8, 1860, Wilkes Family Papers, Duke University, Durham, N.C.

40. Linder, *Atlas,* 306.

41. Stephen B. Barnwell, *American Family,* 165; Rhett, Memoir, Aiken Rhett Collection, CM.

42. Rhett, Memoir, Aiken Rhett Collection, CM.

43. Ordinance, December 27, 1860, Langdon Cheves Papers, SCHS.

44. Robert Barnwell Rhett Jr. to Edward C. Wharton, August 2, 1886, Edward C. Wharton Papers, Louisiana State University, Baton Rouge.

45. Notes on the back of *List of the Committees of the South Carolina Convention, December 17th, 1860,* Langdon Cheves Papers, SCHS.

46. A plan for a provisional government, Rhett Papers, SCHS.

47. Notes on reverse of citizenship ordinance, December 1860, Langdon Cheves Papers, SCHS.

48. John Witherspoon DuBose, "Alabama—The Relation of the State to the Birth of the Southern Confederacy," *Confederate Veteran* 24 (May 1916), 206.

49. *Charleston Mercury,* January 8, 1861; Charles E. Cauthen, *South Carolina Goes to War* (Chapel Hill, N.C., 1950), 84–85; Gerson, "Montgomery Convention," 183–84.

50. Undated convention notes, December 1860, Langdon Cheves Papers, SCHS; Rhett, Memoir, Aiken Rhett Collection, CM.

51. Rhett, Memoir, Aiken Rhett Collection, CM.

52. In his Memoir and elsewhere Rhett repeatedly claimed that he was head of this delegation, though there is no record of his being either elected or appointed as such. However, Christopher G. Memminger to Joseph B. Campbell, February 11, 1861, Joseph B. Campbell Papers, SCHS, refers to him as "Chief of our Delegation," and in the book titled "Index Rerum" in the Aiken Rhett Collection, CM, Rhett says that the convention placed him at the head, though the proceedings of the convention show no such action. Thus it seems probable that the mere fact of his finishing with the most votes in the ballot for delegates was generally acknowledged to entitle him to lead the delegation.

53. Rhett, Memoir, Aiken Rhett Collection, CM.

54. Charles E. Cauthen, ed., *Journal of the South Carolina Executive Councils of 1861 and 1862* (Columbia, S.C.; 1956), 8.

55. Doubleday, *Reminiscences,* n 100.

56. Henry Benning to Rhett, n.d., Rhett Papers, SCL; Scarborough, *Diary of Edmund Ruffin,* 1:530.

57. *Charleston Mercury,* January 21, 28, 1861; Robert Barnwell Rhett Jr. to George W. Bagby, January 11, 12, 31, 1861, Bagby Family Papers, Virginia Historical Society, Richmond.

58. *Charleston Mercury,* January 22, 1861.

59. Doubleday, *Reminiscences,* 114.

60. Robert Barnwell Rhett Jr. to George W. Bagby, January 31, 1861, Bagby Family Papers, Virginia Historical Society, Richmond.

61. John Witherspoon DuBose, "Confederate Diplomacy," *Southern Historical Society Papers* 32 (January–December 1904), 105–6.

62. A plan for a provisional government, Rhett Papers, SCHS.

63. Barnwell to Rhett, January 28, 1861, Rhett Papers, SCL; Robert Barnwell Rhett Jr. to Josephine Bacot, February 23, 1896, Bacot-Huger Collection, SCHS.

64. Rhett to Robert Barnwell Rhett Jr., January 28, 1861, Rhett Papers, SCL.

Chapter Twenty

1. *Charleston Mercury,* February 5, 1861. As is evident in Rhett to Robert Barnwell Rhett Jr., February 12, 1861, Rhett Papers, SCL, there was no *Mercury* reporter in Montgomery until at least the middle or latter part of February, meaning that virtually all of the unsigned letters and reports sent from there in the first weeks of the convention were written by Rhett himself. Despite later public denials, Rhett's own later correspondence makes it clear that he wrote some *Mercury* reports himself, and undeniable inside information contained in some reports confirms him as their writer.

2. *Montgomery* (Ala.) *Daily Post,* February 22, 1861; Robert S. Tharin, *Arbitrary Arrests in the South; or, Scenes from the Experiences of an Alabama Unionist* (New York, 1863), 198; Thomas R. R. Cobb to Marion Cobb, February 4, 1861, Thomas R. R. Cobb Letters, University of Georgia, Athens. The Cobb letters have been published incompletely, and with some inaccurate transcription, in "The Correspondence of Thomas Reade Rootes Cobb, 1861–1862," *Publications of the Southern History Association* 11, in the May, July, and September–November 1907 issues, and also as "Thomas R. R. Cobb . . . Extracts from Letters to His Wife, February 3, 1861–December 10, 1862," *Southern Historical Society Papers* 18 (January–December 1900), but it has been deemed best to use and cite the original typescripts.

3. *Charleston Mercury,* February 5, 6, 1861.

4. Christopher G. Memminger to William Porcher Miles, March 19, 1861, William Porcher Miles Papers, SHC.

5. William C. Davis, *"A Government of Our Own": The Making of the Confederacy* (New York, 1994), 45–54.

6. *Charleston Mercury,* February 6, 1861.

7. James Chesnut to William T. Walthall, January 24, 1880, William T. Walthall Papers, Mississippi Department of Archives and History, Jackson; Richard M. Johnston and William Browne, *Life of Alexander H. Stephens* (Philadelphia, 1878), 389–90.

8. Woodward, *Mary Chesnut,* 6. While there is abundant evidence that Rhett thought he should be selected secretary of state, no document has been found to date explicitly stating Rhett's wish to be president, but the case for it is at least circumstantially strong. It was widely assumed by people in his time, including Mary Chesnut, who knew Rhett and his associates well, and it is certainly in keeping with his own ambitions. His later rationalization in his Memoir that he could have won the presidency but for South Carolina's action, certainly suggests that he had the presidency on his mind, while his February 11, 1861 letter to Elise Rhett (White, *Rhett,* n 194) mentioning "disappointment" most likely refers to chagrin over losing the top office, since his only other disappointment for office lay several days in the future when he failed to get the secretary of state appointment.

9. Reynolds, *Editors Make War,* 181.

10. Alexander H. Stephens to Richard M. Johnston, February 2, 1861, Johnston and Browne, *Stephens,* 383–84.

11. James H. Hammond to Simms, February 6, 1861, James Henry Hammond Papers, LC.

12. Alexander H. Stephens to Linton Stephens, February 4, 1861, Alexander H. Stephens Papers, Manhattanville College of the Sacred Heart, Purchase, N.Y.

13. *Charleston Mercury,* February 5, 1861.

14. Lawrence Keitt to David F. Jamison, February 9, 1861, David F. Jamison Papers, Washington and Lee University, Lexington, Va.; *Charleston Mercury,* February 5, 1861.

15. *Charleston Mercury,* February 5, 6, 1861.

16. Ibid., February 5, 6, 1861.

17. Barnwell to James L. Orr, February 9, 1861, Orr-Patterson Papers, SHC.

18. Rhett to Robert Barnwell Rhett Jr., n.d. [February 3, 1861], Rhett Papers, SCL. Though undated, the content and context of the letter clearly establish that it was written after the discussions of February 3 and to accompany the February 3 report published in the February 5 *Mercury.*

19. Thomas R. R. Cobb to Marion Cobb, February 3, 1861, Thomas R. R. Cobb Letters, University of Georgia, Athens.

20. *Charleston Mercury,* February 5, 1861.

21. Ibid., February 5, 8, 1861.

22. Alexander H. Stephens to Lincoln Stephens, February 4, 1861, Alexander H. Stephens Papers, Manhattanville College of the Sacred Heart, Purchase, N.Y.; United States Congress, *Journal of the Congress of the Confederate States of America, 1861–1865* (Washington, D.C., 1904), 1:16 (hereafter cited as *Journal*).

23. Thomas R. R. Cobb to Marion Cobb, February 4, 1861, Thomas R. R. Cobb Letters, University of Georgia, Athens; Rhett to Robert Barnwell Rhett Jr., February 11, 1861, Rhett Papers, SCL.

24. *Journal,* 1:19–22; Rhett to Robert Barnwell Rhett Jr., February 11, 1861, Rhett Papers, SCL.

25. Cauthen, *South Carolina,* n 85, 85.

26. *Charleston Mercury,* February 8, 1861. One report says that a member of the South Carolina delegation had proposed a new scheme for organization, and since Memminger is known to have had his own, and had just that day been appointed to the appropriate committee, it seems most logical that Rhett was referring to him. A separate report refers to Boyce's proposal by name.

27. Rhett to Robert Barnwell Rhett Jr., February 9, 1861, in possession of Shinaan Krakowsky, Encino, Calif.

28. Rhett to "Mr. Editor," n.d. [February 1862], Rhett Papers, SCL.

29. *Charleston Mercury,* February 9, 1861.

30. William H. Trescot to William Porcher Miles, February 6, 1861, William Porcher Miles Papers, SHC.

31. James Chesnut to William T. Walthall, January 24, 1880, William T. Walthall Papers, Jackson Mississippi Department of Archives and History.

32. Christopher G. Memminger to Joseph B. Campbell, February 11, 1861, Joseph B. Campbell Papers, SCHS.

33. Rhett to Robert Barnwell Rhett Jr., February 11, 1861, Rhett Papers, SCL; *Journal,* 1:25.

34. *Journal,* 1:33–39; Rhett to Robert Barnwell Rhett Jr., February 11, 1861, Rhett Papers, SCL; Rhett to Robert Barnwell Rhett Jr., February 9, 1861, in possession of Shinaan Krakowsky, Encino, Calif.; *Charleston Mercury,* February 12, 1861.

35. *Charleston Mercury,* February 6, 1861; Duncan Kenner to William T. Walthall, July 28, 1879, William T. Walthall Papers, Mississippi Department of Archives and History; *Columbus* (Ga.) *Daily Times,* February 5, 1861; Alfred B. Roman to Duncan Kenner, February 3, 1861, La Villebeuvre Family Papers, Louisiana State University, Baton Rouge; *Mobile Daily Advertiser,* February 9, 1861.

36. *Charleston Mercury,* February 9, 1861; W. S. Wilson to H. T. Ellett, February 9, 1861, Charles Colcock Jones Collection, Duke University, Durham, N.C.; Rhett, Memoir, Aiken Rhett Collection, CM; William Porcher Miles to William T. Walthall, January 27, 1880, Chesnut to William T. Walthall, January 24, 1880, William T. Walthall Papers, Mississippi Department of Archives and History; C. Vann Woodward and Elizabeth Muhlenfeld, eds., *The Private Mary Chesnut: The Unpublished Civil War Diaries* (New York, 1984), 16; Rhett to Robert Barnwell Rhett Jr., February 11, 1861, Rhett Papers, SCL; *Philadelphia Times,* July 12, 1879.

37. Rhett, Memoir, Aiken Rhett Collection, CM.

38. *Charleston Mercury,* February 8, 1861.

39. Rhett, Memoir, Aiken Rhett Collection, CM; Rhett to Louis T. Wigfall, April 15, 1864, Louis T. Wigfall Papers, LC.

40. Thomas R. R. Cobb to Marion Cobb, February 15, 1861, Thomas R. R. Cobb Letters, University of Georgia, Athens.

41. Barnwell to Orr, February 9, 1861, Orr-Patterson Papers, SHC.

42. Rhett, Memoir, Aiken Rhett Collection, CM. For a full discussion of the problems with Toombs and Howell Cobb, see William C. Davis, *Government of Our Own*, 91–95, 100–101.

43. Rhett's account of the interviews with Barnwell is found in a bound volume titled "Index Rerum" in the Aiken Rhett Collection, CM, under the heading "Davis-Presidency."

44. Rhett to Louis T. Wigfall, April 15, 1864, Louis T. Wigfall Papers, LC.

45. Undated essay "R B Rhett Jr. gives data *vs*, Jeffn Davis to Beauregard," Rhett Papers, SCL; Heyward, Rhett, Smith-Rhett Genealogy, Barnwell Rhett Heyward Papers, SCHS; "Davis-Presidency," "Index Rerum", Aiken Rhett Collection, CM.

46. Rhett to Robert Barnwell Rhett Jr., February 9, 1861, in possession of Shinaan Krakowsky, Encino, Calif.; *Charleston Mercury*, February 12, 1861.

47. *Rome (Ga.) Tri-Weekly Courier*, February 12, 1861.

48. Woodward and Muhlenfeld, *Chesnut Diaries*, 85; "Davis-Presidency," "Index Rerum," Aiken Rhett Collection, CM. Rhett remains the only firsthand source to claim that Georgia cast its initial vote for Howell Cobb. As discussed in William C. Davis, *Government of Our Own*, 94–95, 100–101, all evidence suggests that there was not a majority in the Georgia delegation that wanted Cobb, or even respected him, yet in two accounts, the Memoir, and "Davis-Presidency," Rhett makes this claim. The only explanation seems to be either that Rhett invented it, which is possible since it would shatter the idea that his by-then-hated enemy Davis had received a unanimous vote the first time around, or else that Georgia made the vote as a meaningless gesture since Cobb was president of the convention. Knowing that all the other states were already solidly behind Davis, Georgia could then switch its vote.

49. DuBose, *Yancey*, 2:586; Alexander H. Stephens, *A Constitutional View of the Late War Between the States* (Philadelphia, 1870), 2:331,

50. Robert A. Toombs, Rhett, and Jackson Morton to Jefferson Davis, February 9, 1861, Crist and Dix, *Papers of Jefferson Davis*, 7:36.

51. Rhett to Elise Rhett, February 11, 1861, in White, *Rhett*, n 194.

52. *Journal*, 1:40–42.

53. Ibid., 1:49.

54. Ibid., 1:44.

55. William W. Freehling, *The Road to Disunion, Volume I: Secessionists at Bay, 1776–1854* (New York, 1990), 3–7, makes much of Rhett being in black, seeing it as a contrast with Southern and now Confederate preoccupation with being white, a strained rationale at best, and then goes on to declare that the new Confederacy was founded on Thomas Jefferson being "a fool" for championing equal rights, when of course Jefferson was never speaking of blacks. Despite this and other weaknesses in his account, Freehling does gauge Rhett well on the occasion.

56. *Journal*, 1:54; Rhett, Memoir, Aiken Rhett Collection, CM.

57. Rhett to Robert Barnwell Rhett Jr., February 11, 1861, Rhett Papers, SCL.

58. *Montgomery* (Ala.) *Daily Post,* February 13, 19, 1861; James P. Jones and William Warren Rogers, eds., "Montgomery as the Confederate Capital: View of a New Nation," *Alabama Historical Quarterly* 26 (spring 1964), 22; DuBose, *Yancey,* 2:588; A. W. Putnam to Andrew Johnson, February 11, 1861, Leroy P. Graf and Ralph W. Hoskins, eds., *The Papers of Andrew Johnson* (Knoxville, 1976), 4:278.

59. Rhett to Robert Barnwell Rhett Jr., February 11, 1861, Rhett Papers, SCL.

60. Rhett to Robert Barnwell Rhett Jr., February 25, 1861, in possession of Shinaan Krakowsky, Encino, Calif.

61. *Charleston Mercury,* February 26, 1861.

62. Christopher G. Memminger to Joseph B. Campbell, February 11, 1861, Joseph B. Campbell Papers, SCHS.

63. Years of research for writing *A Government of Our Own,* the story of the Montgomery convention, failed to produce a single example of Rhett engaging in any social life in the city, or of the citizens and visitors making any demonstration of interest in hearing from or seeing him. See, for instance, the *Montgomery Confederation,* February 15, 1861.

64. *Charleston Mercury,* February 16, 1861.

65. Woodward, *Mary Chesnut,* 242; Thomas R. R. Cobb to Marion Cobb, February 12, 1861, Thomas R. R. Cobb Letters, University of Georgia, Athens; Robert Barnwell Rhett Jr. to Josephine Bacot, August 14, 1885, Bacot-Huger Collection, SCHS.

66. *Charleston Mercury,* February 26, 1861.

67. White, *Rhett,* 196. Walther, *Fire-Eaters,* 301–2, argues that recent historians are wrong in asserting that moderates forced the fire-eaters out of the government. To the extent that fire-eaters were not *forced* out of existing offices, he is right, for none of them but Rhett, Miles, and Keitt were actually in office in the first place when the government was created (Wigfall not participating in the formation at all). But the salient point, surely, is that the fire-eaters were *frozen* out of office from the first. Davis and Stephens were never ardent secessionists, especially Stephens, and there was not one radical in the cabinet. Howell Cobb, president of the provisional congress, was no fire-eater, and neither were any of the committee chairmen except Rhett. Further evidence of the dominance of the moderates is in the permanent constitution in, among other things, the failure to reopen the slave trade and the refusal to include an explicit statement of the right to secede. It was certainly a reforming document, in which Rhett's strong influence represents probably the only substantial impact the fire-eaters were to have on the new government, but it was not a radical charter. Only Yancey of all the fire-eaters received a significant appointment, and that soon proved to be a cipher.

68. Rhett to Edmund Rhett, March 5, 1861, Rhett Papers, SCL; Rhett, Memoir, Aiken Rhett Collection, CM.

69. Rhett to Robert Barnwell Rhett Jr., February 25, 1861, in possession of Shinaan Krakowsky, Encino, Calif.

70. Rhett to Robert Barnwell Rhett Jr., February 9, 1861, in possession of Shinaan Krakowsky, Encino, Calif.

71. Ibid.; Christopher G. Memminger to Francis W. Pickens, February 9, 1861, Cauthen, *Journal,* 46; William Porcher Miles to Francis W. Pickens, February 9, 1861, William Porcher Miles Papers, LC; Rhett to Robert Barnwell Rhett Jr., February 11, 1861, Rhett Papers, SCL.

72. Christopher G. Memminger to Joseph B. Campbell, February 11, 1861, Joseph B. Campbell Papers, SCHS.

73. Doubleday, *Reminiscences,* 123–24.

74. Louis T. Wigfall to Jefferson Davis, February 18, 1861, Crist and Dix, *Papers of Jefferson Davis,* 7:51.

75. *Charleston Mercury,* February 13, 1861.

76. Rhett to Robert Barnwell Rhett Jr., February 11, 1861, Rhett Papers, SCL; Woodward and Muhlenfeld, *Chesnut Diaries,* 13, 15–17; Woodward, *Mary Chesnut,* 10–11, 14.

77. David S. Fraley to Andrew Johnson, February 17, 1861, Graf and Hoskins, *Papers of Andrew Johnson,* 4:303.

78. *Charleston Mercury,* February 16, 1861.

79. Rhett to Robert Barnwell Rhett Jr., February 11, 12, 1861, Rhett Papers, SCL.

80. Rhett to T. Stuart Rhett, April 15, 1867, Rhett Papers, SCHS; Rhett, Memoir, Rhett, "Political Parties," Aiken Rhett Collection, CM.

81. Constitution & amendments proposed for Confederate States, Rhett Papers, SCHS.

82. *Charleston Mercury,* February 20, 1861.

83. *Journal,* 1:851–58.

84. Rhett to Robert Barnwell Rhett Jr., February 20, 1861, Rhett Papers, SCL; Rhett to Robert Barnwell Rhett Jr., February 25, 1861, in possession of Shinaan Krakowsky, Encino, Calif.

85. *Montgomery Weekly Advertiser,* February 27, 1861; Thomas R. R. Cobb to Marion Cobb, February 25, 1861, Thomas R. R. Cobb Letters, University of Georgia, Athens.

86. *Journal,* 1:87, 92; *Montgomery Weekly Advertiser,* February 26, 1861.

87. There is some uncertainty about the precise dates of death of Ann "Nannie" Rhett and Katherine. Stephen B. Barnwell, *American Family,* 172, says that both died on the same day, March 10, 1861. This cannot be correct, for Rhett wrote his first letter referring to Ann's death on February 20, which should place it within no more than a day or two previously and would obviously be the occasion of his wife coming to be with him. None of his surviving correspondence makes reference to the death of Katherine, however. "Genealogy of the Rhett Family," Rhett Genealogy Notes, SCHS, clearly compiled years later by someone other than Rhett, says only that Katherine died in February–March. However, the Rhett-Dent Family marriage notes, undated, in the Rhett Papers, SCHS, state that she died on February 27, and in the absence of better authority, this must be taken to be correct.

88. Woodward and Muhlenfeld, *Chesnut Diaries,* 5.

Chapter Twenty-One

1. Montgomery, *Daily Post,* February 22, 1861.
2. *Journal,* 1:74; Rhett, Memoir, Aiken Rhett Collection, CM.
3. *Charleston Mercury,* February 26, 1861.
4. Rhett outlined his goals in many places, but most succinctly in his Memoir, Aiken Rhett Collection, CM.
5. *Journal,* 1:87.
6. Rhett, Memoir, Aiken Rhett Collection, CM; DuBose, *Yancey,* 599–600.
7. Charles M. Hubbard, *The Burden of Confederate Diplomacy* (Knoxville, 1998), 25, argues that Rhett's plan had "the best chance of success" but foundered on the rocks of Davis's antipathy and the congress's adherence to protectionism to foster Southern industry. Neither reason is entirely convincing, though surely the latter, at least, worked against Rhett. At this stage Davis had not really had time to develop a dislike for Rhett sufficient to let it influence his judgment on policy, as he would later.
8. Robert A. Toombs to William Lowndes Yancey, Pierre Rost, and Ambrose Dudley Mann, March 16, 1861, United States Navy Department, *Official Records of the Union and Confederate Navies in the War of the Rebellion* (Washington, D.C., 1904–22), series 2, 3:191–95.
9. Ambrose Dudley Mann to Rhett, September 30, 1861, Rhett Papers, SCHS.
10. Rhett, Memoir, Aiken Rhett Collection, CM.
11. Rhett to Robert Barnwell Rhett Jr., February 25, 1861, in possession of Shinaan Krakowsky, Encino, Calif.
12. Keitt to James H. Hammond, February 11, 1861, James Henry Hammond Papers, LC.
13. *Charleston Mercury,* October 23, 1861.
14. William S. Barry to John Pettus, February 12, 1861, Record Group 27, vol. 36, Mississippi Department of Archives and History.
15. *New York Herald,* February 20, 1861.
16. Rhett, Memoir, Aiken Rhett Collection, CM; Heyward, Rhett, Smith-Rhett Genealogy, Barnwell Rhett Heyward Papers, SCHS.
17. Rhett, Memoir, Aiken Rhett Collection, CM.
18. Heyward, Rhett, Smith-Rhett Genealogy, Barnwell Rhett Heyward Papers, SCHS.
19. Rhett, Memoir, Aiken Rhett Collection, CM; *Charleston Mercury,* March 26, 1862.
20. Rhett, Memoir, Aiken Rhett Collection, CM, is the only source for this and probably overstates the case.
21. Robert Barnwell Rhett Jr. to Edward C. Wharton, August 18, 1886, Edward C. Wharton Papers, Louisiana State University, Baton Rouge.
22. Rhett to William Porcher Miles, n.d. [February 1861], William Porcher Miles Papers, SHC; Rhett to Leroy P. Walker, March 9, 1861, Alfred Rhett Compiled Service Record, Record Group 109, National Archives.
23. Rhett to Robert Barnwell Rhett Jr., February 11, 1861, Rhett Papers, SCL.

24. Paul H. Hayne to Jefferson Davis, February 18, 1861, G. A. Baker Catalogue #34 (N.p., 1939), 8; Paul H. Hayne to William Porcher Miles, February 19, 1861, William Porcher Miles Papers, SHC.

25. Barnwell to his wife, February 18, 1861, Jones Papers, Duke University, Durham, N.C.; Francis W. Pickens to William Porcher Miles, February 19, 1861, William Porcher Miles Papers, SHC.

26. Jefferson Davis to William H. T. Whiting, February 23, 1861, Rowland, *Davis*, 5:57, Francis W. Pickens to Jefferson Davis, February 27, 1861, 58; Alfred Roman, *The Military Operations of General Beauregard in the War Between the States* (New York, 1884), 1:20–21.

27. *Charleston Mercury*, 20, February 25, March 1, 1861.

28. Woodward, *Mary Chesnut*, 142.

29. *New Orleans Daily Delta*, February 22, 1861.

30. William H. Trescot to William Porcher Miles, February 17, 1861, William Porcher Miles Papers, SHC.

31. *Charleston Mercury*, February 27, March 1, 1861; Rhett to Robert Barnwell Rhett Jr., n.d. [February–March 1861], Rhett Papers, SCL.

32. Osthaus, *Partisans*, 83.

33. *Journal*, 1:52, 78, 91, 92, 98, 121, 122, 144.

34. Thomas R. R. Cobb to Marion Cobb, February 22, 1861, Thomas R. R. Cobb Letters, University of Georgia, Athens.

35. Woodward, *Mary Chesnut*, 17.

36. Poem, Alexander B. Clitherall Papers, Alabama Department of Archives and History, Montgomery. A variant of the poem is in Philip Clayton to Mrs. Howell Cobb, March 28, 1861, Howell Cobb Papers, University of Georgia.

37. *New York Citizen*, April 27, 1867.

38. Alexander H. Stephens to Linton Stephens, March 3, 1861, Alexander H. Stephens Papers, Manhattanville College of the Sacred Heart, Purchase, N.Y.

39. Woodward and Muhlenfeld, *Chesnut Diaries*, 46.

40. Alexander H. Stephens to Linton Stephens, March 8, 1861, Alexander H. Stephens Papers, Manhattanville College of the Sacred Heart, Purchase, N.Y.

41. *Journal*, 1:92.

42. Ibid., 1:94; Thomas R. R. Cobb to Marion Cobb, March 4, 1861, Thomas R. R. Cobb Letters, University of Georgia, Athens.

43. *Journal*, 1:861.

44. Ibid., 1:868, 874, 882–84, 892–93.

45. Ibid., 1:870–71, 878, 880–81, 891; Rhett to T. Stuart Rhett, April 15, 1867, Aiken Rhett Collection, CM.

46. *Charleston Mercury*, October 22, 1861.

47. *Journal*, 1:872–73, 875–77, 880, 882, 890, 894.

48. Rhett to T. Stuart Rhett, April 15, 1867, Aiken Rhett Collection, CM.

49. *Charleston Mercury*, March 6, 1861.

50. Rhett to T. Stuart Rhett, April 15, 1867, Aiken Rhett Collection, CM.

51. Alexander H. Stephens to Linton Stephens, March 8, 1861, Alexander H. Stephens Papers, Manhattanville College of the Sacred Heart, Purchase, N.Y.

52. Stephens, *Constitutional View,* 2:338; Jabez L. M. Curry, *Civil History of the Government of the Confederate States with Some Personal Reminiscences* (Richmond, 1901), 63–64.

53. Rhett to T. Stuart Rhett, April 15, 1867, Aiken Rhett Collection, CM. Rhett's nephew Barnwell R. Burnet to Joseph Huger, November 8, 1899, Bacot-Huger Collection, SCHS, claims that Rhett also authored the provision requiring appropriations to originate in the executive departments, though Rhett did not claim such authorship.

54. White, *Rhett,* 197–201, argues that Rhett failed almost completely in the permanent constitution, a judgment that seems unwarrantedly harsh.

55. George C. Rable, *The Confederate Republic, a Revolution Against Politics* (Chapel Hill, N.C., 1994), 51.

56. *Charleston Mercury,* March 15, 1861.

57. *Journal,* 1:896. The *Charleston Mercury,* April 11, 1862, outlines the specific deficiencies of the permanent constitution, and it may be assumed that in so doing it spoke for Rhett Sr. as well as his son, if he did not in fact author the editorial himself.

58. Rhett, Memoir, Aiken Rhett Collection, CM. Apparently Rhett made this motion on March 9, but no record of Rhett's motion or of the convention's denial appears in the *Journal,* though the substitute partial relaxation does, on p. 896. A subcommittee report delivered immediately beforehand is missing from the *Journal* record, and perhaps this contained Rhett's unsuccessful proposal.

59. David F. Jamison to William Porcher Miles, March 13, 1861, William Porcher Miles Papers, SHC.

60. *Journal,* 1:131, 150, 152–53.

61. Robert Barnwell Rhett Jr., "The Confederate Government at Montgomery," in *Battles and Leaders of the Civil War,* ed. Clarence C. Buel and Robert U. Johnson (New York, 1887), 1:104. With the exception of a few additions by the son, this article is almost entirely drawn from his father's Memoir and a few other recollections.

62. Barnwell R. Burnet to Joseph Huger, November 8, 1913, Bacot-Huger Collection, SCHS. The fact that this account was written fifty-two years after the event must allow for some inaccuracy or invention in recalling Rhett's precise words.

63. *Vicksburg Daily Evening Citizen,* March 30, 1861.

64. Scarborough, *Diary of Edmund Ruffin,* 1:575.

65. John Manning to his wife, April 2, 1861, Williams-Chesnut-Manning Papers, SCL; Cauthen, *South Carolina,* 87; Rable, *Confederate Republic,* 53; Rhett to Nat M. Burford, March 1861, *Dallas Herald,* April 3, 1861; *Charleston Mercury,* March 25–10 April, 1861.

66. Doubleday, *Reminiscences,* 125; *Athens* (Ga.) *Southern Watchman,* April 3, 1861; *Charleston Mercury,* April 4, 1861.

67. Ralph A. Wooster, *The Secession Conventions of the South* (Princeton, N.J., 1962), 23–24, 48, 74.

68. White, *Rhett,* n 204.

69. James H. Hammond to J. D. Ashmore, April 8, 1861, James Henry Hammond Papers, LC.

70. *Report of the Special Committee of Twenty-One,* n.d. [1861], Langdon Cheves Papers, SCHS; Robert Barnwell Rhett Jr. to George W. Bagby, April 2, 1861, Bagby Family Papers, Virginia Historical Society, Richmond.

71. John D. Williams to Rhett, January 14, 1868, Rhett Papers, SCHS.

72. Sketch of Alfred Rhett, Alfred Rhett Papers, Museum of the Confederacy, Richmond, Va.

73. S. Courtney to William Porcher Miles, April 23, 1861, William Porcher Miles Papers, SHC.

74. Russell, *My Diary,* 69, 79.

75. Rhett, "Political Parties," Aiken Rhett Collection, CM; Robert Barnwell Rhett, Essay on the Money Power in United States, n.d. [post-1866], Rhett Papers, SCHS.

76. Conversation occurring during the war, Rhett Papers, SHC. There are two almost identical versions of this dialogue in the Rhett Papers, the first written as a conversation between an Englishman and a "Confederate," showing that it was written between 1861 and 1865. The second changes "Confederate" to "Southerner," showing it to be postwar.

77. Rhett, "Political Parties," Aiken Rhett Collection, CM.

78. Woodward, *Mary Chesnut,* 232.

Chapter Twenty-Two

1. *New Orleans Daily Picayune,* May 3, 1861; *Journal,* 1:169; *Montgomery Daily Post,* May 1, 1861.

2. Rhett, Memoir, Aiken Rhett Collection, CM.

3. *Journal,* 1:173, 181.

4. Woodward and Muhlenfeld, *Chesnut Diaries,* 67.

5. Robert A. Toombs to William Lowndes Yancey et al., March 16, 1861, *Official Records . . . Navies,* series 2, 3:191–95; Rhett, Memoir, Aiken Rhett Collection, CM. Of course, Rhett's claim in his Memoir that he predicted failure for the Yancey mission may also be simple invention through hindsight, of which there is much in his reminiscences.

6. Russell, *My Diary,* 90.

7. Rhett, Memoir, Aiken Rhett Collection, CM.

8. *Journal,* 1:214, 225, 253; Rhett, Memoir, Aiken Rhett Collection, CM; Barnwell R. Burnet to Joseph Huger, November 8, 1913, Bacot-Huger Collection, SCHS. The Memoir seems to suggest that Perkins made his amendment in regular debate. However, the only such amendment was proposed by Thomas Cobb on May 20, and it was for five and not six years. Since Perkins sat on the foreign affairs committee, it is more likely that in the Memoir, Rhett is describing discussion and amendment that took

place within the committee itself. John Witherspoon DuBose, "William L. Yancey in History," *Southern Historical Society Papers* 27 (January–December 1899), 101, argues that Rhett refused to accept the Perkins amendment and thus killed the bill himself, but DuBose was basing this, as he did his similar account in *Yancey,* 2:600, on Rhett's Memoir, which had been loaned to him by Robert Barnwell Rhett Jr.

9. Rhett, Memoir, Aiken Rhett Collection, CM.

10. *Charleston Mercury,* July 12, 1861; *Journal,* 1:222; Rhett, Memoir, Aiken Rhett Collection, CM. It should be noted that in his Memoir, Rhett complained that Davis was dilatory in securing sufficient arms abroad and also that he failed to act on the offer of the purchase of a fleet of modern warships from the East India Company, which had just been absorbed by the British government. In both instances Rhett was merely incorporating what he was told and shown by P. G. T. Beauregard in the 1870s, whereas there is no evidence that in 1861 Rhett was finding any fault in these areas. Indeed, the East India Fleet affair may never have taken place at all, or if the offer were made, there is no evidence that it ever reached Davis, and there is plenty of evidence that he would have acted upon it if it had. See William C. Davis, *Government of Our Own,* 350–51, n 504.

11. Woodward and Muhlenfeld, *Chesnut Diaries,* 67.

12. *Journal,* 1:219, 220–21, 242; Johnston and Browne, *Stephens,* 424.

13. *Journal,* 1:192, 229, 244; *Charleston Mercury,* May 18, 1861; *New York Citizen,* April 27, 1861.

14. Woodward, *Mary Chesnut,* 57; Thomas R. R. Cobb to Marion Cobb, May 10, 1861, Thomas R. R. Cobb Letters, University of Georgia, Athens; Rhett to Katherine Rhett, May 14, 1861, Rhett Papers, SCHS.

15. Rhett, Memoir, Aiken Rhett Collection, CM; *Journal,* 1:247.

16. Rhett, Memoir, Aiken Rhett Collection, CM; *Journal,* 1:209, 211–13, 243, 262, 264; *Charleston Mercury,* July 3, 1861.

17. Robert Barnwell Rhett Jr. to William B. Phillips, July 10, 1861, William B. Phillips Papers, Virginia Historical Society, Richmond.

18. Rhett to Katherine Rhett, May 14, 1861, Rhett Papers, SCHS; Simms to William Porcher Miles, June 8, 1861, William Porcher Miles Papers, SHC; Woodward and Muhlenfeld, *Chesnut Diaries,* 83.

19. *Charleston Mercury,* June 3, July 2, 8, 1861.

20. Ibid., July 3, 12, 13, 15, 1861.

21. Rhett to Robert Barnwell Rhett Jr., July 25, 1861, Civil War Collection, Henry E. Huntington Library and Art Gallery, San Marino, Calif.

22. Ibid.

23. Ibid.

24. Perry, *Reminiscences,* 132; *Charleston Mercury,* July 30, 1861.

25. *Charleston Mercury,* July 25, 27, 30, 1861.

26. Rhett to Robert Barnwell Rhett Jr., July 25, 1861, Civil War Collection, Henry E. Huntington Library and Art Gallery, San Marino, Calif.; *Journal,* 1:285, 286, 293–94, 308, 314, 377, 389–90; Rhett, Memoir, Aiken Rhett Collection, CM.

27. *Journal,* 1:329–30, 334–35, 339, 342, 359, 409, 455; Thomas R. R. Cobb to Marion Cobb, September 11, 1861, Thomas R. R. Cobb Letters, University of Georgia, Athens.

28. *Charleston Mercury,* October 11, 12, 1861; *Journal,* 1:358, 385, 391, 395, 402, 421, 428, 441–43.

29. *Charleston Mercury,* July 30, 31, August 10, 13, 28, 1861.

30. Woodward and Muhlenfeld, *Chesnut Diaries,* 122,

31. J. Dickson Burns to William Porcher Miles, August 4, 1861, William Porcher Miles Papers, SHC.

32. *Charleston Mercury,* August 10, 28, 1861; *Journal,* 1:415.

33. *Journal,* 1:383, 413.

34. Ibid., 1:465–66.

35. *Charleston Mercury,* September 7, 19, 1861.

36. Thomas Rhett to William Porcher Miles, August 13, 1861, William Porcher Miles Papers, SHC.

37. *Charleston Mercury,* September 19, 28, October 21, 22, November 1, 1861.

38. Ibid., September 26, 1861.

39. Woodward and Muhlenfeld, *Chesnut Diaries,* 163.

40. *Charleston Mercury,* October 1, 7, 18, 21, 1861.

41. Ibid., September 17, October 8, 16, 23, 1861.

42. Ibid., October 9, 10, 1861.

43. Ambrose Dudley Mann to Rhett, September 30, 1861, Rhett Papers, SCHS; *Charleston Mercury,* October 29, 1861.

44. Rhett, Memoir, Aiken Rhett Collection, CM.

45. *Charleston Mercury,* November 1, 1861.

46. Ibid., October 29, 1861.

47. D. G. Duncan to Robert Barnwell Rhett Jr., October 29, 1861, Rhett Papers, SCL; *Charleston Mercury,* October 29, 30, November 4, 1861.

48. Woodward and Muhlenfeld, *Chesnut Diaries,* 169, 183; Woodward, *Mary Chesnut,* 206, 215.

49. Samuel McGowan to Milledge L. Bonham, September 16, 1861, Milledge L. Bonham Papers, SCL; Barnwell to J. H. Thornwall, October 12, 1861, Robert Barnwell Papers, SCL; Ellison Capers to his wife, August 2, 1862, Ellison Capers Papers, Duke University, Durham, N.C.; Simms to James H. Hammond, November 18, 1861, James Henry Hammond Papers, LC.

50. Simms to James H. Hammond, November 18, 1861, Oliphant et al., *Letters,* 4:385.

51. *Charleston Mercury,* November 6, 1861.

52. Woodward, *Mary Chesnut,* 215.

53. Woodward and Muhlenfeld, *Chesnut Diaries,* 194, 206; Robert Barnwell Rhett Jr. to Edmund Rhett, October 29, 1861, Rhett Papers, SHC.

54. Robert Barnwell Rhett Jr. to George W. Bagby, November 25, 1861, Bagby Family Papers, Virginia Historical Society, Richmond.

55. *Charleston Mercury,* November 1, 1861.

Chapter Twenty-Three

1. Scarborough, *Diary of Edmund Ruffin,* 2:177; Woodward, *Mary Chesnut,* 244, 272; Rhett to Sallie Rhett, 1863, Nancy Dixon, *Fortune and Misery: Sallie Rhett Roman of New Orleans* (Baton Rouge, La., 1999), 12.

2. Rhett to Robert Barnwell Rhett Jr., November 28, 1861, Rhett Papers, SCL; *Charleston Mercury,* November 19, 23, 1861.

3. *Journal,* 1: 489.

4. Littleton B. Washington Diary, August 21, 1863, copy in possession of Douglas L. Gibboney, Carlisle, Pa.; Rhett to Robert Barnwell Rhett Jr., November 28, 1861, Rhett Papers, SCL; Rhett, Memoir, Aiken Rhett Collection, CM.

5. *Journal,* 1:478.

6. *Charleston Mercury,* November 4, 1861.

7. *Journal,* 1:476, 493, 518, 568; Rhett, Memoir, Aiken Rhett Collection, CM.

8. *Journal,* 1:483.

9. In Rhett, Memoir, Aiken Rhett Collection, CM, he says that he met delegates George Vest and Thomas Harris the day after they took their seats. Vest and Harris were not both in the congress until December 6, which would suggest December 7 as the day they met with Rhett, but Crist and Dix, *Papers of Jefferson Davis,* 7:n 435, seems to establish that they must have met Rhett on December 2.

10. Rhett to Robert Barnwell Rhett Jr., December 17, 1861, Rhett Papers, SCL; *Charleston Mercury,* March 25, 1862.

11. G. W. B. [George W. Bagby] to Robert Barnwell Rhett Jr., n.d. [December 1861–February 1862], Rhett Papers, SCL.

12. *Journal,* 1:584; Alexander Galt to Robert Barnwell Rhett Jr., September 20, 1862, Rhett Papers, SCL.

13. *Journal,* 1:561.

14. White, *Rhett,* n 220.

15. Thomas Bocock to Rhett, January 19, 1862, Rhett Papers, SCL; *Journal,* 1:546, 549, 588; United States War Department, *War of the Rebellion: Official Records of the Union and Confederate Armies* (Washington, D.C., 1880–1901), series 4, 1:868.

16. *Journal,* 1:478, 528, 553, 557, 563; Robert Barnwell Rhett, Johnson, Trenholm and the Confederate finances, 1873–74, Aiken Rhett Collection, CM.

17. *Journal,* 1:747, 796.

18. Ibid., 1:548, 577, 733–34, 762, 766, 781–82, 819.

19. Rhett statement, February 8, 1862, Rhett Papers, SCL; *Journal,* 1:603; Rhett, Memoir, Aiken Rhett Collection, CM; *Charleston Mercury,* February 27, March 26, 1862.

20. Joseph B. Kershaw to William Porcher Miles, March 1, 1862, Milledge L. Bonham to William Porcher Miles, December 25, 1861, William Porcher Miles Papers, SHC.

21. *Journal,* 1:691, 765; Robert Barnwell Rhett Jr. to Milledge L. Bonham, February 11, 1862, Milledge L. Bonham Papers, SCL; *Charleston Mercury,* February 1, 11, March 21, 1862.

22. *Charleston Mercury*, January 25, February 12, 1862; A. Burnet Rhett to Thomas Rhett, February 24, 1861, Rhett Papers, SCL.

23. *Charleston Mercury*, February 11, 1862.

24. *Journal,* 1:512, 686, 737, 741, 759.

25. Ibid., 1:521, 552, 556, 825; *Charleston Mercury*, September 23, 1862; Thomas R. R. Cobb to Marion Cobb, February 1, 1862, Thomas R. R. Cobb Letters, University of Georgia, Athens; Rhett, Memoir, Aiken Rhett Collection, CM; Barnwell R. Burnet to Joseph Huger, November 8, 1913, Bacot-Huger Collection, SCHS.

26. *Journal,* 1:757; *Charleston Mercury*, September 23, 1862, September 23, 1863; Rhett, Memoir, Aiken Rhett Collection, CM.

27. *Journal,* 1:757, 813; *Charleston Mercury*, September 23, 1862, September 23, 1863; Rhett, Memoir, Aiken Rhett Collection, CM.

28. Rhett, Memoir, Aiken Rhett Collection, CM. Albert B. Moore, *Conscription and Conflict in the Confederacy* (New York, 1924), 230, maintains without citing any source that Rhett took credit for starting conscription, but there seems to be no evidence for the claim.

29. *Charleston Mercury*, January 23, 1862.

30. Ibid., January 15, 21, 27, 31, February 26, 1862.

31. Ibid., March 26, 1862.

32. Rhett to Mr. Editor, n.d. [February 1862], Rhett Papers, SCL.

33. *Journal,* 1:287, 291, 355, 443, 460, 708.

34. Ibid., 1:710, 730.

35. *Charleston Mercury*, February 14, 1862.

36. *Journal,* 1:575.

37. Rhett, Memoir, Aiken Rhett Collection, CM; partial text of speech, February 5, 1862, cited in Perritt, "Rhett," 345–46, as being from the Rhett Papers currently in SCHS but not found among them. Jackson's December 6, 1832 veto of a War of 1812 debt bill is one example of a veto based on something other than constitutionality.

38. *Journal,* 1:809; *Charleston Mercury*, February 14, 1862.

39. *Charleston Mercury*, February 14, March 7, 24, 1862.

40. Woodward, *Mary Chesnut,* 289; Scarborough, *Diary of Edmund Ruffin,* 2:229.

41. *Journal,* 1:709, 757, 821, 823, 829, 831; *Charleston Mercury*, February 5, 1862; Rhett, "Confederate Government," 110; Littleton B. Washington Diary, August 21, 1863, copy in possession of Douglas L. Gibboney, Carlisle, Pa.

42. Russell, *My Diary,* 79.

43. Thomas B. Alexander and Richard E. Beringer, *The Anatomy of the Confederate Congress* (Nashville, 1972), 396, 404, conclude that while Rhett's voting record was moderately strong on economic issues and in the mainstream on the military, he was weak on others such as state rights, sequestration, race and state rights, and more. In fact, his voting record shows him consistently very strong on state rights and slavery, and where the authors charge him with being weak on support of railroads, they fail to appreciate that his opposition reflected only the strength of his state rights position

against internal improvements. As for slavery, no member of the congress had a stronger record in its protection and expansion, including reopening the slave trade.

44. Rhett to Mr. Editor, n.d. [February 1862], Rhett Papers, SCL.
45. *Charleston Mercury*, February 27, March 25, 26, 1862; Rhett to Robert Barnwell Rhett Jr., n.d. [late February 1862], Rhett Papers, SCL.
46. *Charleston Mercury*, October 30, 1861, March 22, April 25, 5, 11, 22, 23, June 13, July 28, 1862.
47. The correspondence between the younger Rhett and Bagby in March 1862 will be found in Crosby; Robert Barnwell Rhett to George W. Bagby, April 9, 1862, Bagby Family Papers, Virginia Historical Society, Richmond.
48. *Charleston Mercury*, April 28, June 3, 1862; Robert Barnwell Rhett Jr. to Barnwell, May 22, 1862, Rhett Papers, SCL.
49. Woodward, *Mary Chesnut*, 318.
50. "Thomas R. R. Cobb," 291; *Charleston Mercury*, May 23, June 13, August 21, 1862.
51. Ellison Capers to his wife, August 1, 1862, Ellison Capers Papers, Duke University, Durham, N.C.
52. *Charleston Mercury*, June 6, 1862.
53. Rhett to Robert Barnwell Rhett Jr., n.d. [February 1862], April 14, August 10, 1862, Rhett Papers, SCL; Rhett, Memoir, Aiken Rhett Collection, CM; Elise Rhett Lewis to Laura White, March 2, 1913, White, *Rhett*, n 226; Edmund Rhett to John C. Pemberton, July 9, 1862, Department of South Carolina and Georgia Collection, Museum of the Confederacy, Richmond, Va.
54. Robert Barnwell Rhett Jr. to John C. Pemberton, June 18, 1862, Department of South Carolina and Georgia Collection, Museum of the Confederacy, Richmond, Va.
55. Rhett Genealogy Notes, Rhett Family Papers, SCHS; Edmund Rhett to Claudia Stuart, June 27, 1862, Stuart Family Papers, SCHS. Charles S. Colcock to Rhett, July 11, 1862, Rhett Papers, SCL.
56. Commission, July 23, 1862, Rhett Papers, SHC.
57. *Testimony Collated and Arranged from the Proceedings of the Court of Inquiry in the Case of Major Alfred Rhett for Fighting a Duel with Colonel W. R. Calhoun* (Charleston, S.C., 1862), in possession of Leslie Crosby, Huntsville, Ala.; *Correspondence Concerning Occurrences of April 23, 1862 Between Col. W. R. Calhoun and Major Alfred Rhett* (Charleston, S.C., 1862), 2–5; Notice, August 8, 1862, Rhett Papers, SCL. "Robert Barnwell Rhett on the Biography of Calhoun, " 310, states erroneously that Robert Barnwell Rhett killed an opponent in a duel. Its author confuses him with his son Alfred.

Chapter Twenty-Four

1. Laura White, "The Fate of Calhoun's Sovereign Convention in South Carolina," *American Historical Review* 34 (July 1929), 575ff, n 762.
2. *Charleston Mercury*, September 23, 1862.

3. Ibid., September 24, 1862.

4. Ibid., October 2, 29, 1862.

5. P. G. T. Beauregard to William Porcher Miles, April 1863, War Department, *Official Records,* series 1, 53:288.

6. *Charleston Mercury,* September 23, 1862.

7. Rhett to Robert Barnwell Rhett Jr., September 18, October 19, 1862, Rhett Papers, SCL; *Charleston Mercury,* October 23, 1862.

8. Rhett to Robert Barnwell Rhett Jr., September 18, 1862, Rhett Papers, SCL; *Charleston Mercury,* October 17, 1862.

9. Rhett to Robert Barnwell Rhett Jr., October 19, 1862, Rhett Papers, SCL.

10. *Charleston Mercury,* February 21, 1863; P. J. Staudenraus, ed., "Occupied Beaufort, 1863: A War Correspondent's View," *South Carolina Historical Magazine* 64 (July 1963), 137.

11. Robert Barnwell Rhett Jr. to Josephine Bacot, February 9, 1896, Bacot-Huger Collection, SCHS; *Memorial of the Late James L. Petigru,* 19.

12. Rhett to Lewis M. Ayer, April 15, 1863, Lewis M. Ayer Papers, SCL; *Charleston Mercury,* February 11, 1863; Receipts, November 10, 1862, October 3, 1863, Robert Barnwell Rhett Sr. File, Confederate Papers Relating to Citizens or Business Firms, M346, National Archives; Rhett to Robert J. Jeffords, May 30, 1863, Robert J. Jeffords Papers, Duke University, Durham, N.C.

13. Rhett to Claudia Stuart, January 9, 1866, April 25, 1868, Stuart Family Papers, SCHS; Rhett to Robert Barnwell Rhett Jr., October 30, 1869, Crosby; Jonathan H. Poston, *The Buildings of Charleston. A Guide to the City's Architecture* (Columbia: University of South Carolina Press, 1997), 638–39. In his 1868 letter to Claudia, Rhett says he sold the house for thirty-three thousand dollars, ten thousand dollars more than he paid for it, which would mean that he had paid twenty-three thousand dollars. However, in his 1869 letter to his son Robert he states that he actually paid ten thousand dollars for the house.

14. *Charleston Mercury,* September 26, 1862; Robert Barnwell Rhett Jr. to William Porcher Miles, December 28, 1862, Rhett Papers, SHC; Ellison Capers to his wife, February 26, 1863, Ellison Capers Papers, Duke University, Durham, N.C.

15. Benjamin Rhett to Milledge L. Bonham, February 5, 1863, Milledge L. Bonham Papers, SCL.

16. Rhett to Robert Minor, July 25, 1863, Minor Family Papers, Virginia Historical Society, Richmond.

17. Rhett to Robert Barnwell Rhett Jr., October 19, 1862, Rhett Papers, SCL; *Charleston Mercury,* January 1, 1863. In the set of the *Mercury* that belonged to the younger Rhett, and which is now in the Charleston Library Society, he has annotated editorials starting in January 1863 with the initials "R.B.R.Jr.," indicating that he wrote them.

18. *Charleston Mercury,* January 3, 5, 20, 26, March 26, 1863; Rhett, "For the Mercury," n.d. [1863], Rhett Papers, SCL.

19. Rhett to Robert J. Jeffords, May 30, 1863, Robert J. Jeffords Papers, Duke University, Durham, N.C.; Rhett to Robert Barnwell Rhett Jr., March 10, 1863, Rhett

Papers; Rhett to Lewis M. Ayer, April 15, 1863, Lewis M. Ayer Papers, SCL; *Charleston Mercury,* March 12, April 18, 1863.

20. *Charleston Mercury,* May 25, 1863; Rhett to Robert Barnwell Rhett Jr., March 10, 1863, Rhett Papers, SCL.

21. Sketch of Alfred Rhett, Alfred Rhett Papers, Museum of the Confederacy, Richmond, Va.; Miles, Orr, Ayer, Boyce, et al., recommendation, n.d. [1863], Alfred Rhett Compiled Service Record, Record Group 109; Rhett to James A. Seddon, September 24, 1863, James A. Seddon to Rhett, October 1, 1863, Letters Received by the Confederate Secretary of War, File R (WD) 317–1863, Record Group 109, National Archives.

22. *Charleston Mercury,* May 14, June 23, 24, July 9, 16, 30, September 23, 1863; Rhett, Memoir, Aiken Rhett Collection, CM; Robert Barnwell Rhett Jr. to Alfred B. Roman, May 14, 1889, Alfred B. Roman Papers, LC.

23. *Charleston Mercury,* July 31, 1863.

24. Robert Barnwell Rhett Jr. to Josephine Bacot, February 1, 1905, Bacot-Huger Collection, SCHS; *Charleston Mercury,* August 11, 1863.

25. Rhett, Memoir, Aiken Rhett Collection, CM.

26. *Charleston Mercury,* September 8, October 29, 1863.

27. Ibid., September 23, 1863; Rhett to James A. Seddon, September 24, 1863, Letters Received by the Confederate Secretary of War, File R (WD), 317–1863, Record Group 109, National Archives.

28. White, *Rhett,* 233; Milton Maxcy Leverett to his mother, October 10, 1863, Leverett Family Papers, SCL.

29. *Charleston Courier,* September 24, October 6, 1863.

30. *Charleston Courier,* October 26, November 10, 1863.

31. Rhett, Memoir, Aiken Rhett Collection, CM.

32. *Charleston Mercury,* October 29, 1863.

33. Heyward, Rhett, Smith-Rhett Genealogy, Barnwell Rhett Heyward Papers, SCHS.

34. Rhett Genealogy Notes, Rhett Family Papers, SCHS; Rhett to Sallie Rhett, 1863, in Dixon, *Fortune and Misery,* 12.

35. *Charleston Mercury,* November 3, 1863; *Charleston Daily Courier,* November 3, 1863. Several historians have assumed that Rhett and his editor son participated in the ceremonies for Davis in Charleston, but there seems not to be a shred of evidence of this, and such conclusions must be mistaking references to "Colonel Rhett" in the press for one or the other of them, when clearly Alfred is meant. See for instance, Hudson Strode, *Jefferson Davis, Confederate President* (New York, 1959), 492.

36. R B Rhett Jr. gives data *vs.* Jeffn Davis to P. G. T. Beauregard, n.d., Rhett Papers, SCL.

37. Keitt to James H. Hammond, December 11, 1863, James Henry Hammond Papers, LC.

38. *Charleston Mercury,* November 12, 1863.

39. Rhett to P. G. T. Beauregard, December 9, 1863, R. B. Rhett file, Confederate Papers Relating to Citizens or Business Firms, M346, National Archives; P. G. T.

Beauregard to Rhett, December 12, 1863, War Department, *Official Records,* series 1, vol. 28, part 2, 547.

40. Rhett to Beverly Robertson, April 18, 1864, Elizabeth Byrd Nicholas Papers, Virginia Historical Society, Richmond; Rhett to James A. Seddon, April 17, 1864, Letters Received by the Confederate Secretary of War, File R (WD), 124–1864, Record Group 109, Receipt, January 9, 1864, Robert Barnwell Rhett Jr. File, Confederate Papers Relating to Citizens or Business Firms, M346, National Archives.

41. Rhett to Claudia Stuart, January 9, 1866, Stuart Family Papers, SCHS; Receipts, December 20, 31, 1863, March 31, April 6, 7, 1864, Rhett file, Confederate Papers Relating to Citizens or Business Firms, M346, National Archives.

42. Heyward, Rhett, Smith-Rhett Genealogy, Barnwell Rhett Heyward Papers, SCHS. Heyward mistakenly says that Rhett had 350 slaves, but Rhett in his January 9, 1866 letter to his sister Claudia specifically says he only had 170. While it is perhaps impolitic to suggest that Rhett's slaves did not run away to Union lines during the war because they were content as they were, it must be considered that no doubt one of the reasons he did not prosper as a planter was that he did not work his slaves hard nor did he mistreat them. More persuasive, however, is the fact that even after the war all but a few of his former slaves remained with him at a time when they were at perfect liberty to leave.

43. Navy Department, *Official Records,* series 1, 15:515; Rhett, Memoir, Aiken Rhett Collection, CM; *Charleston Mercury,* April 8, 1864. There is no further record of the Hammond ram or the cotton shipment other than this April 30, 1864 statement of the plan, but the fact that in Rhett to Claudia Stuart, January 9, 1866, Stuart Family Papers, SCHS, he makes no mention of any cotton sale while detailing to her his several other sources of substantial income during the war, suggests that the cotton was never sold.

44. Rhett to Louis T. Wigfall, April 15, 1864, Louis T. Wigfall Papers, LC; Rhett to Claudia Stuart, January 9, 1866, Stuart Family Papers, SCHS; *Charleston Mercury,* January 8, 1864.

45. Rhett to Louis T. Wigfall, April 15, 1864, Louis T. Wigfall Papers, LC.

46. *Charleston Mercury,* March 12, May 7, 21, June 30, July 15, 1864.

47. Ibid., April 8, 25, May 27, July 20, 1864.

Chapter Twenty-Five

1. Rhett to Elise Rhett, September 14, 1862, August 28, 1864, cited in White, *Rhett,* 235.

2. Rhett, Memoir, Aiken Rhett Collection, CM; Woodward, *Mary Chesnut,* 621.

3. *Charleston Mercury,* August 5, 15, 24, 1864.

4. Ibid., October 13, November 5, 7, 1864.

5. Ibid., November 3, 1864.

6. Ibid., November 19, 1864.

7. White, *Rhett,* 239–40.

8. Act, December 23, 1864, War Department, *Official Records,* series 1, 44:981–84, Act, December 1864, series 4, 3: 980.
9. William C. Preston to James A. Seddon, December 29, 1864, War Department, *Official Records,* series 4, 3:979.
10. Robert Barnwell Rhett Jr., "Government," 110.
11. *Charleston Mercury,* January 6, 10, 11, 16, 17, 19, 1865.
12. Edward K. Eckert, *"Fiction Distorting Fact": The Prison Life, Annotated by Jefferson Davis* (Macon, Ga., 1987), 66.
13. *Charleston Mercury,* January 10, 11, 16, 1865.
14. Ibid., November 23, 27, 1864, January 3, 4, 7, 1865.
15. Alfred P. Aldrich to Lewis M. Ayer, January 9, 1865, Lewis M. Ayer Papers, SCL.
16. Rhett, Memoir, Aiken Rhett Collection, CM; *Charleston Mercury,* February 7, 1865.
17. Rhett, Memoir, Aiken Rhett Collection, CM.
18. *Charleston Mercury,* February 1, 1865.
19. Conversation occurring during the war, n.d., Rhett Papers, SHC. This undated document was certainly written during the war because Rhett has noted in the title that "since the war, the language must be modified and 'Confederate' must be 'Southerner.'" This also suggests that it was written late enough in the war that the probability of defeat was substantial, arguing for late 1864 or early 1865. This same collection has a later draft titled "Conversation concerning the late war in the United States," in which he has made the changes he anticipated.
20. *Charleston Mercury,* January 3, 26, February 1, 3, 5, 1865.
21. Ibid., January 7, February 1, 5, 1865.
22. Ibid., February 7, 11, 1865.
23. Robert Barnwell Rhett Jr. to J. Franklin Jameson, May 19, 1899, J. Franklin Jameson Papers, LC; Rhett, Memoir, Aiken Rhett Collection, CM.
24. This date is conjectural. The only Rhett source for his departure is the Memoir, in which he merely says that he abandoned his plantation when Sherman started crossing the Savannah. The Katherine Rhett account, cited below, says that they left the morning after "the enemies gun boat" had come up the river. The most likely river is the Ashepoo, and Navy Department, *Official Records,* series 1,16:195, carries the only report of a Union ship passing up the Ashepoo, the *Pawnee* on January 26. This dating also makes sense given Sherman's path of invasion, for if Rhett had waited any longer, he and his party would have been cut off by the advancing Federals.
25. Rhett to Claudia Stuart, January 9, 1866, Stuart Family Papers, SCHS.
26. Katherine Rhett account of flight from Charleston, n.d., Rhett Papers, SCHS. Her memory was perhaps somewhat inventive, in that magnolias usually do not bloom in February.
27. Joseph LeConte, *"Ware Sherman": A Journal of Three Months' Personal Experience in the Last Days of the Confederacy* (Berkeley, Calif., 1938), 90. Rhett's route from the Ashepoo to Aiken is somewhat conjectural, and the LeConte account is the only hint that he came close to Columbia before turning west. It is in fact possible that he actually went to Columbia first, before turning toward Georgia.

28. Ibid., 90; Robert Barnwell Rhett to J. Franklin Jameson, May 19, 1899, J. Franklin Jameson Papers, LC; William R. Nordin to Benson J. Lossing, March 1, 1865, Benson J. Lossing Papers, Duke University, Durham, N.C.; Rhett to Robert Barnwell Rhett Jr., December 15, 1850, Crosby.

29. Rhett to Robert Barnwell Rhett Jr., February 21, May 3, 1865, Crosby; Rhett, Memoir, Aiken Rhett Collection, CM; White, *Rhett,* 240; Sketch of Alfred Rhett, Alfred Rhett Papers, Museum of the Confederacy, Richmond, Va.

30. Woodward and Muhlenfeld, *Chesnut Diaries,* 232; Woodward, *Mary Chesnut,* 827–28.

31. Rhett to Claudia Stuart, January 9, 1866, Stuart Family Papers, SCHS; undated fragment on Henry Wirz, Rhett Papers, SCHS; White, *Rhett,* 241; Robert Barnwell Rhett Jr. to Quincy A. Gillmore, September 7, 1865, quoted in White, *Rhett,* n 240.

32. Rhett, Memoir, Aiken Rhett Collection, CM.

33. Rhett to Claudia Stuart, January 9, 1866, Stuart Family Papers, SCHS; Heyward, Rhett, Smith-Rhett Genealogy, Barnwell Rhett Heyward Papers, SCHS; McConaghy, "Ordinary White Folk," 475; Rhett to Robert Barnwell Rhett Jr., April 28, May 21, 1866, Crosby.

34. Rhett to Robert Barnwell Rhett Jr., January 9, 1866, Crosby.

35. Rhett to Claudia Stuart, January 9, April 25, 1866, Stuart Family Papers, SCHS; Rhett to Robert Barnwell Rhett Jr., January 9, April 28, 1866, Crosby.

36. Rhett to Robert Barnwell Rhett Jr., May 2, 1866, Crosby; Mortgage, March 8, 1866, Conner Family Papers, SCHS; Linder, *Atlas,* 176–77; Plantation Account Book 1854–57, Rhett Papers, Duke University, Durham, N.C.

37. Edmund Rhett to Porter and Conner, July 27, 1869, Conner Family Papers, SCHS; Robert Barnwell to Rhett, July 6, 1866, A. J. Samson to Rhett, March 16, 1866, Robert Barnwell Rhett, History of a Cup of Tea, n.d., Rhett Papers, SCHS.

38. Mortgage, August 1, 1866, Conner Family Papers, SCHS; Robert Barnwell Rhett Jr. to Joseph B. Campbell, August 4, 1866, Joseph B. Campbell Papers, SCHS; E. Culpepper Clark, *Francis Warrington Dawson and the Politics of Restoration: South Carolina, 1874–1889* (Tuscaloosa, Ala., 1980), 21; Robert Barnwell Rhett Jr. to George W. Bagby, November 15, December 17, 1866, Bagby Family Papers, Virginia Historical Society, Richmond; *Charleston Mercury,* November 19, 23, 24, 1866.

39. Rhett to James Buchanan, April 2, 1867, James Buchanan Papers, Historical Society of Pennsylvania, Philadelphia; *Charleston Mercury,* December 31, 1866, 30, March 31, April 15, 1867; Rhett to Robert Barnwell Rhett Jr., January 6, 1867, Crosby; Heyward, Rhett, Smith-Rhett Genealogy, Barnwell Rhett Heyward Papers, SCHS; Conversation concerning the late war, Rhett Papers, SHC.

40. Promissory note, April 8, 1867, Rhett Papers, SCHS; Robert Barnwell Rhett Jr. to Joseph B. Campbell, May 8, 1867, Joseph B. Campbell Papers, SCHS; Robert Barnwell Rhett Jr. to George W. Bagby, May 29, 1867, Bagby Family Papers, Virginia Historical Society, Richmond; Clark, *Dawson,* 22–23; Rhett to Robert Barnwell Rhett Jr., January 8, 1867, Crosby.

41. Rhett to Claudia Stuart, April 25 1868, Stuart Family Papers, SCHS; Rhett, "Political Parties," Aiken Rhett Collection, CM.
42. Rhett, Memoir, Aiken Rhett Collection, CM; Rhett to Robert Barnwell Rhett Jr., April 28, 1866, Crosby; John G. Shorter to Rhett, July 25, 1866, Rhett Papers, SCHS. White, *Rhett,* 241, maintains that he started working on the memoir in 1864, though this appears to be a misreading of the date on the 1867 letter he wrote to Stuart Rhett explaining his role in framing the Confederate constitution. However, White also cites several letters of Rhett to his daughter Elise, 1865–68, that are not now available, and it is possible that Rhett may have mentioned the memoir idea in one of them as early as 1865.
43. Rhett to James Buchanan, April 2, 1867, James Buchanan Papers, Historical Society of Pennsylvania, Philadelphia; Robert Barnwell Rhett Jr. to S. L. M. Barlow, April 23, 1867, S. L. M. Barlow Papers, Henry E. Huntington Library and Art Gallery, San Marino, Calif.; Rhett to Katherine Rhett, n.d. [June 1867], Rhett Papers, SCHS.

Chapter Twenty-Six

1. Robert Barnwell Rhett Jr. to Barlow, April 23, 1867, Rhett to S. L. M. Barlow, May 4, 1867, S. L. M. Barlow Papers, Henry E. Huntington Library and Art Gallery, San Marino, Calif.
2. Rhett to Katherine Rhett, n.d. [May–June 1867], June 9, 1867, Rhett Papers, SCHS; White, *Rhett,* 241.
3. Robert Barnwell Rhett Jr. to Richard Lathers, August 10, 1867, Robert Barnwell Rhett Jr. Papers, SCL; *Edward Lafitte* vs. *Robert Barnwell Rhett Jr., et al.,* July 30, 1869, Conner Family Papers, SCHS.
4. Rhett to Claudia Stuart, October 21, 1867, April 25, 1868, Stuart Family Papers, SCHS; Rhett to Katherine Rhett, June 9, 1867, Rhett Papers, SCHS; Rhett to Robert Barnwell Rhett Jr., January 8, 1867, Rhett to Katherine Rhett, September 2, 1867, Crosby.
5. Rhett to Claudia Stuart, October 21, 1867, 25 April 1868, Stuart Family Papers, SCHS.
6. Conversation concerning the late war, Rhett Papers, SHC; A. R. Stuart to Claudia Stuart, February 7, 1868, Stuart Family Papers, SCHS.
7. Rhett to Armistead L. Burt, April 3, 1868, Armistead L. Burt Papers, Duke University, Durham, N.C.; Statement on R. B. Rhett Jr., & Bro., April 14, 1868, South Carolina, 7:528, R. G. Dun & Company Collection, Harvard University Graduate School of Business Administration, Boston, Mass.
8. Clark, *Dawson,* n 64.
9. Rhett to Claudia Stuart, April 25, 1868, Stuart Family Papers, SCHS; White, *Rhett,* 241.
10. Rhett to Claudia Stuart, April 25, 1868, Stuart Family Papers, SCHS; Claudia Stuart to Rhett, May 6, 1865, Rhett Papers, SCHS.
11. Rhett to Katherine Rhett, August 20, 28, 1868, Rhett Papers, SCHS.

12. Ibid., n.d. [July 1868], July 6, 18, 1868, SCHS.

13. Ibid., August 8, 1868, Rhett Papers, SCHS; Perry, *Reminiscences, 32.*

14. Rhett to Katherine Rhett, August 8, 11, 14, 1868, Rhett Papers, SCHS.

15. Ibid., August 20, 28, n.d. [September], 1868, Rhett Papers, SCHS; Rhett to Francis Porcher, October 8, 1868, Wickham Family Papers, Virginia Historical Society, Richmond.

16. Rhett to Armistead L. Burt, April 3, 1868, Armistead L. Burt Papers, Duke University, Durham, N.C.; *Charleston Mercury,* June 25, July 1, 30, August 3, 1868; Rhett to Katherine Rhett, August 28, 1868, Rhett Papers, SCHS; Rhett to Manton Marble, May 24, 1868, Crosby.

17. Rhett to Robert Barnwell Rhett Jr., n.d. [fall 1868], Edmund Rhett to Rhett, n.d. [fall 1868], Crosby.

18. Rhett to Robert Barnwell Rhett Jr., November 24, 1868, Crosby. A copy of the Farewell in the Aiken Rhett Collection, CM, has a notation by Rhett that he wrote it for his son.

19. A Farewell to the Subscribers of the Charleston Mercury, n.d. [November 1868], Rhett Papers, SCL.

20. Rhett to Robert Barnwell Rhett Jr., May 21, 1866, January 24, 1869, Crosby; Rhett to Katherine Rhett, February 1, 1869, Rhett Papers, SHC.

21. Edmund Rhett to Porter and Conner, July 27, August 9, 1869, Rhett endorsement on Edmund Rhett to Harry Shields, July 27, 1869, Conner Family Papers, SCHS.

22. *Lafitte* vs. *Robert Barnwell Rhett Jr. et al.,* July 30, 1869, Rhett to Porter and Conner, August 9, 1869, Report in *Shields* vs. *Rhett,* December 7, 1869, Edmund Rhett to Porter and Conner, December 9, 1869, *Hamilton Shields* vs. *R. Barnwell Rhett,* decree, December 31, 1869, decree, n.d. [January 1870], Conner Family Papers, SCHS.

23. Rhett to Robert Barnwell Rhett Jr., April 2, 30, 1870, Crosby; Rhett to Herbert Rhett, May 27, June 19, November 29, 1870, Rhett Papers, SHC; Rhett to Katherine Rhett, December 3, 1869, Rhett Papers, SCHS.

24. Clipping on end sheet of "Index Rerum" volume in the Aiken Rhett Collection, CM; Katherine Rhett to Herbert Rhett, June 11, 1870, Rhett Papers, SHC.

25. Rhett to Herbert Rhett, July 12, 1869, March 1, May 27, June 19, n.d. [1870], Rhett Papers, SHC.

26. Rhett to Herbert Rhett, n.d. [1870], May 27, June 19, November 29, 1870, Rhett Papers, SHC; Three Articles on Free Government, 1870, Aiken Rhett Collection, CM; Rhett to Robert Barnwell Rhett Jr., March 23, 1870, Crosby.

27. Barnwell Rhett Heyward, "The Descendants of Col. William Rhett of South Carolina," *South Carolina Historical and Genealogical Magazine* 4 (January 1903), 62; Rhett to Robert Barnwell Rhett Jr., July 22,1871, Crosby; Sheriff's sale records, January 25, 1870, February 11, 1871, John K. Terry to R. B. Grant, March 18, 1873, Records of the Sheriff, Mixed Provenance, Colleton County, S.C., SCDAH.

28. Robert Barnwell Rhett Jr. to Josephine Bacot, 22 July 1903, Bacot-Huger Collection, SCHS; Bill of sale, October 13, 1871, Rhett Papers, SCHS.

29. Rhett to Robert Barnwell Rhett Jr., January 3, 1868, October 30, 1869, Crosby; Rhett to John Lewis, n.d. [July 1872], Rhett Papers, SCHS.

30. Undated note, Rhett Papers, SCHS.

31. Alfred B. Roman to P. G. T. Beauregard, June 23, 1872, Alfred B. Roman Papers, LC; White, *Rhett,* 242; Rhett to Robert Barnwell Rhett Jr., February 5, 1872, Crosby.

32. *Charleston Mercury,* October 22, 1868; Rhett, Memoir, Aiken Rhett Collection, CM.

33. Rhett to William Porcher Miles, March 22, 1871, William Porcher Miles Papers, SHC; Rhett, Genl Johnson, Mr. George Trenholm and the Confederate finances, undated fragment 1873–74, Aiken Rhett Collection, CM; Rhett to Robert Barnwell Rhett Jr., January 7, 1869, May 22, 1870, Crosby.

34. Rhett to Robert Barnwell Rhett Jr., April 18, 30, 1870, Crosby.

35. Rhett, "Political Parties," Aiken Rhett Collection, CM.

36. Robert Barnwell Rhett, Northern Civilization in the United States, Aiken Rhett Collection, CM.

37. Rhett, "Political Parties," and various unsigned editorials, Aiken Rhett Collection, CM; Rhett to Josephine Rhett, July 27, 1874, Bacot-Huger Collection, SCHS.

38. Diary, February 28, 1873, Rhett Papers, SCHS. Dixon, *Fortune and Misery,* 5–6, concludes erroneously that Rhett and Katherine did not live together from 1872 to 1876.

39. Rhett to Josephine Rhett, May 29, July 24, 1873, Bacot-Huger Collection, SCHS.

40. Robert Barnwell Rhett, Sonnet to my wife on our twentieth year marriage Day, April 26, 1874, Rhett Papers, SCHS.

41. Rhett to Josephine Rhett, July 27, 1874, Bacot-Huger Collection, SCHS.

42. Essay on Money Power in United States, n.d. [1875], Rhett Papers, SCHS; Robert Barnwell Rhett, "Fears for Democracy," *Southern Magazine* 17 (September 1875), 306–32 *passim.* The original draft of the article is in the Rhett Papers, SCHS.

43. Drafts of these essays and outlines are to be found in the Rhett Papers, SCHS, and in the Aiken Rhett Collection, CM. Rhett's copy of the Wallace biography is in the Crosby.

44. An undated letter fragment in the Aiken Rhett Collection, CM, makes it clear that Rhett had access to a portion of Johnston's manuscript of his *Narrative of Military Operations,* and internal evidence suggests that the letter was written in the spring of 1874. Johnston's book appeared later that same year.

45. The several drafts of the Memoir are to be found in the Aiken Rhett Papers, CM, and in the Rhett Papers, SCHS. The Memoir has been edited for publication by the author as *A Fire-Eater Remembers: The Confederate Memoir of Robert Barnwell Rhett* (Columbia: University of South Carolina Press, 2000).

46. Rhett to Elise Rhett, January 8, 1875, cited in White, *Rhett,* 242.

47. Robert Barnwell Rhett Jr. to Rhett, January 7, 1876, Rhett Papers, SCHS.

48. Perry, *Reminiscences,* 134.

49. Barnwell R. Burnet to Joseph Huger, November 8, 1913, Bacot-Huger Collection, SCHS.

50. Paul H. Hayne to Mary Hayne, July 8, 1873, Paul H. Hayne Papers, Duke University, Durham, N.C.; Clark, *Dawson*, 64–65.

51. Heyward, Rhett, Smith-Rhett Genealogy, Barnwell Rhett Heyward Papers, SCHS; Rhett, Sketch of James Smith, Crosby.

52. Undated poem in Rhett Papers, SCHS.

Chapter Twenty-Seven

1. George Ward Nichols, "The Story of the Great March," *Confederate Veteran* 22 (November 1914), 509.

2. George S. Bernard Scrapbook, Duke University, Durham, N.C.

3. Robert Barnwell Rhett Jr. to Josephine Bacot, February 12, 1903, Bacot-Huger Collection, SCHS.

4. Katherine Rhett to Herbert Rhett, three letters, one with no date, and two with fragmentary dates of January 24 and 16 May, Rhett Papers, SHC. The precise date that Rhett's body was brought to Magnolia Cemetery has not been determined, but it would appear to have been January 1877.

5. *Charleston News and Courier,* September 18, 1876; *Charleston Daily Journal of Commerce,* September 16, 1876.

6. Perry, *Reminiscences,* 133; Bass, "Grayson," 291; McCarter Journal, n.d., LC.

7. "Conceit," in "Index Rerum," Aiken Rhett Collection, CM.

8. A surprising number of historians confuse the two. Recent examples are Niven, *Calhoun,* 163, 231, which identifies him as editor of the *Mercury* in 1828; Nichols, *Disruption,* 52; Channing, *Crisis of Fear,* throughout; and Rable, *Confederate Republic,* 134. Of course it is not always possible to tell whether father or son was speaking, since the views of the former were adopted wholesale by the latter. For this biography it has been assumed, unless otherwise noted, that whichever was actually writing, the views reflected were those of Rhett Sr.

9. As just one example of Rhett's being largely ignored, whereas some historians have given him great credit for realizing secession, he does not appear at all in the index of Dumond, *Secession Movement,* one of the mainstays of the literature, and is mentioned only twice in passing in the book, which regards Yancey as the prime mover of secession.

10. Autobiographical fragment, n.d., Rhett Papers, SCHS.

11. An excellent essay on conservatism will be found in Alan Wolfe, "The Revolution That Never Was," *The New Republic,* June 7, 1999, 34–41.

12. Matthew Parris, "Another Voice," *The Spectator,* September 26, 1998.

13. Students of Rhett have expressed widely diverging opinions on his effectiveness as a politician and his role in secession. White, *Rhett,* 243 and elsewhere, accepts that Rhett played a possibly decisive role. Heidler, *Pulling the Temple Down,* 183, 186, and in a photo caption, maintains that he was a loner who contributed little but divisiveness in 1860 and that his inflexibility made him an ineffectual failure as a politician. Perritt, "Rhett," 381, regards him unwarrantedly as a "near great" who had

all the attributes of a first-class leader but stubbornness and "his own natural exuberance," going so far as to maintain that if the Confederacy had succeeded, his reputation would have been much greater despite his personal unpopularity. On p. 367 Perritt admits, however, that Rhett was unable to give real leadership, thanks to his personality. Cauthen, *South Carolina,* 32, credits him with a leadership that kept the people in a mood for secession, which is clearly in error. John C. Roberson, "The Foundations of Southern Nationalism: Charleston and the Lowcountry, 1847–1861," Ph.D. diss., University of South Carolina, 1991, 2:438–39, astutely credits Rhett only with leadership of a "vocal and persevering minority," while the state never really accepted him or his doctrine. Roberson's statement that "the final act of secession in 1860 and the creation of a Southern nation in 1861 can be described as a manifestation of the political ideology of Robert Barnwell Rhett more than any other one individual," however, seems to miss an important point. As evidenced by what happened in Montgomery in February 1861, the idea that a new nation would be the inevitable concomitant of secession was practically universal except among those clinging to the hope of reconstruction. In short, almost everyone who favored secession as a permanent act, which was a large plurality among the divergent opinions in the South at the time, if not a majority, foresaw the Confederacy as the natural—indeed vital—next step. Thus to credit those events as representing Rhett's ideology any more than that of hundreds of other political leaders, and hundreds of thousands of Southerners, seems a bit overstated. Though not crediting Rhett with being a deep thinker, which he was not, Roberson also (449–50) argues that by maintaining a consistent stand for secession over a prolonged period of time he gradually gained adherents, laying the groundwork for Southern nationalist ideology. Thus "by his persistence in advocating the radical themes of resistance and revolution, Robert Barnwell Rhett can legitimately be considered 'the father of secession.'" Yet Yancey was just as consistent, if not for as long a time, and was far more actively involved in bringing about the breakup of the Democratic Party that helped lead to Lincoln's election and the final impetus for secession, which would seem to give him claim to equal paternity at least. Walther, *Fire-Eaters,* 6, 121, credits Rhett with being an adroit "political tactician," "a driven and vastly influential disunionist who stopped at nothing to achieve his prize," which is certainly true, but he is much more judicious in his assessment of Rhett's real impact on the moment of secession itself, making no claims at all of any decisive influence.

14. Walther, *Fire-Eaters,* 2–4, addresses the problem of defining a fire-eater, and determining how many of them there really were.

15. Myrta Lockett Avary, ed., *Recollections of Alexander H. Stephens* (New York, 1910), 334.

16. David Donald, "The Proslavery Argument Reconsidered," *Journal of Southern History* 37 (February 1971), 12, while raising the call for analysis of the lives of Rhett and Yancey in particular, perceives a "general pattern" among the fire-eaters: "All were unhappy men who had severe personal problems relating to their place in southern society. Though ambitious and hardworking, all failed in the paths normally open

to the enterprising in the South; planting, practicing law, and politics. Few of them had any large personal stake in the system which they defended." With the exception of his professional failures, Rhett did not at all fit such a profile. He knew precisely his place in his society, and his nearly four hundred slaves in the 1850s gave him a larger than normal stake in the system he defended.

17. The debate over the influence, or lack of it, of the fire-eaters continues to the present. The conventional view that the extremists were forgotten once the Confederacy was formed is examined in Freehling, *Road to Disunion,* 3–7, and most persuasively in Heidler, *Pulling the Temple Down,* 186–88. Dissenting opinions will be found in Rable, *Confederate Republic,* n 316, and Walther, *Fire-Eaters,* 298–302. Walther's assertion that "more moderate southerners did not force out the fire-eaters from the government they helped create," is correct in that fire-eaters were not, literally, "forced out" of offices they already held. But inarguably they were "frozen out" of positions of active influence in the new government, whether appointive or elective, and from any significant influence in shaping policy. Their carping and criticism, even their flirtation with plotting, may have been an annoyance and irritant to Davis and the administration, but to call that "influence" in the conventional acceptance of the term would be to say that a brick wall is "influenced" by a rubber ball bouncing off of it.

18. "The wreck of the Confederacy," in "Index Rerum", Aiken Rhett Collection, CM.

19. C. Vann Woodward, "The Irony of Southern History," *Journal of Southern History* 19 (February 1953), 8, makes this point ably.

20. Katherine Rhett to Herbert Rhett, May 20, 18—, Rhett Papers, SHC.

21. Essay, "R B Rhett Jr. gives data vs. Jeffn Davis to Beauregard," Robert Barnwell Rhett Jr. to Alfred B. Roman, January 9, 1883, Rhett Papers, SCL; Robert Barnwell Rhett Jr. to R. B. Rhett, January 27, 1884, Robert Barnwell Rhett Jr. to Josephine Rhett, January 28, 1883, Bacot-Huger Collection, SCHS.

22. P. G. T. Beauregard to Alfred B. Roman, January 4, 1882, Alfred B. Roman Papers, LC; Robert Barnwell Rhett Jr., "Confederate Government," 110.

23. Robert Barnwell Rhett Jr. to Alfred B. Roman, May 14, 23, 1889, P. G. T. Beauregard to Alfred B. Roman, November 26, 1889, Alfred B. Roman Papers, LC; Robert Barnwell Rhett Jr. to Robert A. Brock, August 25, September 12, 1889, Robert A. Brock Papers, Henry E. Huntington Library and Art Gallery, San Marino, Calif.; Robert Barnwell Rhett Jr. to Josephine Bacot, August 31, September 14, 1890, February 23, 1896, Bacot-Huger Collection, SCHS.

24. DuBose, *Yancey,* 596–97, n 602.

25. Robert Barnwell Rhett Jr. to J. Franklin Jameson, May 19, 1899, J. Franklin Jameson Papers, LC; J. Franklin Jameson to Josephine Bacot, February 26, March 7, 1908, Bacot-Huger Collection, SCHS.

26. Stephen B. Barnwell, *American Family,* 171–72.

27. Among the host of supporting characters in the film version of *Gone with the Wind* was the sister of Ashley Wilkes, young India, a beautiful Southern flower in full bloom. The actress who played her was little known as yet but talented and lovely,

the perfect lady to play in such a romance of an Old South that never was. She was Alicia Rhett, great-granddaughter of Robert Barnwell Rhett. See *Charleston News and Courier,* January 23, 1937, January 29, 1984.

Bibliography

UNFORTUNATELY, ROBERT BARNWELL RHETT'S own collection of his papers was dispersed or destroyed with the fall of Charleston in February 1865. A few letters found their way into public archives, and his children and descendants placed important, though small, collections of his papers in the South Carolina Historical Society, the Charleston Museum, and the South Caroliniana Library at the University of South Carolina. Fortunately, these collections consist predominantly of letters by Rhett, but much has undoubtedly been lost by the dispersal of almost all of the correspondence written to him, most especially that for the Civil War years. Consequently, much more is known of what he was saying to others than of what they were telling him. The impact of this imbalance is that much probable favorable comment on him and his activities is missing, while most of the commentary that survives from his contemporaries comes from his opponents such as James Henry Hammond, whose papers at the Library of Congress are invaluable but present an almost unrelentingly negative viewpoint on Rhett. Since historians can only write based on the sources they have, anyone working on Rhett must inevitably deal with an overwhelming body of negative opinion and precious little that is positive. Thus it is something of a struggle to present a balanced portrait of the man, especially since out of his own mouth he so often offends.

The starting place among published works is Laura White's outstanding 1931 *Robert Barnwell Rhett: Father of Secession*. Despite being now seventy years old and having started as that often most unpublishable of species, a doctoral dissertation, White's book has been the standard life of Rhett—indeed, the only life—and still rewards reading today. Some of her conclusions may be questioned, and certainly her research did not include a great deal of material that has come to light since she wrote, but other than that her book suffers from nothing but age. She had access to Rhett's elderly daughter Elise, who made available to her recollections and Rhett letters and other documents that cannot today be located, which alone would be enough to make her biography invaluable. Supplementing White is Daniel Wallace's *The Political Life and Services of the Hon. R. Barnwell Rhett, of South Carolina. By "A Cotemporary."* Published in a newspaper in 1857 and again in 1859 as a campaign biography book to boost Rhett's chances for a Senate seat, it is quite possible that he was in whole or part its author. In any case he clearly provided much of the information and approved of the content, making this a reliable outline and providing some insights and anecdotal material not otherwise available. For a good, though occasionally inaccurate, guide to the labyrinthine family connections of the Rhetts and their kin, Stephen B. Barnwell's 1969 *The Story of an American Family* is generally reliable.

Among more recent works, John Coussons's 1971 dissertation, "Thirty Years with Calhoun, Rhett, and the Charleston Mercury: A Chapter in South Carolina Politics," is not really a biography but is an excellent examination of the inextricable relationship between Rhett and the newspaper that became his organ. H. Hardy Perritt's dissertation, "Robert Barnwell Rhett: South Carolina Secession Spokesman," dating from 1954, is a more conventional biography that is useful, though its account of the years from 1861 onward offers nothing not available elsewhere. Perritt, like White, had access to some family papers that are not today in any of the collections in public archives. Perritt's several articles on Rhett, largely drawn from his dissertation, are also useful, especially in evaluating Rhett as a public speaker. Rhett's own numerous articles in the *Southern Quarterly Review* and the *Southern Magazine* are, of course, essential.

Excellent background on Rhett's years of partnership with John C. Calhoun will be found in the standard biographies of Calhoun by Margaret Coit, John Niven, and Charles Wiltse, though the best portrait of their relationship emerges in the numerous volumes of Clyde N. Wilson's excellent edition of *The Papers of John C. Calhoun*, now approaching completion. Rhett's relationship with his rivals for Calhoun's favor is illuminated in Drew Gilpin Faust's *James Henry Hammond and the Old South*, Carol Bleser's edition of *Secret and Sacred: The Diaries of James Henry Hammond*, and John B. Edmunds Jr.'s fine biography, *Francis W. Pickens and the Politics of Destruction*.

Though Rhett is not himself treated extensively in Charles E. Cauthen's *South Carolina Goes to War* or Steven A. Channing's *Crisis of Fear: Secession in South Carolina*, they are both important for background and context on Rhett's activities in 1860. Two differing viewpoints on the fire-eaters—though not much different on Rhett himself—are to be found in David S. Heidler's *Pulling the Temple Down: The Fire-Eaters and the Destruction of the Union* and Eric H. Walther's *The Fire-Eaters*. Because of their differences and because each has its special strengths, both need to be consulted for any balanced view of those turbulent men. Of course, no serious study can be done on Rhett without immersion in the files of the *Charleston Mercury*. The complete run at the Charleston Library Society is apparently Robert Barnwell Rhett Jr.'s, which has the added benefit of marginal notations by him that help identify which editorials were written by him and which by his father, as well as providing a few other useful bits of marginalia. Rhett's role in the formation of the Confederacy and framing the Constitution is most fully explored in William C. Davis's *"A Government of Our Own": The Making of the Confederacy,* while for study of his service in the Provisional Congress, the United States Congress's 1904 edition of the *Journal of the Congress of the Confederate States of America* is indispensable.

Full details on these and all other sources actually used for this study follow. It should be noted that scores of others have been consulted. However, most of the literature on secession is repetitive where Rhett is concerned, being drawn almost exclusively from White's biography, and therefore no works are included unless they have actually been cited in the notes.

Primary Sources

MANUSCRIPTS

Alabama Department of Archives and History, Montgomery
    Clitherall, Alexander B., Papers
    Yancey, William Lowndes, Papers
British Museum, London, England
    Gladstone, William, Papers
Charleston Library Society, Charleston, S.C.
    Burt, Armistead L., Papers
    Conner, Henry L., Papers
Charleston Museum, Charleston, S.C.
    Aiken Rhett Collection
Crosby, Leslie, Huntsville, Ala.
    Rhett, Robert Barnwell, Jr., Papers
Dallas Historical Society, Dallas, Tex.
    Reagan, John H., "Judge Reagan on Davis"
Duke University, Durham, N.C.
    Bernard, George S., Scrapbook
    Burt, Armistead L., Papers
    Calhoun, John C., Papers
    Campbell Family Papers
    Capers, Ellison, Papers
    Chesnut, James, Jr., Papers
    Gordon, George A., Papers

Hayne, Paul H., Papers
Holmes, George Frederick, Letterbook
Huger, Alfred, Papers
Jeffords, Robert J., Papers
Jones, Charles Colcock, Papers
Lossing, Benson J., Papers
Pickens, Francis W., Papers
Planters & Mechanics Bank of South Carolina Letter Book
Rhett, Robert Barnwell, Papers
Toombs, Robert A., Papers
Wilkes Family Papers
Emory University, Atlanta, Ga.
Burke, Joseph F., Papers
Stephens, Alexander H., Papers
Gibboney, Douglas L., Carlisle, Pa.
Washington, Littleton B., Diary (copy)
Harvard University Graduate School of Business Administration, Boston, Mass.
Dun, R. G., & Company Collection
Henry E. Huntington Library and Art Gallery, San Marino, Calif.
Barlow, Samuel Latham Mitchell, Papers
Brock, Robert Alonzo, Papers
Civil War Collection
General Holdings
Hunter, Robert Mercer Taliaferro, Letter
Historical Society of Pennsylvania, Pa.
Buchanan, James, Papers
Gratz, Simon, Autograph Collection
Krakowsky, Shinaan, Encino, Calif.
Rhett, Robert Barnwell, Letters
Library of Congress, Washington, D.C.
Blair Family Papers
Elmore, Francis H., Papers
Hammond, James Henry, Papers
Jameson, J. Franklin, Calhoun Correspondence
McCarter Journal, 1860–66
Miles, William Porcher, Papers
Petigru, James L., Papers
Rives, William C., Papers
Roman, Alfred, Papers

Seabrook, Whitemarsh B., Papers
Stephens, Alexander H., Papers
Trescot, William H., Papers
Van Buren, Martin, Papers
Wigfall, Louis T., Papers
Louisiana State University, Baton Rouge
La Villebeuvre Family Papers
Wharton, Edward C., Papers
Manhattanville College of the Sacred Heart, Purchase, N.Y.
Stephens, Alexander H., Papers
Mississippi Department of Archives and History, Jackson
Claiborne, J. F. H., Papers
Governors Record Group, Record Group 27, Volume 36
Walthall, William T., Papers
Museum of the Confederacy, Richmond, Va.
Department of South Carolina and Georgia Collection
Provisional Constitution of the Confederate States of America
Rhett, Alfred, Papers
National Archives, Washington, D.C.
Confederate Papers Relating to Citizens or Business Firms, M346
Rhett, Robert Barnwell, File
Rhett, Robert Barnwell, Jr., File
Letters Received by the Confederate Secretary of War, Record Group 109
Files R (WD) 1863, 1864
Thompson, Jacob, Letterbooks, Entry 467, Record Group 109
Public Record Office, London, England
Board of Trade Records, Volume 10
South Carolina, Records Relating to, 1663–1782
South Carolina Department of Archives and History, Columbia
Executive Council Journal Letter-Book, 1861
Journals of the House of Representatives of the Legislature of the State of
South Carolina
27th, 28th, 29th, 30th General Assemblies
Records of the Sheriff, Mixed Provenance
Colleton County
South Carolina Historical Society, Charleston
Bacot-Huger Collection
Barnwell Family Papers
Campbell, Joseph B., Papers

Charleston County Court of Probate Deed Book 1694–1704
Chesnut-Miller-Manning Papers
Cheves, Langdon, Papers
Conner Family Papers
Glover, Joseph, Papers
Heyward, Barnwell Rhett, Papers and Smith-Rhett Genealogy
Pope Family Papers
Poyas, Elizabeth A., "The Olden Time in Carolina"
Rhett, Robert Barnwell, Papers
Rhett Family Papers
Rhett Genealogy Notes
Stuart Family Papers
Vanderhorst, Ann M., Diary
South Caroliniana Library, University of South Carolina, Columbia
Ayer, Lewis M., Papers
Barnwell, Robert W., Papers
Bonham, Milledge L., Papers
Elmore, Franklin H., Papers
Grayson, William J., Autobiography
Gregg, Maxcy, Papers
Longstreet, Augustus, Papers
McGowan, Samuel, Papers
Perry, Benjamin Franklin, Papers
Petigru, James L., Papers
Preston, William Campbell, Papers
Rhett, Robert Barnwell, Papers
Rhett, Robert Barnwell, Jr., Papers
Simpson, Richard, Papers
Stapleton, John, Papers
Sumter District Broadside, 1851
Thornwell, James H., Papers
Williams-Chesnut-Manning Family Papers
Southern Historical Collection, University of North Carolina, Chapel Hill
Elliott and Gonzales Family Papers
Miles, William Porcher, Papers
Orr-Patterson Papers
Rhett, Robert Barnwell, Papers
Ruffin, Edmund, Papers
Yancey, Benjamin C., Papers

University of Georgia, Athens
    Cobb, Howell, Papers
    Cobb, Thomas R. R., Letters
University of Virginia, Charlottesville
    Hunter, Robert Mercer Taliaferro, Papers
Virginia Historical Society, Richmond
    Bagby, George W., Papers
    Bagby Family Papers
    Hunter, Robert Mercer Taliaferro, Letter
    Hunter Family Papers
    London, Daniel H., Papers
    Minor Family Papers
    Nicholas, Elizabeth Byrd, Papers
    Phillips, William B., Papers
    Ruffin, Edmund, Papers
    Wickham Family Papers
Washington and Lee University, Lexington, Va.
    Jamison, David F., Papers

NEWSPAPERS

Athens, Ga., *Southern Watchman,* 1861
Atlanta, Ga., *Daily Constitution,* 1880
Atlanta, Ga., *Daily Intelligencer,* 1861
Augusta, Ga., *Daily Constitutionalist,* 1861
Baltimore, Md., *Nile's National Register,* 1838
Charleston, S.C., *Courier,* 1861–65
Charleston, S.C., *Daily Courier,* 1863
Charleston, S.C., *Journal of Commerce,* 1876
Charleston, S.C., *Mercury,* 1828–68
Charleston, S.C., *News and Courier,* 1876, 1937, 1984
Charleston, S.C., *Sunday News,* 1896, 1897
Columbia, S.C., *Daily South Carolinian,* 1852, 1861
Columbus, Ga., *Daily Times,* 1861
Dallas, Tex., *Herald,* 1861
Edgefield, S.C., *Advertiser,* 1840
Huntsville, Ala., *Southern Advocate,* 1861
London, England, *Times of London,* 1861
Mobile, Ala., *Daily Advertiser,* 1861
Montgomery, Ala., *Confederation,* 1861

Montgomery, Ala., *Daily Post,* 1861
Montgomery, Ala., *Weekly Advertiser,* 1861
Montgomery, Ala., *Weekly Mail,* 1861
Nashville, Tenn., *Union & American,* 1861
Natchez, Miss., *Daily Courier,* 1861
Natchez, *Daily Free-Trader,* 1861
New Orleans, La., *Daily Delta,* 1861
New Orleans, La. *Daily Picayune,* 1861
New York, N.Y., *Citizen,* 1861, 1867
New York, N.Y., *Frank Leslie's Illustrated Newspaper,* 1861
New York, N.Y., *Herald,* 1861
Philadelphia, Pa., *Times,* 1879
Rome, Ga., *Tri-Weekly Courier,* 1861
Spartanburg, S.C., *Spartan,* 1857
Vicksburg, Miss., *Daily Evening Citizen,* 1861
Vicksburg, Miss., *Sentinel,* 1851

OFFICIAL PUBLICATIONS

Cauthen, Charles E., ed. *Journal of the South Carolina Executive Councils of 1861 and 1862.* Columbia, S.C.: South Carolina Department of Archives and History, 1956.

Correspondence Concerning Occurrences of April 23, 1862 between Col. W. R. Calhoun and Major Alfred Rhett. Charleston, S.C.: A. S. Johnston, 1862.

Journal of the Convention of the People of South Carolina: Assembled at Columbia on the 19th November, 1832, and Again, on the 11th March, 1833. Columbia, S.C., 1833.

Kennedy, Joseph C., ed. *Preliminary Report on the Eighth Census, 1860.* Washington, D.C.: Government Printing Office, 1862.

Speeches Delivered in the Convention of the State of South Carolina, Held in Columbia in March, 1833. Charleston, S.C., 1833.

United States Congress. *Congressional Globe.* 25th–32nd Congresses. Washington, D.C., 1837–52.

United States Congress. *Journal of the Congress of the Confederate States of America.* 7 vols. Washington, D.C.: Government Printing Office, 1904.

United States Navy Department. *Official Records of the Union and Confederate Navies in the War of the Rebellion.* 31 vols. Washington, D.C.: Government Printing Office, 1894–1922.

United States War Department. *War of the Rebellion: Official Records of the Union and Confederate Armies.* 128 vols. Washington, D.C.: Government Printing Office, 1880–1901.

LETTERS, DIARIES, SPEECHES, AND MEMOIRS

Adams, Charles Francis, ed. *Memoirs of John Quincy Adams.* 12 vols. Philadelphia, Pa.: J. B. Lippincott, 1874–77.

An Address from the Hon. R. Barnwell Rhett to the People of Beaufort and Colleton Districts. Washington, D.C., 1841.

Address of Hon. R. Barnwell Rhett, to His Constituents, the Citizens of Beaufort, Colleton, Orangeburgh and Barnwell Districts. N.p., 1843.

Address to the People of Beaufort and Colleton Districts, upon the Subject of Abolition, by Robert Barnwell Rhett, January 15, 1838. N.p., 1838.

Ambler, Charles Henry, ed. *Correspondence of Robert M. T. Hunter, 1826–1876. Annual Report of the American Historical Association for the Year 1916, Vol. II.* Washington, D.C.: American Historical Association, 1918.

American Annual Cyclopedia and Register of Important Events of the Year 1861. New York, 1864.

Argument of R. Barnwell Smith, Esq. Delivered in the Court of Appeals of the State of South Carolina, Before the Hon. David Johnson & William Harper; on the Third April, 1834; in the Case of the State, Ex Relatione *Edward McCrady, Against Col. B. F. Hunt; on the Constitutionality of the Oath in the Act for the Military Organization of This State, Passed 19th December, 1833.* Charleston, S.C., 1834.

Avary, Myrta Lockett, ed. *Recollections of Alexander H. Stephens.* New York: Doubleday, Page, 1910.

Baker, G. A. *Catalog #34.* N.p., 1939.

Basler, Roy P., ed. *The Collected Works of Abraham Lincoln.* 9 vols. New Brunswick, N.J.: Rutgers University Press, 1953.

Bleser, Carol, ed. *Secret and Sacred: The Diaries of James Henry Hammond, Southern Slaveholder.* New York: Oxford University Press, 1988.

The Book of Allegiance; or, A Report of the Arguments of Counsel, Opinions of the Court of Appeals of South Carolina on the Oath of Allegiance. Columbia, S.C.: Office of the Telescope, 1834.

Bulloch, James D. *The Secret Service of the Confederate States in Europe.* 2 vols. Liverpool, England: G. P. Putnam, 1883.

Butterfield, L. H., Marc Friedlaender, and Mary-Jo Kline, eds. *The Book of Abigail and John: Selected Letters of the Adams Family, 1762–1784.* Cambridge, Mass.: Harvard University Press, 1975.

Calhoun, Richard J., ed. *Witness to Sorrow: The Antebellum Autobiography of William J. Grayson.* Columbia: University of South Carolina Press, 1990.

Capers, Henry D. *The Life and Times of C. G. Memminger.* Richmond, Va.: Everett Waddey, 1893.

Carson, James Petigru, ed. *Life, Letters and Speeches of James Louis Petigru.* Washington, D.C.: W. H. Loudermilk and Co., 1920.

Chittenden, Lucius E. *Recollections of President Lincoln and His Administration.* New York: Harper and Bros., 1891.

Claiborne, J. F. H. *Life and Correspondence of John A. Quitman.* 2 vols. New York: Harper and Bros., 1860.

Clay-Clopton, Virginia. *A Belle of the Fifties.* New York: Doubleday, Page, 1905.

Crist, Lynda Lasswell, and Mary Seaton Dix, eds. *The Papers of Jefferson Davis. Vols. 5–7.* Baton Rouge: Louisiana State University Press, 1985–1992.

Curry, Jabez L. M. *Civil History of the Government of the Confederate States with Some Personal Reminiscences.* Richmond, Va.: Johnson Publishing Co., 1901.

Cutler, Wayne, ed. *The Correspondence of James K. Polk, Volume V, 1839–1841.* Nashville, Tenn.: Vanderbilt University Press, 1979.

Davis, Jefferson. *The Rise and Fall of the Confederate States Government.* 2 vols. New York: D. Appleton, 1881.

The Death and Funeral Ceremonies of John Caldwell Calhoun. Columbia, S.C.: A. S. Johnston, 1850.

Deems, Charles F., ed. *Annals of Southern Methodism for 1856.* Nashville: privately printed, 1857.

Doubleday, Abner. *Reminiscences of Forts Sumter and Moultrie in 1860–61.* New York: Harper and Bros., 1876.

Eckert, Edward K. *"Fiction Distorting Fact": The Prison Life, Annotated by Jefferson Davis.* Macon, Ga.: Mercer University Press, 1987.

Graf, Leroy P., and Ralph W. Hoskins, eds. *The Papers of Andrew Johnson, IV.* Knoxville: University of Tennessee Press, 1976.

Grayson, William J. *James Louis Petigru. A Biographical Sketch.* New York: Harper and Bros., 1866.

Grimké, Thomas. *An Oration, on the Practicability and Expediency of Reducing the Whole Body of the Law to the Simplicity and Order of A Code.* Charleston, S.C.: A. E. Miller, 1827.

Hesseltine, William B., ed. *Three Against Lincoln: Murat Halstead Reports the Caucuses of 1860.* Baton Rouge: Louisiana State University Press, 1960.

Jameson, J. Franklin, ed. *Correspondence of John C. Calhoun.* Washington, D.C.: American Historical Association, 1900.

Johnston, Joseph E. *Narrative of Military Operations.* New York: D. Appleton & Co., 1874.

Johnston, Richard M., and William Browne. *Life of Alexander H. Stephens.* Philadelphia, Pa.: J. B. Lippincott, 1878.

Lawrence, William, ed. *Extracts from the Diary and Correspondence of the Late Amos Lawrence.* Boston: D. Lathrop and Co., 1855.

LeConte, Joseph. *"Ware Sherman": A Journal of Three Months' Personal Experience in the Last Days of the Confederacy.* Berkeley: University of California Press, 1938.

McIntosh, James T., ed. *The Papers of Jefferson Davis. Vol. 2.* Baton Rouge: Louisiana State University Press, 1974.

Meats, Stephen, and Edwin T. Arnold, eds. *The Writings of Benjamin F. Perry.* 3 vols. Spartanburg, S.C.: Reprint Company, 1980.

[Memminger, Christopher G.] *Declaration of the Immediate Causes Which Induce and Justify the Secession of South Carolina from the Federal Union; and the Ordinance of Secession.* Charleston, S.C., 1860.

————. *Plan of a Provisional Government for the Southern Confederacy.* Charleston, S.C., 1861.

Memorial of the Late James L. Petigru. Proceedings of the Bar of Charleston, S.C., March 25, 1863. New York: Richardson and Company, 1866.

Moore, John Bassett, ed. *The Works of James Buchanan.* 12 vols. Philadelphia, Pa.: J. B. Lippincott, 1908–11.

Oliphant, Mary C. Simms, Alfred Taylor Odell, and T. C. Duncan Eaves, eds. *The Letters of William Gilmore Simms.* 5 vols. Columbia: University of South Carolina Press, 1956.

O'Neall, John B. *Biographical Sketches of the Bench and Bar of South Carolina.* 2 vols. Charleston, S.C.: S. G. Courtenay, 1859.

Perry, Benjamin Franklin. *Reminiscences of Public Men, with Speeches and Addresses.* Greenville, S.C.: Shannon and Company, 1889.

Perry, Hext M. *Reminiscences of Public Men, by Ex-Gov. B. F. Perry.* Philadelphia, Pa.: J. D. Avil & Co., 1883.

Phillips, Ulrich B., ed. *The Correspondence of Robert Toombs, Alexander H. Stephens, and Howell Cobb. Annual Report of the American Historical Association for the Year 1911, Vol. II.* Washington, D.C.: American Historical Association, 1913.

Proceedings of the Celebration of the 4th July, 1831, at Charleston, S.C. by the State Rights and Free Trade Party: Containing the Speeches & Toasts, Delivered on the Occasion. Charleston, S.C., 1831.

Quaife, Milo M., ed. *The Diary of James K. Polk.* 4 vols. Chicago: A. C. McClurg, 1910.

Remarks of Messrs. Rhett, Belser, and A. V. Brown, on the Constitutional Power of Congress To Receive or Reject Petitions; and in Favor of the Retention of the 25th Rule, Prohibiting the Reception of Abolition Petitions. Washington, D.C., 1844.

[Rhett, Robert Barnwell]. *The Compromises of the Constitution Considered in the Organization of A National Convention.* N.p., n.d. [Washington ca. 1843].

————. *The Right of Debate, Considered in Three Letters, Addressed to the Editors of the National Intelligencer.* Washington, D.C., 1841.

Roman, Alfred. *The Military Operations of General Beauregard in the War Between the States 1861 to 1865.* 2 vols. New York: Harper & Bros., 1884.

Rosengarten, Theodore. *Tombee, Portrait of a Cotton Planter.* New York: Oxford University Press, 1986.

Rowland, Dunbar, comp. *Jefferson Davis, Constitutionalist: His Letters, Papers and Speeches.* 10 vols. Jackson, Miss.: Mississippi Department of Archives and History, 1923.

Russell, William Howard. *My Diary North and South.* New York: Harper & Bros., 1954.

Sabine, Lorenzo. *Notes on Duels and Duelling.* Boston: Crosby, Nichols, 1855.

Scarborough, William K. *The Diary of Edmund Ruffin.* 3 vols. Baton Rouge: Louisiana State University Press, 1972–89.

Speech of Robert Barnwell Rhett, to His Constituents on the Salt Ketcher River, at a Dinner Given on the 4th Day of July, 1839. Charleston, S.C., 1839.

Stephens, Alexander H. *A Constitutional View of the Late War between the States.* 2 vols. Philadelphia, Pa.: J. B. Lippincott, 1870.

Tharin, Robert S. *Arbitrary Arrests in the South; or, Scenes from the Experiences of an Alabama Unionist.* New York: J. Bradburn, 1863.

Thomas, J. P., ed. *The Carolina Tribute to Calhoun.* Columbia, S.C.: Richard L. Bryan, 1857.

Wallace, Daniel. *The Political Life and Services of the Hon. R. Barnwell Rhett, of South Carolina.* By "A Cotemporary." Cahaba, Ala., 1859.

Wiggins, Sarah Woolfolk, ed. *The Journals of Josiah Gorgas, 1857–1878.* Tuscaloosa: University of Alabama Press, 1995.

Wilson, Clyde N., ed. *The Papers of John C. Calhoun. Vols. 14–22.* Columbia: University of South Carolina Press, 1981–95.

Wilson, Clyde N., and Shirley Bright Cook, eds. *The Papers of John C. Calhoun.* Vols. 23–24. Columbia: University of South Carolina Press, 1996–98.

Wilson, Henry. *History of the Rise and Fall of the Slave Power in America.* 3 vols. Boston: Houghton Mifflin, 1872.

Woodward, C. Vann, ed. *Mary Chesnut's Civil War.* New Haven, Conn.: Yale University Press, 1981.

Woodward, C. Vann, and Elisabeth Muhlenfeld, eds. *The Private Mary Chesnut: The Unpublished Civil War Diaries.* New York: Oxford University Press, 1984.

ARTICLES

Barnwell, John, ed. "Hamlet to Hotspur: Letters of Robert Woodward Barnwell to Robert Barnwell Rhett." *South Carolina Historical Magazine* 77 (October 1976), 236–56.

Barnwell, Joseph W., and Mabel L. Webber, comps. "St. Helena's Parish Register." *South Carolina Historical and Genealogical Magazine* 23 (October 1922), 171–204.

Boucher, Chauncey Samuel, and Robert P. Brooks, eds. "Correspondence Addressed to John C. Calhoun 1837–1849." In *Annual Report of the American Historical Association for the Year 1929*. Washington, D.C., 1930.

Childs, Margaretta, and Isabella G. Leland, comps. "South Carolina Episcopal Church Records." *South Carolina Historical Magazine* 84 (October 1983), 250–63.

"Correspondence of Thomas Reade Roote Cobb, 1861–1862." *Publications of the Southern History Association* 9 (May 1907), 148–85; (July 1907), 233–60; (September–November 1907), 312–28.

"Despatch from the British Consul at Charleston to Lord John Russell, 1860." *American Historical Review* 18 (July 1913), 783–87.

Jones, James P., and William Warren Rogers, eds. "Montgomery as the Confederate Capital: View of a New Nation." *Alabama Historical Quarterly* 26 (Spring 1964), 1–125.

"Letters of Dr. Thomas Cooper, 1825–1832." *American Historical Review* 6 (July 1901), 725–36.

"The Lower Country of South Carolina." *The Land We Love* 1 (October 1866), 382–92; 2 (November 1866), 5–11.

Nichols, George Ward. "The Story of the Great March." *Confederate Veteran* 22 (November 1914), 508–9.

"Nullification Resolutions of 1828." *Publications of the Southern History Association* 3 (1899), 212–20.

"Papers of the Hon. John A. Campbell—1861–1865." *Southern Historical Society Papers* 42 (September 1917), 3–81.

Rhett, Robert Barnwell. "The Democratic Presidential Nomination." *United States Magazine and Democratic Review* 14 (January 1844), 89–94.

———. "Fears for Democracy." *Southern Magazine* 17 (September 1875), 306–32.

———. "Inquiry into the Origin and Course of the Political Parties in the United States." *Southern Review* 20 (October 1871), 776–812.

———. "The Issue at Stake." *United States Magazine and Democratic Review* 13 (November 1843), 542–47.

———. "The Memphis Convention." *Southern Quarterly Review* 10 (October 1846), 377–417.

———. "Mr. Calhoun and the Mississippi." *Southern Quarterly Review* 10 (October 1846), 441–512.

———. "Tract on Government." *Southern Quarterly Review* 18 (April 1854), 486–520.

———. "The Wilmot Proviso." *Southern Quarterly Review* 11 (April 1847), 377–406.

Rhett, Robert Barnwell, Jr. "The Confederate Government at Montgomery." In *Battles and Leaders of the Civil War,* vol. 1, edited by Clarence C. Buel and Robert U. Johnson. 4 vols. New York, 1887, 99–110.

"Robert Barnwell Rhett on the Biography of Calhoun, 1854." *American Historical Review* 13 (January 1908), 310–12.

"The Southern Convention." *Southern Quarterly Review* 18 (September 1850), 191–232.

Staudenraus, P. J., ed. "Occupied Beaufort, 1863: A War Correspondent's View." *South Carolina Historical Magazine* 64 (July 1963), 136–44.

Steiner, Bernard C., ed. "The South Atlantic States in 1833, as Seen by a New Englander." *Maryland Historical Magazine* 13 (December 1918), 295–386.

"Thomas R. R. Cobb . . . Extracts from Letters to His Wife, February 3, 1861–December 10, 1862." *Southern Historical Society Papers* 28 (January –December 1900), 280–301.

Waring, Alice Noble. "Five Letters from Francis W. Pickens to Patrick Noble, 1835– 1836." *South Carolina Historical Magazine* 54 (April 1953), 75–82.

Secondary Sources

THESES AND DISSERTATIONS

Bass, Robert D., ed. "Autobiography of William J. Grayson." Ph.D. diss., University of South Carolina, 1933.

Betts, Rose Miller. "William Henry Trescot." Master's thesis, University of South Carolina, 1929.

Coussons, John S. "Thirty Years with Calhoun, Rhett, and the Charleston Mercury: A Chapter in South Carolina Politics." Ph.D. diss., Louisiana State University, 1971.

Glenn, Virginia Louise. "James Hamilton, Jr., of South Carolina: A Biography." Ph.D. diss., University of North Carolina, 1964.

Kemp, Paige Holliman. "Montgomery, Alabama, 1861: A Social History of the Cradle of the Confederacy." Master's thesis, Auburn University, 1978.

McConaghy, Mary Delaney. "Ordinary White Folk in a Lowcountry Community: The Structure and Dynamics of St. Bartholomew's Parish, South Carolina, 1850– 1870." Ph.D. diss., University of Pennsylvania, 1996.

Olsberg, Robert Nicholas. "William Henry Trescot: The Crisis of 1860." Master's thesis, University of South Carolina, 1967.

Perritt, Henry H. "Robert Barnwell Rhett: South Carolina Secession Spokesman." Ph.D. diss., University of Florida, 1954.

Roberson, John C. "The Foundations of Southern Nationalism: Charleston and the Lowcountry, 1847–1861." 2 vols. Ph.D. diss., University of South Carolina, 1991.

Segars, Ernest B. "A Study of the *Charleston* (S.C.) *Mercury* during Robert Barnwell Rhett, Senior's Tenure As an Editorial Writer, 1861–1863." Master's thesis, University of South Carolina, 1974.

Williamson, Joel R. "The Disruption of State Government in South Carolina during the Magrath Administration." Master's thesis, University of South Carolina, 1951.

BOOKS

Alexander, Thomas B., and Richard E. Beringer. *The Anatomy of the Confederate Congress.* Nashville: Vanderbilt University Press, 1972.

Bailey, N. Louise, et al. *Biographical Directory of the South Carolina Senate 1776–1985.* 3 vols. Columbia: South Carolina Department of Archives and History, 1986.

Barnwell, John. *Love of Order: South Carolina's First Secession Crisis.* Chapel Hill: University of North Carolina Press, 1982.

Barnwell, Stephen B. *The Story of an American Family.* Marqette, Mich., 1969.

Boucher, Chauncey Samuel. *The Nullification Controversy in South Carolina.* New York: Greenwood Press, 1969.

Braden, Waldo W., ed. *Oratory in the Old South 1828–1860.* Baton Rouge: Louisiana State University Press, 1970.

Campbell, Stanley W. *The Slave Catchers: Enforcement of the Fugitive Slave Law, 1850–1860.* Chapel Hill: University of North Carolina Press, 1970.

Carpenter, Jesse T. *The South as a Conscious Minority 1789–1861.* New York: New York University Press, 1930.

Cauthen, Charles E. *South Carolina Goes to War.* Chapel Hill: University of North Carolina Press, 1950.

Channing, Steven A. *Crisis of Fear: Secession in South Carolina.* New York: Simon and Schuster, 1970.

Clark, E. Culpepper. *Francis Warrington Dawson and the Politics of Restoration: South Carolina, 1874–1889.* Tuscaloosa: University of Alabama Press, 1980.

Clowse, Converse D. *Economic Beginnings in Colonial South Carolina, 1670–1730.* Columbia: University of South Carolina Press, 1971.

Coit, Margaret L. *John C. Calhoun, American Patriot.* Boston: Little, Brown, 1950.

Coulter, E. Merton. *The Confederate States of America 1861–1865.* Baton Rouge: Louisiana State University Press, 1950.

Crenshaw, Ollinger. *The Slave States in the Presidential Election of 1860*. Baltimore, Md.: Johns Hopkins University Press, 1945.

Davis, Burke. *Sherman's March*. New York: Random House, 1980.

Davis, William C. *"A Government of Our Own": The Making of the Confederacy*. New York: Free Press, 1994.

———. *Jefferson Davis, the Man and His Hour*. New York: HarperCollins, 1991.

DeRosa, Marshall L. *The Confederate Constitution of 1861*. Columbia: University of Missouri Press, 1991.

Dixon, Nancy. *Fortune and Misery: Sallie Rhett Roman of New Orleans*. Baton Rouge: Louisiana State University Press, 1999.

DuBose, John Witherspoon. *The Life and Times of William Lowndes Yancey*. Birmingham, Ala.: Roberts & Son, 1892.

Dumond, Dwight Lowell. *The Secession Movement 1860–1861*. New York: Macmillan, 1931.

Edmunds, John B., Jr. *Francis W. Pickens and the Politics of Destruction*. Chapel Hill: University of North Carolina Press, 1986.

Faust, Drew Gilpin. *James Henry Hammond and the Old South*. Baton Rouge: Louisiana State University Press, 1982.

Ford, Lacy K., Jr. *Origins of Southern Radicalism: The South Carolina Upcountry, 1800–1860*. New York: Oxford University Press, 1988.

Freehling, William W. *The Road to Disunion, Volume 1: Secessionists at Bay, 1776– 1854*. New York: Oxford University Press, 1990.

Greenberg, Kenneth S. *Masters and Statesmen: The Political Culture of American Slavery*. Baltimore, Md.: Johns Hopkins University Press, 1985.

Guess, Francis William. *South Carolina, Annals of Pride and Protest*. New York: Harper & Bros., 1960.

Hamer, Philip M. *The Secession Movement in South Carolina 1847–1852*. Allentown, Pa.: H. R. Haas & Co., 1918.

Heidler, David S. *Pulling the Temple Down: The Fire-Eaters and the Destruction of the Union*. Harrisburg, Pa.: Stackpole, 1994.

Hennig, Helen Kohn. *Great South Carolinians*. Chapel Hill: University of North Carolina Press, 1940.

Hubbard, Charles M. *The Burden of Confederate Diplomacy*. Knoxville: University of Tennessee Press, 1998.

Johannsen, Robert W. *Stephen A. Douglas*. New York: Oxford University Press, 1973.

Lee, Charles R. *The Confederate Constitution*. Chapel Hill: University of North Carolina Press, 1963.

Lesser, Charles H. *Relic of the Lost Cause: The Story of South Carolina's Ordinance of Secession*. Columbia: South Carolina Department of Archives and History, 1996.

Linder, Suzanne Cameron. *Historical Atlas of the Rice Plantations of the ACE River Basin—1860.* Columbia: University of South Carolina Press, 1995.

May, Robert E. *John A. Quitman, Old South Crusader.* Baton Rouge: Louisiana State University Press, 1985.

McCardell, John. *The Idea of a Southern Nation: Southern Nationalists and Southern Nationalism, 1830–1860.* New York: W. W. Norton, 1979.

McCurry, Stephanie. *Masters of Small Worlds: Yeoman Households, Gender Relations, & the Political Culture of the Antebellum South Carolina Low Country.* New York: Oxford University Press, 1995.

Moore, Albert B. *Conscription and Conflict in the Confederacy.* New York: Macmillan, 1924.

Moore, Alexander. *Biographical Directory of the South Carolina House of Representatives, Volume V 1816–1828.* Columbia: South Carolina Department of Archives and History, 1992.

Nichols, Roy F. *The Disruption of American Democracy.* New York: Macmillan, 1948.

Niven, John. *John C. Calhoun and the Price of Union.* Baton Rouge: Louisiana State University Press, 1988.

Osthaus, Carl R. *Partisans of the Southern Press: Editorial Spokesmen of the Nineteenth Century.* Lexington: University Press of Kentucky, 1994.

Owsley, Frank L. *King Cotton Diplomacy.* Chicago: University of Chicago Press, 1959.

Poston, Jonathan H. *The Buildings of Charleston. A Guide to the City's Architecture.* Columbia: University of South Carolina Press, 1997.

Rable, George C. *The Confederate Republic, a Revolution against Politics.* Chapel Hill: University of North Carolina Press, 1994.

Remini, Robert. *Andrew Jackson and the Course of American Democracy, 1883–1845.* New York: Harper & Row, 1984.

Reynolds, Donald E. *Editors Make War: Southern Newspapers in the Secession Crisis.* Nashville: Vanderbilt University Press, 1970.

Rowland, Dunbar. *Courts, Judges, and Lawyers in Mississippi 1795–1935.* Jackson: Mississippi Department of Archives and History, 1935.

Rowland, Lawrence S., Alexander Moore, and George C. Rogers Jr. *The History of Beaufort County, South Carolina: Volume 1, 1514–1861.* Columbia: University of South Carolina Press, 1996.

Russel, Robert R. *Critical Studies in Antebellum Sectionalism.* Westport, Conn.: Greenwood Press, 1972.

Schultz, Harold S. *Nationalism and Sectionalism in South Carolina, 1852–1860: A Study of the Movement for Southern Independence.* Durham, N.C.: Duke University Press, 1950.

Shryock, Richard Harrison. *Georgia and the Union in 1850.* Durham, N.C.: Duke University Press, 1926.

Takaki, Ronald T. *A Pro-Slavery Crusade: The Agitation to Reopen the African Slave Trade.* New York: Free Press, 1971.

Walther, Eric H. *The Fire-Eaters.* Baton Rouge: Louisiana State University Press, 1992.

White, Laura A. *Robert Barnwell Rhett: Father of Secession.* Washington, D.C.: American Historical Association, 1931.

Whitridge, Arnold. *No Compromise! The Story of the Fanatics Who Paved the Way to the Civil War.* New York: Farrar, Strauss, 1960.

Wooster, Ralph A. *The Secession Conventions of the South.* Princeton, N.J.: Princeton University Press, 1962.

Yearns, Wilfred Buck. *The Confederate Congress.* Athens: University of Georgia Press, 1960.

ARTICLES

Anderson, James L., and W. Edwin Hemphill. "The 1843 Biography of John C. Calhoun: Was R. M. T. Hunter Its Author?" *Journal of Southern History* 38 (August 1972), 469–74.

Boucher, Chauncey Samuel. "The Annexation of Texas and the Bluffton Movement in South Carolina." *Mississippi Valley Historical Review* 6 (June 1919), 3–33.

———. "The Secession and Co-operation Movements in South Carolina, 1848 to 1852." *Washington University Studies* 5 (April 1918), 65–138.

———. "South Carolina and the South on the Eve of Secession, 1852 to 1860." *Washington University Studies* 6 (April 1919), 79–144.

Craven, Avery. "The 1840's and the Democratic Process." *Journal of Southern History* 16 (May 1950), 160–76.

Donald, David. "The Proslavery Argument Reconsidered." *Journal of Southern History* 37 (February 1971), 3–18.

DuBose, John Witherspoon. "Alabama—The Relation of the State to the Birth of the Southern Confederacy." *Confederate Veteran* 24 (May 1916), 201–8.

———. "Confederate Diplomacy." *Southern Historical Society Papers* 32 (January–December 1904), 102–16.

———. "William L. Yancey in History." *Southern Historical Society Papers* 27 (January–December 1899), 98–101.

Fitts, Albert N. "The Confederate Convention." *Alabama Review* 2 (April 1949), 83–101.

Gerson, Armand J. "The Inception of the Montgomery Convention." In *American Historical Association Annual Report.* Washington, D.C., 1910, 179–87.

Heyward, Barnwell Rhett. "The Descendants of Col. William Rhett of South Carolina." *South Carolina Historical and Genealogical Magazine* 4 (January 1903), 36–74.

Higginbotham, Don. "Fomenters of Revolution: Massachusetts and South Carolina." *Journal of the Early Republic* 14 (Spring 1994), 1–33.

"Historical Notes: The Date of the Changing of the Name Smith to Rhett." *South Carolina Historical and Genealogical Magazine* 30 (October 1929), 257–58.

Lander, Ernest M., Jr. "The Calhoun-Preston Feud, 1836–1842." *South Carolina Historical Magazine* 59 (January 1958), 24–37.

"Last Survivor of the Original Confederate Congress." *Confederate Veteran* 25 (February 1917), 54.

Millard, Flora J. "The Foreign Policy of the Confederate States." *Confederate Veteran* 26 (June 1918), 241–46.

Parris, Matthew. "Another Voice." *The Spectator,* September 26, 1998.

Perritt, H. Hardy. "Robert Barnwell Rhett: Disunionist Heir of Calhoun, 1850–1852." *Southern Speech Journal* 24 (Fall 1958), 38–55.

———. "Robert Barnwell Rhett: Prophet of Resistance, 1828–1834." *Southern Speech Journal* 21 (Winter 1955), 103–19.

Rogers, George C., Jr. "South Carolina Federalists and the Origins of the Nullification Movement." *South Carolina Historical Magazine* 71 (January 1970), 17–32.

Salley, A. S. "The Family of the First Landgrave Thomas Smith." *South Carolina Historical and Genealogical Magazine* 28 (July 1927), 169–75.

———. "More on Landgrave Smith's Family." *South Carolina Historical and Genealogical Magazine* 30 (October 1929), 255–58.

Sioussat, St. George L. "Tennessee, the Compromise of 1850, and the Nashville Convention." *Mississippi Valley Historical Review* 2 (December 1915), 313–47.

Walther, Eric H. "The Fire-Eaters and the Riddle of Southern Nationalism." *Southern Studies* n.s. 3 (Spring 1992), 67–77.

White, Laura. "The Fate of Calhoun's Sovereign Convention in South Carolina." *American Historical Review* 34 (July 1929), 757–71.

Wolfe, Alan. "The Revolution That Never Was." *The New Republic,* June 7, 1999, 34–42.

Woodward, C. Vann. "The Irony of Southern History." *Journal of Southern History* 19 (February 1953), 3–19.

Index

Even though Rhett is referred to as Robert Barnwell Smith in the text up to the time when he changed his name, to avoid unnecessary confusion, all index references to him are to Rhett, regardless of whether before or after the name change. His brothers who changed their names are also so handled in the index.

109, 118, 122, 125–26, 129–30, 132,
147, 153, 161–62, 179; and Dred
Scott decision, 385; on emancipation,
113, 191; and expansionism, 377,
402; and fiscal policy, 103ff, 130ff;
and gag rule, 92, 110ff, 127–28,
130–31, 153–55, 191–92, 194, 215;
on government, 71–72, 83–84,
341–43, 376–77; on impeachment,
34–35, 51; and Independent Treasury,
102ff, 119ff, 148; and internal
improvements, 29, 32, 51, 105, 128,
157, 190, 227–28, 244; as Jeffersonian Republican, 24–26, 101; on the
judiciary, 33–36, 51; and Kansas
controversy, 375–76; on labor versus
capital, 113–14, 116–17, 122–23;
and loyalty to Union, 32, 54, 74–75,
77, 78, 82–83, 205; libertarianism,
578; and majority rule, 116, 155–56,
183, 190, 274, 537–38, 577, 586;
and National Bank, 18, 98, 101,
103–105; and National Road, 118;
and nullification, 43ff, 58, 61, 64–65,
69–70, 75–76, 105–6, 222, 228, 236,
252; on oligarchy, 20–21, 25, 116,
132, 576; on political parties, 25, 54,
101, 118, 125–26, 306; as populist,
579–80; as secessionist, 31–32,
37–38, 39–42, 46–48, 52–53, 61, 62,
64, 69, 74–75, 110, 112, 124–25,
127, 133–35, 148, 153, 158–59, 162,
183, 192, 198, 200–201, 206–208,
211, 220, 222, 228, 236, 237, 249,
252, 267, 277–78, 281–82, 284–85,
297–98, 309–10, 325–31, 341, 342,
344, 351, 352–53, 367, 398ff, 618n,
667–68n; on slave trade reopening,
356–57, 370–73; on separate state
secession, 204–5, 210, 253, 263, 278,
290, 292, 297–98, 300–301, 393,
396, 409; and slavery, 15, 27–28, 64,
66, 92, 110, 112, 113–14, 116–17,

122–25, 158–59, 190, 191–92, 218,
233ff, 239, 244, 250, 253–54,
273–76, 292ff, 306, 343, 377, 406,
465–66, 479, 494, 509–10, 531, 537,
539, 577, 582; as strict construction-
ist, 29; on Southern nationhood, 75,
78, 116, 280, 281, 283, 352, 376,
396, 399–400, 411, 414; and tariff,
16–17, 19, 25, 28–29, 30, 32, 38;
and Tariff of 1828, 38–42, 49, 52,
63; and Tariff of 1832, 73–75, 106,
114–15, 132–35, 136, 145; and
Tariff of 1842, 153ff, 157, 158–59,
161ff, 185–86, 188, 190, 195, 222ff,
227; and Texas annexation, 109–10,
183–84, 197, 200, 215ff; and Wilmot
Proviso, 233ff, 248ff
—personal attitudes: on character,
24; on dueling, 58–59, 269, 314,
321–25, 349–50, 567–73; on education, 253–60, 265–66, 567; on the
Enlightenment, 20; on greatness, 13;
on history, 576; on Negroes, 51, 90,
116, 253, 343, 391, 538–39; on
oratory, 14, 375–76
—personal relationships: John Quincy
Adams, 141; Robert W. Barnwell,
23; John C. Calhoun, 22, 32, 43,
56, 60, 61, 102–4, 107ff, 126, 128,
138, 144, 163–64, 175, 189, 196ff,
202–3, 212, 214, 219, 223ff, 227,
229, 230, 237, 249–50, 262, 270–71,
341; Lewis Cass, 250–51, 260;
Charleston *Mercury*, 79, 122, 129,
156, 166, 175, 264, 272, 364ff,
391ff, 545–47, 551–53, 556; Jeremiah
Clemens, 317ff; Jefferson Davis, 291,
341, 344, 367, 402, 418, 424–25,
429, 430–33, 435, 437, 439, 444–46,
447ff, 459–60, 462, 468–69, 471–72,
474–76, 480, 481–87, 489–92,
494–96, 498, 500, 502–6, 509–16,
518–19, 521–22, 525–28, 531–34,